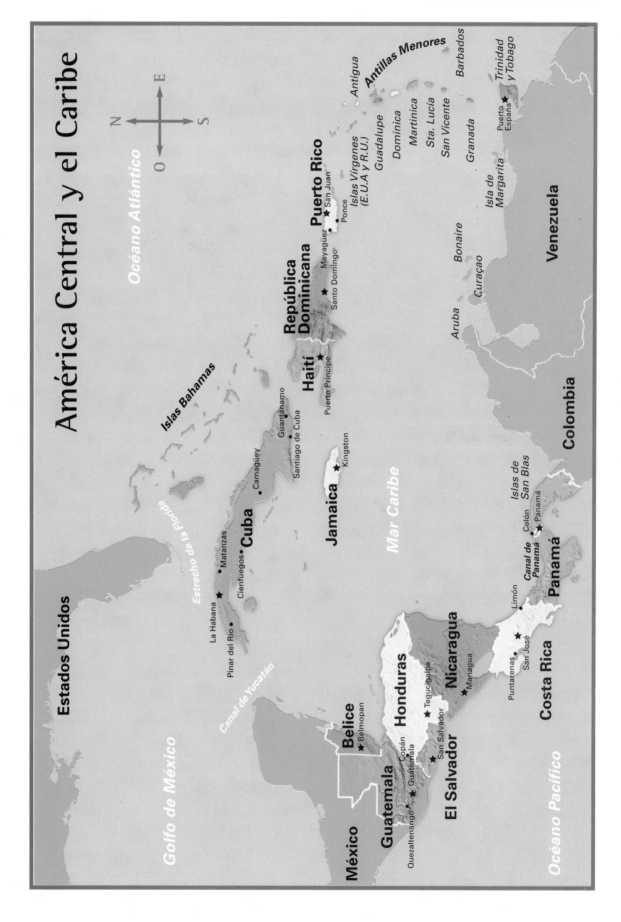

América Central y el Caribe

PANORAMA

Introducción a la lengua española

PANORAMA
Introducción a la lengua española

José A. Blanco

Mary Ann Dellinger
Virginia Military Institute

Philip Donley
Austin Community College

María Isabel García
Boston University

• • •

Elaine K. Horwitz
Senior Consulting Editor
University of Texas

VISTA
HIGHER LEARNING

Boston, Massachusetts • Auburn, California

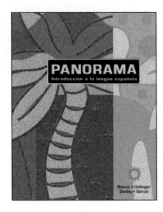

Award-winning cover Illustrator, **José Ortega** was born in Ecuador and studied at New York's prestigious School of Visual Arts. His work has appeared in magazines and advertisements throughout the world.

Publisher: José A. Blanco

Editorial Director of College Publishing: Denise St. Jean

Director of Manufacturing: Stephen Pekich

Staff Editors: María Cinta Aparisi, Gustavo Cinci, Mark Porter,

Contributing Writers: Sharon Alexander, María Elena Alvarado, Karin Fajardo, Ana M. Fores, Francisco de la Rosa, Gregory Garretson, Jane Ann Johnson, Norah L. Jones, Ralph Kite, Susan Lake, Ann Morrill, Lourdes M. Murray, Isabel Picado, Beatriz Pojman, Teresa Shu, Marcia Tugendhat

Art Director: Linda Jurras

Design Team: Polo Barrera, Martin Beveridge, Ianka de la Rosa, Barbara Gazley, Suzanne Korschun, Susan Prentiss

Photographer: Martin Bernetti

Production Team: Ted Cantrell, Oscar Díez, Holly Kersey, Greg Moutafis, Eric Murphy, Janet Spicer

Student Text ISBN 1-931100-64-0

Instructor's Annotated Edition ISBN 1-931100-65-9

Library of Congress Card Number: 2001095415

3 4 5 6 7 8 9 VH 05 04 03

Introduction

Welcome to **PANORAMA**, the brief version of VISTAS, Vista Higher Learning's highly successful, widely adopted introductory college Spanish program. Combining VISTAS' fresh, student-friendly approach with pared-down content, **PANORAMA** is intended for courses with reduced contact hours or those in which instructors prefer to cover fewer lessons in an academic year.

Like VISTAS, **PANORAMA** was written with you, the student, in mind. In light of this, here are some of the elements you will encounter:

- Practical, high-frequency vocabulary that will allow you to communicate in everyday situations

- Clear, comprehensive grammar explanations with special features that make it easier to learn and to use

- Ample guided, focused practice to make you comfortable with the vocabulary and grammar you are learning and to give you a solid foundation for communication

- An emphasis on communicative interactions with a classmate, small groups, the full class and your instructor

- Careful development of reading, writing, and listening skills incorporating learning strategies and a process approach

- Integration of the culture of the everyday lives of Spanish speakers and coverage of the entire Spanish-speaking world

- A complete set of print and technology ancillaries to help you learn Spanish more easily

And like VISTAS, **PANORAMA** offers some elements that set it apart from other college-level introductory Spanish textbooks:

- A different and more cohesive way of integrating video with the student textbook

- Student annotations with handy point-of-use information on virtually every page

- An abundance of drawings, photos, charts, and graphs, all designed to help you learn

- A highly structured, easy-to-navigate design and organization

To familiarize yourself with how the lessons in **PANORAMA** are organized, turn to page xii and take the at-a-glance tour.

table of contents

	contexts	fotonovela

estructura	**adelante**	**panorama**

table of contents

	contextos	**fotonovela**

estructura	adelante	panorama

table of contents

	contexts	fotonovela

estructura	adelante	panorama

table of contents

	contexts	fotonovela

Consulta (Reference)

Lesson Openers
outline the content and features of each lesson.

Hola, ¿qué tal?

1

Communicative Goals

You will learn how to:
- Greet people in Spanish
- Say goodbye
- Identify yourself and others
- Talk about the time of day

pages 2-5
- Words and phrases related to greetings and leave-takings
- Terms to identify yourself and others
- Expressions of courtesy

contextos

pages 6-9
- Mrs. Ramos, from the travel agency Ecuatur, greets the students and hands out their travel papers. Don Francisco, the driver, introduces himself and asks the students to board the bus.
- **Pronunciación:** The Spanish alphabet

fotonovela

pages 10-25
- Nouns and articles
- Numbers 0-30
- Present tense of the verb **ser**
- Telling time

estructura

pages 26-27
- **Lectura:** Read a telephone list.

adelante

pages 28-29
Featured Country: United States
- Cities and states with the largest Hispanic populations
- Influence of Hispanic culture in the U.S.

panorama

Contextos
presents vocabulary in meaningful contexts.

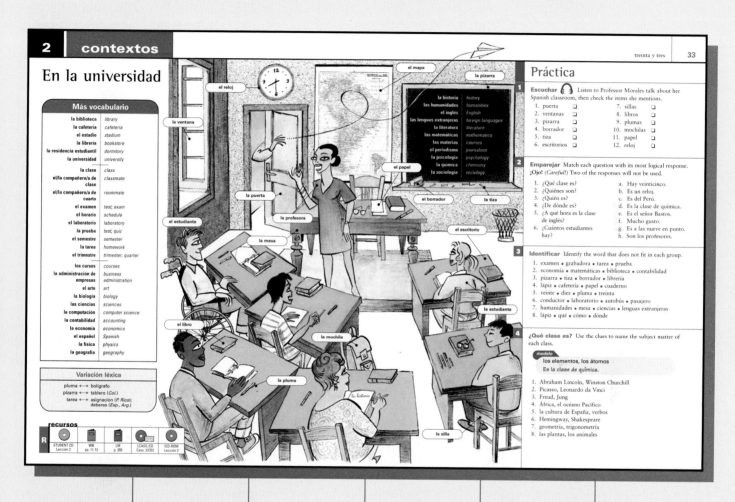

Más vocabulario boxes call out other important theme-related vocabulary in easy-to-reference Spanish-English lists.

Illustrations High-frequency vocabulary is introduced through expansive, full-color illustrations.

Práctica This section always begins with a listening exercise and continues with activities that practice the new vocabulary in meaningful contexts.

Variación léxica presents alternate words and expressions used throughout the Spanish-speaking world.

Recursos boxes let you know exactly what ancillaries you can use to reinforce or expand on the section.

PANORAMA-at-a-glance

Contextos
practices vocabulary in a variety of formats.

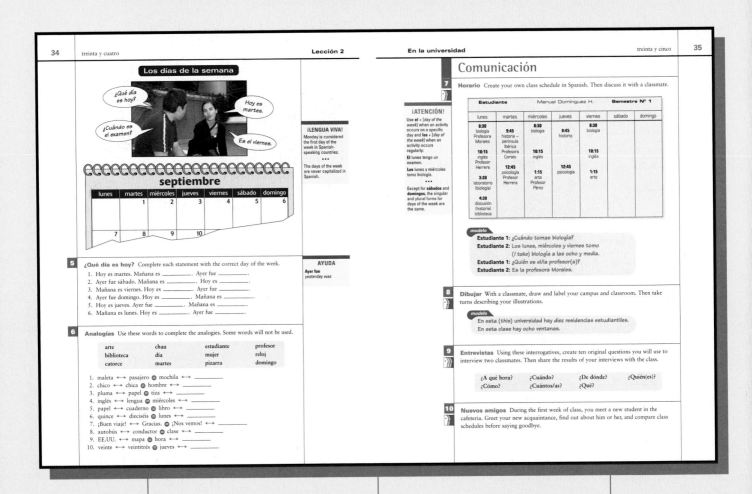

Práctica exercises reinforce the vocabulary through varied and engaging formats.

Student Sidebars provide handy, on-the-spot information that helps you complete the activities.

Comunicación activities get you using the vocabulary creatively in interactions with a partner, a small group, or the entire class.

Fotonovela
tells the story of four students traveling in Ecuador.

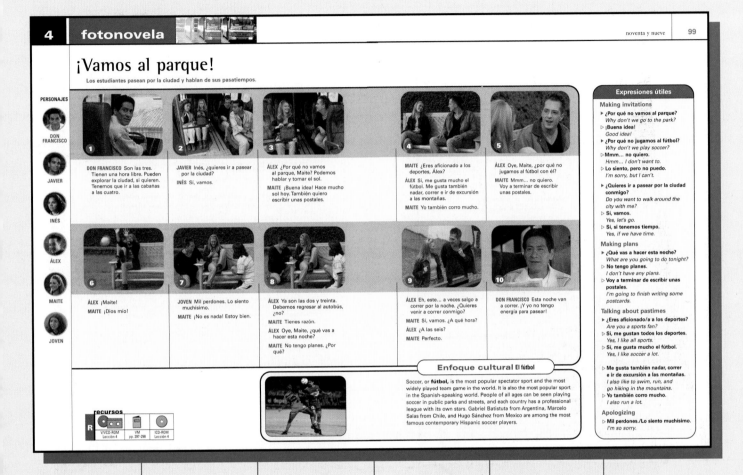

Personajes The photo-based conversations take place among a cast of recurring characters—four college students on vacation in Ecuador and the bus driver who accompanies them.

PANORAMA Video The **Fotonovela** episode appears in the textbook's Video Program. To learn more about the video, turn to pages xxiv and xxv in this at-a-glance tour.

Dialogues use vocabulary from **Contextos** and introduce in a comprehensible way examples of the grammar points you will study in the **Estructura** section.

Enfoque cultural provides detailed cultural information on a topic related to the **Fotonovela** conversation.

Expresiones útiles organizes new, active words and expressions by language function so you can focus on using them for real-life, practical purposes.

PANORAMA-at-a-glance

Pronunciación & Ortografía
present the rules of Spanish pronunciation and spelling.

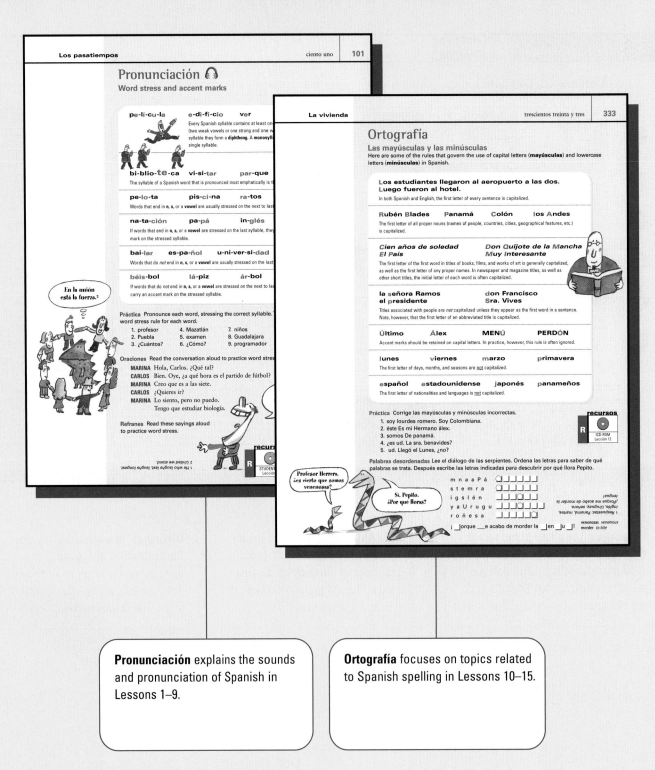

Pronunciación explains the sounds and pronunciation of Spanish in Lessons 1–9.

Ortografía focuses on topics related to Spanish spelling in Lessons 10–15.

Estructura
presents Spanish grammar in a graphic-intensive format.

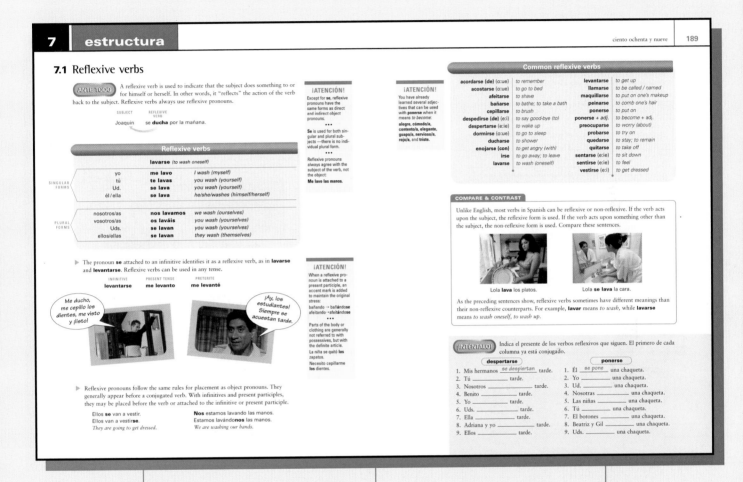

Ante todo eases you into the grammar with definitions of grammatical terms and reminders about what you already know of English grammar or have learned in earlier lessons.

Compare & contrast homes in on aspects of grammar that native speakers of English could find difficult, clarifying similarities and differences between Spanish and English.

Diagrams To clarify concepts, clear and easy-to-grasp grammar explanations are reinforced by diagrams that colorfully present sample words, phrases, and sentences.

Charts To help you learn, colorful, easy-to-use charts call out key grammatical structures and forms, as well as important related vocabulary.

Student sidebars provide you with on-the-spot linguistic, cultural, or language-learning information directly related to the materials in front of you.

¡Inténtalo! exercises offer an easy first step in your practice of each new grammar point. They get you working with the grammar right away in simple, easy-to-understand formats.

PANORAMA-at-a-glance

Estructura
provides directed and communicative practice.

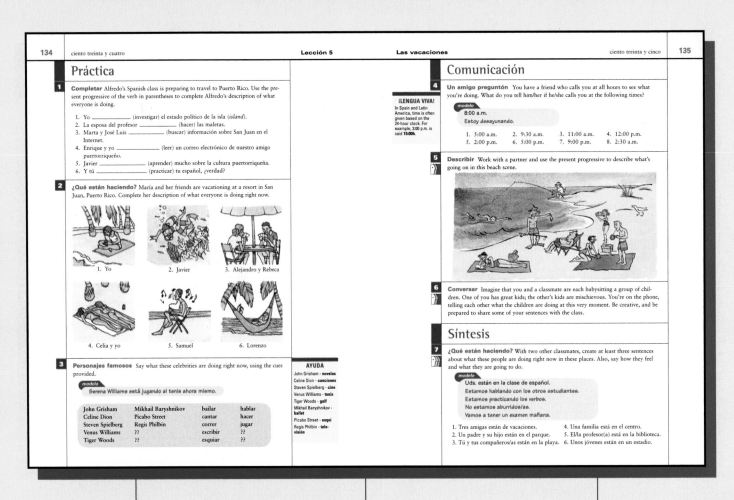

Práctica

1 Completar Alfredo's Spanish class is preparing to travel to Puerto Rico. Use the present progressive of the verb in parentheses to complete Alfredo's description of what everyone is doing.

1. Yo _____ (investigar) el estado político de la isla (*island*).
2. La esposa del profesor _____ (hacer) las maletas.
3. Marta y José Luis _____ (buscar) información sobre San Juan en el Internet.
4. Enrique y yo _____ (leer) un correo electrónico de nuestro amigo puertorriqueño.
5. Javier _____ (aprender) mucho sobre la cultura puertorriqueña.
6. Y tú _____ (practicar) tu español, ¿verdad?

2 ¿Qué están haciendo? María and her friends are vacationing at a resort in San Juan, Puerto Rico. Complete her description of what everyone is doing right now.

1. Yo   2. Javier   3. Alejandro y Rebeca

4. Celia y yo   5. Samuel   6. Lorenzo

3 Personajes famosos Say what these celebrities are doing right now, using the cues provided.

modelo
Serena Williams está jugando al tenis ahora mismo.

John Grisham	Mikhail Baryshnikov	bailar	hablar
Celine Dion	Picabo Street	cantar	hacer
Steven Spielberg	Regis Philbin	correr	jugar
Venus Williams	??	escribir	??
Tiger Woods	??	esquiar	??

AYUDA
John Grisham - novelas
Celine Dion - canciones
Steven Spielberg - cine
Venus Williams - tenis
Tiger Woods - golf
Mikhail Baryshnikov - ballet
Picabo Street - esquí
Regis Philbin - televisión

Comunicación

¡LENGUA VIVA!
In Spain and Latin America, time is often given based on the 24-hour clock. For example, 3:00 p.m. is said **15:00h.**

4 Un amigo preguntón You have a friend who calls you at all hours to see what you're doing. What do you tell him/her if he/she calls you at the following times?

modelo
8:00 a.m.
Estoy desayunando.

1. 5:00 a.m.   2. 9:30 a.m.   3. 11:00 a.m.   4. 12:00 p.m.
5. 2:00 p.m.   6. 5:00 p.m.   7. 9:00 p.m.   8. 2:30 a.m.

5 Describir Work with a partner and use the present progressive to describe what's going on in this beach scene.

6 Conversar Imagine that you and a classmate are each babysitting a group of children. One of you has great kids; the other's kids are mischievous. You're on the phone, telling each other what the children are doing at this very moment. Be creative, and be prepared to share some of your sentences with the class.

Síntesis

7 ¿Qué están haciendo? With two other classmates, create at least three sentences about what these people are doing right now in these places. Also, say how they feel and what they are going to do.

modelo
Uds. están en la clase de español.
Estamos hablando con los otros estudiantes.
Estamos practicando los verbos.
No estamos aburridos/as.
Vamos a tener un examen mañana.

1. Tres amigas están de vacaciones.   4. Una familia está en el centro.
2. Un padre y su hijo están en el parque.   5. El/la profesor(a) está en la biblioteca.
3. Tú y tus compañeros/as están en la playa.   6. Unos jóvenes están en un estadio.

Práctica exercises provide a wide range of guided, yet meaningful exercises that weave current and previously learned vocabulary together with the current grammar point.

Comunicación offers opportunities for creative expression using the lesson's grammar and vocabulary. These take place with a partner, in small groups, or with the whole class.

Síntesis integrates the current grammar point with previously learned points, providing built-in, consistent review and recycling as you progress through the text.

Adelante
In every lesson, *Lectura* develops reading skills in the context of the lesson theme.

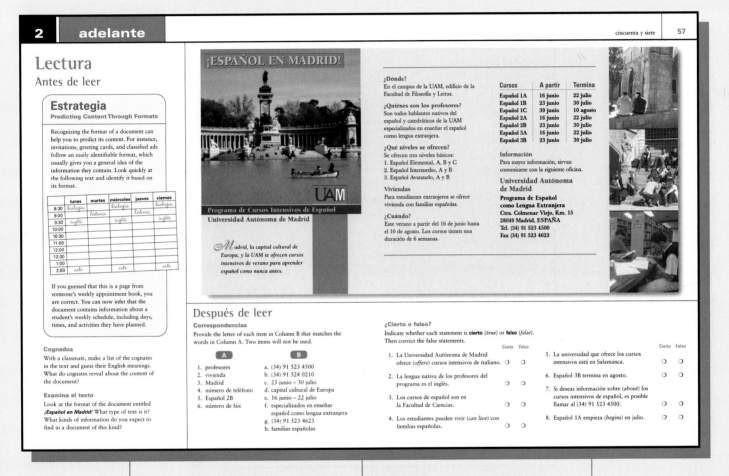

2 | **adelante**

cincuenta y siete | **57**

Lectura
Antes de leer

Estrategia
Predicting Content Through Formats

Recognizing the format of a document can help you to predict its content. For instance, invitations, greeting cards, and classified ads follow an easily identifiable format, which usually gives you a general idea of the information they contain. Look quickly at the following text and identify it based on its format.

	lunes	martes	miércoles	jueves	viernes
8:30	biología		biología		biología
9:00		historia		historia	
9:30	inglés		inglés		inglés
10:00					
10:30					
11:00					
12:00					
12:30					
1:00					
2:00	arte		arte		arte

If you guessed that this is a page from someone's weekly appointment book, you are correct. You can now infer that the document contains information about a student's weekly schedule, including days, times, and activities they have planned.

Cognados

With a classmate, make a list of the cognates in the text and guess their English meanings. What do cognates reveal about the content of the document?

Examina el texto

Look at the format of the document entitled *¡Español en Madrid!* What type of text is it? What kinds of information do you expect to find in a document of this kind?

¡ESPAÑOL EN MADRID!

Programa de Cursos Intensivos de Español
Universidad Autónoma de Madrid

Madrid, la capital cultural de Europa, y la UAM te ofrecen cursos intensivos de verano para aprender español como nunca antes.

¿Dónde?
En el campus de la UAM, edificio de la Facultad de Filosofía y Letras.

¿Quiénes son los profesores?
Son todos hablantes nativos del español y catedráticos de la UAM especializados en enseñar el español como lengua extranjera.

¿Qué niveles se ofrecen?
Se ofrecen tres niveles básicos:
1. Español Elemental, A, B y C
2. Español Intermedio, A y B
3. Español Avanzado, A y B

Viviendas
Para estudiantes extranjeros se ofrece vivienda con familias españolas.

¿Cuándo?
Este verano a partir del 16 de junio hasta el 10 de agosto. Los cursos tienen una duración de 6 semanas.

Cursos	A partir	Termina
Español 1A	16 junio	22 julio
Español 1B	23 junio	30 julio
Español 1C	30 junio	10 agosto
Español 2A	16 junio	22 julio
Español 2B	23 junio	30 julio
Español 3A	16 junio	22 julio
Español 3B	23 junio	30 julio

Información
Para mayor información, sirvan comunicarse con la siguiente oficina.

Universidad Autónoma de Madrid
Programa de Español como Lengua Extranjera
Ctra. Colmenar Viejo, Km. 15
28049 Madrid, ESPAÑA
Tel. (34) 91 523 4500
Fax (34) 91 523 4623

Después de leer

Correspondencias

Provide the letter of each item in Column B that matches the words in Column A. Two items will not be used.

A
1. profesores
2. vivienda
3. Madrid
4. número de teléfono
5. Español 2B
6. número de fax

B
a. (34) 91 523 4500
b. (34) 91 524 0210
c. 23 junio – 30 julio
d. capital cultural de Europa
e. 16 junio – 22 julio
f. especializados en enseñar español como lengua extranjera
g. (34) 91 523 4623
h. familias españolas

¿Cierto o falso?

Indicate whether each statement is **cierto** (*true*) or **falso** (*false*). Then correct the false statements.

	Cierto	Falso
1. La Universidad Autónoma de Madrid ofrece (*offers*) cursos intensivos de italiano.	○	○
2. La lengua nativa de los profesores del programa es el inglés.	○	○
3. Los cursos de español son en la Facultad de Ciencias.	○	○
4. Los estudiantes pueden vivir (*can live*) con familias españolas.	○	○
5. La universidad que ofrece los cursos intensivos está en Salamanca.	○	○
6. Español 3B termina en agosto.	○	○
7. Si deseas información sobre (*about*) los cursos intensivos de español, es posible llamar al (34) 91 523 4500.	○	○
8. Español 1A empieza (*begins*) en julio.	○	○

Antes de leer presents valuable reading strategies and pre-reading activities that strengthen your reading abilities in Spanish.

Readings are specifically related to the lesson theme and recycle vocabulary and grammar you have learned.

Después de leer Includes post-reading exercises that review and check your comprehension of the reading.

Adelante

In Lessons 3, 6, 9, 12, and 15, *Escritura* develops writing skills in the context of the lesson theme.

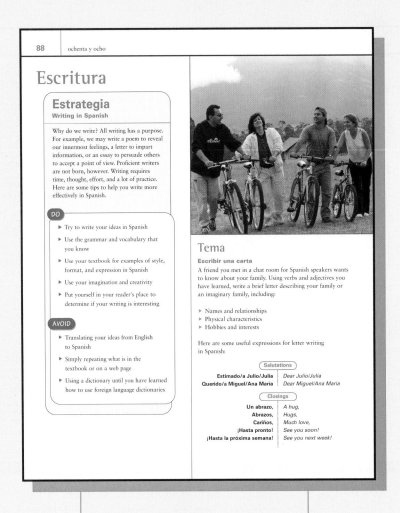

Estrategia provides strategies that help you prepare for the writing task presented in the next section.

Tema describes the writing topic and includes suggestions for approaching it.

Adelante
Like *Escritura, Escuchar* appears every three lessons and develops listening skills using a process approach.

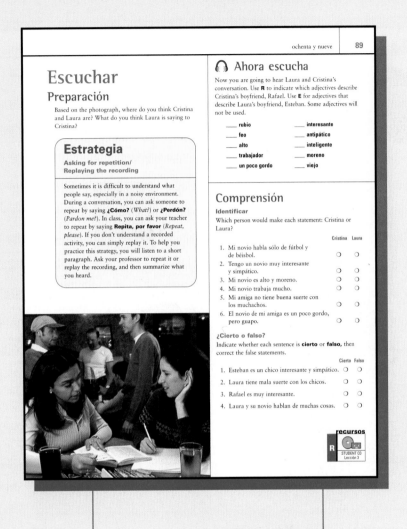

Escuchar
Preparación

Based on the photograph, where do you think Cristina and Laura are? What do you think Laura is saying to Cristina?

Estrategia

**Asking for repetition/
Replaying the recording**

Sometimes it is difficult to understand what people say, especially in a noisy environment. During a conversation, you can ask someone to repeat by saying **¿Cómo?** (*What?*) or **¿Perdón?** (*Pardon me?*). In class, you can ask your teacher to repeat by saying **Repita, por favor** (*Repeat, please*). If you don't understand a recorded activity, you can simply replay it. To help you practice this strategy, you will listen to a short paragraph. Ask your professor to repeat it or replay the recording, and then summarize what you heard.

Ahora escucha

Now you are going to hear Laura and Cristina's conversation. Use **R** to indicate which adjectives describe Cristina's boyfriend, Rafael. Use **E** for adjectives that describe Laura's boyfriend, Esteban. Some adjectives will not be used.

____ rubio   ____ interesante
____ feo   ____ antipático
____ alto   ____ inteligente
____ trabajador   ____ moreno
____ un poco gordo   ____ viejo

Comprensión

Identificar

Which person would make each statement: Cristina or Laura?

	Cristina	Laura
1. Mi novio habla sólo de fútbol y de béisbol.	○	○
2. Tengo un novio muy interesante y simpático.	○	○
3. Mi novio es alto y moreno.	○	○
4. Mi novio trabaja mucho.	○	○
5. Mi amiga no tiene buena suerte con los muchachos.	○	○
6. El novio de mi amiga es un poco gordo, pero guapo.	○	○

¿Cierto o falso?

Indicate whether each sentence is **cierto** or **falso,** then correct the false statements.

	Cierto	Falso
1. Esteban es un chico interesante y simpático.	○	○
2. Laura tiene mala suerte con los chicos.	○	○
3. Rafael es muy interesante.	○	○
4. Laura y su novio hablan de muchas cosas.	○	○

recursos

R | STUDENT CD | Lección 3

Escuchar presents a recorded conversation or narration to develop your listening skills in Spanish. **Preparación** and **Estrategia** prepare you for the listening passage.

Ahora escucha tracks you through the passage, and **Comprensión** checks your understanding of what you heard.

PANORAMA-at-a-glance

Panorama
presents the countries of the Spanish-speaking world.

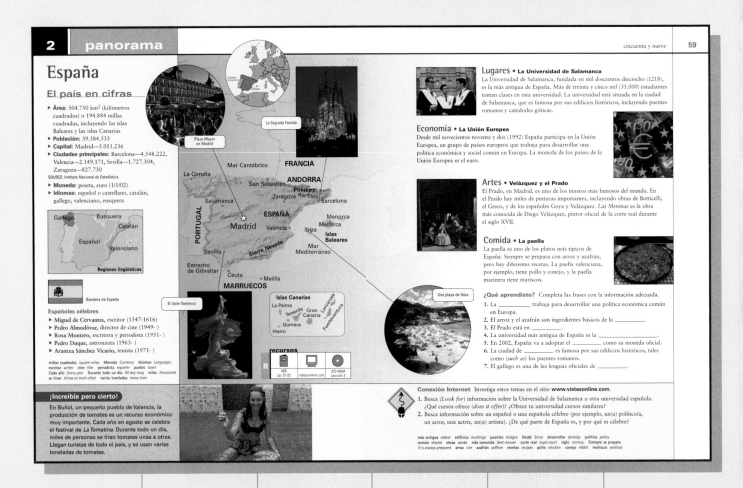

El país en cifras presents interesting, key facts about the featured country.

Maps point out major cities, rivers, and geographical features and situate the country in the context of its immediate surroundings and the world.

Readings A series of brief paragraphs explores facets of the country's culture such as history, places, fine arts, literature, and aspects of everyday life.

¡Increíble pero cierto! highlights an intriguing fact about the country or its people.

Conexión Internet offers Internet activities on the program's Web Site for additional avenues of discovery.

Vocabulario
summarizes all the active vocabulary of the lesson.

3 vocabulario

La familia

el/la abuelo/a	grandfather/grandmother
el/la cuñado/a	brother-in-law/sister-in-law
el/la esposo/a	husband; wife; spouse
la familia	family
el/la hermanastro/a	stepbrother/stepsister
el/la hermano/a	brother/sister
el/la hijastro/a	stepson/stepdaughter
el/la hijo/a	son/daughter
los hijos	children
la madrastra	stepmother
la madre	mother
el/la medio/a hermano/a	half-brother/half-sister
el/la nieto/a	grandson/granddaughter
la nuera	daughter-in-law
el padrastro	stepfather
el padre	father
los padres	parents
los parientes	relatives
el/la primo/a	cousin
el/la sobrino/a	nephew/niece
el/la suegro/a	father-in-law/mother-in-law
el/la tío/a	uncle/aunt
el yerno	son-in-law

Otras personas

el/la amigo/a	friend
la gente	people
el/la muchacho/a	boy/girl
el/la niño/a	child
el/la novio/a	boyfriend/girlfriend
la persona	person

Profesiones

el/la artista	artist
el/la doctor(a), el/la médico/a	doctor; physician
el/la ingeniero/a	engineer
el/la periodista	journalist
el/la programador(a)	computer programmer

Verbos

abrir	to open
aprender	to learn
asistir (a)	to attend
beber	to drink
comer	to eat
compartir	to share
comprender	to understand
correr	to run
creer (en)	to believe (in)
deber (+ *inf.*)	to have to; should
decidir	to decide
describir	to describe
escribir	to write
leer	to read
recibir	to receive
tener (*irreg.*)	to have
venir (*irreg.*)	to come
vivir	to live

Adjetivos

alto/a	tall
antipático/a	unpleasant
bajo/a	short (in height)
bonito/a	pretty
buen, bueno/a	good
delgado/a	thin; slender
difícil	difficult; hard
fácil	easy
feo/a	ugly
gordo/a	fat
gran, grande	big
guapo/a	handsome; good-looking
importante	important
inteligente	intelligent
interesante	interesting
joven	young
mal, malo/a	bad
mismo/a	same
moreno/a	brunet(te)
mucho/a	much; many; a lot of
pelirrojo/a	red-headed
pequeño/a	small
rubio/a	blond(e)
simpático/a	nice; likeable
tonto/a	silly; foolish
trabajador(a)	hard-working
viejo/a	old

Nacionalidades

alemán, alemana	German
canadiense	Canadian
chino/a	Chinese
ecuatoriano/a	Ecuadorian
español(a)	Spanish
estadounidense	from the United States
francés, francesa	French
inglés, inglesa	English
italiano/a	Italian
japonés, japonesa	Japanese
mexicano/a	Mexican
norteamericano/a	(North) American
puertorriqueño/a	Puerto Rican
ruso/a	Russian

Expresiones con tener

tener... años	to be... years old
tener (mucho) calor	to be (very) hot
tener (mucho) cuidado	to be (very) careful
tener (mucho) frío	to be (very) cold
tener ganas de + (*inf.*)	to feel like doing something
tener (mucha) hambre	to be (very) hungry
tener (mucho) miedo	to be (very) afraid/scared
tener (mucha) prisa	to be in a (big) hurry
tener que + (*inf.*)	to have to do something
tener razón	to be right
no tener razón	to be wrong
tener (mucha) sed	to be (very) thirsty
tener (mucho) sueño	to be (very) sleepy
tener (mucha) suerte	to be (very) lucky

Possessive adjectives	See page 75.
Expresiones útiles	See page 67.

recursos

| R | LCASS./CD Cass. 3/CD3 | LM p. 214 |

Video Program

Fully integrated with your textbook, the **PANORAMA** video contains fifteen episodes, one for each lesson of the text. The episodes present the adventures of four college students who are studying at the **Universidad de San Francisco** in Quito, Ecuador. They each decide to spend their vacation break on a bus tour of the Ecuadorian countryside with the ultimate goal of hiking up a volcano. The video, shot in various locations in Ecuador, tells their story and the story of don Francisco, the tour bus driver who accompanies them.

The **Fotonovela** section in each textbook lesson is actually an abbreviated version of the dramatic episode featured in the video. Therefore, each **Fotonovela** section can be done before you see the corresponding video episode, after it, or as a section that stands alone in its own right.

The Cast

Here are the main characters you will meet when you watch the video:

From México,
Alejandro (Álex)
Morales Paredes

From Ecuador,
Inés Ayala Loor

From Puerto Rico,
Javier Gómez
Lozano

From Spain,
María Teresa (Maite)
Fuentes de Alba

And, also from Ecuador,
don Francisco
Castillo Moreno

As you watch each video episode, you will first see a live segment in which the characters interact using vocabulary and grammar you are studying. As the video progresses, the live segments carefully combine new vocabulary and grammar with previously taught language. You will then see a **Resumen** section in which one of the main video characters recaps the live segment, emphasizing the grammar and vocabulary you are studying within the context of the episode's key events.

In addition, in most of the video episodes, there are brief pauses to allow the characters to reminisce about their home country. These flashbacks—montages of real-life images shot in Spain, México, Puerto Rico, and various parts of Ecuador—connect the theme of the video to everyday life in various parts of the Spanish-speaking world.

Student Ancillaries

Student Audio CD
Free-of-charge with each copy of **PANORAMA**, the Student Audio CD contains the audio recordings for the following materials in your textbook: the first **Práctica** exercise in each **Contextos** section (Lessons 1–15), the **Pronunciación** exercises (Lessons 1–9), and the **Estrategia** and **Ahora escucha** activities in each **Escuchar** section (Lessons 3, 6, 9, 12, and 15).

Student Activities Manual (SAM)
The Workbook, Lab Manual, and Video Manual are all contained in one convenient booklet.

Electronic Student Activities Manual (E-SAM)
The E-SAM is an online version of the printed SAM that includes the complete Lab Audio Program and automatic scoring. Special features allow tracking and analysis of your progress.

Lab Audio Program
The Lab Audio Program contains the recordings to be used in conjunction with the laboratory activities of the Student Activities Manual. It comes in three versions: 15 audiocassettes, 15 audio CDs, or 2 audio CD-ROMs that can be played in the CD-ROM drive of your computer.

Video Program
This text-specific video provides dramatic vignettes, cultural footage, and unique summary features that are fully integrated with the lessons in your textbook.

Interactive CD-ROMs
Free-of-charge with each copy of **PANORAMA,** these two dual-platform CD-ROMs provide useful reference tools and highly interactive, visually captivating multimedia materials and activities.

Video CD-ROM
Free-of-charge with each SAM, the Video CD-ROM offers you the complete Video Program with videoscripts, note-taking capabilities, and enhanced navigation tools.

Web Site (vistasonline.com)
The entire **vistasonline** Web site, including the special **PANORAMA** channel, supports you and your instructor with a wide range of online resources—cultural information and links, Internet activities, teaching suggestions, lesson plans, course syllabi, and more—that directly correlate to your textbook and go beyond it.

Instructor Ancillaries

In addition to the student ancillaries, all of which are available to the instructor, the following supplements are also available.

Instructor's Annotated Edition

The Instructor's Annotated Edition (IAE) provides a wealth of information designed to support classroom teaching and management. The same size as the student text, the IAE contains slightly reduced student text pages on which answers have been provided. Side and bottom panels offer resources for implementing and extending student text activities.

Instructor's Resource Manual

The Instructor's Resource Manual (IRM) offers materials that reinforce and expand on the lessons in the student text. The **Hojas de actividades** are reproducible charts, grids, and handouts correlated to the textbook's pair, small group, class circulation, and information gap activities. **Vocabulario adicional** sheets contain reproducible supplementary vocabulary lists related to the themes of selected textbook lessons. Additional materials, such as the answers to the **¡Inténtalo!** and **Práctica** exercises in the student textbook, are also included.

Testing Program with Audio CD

The Testing Program contains versions A and B of the following: a test for each of the textbook's 15 lessons, semester exams for Lessons 1–7 and 8–15, and quarter exams for Lessons 1–5, 6–10, and 11–15. All tests and exams include sections on listening comprehension, vocabulary, grammar, and communication. Listening scripts, answer keys, suggestions for oral tests, and an audio CD of the listening sections are also provided.

Computerized Test files CD-ROM for Windows® and Macintosh®

This CD-ROM contains the tests, exams, listening scripts, and answer keys of the printed Testing Program as Microsoft Word® files.

Tapescript/Videoscript

The Tapescript/Videoscript contains the complete written transcripts of the audio tracks of the Lab Audio Program, the Student Audio CD, and the Video Program.

Overhead Transparencies

The Overhead Transparencies consist of the maps of the countries of the Spanish-speaking world, the **Contextos** vocabulary drawings, and other selected illustrations from the student text.

acknowledgments

On behalf of its authors and editors, Vista Higher Learning expresses its sincere appreciation to the many college professors nationwide who contributed their ideas and suggestions to **VISTAS,** our flagship program from which **PANORAMA** is derived. We are grateful to the members of the Spanish-teaching community who participated in the focus groups held at the program's initial stages. We are also indebted to the teaching professionals who reviewed manuscript and class-tested materials. Their insights and detailed comments were invaluable to **VISTAS** and **PANORAMA** in their final published form.

VISTAS Focus Group Participants

Helga Barkemeyer
Montclair State University, NJ

Kathy P. Barton
Indiana University of Pennsylvania

Christine Bennett
College of Notre Dame, CA

Mara-Lee Bierman
Rockland County Community College, NY

Arthur Brady
Mercy College, NY

Elizabeth C. Calvera
Virginia Polytechnic Institute and State University

Richard P. Castillo
College of San Mateo, CA

William Chace
Hunter College, NY

Robert Chávez
West Valley College, CA

María Costa
California State University at Los Angeles

Frances Diccicco
Bucks County Community College, PA

Ronna Feit
Nassau County Community College, NY

Judith Gale
Pace University, NY

Javier Gallvan
Rancho Santiago College, CA

Susan C. Giráldez
University of the Pacific, CA

Jacquelyn W. Green
City College of San Francisco, CA

Josef Hellebrandt
Santa Clara University, CA

Librada Hernández
Los Angeles Valley College, CA

Steven Hess
Long Island University, NY

Juergen Kempff
University of California at Irvine

Denis Murphy
College of New Jersey

José Ramón Núñez
Long Beach City College, CA

Tyrone Parker
Catonsville Community College, MD

Bernardo García Pondavenes
Laney College, CA

Carmen I. Román
University of Maryland

Tony Ruiz
Gavilan Community College, CA

Monica F. Sasscer
Northern Virginia Community College

Lynn Sekelick
George Mason University, VA

Billy Bussell Thompson
Hofstra University, NY

Mercedes A. Thompson
El Camino College, CA

Elizabeth Turner
Dutchess County College, NY

J. Francisco Zermeño
Chabot College, CA

VISTAS Class Testing Participants

Pat Brady
Tidewater Community College, VA

José Carmona
Daytona Beach Community College, FL

Richard K. Curry
Texas A&M University, TX

Marcella Fierro
Mesa Community College, AZ

Carmen Forner
Community College of Southern Nevada, NV

Mari Carmen Gracia
Modesto Junior College, CA

Jorge Gracia
De Anza College, CA

Josef Hellebrandt
Santa Clara University, CA

Tania Hering
Alabama A&M University, AL

Shelly A. Moorman
University of St. Thomas, MN

Claire L. Reetz
Florida Community College at Jacksonville, FL

Monica Rivas
Mission College, CA

Joaquín Rodríguez-Barberá
Sam Houston State University, TX

Rosa Salinas Samelson
Palo Alto College, TX

José Alejandro Sandoval Erosa
Des Moines Area Community College, IA

Roy L. Tanner
Truman State University, MO

Evelyn F. Trujillo
Florida A&M University, FL

Fausto G. Vergara
Houston Community College, TX

VISTAS Reviewers

Luz María Álvarez
Johnson County Community
College, KS

Pilar B. Ara
Pasadena City College, CA

Enrica J. Ardemagni
Indiana University-Purdue University
Indianapolis

Barbara Ávila-Shah
State University of New York at Buffalo

Helga Barkemeyer
Montclair State University, NJ

Clementina L. Bassi
Santa Fe Community College, FL

Kevin E. Beard
Richland College, TX

Nuria Bustamante
Los Angeles Community College, CA

Jeremy W. Cole
University of Kansas

Richard K. Curry
Texas A & M University (10)

William O. Deaver, Jr.
Armstrong Atlantic State University, GA

Octavio Delasuaree
William Paterson College, NJ

Humberto Delgado-Jenkins
Georgia Perimeter College

John J. Deveny, Jr.
Oklahoma State University

Susana Durán
Gulf Coast Community College, FL

Ronna S. Feit
Nassau Community College, NY

José A. Feliciano-Butler
University of South Florida

Marcella Fierro
Mesa Community College, AZ

John L. Finan
William Rainey Harper College, IL

Melissa Anne Fitch
University of Arizona

Ken Fleak
University of South Carolina

Marianne Franco
Modesto College, CA

Kathleen Gallivan
West Virginia University

Barbara N. Gantt
Northern Arizona University

David Ross Gerling
Sam Houston State University, TX

Yolanda L. González
Valencia Community College, FL

Jorge Gracia
De Anza College, CA

Jacquelyn W. Green
City College of San Francisco, CA

Margaret B. Haas
Kent State University, OH

Ellen Haynes
University of Colorado

Eda Henao
Borough of Manhattan Community
College, NY

Steven Konopacki
Palm Beach Community College, FL

Roxana Levin
St. Petersburg Junior College, FL

María Helena López
Okaloosa-Walton Community
College, FL

Melina L. Lozano
Madison Area Technical College, WI

Nelson I. Madera
Tallahassee Community College, FL

Verónica Mejía Noguer
Chaffey College, CA

Alfonso Millet
Oakland Community Collge, MI

James E. Palmer
Tarrant County College
(Northeast Campus), TX

Monserrat Piera
Temple University, PA

Alcibiades Policarpo
Sam Houston State University, TX

Claire L. Reetz
Florida Community College
at Jacksonville

Duane Rhoades
University of Wyoming

Charisse Richarz
Blinn College, TX

Karen L. Robinson
University of Nebraska at Omaha

Joaquín Rodríguez-Barberá
Sam Houston State University, TX

Paul Roggendorff
The University of Kentucky

Carmen I. Román
University of Maryland

Dora Marrón Romero
Broward Community College
(North Campus), FL

S. Louise Roswell
Monroe Community College, NY

Rosa Salinas Samelson
Palo Alto College, TX

Vernon C. Smith
Rio Salado College, AZ

Jorge W. Suazo
Georgia Southern University

Roy L. Tanner
Truman State University, MO

Lourdes María Torres
De Paul University, IL

Ana Torres-Smith
Florida State University

Edith Valladares
Central Piedmont Community
College, NC

Mayela Vallejos-Ramírez
University of Nebraska-Lincoln

Fausto G. Vergara
Houston Community Collge, TX

Virginia Vigil, deceased
Austin Community College, TX

Nancy Virumbrales
Waubsonsee Community College, IL

Alicia J. von Lehe
Santa Fe Community College, FL

Gloria Yampey-Jörg
Houston Community College
Central Campus, TX

Gerald P. Young
Indian River Community College, FL

Additional Acknowledgments

We are especially grateful to our Senior Consulting Editor, Professor Elaine Horwitz, for her critical reading of the manuscript and her contributions to the student sidebars and the Instructor's Annotated Edition.

We also would like to express our gratitude to the entire staff of Vista Higher Learning—past and present—that worked on **VISTAS** and **PANORAMA**. Without the hard work and tenacity of these individuals, these programs would have never seen the light. In alphabetical order they are:

María Cinta Aparisi

Martin Beveridge

Ted Cantrell

Gustavo Cinci

Ianka De La Rosa

Linda Jurras

Holly Kersey

Suzanne Korschun

Pam Mishkin

Greg Moutafis

Eric Murphy

Peter O'Faherty

Stephen Pekich

Mark Porter

Sonny Regelman

Janet Spicer

Denise St. Jean

Daniella Tourgeman

Bruce Zimmerli

José Blanco

Mary Ann Dellinger

Philip Donley

María Isabel García

Hola, ¿qué tal?

1

Communicative Goals

You will learn how to:

- Greet people in Spanish
- Say goodbye
- Identify yourself and others
- Talk about the time of day

contextos

fotonovela

estructura

adelante

panorama

Hola, ¿qué tal?

Más vocabulario

Buenos días.	*Good morning.*
Buenas noches.	*Good evening.; Good night.*
Hasta la vista.	*See you later.*
Hasta pronto.	*See you soon.*
¿Cómo se llama usted?	*What's your name?*
Le presento a…	*(formal) I would like to introduce (name) to you.*
Te presento a…	*(familiar) I would like to introduce (name) to you.*
¿Cómo estás?	*How are you?*
No muy bien.	*Not very well.*
¿Qué pasa?	*What's happening?; What's going on?*
Por favor	*Please*
De nada.	*You're welcome.*
No hay de qué.	*You're welcome.*
Lo siento.	*I'm sorry.*
Muchas gracias.	*Thank you very much; Thanks a lot.*

Variación léxica

Items are presented for recognition purposes only.

Buenos días. ←→ Buenas.

De nada. ←→ A la orden.

Lo siento. ←→ Perdón.

¿Qué tal? ←→ ¿Qué hubo? *(Col.)*

ELENA Patricia, éste es el señor Perales.

PATRICIA Encantada.

SEÑOR PERALES Igualmente. ¿De dónde es usted, señorita?

PATRICIA Soy de México. ¿Y usted?

SEÑOR PERALES De Puerto Rico.

TOMÁS ¿Qué tal, Alberto?

ALBERTO Regular. ¿Y tú?

TOMÁS Bien. ¿Qué hay de nuevo?

ALBERTO Nada.

SEÑOR VARGAS Buenas tardes, señora Wong. ¿Cómo está usted?

SEÑORA WONG Muy bien, gracias. ¿Y usted, señor Vargas?

SEÑOR VARGAS Bien, gracias.

SEÑORA WONG Hasta mañana, señor Vargas. Saludos a la señora Vargas.

SEÑOR VARGAS Adiós.

recursos

BERTA Hasta luego, Tere.
TERESA Chau, Berta. Nos vemos mañana.

CARMEN Buenas tardes. Me llamo Carmen.
¿Cómo te llamas tú?
ANTONIO Buenas tardes. Me llamo Antonio.
Mucho gusto.
CARMEN El gusto es mío. ¿De dónde eres?
ANTONIO Soy de los Estados Unidos, de California.

Práctica

1 Escuchar Listen to each question or statement, then choose the correct response.

1. a. Muy bien, gracias.   b. Me llamo Graciela.
2. a. Lo siento.   b. Mucho gusto.
3. a. Soy de Puerto Rico.   b. No muy bien.
4. a. No hay de qué.   b. Regular.
5. a. Mucho gusto.   b. Hasta pronto.
6. a. Nada.   b. Igualmente.
7. a. Me llamo Guillermo Montero. b. Muy bien, gracias.
8. a. Buenas tardes. ¿Cómo estás? b. El gusto es mío.
9. a. Saludos a la Sra. Ramírez. b. Encantada.
10. a. Adiós.   b. Regular.

2 Escoger For each expression, write another word or phrase that expresses a similar idea.

> **modelo**
>
> ¿Cómo estás?
> ¿Qué tal?

1. De nada. _____
2. Encantado. _____
3. Adiós. _____
4. Te presento a Antonio. _____
5. ¿Cómo estás? _____
6. Mucho gusto. _____

3 Ordenar Work with a classmate to put this scrambled conversation in order. Then act it out.

—Muy bien, gracias. Soy Rosabel.
—Soy del Ecuador. ¿Y tú?
—Mucho gusto, Rosabel.
—Hola. Me llamo Carlos. ¿Cómo estás?
—Soy de Argentina.
—Igualmente. ¿De dónde eres, Carlos?

CARLOS _____
ROSABEL _____
CARLOS _____
ROSABEL _____
CARLOS _____
ROSABEL _____

4   **Completar**   Work with a partner to complete these exchanges.

> **modelo**
>
> **Estudiante 1:** ¿Cómo estás?
> **Estudiante 2:** _____Muy bien, gracias._____

1. **Persona 1:** _____
   Persona 2: Buenos días. ¿Qué tal?

2. **Persona 1:** _____
   Persona 2: Me llamo Carmen Sánchez.

3. **Persona 1:** _____
   Persona 2: De México.

4. **Persona 1:** Te presento a Marisol.
   Persona 2: _____

5. **Persona 1:** Gracias.
   Persona 2: _____

6. **Persona 1:** _____
   Persona 2: Regular

7. **Persona 1:** _____
   Persona 2: Nada.

8. **Persona 1:** ¡Hasta la vista!
   Persona 2: _____

5   **Cambiar**   Work with a partner and correct the second part of each conversation to make it logical.

> **modelo**
>
> **Estudiante 1:** ¿Qué tal?
> **Estudiante 2:** ~~No hay de qué.~~ Bien. ¿Y tú?

1. **Estudiante 1:** Hasta mañana, señora Ramírez. Saludos al señor Ramírez.
   Estudiante 2: *Muy bien, gracias.*

2. **Estudiante 1:** ¿Qué hay de nuevo, Alberto?
   Estudiante 2: *Sí, me llamo Alberto. ¿Cómo te llamas tú?*

3. **Estudiante 1:** Gracias, Tomás.
   Estudiante 2: *Regular. ¿Y tú?*

4. **Estudiante 1:** Miguel, ésta es la señorita Perales.
   Estudiante 2: *No hay de qué, señorita.*

5. **Estudiante 1:** ¿De dónde eres, Antonio?
   Estudiante 2: *Muy bien, gracias. ¿Y tú?*

6. **Estudiante 1:** ¿Cómo se llama usted?
   Estudiante 2: *El gusto es mío.*

7. **Estudiante 1:** ¿Qué pasa?
   Estudiante 2: *El gusto es mío.*

8. **Estudiante 1:** Buenas tardes, señor. ¿Cómo está usted?
   Estudiante 2: *Soy de Puerto Rico.*

¡LENGUA VIVA!

Titles of Respect
The titles **señor, señora,** and **señorita** are abbreviated **Sr., Sra.** and **Srta.** Note that these abbreviations are capitalized.

•••

There is no Spanish equivalent for the English title *Ms.;* women are addressed as **señora** or **señorita.**

Comunicación

6   **Diálogos**   With a partner, complete and act out these conversations.

Conversación 1   —Hola. Me llamo Teresa. ¿Cómo te llamas tú?

—_____

—Soy de Puerto Rico. ¿Y tú?

—_____

Conversación 2   —_____

—Muy bien. gracias. ¿Y usted, señora López?

—_____

—Hasta luego, señora. Saludos al señor López.

—_____

Conversación 3   —_____

—Regular. ¿Y tú?

—_____

—Nada.

7   **Conversaciones**   This is the first day of class. Write four conversations based on what the people in this scene would say.

8   **Situaciones**   Work with two classmates to write and act out these situations.

1. On your way out of class on the first day of school, you strike up a conversation with the two students who were sitting next to you. You find out each student's name and where he or she is from before you say goodbye and go to your next class.
2. At the next class you meet up with a friend and find out how he or she is doing. As you are talking, your friend Elena enters. Introduce her to your friend.
3. As you're leaving the bookstore, you meet your parents' friends Mrs. Sánchez and Mr. Rodríguez. You greet them and ask how each person is. As you say goodbye, you send greetings to Mrs. Rodríguez.
4. Make up and act out a real-life situation that you and your classmates can imagine yourselves in.

¡Todos a bordo!

Los cuatro estudiantes, don Francisco y la Sra. Ramos se reúnen (*meet*) en la universidad.

PERSONAJES

DON FRANCISCO

SRA. RAMOS

ÁLEX

JAVIER

INÉS

MAITE

1

SRA. RAMOS Buenos días, chicos. Yo soy Isabel Ramos de la agencia Ecuatur.

DON FRANCISCO Y yo soy don Francisco, el conductor.

2

SRA. RAMOS Bueno, ¿quién es María Teresa Fuentes de Alba?

MAITE ¡Soy yo!

SRA. RAMOS Ah, bien. Aquí tienes los documentos de viaje.

MAITE Gracias.

3

SRA. RAMOS ¿Javier Gómez Lozano?

JAVIER Aquí... soy yo.

6

JAVIER ¿Qué tal? Me llamo Javier.

ÁLEX Mucho gusto, Javier. Yo soy Álex. ¿De dónde eres?

JAVIER De Puerto Rico. ¿Y tú?

ÁLEX Yo soy de México.

7

DON FRANCISCO Bueno, chicos, ¡todos a bordo!

8

INÉS Con permiso.

recursos

| R | V/VCD-ROM Lección 1 | VM pp. 291-292 | ICD-ROM Lección 1 |

SRA. RAMOS Y tú eres Inés Ayala Loor, ¿verdad?

INÉS Sí, yo soy Inés.

SRA. RAMOS Y tú eres Alejandro Morales Paredes, ¿no?

ÁLEX Sí, señora.

INÉS Hola. Soy Inés.

MAITE Encantada. Yo me llamo Maite. ¿De dónde eres?

INÉS Soy del Ecuador, de Portoviejo. ¿Y tú?

MAITE De España. Soy de Madrid, la capital. Oye, ¿qué hora es?

INÉS Son las diez y tres minutos.

ÁLEX Perdón.

DON FRANCISCO ¿Y los otros?

SRA. RAMOS Son todos.

DON FRANCISCO Está bien.

Enfoque cultural Saludos y presentaciones

In the Hispanic world, it is customary for men and women to shake hands when meeting someone for the first time and when saying hello and goodbye to people they already know. Men greet female friends and family members with a brief kiss, and they greet males they know well with an **abrazo**—a quick hug and pat on the back. Women of all ages frequently greet good friends, family members, and other loved ones with a brief kiss on one or both cheeks.

Expresiones útiles

Identifying yourself and others

▶ **¿Cómo se llama usted?**
What's your name?

▷ **Yo soy don Francisco, el conductor.**
I'm don Francisco, the driver.

▶ **¿Cómo te llamas?**
What's your name?

▷ **Me llamo Javier.**
My name is Javier.

▶ **¿Quién es… ?**
Who is… ?

▷ **Aquí… soy yo.**
Here… that's me.

▶ **Tú eres… , ¿verdad?/¿no?**
You are …, right?/no?

▷ **Sí, señora.**
Yes, ma'am.

Saying what time it is

▶ **¿Qué hora es?**
What time is it?

▷ **Es la una.**
It's one o'clock.

▷ **Son las dos.**
It's two o'clock.

▷ **Son las diez y tres minutos.**
It's 10:03.

Saying "excuse me"

▷ **Con permiso.**
Pardon me; Excuse me.
(to request permission)

▷ **Perdón.**
Pardon me; Excuse me.
(to get someone's attention or to ask forgiveness)

When starting a trip

▷ **¡Todos a bordo!**
All aboard!

▷ **¡Buen viaje!**
Have a good trip!

Getting a friend's attention

▷ **Oye…**
Listen…

Reacciona a la fotonovela

1 **¿Cierto o falso?** Indicate if each statement is **cierto** or **falso**. Then correct the false statements.

	Cierto	Falso
1. Javier y Álex son pasajeros (*passengers*).	○	○
2. Javier Gómez Lozano es el conductor.	○	○
3. Inés Ayala Loor es de la agencia Ecuatur.	○	○
4. Inés es del Ecuador.	○	○
5. Maite es de España.	○	○
6. Javier es de Puerto Rico.	○	○
7. Álex es del Ecuador.	○	○

2 **Identificar** Indicate which person would make each statement. One name will be used twice.

1. Yo soy de México. ¿De dónde eres tú?
2. ¡Atención! ¡Todos a bordo!
3. ¿Yo? Soy de la capital de España.
4. Y yo soy del Ecuador.
5. ¿Qué hora es, Inés?
6. Yo soy de Puerto Rico. ¿Y tú?

ÁLEX   INÉS   MAITE

DON FRANCISCO   JAVIER

3 **Completar** Complete this slightly altered version of the conversation that Inés and Maite had.

INÉS   Hola. ¿Cómo te _____?

MAITE Me llamo Maite. ¿Y _____?

INÉS   Inés. Mucho _____.

MAITE _____ gusto es mío.

INÉS   ¿De _____ eres?

MAITE _____ España. ¿Y _____?

INÉS   Del _____.

4 **Conversar** Imagine that you are chatting with a traveler you just met at the airport. With a partner, prepare a conversation using these cues.

Estudiante 1	Estudiante 2
Say "good afternoon" to your partner and ask for his or her name.	Say hello and what your name is. Then ask what your partner's name is.
Say what your name is and that you are glad to meet your partner.	Say that the pleasure is yours.
Ask how your partner is.	Say that you're doing well, thank you.
Ask where your partner is from.	Say where you're from.
Wish your partner a good trip.	Say thank you and goodbye.

Pronunciación

The Spanish alphabet

The Spanish alphabet consisted of 30 letters until 1994, when the **Real Academia Española** (Royal Spanish Academy) removed **ch (che)** and **ll (elle)**. You may still see **ch** and **ll** listed as separate letters in reference works printed before 1994. Two Spanish letters, **ñ (eñe)** and **rr (erre)**, don't appear in the English alphabet. The letters **k (ka)** and **w (doble ve)** are used only in words of foreign origin.

Letra	Nombre(s)	Ejemplos	Letra	Nombre(s)	Ejemplos
a	a	adiós	ñ	eñe	mañana
b	be	bien, problema	o	o	once
c	ce	cosa, cero	p	pe	profesor
d	de	diario, nada	q	cu	qué
e	e	estudiante	r	ere	regular, señora
f	efe	foto	rr	erre	carro
g	ge	gracias, Gerardo, regular	s	ese	señor
h	hache	hola	t	te	tú
i	i	igualmente	u	u	usted
j	jota	Javier	v	ve	vista, nuevo
k	ka, ca	kilómetro	w	doble ve	*walkman*
l	ele	lápiz	x	equis	existir, México
m	eme	mapa	y	i griega, ye	yo
n	ene	nacionalidad	z	zeta, ceta	zona

El alfabeto Repeat the Spanish alphabet and example words after your instructor.

Práctica Spell these words aloud in Spanish.

1. nada
2. maleta
3. quince
4. muy
5. hombre
6. por favor
7. San Fernando
8. Estados Unidos
9. Puerto Rico
10. España
11. Javier
12. Ecuador
13. Maite
14. gracias
15. Nueva York

Refranes Read these sayings aloud after your instructor.

Ver es creer.[1]

En boca cerrada no entran moscas.[2]

1 *Seeing is believing.*
2 *Silence is golden.*

recursos

R	STUDENT CD Lección 1	LM p. 198	LCASS./CD Cass. 1/CD1	ICD-ROM Lección 1

1.1 Nouns and articles

Spanish nouns

ANTE TODO A noun is a word used to identify people, animals, places, things, or ideas. Unlike English, all Spanish nouns, even those that refer to non-living things, have gender; that is, they are considered either masculine or feminine. As in English, nouns in Spanish also have number, meaning that they are either singular or plural.

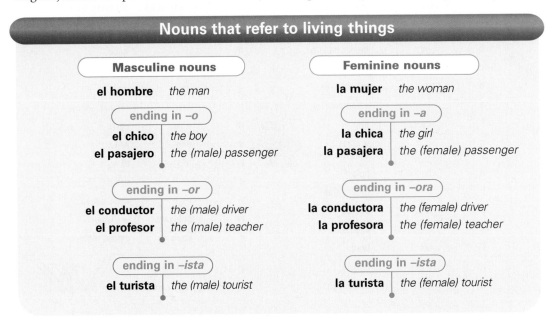

Nouns that refer to living things

Masculine nouns		Feminine nouns	
el hombre	*the man*	**la mujer**	*the woman*
ending in –o		*ending in –a*	
el chico	*the boy*	**la chica**	*the girl*
el pasajero	*the (male) passenger*	**la pasajera**	*the (female) passenger*
ending in –or		*ending in –ora*	
el conductor	*the (male) driver*	**la conductora**	*the (female) driver*
el profesor	*the (male) teacher*	**la profesora**	*the (female) teacher*
ending in –ista		*ending in –ista*	
el turista	*the (male) tourist*	**la turista**	*the (female) tourist*

▶ As shown above, nouns that refer to males, like **el hombre**, are generally masculine, while nouns that refer to females, like **la mujer**, are generally feminine.

▶ Many nouns that refer to male beings end in **–o** or **–or**. Their corresponding feminine forms end in **–a** and **–ora**, respectively.

el conductor

la profesora

▶ The masculine and feminine forms of nouns that end in **–ista** are the same, so gender is indicated by the article **el** (masculine) or **la** (feminine). Some other nouns have identical masculine and feminine forms.

el joven
the youth; the young man

la joven
the youth; the young woman

el estudiante
the (male) student

la estudiante
the (female) student

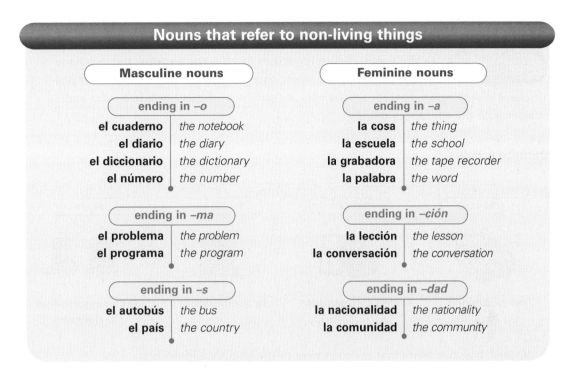

CONSEJOS

Since **la fotografía** is feminine, so is its short-ened form, **la foto,** even though it ends in **–o.**

▶ As shown above, certain noun endings are strongly associated with a specific gender, so you can use them to determine if a noun is masculine or feminine.

▶ Because the gender of nouns that refer to non-living things cannot be determined by fool-proof rules, you should memorize the gender of each noun you learn. It is helpful to memorize each noun with its corresponding article, **el** for masculine and **la** for feminine.

▶ Another reason to memorize the gender of every noun is that there are common exceptions to the rules of gender. For example, **el mapa** (*map*) and **el día** (*day*) end in **–a,** but are masculine. **La mano** (*hand*) ends in **-o,** but is feminine.

Plural of nouns

¡ATENCIÓN!

When a singular noun has an accent mark on the last syllable, the accent is dropped from the plural form:

la lección →
      las lecciones
el autobús →
      los autobuses

You will learn more about accent marks in Lesson 4, **Pronuncia-ción,** p. 101.

▶ In Spanish, nouns that end in a vowel form the plural by adding **–s.** Nouns that end in a consonant add **–es.** Nouns that end in **–z** change the **–z** to **–c,** then add **–es.**

el chic**o** ➤ los chic**os**   la nacionalida**d** ➤ las nacionalida**des**

el diari**o** ➤ los diari**os**   el país ➤ los país**es**

la palabr**a** ➤ las palabr**as**   el profesor ➤ los profeso**res**

el problem**a** ➤ los problem**as**   el lápi**z** ➤ los lápi**ces**

▶ You use the masculine plural form of the noun to refer to a group that includes both males and females.

1 pasajer**o** + 2 pasajer**as** = 3 pasajer**os**

2 chic**os** + 2 chic**as** = 4 chic**os**

Spanish articles

ANTE TODO   As you know, English often uses definite articles (**the**) and indefinite articles (**a, an**) before nouns. Spanish also has definite and indefinite articles. Unlike English, Spanish articles vary in form because they agree in gender and number with the nouns they modify.

Definite articles

| **el** diccionario | **los** diccionarios | **la** computadora | **las** computadoras |
| *the dictionary* | *the dictionaries* | *the computer* | *the computers* |

▶ Spanish has four forms that are equivalent to the English definite article *the*. You use definite articles to refer to specific nouns.

Indefinite articles

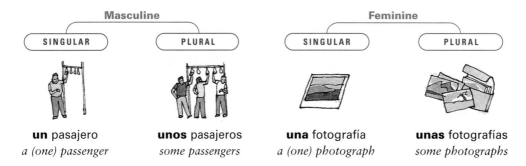

| **un** pasajero | **unos** pasajeros | **una** fotografía | **unas** fotografías |
| *a (one) passenger* | *some passengers* | *a (one) photograph* | *some photographs* |

▶ Spanish has four forms that are equivalent to the English indefinite article, which according to context may mean *a, an,* or *some.* You use indefinite articles to refer to unspecified persons or things.

¡INTÉNTALO!   Provide a definite article for each noun in the first column and an indefinite article for each noun in the second column. The first item has been done for you.

¿el, la, los o las?

1. ___la___ chica
2. _____ chico
3. _____ maleta
4. _____ cuadernos
5. _____ lápiz
6. _____ mujeres

¿un, una, unos o unas?

1. ___un___ autobús
2. _____ escuelas
3. _____ computadora
4. _____ hombres
5. _____ señora
6. _____ lápices

Práctica

1   **¿Singular o plural?** If the word is singular, make it plural. If it is plural, make it singular.

1. el número
2. un diario
3. la estudiante
4. el conductor
5. el país
6. las cosas
7. unos turistas
8. las nacionalidades

9. unas computadoras
10. los problemas
11. una fotografía
12. los profesores
13. unas señoritas
14. el hombre
15. la grabadora
16. la señora

2   **Identificar** For each drawing, provide the noun with its corresponding definite and indefinite articles.

> **modelo**
> las maletas, unas maletas

1. _____

2. _____

3. _____

4. _____

5. _____

6. _____

7. _____

8. _____

Comunicación

3

Charadas In groups, play a game of charades. Individually, think of two nouns for each charade, for example, a boy using a computer (**un chico; una computadora**). The first person to guess correctly acts out the next charade.

1.2 Numbers 0–30

Los números 0 a 30					
0	cero				
1	uno	**11**	once	**21**	veintiuno
2	dos	**12**	doce	**22**	veintidós
3	tres	**13**	trece	**23**	veintitrés
4	cuatro	**14**	catorce	**24**	veinticuatro
5	cinco	**15**	quince	**25**	veinticinco
6	seis	**16**	dieciséis	**26**	veintiséis
7	siete	**17**	diecisiete	**27**	veintisiete
8	ocho	**18**	dieciocho	**28**	veintiocho
9	nueve	**19**	diecinueve	**29**	veintinueve
10	diez	**20**	veinte	**30**	treinta

▶ The number **uno** (*one*) and numbers ending in **–uno**, such as **veintiuno**, have more than one form. Before masculine nouns, **uno** shortens to **un**. Before feminine nouns, **uno** changes to **una**.

> **un** hombre ➤ veinti**ún** hombres   **una** mujer ➤ veinti**una** mujeres

▶ To ask *how many* people or things there are, use **cuántos** before masculine nouns and **cuántas** before feminine nouns.

▶ The Spanish equivalent of both *there is* and *there are* is **hay**. Use **¿Hay...?** to ask *Is there...?* or *Are there...?* Use **no hay** to express *there is not* or *there are not*.

¡ATENCIÓN!

The numbers sixteen through nineteen can also be written as three words: **diez y seis, diez y siete**...

• • •

The forms **uno** and **veintiuno** are used when counting (**uno, dos, tres...veinte, veintiuno, veintidós...**) and when the number *follows* a noun, even if the noun is feminine: **la lección uno**.

—¿Cuántos estudiantes **hay**?
How many students are there?

—¿**Hay** chicas en la fotografía?
Are there girls in the picture?

—Hay tres estudiantes en la foto.
There are three students in the photo.

—**Hay** cuatro chicos, y **no hay** chicas.
There are four guys, and there are no girls.

¡INTÉNTALO! Provide the Spanish words for these numbers.

1. **7**	6. **15**	11. **30**	16. **10**
2. **16**	7. **21**	12. **4**	17. **2**
3. **29**	8. **9**	13. **12**	18. **5**
4. **1**	9. **23**	14. **28**	19. **22**
5. **0**	10. **11**	15. **14**	20. **13**

Práctica

1   **Contar**   Following the pattern, provide the missing numbers in Spanish.

1. 1, 3, 5, .., 29
2. 2, 4, 6, .., 30
3. 3, 6, 9, .., 30
4. 30, 28, 26, .., 0
5. 30, 25, 20, .., 0
6. 28, 24, 20, .., 0

2   **Resolver**   Solve these math problems with a partner.

modelo

> 5 + 3 =
> **Estudiante 1:** *cinco más tres son…*
> **Estudiante 2:** *ocho*

1. **2 + 15 =**
2. **20 – 1 =**
3. **5 + 7 =**
4. **18 + 12 =**
5. **3 + 22 =**

6. **6 – 3 =**
7. **11 + 12 =**
8. **7 – 7 =**
9. **8 + 5 =**
10. **23 – 14 =**

3   **¿Cuántos hay?**   How many persons or things are there in these drawings?

modelo

> Hay cuatro maletas.

1. _____
2. _____

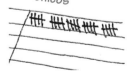
Chicos

3. _____
4. _____
5. _____

Chicas

6. _____
7. _____
8. _____

Comunicación

4

En la clase With a classmate, take turns asking and answering these questions about your classroom.

1. ¿Cuántos estudiantes hay?
2. ¿Cuántos profesores hay?
3. ¿Hay una computadora?
4. ¿Hay una maleta?
5. ¿Cuántos mapas hay?

6. ¿Cuántos lápices hay?
7. ¿Hay cuadernos?
8. ¿Cuántas grabadoras hay?
9. ¿Hay hombres?
10. ¿Cuántas mujeres hay?

5

Preguntas With a classmate, take turns asking and answering questions about the drawing. Talk about:

1. How many children there are
2. How many women there are
3. If there are some photographs
4. If there is a boy
5. How many notebooks there are

6. If there is a bus
7. If there are tourists
8. How many pencils there are
9. If there is a man
10. How many computers there are

1.3 Present tense of the verb **ser** (*to be*)

Subject pronouns

ANTE TODO In order to use verbs, you will need to learn about subject pronouns. A subject pronoun replaces the name or title of a person or thing and acts as the subject of a verb. In both Spanish and English, subject pronouns are divided into three groups: first person, second person, and third person.

Subject pronouns			
	SINGULAR		**PLURAL**
FIRST PERSON	**yo** / *I*	**nosotros** *we* (masculine)
		nosotras *we* (feminine)
SECOND PERSON	**tú** *you* (familiar)	**vosotros** *you* (masc., fam.)
	usted (Ud.) *you* (formal)	**vosotras** *you* (fem., fam.)
		ustedes (Uds.) *you* (form.)
THIRD PERSON	**él** *he*	**ellos** *they* (masc.)
	ella *she*	**ellas** *they* (fem.)

¡LENGUA VIVA!
In Latin America, **ustedes** is used as the plural for both **tú** and **usted**. In Spain, however, **vosotros** and **vosotras** are used as the plural of **tú**, and **ustedes** is used only as the plural of **usted**.

• • •

Usted and **ustedes** are abbreviated as **Ud.** and **Uds.**, or occasionally as **Vd.** and **Vds.**

▶ Spanish has two subject pronouns that mean *you* (singular). Use **tú** when addressing a friend, a family member, or a child you know well. Use **usted** to address a person with whom you have a formal or more distant relationship, such as a superior at work, a professor, or an older person.

▶ The masculine plural forms **nosotros**, **vosotros**, and **ellos** refer to a group of males or to a group of males and females. The feminine plural forms **nosotras**, **vosotras**, and **ellas** can refer only to groups made up exclusively of females.

nosotros, vosotros, ellos

nosotros, vosotros, ellos

nosotras, vosotras, ellas

▶ There is no Spanish equivalent of the English subject pronoun *it*. Generally it is not expressed in Spanish.

Es un problema.
It's a problem.

Es una computadora.
It's a computer.

The present tense of *ser*

ANTE TODO In **Contextos** and **Fotonovela**, you have already used several forms of the present tense of **ser** (*to be*) to identify yourself and others and to talk about where you and others are from. **Ser** is an irregular verb, which means its forms don't follow the regular patterns that most verbs follow. You need to memorize the forms, which appear in the following chart.

The present tense of *ser*		
ser *(to be)*		
SINGULAR FORMS		
yo	**soy**	*I am*
tú	**eres**	*you are* (fam.)
Ud./él/ella	**es**	*you are* (form.); *he/she is*
PLURAL FORMS		
nosotros/as	**somos**	*we are*
vosotros/as	**sois**	*you are* (fam.)
Uds./ellos/ellas	**son**	*you are* (form.); *they are*

Uses of *ser*

▶ To identify people and things

—¿Quién **es** él?
Who is he?

—**Es** Javier Gómez Lozano.
He's Javier Gómez Lozano.

—¿Qué **es**?
What is it?

—**Es** un mapa de España.
It's a map of Spain.

Es Maite.

Es un autobús.

▶ To express possession, with the preposition **de**

—¿**De** quién **es**?
Whose is it?

—**Es** el diario **de** Maite.
It's Maite's diary.

—**Es** la computadora **de** Álex.
It's Alex's computer.

—¿**De** quiénes **son**?
Whose are they?

—**Son** los lápices **de** la chica.
They are the girl's pencils.

—**Son** las maletas **del** chico.
They are the boy's suitcases.

¡ATENCIÓN!

When **de** is followed by the article **el**, the two combine to form the contraction **del**. **De** does *not* contract with **la**, **las**, or **los**.

• • •

There is no Spanish equivalent of the English construction [*noun*] +'s (*Maite's*). In its place, Spanish uses [*noun*] + **de** + [*owner*]: **el diario de Maite**.

▶ To express origin, with the preposition **de**

—¿**De** dónde **es** Javier?
Where is Javier from?

—Es **de** Puerto Rico.
He's from Puerto Rico.

—¿**De** dónde **es** Inés?
Where is Inés from?

—**Es del** Ecuador.
She's from Ecuador.

▶ To express profession or occupation

Don Francisco **es conductor**.
Don Francisco is a driver.

Yo **soy estudiante**.
I am a student.

¡INTÉNTALO! Provide the correct subject pronouns in Column 1, and the correct present forms of **ser** in Column 2. The first item has been done for you.

1. Gabriel ____él____ ____es____
2. Juan y yo (*m.*) _____ _____
3. Óscar y Flora _____ _____
4. Adriana _____ _____
5. las turistas _____ _____
6. el chico _____ _____
7. los conductores _____ _____
8. el señor y la señora Ruiz _____ _____

Práctica

1 **Pronombres** What subject pronouns would you use to a) talk to these people directly and b) talk about them?

1. una chica
2. el presidente de México
3. tres chicas y un chico
4. un estudiante
5. la señora Ochoa
6. dos profesoras

2 **Identidad y origen** With a partner, take turns asking and answering questions about these people: **¿Quién es?/¿Quiénes son?** and **¿De dónde es?/¿De dónde son?**

> **modelo**
> Ricky Martin
> **Estudiante 1:** ¿Quién es?　　　**Estudiante 1:** ¿De dónde es?
> **Estudiante 2:** Es Ricky Martin.　　**Estudiante 2:** Es de Puerto Rico.

1. Enrique Iglesias
2. Sammy Sosa
3. Rebecca Lobo y Robert Rodríguez
4. Laura Esquivel y Salma Hayek
5. Gabriel García Márquez
6. Antonio Banderas y Sergio García
7. Edward James Olmos y Jimmy Smits
8. Octavio Paz

3 **¿Qué es?** Ask your partner what each object is and to whom it belongs.

> **modelo**
> **Estudiante 1:** ¿Qué es?　　　**Estudiante 1:** ¿De quién es?
> **Estudiante 2:** Es una grabadora.　**Estudiante 2:** Es del profesor.

 1.　　 2.　　 3.　　 4.

Comunicación

4

En la oficina Using the items in the word bank, ask your partner questions about this businessman's office. Be imaginative in your responses.

¿Quién?	¿De dónde?	¿Cuántos?
¿Qué?	¿De quién?	¿Cuántas?

COMPUTADORAS DEL ECUADOR, S.A

5

¿Quién es? In small groups, take turns pretending to be individuals or groups from Spain, Mexico, Puerto Rico, Cuba, or the United States who are famous for their work in the following professions. The others will ask questions using the verb **ser** until they guess the identity of each person or group.

actor *actor*	deportista *athlete*	escritor(a) *writer*
actriz *actress*	cantante *singer*	músico/a *musician*

modelo

Estudiante 3: ¿Eres de los Estados Unidos?
Estudiante 1: Sí.
Estudiante 2: ¿Eres hombre?
Estudiante 1: No. Soy mujer.
Estudiante 3: ¿Eres escritora?
Estudiante 1: No. Soy actriz.
Estudiante 2: ¿Eres Rita Moreno?
Estudiante 1: ¡Sí! ¡Sí!

NOTA CULTURAL

Rita Moreno, a Puerto Rican actress, is the only female performer to have won all four prestigious entertainment awards: the Oscar, the Emmy, the Grammy, and the Tony. She played Anita in *West Side Story,* a role for which she won an Oscar.

1.4 Telling time

 In both English and Spanish, the verb *to be* (**ser**) and numbers are used to tell time.

▶ To ask what time it is, use **¿Qué hora es?** When telling time, use **es + la** with **una** and **son + las** with all other hours.

Es la una. **Son las** dos. **Son las** seis.

▶ As in English, you express time from the hour to the half-hour in Spanish by adding minutes.

Son las cuatro **y cinco**. Son las once **y veinte**.

▶ You may use either **y cuarto** or **y quince** to express fifteen minutes or quarter past the hour. For thirty minutes or half past the hour, you may use either **y media** or **y treinta**.

Es la una **y cuarto**. Son las nueve **y quince**.

Son las doce **y media**. Son las siete **y treinta**.

▶ You express time from the half-hour to the hour in Spanish by subtracting minutes or a portion of an hour from the next hour.

Es la una menos **cuarto.**

Son las tres menos **quince.**

Son las ocho **menos veinte.**

Son las tres **menos diez.**

▶ Here are some useful words and phrases associated with telling time:

¿A qué hora es la clase de biología?
(At) what time is biology class?

Son las ocho **en punto.**
It's 8 o'clock on the dot/sharp.

Es **el mediodía.**
It's noon.

Es **la medianoche.**
It's midnight.

La clase es **a la una/a las dos.**
The class is at 1 o'clock/at two o'clock.

Son las nueve **de la mañana.**
It's 9 a.m. (in the morning).

Son las cuatro y cuarto **de la tarde.**
It's 4:15 p.m. (in the afternoon).

Son las diez y media **de la noche.**
It's 10:30 p.m. (at night).

Oye, ¿qué hora es?

Son las diez y tres minutos.

Oiga, ¿qué hora es?

Son las diez.

¡INTÉNTALO! Practice telling time by completing these sentences. The first item has been done for you.

1. (1:00 a.m.) Es la _____ una _____ de la mañana.
2. (2:50 a.m.) Son las tres _____ diez de la mañana.
3. (4:15 p.m.) Son las cuatro y _____ de la tarde.
4. (8:30 p.m.) Son las ocho y _____ de la noche.
5. (9:15 a.m.) Son las nueve y quince de la _____.
6. (12:00 p.m.) Es el _____.
7. (6:00 a.m.) Son las seis de la _____.
8. (4:05 p.m.) Son las cuatro y cinco de la _____.
9. (12:00 a.m.) Es la _____.
10. (3:45 a.m.) Son las cuatro menos _____ de la mañana.
11. (9:55 p.m.) Son las _____ menos cinco de la noche.

Práctica

1   **Ordenar**   Put these times in order, from the earliest to the latest.

  a. Son las dos de la tarde.   d. Son las seis menos cuarto de la tarde.

  b. Son las once de la mañana.   e. Son las dos menos diez de la tarde.

  c. Son las siete y media de la noche.   f. Son las ocho y veintidós de la mañana.

2   **¿Qué hora es?**   Give the times shown on each clock or watch.

> **modelo**
>
> Son las cuatro y cuarto/quince de la tarde.

1. _____   2. _____   3. _____   4. _____   5. _____

6. _____   7. _____   8. _____   9. _____   10. _____

3   **¿A qué hora?**   Ask your partner at what time these events take place. Your partner will answer according to the cues provided.

> **modelo**
>
> la clase de matemáticas (2:30 p.m.)
>
> **Estudiante 1:** ¿A qué hora es la clase de matemáticas?
>
> **Estudiante 2:** Es a las dos y media de la tarde.

1. el programa *Las cuatro amigas* (*11:30 a.m.*)
2. el drama *La casa de Bernarda Alba* (*7:00 p.m.*)
3. el programa *Las computadoras* (*8:30 a.m.*)
4. la clase de español (*10:30 a.m.*)
5. la clase de biología (*9:40 a.m. sharp*)
6. la clase de historia (*10:50 a.m.*)
7. el partido (*game*) de béisbol (*5:15 p.m.*)
8. el partido de tenis (*12:45 p.m. sharp*)
9. el partido de baloncesto (*basketball*) (*7:45 p.m.*)
10. la fiesta (*8:30 p.m.*)

Comunicación

4

En la televisión With a partner, take turns asking and answering questions about these television listings.

> **modelo**
>
> **Estudiante 1:** ¿A qué hora es *Las computadoras?*
> **Estudiante 2:** Es a las nueve en punto de la noche.

TV Hoy – Programación

11:00 am Telenovela: *Cuatro viajeros y un autobús*

12:00 pm Película: *El cóndor* (drama)

2:00 pm Telenovela: *Dos mujeres y dos hombres*

3:00 pm Programa juvenil: *Fiesta*

3.30 pm Telenovela: *¡Sí, sí, sí!*

4:00 pm Telenovela: *El diario de la Sra. González*

5:00 pm Telenovela: *Tres mujeres*

6:00 pm Noticias

7:00 pm Especial musical: *Música folklórica de México*

7:30 pm La naturaleza: *Jardín secreto*

8:00 pm Noticiero: *Veinticuatro horas*

9:00 pm Documental: *Las computadoras*

5

Preguntas With a partner, answer these questions based on your own knowledge.

1. Son las tres de la tarde en Nueva York. ¿Qué hora es en Los Ángeles?

2. Son las ocho y media en Chicago. ¿Qué hora es en Miami?

3. Son las dos menos cinco en San Francisco. ¿Qué hora es en San Antonio?

4. ¿A qué hora es el programa *60 Minutes*?

5. ¿A qué hora es el programa *Today Show*?

Síntesis

6

Situación With two classmates, play the roles of university journalism students and a visiting literature professor (**profesor(a) de literatura**) from Venezuela whom they are interviewing. The students arrive early for the interview, introduce themselves, and find out about each other. When the professor arrives, the students ask what his/her name is, where he/she is from, what time his/her literature class is, and how many students are in the class. The professor asks a few questions to find out about the students. The professor ends the interview by looking at the clock and saying that the class begins in five minutes. The students say thank you and goodbye.

recursos

R	WB pp. 3-8	LM p. 199-202	LCASS./CD Cass. 1/CD1	ICD-ROM Lección 1

Lectura
Antes de leer

Estrategia
Recognizing cognates

As you learned earlier in this lesson, cognates are words that share similar meanings and spellings in two or more languages. When reading in Spanish, it's helpful to look for cognates and use them to guess the meaning of what you're reading. But watch out for false cognates. For example, **librería** means *bookstore,* not *library,* and **embarazada** means *pregnant,* not *embarrassed.* Look at this list of Spanish words, paying special attention to prefixes and suffixes. Can you guess the meaning of each word?

importante	oportunidad
farmacia	cultura
inteligente	activo
dentista	sociología
decisión	espectacular
televisión	restaurante
médico	policía

Examinar el texto
Glance quickly at the reading selection and guess what type of document it is. Explain your answer.

Cognados
Read the document and make a list of the cognates you find. Guess their English equivalents, then compare your answers with those of a classmate.

Teléfonos importantes

Policía

Médico

Dentista

Pediatra

Farmacia

Banco Central

Aerolíneas Nacionales

Cine Metro

Hora/Temperatura

Profesora Salgado
(universidad)

Felipe (oficina)

Gimnasio Gente Activa

Restaurante Roma

Supermercado Famoso

Librería El Inteligente

54.11.11

54.36.92

54.87.11

53.14.57

54.03.06

54.90.83

54.87.40

53.45.96

53.24.81

54.15.33

54.84.99

54.36.04

53.75.44

54.77.23

54.66.04

Después de leer

¿Cierto o falso?

Indicate whether each statement is **cierto** or **falso**. Then correct the false statements.

1. There is a child in this household.
   _____
   _____

2. To renew a prescription you would dial 54.90.83.
   _____
   _____

3. If you wanted the exact time and information about weather you'd dial 53.24.81.
   _____
   _____

4. Felipe probably works outdoors.
   _____
   _____

5. This household probably orders a lot of Chinese food.
   _____
   _____

6. If you had a toothache, you would dial 54.87.11.
   _____
   _____

7. You would dial 54.87.40 to make a flight reservation.
   _____
   _____

8. To find out if a best-selling book was in stock, you would dial 54.66.04.
   _____
   _____

9. If you needed information about aerobics classes, you would dial 54.15.33.
   _____
   _____

10. You would call **Cine Metro** to find out what time a movie starts.
    _____
    _____

Hacer una lista

Make your own list of phone numbers like the one shown in this reading. Include emergency phone numbers as well as frequently called numbers. Use as many cognates from the reading as you can.

Estados Unidos
Influencia de la cultura hispánica

El país en cifras

▶ **Población de origen hispano:** 35.306.000

▶ **País de origen de hispanos en EE.UU.:**

- 19,8% otros
- 3,5% Cuba
- 9,6% Puerto Rico
- 8,6% Centroamérica y Sudamérica
- 58,5% México

SOURCE: U.S. Census Bureau

▶ **Estados con la mayor población hispana:**

- **California** 10.967.000
- **Texas** 6.670.000
- **Nueva York** 2.868.000
- **Florida** 2.683.000
- **Illinois** 1.530.000

SOURCE: U.S. Census Bureau

▶ **Ciudades de mayor población hispana:**

S. Antonio	N.Y.C.	L.A.	Chicago	Houston
0.65	2.2	1.7	0.75	0.73

Figures in millions

▶ **Lugares con nombres españoles:**

Nombre	Significado
Nevada	tormenta de nieve (*snowstorm*)
Colorado	de color rojo (*of reddish color*)
Montana	montaña (*mountain*)
Florida	tierra de flores (*land of flowers*)
Cape Canaveral	cañaveral (*sugar-cane plantation*)
El Paso	paso (*pass*)
Las Vegas	vega (*fertile plain*)

en cifras *in figures* mayor *biggest* van a ser *are going to be*
más grande *largest* se duplicará *will double*

Mission District, en San Francisco

AK   HI

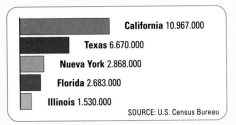
Tito Puente (1925-2000), músico

CANADÁ

San Francisco · Chicago · Ciudad de Nueva York · Los Ángeles · Las Vegas · San Diego · Washington DC · San Antonio · Miami · Océano Atlántico · Golfo de México · MÉXICO · Mar Caribe

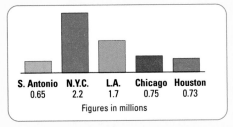
El Álamo, en San Antonio, Texas

recursos

R | WB pp. 9-10 | vistasonline.com | ICD-ROM Lección 1

¡Increíble pero cierto!

Se estima que en el año 2015 los hispanos van a ser el grupo minoritario más grande de los Estados Unidos. En 10 años el número de hispanos se duplicará en los estados de California, Texas, Nueva York, Florida e Illinois.

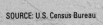

SOURCE: U.S. Census Bureau

Comida • **La comida mexicana**

La comida mexicana es muy popular en los Estados Unidos. Los tacos, las enchiladas, los burritos y los frijoles, entre otros, son platos mexicanos que frecuentemente forman parte de las comidas de muchos norteamericanos. También son populares las variaciones estadounidenses de la comida mexicana... el tex-mex y el cali-mex.

Lugares • **La Pequeña Habana**

Una de las joyas de la Florida es la Pequeña Habana, un barrio de Miami donde viven muchos cubanoamericanos. En todas sus calles se encuentran las costumbres de la cultura cubana, los aromas y sabores de su comida y la música salsa. La Pequeña Habana es un verdadero trozo de Cuba en los Estados Unidos.

Costumbres • **Desfile puertorriqueño**

Cada junio desde mil novecientos cincuenta y uno (1951), mucha gente de origen puertorriqueño celebra su orgullo latino con un desfile en la ciudad de Nueva York. El desfile es un gran espectáculo con carrozas y música salsa, flamenco y hip-hop. Muchos espectadores participan llevando la bandera de Puerto Rico en su ropa o pintándose los colores de la bandera en la cara.

¿Qué aprendiste? Completa las frases con la información adecuada (*appropriate*).

1. Hay _____ personas de origen hispano en los Estados Unidos.
2. Los cuatro estados con las poblaciones hispanas más grandes son (en orden) _____, Texas, _____ y Florida.

3. Los burritos y las enchiladas son platos _____.
4. El tex-mex y el _____ son variaciones de la comida mexicana.
5. La Pequeña _____ es un barrio de Miami.
6. En Miami hay muchas personas de origen _____.
7. Cada junio se celebra en Nueva York un gran desfile para personas de origen _____.
8. El estado de _____ tiene una gran población puertorriqueña.

Una partida de ajedrez en un parque de Miami

Conexión Internet Investiga estos temas en el sitio **www.vistasonline.com**.

1. Haz (*Make*) una lista de seis hispanoamericanos célebres: dos mexicoamericanos, dos puertorriqueños y dos cubanoamericanos. Explica (*Explain*) por qué (*why*) son célebres.
2. Escoge (*Choose*) seis lugares en los Estados Unidos con nombres hispanos y busca información sobre el origen y el significado (*meaning*) de cada nombre.

Comida *Food* entre otros *among others* platos *dishes* También *Also* Lugares *Places* La Pequeña Habana *Little Havana* joyas *jewels* barrio *neighborhood* viven *live* todas sus calles *all of its streets* se encuentran *are found* costumbres *customs* sabores *flavors* verdadero trozo *true slice* Desfile *Parade* Cada junio desde *Each June since* gente *people* orgullo *pride* ciudad *city* con carrozas *with floats* llevando *wearing* bandera *flag* ropa *clothing* pintándose *painting* cara *face*

Saludos

Hola.	*Hello; Hi.*
Buenos días.	*Good morning.*
Buenas tardes.	*Good afternoon.*
Buenas noches.	*Good evening; Good night.*

Despedidas

Adiós.	*Good-bye.*
Nos vemos.	*See you.*
Hasta luego.	*See you later.*
Hasta la vista.	*See you later.*
Hasta pronto.	*See you soon.*
Hasta mañana.	*See you tomorrow.*
Saludos a...	*Greetings to …*
Chau.	*Bye.*

¿Cómo está?

¿Cómo está usted?	*How are you?* (form.)
¿Cómo estás?	*How are you?* (fam.)
¿Qué hay de nuevo?	*What's new?*
¿Qué pasa?	*What's happening?; What's going on?*
¿Qué tal?	*How are you?; How is it going?*
(Muy) bien, gracias.	*(Very) well, thanks.*
Nada.	*Nothing.*
No muy bien.	*Not very well.*
Regular.	*So so; OK.*

¿A qué hora?

¿A qué hora...?	*(At) what time …?*
¿Qué hora es?	*What time is it?*
Es la una.	*It's one o'clock.*
Son las...	*It's … o'clock.*
la medianoche	*midnight*
el mediodía	*noon*
de la mañana	*in the morning; A.M.*
de la noche	*in the evening; at night; P.M.*
de la tarde	*in the afternoon; in the early evening; P.M.*
en punto	*on the dot; exactly; sharp*
menos cuarto/ menos quince	*quarter to*
y cuarto/y quince	*quarter after*
y media/y treinta	*thirty (minutes past the hour)*

Presentaciones

¿Cómo se llama usted?	*What's your name?* (form.)
¿Cómo te llamas (tú)?	*What's your name?* (fam.)
Me llamo...	*My name is …*
¿Y tú?	*And you?* (fam.)
¿Y Ud.?	*And you?* (form.)
Mucho gusto.	*Pleased to meet you.*
El gusto es mío.	*The pleasure is mine.*
Encantado/a.	*Delighted; Pleased to meet you.*
Igualmente.	*Likewise.*
Éste/ésta es...	*This is …*
Le presento a...	*I would like to introduce you to… (form.)*
Te presento a...	*I would like to introduce to you… (fam.)*

Expresiones de cortesía

Con permiso.	*Pardon me; Excuse me.*
De nada.	*You're welcome.*
Lo siento.	*I'm sorry.*
(Muchas) gracias.	*Thank you (very much); Thanks (a lot).*
No hay de qué.	*You're welcome.*
Perdón.	*Pardon me; Excuse me.*

Títulos

señor (Sr.)	*Mr.; sir*
señora (Sra.)	*Mrs.; ma'am*
señorita (Srta.)	*Miss*

Países

Ecuador	*Ecuador*
España	*Spain*
Estados Unidos (EE.UU.; E.U.)	*United States*
México	*Mexico*
Puerto Rico	*Puerto Rico*

Verbos

ser	*to be*

Sustantivos

el autobús	*bus*
la capital	*capital city*
la chica	*girl*
el chico	*boy*
la computadora	*computer*
la comunidad	*community*
el/la conductor(a)	*chauffeur; driver*
la conversación	*conversation*
la cosa	*thing*
el cuaderno	*notebook*
el día	*day*
el diario	*diary*
el diccionario	*dictionary*
la escuela	*school*
el/la estudiante	*student*
la foto(grafía)	*photograph*
la grabadora	*tape recorder*
el hombre	*man*
el/la joven	*youth; young person*
el lápiz	*pencil*
la lección	*lesson*
la maleta	*suitcase*
la mano	*hand*
el mapa	*map*
la mujer	*woman*
la nacionalidad	*nationality*
el número	*number*
el país	*country*
la palabra	*word*
el/la pasajero(a)	*passenger*
el problema	*problem*
el/la profesor(a)	*teacher*
el programa	*program*
el/la turista	*tourist*

¿De dónde es?

¿De dónde es Ud.?	*Where are you from?* (form.)
¿De dónde eres?	*Where are you from?* (fam.)
Soy de...	*I'm from …*

Palabras adicionales

¿cuánto(s)/a(s)?	*how much/many?*
¿de quién...?	*whose …?* (sing.)
¿de quiénes...?	*whose …?* (plural)
(no) hay	*there is (not); there are (not)*

En la universidad

2

Communicative Goals

You will learn how to:

- Talk about your classes and school life
- Discuss everyday activities
- Ask questions in Spanish
- Describe the location of people and things

En la universidad

Más vocabulario

la biblioteca	library
la cafetería	cafeteria
el estadio	stadium
la librería	bookstore
la residencia estudiantil	dormitory
la universidad	university
la clase	class
el/la compañero/a de clase	classmate
el/la compañero/a de cuarto	roommate
el examen	test; exam
el horario	schedule
el laboratorio	laboratory
la prueba	test; quiz
el semestre	semester
la tarea	homework
el trimestre	trimester; quarter
los cursos	courses
la administración de empresas	business administration
el arte	art
la biología	biology
las ciencias	sciences
la computación	computer science
la contabilidad	accounting
la economía	economics
el español	Spanish
la física	physics
la geografía	geography

Variación léxica

pluma ⟷ bolígrafo
pizarra ⟷ tablero (*Col.*)
tarea ⟷ asignación (*P. Rico*);
        deberes (*Esp., Arg.*)

el reloj

la ventana

la puerta

la profesora

el estudiante

la mesa

el libro

la mochila

la pluma

recursos

STUDENT CD Lección 2	WB pp. 11-12	LM p. 203	LCASS./CD Cass. 2/CD2	ICD-ROM Lección 2

Práctica

el mapa

la pizarra

la historia	*history*
las humanidades	*humanities*
el inglés	*English*
las lenguas extranjeras	*foreign languages*
la literatura	*literature*
las matemáticas	*mathematics*
las materias	*courses*
el periodismo	*journalism*
la psicología	*psychology*
la química	*chemistry*
la sociología	*sociology*

el papel

el borrador

la tiza

el escritorio

la estudiante

la silla

1

Escuchar Listen to Professor Morales talk about her Spanish classroom, then check the items she mentions.

1. puerta ❑
2. ventanas ❑
3. pizarra ❑
4. borrador ❑
5. tiza ❑
6. escritorios ❑
7. sillas ❑
8. libros ❑
9. plumas ❑
10. mochilas ❑
11. papel ❑
12. reloj ❑

2

Emparejar Match each question with its most logical response. **¡Ojo!** (*Careful!*) Two of the responses will not be used.

1. ¿Qué clase es?
2. ¿Quiénes son?
3. ¿Quién es?
4. ¿De dónde es?
5. ¿A qué hora es la clase de inglés?
6. ¿Cuántos estudiantes hay?

a. Hay veinticinco.
b. Es un reloj.
c. Es del Perú.
d. Es la clase de química.
e. Es el señor Bastos.
f. Mucho gusto.
g. Es a las nueve en punto.
h. Son los profesores.

3

Identificar Identify the word that does not fit in each group.

1. examen • grabadora • tarea • prueba
2. economía • matemáticas • biblioteca • contabilidad
3. pizarra • tiza • borrador • librería
4. lápiz • cafetería • papel • cuaderno
5. veinte • diez • pluma • treinta
6. conductor • laboratorio • autobús • pasajero
7. humanidades • mesa • ciencias • lenguas extranjeras
8. lápiz • qué • cómo • dónde

4

¿Qué clase es? Use the clues to name the subject matter of each class.

> **modelo**
> los elementos, los átomos
> *Es la clase de química.*

1. Abraham Lincoln, Winston Churchill
2. Picasso, Leonardo da Vinci
3. Freud, Jung
4. África, el océano Pacífico
5. la cultura de España, verbos
6. Hemingway, Shakespeare
7. geometría, trigonometría
8. las plantas, los animales

Los días de la semana

¿Qué día es hoy?

Hoy es martes.

¿Cuándo es el examen?

Es el viernes.

septiembre

lunes	martes	miércoles	jueves	viernes	sábado	domingo
	1	2	3	4	5	6
7	8	9	10			

¡LENGUA VIVA!

Monday is considered the first day of the week in Spanish-speaking countries.

• • •

The days of the week are never capitalized in Spanish.

---

5   **¿Qué día es hoy?**   Complete each statement with the correct day of the week.

1. Hoy es martes. Mañana es _____. Ayer fue _____.
2. Ayer fue sábado. Mañana es _____. Hoy es _____.
3. Mañana es viernes. Hoy es _____. Ayer fue _____.
4. Ayer fue domingo. Hoy es _____. Mañana es _____.
5. Hoy es jueves. Ayer fue _____. Mañana es _____.
6. Mañana es lunes. Hoy es _____. Ayer fue _____.

AYUDA

Ayer fue
yesterday was

---

6   **Analogías**   Use these words to complete the analogies. Some words will not be used.

arte	chau	estudiante	profesor
biblioteca	día	mujer	reloj
catorce	martes	pizarra	domingo

1. maleta ⟷ pasajero ⊜ mochila ⟷ _____
2. chico ⟷ chica ⊜ hombre ⟷ _____
3. pluma ⟷ papel ⊜ tiza ⟷ _____
4. inglés ⟷ lengua ⊜ miércoles ⟷ _____
5. papel ⟷ cuaderno ⊜ libro ⟷ _____
6. quince ⟷ dieciséis ⊜ lunes ⟷ _____
7. ¡Buen viaje! ⟷ Gracias. ⊜ ¡Nos vemos! ⟷ _____
8. autobús ⟷ conductor ⊜ clase ⟷ _____
9. EE.UU. ⟷ mapa ⊜ hora ⟷ _____
10. veinte ⟷ veintitrés ⊜ jueves ⟷ _____

Comunicación

7 **Horario** Create your own class schedule in Spanish. Then discuss it with a classmate.

Estudiante		Manuel Domínguez H.			Semestre Nº 1	
lunes	martes	miércoles	jueves	viernes	sábado	domingo
8:30 biología Profesora Morales	**9:45** historia – península Ibérica Profesora Cortés	**8:30** biología	**9:45** historia	**8:30** biología		
10:15 inglés Profesor Herrera	**10:15**	**10:15** inglés		**10:15** inglés		
3:30 laboratorio (biología)	**12:45** psicología Profesor Herrera	**12:45** **1:15** arte Profesor Pérez	**12:45** psicología	**1:15** arte		
4:30 discusión (historia) biblioteca						

modelo

Estudiante 1: ¿Cuándo tomas biología?

Estudiante 2: Los lunes, miércoles y viernes tomo (*I take*) biología a las ocho y media.

Estudiante 1: ¿Quién es el/la profesor(a)?

Estudiante 2: Es la profesora Morales.

8 **Dibujar** With a classmate, draw and label your campus and classroom. Then take turns describing your illustrations.

modelo

En esta (*this*) universidad hay diez residencias estudiantiles.
En esta clase hay ocho ventanas.

9 **Entrevistas** Using these interrogatives, create ten original questions you will use to interview two classmates. Then share the results of your interviews with the class.

¿A qué hora?	¿Cuándo?	¿De dónde?	¿Quién(es)?
¿Cómo?	¿Cuántos/as?	¿Qué?	

10 **Nuevos amigos** During the first week of class, you meet a new student in the cafeteria. Greet your new acquaintance, find out about him or her, and compare class schedules before saying goodbye.

¿Qué clases tomas?

Maite, Inés, Javier y Álex hablan de las clases.

PERSONAJES

MAITE

INÉS

ÁLEX

JAVIER

ÁLEX Hola, Ricardo...
Aquí estamos en la Mitad del Mundo. ¿Qué tal las clases en la UNAM?

MAITE Es exactamente como las fotos en los libros de geografía.

INÉS ¡Sí! ¿También tomas tú geografía?

MAITE Yo no. Yo tomo inglés y literatura. También tomo una clase de periodismo.

MAITE Muy buenos días. María Teresa Fuentes, de Radio Andina FM 93. Hoy estoy con estudiantes de la Universidad San Francisco de Quito.
¡A ver! La señorita que está cerca de la ventana... ¿Cómo te llamas y de dónde eres?

MAITE ¿En qué clase hay más chicos?

INÉS Bueno, eh... en la clase de historia.

MAITE ¿Y más chicas?

INÉS En la de sociología hay más chicas, casi un ochenta y cinco por ciento.

MAITE Y tú, joven, ¿cómo te llamas y de dónde eres?

JAVIER Me llamo Javier Gómez y soy de San Juan, Puerto Rico.

MAITE ¿Tomas muchas clases este semestre?

JAVIER Sí, tomo tres: historia y arte los lunes, miércoles y viernes y computación los martes y jueves.

MAITE ¿Te gustan las computadoras, Javier?

JAVIER No me gustan nada. Me gusta mucho más el arte... y sobre todo me gusta dibujar.

ÁLEX ¿Cómo que no? ¿No te gustan las computadoras?

recursos

| R | V/VCD-ROM Lección 2 | VM pp. 293-294 | ICD-ROM Lección 2 |

INÉS Hola. Me llamo Inés Ayala Loor y soy del Ecuador... de Portoviejo.

MAITE Encantada. ¿Qué clases tomas en la universidad?

INÉS Tomo geografía, inglés, historia, sociología y arte.

MAITE Tomas muchas clases, ¿no?

INÉS Pues sí, me gusta estudiar mucho.

ÁLEX Pero si son muy interesantes, hombre.

JAVIER Sí, ¡muy interesantes!

Enfoque cultural La vida universitaria

Universities in Spanish-speaking countries differ from those in the United States. In most cases students enroll in programs that prepare them for a specific career, rather than choosing a major. The courses for these programs are standardized within each country, so students take few elective courses. The classes themselves are also taught differently. Most are conducted as lectures that meet one or two times weekly. Grades are often based on a scale of one to ten, where five is passing.

Expresiones útiles

Talking about classes

▶ **¿Qué tal las clases en la UNAM?**
How are classes going at UNAM?

▶ **¿También tomas tú geografía?**
Are you also taking geography?

▷ **No, tomo inglés y literatura.**
No, I'm taking English and literature.

▶ **Tomas muchas clases, ¿no?**
You're taking lots of classes, aren't you?

▷ **Pues sí.** *Well, yes.*

▶ **¿En qué clase hay más chicos?**
In which class are there more guys?

▷ **En la clase de historia.**
In history class.

Talking about likes/dislikes

▶ **¿Te gusta estudiar?**
Do you like to study?

▷ **Sí, me gusta mucho. Pero también me gusta mirar la televisión.**
Yes, I like it a lot. But I also like to watch television.

▶ **¿Te gusta la clase de sociología?**
Do you like sociology class?

▷ **Sí, me gusta muchísimo.**
Yes, I like it very much.

▶ **¿Te gustan las computadoras?**
Do you like computers?

▷ **No, no me gustan nada.**
No, I don't like them at all.

Talking about location

▷ **Aquí estamos en...**
Here we are at/in...

▶ **¿Dónde está la señorita?**
Where is the young woman?

▷ **Está cerca de la ventana.**
She's near the window.

Expressing hesitation

▷ **A ver...**
Let's see...

▷ **Bueno...**
Well...

Reacciona a la fotonovela

1   **Escoger** Choose the answer that best completes each sentence.

1. Maite toma (*is taking*) _____ en la universidad.
   a. geografía, inglés y periodismo   b. inglés, periodismo y geografía
   c. periodismo, inglés y literatura

2. Inés toma sociología, geografía, _____.
   a. inglés, historia y arte   b. periodismo, computación y arte
   c. historia, literatura y biología

3. Javier toma _____ clases este semestre.
   a. cuatro   b. tres   c. dos

4. Javier toma historia y _____ los _____.
   a. computación; martes y jueves   b. arte; lunes, martes y miércoles
   c. arte; lunes, miércoles y viernes

2   **Identificar** Indicate which person would make each statement. The names may be used more than once.

1. Sí, me gusta estudiar.
2. ¡Hola! ¿Te gustan las clases en la UNAM?
3. ¿La clase de periodismo? Sí, me gusta mucho.
4. Hay más chicas en la clase de sociología.
5. Buenos días. Yo soy de Radio Andina FM 93.
6. ¡Uf! ¡No me gustan las computadoras!
7. Las computadoras son muy interesantes.
   Me gustan muchísimo.
8. Me gusta dibujar en la clase de arte.

INÉS

JAVIER   MAITE

ÁLEX

NOTA CULTURAL

Álex is a student at **la UNAM,** or **Universidad Nacional Autónoma de México** (*National Autonomous University of Mexico*). Founded in 1551, it is now the largest university in the world, with an annual enrollment of 280,000 students.

3   **Completar** These sentences are similar to things said in the **Fotonovela.** Complete each sentence with the correct word(s).

| la sociología | el arte | la Universidad San Francisco de Quito |
| la clase de historia | geografía | la Mitad del Mundo |

1. Maite, Javier, Inés y yo estamos en...
2. Hay fotos impresionantes de la Mitad del Mundo en los libros de...
3. Me llamo María Teresa Fuentes. Estoy aquí con estudiantes de...

4. Hay muchos chicos en...
5. No me gustan las computadoras. Me gusta más...

NOTA CULTURAL

In the **Fotonovela,** Álex, Maite, Javier, and Inés visit **la Mitad del Mundo** (*Center of the World*), a monument north of Quito, Ecuador. It marks the line at which the equator divides the Earth's northern and southern hemispheres.

4   **Conversar** Prepare a conversation in which you greet a classmate, introduce yourself, and find out where he/she is from. Find out if he or she likes to study, how many classes he/she is taking this semester, and which classes he/she likes and doesn't like.

Pronunciación

Spanish vowels

a   e   i   o   u

Spanish vowels are never silent; they are always pronounced in a short, crisp way without the glide sounds used in English.

Álex	**clase**	**nada**	**encantada**

The letter **a** is pronounced like the *a* in *father*, but shorter.

el	**ene**	**mesa**	**elefante**

The letter **e** is pronounced like the *e* in *they*, but shorter.

Inés	**chica**	**tiza**	**señorita**

The letter **i** sounds like the *ee* in *beet*, but shorter.

hola	**con**	**libro**	**don Francisco**

The letter **o** is pronounced like the *o* in *tone*, but shorter.

uno	**regular**	**saludos**	**gusto**

The letter **u** sounds like the *oo* in *room*, but shorter.

Práctica Practice the vowels by saying the names of these places in Spain.

1. Madrid   3. Tenerife   5. Barcelona   7. Burgos
2. Alicante   4. Toledo   6. Granada   8. La Coruña

Oraciones Read the sentences aloud, focusing on the vowels.

1. Hola. Me llamo Ramiro Morgado.
2. Estudio arte en la Universidad de Salamanca.
3. Tomo también literatura y contabilidad.
4. Ay, tengo clase en cinco minutos. ¡Nos vemos!

Refranes Practice the vowels by reading these sayings aloud.

Del dicho al hecho hay un gran trecho.[1]

Cada loco con su tema.[2]

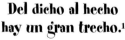
1 Easier said than done.
2 To each his own.

recursos

| R | STUDENT CD Lección 2 | LM p. 204 | LCASS./CD Cass. 2/CD2 | ICD-ROM Lección 2 |

2.1 The present tense of regular –ar verbs

ANTE TODO In order to talk about activities, you need to use verbs. Verbs express actions or states of being. In English and Spanish, the infinitive is the base form of the verb. In English, the infinitive is preceded by the word *to*: *to study*, *to be*. The infinitive in Spanish is a one-word form and can be recognized by its endings: **–ar, –er,** or **–ir.** In this lesson, you will learn the forms of **–ar** verbs.

–ar verb		–er verb		–ir verb	
estudiar	*to study*	**comer**	*to eat*	**escribir**	*to write*

Present tense of *estudiar*

estudiar *(to study)*

SINGULAR FORMS	yo	estudi**o**	*I study*
	tú	estudi**as**	*you (fam.) study*
	Ud./él/ella	estudi**a**	*you (form.) study; he/she studies*
PLURAL FORMS	nosotros/as	estudi**amos**	*we study*
	vosotros/as	estudi**áis**	*you (fam.) study*
	Uds./ellos/ellas	estudi**an**	*you (form.)/they study*

¿Tomas muchas clases este semestre?

Sí, tomo tres.

▶ To create the forms of most regular verbs in Spanish, you drop the infinitive endings (**–ar, –er, –ir**). You then add to the stem the endings that correspond to the different subject pronouns. The following diagram will help you visualize the process by which verb forms are created.

Conjugation of –ar verbs

INFINITIVE	VERB STEM	CONJUGATED FORM
estudi**ar**	estudi-	yo estudi**o**
bail**ar**	bail-	tú bail**as**
trabaj**ar**	trabaj-	nosotros trabaj**amos**

Common –ar verbs

bailar	to dance	**explicar**	to explain
buscar	to look for	**hablar**	to talk; to speak
caminar	to walk	**llegar**	to arrive
cantar	to sing	**llevar**	to carry
comprar	to buy	**mirar**	to look (at); to watch
contestar	to answer	**necesitar**	to need
conversar	to converse	**practicar**	to practice
descansar	to rest	**preguntar**	to ask (a question)
desear	to want; to wish	**preparar**	to prepare
dibujar	to draw	**regresar**	to return
enseñar	to teach	**terminar**	to end; to finish
escuchar	to listen (to)	**tomar**	to take; to drink
esperar	to wait (for); to hope	**trabajar**	to work
estudiar	to study	**viajar**	to travel

COMPARE & CONTRAST

Compare the verbs in the English sentences to the verb in the Spanish equivalent.

Paco **trabaja** en la cafetería.

1. *Paco works in the cafeteria.*
2. *Paco is working in the cafeteria.*
3. *Paco does work in the cafeteria.*

English uses three sets of forms to talk about the present: 1) the simple present (*Paco works*), 2) the present progressive (*Paco is working*), and 3) the emphatic present (*Paco does work*). In Spanish, the simple present can be used in all three cases.

In both Spanish and English, the present tense is also sometimes used to express future action.

Marina **viaja** a Madrid mañana.

1. *Marina travels to Madrid tomorrow.*
2. *Marina will travel to Madrid tomorrow.*
3. *Marina is traveling to Madrid tomorrow.*

▶ In Spanish, as in English, when two verbs are used together with no change of subject, the second verb is generally in the infinitive.

Deseo hablar con don Francisco.
I want to speak with don Francisco.

Necesitamos comprar cuadernos
We need to buy notebooks.

▶ To make a sentence negative in Spanish, the word **no** is placed before the conjugated verb. In this case, **no** means *not*.

Ellos **no** miran la televisión.
They don't watch television.

Alicia **no** desea bailar ahora.
Alicia doesn't want to dance now.

¿Hablas español?

No, no hablo español.

▶ Note that no subject pronouns were used in the Spanish conversation depicted above. Spanish speakers often omit them because the verb endings indicate who the subject is. In Spanish, subject pronouns are used for emphasis, clarification, or contrast, as in the examples below.

Clarification/Contrast

—¿Qué enseñan **ellos**?
What do they teach?

—**Ella** enseña arte y **él** enseña física.
She teaches art, and he teaches physics.

Emphasis

—¿Quién desea trabajar hoy?
Who wants to work today?

—**Yo** no deseo trabajar hoy.
I don't want to work today.

¡INTÉNTALO! Provide the present tense forms of these verbs. The first items have been done for you.

hablar

1. Yo ___hablo___ español.
2. Ellos _____ español.
3. Inés _____ español.
4. Nosotras _____ español.
5. Tú _____ español.
6. Los estudiantes _____ español.
7. Ud. _____ español.
8. Javier y yo _____ español.

trabajar

1. Uds. ___trabajan___ mucho.
2. Juanita y yo _____ mucho.
3. Nuestra profesora _____ mucho.
4. Tú _____ mucho.
5. Yo _____ mucho.
6. Las chicas _____ mucho.
7. Él _____ mucho.
8. Tú y Álex _____ mucho.

desear

1. Ud. ___desea___ viajar.
2. Yo _____ viajar.
3. Nosotros _____ viajar.
4. Lourdes y Luz _____ viajar.
5. Tú _____ viajar.
6. Ella _____ viajar.
7. Marco y yo _____ viajar.
8. Uds. _____ viajar.

Práctica

1

Me gusta... Get together with a classmate and take turns asking each other if you like these activities.

¿Te gusta...? *Do you like...?*   **Sí, me gusta...** *Yes, I like...*

bailar	escuchar música rock	trabajar
cantar	mirar la televisión	viajar
dibujar	practicar el español	estudiar

modelo

tomar el autobús
Estudiante 1: ¿Te gusta tomar el autobús?
Estudiante 2: Sí, me gusta tomar el autobús. /
          No, no me gusta tomar el autobús.

AYUDA

Spanish **no** translates to both *no* and *not* in English. In negative answers to questions, you will need to use **no** twice:

¿Estudias geografía?

No, no estudio geografía.

2

Completar Complete the conversation with the appropriate forms of the verbs. Then act it out with a partner.

JUAN ¡Hola, Linda! ¿Qué tal las clases?

LINDA Bien. _____ (tomar) tres clases... química, biología y computación. Y tú, ¿cuántas clases _____ (tomar)?

JUAN _____ (tomar) cuatro... sociología, biología, arte y literatura. Yo _____ (tomar) biología a las cuatro con el doctor Cárdenas. ¿Y tú?

LINDA Lily, Alberto y yo _____ (tomar) biología a las diez, con la profesora Garza.

JUAN ¿_____ (estudiar) ustedes mucho?

LINDA Sí, porque hay muchos exámenes. Alberto y yo _____ (estudiar) dos horas juntos todos los días (*together every day*).

JUAN ¿Lily no _____ (estudiar) con ustedes?

LINDA Shhh... no... ella _____ (estudiar) con su novio (*boyfriend*), Arturo.

3

Oraciones Form sentences using the words provided. Remember to conjugate the verbs and add any other necessary words.

1. Uds. / practicar/ vocabulario
2. (Yo) desear / practicar / verbos / hoy
3. ¿Preparar (tú) / tarea?
4. clase de español / terminar / once
5. ¿Qué / buscar / Uds.?
6. (Nosotros) buscar / pluma
7. (Yo) comprar / computadora
8. Mi (*My*) compañera de cuarto desear / regresar / lunes
9. Ella / bailar / y / cantar / muy bien
10. jóvenes / desear / descansar / ahora

Comunicación

4 **Describir** With a partner, describe what you see in the pictures using the given verbs.

 modelo
enseñar
La profesora enseña química.

1. caminar, hablar, llevar

2. buscar, descansar, estudiar

3. dibujar, cantar, escuchar

4. llevar, tomar, viajar

5 **Charadas** In groups of three students, play a game of charades using the verbs in the word bank. For example, if someone is studying, you say "**Estudias.**" The first person to guess correctly acts out the next charade.

mirar	conversar	enseñar	caminar	preguntar
bailar	dibujar	descansar	escuchar	cantar

Síntesis

6 **Conversación** Get together with a classmate and pretend that you are friends who have not seen each other on campus for a few days. Have a conversation in which you catch up on things. Mention how you're feeling, what classes you're taking, what days and times you have classes, and what classes you like and don't like.

2.2 Forming questions in Spanish

 **ANTE TODO**   There are three basic ways to ask questions in Spanish. Can you guess what they are by looking at the photos and photo captions on this page?

¿Dibujas mucho?

Las computadoras son muy interesantes, ¿no?

¿También tomas tú geografía?

▶ One way to form a question is to raise the pitch of your voice at the end of a declarative sentence. When writing any question in Spanish, be sure to use an upside down question mark (**¿**) at the beginning and a regular question mark (**?**) at the end of the sentence.

Statement	Question
Uds. trabajan los sábados.	¿Uds. trabajan los sábados?
You work on Saturdays.	*Do you work on Saturdays?*
Miguel busca un mapa.	¿Miguel busca un mapa?
Miguel is looking for a map.	*Is Miguel looking for a map?*

▶ As in English, you can form a question by inverting the order of the subject and the verb of a declarative statement. The subject may even be placed at the end of the sentence.

Statement	Question
SUBJECT VERB	VERB SUBJECT
Uds. trabajan los sábados.	**¿Trabajan Uds.** los sábados?
You work on Saturdays.	*Do you work on Saturdays?*
SUBJECT VERB	VERB SUBJECT
Carlota regresa a las seis.	**¿Regresa** a las seis **Carlota**?
Carlota returns at six.	*Does Carlota return at six?*

▶ Questions can also be formed by adding the tags **¿no?** or **¿verdad?** at the end of a statement.

Statement	Question
Uds. trabajan los sábados.	Uds. trabajan los sábados, **¿verdad?**
You work on Saturdays.	*You work on Saturdays, right?*
Carlota regresa a las seis.	Carlota regresa a las seis, **¿no?**
Carlota returns at six.	*Carlota returns at six, doesn't she?*

Question words

Interrogative words

¿Cómo?	How?	**¿Adónde?**	Where (to)?
¿Cuál?, ¿Cuáles?	Which?; Which one(s)?	**¿De dónde?**	From where?
¿Cuándo?	When?	**¿Por qué?**	Why?
¿Qué?	What?; Which?	**¿Cuánto/a?**	How much?
¿Dónde?	Where?	**¿Cuántos/as?**	How many?
		¿Quién?, ¿Quiénes?	Who?

▶ To ask a question that requires more than a simple *yes* or *no* answer, an interrogative word is used.

¿Cuál de ellos estudia en la biblioteca?
Which of them studies in the library?

¿Cuándo descansan Uds.?
When do you rest?

¿Cuántos estudiantes hablan español?
How many students speak Spanish?

¿Dónde trabaja Ricardo?
Where does Ricardo work?

¿Qué clases tomas?
What classes are you taking?

¿Adónde caminamos?
Where are we walking?

¿De dónde son Álex y Javier?
Where are Alex and Javier from?

¿Por qué necesitas hablar con ella?
Why do you need to talk to her?

¿Quién enseña la clase de arte?
Who teaches the art class?

¿Cuánta tarea hay?
How much homework is there?

CONSÚLTALO

¿Qué? and ¿cuál(es)?
You will learn more about the difference between **qué** and **cuál** in Lesson 9, p. 258.

▶ When pronouncing this type of question, the pitch of your voice falls at the end of the sentence.

¿Cómo llegas a clase?
How do you get to class?

¿Por qué necesitas estudiar?
Why do you need to study?

 **¡INTÉNTALO!** Make questions out of these statements. Use intonation in column 1 and the tag **¿no?** in column 2. The first item has been done for you.

Statement	Intonation	Tag questions
1. Hablas inglés.	¿Hablas inglés?	Hablas inglés, ¿no?
2. Trabajamos mañana.		
3. Uds. desean bailar.		
4. Raúl estudia mucho.		
5. Enseño a las nueve.		
6. Luz mira la televisión.		
7. Los chicos descansan.		
8. Él prepara la prueba.		
9. Tomamos el autobús.		
10. Necesito una pluma.		

Práctica

1 **Preguntas** Change these sentences into questions by inverting the word order.

> **modelo**
>
> Ernesto habla con el señor Gómez.
> ¿Habla Ernesto con el señor Gómez? /
> ¿Habla con el señor Gómez Ernesto?

1. La profesora prepara la prueba.

2. Sandra y yo necesitamos estudiar.

3. Los chicos practican el vocabulario.

4. Jaime termina la tarea.

5. Tú escuchas la radio.

2 **El escritorio** Get together with a partner and take turns asking questions about each other's desks.

> **modelo**
>
> **Estudiante 1:** Hay un libro en el escritorio, ¿verdad?
> **Estudiante 2:** No, no hay un libro en el escritorio.
>
> **Estudiante 1:** ¿Cuántos cuadernos hay en el escritorio?
> **Estudiante 2:** Hay un cuaderno en el escritorio.

3 **Completar** Irene and Manolo are chatting in the library. Complete their conversation with the appropriate questions.

AYUDA

Notice the difference between **¿por qué?**, which is written as two words and has an accent, and **porque**, which is written as one word:

¿por qué? *why?*

porque *because*

IRENE	Hola, Manolo. _____
MANOLO	Bien, gracias. _____
IRENE	Muy bien. _____
MANOLO	Son las nueve.
IRENE	_____
MANOLO	Estudio historia.
IRENE	_____
MANOLO	Porque hay un examen mañana.
IRENE	_____
MANOLO	Sí, me gusta mucho la clase.
IRENE	_____
MANOLO	El profesor Padilla enseña la clase.
IRENE	_____
MANOLO	No, no tomo psicología este semestre.
IRENE	_____
MANOLO	Regreso a la residencia a las once.
IRENE	_____
MANOLO	No, no deseo tomar una soda. ¡Deseo estudiar!

Comunicación

4

Encuesta Your instructor will give you a worksheet. Change the categories in the first column into questions, then use them to survey your classmates. Find at least one person for each category. Be prepared to report the results of your survey to the class.

Categorías	Nombres
1. Estudiar computación	
2. Tomar una clase de psicología	
3. Dibujar bien	
4. Cantar bien	
5. Escuchar música clásica	
6. Escuchar jazz	
7. Hablar mucho en clase	
8. Desear viajar a España	

5

Un juego (*A game*) In groups of four or five, play a game of *Jeopardy.*® Each person has to write two clues. Then take turns reading the clues and guessing the questions. The person who guesses correctly reads the next clue.

Es algo que...	**Es un lugar donde...**	**Es una persona que...**
It's something that…	*It's a place where…*	*It's a person that…*

modelo

Estudiante 1: Es un lugar donde estudiamos.
Estudiante 2: ¿Qué es la biblioteca?

Estudiante 1: Es algo que escuchamos.
Estudiante 2: ¿Qué es la música?

Estudiante 1: Es un director de España.
Estudiante 2: ¿Quién es Pedro Almodóvar?

NOTA CULTURAL

Pedro Almodóvar is an award-winning film director from Spain. His films are full of both humor and melodrama, and their controversial subject matter has often sparked great debate. His 1999 film **Todo sobre mi madre** (*All About My Mother*) received an Oscar for Best Foreign Film and Best Director at the Cannes Film Festival.

Síntesis

6

Entrevista Imagine that you are a reporter for the school newspaper. Write five questions about student life at your school and use them to interview two classmates. Be prepared to report your findings to the class.

2.3 The present tense of **estar**

CONSÚLTALO

Present tense of *ser*
To review forms of **ser**,
see Lesson 1, pp. 17-18.

ANTE TODO In Lesson 1, you learned how to conjugate and use the ver **ser** (*to be*). You will now learn a second verb which means *to be*, the verb **estar**. Although **estar** ends in **–ar**, it does not follow the pattern of regular **–ar** verbs. The **yo** form (**estoy**) is irregular. Also, all forms but the **yo** and **nosotros/as** forms have an accented **á**.

Present tense of *estar*

estar *(to be)*

SINGULAR FORMS		
yo	est**oy**	*I am*
tú	est**ás**	*you* (fam.) *are*
Ud./él/ella	est**á**	*you* (form.) *are; he/she is*
PLURAL FORMS		
nosotros/as	est**amos**	*we are*
vosotros/as	est**áis**	*you* (fam.) *are*
Uds./ellos/ellas	est**án**	*you* (form.)/*they are*

Hola, Ricardo…
Aquí estamos en
la Mitad del
Mundo.

María está en
la biblioteca.

COMPARE & CONTRAST

In the following chart, compare the uses of the verb **estar** to those of the verb **ser**.

Uses of *estar*

Location
Estoy en el Ecuador.
I am in Ecuador.

Inés **está** al lado de Javier.
Inés is next to Javier.

Health
Álex **está** enfermo hoy.
Álex is sick today.

Well-being
—¿Cómo **estás**, Maite?
How are you, Maite?

—**Estoy** muy bien, gracias.
I'm very well, thank you.

Uses of *ser*

Identity
Hola, **soy** Maite.
Hello, I'm Maite.

Occupation
Soy estudiante.
I'm a student.

Origins
—¿**Eres** de España?
Are you from Spain?

—Sí, **soy** de España.
Yes, I'm from Spain.

Time-telling
Son las cuatro.
It's four o'clock.

Prepositions of location

al lado de	*next to; beside*	**delante de**	*in front of*
a la derecha de	*to the right of*	**detrás de**	*behind*
a la izquierda de	*to the left of*	**encima de**	*on top of*
en	*in; on*	**entre**	*between; among*
cerca de	*near*	**lejos de**	*far from*
con	*with*	**sobre**	*on; over*
debajo de	*below*		

▶ **Estar** is often used with certain prepositions to describe the location of a person or an object.

La clase **está al lado de** la biblioteca.
The class is next to the library.

Los libros **están encima del** escritorio.
The books are on top of the desk.

El laboratorio **está cerca de** la clase.
The lab is near the classroom.

Maribel está **delante de** José.
Maribel is in front of José.

El estadio no **está lejos de** la librería.
The stadium isn't far from the bookstore.

Estamos **entre** amigos.
We're among friends.

Hay muchos estudiantes **en** la clase.
There are a lot of students in the class.

El libro está **sobre** la mesa.
The book is on the table.

¡A ver! La señorita que está cerca de la ventana...

Aquí estoy con cuatro estudiantes de la universidad... ¡Qué aventura!

¡INTÉNTALO! Provide the present tense forms of **estar**. The first item has been done for you.

1. Uds. ___están___ en la clase.
2. José _____ en la biblioteca.
3. Yo _____ en el estadio.
4. Nosotras _____ en la cafetería.
5. Tú _____ en el laboratorio.
6. Elena _____ en la librería.
7. Ellas _____ en la clase.
8. Ana y yo _____ en la clase.
9. Ud. _____ en la biblioteca.
10. Javier y Maribel _____ en el estadio.
11. Nosotros _____ en la cafetería.
12. Yo _____ en el laboratorio.
13. Carmen y María _____ en la librería.
14. Tú _____ en la clase.

Práctica

1   **Completar**   Complete this phone conversation between Daniela and her mother with the appropriate forms of **ser** or **estar**.

MAMÁ	Hola, Daniela. ¿Cómo _____?
DANIELA	Hola, mamá. _____ bien. ¿Dónde _____ papá? ¡Ya (*already*) _____ las ocho de la noche!
MAMÁ	No _____ aquí. _____ en la oficina.
DANIELA	Y Andrés y Margarita, ¿dónde _____ ellos?
MAMÁ	_____ en el Restaurante García con Martín.
DANIELA	¿Quién _____ Martín?
MAMÁ	_____ un compañero de clase. _____ de México.
DANIELA	Ah. Y el restaurante García, ¿dónde _____?
MAMÁ	_____ cerca de la Plaza Mayor, en San Modesto.
DANIELA	Gracias, mamá. Voy (*I'm going*) al restaurante. ¡Hasta pronto!

2   **Escoger**   Choose the preposition that best completes each sentence.

1. La pluma está (encima de / detrás de) la mesa.
2. La ventana está (a la izquierda de / debajo de) la puerta.
3. La pizarra está (debajo de / delante de) los estudiantes.
4. Las sillas están (encima de / detrás de) los escritorios.
5. Los estudiantes llevan los libros (en / sobre) la mochila.
6. La biblioteca está (sobre / al lado de) la residencia estudiantil.
7. España está (cerca de / lejos de) Puerto Rico.
8. Cuba está (cerca de / lejos de) los Estados Unidos.
9. Felipe trabaja (con / en) Ricardo en la cafetería.

3   **¿Dónde está...?**   Imagine that you are in the school bookstore and can't find various items. Ask the clerk (your partner) where the items in the drawing are located. Then switch roles.

> **modelo**
>
> **Estudiante 1:** ¿Dónde están los diccionarios?
> **Estudiante 2:** Los diccionarios están debajo de los libros de literatura.

Comunicación

4

¿Dónde estás...? Get together with a partner and take turns asking each other where you are at these times.

> **modelo**
>
> lunes / 10:00 a.m.
>
> **Estudiante 1:** ¿Dónde estás los lunes a las diez de la mañana?
>
> **Estudiante 2:** Estoy en la clase de español.

1. sábado / 6:00 a.m.
2. miércoles / 9:15 a.m.
3. lunes / 11:10 a.m.
4. jueves / 12:30 a.m.

5. viernes / 2:25 p.m.
6. martes / 3:50 p.m.
7. jueves / 5:45 p.m.
8. miércoles / 8:20 p.m.

5

La ciudad universitaria Imagine you are an exchange student at a Spanish university. Tell a classmate which buildings you are looking for and ask if they are near or far away. Your classmate will respond according to the campus map.

> **modelo**
>
> **Estudiante 1:** ¿La Facultad (School) de Medicina está lejos?
>
> **Estudiante 2:** No, está cerca. Está a la izquierda de la Facultad de Administración de Empresas.

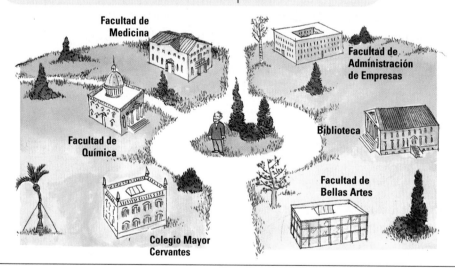

Facultad de Medicina

Facultad de Administración de Empresas

Biblioteca

Facultad de Química

Facultad de Bellas Artes

Colegio Mayor Cervantes

Síntesis

6

Entrevista Use these questions to interview two classmates. Then switch roles.

1. ¿Cómo estás?
2. ¿Dónde estamos ahora?
3. ¿Dónde está tu (*your*) compañero/a de cuarto ahora?
4. ¿Cuántos estudiantes hay en la clase de español?
5. ¿Quiénes no están en la clase hoy?
6. ¿A qué hora termina la clase hoy?
7. ¿Estudias mucho?
8. ¿Cuántas horas estudias para (*for*) una prueba?

2.4 Numbers 31–100

Los números 31 – 100		
31 treinta y uno	**37** treinta y siete	**50** cincuenta
32 treinta y dos	**38** treinta y ocho	**60** sesenta
33 treinta y tres	**39** treinta y nueve	**70** setenta
34 treinta y cuatro	**40** cuarenta	**80** ochenta
35 treinta y cinco	**41** cuarenta y uno	**90** noventa
36 treinta y seis	**42** cuarenta y dos	**100** cien, ciento
	(and so on)	

▶ The word **y** is used in most numbers from **31** through **99**. Also, beginning with **31**, most numbers are written as three words.

Hay **ochenta y cinco** exámenes.
There are eighty-five exams.

Hay **cuarenta y dos** estudiantes.
There are forty-two students.

¿En qué clase hay más chicas?

En la de sociología... casi un ochenta y cinco por ciento.

▶ With numbers that end in **uno** (31, 41, etc.), **uno** becomes **un** before a masculine noun and **una** before a feminine noun.

Hay **treinta y un** chicos.
There are thirty-one guys.

Hay **treinta y una** chicas.
There are thirty-one girls.

▶ **Cien** is used before nouns and in counting. The words **un, una,** and **uno** are never used before **cien** in Spanish. **Ciento** is used for numbers over one hundred.

¿Cuántos libros hay? **Cientos.**
How many books are there?
Hundreds.

Hay **cien** libros y **cien** sillas.
There are one hundred books
and one hundred chairs.

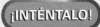 **¡INTÉNTALO!**   Provide the words for these numbers.

1. **56** _____
2. **31** _____
3. **84** _____
4. **99** _____
5. **43** _____
6. **68** _____
7. **72** _____
8. **35** _____
9. **87** _____
10. **59** _____
11. **100** _____
12. **61** _____
13. **96** _____
14. **74** _____
15. **42** _____

Práctica

1 **Baloncesto** Provide these basketball scores in Spanish.

1. Ohio State 76, Michigan 65
2. Florida 92, Florida State 84
3. Stanford 58, UCLA 49
4. Purdue 81, Indiana 78
5. Princeton 67, Harvard 55
6. Duke 100, Virginia 91
7. Kansas 95, Colorado 53
8. Texas 79, Oklahoma 47
9. Army 86, Navy 71
10. Kentucky 98, Tennessee 74

NOTA CULTURAL

Basketball (called **baloncesto** or **básquetbol**) is also a popular sport in many Spanish-speaking countries. Spain, Puerto Rico, Argentina, and Mexico, for example, have national leagues and champion teams often go on to international competitions.

2 **Números de teléfono** Imagine that you are a telephone operator in Spain. Give the appropriate phone numbers when callers ask for them.

modelo

Estudiante 1: ¿Cuál es el número de teléfono de José Morales Ballesteros, por favor?

Estudiante 2: Es el noventa y uno, noventa y cuatro, cuatro, sesenta y seis, sesenta y dos.

NOTA CULTURAL

In Spanish-speaking countries, the number of digits in phone numbers may vary from four to seven; they are often said in pairs. In the past, telephones were not as common as they are today, and smaller towns didn't need many digits in their phone numbers.

122 MOR

Morales Ballesteros, José	Venerable Centenares, 22	(91) 944-6662
Morales Benito, Francisco	Plaza Ahorro, 16	(91) 773-1216
Morales Borrego, Flora	Mayor, 51	(91) 634-3211
Morales Calvo, Emilio	Villafuerte, 49	(91) 472-2350
Morales Campos, María Josefa	Toledo, 35	(91) 419-7660
Morales Cid, Pedro	Rosal, 98	(91) 773-1382
Morales Conde, Ángel	Alameda, 67	(91) 944-3915
Morales Crespo, José Pascual	Fernando de la Peña, 13	(91) 634-7148
Morales de la Iglesia, Juliana	Buenavista, 80	(91) 834-5238
Morales Fraile, María Rosa	Plaza March, 74	(91) 834-3371

3 **Direcciones** With a partner, practice requesting people's addresses using the list of phone numbers in Activity 2. Note that in Spanish address numbers are usually written after the name of the street.

modelo

Estudiante 1: ¿Cuál es la dirección (address) de José Morales?

Estudiante 2: Es Venerable Centenares, número veintidós.

Comunicación

4

Precios (*Prices*) With a partner, take turns asking how much the items in the ad cost.

> **modelo**
>
> **Estudiante 1:** *Deseo comprar papel.*
> *¿Cuánto cuesta (How much does it cost)?*
> **Estudiante 2:** *Un paquete cuesta (it costs) cuatro dólares*
> *y cuarenta y un centavos.*

AYUDA AL INSTANTE

una caja de *a box of*

un paquete de *a package of*

• • •

Note that in Spanish, a comma is used in place of a decimal period, which is the standard in the U.S.

U.S.	Spanish
$4.95	$4,95
$12.50	$12,50

Conversely, Spanish uses a period instead of a comma to indicate thousands.

U.S.	Spanish
1,500	1.500
50,000	50.000

5

Entrevista Find out the telephone numbers and e-mail addresses of four classmates.

> **modelo**
>
> **Estudiante 1:** *¿Cuál es tu (your) número de teléfono?*
> **Estudiante 2:** *Es el 6-35-19-51.*
> **Estudiante 1:** *¿Y tu dirección de correo electrónico?*
> **Estudiante 2:** *Es jota-Smith-arroba-pe-ele-punto-*
> *e-de-u. (jsmith@pl.edu)*

AYUDA

arroba = @

punto = . (*dot*)

Síntesis

6

¿A qué distancia...? Your instructor will give you and a partner incomplete charts that indicate the distances between Madrid and various locations. Fill in the missing information on your chart by asking your partner questions.

> **modelo**
>
> **Estudiante 1:** *¿A qué distancia está Arganda del Rey?*
> **Estudiante 2:** *Está a veintisiete kilómetros de Madrid.*

recursos

R	WB pp. 13-20	LM p. 205-208	LCASS./CD Cass. 2/CD2	ICD-ROM Lección 2

Lectura

Antes de leer

Estrategia

Predicting Content Through Formats

Recognizing the format of a document can help you to predict its content. For instance, invitations, greeting cards, and classified ads follow an easily identifiable format, which usually gives you a general idea of the information they contain. Look quickly at the following text and identify it based on its format.

	lunes	martes	miércoles	jueves	viernes
8:30	biología		biología		biología
9:00		historia		historia	
9:30	inglés		inglés		inglés
10:00					
10:30					
11:00					
12:00					
12:30					
1:00					
2:00	arte		arte		arte

If you guessed that this is a page from someone's weekly appointment book, you are correct. You can now infer that the document contains information about a student's weekly schedule, including days, times, and activities they have planned.

Cognados

With a classmate, make a list of the cognates in the text and guess their English meanings. What do cognates reveal about the content of the document?

Examina el texto

Look at the format of the document entitled *¡Español en Madrid!* What type of text is it? What kinds of information do you expect to find in a document of this kind?

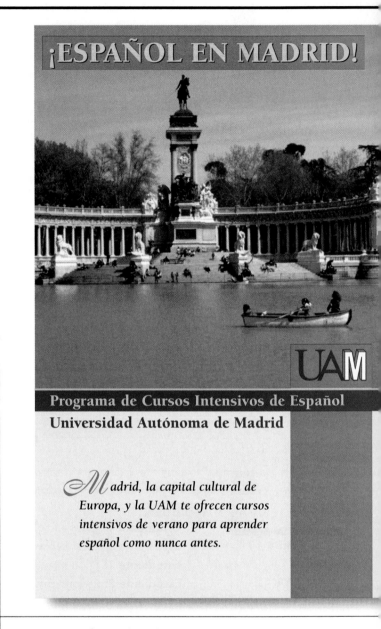

¡ESPAÑOL EN MADRID!

UAM

Programa de Cursos Intensivos de Español
Universidad Autónoma de Madrid

M adrid, la capital cultural de Europa, y la UAM te ofrecen cursos intensivos de verano para aprender español como nunca antes.

Después de leer

Correspondencias

Provide the letter of each item in Column B that matches the words in Column A. Two items will not be used.

A	B
1. profesores	a. (34) 91 523 4500
2. vivienda	b. (34) 91 524 0210
3. Madrid	c. 23 junio – 30 julio
4. número de teléfono	d. capital cultural de Europa
5. Español 2B	e. 16 junio – 22 julio
6. número de fax	f. especializados en enseñar español como lengua extranjera
	g. (34) 91 523 4623
	h. familias españolas

¿Dónde?

En el campus de la UAM, edificio de la Facultad de Filosofía y Letras.

¿Quiénes son los profesores?

Son todos hablantes nativos del español y catedráticos de la UAM especializados en enseñar el español como lengua extranjera.

¿Qué niveles se ofrecen?

Se ofrecen tres niveles básicos:
1. Español Elemental, A, B y C
2. Español Intermedio, A y B
3. Español Avanzado, A y B

Viviendas

Para estudiantes extranjeros se ofrece vivienda con familias españolas.

¿Cuándo?

Este verano a partir del 16 de junio hasta el 10 de agosto. Los cursos tienen una duración de 6 semanas.

Cursos	A partir	Termina
Español 1A	16 junio	22 julio
Español 1B	23 junio	30 julio
Español 1C	30 junio	10 agosto
Español 2A	16 junio	22 julio
Español 2B	23 junio	30 julio
Español 3A	16 junio	22 julio
Español 3B	23 junio	30 julio

Información

Para mayor información, sirvan comunicarse con la siguiente oficina.

Universidad Autónoma de Madrid

Programa de Español como Lengua Extranjera
Ctra. Colmenar Viejo, Km. 15
28049 Madrid, ESPAÑA
Tel. (34) 91 523 4500
Fax (34) 91 523 4623

¿Cierto o falso?

Indicate whether each statement is **cierto** (*true*) or **falso** (*false*).
Then correct the false statements.

	Cierto	Falso
1. La Universidad Autónoma de Madrid ofrece (*offers*) cursos intensivos de italiano.	○	○
2. La lengua nativa de los profesores del programa es el inglés.	○	○
3. Los cursos de español son en la Facultad de Ciencias.	○	○
4. Los estudiantes pueden vivir (*can live*) con familias españolas.	○	○

	Cierto	Falso
5. La universidad que ofrece los cursos intensivos está en Salamanca.	○	○
6. Español 3B termina en agosto.	○	○
7. Si deseas información sobre (*about*) los cursos intensivos de español, es posible llamar al (34) 91 523 4500.	○	○
8. Español 1A empieza (*begins*) en julio.	○	○

España

El país en cifras

▶ **Área:** 504.750 km² (kilómetros cuadrados) o 194.884 millas cuadradas, incluyendo las islas Baleares y las islas Canarias

▶ **Población:** 39.584.533

▶ **Capital:** Madrid—5.051.236

▶ **Ciudades principales:** Barcelona—4.548.222, Valencia—2.149.171, Sevilla—1.727.304, Zaragoza—827.730

SOURCE: Instituto Nacional de Estadística

▶ **Moneda:** peseta, euro (1/1/02)

▶ **Idiomas:** español o castellano, catalán, gallego, valenciano, eusquera

Gallego
Eusquera
Catalán
Español
Valenciano

Regiones lingüísticas

Bandera de España

Españoles célebres

▶ **Miguel de Cervantes,** escritor (1547-1616)

▶ **Pedro Almodóvar,** director de cine (1949-)

▶ **Rosa Montero,** escritora y periodista (1951-)

▶ **Pedro Duque,** astronauta (1963-)

▶ **Arantxa Sánchez Vicario,** tenista (1971-)

millas cuadradas *square miles* Moneda *Currency* Idiomas *Languages*
escritor *writer* cine *film* periodista *reporter* pueblo *town*
Cada año *Every year* Durante todo un día *All day long* miles *thousands*
se tiran *throw at each other* varias toneladas *many tons*

La Sagrada Familia

Mar Cantábrico

FRANCIA

La Coruña

San Sebastián

ANDORRA

Pirineos

Zaragoza   Río Ebro

Salamanca

ESPAÑA

Barcelona

PORTUGAL

Madrid

Valencia

Menorca

Mallorca

Ibiza

Islas Baleares

Sevilla

Sierra Nevada

Mar Mediterráneo

Estrecho de Gibraltar

Ceuta

Melilla

MARRUECOS

Plaza Mayor en Madrid

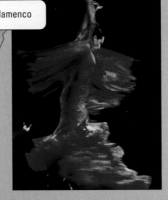

El baile flamenco

Islas Canarias

La Palma
Tenerife   Gran Canaria   Lanzarote
Gomera   Fuerteventura
Hierro

recursos

R | WB pp. 21-22 | vistasonline.com | ICD-ROM Lección 2

¡Increíble pero cierto!

En Buñol, un pequeño pueblo de Valencia, la producción de tomates es un recurso económico muy importante. Cada año en agosto se celebra el festival de *La Tomatina.* Durante todo un día, miles de personas se tiran tomates unas a otras. Llegan turistas de todo el país, y se usan varias toneladas de tomates.

Lugares • La Universidad de Salamanca

La Universidad de Salamanca, fundada en mil doscientos dieciocho (1218), es la más antigua de España. Más de treinta y cinco mil (35.000) estudiantes toman clases en esta universidad. La universidad está situada en la ciudad de Salamanca, que es famosa por sus edificios históricos, incluyendo puentes romanos y catedrales góticas.

Economía • La Unión Europea

Desde mil novecientos noventa y dos (1992) España participa en la Unión Europea, un grupo de países europeos que trabaja para desarrollar una política económica y social común en Europa. La moneda de los países de la Unión Europea es el euro.

Artes • Velázquez y el Prado

El Prado, en Madrid, es uno de los museos más famosos del mundo. En el Prado hay miles de pinturas importantes, incluyendo obras de Botticelli, el Greco, y de los españoles Goya y Velázquez. *Las Meninas* es la obra más conocida de Diego Velázquez, pintor oficial de la corte real durante el siglo XVII.

Comida • La paella

La paella es uno de los platos más típicos de España. Siempre se prepara con arroz y azafrán, pero hay diferentes recetas. La paella valenciana, por ejemplo, tiene pollo y conejo, y la paella marinera tiene mariscos.

Una playa de Ibiza

¿Qué aprendiste? Completa las frases con la información adecuada.

1. La _____ trabaja para desarrollar una política económica común en Europa.
2. El arroz y el azafrán son ingredientes básicos de la _____.
3. El Prado está en _____.
4. La universidad más antigua de España es la _____.
5. En 2002, España va a adoptar el _____ como su moneda oficial.
6. La ciudad de _____ es famosa por sus edificios históricos, tales como (*such as*) los puentes romanos.
7. El gallego es una de las lenguas oficiales de _____.

Conexión Internet Investiga estos temas en el sitio **www.vistasonline.com**.

1. Busca (*Look for*) información sobre la Universidad de Salamanca u otra universidad española. ¿Qué cursos ofrece (*does it offer*)? ¿Ofrece tu universidad cursos similares?
2. Busca información sobre un español o una española célebre (por ejemplo, un(a) político/a, un actor, una actriz, un(a) artista). ¿De qué parte de España es, y por qué es célebre?

más antigua *oldest* **edificios** *buildings* **puentes** *bridges* **Desde** *Since* **desarrollar** *develop* **política** *policy*
común *shared* **obras** *works* **más conocida** *best-known* **corte real** *royal court* **siglo** *century* **Siempre se prepara**
It is always prepared **arroz** *rice* **azafrán** *saffron* **recetas** *recipes* **pollo** *chicken* **conejo** *rabbit* **mariscos** *seafood*

La clase y la universidad

el borrador	eraser
la clase	class
el/la compañero/a de clase	classmate
el/la compañero/a de cuarto	roommate
el escritorio	desk
el libro	book
la mesa	table
la mochila	backpack
el papel	paper
la pizarra	blackboard
la pluma	pen
la puerta	door
el reloj	clock; watch
la silla	seat
la tiza	chalk
la ventana	window
la biblioteca	library
la cafetería	cafeteria
el estadio	stadium
el laboratorio	laboratory
la librería	bookstore
la residencia estudiantil	dormitory
la universidad	university; college
el curso, la materia	course
el examen	test; exam
el horario	schedule
la prueba	test; quiz
el semestre	semester
la tarea	homework
el trimestre	trimester; quarter

Los días de la semana

¿Cuándo?	When
¿Qué día es hoy?	What day is it?
Hoy es…	Today is …
la semana	week
lunes	Monday
martes	Tuesday
miércoles	Wednesday
jueves	Thursday
viernes	Friday
sábado	Saturday
domingo	Sunday

Las materias

la administración de empresas	business administration
el arte	art
la biología	biology
las ciencias	sciences
la computación	computer science
la contabilidad	accounting
la economía	economics
el español	Spanish
la física	physics
la geografía	geography
la historia	history
las humanidades	humanities
el inglés	English
las lenguas extranjeras	foreign languages
la literatura	literature
las matemáticas	mathematics
el periodismo	journalism
la psicología	psychology
la química	chemistry
la sociología	sociology

Preposiciones

al lado de	beside
a la derecha de	to the right of
a la izquierda de	to the left of
en	in; on
cerca de	near
con	with
debajo de	below; under
delante de	in front of
detrás de	behind
encima de	on top of
entre	between; among
lejos de	far from
sobre	on; over

Verbos

bailar	to dance
buscar	to look for
caminar	to walk
cantar	to sing
comprar	to buy
contestar	to answer
conversar	to converse, to chat
descansar	to rest
desear	to wish; to desire
dibujar	to draw
enseñar	to teach
escuchar la radio/música	to listen (to) the radio/music
esperar	to wait (for); to hope
estar (irreg.)	to be
estudiar	to study
hablar	to talk; to speak
llegar	to arrive
llevar	to carry
mirar (la) televisión	to watch television
necesitar	to need
practicar	to practice
preguntar	to ask (a question)
preparar	to prepare
regresar	to return
terminar	to end; to finish
tomar	to take; to drink
trabajar	to work
viajar	to travel

Palabras adicionales

¿adónde?	(to) where?
ahora	now
¿cuál?, ¿cuáles?	which?; which one(s)?
¿por qué?	why?
porque	because

Los números 31-100	See page 53.
Expresiones útiles	See page 37.

recursos

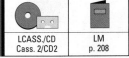

R | LCASS./CD Cass. 2/CD2 | LM p. 208

La familia

3

Communicative Goals

You will learn how to:
- Talk about your family and friends
- Describe people and things
- Express ownership

La familia

La familia de
José Miguel
Pérez Santoro

Juan Santoro Sánchez

mi abuelo (*my grandfather*)

Más vocabulario

la familia	*family*
el/la hermanastro/a	*stepbrother/stepsister*
el/la hijastro/a	*stepson/stepdaughter*
la madrastra	*stepmother*
el medio hermano/ la media hermana	*half-brother/ half-sister*
el padrastro	*stepfather*
los parientes	*relatives*
el/la cuñado/a	*brother-in-law/ sister-in-law*
la nuera	*daughter-in-law*
el/la suegro/a	*father-in-law/ mother-in-law*
el yerno	*son-in-law*
el/la amigo/a	*friend*
la gente	*people*
el/la muchacho/a	*boy/girl*
el/la niño/a	*child*
el/la novio/a	*boyfriend/girlfriend*
la persona	*person*
el/la artista	*artist*
el/la ingeniero/a	*engineer*
el/la doctor(a), el/la médico(a)	*doctor; physician*
el/la periodista	*journalist*
el/la programador(a)	*computer programmer*

Ernesto Santoro González

mi tío (*uncle*)
hijo (*son*) **de Juan y Socorro**

Marina Gutiérrez de Santoro

mi tía (*aunt*)
esposa (*wife*) **de Ernesto**

Silvia Socorro Santoro Gutiérrez

mi prima (*cousin*)
hija (*daughter*) **de Ernesto y Marina**

Héctor Manuel Santoro Gutiérrez

mi primo (*cousin*)
nieto (*grandson*) **de Juan y Socorro**

Carmen Santoro Gutiérrez

mi prima
hija de Ernesto y Marina

Variación léxica

madre ←→ mamá, mami (*colloquial*)
padre ←→ papá, papi (*colloquial*)
muchacho/a ←→ chico/a

¡LENGUA VIVA!

Middle names and last names are used differently in Spanish than in English:
• It is common to go by both first name and middle name, such as **José Miguel**.
• Spanish speakers have two last names: first the father's, then the mother's (the first last name of each parent).
• Wives sometimes replace their second last name with their husband's first last name, preceded by **de**: **Mirta Santoro de Pérez**.

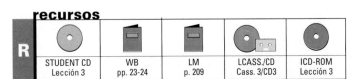

Socorro González de Santoro

mi abuela (*my grandmother*)

Mirta Santoro de Pérez

mi madre (*mother*)
hija de Juan y Socorro

Rubén Ernesto Pérez Gómez

mi padre (*father*)
esposo de mi madre

José Miguel Pérez Santoro

hijo de Rubén y de Mirta

Beatriz Alicia Pérez de Morales

mi hermana (*sister*)

Felipe Morales Zapata

esposo (*husband*) **de Beatriz Alicia**

Víctor Miguel Morales Pérez

mi sobrino (*nephew*)
hermano (*brother*)
de Anita

Anita Morales Pérez

mi sobrina (*niece*)
nieta (*granddaughter*)
de mis padres (*parents*)

los hijos (*children*) **de Beatriz Alicia y de Felipe**

Práctica

1 **Escuchar** 🎧 Listen to each statement made by José Miguel Pérez Santoro, then indicate whether it is **cierto** or **falso,** based on his family tree.

	Cierto	Falso		Cierto	Falso
1.	○	○	6.	○	○
2.	○	○	7.	○	○
3.	○	○	8.	○	○
4.	○	○	9.	○	○
5.	○	○	10.	○	○

2 **Emparejar** Provide the letter of the phrase that matches each description. Two items will not be used.

1. Es un hombre que programa las computadoras.
2. Son los padres de mi esposo.
3. Son los hijos de mis (*my*) tíos.
4. Es una mujer que trabaja en un hospital.
5. Es el hijo de mi madrastra y el hijastro de mi padre.
6. Es el esposo de mi hija.
7. Es el hijo de mi hermana.
8. Es un hombre que dibuja y pinta mucho.
9. Es una mujer que da (*gives*) clases en la universidad.
10. Es un hombre que trabaja con planos (*blueprints*).

a. Es una médica. o doctora
b. Es mi hermanastro.
c. Es un programador.
d. Es un ingeniero.
e. Son mis suegros.
f. Es mi novio.
g. Es mi padrastro.
h. Son mis primos.
i. Es un artista.
j. Es una profesora.
k. Es mi sobrino.
l. Es mi yerno.

3 **Completar** Complete these sentences with the correct family terms.

1. La madre de mi madre es mi _____.
2. La hija de mi tío es mi _____.
3. El hijo de mi hermana es mi _____.
4. La esposa de mi hermano es mi _____.
5. La hermana de mi padre es mi _____.
6. Mi madre y mi padre son mis _____.
7. El hijo de mi padre pero no de mi madre es mi _____.
8. Mi hija es la _____ de mi padre.
9. Mi esposa es la _____ de mis padres.
10. El hijo de mi esposo no es hijo mío; es mi _____.
11. El esposo de mi hija es mi _____.
12. Mi _____ es la hija de mi padrastro pero no de mi madre.
13. El padre de mi madre es mi _____.
14. Los padres de mi esposa son mis _____.

4   **Escoger** Complete the description of each photo using words you have learned in **Contextos**.

1. La _____ de Sara es muy grande.

2. Héctor y Lupita son _____.

3. Alberto Díaz es _____.

4. Elena Vargas Soto es _____.

5. Los dos _____ juegan al fútbol.

6. Don Manuel es el _____ de Martín.

7. Rubén camina con su _____.

8. Irene es _____.

Comunicación

CONSÚLTALO

Panorama Cities and towns where family members are from can be seen on p. 90.

5

Una familia With a classmate, identify the members in the family tree by asking questions about how each family member is related to Graciela Vargas García.

> **modelo**
>
> **Estudiante 1:** ¿Quién es Beatriz Pardo de Vargas?
> **Estudiante 2:** Es la abuela de Graciela.

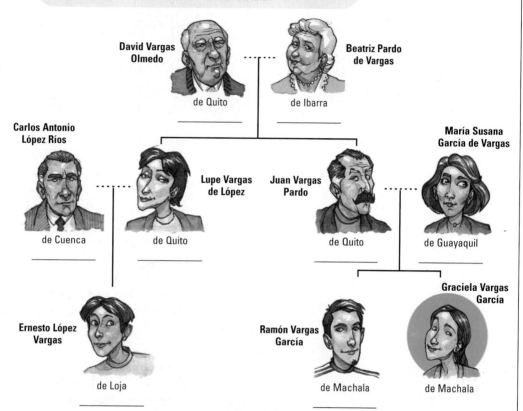

David Vargas Olmedo
de Quito

Beatriz Pardo de Vargas
de Ibarra

Carlos Antonio López Ríos
de Cuenca

Lupe Vargas de López
de Quito

Juan Vargas Pardo
de Quito

María Susana García de Vargas
de Guayaquil

Ernesto López Vargas
de Loja

Ramón Vargas García
de Machala

Graciela Vargas García
de Machala

Now take turns asking each other these questions.

1. ¿Cómo se llama el primo de Graciela?
2. ¿Cómo se llama la hija de David y de Beatriz?
3. ¿De dónde es María Susana?
4. ¿De dónde son Ramón y Graciela?
5. ¿Cómo se llama el yerno de David y de Beatriz?
6. ¿De dónde es Carlos Antonio?
7. ¿De dónde es Ernesto?
8. ¿Cómo se llama el sobrino de Lupe?

6

Preguntas personales With a classmate, take turns asking each other the following questions.

1. ¿Cuántas personas hay en tu familia?
2. ¿Cómo se llaman tus padres? ¿De dónde son? ¿Dónde trabajan?
3. ¿Cuántos hermanos tienes? ¿Cómo se llaman? ¿Dónde estudian o trabajan?
4. ¿Cuántos primos tienes? ¿Cuántos son niños y cuántos son adultos? ¿Hay más chicos o más chicas en tu familia?
5. ¿Eres tío/a? ¿Cómo se llaman tus sobrinos/as? ¿Dónde estudian o trabajan?
6. ¿Quién es tu pariente favorito?
7. ¿Tienes novio/a? ¿Tienes esposo/a? ¿Cómo se llama?

AYUDA

tengo *I have*
tienes *you have*
tu *your* (sing.)
tus *your* (plural)
mi *my* (sing.)
mis *my* (plural)

¿Es grande tu familia?

Los chicos hablan de sus familias en el autobús.

PERSONAJES

MAITE

INÉS

DON FRANCISCO

ÁLEX

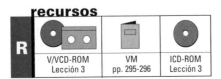

JAVIER

1

MAITE Inés, ¿tienes una familia grande?

INÉS Pues, sí... mis papás, mis abuelos, cuatro hermanas y muchos tíos y primos.

2

INÉS Sólo tengo un hermano mayor, Pablo. Su esposa, Francesca, es médica. No es ecuatoriana, es italiana. Sus papás viven en Roma, creo. Vienen de visita cada año. Ah... y Pablo es periodista.

MAITE ¡Qué interesante!

3

INÉS ¿Y tú, Javier? ¿Tienes hermanos?

JAVIER No, pero aquí tengo unas fotos de mi familia.

INÉS ¡Ah! ¡Qué bien! ¡A ver!

6

INÉS ¿Y cómo es él?

JAVIER Es muy simpático. Él es viejo pero es un hombre muy trabajador.

7

MAITE Oye, Javier, ¿qué dibujas?

JAVIER ¿Eh? ¿Quién? ¿Yo? ¡Nada!

MAITE ¡Venga! ¡No seas tonto!

8

MAITE Jaaavieeer... Oye, pero ¡qué bien dibujas!

JAVIER Este... pues... ¡Sí! ¡Gracias!

recursos

R			
	V/VCD-ROM Lección 3	VM pp. 295-296	ICD-ROM Lección 3

JAVIER ¡Aquí están!

INÉS ¡Qué alto es tu papá!
Y tu mamá, ¡qué bonita!

JAVIER Mira, aquí estoy yo.
Y éste es mi abuelo. Es el
padre de mi mamá.

INÉS ¿Cuántos años tiene tu
abuelo?

JAVIER Noventa y dos.

MAITE Álex, mira, ¿te gusta?

ÁLEX Sí, mucho. ¡Es muy bonito!

DON FRANCISCO Epa, ¿qué pasa
con Inés y Javier?

Enfoque cultural La familia hispana

It is difficult to generalize about families in any culture, not just among
Spanish speakers. There are many kinds of Hispanic families—large
and small, close-knit and distant, loving and contentious. Traditionally,
however, the family is one of the most important social institutions for
Spanish speakers. Extended families, consisting of nuclear families
and grandparents, aunts, and uncles, may reside in the same dwelling.
Unmarried children often may live with their parents while attending
college or working full-time.

Expresiones útiles

Talking about your family

▶ **¿Tienes una familia grande?**
Do you have a large family?

▷ **Sí... mis papás, mis abuelos,
cuatro hermanas y muchos tíos.**
*Yes... my parents, my grandparents, four sisters, and many (aunts
and) uncles.*

▷ **Sólo tengo un hermano mayor/
menor.**
*I only have one older/younger
brother.*

▶ **¿Tienes hermanos?**
*Do you have siblings (brothers
or sisters)?*

▷ **No, soy hijo único.**
No, I'm an only (male) child.

▷ **Su esposa, Francesca, es médica.**
His wife, Francesca, is a doctor.

▷ **No es ecuatoriana, es italiana.**
She's not Ecuadorian; she's Italian.

▷ **Pablo es periodista.**
Pablo is a journalist.

▷ **Es el padre de mi mamá.**
He is my mother's father.

Describing people

▷ **¡Qué alto es tu papá!**
How tall your father is!

▷ **Y tu mamá, ¡qué bonita!**
And your mother, how pretty!

▶ **¿Cómo es tu abuelo?**
What is your grandfather like?

▷ **Es simpático.**
He's nice.

▷ **Es viejo.**
He's old.

▷ **Es un hombre muy trabajador.**
He's a very hard-working man.

Saying how old people are

▶ **¿Cuántos años tienes?**
How old are you?

▶ **¿Cuántos años tiene tu abuelo?**
How old is your grandfather?

▷ **Noventa y dos.**
Ninety-two.

Reacciona a la fotonovela

1 **¿Cierto o falso?** Indicate whether each sentence is **cierto** or **falso.** Correct the false statements.

	Cierto	Falso
1. Inés tiene una familia grande.	○	○
2. El hermano de Inés es médico.	○	○
3. Francesca es de Italia.	○	○
4. Javier tiene cuatro hermanos.	○	○
5. El abuelo de Javier tiene ochenta años.	○	○
6. Javier habla del padre de su (*his*) padre.	○	○

2 **Identificar** Indicate which person would make each statement. The names may be used more than once. **¡Ojo!** One name will not be used.

1. ¡Tengo una familia grande! ¡Tengo un hermano, cuatro hermanas y muchos primos!
2. Mi abuelo tiene mucha energía. Trabaja mucho.
3. ¿Es tu mamá? ¡Es muy bonita!
4. Oye, chico… ¿qué dibujas?
5. ¿Fotos de mi familia? ¡Tengo muchas!
6. Mmm… Inés y Javier… ¿qué pasa con ellos?
7. ¡Dibujas muy bien! Eres un artista excelente.
8. Mmm… ¿Yo? ¡No dibujo nada!

ÁLEX   JAVIER

INÉS   MAITE

DON FRANCISCO

3 **Completar** These sentences are based on the **Fotonovela.** Complete each sentence with the correct word from the box. Two words won't be used.

simpático	italiana	Roma	americana
esposa	primos	hermanos	gente

1. Tengo cuatro hermanas y muchos tíos y _____.
2. La esposa de mi hermano no es ecuatoriana, es _____.
3. ¿Cómo es mi abuelo? Es muy _____.
4. Soy hijo único. No tengo _____.
5. Los papás de Francesca viven (*live*) en _____.
6. Francesca es la _____ de Pablo.

4 **Conversar** With a partner, use these questions to talk about your families.

1. ¿Cuántos años tienes?
2. ¿Tienes una familia grande?
3. ¿Tienes hermanos o hermanas?
4. ¿Cuántos años tiene tu abuelo (tu hermana, tu primo, etc.)?
5. ¿Cómo son tus padres?

AYUDA

Yo tengo… años.
Mi abuelo tiene… años.

Pronunciación

Diphthongs and linking

hermano   **niña**   **cuñado**

In Spanish, **a**, **e**, and **o** are considered strong vowels. The weak vowels are **i** and **u**.

ruido   **parientes**   **periodista**

A diphthong is a combination of two weak vowels or of a strong vowel and a weak vowel. Diphthongs are pronounced as a single syllable.

mi hijo   **una clase excelente**

Two identical vowel sounds that appear together are pronounced like one long vowel.

la abuela

con Natalia   **sus sobrinos**   **las sillas**

Two identical consonants together sound like a single consonant.

es ingeniera   **mis abuelos**   **sus hijos**

A consonant at the end of a word is linked with the vowel at the beginning of the next word.

mi hermano   **su esposa**   **nuestro amigo**

A vowel at the end of a word is linked with the vowel at the beginning of the next word.

Práctica   Say these words aloud, focusing on the diphthongs.

1. historia	5. residencia	9. lenguas
2. nieto	6. prueba	10. estudiar
3. parientes	7. puerta	11. izquierda
4. novia	8. ciencias	12. ecuatoriano

Refranes   Read these sayings aloud to practice diphthongs and linking sounds.

Cuando una puerta se cierra, otra se abre.[1]

Hablando del rey de Roma, por la puerta se asoma.[2]

1 When one door closes, another opens.
2 Speak of the devil and he will appear.

3.1 Descriptive adjectives

ANTE TODO Adjectives are words that describe people, places, and things. In Spanish, descriptive adjectives are often used with the verb **ser** to point out the characteristics or qualities of nouns or pronouns, such as nationality, size, color, shape, personality, and appearance.

NOUN   ADJECTIVE   PRONOUN   ADJECTIVE

El abuelo de Maite es **alto.**   **Él** es muy **simpático** también.

Forms and agreement of adjectives

COMPARE & CONTRAST

In English, the forms of descriptive adjectives do not change to reflect the gender (masculine/feminine) and number (singular/plural) of the noun or pronoun they describe.

*Juan is **nice.*** *Elena is **nice.*** *They are **nice.***

In Spanish, the forms of descriptive adjectives agree in gender and/or number with the nouns or pronouns they describe.

Juan es simpátic**o**.   Elena es simpátic**a**.   Ellos son simpátic**os**.

▶ Adjectives that end in **–o** have four different forms. The feminine singular is formed by changing the **–o** to **–a.** The plural is formed by adding **–s** to the singular forms.

Masculine		Feminine	
SINGULAR	PLURAL	SINGULAR	PLURAL
el muchach**o** alt**o**	los muchach**os** alt**os**	la muchach**a** alt**a**	las muchach**as** alt**as**

Mi abuelo es muy simpático.

¡Qué alto es tu papá! Y tu mamá, ¡qué bonita!

▶ Adjectives that end in **–e** or a consonant have the same masculine and feminine forms.

Masculine		Feminine	
SINGULAR	PLURAL	SINGULAR	PLURAL
el muchacho inteligent**e**	los muchachos inteligent**es**	la muchacha inteligent**e**	las muchachas inteligent**es**
el examen difíci**l**	los exámenes difíci**les**	la clase difíci**l**	las clases difíci**les**

▶ Adjectives that end in **–or** are variable in both gender and number.

Masculine		**Feminine**	
SINGULAR	PLURAL	SINGULAR	PLURAL
el hombre trabajad**or**	los hombres trabajad**ores**	la mujer trabajad**ora**	las mujeres trabajad**oras**

▶ Adjectives that refer to nouns of different genders use the masculine plural form.

Manuel es alt**o**.　　　Lola es alt**a**.　　　Manuel y Lola son alt**os**.

Common adjectives

alto/a	tall	**gordo/a**	fat	**moreno/a**	brunet(te)
antipático/a	unpleasant	**grande**	big; large	**mucho/a**	much; many; a lot of
bajo/a	short (in height)	**guapo/a**	handsome; good-looking	**pelirrojo/a**	red-haired
bonito/a	pretty	**importante**	important	**pequeño/a**	small
bueno/a	good	**inteligente**	intelligent	**rubio/a**	blond
delgado/a	thin; slender	**interesante**	interesting	**simpático/a**	nice; likeable
difícil	hard; difficult	**joven**	young	**tonto/a**	silly; foolish
fácil	easy	**malo/a**	bad	**trabajador(a)**	hard-working
feo/a	ugly	**mismo/a**	same	**viejo/a**	old

Adjectives of nationality

¡ATENCIÓN!

Unlike in English, Spanish adjectives of nationality are **not** capitalized. Proper names of countries, however, are capitalized.

México　**Canadá**
China　**Perú**

• • •

Note that adjectives of nationality which carry an accent mark on the last syllable, drop it in the feminine and plural forms.

inglés → inglesa
alemán → alemanes

▶ Adjectives of nationality are formed like other descriptive adjectives. Adjectives of nationality that end in **–o** form the feminine by changing the **–o** to **–a**.

chin**o** ⟶ chin**a**　　　　　mexican**o** ⟶ mexican**a**

The plural is formed by adding an **–s** to the masculine or feminine form.

chin**o** ⟶ chin**os**　　　　　mexican**a** ⟶ mexican**as**

▶ Adjectives of nationality that end in **–e** have only two forms, singular and plural.

canadiens**e** ⟶ canadiens**es**　　　estadounidens**e** ⟶ estadounidens**es**

▶ Adjectives of nationality that end in a consonant form the feminine by adding **–a**.

alem**án** ⟶ alem**ana**　　　español ⟶ español**a**
japon**és** ⟶ japon**esa**　　　inglés ⟶ ingle**sa**

Some adjectives of nationality

alemán, alemana	German	**japonés, japonesa**	Japanese
canadiense	Canadian	**inglés, inglesa**	English
chino/a	Chinese	**italiano/a**	Italian
ecuatoriano/a	Ecuadorian	**mexicano/a**	Mexican
español(a)	Spanish	**norteamericano/a**	(North) American
estadounidense	from the United States	**puertorriqueño/a**	Puerto Rican
francés, francesa	French	**ruso/a**	Russian

Position of adjectives

▶ Descriptive adjectives and adjectives of nationality generally follow the nouns they modify.

El chico **rubio** es de España.
The blond boy is from Spain.

La mujer **española** habla inglés.
The Spanish woman speaks English.

▶ Unlike descriptive adjectives, adjectives of quantity are placed before the modified noun.

Hay **muchos** libros en la biblioteca.
There are many books in the library.

Hablo con **dos** turistas puertorriqueños.
I am talking with two Puerto Rican tourists.

▶ **Bueno/a** and **malo/a** can be placed before or after a noun. When placed before a masculine singular noun, the forms are shortened: **bueno → buen; malo → mal**.

Joaquín es un **buen** amigo.
Joaquín es un amigo **bueno.**   ⟶   *Joaquín is a good friend.*

Hoy es un **mal** día.
Hoy es un día **malo.**   ⟶   *Today is a bad day.*

▶ When **grande** appears before a singular noun, it is shortened to **gran,** and the meaning of the word changes: **gran** = *great* and **grande** = *big, large.*

Nelson Mandela es un **gran** hombre.
Nelson Mandela is a great man.

La familia de Inés es **grande**.
Inés' family is large.

¡LENGUA VIVA!

Like **bueno** and **grande**, **santo** is also shortened before masculine nouns (unless they begin with **To-** or **Do-**): **San Francisco, San José, Santo Tomás. Santa** is used with the names of female saints: **Santa Bárbara, Santa Clara**.

 Provide the appropriate forms of the adjectives. The first item in each column has been done for you.

1. Eres ___simpático___ .
2. Yolanda es _____ .
3. Nosotros somos _____ .
4. Dolores y Pilar son _____ .
5. Diego es _____ .
6. Tomás y yo somos _____ .
7. Ellas son _____ .
8. La médica es _____ .
9. Los niños son _____ .
10. Él es _____ .

1. Soy ___español___ .
2. Ángela es _____ .
3. Los turistas son _____ .
4. Nosotros somos _____ .
5. El periodista es _____ .
6. Ellos son _____ .
7. Clara y Bárbara son _____ .
8. Ella es _____ .
9. Rafael y yo somos _____ .
10. Luis es _____ .

Práctica

1 **Emparejar** Find the words in column B that are the opposite of the words in column A. One word in B will not be used, and another will be used twice.

A	**B**
1. guapo	a. delgado
2. moreno	b. pequeño
3. alto	c. malo
4. gordo	d. feo
5. joven	e. viejo
6. grande	f. rubio
7. simpático	g. antipático
8. bonito	h. bajo

2 **Completar** Indicate the nationalities of the following people by selecting the correct adjectives and changing their forms when necessary.

1. Una persona de Ecuador es _____.
2. Carlos Fuentes es un gran escritor (*writer*) de México; es _____.
3. Los habitantes de Vancouver son _____.
4. Armani es un diseñador de moda (*fashion designer*) _____.
5. Catherine Deneuve es una actriz _____.
6. Tony Blair y Margaret Thatcher son _____.
7. Steffi Graf y Boris Becker son _____.
8. Los habitantes de Puerto Rico son _____.

3 **Describir** Look at the drawing and describe each family member using as many adjectives as possible.

Carlos Romero Sandoval · Josefina Barcos de Romero · Susana Romero Barcos · Tomás Romero Barcos · Alberto Romero Pereda

1. Susana Romero Barcos es _____.
2. Tomás Romero Barcos es _____.
3. Los dos hermanos son _____.
4. Josefina Barcos de Romero es _____.
5. Carlos Romero Sandoval es _____.
6. Alberto Romero Pereda es _____.
7. Tomás y su (*his*) padre son _____.
8. Susana y su (*her*) madre son _____.

Comunicación

4 **¿Cómo es?** With a partner, take turns describing each item on the list. Tell your partner whether you agree (**Estoy de acuerdo.**) or disagree (**No estoy de acuerdo.**) with the descriptions.

> **modelo**
>
> San Francisco
> **Estudiante 1:** San Francisco es una ciudad muy bonita.
> **Estudiante 2:** No estoy de acuerdo. Es muy fea.

1. Nueva York
2. Ben Affleck
3. Madonna
4. El presidente de los Estados Unidos
5. Steven Spielberg
6. La primera dama (*first lady*) de los Estados Unidos
7. El/La profesor(a) de español
8. Los Ángeles
9. Mi universidad
10. Mi clase de español

AYUDA

Here are some tips to help you complete the descriptions:
- **Ben Affleck es actor de cine.**
- **Madonna es cantante y actriz.**
- **Steven Spielberg es director de cine.**

5 **Anuncio personal** Write a personal ad that describes yourself and your ideal boyfriend, girlfriend, or mate. Then compare your ad with a classmate's. How are you similar and how are you different? Are you looking for the same things in a boyfriend, girlfriend, or mate?

SOY ALTA, morena y bonita. Soy ecuatoriana, de Quito, Ecuador. Estudio arte en la universidad. Busco un chico similar. Mi novio ideal es alto, moreno, inteligente y muy simpático.

Síntesis

6 **¿Quién es?** Working in groups, take turns describing a favorite famous person. The description may include physical appearance, personality traits, nationality, profession, and any other information you know. As you give your description, other group members will try to guess who you are describing.

3.2 Possessive adjectives

 **ANTE TODO**   Possessive adjectives, like descriptive adjectives, are words that are used to qualify people, places, or things. Possessive adjectives express the quality of ownership or possession.

Forms of possessive adjectives

SINGULAR FORMS	PLURAL FORMS	
mi	mis	*my*
tu	tus	*your* (fam.)
su	sus	*his, her, its, your* (form.)
nuestro/a	nuestros/as	*our*
vuestro/a	vuestros/as	*your* (fam.)
su	sus	*their, your* (form.)

COMPARE & CONTRAST

In English, possessive adjectives are invariable; that is, they do not agree in gender and number with the nouns they modify. Spanish possessive adjectives, however, do agree in number with the nouns they modify.

my cousin	*my cousins*	*my aunt*	*my aunts*
mi primo	**mis** primos	**mi** tía	**mis** tías

The forms **nuestro** and **vuestro** agree in both gender and number with the nouns they modify.

nuestr**o** prim**o**   nuestr**os** prim**os**   nuestr**a** tí**a**   nuestr**as** tí**as**

CONSEJOS

Look at the context, focusing on nouns and pronouns, to help you determine the meaning of **su(s)**.

▶ Possessive adjectives are always placed before the nouns they modify.

—¿Está **tu novio** aquí?   —No, **mi novio** está en la biblioteca.
Is your boyfriend here?   *No, my boyfriend is in the library.*

▶ Because **su** and **sus** have multiple meanings (*your, his, her, their, its*), you can avoid confusion by using this construction instead: [*article*] + [*noun*] + **de** + [*subject pronoun*].

	los parientes **de él/ella**	*his/her relatives*
sus parientes ◀	los parientes **de Ud./Uds.**	*your relatives*
	los parientes **de ellos/ellas**	*their relatives*

 ¡INTÉNTALO!   Provide the appropriate form of each possessive adjective. The first item in each column has been done for you.

1. Es _____ mi _____ (*my*) libro.
2. _____ (*My*) familia es ecuatoriana.
3. ____ (*Your,* fam.) esposo es italiano.
4. _____ (*Our*) profesor es español.
5. Es _____ (*her*) reloj.
6. Es _____ (*your,* fam.) mochila.
7. Es _____ (*your,* form.) maleta.
8. ____ (*Their*) sobrina es alemana.

1. ____ Sus ____ (*Her*) primos son franceses.
2. _____ (*Our*) primos son canadienses.
3. Son _____ (*their*) lápices.
4. _____ (*Their*) nietos son japoneses.
5. Son _____ (*our*) plumas.
6. Son _____ (*my*) papeles.
7. _____ (*My*) amigas son inglesas.
8. Son _____ (*his*) cuadernos.

Práctica

1

Completar Complete each sentence with the correct possessive adjective. Use the subject of each sentence as a guide.

> **modelo**
>
> Ana busca ____su____ (su, tu, nuestro) libro de español.

1. Marta busca _____ (sus, tus, su) libro de psicología.
2. Los estudiantes necesitan terminar _____ (nuestro, mi, su) tarea.
3. Carlos y yo llegamos a _____ (nuestro, tu, su) apartamento a las nueve.
4. Marta y Susana hablan con _____ (nuestras, sus, tus) amigos del Ecuador.
5. Los lunes y los martes regreso a _____ (mi, su, nuestro) casa a las ocho.
6. Tú estudias con _____ (su, sus, tu) amiga Rafaela, ¿no?
7. ¿Busca Ud. _____ (tu, nuestro, su) maleta?
8. Mi hermano trabaja con _____ (sus, tu, nuestro) tío.

2

Clarificar Clarify each sentence with a prepositional phrase. Follow the model.

> **modelo**
>
> Su hermana es muy bonita. (ella)
> La hermana de ella es muy bonita.

1. Su casa es muy grande. (ellos) _____
2. ¿Cómo se llama su hermano? (ellas) _____
3. Es su computadora. (ella) _____
4. Sus abuelos son muy simpáticos. (él) _____
5. Maribel es su prima. (ella) _____
6. Son sus libros. (ellos) _____

3

¿Dónde está? With a partner, imagine that you can't remember where you put some of the belongings you see in the pictures. Your partner will help you by reminding you where your things are. Take turns playing each role.

> **modelo**
>
> **Estudiante 1:** ¿Dónde está mi mochila?
> **Estudiante 2:** Tu mochila está en el escritorio.

1.

2.

3.

4.

5.

6.

Comunicación

4

Describir Get together with a partner and describe the people and places on the list.

> **modelo**
>
> La biblioteca de tu universidad
> La biblioteca de nuestra universidad es muy grande. Hay muchos libros
> en la biblioteca. Mis amigos y yo estudiamos en la biblioteca.

1. Tu profesor favorito
2. Tu profesora favorita
3. Tu clase de español
4. La librería de tu universidad
5. Tus padres
6. Tus abuelos
7. Tu mejor (*best*) amigo
8. Tu mejor amiga
9. Tu universidad
10. Tu país de origen

5

Una familia Working with two classmates, imagine that you are an elderly couple showing a photograph of your son's family to a friend. Look at the photograph and take turns describing it as the friend asks questions. After you've acted out the situation once, switch roles.

Síntesis

6

Describe a tu familia Get together with two classmates and describe your family to them in several sentences (**Mi padre es alto y moreno. Mi madre es delgada y muy bonita. Mis hermanos son...**). They will work together to try to repeat your description (**Su padre es alto y moreno. Su madre...**). If they forget any details, they will ask you questions (**¿Es alto tu hermano?**). Alternate roles until all of you have described your families.

3.3 Present tense of regular **–er** and **–ir** verbs

ANTE TODO In Lesson 2, you learned how to form the present tense of regular **–ar** verbs. You also learned about the importance of verb forms, which change to show who is performing the action. The chart below contains the forms of the regular **–ar** verb **trabajar**, which is conjugated just like **hablar, enseñar, comprar, estudiar,** and other **–ar** verbs you have learned. The chart also shows the forms of an **–er** verb and an **–ir** verb.

CONSÚLTALO
Present tense of regular –ar verbs. To review the conjugation of –ar verbs, see Lesson 2, pp. 40-42.

Present tense of *–ar*, *–er*, and *–ir* verbs

		trabajar *(to work)*	**comer** *(to eat)*	**escribir** *(to write)*
SINGULAR FORMS	yo	trabaj**o**	com**o**	escrib**o**
	tú	trabaj**as**	com**es**	escrib**es**
	Ud./él/ella	trabaj**a**	com**e**	escrib**e**
PLURAL FORMS	nosotros/as	trabaj**amos**	com**emos**	escrib**imos**
	vosotros/as	trabaj**áis**	com**éis**	escrib**ís**
	Uds./ellos/ellas	trabaj**an**	com**en**	escrib**en**

▶ **–Ar, –er,** and **–ir** verbs have very similar endings. Study the preceding chart to detect the patterns that make it easier for you to learn the forms of these verbs and to use them to communicate in Spanish.

Inés y Javier comen.

Maite escribe.

CONSEJOS
Here are some tips on learning Spanish verbs:
1) Learn to identify the stem of each verb, to which all endings attach.
2) Memorize the endings that go with each verb and verb tense.
3) As often as possible, practice using different forms of each verb in speech and writing.
4) Devote extra time to learning irregular verbs, such as **ser** and **estar.**

▶ The **yo** forms of all three types of verbs end in **–o.**

yo trabaj**o**   yo com**o**   yo escrib**o**

▶ Except for the **yo** form, all of the verb endings for **–ar** verbs begin with **–a.**

–as	**–amos**	**–an**
–a	**–áis**	

▶ Except for the **yo** form, all of the verb endings for **–er** verbs begin with **–e.**

–es	**–emos**	**–en**
–e	**–éis**	

▶ **–Er** and **–ir** verbs have the exact same endings, except in the **nosotros/as** and **vosotros/as** forms.

nosotros  com**emos** / escrib**imos**   vosotros  com**éis** / escrib**ís**

Common *–er* and *–ir* verbs

–er verbs		–ir verbs	
aprender	to learn	**abrir**	to open
beber	to drink	**asistir (a)**	to attend
comer	to eat	**compartir**	to share
comprender	to understand	**decidir**	to decide
correr	to run	**describir**	to describe
creer (en)	to believe (in)	**escribir**	to write
deber (+ *inf.*)	should; must; ought to	**recibir**	to receive
leer	to read	**vivir**	to live

Ellos **corren** en el parque.

Él **escribe** una carta.

¡INTÉNTALO! Provide the appropriate present tense forms of these verbs. The first item in each column has been done for you.

correr

1. Graciela ___corre___.
2. Tú _____.
3. Nosotros _____.
4. Yo _____.
5. Ellos _____.
6. Ud. _____.
7. Uds. _____.
8. La gente _____.
9. Marcos y yo _____.

abrir

1. Ellos ___abren___ la puerta.
2. Carolina _____ la maleta.
3. Yo _____ las ventanas.
4. Nosotras _____ los libros.
5. Ud. _____ el cuaderno.
6. Tú _____ la ventana.
7. Uds. _____ las maletas.
8. Él _____ el libro.
9. Los muchachos _____ los cuadernos.

aprender

1. Él ___aprende___ español.
2. Uds. _____ español.
3. Maribel y yo _____ inglés.
4. Tú _____ japonés.
5. Uds. _____ francés.
6. Mi hijo _____ chino.
7. Yo _____ alemán.
8. Ud. _____ inglés.
9. Nosotros _____ italiano.

Práctica

1   **Completar**   Complete Susana's sentences about her family with the correct forms of the verbs in parentheses. One of the verbs will remain in the infinitive.

1. Mi familia y yo _____ (vivir) en Guayaquil.
2. Tengo muchos libros. Me gusta _____ (leer).
3. Mi hermano Alfredo es muy inteligente. Alfredo _____ (asistir) a clases los lunes, miércoles y viernes.
4. Los martes y jueves Alfredo y yo _____ (correr).
5. Mis padres _____ (comer) mucho.
6. Yo _____ (creer) que (*that*) mis padres deben comer menos (*less*).

2   **Oraciones**   Form complete sentences using the clues provided.

> **modelo**
>
> Yo / correr / amigos / lunes y miércoles
> *Yo corro con mis amigos los lunes y miércoles.*

1. Manuela / asistir / universidad / Quito
2. Eugenio / abrir / puerta / ventanas
3. Isabel y yo / leer / biblioteca
4. Sofía y Roberto / aprender / hablar / español
5. Tú / comer / cafetería / universidad / ¿no?
6. Yo / no desear / compartir / libro de español

3   **Consejos**   Get together with a partner and give him or her advice based on these clues. Your partner will respond by agreeing or disagreeing with your advice. Then switch roles.

> **modelo**
>
> Correr
> **Estudiante 1:** *Debes correr más (more).*
> **Estudiante 2:** *Sí, debo correr más.*
>   *No, no debo correr más. Debo correr menos (less).*

1. Asistir a clase todos los días (*every day*)
2. Escribir a tu familia
3. Decidir tus cursos para el próximo (*next*) semestre
4. Beber menos café (*coffee*)
5. Leer más y mirar menos la televisión
6. Estudiar más
7. Hablar más en clase
8. Aprender a hablar japonés

Comunicación

4 **Entrevista** Get together with a classmate and use these questions to interview each other. Be prepared to report the results of your interviews to the class.

1. ¿Dónde comes al mediodía? ¿Comes mucho?
2. ¿Debes comer más (*more*) o menos (*less*)?
3. ¿Cuándo asistes a tus clases?
4. ¿Cuál es tu clase favorita? ¿Por qué?
5. ¿Dónde vives?
6. ¿Con quién vives?
7. ¿Qué cursos debes tomar el próximo (*next*) semestre?
8. ¿Lees el periódico (*newspaper*)? ¿Qué periódico lees y cuándo?
9. ¿Recibes muchas cartas (*letters*)? ¿De quiénes?
10. ¿Escribes poemas?

5 **Encuesta** Your instructor will give you a worksheet. Walk around the class and ask your classmates if they do (or should do) the things mentioned on the questionnaire. Try to find at least two people for each item. Be prepared to report the results of your survey to the class.

Actividades	Nombres
1. Vivir en una residencia estudiantil	
2. Asistir a una clase de arte	
3. Correr todos los días (*every day*)	
4. Escribir muchos mensajes electrónicos (*e-mails*)	
5. Recibir muchos mensajes electrónicos	
6. Comprender tres lenguas	
7. Deber estudiar más (*more*)	
8. Deber leer más libros	

Síntesis

6 **Conversación** Get together with a partner and talk about your Spanish class. Don't forget to include the following topics:

▶ What the teacher is like

▶ What the students are like

▶ Things that happen in class

▶ What the homework is like

▶ Things you should do before the next test (**antes del próximo examen**)

3.4 Present tense of **tener** and **venir**

The verbs **tener** (*to have*) and **venir** (*to come*) are among the most frequently used in Spanish. Because most of their forms are irregular, you will have to learn each one individually.

		tener *(to have)*	**venir** *(to come)*
Present tense of *tener* and *venir*			
SINGULAR FORMS	yo	ten**go**	ven**go**
	tú	tien**es**	vien**es**
	Ud./él/ella	tien**e**	vien**e**
PLURAL FORMS	nosotros/as	ten**emos**	ven**imos**
	vosotros/as	ten**éis**	ven**ís**
	Uds./ellos/ellas	tien**en**	vien**en**

▶ The endings are the same as those of regular **–er** and **–ir** verbs, except for the **yo** forms, which are irregular: **tengo, vengo.**

▶ In the **tú, Ud.,** and **Uds.** forms, the **e** of the stem changes to **ie.**

INFINITIVE	VERB STEM	VERB FORM
tener	→ ten- →	tú t**ie**nes
		él/ella/Ud. t**ie**ne
		ellos/ellas/Uds. t**ie**nen
venir	→ ven- →	tú v**ie**nes
		él/ella/Ud. v**ie**ne
		ellos/ellas/Uds. v**ie**nen

CONSEJOS

Use what you already know about regular **–er** and **–ir** verbs to identify the irregularities in **tener** and **venir**:
1) Which verb forms use a regular stem? Which use an irregular stem?
2) Which verb forms use the regular endings? Which use irregular endings?

¿Tienes hermanos?

Sí, tengo cuatro hermanas y un hermano mayor.

▶ The **nosotros** and **vosotros** forms are the only ones which are regular. Compare them to the forms of **comer** and **escribir** that you learned on page 86.

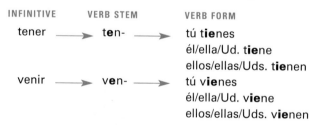

	tener	**comer**	**venir**	**escribir**
nosotros/as	ten**emos**	com**emos**	ven**imos**	escrib**imos**
vosotros/as	ten**éis**	com**éis**	ven**ís**	escrib**ís**

Expressions with *tener*

tener... años	*to be... years old*	tener (mucha) prisa	*to be in a (big) hurry*
tener (mucho) calor	*to be (very) hot*	tener razón	*to be right*
tener (mucho) cuidado	*to be (very) careful*	no tener razón	*to be wrong*
		tener (mucha) sed	*to be (very) thirsty*
tener (mucho) frío	*to be (very) cold*	tener (mucho) sueño	*to be (very) sleepy*
tener (mucha) hambre	*to be (very) hungry*		
tener (mucho) miedo (de)	*to be (very) afraid/ scared (of)*	tener (mucha) suerte	*to be (very) lucky*

▶ In certain idiomatic or set expressions in Spanish, you use the construction **tener** + [*noun*] instead of **ser** or **estar** to express *to be* + [*adjective*]. The chart above contains a list of the most common expressions with **tener.**

▶ To express an obligation, use **tener que** (*to have to*) + [*infinitive*].

—¿Qué **tienes que** estudiar hoy?　　—**Tengo que** estudiar biología.
What do you have to study today?　　*I have to study biology.*

▶ To ask people if they feel like doing something, use **tener ganas de** (*to feel like*) + [*infinitive*].

—¿**Tienes ganas de** comer?　　—No, **tengo ganas de** dormir.
Do you feel like eating?　　*No, I feel like sleeping.*

LaciUDAD.com

Ud. tiene que visitarnos.

¡INTÉNTALO! Provide the appropriate forms of **tener** and **venir**. The first item in each column has been done for you.

tener	**venir**
1. Ellos ___*tienen*___ dos hermanos.	1. Mis padres ___*vienen*___ de México.
2. Yo _____ una hermana.	2. Tú _____ de España.
3. El artista _____ tres primos.	3. Nosotras _____ de Cuba.
4. Nosotros _____ diez tíos.	4. Pepe _____ de Italia.
5. Eva y Diana _____ un sobrino.	5. Yo _____ de Francia.
6. Ud. _____ cinco nietos.	6. Uds. _____ de Canadá.
7. Tú _____ dos hermanastras.	7. Alfonso y yo_____ de Portugal.
8. Uds. _____ cuatro hijos.	8. Ellos _____ de Alemania.
9. Ella _____ una hija.	9. Ud. _____ de Venezuela.

Práctica

1 **Emparejar** Find the phrase in column B that matches best with the phrase in column A. One phrase in column B will not be used.

A	**B**
1. el Polo Norte	a. tener calor
2. una sauna	b. tener sed
3. la comida salada (*salty food*)	c. tener frío
4. una persona muy inteligente	d. tener razón
5. un abuelo	e. tener ganas de
6. una dieta	f. tener hambre
	g. tener 75 años

2 **Completar** Complete each sentence with the forms of **tener** or **venir**.

1. Manolo y Laura vienen a las ocho. Carlos _____ a las nueve.
2. Cristian tiene cinco hermanos, pero yo _____ ocho.
3. Clara y yo no venimos a la fiesta, pero Sandra sí _____.
4. Tú y Ricardo tienen mucha hambre, pero yo sólo (*only*) _____ sed.
5. Uds. no tienen razón; nosotros sí _____ razón.
6. Yo no vengo a clase mañana. ¿_____ tú?
7. Yo tengo que estudiar para un examen, pero mis amigos _____ que trabajar.
8. Muchos estudiantes tienen miedo de los exámenes; Sandra y yo _____ miedo de los profesores.

3 **Describir** Look at the drawings and describe what people are doing using an expression with **tener.**

1. _____

2. _____

3. _____

4. _____

5. _____

6. _____

Comunicación

4 **¿Sí o no?** Using complete sentences, indicate whether these statements apply to you.

1. Mi padre tiene 50 años.
2. Mis amigos vienen a mi casa todos los días (*every day*).
3. Vengo a la universidad los martes.
4. Tengo hambre.
5. Tengo dos computadoras.
6. Tengo sed.
7. Tengo que estudiar los domingos.
8. Tengo una familia grande.

Now interview a classmate by transforming each statement into a question. Be prepared to report the results of your interview to the class.

modelo
Estudiante 1: ¿Tiene tu padre 50 años?
Estudiante 2: No, no tiene 50 años. Tiene 65.

5 **Preguntas** Get together with a classmate and ask each other the following questions.

1. ¿Tienes que estudiar hoy?
2. ¿Cuántos años tienes? ¿Y tus hermanos/as?
3. ¿Cuándo vienes a la clase de español?
4. En tu opinión, ¿quién siempre (*always*) tiene razón?
5. ¿Cuándo vienen tus amigos a tu casa, apartamento o residencia estudiantil?
6. ¿De qué tienes miedo? ¿Por qué?
7. ¿Qué tienes ganas de hacer esta noche (*tonight*)?

6 **Conversación** Working with a partner, continue the conversation between Juana and Carlos, based on the drawing. Use your imagination!

modelo
Carlos: ¿No tienes ganas de comer, Juana?
Juana: No, porque tengo que...

recursos

| R | WB pp. 25-32 | LM p. 211-214 | LCASS./CD Cass. 3/CD3 | ICD-ROM Lección 3 |

Lectura

Antes de leer

Estrategia

Guessing meaning from context

As you read in Spanish, you'll often come across words you haven't learned. You can guess what they mean by looking at the surrounding words and sentences. Look at the following text and guess what **bisabuela** means, based on the context.

> ¡Hola, Claudia!
>
> ¿Qué hay de nuevo?
>
> ¿Sabes qué? Ayer fui a ver a mi bisabuela, la abuela de mi mamá. Tiene 85 años pero es muy independiente. Vive en un apartamento en Quito con su prima Lorena, quien también tiene 85 años.

If you guessed *great-grandmother*, you are correct, and you can conclude from this word and the format clues that this is a letter about someone's visit with his or her great-grandmother.

Examinar el texto

Quickly read through the paragraphs and find two or three words you don't know. Using the context as your guide, guess what these words mean. Then glance at the paragraphs where these words appear and try to predict what the paragraphs are about.

Examinar el formato

Look at the format of the reading. What clues do the captions, photos, and layout give you about its content?

Gente · · · Las familias

1. Me llamo Armando y tengo setenta años pero no me considero viejo. Tengo seis nietas y un nieto. Vivo con mi hija y tengo la oportunidad de pasar mucho tiempo con ella y con mi nieto. Por las tardes salgo a pasear por el parque con mi nieto y por la noche le leo cuentos.

Armando. Tiene seis nietas y un nieto.

2. Mi prima Victoria y yo nos llevamos muy bien. Estudiamos juntas en la universidad y compartimos un apartamento. Ella es muy inteligente y me ayuda con los estudios. Además, es muy simpática y generosa. Si no tengo dinero, ¡ella me lo presta!

Diana. Vive con su prima.

3. Me llamo Ramona y soy paraguaya, aunque ahora vivo en los Estados Unidos. Tengo tres hijos, uno de nueve años, uno de doce y el mayor de quince. Es difícil a veces, pero mi esposo y yo tratamos de ayudarlos y comprenderlos siempre.

Ramona. Sus hijos son muy importantes para ella.

4. Tengo mucha suerte. Aunque mis padres se divorciaron, tengo una familia muy unida. Tengo dos hermanos y dos hermanas. Me gusta hablar y salir a fiestas con ellos. Ahora tengo novio en la universidad y él no conoce a mis hermanos. ¡Espero que se lleven bien!

Ana María. Su familia es muy unida.

5. Antes quería tener hermanos pero ya no es tan importante. Saco provecho de ser hijo único: no tengo que compartir mis cosas con hermanos, no hay discusiones y, como soy nieto único también, ¡mis abuelos piensan que soy perfecto!

Fernando. Es hijo único.

6. Como soy bastante joven todavía, no tengo ni esposa ni hijos. Pero tengo un sobrino, el hijo de mi hermano, que es muy especial para mí. Se llama Benjamín y tiene diez años. Es un muchacho muy simpático. Siempre tiene hambre y por lo tanto vamos frecuentemente a comer hamburguesas. Nos gusta también ir al cine a ver películas de acción. Hablamos de todo. ¡Creo que ser tío es mejor que ser padre!

Santiago. Ser tío es divertido.

dinero *money* discusiones *arguments*

Después de leer

Emparejar

Glance at the paragraphs and see how the words and phrases in column A are used in context. Then find their definitions in column B.

A	B
1. me lo presta	a. the oldest
2. nos llevamos bien	b. movies
3. no conoce	c. the youngest
4. películas	d. loans it to me
5. mejor que	e. borrows it from me
6. el mayor	f. we see each other
	g. doesn't know
	h. we get along
	i. portraits
	j. better than

Seleccionar

Choose the sentence that best summarizes each paragraph.

1. Párrafo 1
   a. Me gusta mucho ser abuelo.
   b. No hablo mucho con mi nieto.
   c. No tengo nietos.
2. Párrafo 2
   a. Mi prima es antipática.
   b. Mi prima no es muy trabajadora.
   c. Mi prima y yo somos muy buenas amigas.
3. Párrafo 3
   a. Tener hijos es un gran sacrificio pero es muy bonito también.
   b. No comprendo a mis hijos.
   c. Mi esposo y yo no tenemos hijos.
4. Párrafo 4
   a. No hablo mucho con mis hermanos.
   b. Comparto mis cosas con mis hermanos.
   c. Mis hermanos y yo somos como (*like*) amigos.
5. Párrafo 5
   a. Me gusta ser hijo único.
   b. Tengo hermanos y hermanas.
   c. Vivo con mis abuelos.
6. Párrafo 6
   a. Mi sobrino tiene diez años.
   b. Me gusta mucho ser tío.
   c. Mi esposa y yo no tenemos hijos.

Escritura

Estrategia
Writing in Spanish

Why do we write? All writing has a purpose. For example, we may write a poem to reveal our innermost feelings, a letter to impart information, or an essay to persuade others to accept a point of view. Proficient writers are not born, however. Writing requires time, thought, effort, and a lot of practice. Here are some tips to help you write more effectively in Spanish.

DO

▶ Try to write your ideas in Spanish

▶ Use the grammar and vocabulary that you know

▶ Use your textbook for examples of style, format, and expression in Spanish

▶ Use your imagination and creativity

▶ Put yourself in your reader's place to determine if your writing is interesting

AVOID

▶ Translating your ideas from English to Spanish

▶ Simply repeating what is in the textbook or on a web page

▶ Using a dictionary until you have learned how to use foreign language dictionaries

Tema

Escribir una carta

A friend you met in a chat room for Spanish speakers wants to know about your family. Using verbs and adjectives you have learned, write a brief letter describing your family or an imaginary family, including:

▶ Names and relationships
▶ Physical characteristics
▶ Hobbies and interests

Here are some useful expressions for letter writing in Spanish:

Salutations

Estimado/a Julio/Julia	*Dear Julio/Julia*
Querido/a Miguel/Ana María	*Dear Miguel/Ana María*

Closings

Un abrazo,	*A hug,*
Abrazos,	*Hugs,*
Cariños,	*Much love,*
¡Hasta pronto!	*See you soon!*
¡Hasta la próxima semana!	*See you next week!*

Escuchar

Preparación

Based on the photograph, where do you think Cristina and Laura are? What do you think Laura is saying to Cristina?

Estrategia

Asking for repetition/ Replaying the recording

Sometimes it is difficult to understand what people say, especially in a noisy environment. During a conversation, you can ask someone to repeat by saying **¿Cómo?** (*What?*) or **¿Perdón?** (*Pardon me?*). In class, you can ask your teacher to repeat by saying **Repita, por favor** (*Repeat, please*). If you don't understand a recorded activity, you can simply replay it. To help you practice this strategy, you will listen to a short paragraph. Ask your professor to repeat it or replay the recording, and then summarize what you heard.

🎧 Ahora escucha

Now you are going to hear Laura and Cristina's conversation. Use **R** to indicate which adjectives describe Cristina's boyfriend, Rafael. Use **E** for adjectives that describe Laura's boyfriend, Esteban. Some adjectives will not be used.

____ rubio   ____ interesante

____ feo   ____ antipático

____ alto   ____ inteligente

____ trabajador ____ moreno

____ un poco gordo ____ viejo

Comprensión

Identificar

Which person would make each statement: Cristina or Laura?

	Cristina	Laura
1. Mi novio habla sólo de fútbol y de béisbol.	○	○
2. Tengo un novio muy interesante y simpático.	○	○
3. Mi novio es alto y moreno.	○	○
4. Mi novio trabaja mucho.	○	○
5. Mi amiga no tiene buena suerte con los muchachos.	○	○
6. El novio de mi amiga es un poco gordo, pero guapo.	○	○

¿Cierto o falso?

Indicate whether each sentence is **cierto** or **falso,** then correct the false statements.

	Cierto	Falso
1. Esteban es un chico interesante y simpático.	○	○
2. Laura tiene mala suerte con los chicos.	○	○
3. Rafael es muy interesante.	○	○
4. Laura y su novio hablan de muchas cosas.	○	○

Ecuador

El país en cifras

▸ **Área:** 283.560 km² (109.483 millas²), *incluyendo las islas Galápagos, aproximadamente el área de Colorado*

▸ **Población:** 13.112.000

▸ **Capital:** Quito — 1.892.000

▸ **Ciudades principales:**
Guayaquil — 2.452.000, Cuenca — 247.000,
Machala — 191.000, Portoviejo — 164.000

SOURCE: Population Division, UN Secretariat

▸ **Moneda:** sucre

▸ **Idiomas:** español (oficial), quichua

La lengua oficial del Ecuador es el español, pero también se hablan otras lenguas en el país. Aproximadamente unos 4.000.000 de ecuatorianos hablan lenguas indígenas; la mayoría de ellos habla quichua. El quichua es el dialecto ecuatoriano del quechua, la lengua de los incas.

Los indios del Ecuador hablan quichua.

Bandera de Ecuador

Ecuatorianos célebres

▸ Francisco Eugenio De Santa Cruz y Espejo, médico, periodista y patriota (1747-1795)

▸ Juan León Mera, novelista (1832-1894)

▸ Eduardo Kingman, pintor (1911-)

▸ Rosalía Arteaga, abogada, política y ex-vicepresidenta (1956-)

se hablan *are spoken*   otras *other*   mayoría *majority*
abogada *lawyer*   mundo *world*   dos veces más alto *twice as tall*

Las islas Galápagos

ESTADOS UNIDOS
OCÉANO ATLÁNTICO
OCÉANO PACÍFICO
ECUADOR   AMÉRICA DEL SUR

COLOMBIA

Río Esmeraldas

• Ibarra

Quito ☆

Indios amazónicos

Volcán Cotopaxi

Río Napo

Portoviejo •

Volcán Tungurahua

Río Pastaza

Río Daule

Guayaquil •

Cordillera de los Andes

Volcán Chimborazo

Cuenca •

Océano Pacífico

Machala •

• Loja

La ciudad de Quito y la cordillera de los Andes

PERÚ

Catedral de Guayaquil

recursos

R	WB pp. 33-34	WB Repaso pp. 35-36	vistasonline.com	ICD-ROM Lección 3

¡Increíble pero cierto!

El volcán Cotopaxi, situado a unos 60 kilómetros al sur de Quito, es considerado el volcán activo más alto del mundo. Tiene una altura de 5.897 metros (19.340 pies). Es dos veces más alto que el monte St. Helens (2.550 metros o 9.215 pies) en el estado de Washington.

Lugares • **Las islas Galápagos**

Muchas personas de todo el mundo visitan las islas Galápagos porque son un verdadero tesoro ecológico. En estas islas Charles Darwin estudió las especies que inspiraron sus ideas sobre la evolución. Debido a que las islas están lejos del continente, sus plantas y animales son únicos y evolucionaron de una manera diferente. Las islas son famosas por sus tortugas gigantes.

Artes • **Oswaldo Guayasamín**

Oswaldo Guayasamín (1919-1999) fue uno de los pintores latinoamericanos más famosos del mundo. También fue escultor y muralista. Su expresivo estilo muestra la influencia del cubismo y sus temas preferidos son la injusticia y la pobreza sufridas por los indígenas de su país.

Deportes • **El *trekking***

El sistema montañoso de los Andes cruza y divide el Ecuador en dos. La Sierra, que tiene volcanes, grandes valles y una variedad increíble de plantas y animales, es un lugar perfecto para el *trekking*. Miles de turistas visitan el Ecuador todos los años para hacer *trekking* y escalar montañas.

Artesanía • **Los tejidos**

Los tejidos de colores vivos son característicos del Ecuador. Los indígenas, continuando una larga tradición, tejen bolsas, cinturones y tapices apreciados en todo el mundo. Cada pueblo usa colores, figuras y diseños diferentes. Los turistas pueden admirar y comprar los tejidos en tiendas y en mercados como el de Otavalo.

Explosión del volcán
Tungurahua en 1999

¿Qué aprendiste? Completa las frases con la información correcta.

1. La ciudad más grande (*biggest*) del Ecuador es _____.
2. La capital del Ecuador es _____.
3. Unos 4.000.000 de ecuatorianos hablan _____.
4. Darwin estudió el proceso de la evolución en _____.
5. Dos temas del arte de _____ son la pobreza y la _____.
6. Los _____ son característicos del país.
7. Los Andes son un lugar perfecto para el _____.
8. El volcán _____ es el volcán activo más alto del mundo.

Conexión Internet Investiga estos temas en el sitio **www.vistasonline.com**.

1. Busca información sobre una ciudad del Ecuador.
   ¿Te gustaría (*would you like*) visitar la ciudad? ¿Por qué?
2. Haz una lista de tres animales o plantas que viven sólo en las islas Galápagos.
   ¿Dónde hay animales o plantas similares?

verdadero tesoro *true treasure* estudió *studied* inspiraron *inspired* Debido a que *Due to the fact that* evolucionaron *they evolved*
tortugas *tortoises* fue *was* más *most* muestra *shows* pobreza *poverty* cruza *crosses* lugar *place* Miles *Thousands* tejidos *weavings*
vivos *bright* larga *long* tejen *weave* bolsas *bags* cinturones *belts* tapices *tapestries* pueblo *town* diseños *designs* pueden *can*
tiendas *stores* mercados *markets*

La familia

el/la abuelo/a	grandfather/ grandmother
el/la cuñado/a	brother-in-law/ sister-in-law
el/la esposo/a	husband; wife; spouse
la familia	family
el/la hermanastro/a	stepbrother/ stepsister
el/la hermano/a	brother/sister
el/la hijastro/a	stepson/ stepdaughter
el/la hijo/a	son/daughter
los hijos	children
la madrastra	stepmother
la madre	mother
el/la medio/a hermano/a	half-brother/ half-sister
el/la nieto/a	grandson/ granddaughter
la nuera	daughter-in-law
el padrastro	stepfather
el padre	father
los padres	parents
los parientes	relatives
el/la primo/a	cousin
el/la sobrino/a	nephew/niece
el/la suegro/a	father-in-law/ mother-in-law
el/la tío/a	uncle/aunt
el yerno	son-in-law

Otras personas

el/la amigo/a	friend
la gente	people
el/la muchacho/a	boy/girl
el/la niño/a	child
el/la novio/a	boyfriend/girlfriend
la persona	person

Profesiones

el/la artista	artist
el/la doctor(a), el/la médico/a	doctor; physician
el/la ingeniero/a	engineer
el/la periodista	journalist
el/la programador(a)	computer programmer

Verbos

abrir	to open
aprender	to learn
asistir (a)	to attend
beber	to drink
comer	to eat
compartir	to share
comprender	to understand
correr	to run
creer (en)	to believe (in)
deber (+ *inf.*)	to have to; should
decidir	to decide
describir	to describe
escribir	to write
leer	to read
recibir	to receive
tener (*irreg.*)	to have
venir (*irreg.*)	to come
vivir	to live

Adjetivos

alto/a	tall
antipático/a	unpleasant
bajo/a	short (in height)
bonito/a	pretty
buen, bueno/a	good
delgado/a	thin; slender
difícil	difficult; hard
fácil	easy
feo/a	ugly
gordo/a	fat
gran, grande	big
guapo/a	handsome; good-looking
importante	important
inteligente	intelligent
interesante	interesting
joven	young
mal, malo/a	bad
mismo/a	same
moreno/a	brunet(te)
mucho/a	much; many; a lot of
pelirrojo/a	red-headed
pequeño/a	small
rubio/a	blond(e)
simpático/a	nice; likeable
tonto/a	silly; foolish
trabajador(a)	hard-working
viejo/a	old

Nacionalidades

alemán, alemana	German
canadiense	Canadian
chino/a	Chinese
ecuatoriano/a	Ecuadorian
español(a)	Spanish
estadounidense	from the United States
francés, francesa	French
inglés, inglesa	English
italiano/a	Italian
japonés, japonesa	Japanese
mexicano/a	Mexican
norteamericano/a	(North) American
puertorriqueño/a	Puerto Rican
ruso/a	Russian

Expresiones con tener

tener… años	to be… years old
tener (mucho) calor	to be (very) hot
tener (mucho) cuidado	to be (very) careful
tener (mucho) frío	to be (very) cold
tener ganas de + (*inf.*)	to feel like doing something
tener (mucha) hambre	to be (very) hungry
tener (mucho) miedo	to be (very) afraid/ scared
tener (mucha) prisa	to be in a (big) hurry
tener que + (*inf.*)	to have to do something
tener razón	to be right
no tener razón	to be wrong
tener (mucha) sed	to be (very) thirsty
tener (mucho) sueño	to be (very) sleepy
tener (mucha) suerte	to be (very) lucky

Possessive adjectives	See page 75.
Expresiones útiles	See page 67.

recursos

LCASS./CD Cass. 3/CD3	LM p. 214

Los pasatiempos

4

Communicative Goals

You will learn how to:

- Talk about pastimes, weekend activities, and sports
- Make plans and invitations
- Talk about the weather

Los pasatiempos

Más vocabulario

el béisbol	*baseball*
el ciclismo	*cycling*
el equipo	*team*
el esquí (acuático)	*(water) skiing*
el/la excursionista	*hiker*
el fútbol americano	*football*
el golf	*golf*
el hockey	*hockey*
el/la jugador(a)	*player*
la natación	*swimming*
el partido	*game; match*
la pelota	*ball*
la piscina	*swimming pool*
el tenis	*tennis*
el vóleibol	*volleyball*
bucear	*to scuba dive*
escalar montañas	*to climb mountains*
escribir una carta/ un mensaje electrónico/ una tarjeta (postal)	*to write a letter/ an e-mail message/ a postcard*
esquiar	*to ski*
ganar	*to win*
ir de excursión (a las montañas)	*to go on a hike (in the mountains)*
leer correo electrónico	*to read e-mail*
leer una revista	*to read a magazine*
practicar deportes (*m. pl.*)	*to play sports*
ser aficionado/a a	*to be a fan of*
deportivo/a	*sports-related*

Variación léxica

piscina ⟷ pileta (*Arg.*); alberca (*Méx.*)
baloncesto ⟷ básquetbol (*Amér. L.*)
béisbol ⟷ pelota (*P. Rico, Rep. Dom.*)

PARQUE MUNICIPAL

Lee el periódico. (leer)

Pasea en bicicleta. (pasear)

el fútbol

Visitan el monumento. (visitar)

Pasean. (pasean)

Toma el sol. (tomar)

Patina en línea. (patinar)

Nada. (nadar)

el baloncesto

Práctica

1 **Escuchar** 🎧 Indicate the letter of the activity in Column B that best corresponds to each statement you hear. Two items in Column B will not be used.

A	B
1. _____	a. Leer correo electrónico
2. _____	b. Tomar el sol
3. _____	c. Pasear en bicicleta
4. _____	d. Ir a un partido de fútbol americano
5. _____	e. Escribir una tarjeta postal
6. _____	f. Practicar muchos deportes
	g. Nadar
	h. Ir de excursión a las montañas

2 **¿Cierto o falso?** Indicate whether each statement is **cierto** or **falso** based on the illustration.

	Cierto	Falso
1. Un hombre nada en la piscina.	○	○
2. Un hombre lee una revista.	○	○
3. Un chico pasea en bicicleta.	○	○
4. Hay un partido de baloncesto en el parque.	○	○
5. Dos muchachos esquían.	○	○
6. Dos mujeres practican el golf.	○	○
7. Una mujer y dos niños visitan un monumento.	○	○
8. Un hombre bucea.	○	○
9. Hay dos excursionistas.	○	○
10. Una mujer toma el sol.	○	○

3 **Clasificar** Classify the following words as related to **deportes**, **lugares** (places), or **personas**.

1. el hockey _____
2. el ciclismo _____
3. el excursionista _____
4. el esquí acuático _____
5. la jugadora _____
6. la montaña _____
7. la natación _____
8. el parque _____
9. el aficionado _____
10. la piscina _____
11. el béisbol _____
12. la pelota _____

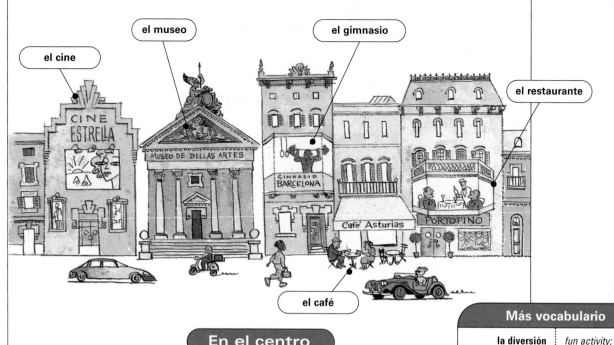

En el centro

Más vocabulario

la diversión	fun activity; entertainment; recreation
el fin de semana	weekend
la iglesia	church
el lugar	place
el pasatiempo	pastime; hobby
los ratos libres	spare (free) time
el tiempo libre	free time
pasar tiempo	to spend time
pasear por la ciudad/el pueblo	to walk around the city/the town
ver películas (f. pl.)	to see movies
favorito/a	favorite

4   **Identificar**   Identify the place where these activities would take place.

> **modelo**
> Esquiamos.
> Es una montaña.

1. Tomamos una limonada.
2. Vemos una película.
3. Nadamos y tomamos el sol.
4. Hay muchos monumentos.
5. Comemos tacos y fajitas.
6. Miramos pinturas (*paintings*) de Diego Rivera y Frida Kahlo.
7. Hay mucho tráfico.
8. Hacemos ejercicio.

5   **Seleccionar**   Working with a partner, select the most logical response to each statement.

1. ¿Dónde está la piscina? ¿Está cerca de aquí?
2. ¿Hay un restaurante bueno en el centro?
3. Me gusta visitar monumentos.
4. ¿Qué tal, Juanita? ¿No corres hoy?
5. ¿Te gusta ir al cine los fines de semana?
6. ¿No te gusta practicar el béisbol?

a. Pues, en el parque hay una estatua (*statue*) de Benito Juárez.
b. Sí, me gusta ver películas los sábados.
c. Sí, me gusta comer en el restaurante Portofino.
d. Sí, está en el parque municipal, cerca del gimnasio.
e. No, hoy no estoy bien.
f. Sí, pero me gusta más practicar el ciclismo.

AYUDA

Me gusta...
I like (to)...

No me gusta...
I don't like (to)...

¿Te gusta...?
Do you like (to)...?

• • •

Gustan is used when the thing liked is plural:

Me gustan los gatos.
I like cats.

No me gustan los insectos.
I don't like insects.

• • •

Gustar and verbs like ***gustar*** For more information on **gustar**, see Lesson 7, pp. 198–199.

Comunicación

6

Preguntar Ask a classmate what he or she does in the places mentioned below. Your classmate will respond using verbs from the word bank.

beber	leer	patinar
correr	mirar	practicar
escalar	nadar	tomar
escribir	pasear	visitar

> **modelo**
>
> un pueblo interesante
> **Estudiante 1:** ¿Qué haces (*do you do*) cuando estás en un pueblo interesante?
> **Estudiante 2:** Paseo por el pueblo y busco lugares interesantes.

1. una biblioteca
2. un estadio
3. una ciudad grande
4. una piscina
5. las montañas
6. un parque
7. un café
8. un museo

7

Conversación Using the words and expressions provided, work with a partner to prepare a short conversation about your pastimes.

¿a qué hora?	¿cuándo?	¿qué?
¿cómo?	¿dónde?	¿con quién(es)?

> **modelo**
>
> **Estudiante 1:** ¿Cuándo patinas en línea?
> **Estudiante 2:** Patino en línea los domingos. Y tú, ¿patinas en línea?
> **Estudiante 1:** No, no me gusta patinar en línea. Me gusta practicar el béisbol.

8

Entrevista Your instructor will give you a worksheet. Working with one or two classmates, interview each other to find how you like to spend your free time and note the responses on your worksheet. Each of you should mention at least five activities and specify where they take place.

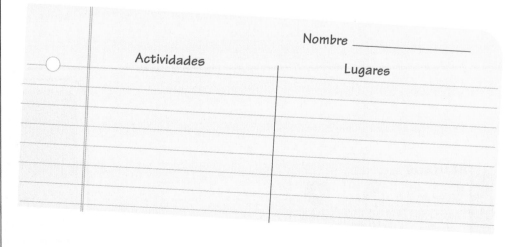

Nombre _____

Actividades   Lugares

¡Vamos al parque!

Los estudiantes pasean por la ciudad y hablan de sus pasatiempos.

1

DON FRANCISCO Tienen una hora libre. Pueden explorar la ciudad, si quieren. Tenemos que ir a las cabañas a las cuatro.

2

JAVIER Inés, ¿quieres ir a pasear por la ciudad?

INÉS Sí, vamos.

3

ÁLEX ¿Por qué no vamos al parque, Maite? Podemos hablar y tomar el sol.

MAITE ¡Buena idea! Hace mucho sol hoy. También quiero escribir unas postales.

6

ÁLEX ¡Maite!

MAITE ¡Dios mío!

7

JOVEN Mil perdones. Lo siento muchísimo.

MAITE ¡No es nada! Estoy bien.

8

ÁLEX Ya son las dos y treinta. Debemos regresar al autobús, ¿no?

MAITE Tienes razón.

ÁLEX Oye, Maite, ¿qué vas a hacer esta noche?

MAITE No tengo planes. ¿Por qué?

MAITE ¿Eres aficionado a los deportes, Álex?

ÁLEX Sí, me gusta mucho el fútbol. Me gusta también nadar, correr e ir de excursión a las montañas.

MAITE Yo también corro mucho.

ÁLEX Oye, Maite, ¿por qué no jugamos al fútbol con él?

MAITE Mmm... no quiero. Voy a terminar de escribir unas postales.

ÁLEX Eh, este... a veces salgo a correr por la noche. ¿Quieres venir a correr conmigo?

MAITE Sí, vamos. ¿A qué hora?

ÁLEX ¿A las seis?

MAITE Perfecto.

DON FRANCISCO Esta noche van a correr. ¡Y yo no tengo energía para pasear!

Enfoque cultural El fútbol

Soccer, or **fútbol,** is the most popular spectator sport and the most widely played team game in the world. It is also the most popular sport in the Spanish-speaking world. People of all ages can be seen playing soccer in public parks and streets, and each country has a professional league with its own stars. Gabriel Batistuta from Argentina, Marcelo Salas from Chile, and Hugo Sánchez from Mexico are among the most famous contemporary Hispanic soccer players.

Reacciona a la fotonovela

1 **Escoger** Choose the answer that best completes each sentence.

1. Inés y Javier _____.
   a. toman el sol b. pasean por la ciudad c. corren por el parque

2. Álex desea _____ en el parque.
   a. hablar y tomar el sol b. hablar y leer el periódico c. nadar y tomar el sol

3. A Álex le gusta nadar, _____.
   a. jugar al fútbol b. escalar montañas c. ir de excursión y correr

4. A Maite le gusta _____.
   a. nadar y correr b. correr y escribir postales c. correr y jugar al fútbol

5. Maite desea _____.
   a. ir de excursión b. jugar al fútbol c. ir al parque

2 **Identificar** Identify the person who would make each statement.

1. No me gusta practicar el fútbol pero me gusta correr. _____

2. ¿Por qué no vamos a pasear por la ciudad? _____

3. ¿Por qué no exploran Uds. la ciudad? Tienen tiempo. _____

4. ¿Por qué no corres conmigo esta noche? _____

5. No voy al parque. Prefiero estar con mi amigo. _____

JAVIER

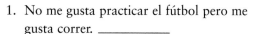
INÉS

MAITE

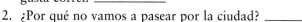
ÁLEX

DON FRANCISCO

3 **Preguntas** Answer the questions using the information from the **Fotonovela.**

1. ¿Qué desean hacer Inés y Javier?

2. ¿Qué desea hacer Álex en el parque?

3. ¿Qué desea hacer Maite en el parque?

4. ¿A qué hora regresan Maite y Álex al autobús?

5. ¿Qué deciden hacer Maite y Álex esta noche?

4 **Conversación** With a partner, prepare a conversation in which you talk about pastimes and invite each other to do some activity together. Use the following expressions:

1. ¿Eres aficionado/a a...?
2. ¿Te gusta...?
3. ¿Qué vas a hacer esta noche...?
4. ¿Por qué no...?
5. ¿Quieres... conmigo?

AYUDA

contigo *with you*
¿A qué hora?
(At) What time?
¿Dónde? *Where?*
No puedo porque...
I can't because...
Nos vemos a las siete.
See you at seven.

Pronunciación

Word stress and accent marks

pe-lí-cu-la   **e-di-fi-cio**   **ver**   **yo**

Every Spanish syllable contains at least one vowel. When two vowels (two weak vowels or one strong and one weak) are joined in the same syllable they form a **diphthong**. A **monosyllable** is a word formed by a single syllable.

---

bi-blio-te-ca   **vi-si-tar**   **par-que**   **fút-bol**

The syllable of a Spanish word that is pronounced most emphatically is the "stressed" syllable.

---

pe-lo-ta   **pis-ci-na**   **ra-tos**   **ha-blan**

Words that end in **n, s,** or a **vowel** are usually stressed on the next to last syllable.

---

na-ta-ción   **pa-pá**   **in-glés**   **Jo-sé**

If words that end in **n, s,** or a **vowel** are stressed on the last syllable, they must carry an accent mark on the stressed syllable.

---

bai-lar   **es-pa-ñol**   **u-ni-ver-si-dad**   **tra-ba-ja-dor**

Words that do *not* end in **n, s,** or a **vowel** are usually stressed on the last syllable.

---

béis-bol   **lá-piz**   **ár-bol**   **Gó-mez**

If words that do *not* end in **n, s,** or a **vowel** are stressed on the next to last syllable, they must carry an accent mark on the stressed syllable.

En la unión está la fuerza.[2]

Práctica Pronounce each word, stressing the correct syllable. Then give the word stress rule for each word.

1. profesor	4. Mazatlán	7. niños	10. México
2. Puebla	5. examen	8. Guadalajara	11. están
3. ¿Cuántos?	6. ¿Cómo?	9. programador	12. geografía

Oraciones Read the conversation aloud to practice word stress.

MARINA Hola, Carlos. ¿Qué tal?

CARLOS Bien. Oye, ¿a qué hora es el partido de fútbol?

MARINA Creo que es a las siete.

CARLOS ¿Quieres ir?

MARINA Lo siento, pero no puedo.
Tengo que estudiar biología.

Quien ríe de último, ríe mejor.[1]

Refranes Read these sayings aloud to practice word stress.

1 *He who laughs last, laughs longest.*
2 *United we stand.*

recursos

R	STUDENT CD Lección 4	LM p. 216	LCASS./CD Cass. 4/CD4	ICD-ROM Lección 4

4.1 The present tense of **ir**

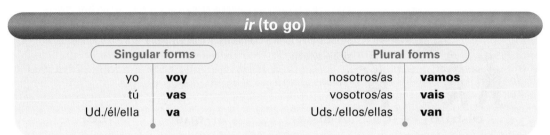

ANTE TODO The verb **ir** (*to go*) is irregular in the present tense. Note that, except for the **yo** form (**voy**) and the lack of a written accent on the **vosotros** form (**vais**), the endings are the same as those for **–ar** verbs.

ir (to go)			
Singular forms		**Plural forms**	
yo	**voy**	nosotros/as	**vamos**
tú	**vas**	vosotros/as	**vais**
Ud./él/ella	**va**	Uds./ellos/ellas	**van**

▶ **Ir** is often used with the preposition **a** (*to*). If **a** is followed by the definite article **el**, they combine to form the contraction **al**. If **a** is followed by the other definite articles (**la, las, los**), there is no contraction.

CONSÚLTALO

Contractions To review the **de** + **el** contraction, see Lesson 1, pp. 18-19.

$$a + el = al$$

Voy **al** parque con Juan.
I'm going to the park with Juan.

Los excursionistas van **a las** montañas.
The hikers are going to the mountains.

▶ The construction **ir a** + [*infinitive*] is used to talk about actions that are going to happen in the future. It is equivalent to the English *to be going to* + [*infinitive*].

Va a leer el periódico.
He is going to read the newspaper.

Van a pasear por el pueblo.
They are going to walk around town.

¡ATENCIÓN!

Remember to use **adónde** instead of **dónde** when asking a question that contains a form of the verb **ir**:

¿Adónde vas?
(To) Where are you going?

Voy a escribir unas postales.

Álex y Maite van a volver al autobús.

▶ **Vamos a** + [*infinitive*] can also express the idea of *let's (do something)*.

Vamos a pasear.
Let's take a stroll.

¡Vamos a ver!
Let's see!

¡INTÉNTALO! Provide the present tense forms of **ir**. The first item has been done for you.

1. Ellos ___van___.
2. Yo _____.
3. Tu novio _____.
4. Adela _____.
5. Mi prima y yo _____.
6. Tú _____.
7. Uds. _____.
8. Nosotros _____.
9. Ud. _____.
10. Nosotras _____.
11. Miguel _____.
12. Ellos _____.

Práctica

1 **¿Adónde van?** Everyone in your neighborhood is dashing off to various places. Say where they are going.

CONSEJOS

Remember that when the subject is a pronoun (**tú**, **nosotros**, etc.) it can be dropped to avoid being repetitive.

1. la señora Castillo / el centro
2. las hermanas Gómez / la piscina
3. tu tío y tu papá / el partido de fútbol
4. yo / el Museo de Arte Moderno
5. nosotros / el restaurante Miramar

2 **¿Qué van a hacer?** These sentences describe what several people are doing today. Use **ir a** + [*infinitive*] to say that they are also going to do the same activities tomorrow.

> **modelo**
>
> Martín y Rodolfo nadan en la piscina.
> **Van a nadar en la piscina mañana también.**

1. Sara lee el periódico.
2. Yo practico deportes.
3. Uds. van de excursión.
4. Mi hermana escribe una carta.
5. Tú tomas el sol.
6. Paseamos con nuestros amigos.
7. Mis amigos ven una película.

3 **Preguntas** With a partner, take turns asking and answering questions about where the people in the drawings are going.

> **modelo**
>
> **Estudiante 1:** ¿Adónde va Estela?
> **Estudiante 2:** Va a la Librería Sol.

1. Álex y Miguel

2. mi amigo

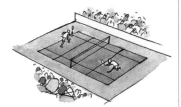

3. tú

4. los estudiantes

5. profesora Torres

6. Uds.

Comunicación

4

Situaciones Work with a partner and say where you and your friends go in the following situations.

1. Cuando deseo descansar...
2. Cuando mi novio/a tiene que estudiar...
3. Si mis compañeros de clase necesitan practicar el español...
4. Si deseo hablar con unos amigos...
5. Cuando tengo dinero (*money*)...
6. Cuando mis amigos y yo tenemos hambre...
7. Si tengo tiempo libre...
8. Cuando mis amigos desean esquiar...
9. Si estoy de vacaciones...
10. Si quiero leer...

5

Encuesta Your instructor will give you a worksheet. Walk around the class and ask your classmates if they are going to do these activities today. Try to find at least two people for each item and note their names on the worksheet. Be prepared to report your findings to the class.

Actividades	Nombres
1. Comer en un restaurante	
2. Mirar la televisión	
3. Leer una revista	
4. Escribir un mensaje electrónico	
5. Correr	
6. Ver una película	
7. Pasear en bicicleta	
8. Estudiar en la biblioteca	

6

Entrevista Interview two classmates to find out where they are going and what they are going to do on their next vacation.

> **modelo**
>
> **Estudiante 1:** ¿Adónde vas de vacaciones (*for vacation*)?
> **Estudiante 2:** Voy a Guadalajara con mis amigos.
> **Estudiante 1:** ¿Y qué van a hacer Uds. en Guadalajara?
> **Estudiante 2:** Vamos a visitar unos monumentos y museos.

Síntesis

7

El fin de semana Create a schedule with your activities for this weekend. For each day, list at least three things you need to do and two things you will do for fun. Then tell a classmate what your weekend schedule is, and he or she will write down what you say. Switch roles to see if you have any plans in common, and then take turns inviting each other to participate in some of the activities you listed.

4.2 Present tense of stem–changing verbs

CONSÚLTALO

The present tense of regular -ar verbs To review, see Lesson 2, section 2.1, p. 44.

• • •

The present tense of regular -er and -ir verbs To review, see Lesson 3, pp. 78-79.

ANTE TODO Stem-changing verbs deviate from the normal pattern of regular verbs in that the stressed vowel of the stem changes when the verb is conjugated. Observe the following diagram:

Present tense of stem-changing verbs			
	e → ie	o → ue	e → i
	empezar (to begin)	**volver** (to return)	**pedir** (to ask for; to request)
SINGULAR FORMS			
yo	empiezo	vuelvo	pido
tú	empiezas	vuelves	pides
Ud./él/ella	empieza	vuelve	pide
PLURAL FORMS			
nosotros/as	empezamos	volvemos	pedimos
vosotros/as	empezáis	volvéis	pedís
Uds./ellos/ellas	empiezan	vuelven	piden

El joven pide perdón.

Álex empieza a enviar mensajes.

COMPARE & CONTRAST

If you compare the *endings* of the stem-changing verbs in the preceding chart with those of regular **–ar**, **–er**, and **–ir** verbs, you will see that they are the same. The difference is that stem-changing verbs have a *stem* change in all of their present tense forms *except* the **nosotros/as** and **vosotros/as** forms, which are regular.

LENGUA VIVA

As you learned in Lesson 2, **preguntar** means *to ask a question.* **Pedir** means *to ask for something*:

Ella me pregunta cuántos años tengo. *She asks me how old I am.*

Él me pide ayuda. *He asks me for help.*

INFINITIVE	VERB STEM	STEM CHANGE	CONJUGATED FORM
empezar	empez-	empiez-	empiezo
volver	volv-	vuelv-	vuelvo
pedir	ped-	pid-	pido

To help you identify stem-changing verbs they will appear as follows throughout the text:

empezar (e:ie), volver (o:ue), pedir (e:i)

Common stem-changing verbs

e:ie		o:ue		e:i	
cerrar	to close	**dormir**	to sleep	**conseguir**	to get; to obtain
comenzar	to begin	**encontrar**	to find	**repetir**	to repeat
entender	to understand	**mostrar**	to show	**seguir**	to follow; to continue
pensar	to think	**poder**	to be able; can		
perder	to lose; to miss	**recordar**	to remember		
preferir	to prefer	**volver**	to return		
querer	to want; to love				

LENGUA VIVA

The verb **perder** can mean *to lose* or *to miss*, in the sense of "to miss a train":

Siempre pierdo mis llaves.
I always lose my keys.

Es importante no perder el autobús.
It's important not to miss the bus.

▶ **Jugar**, which means to play (*a sport or game*), is the only Spanish verb in which the stem change is **u ⟶ ue**. **Jugar** is followed by **a** + [*definite article*] when the name of a sport or game is mentioned.

Oye, Maite, ¿por qué no jugamos al fútbol?

Álex y el joven juegan al fútbol.

¡ATENCIÓN!

Comenzar and **empezar** require the preposition **a** when they are followed by an infinitive:

Ana empieza a estudiar.

Comienzan a trabajar.

● ● ●

Pensar + [*infinitive*] means *to plan* or *to intend to do something*. **Pensar en** means *to think about someone or something*.

¿Piensan ir al partido?
Are you thinking about going to the match?

Pienso mucho en mi novio.
I think about my boyfriend a lot.

▶ In addition to the stem change **e ⟶ i**, **seguir** and **conseguir** have irregular **yo** forms: **sigo, consigo.**

Sigo su plan.
I'm following their plan.

Consigo libros en el Internet.
I get books on the Internet.

¡INTÉNTALO! Provide the present tense forms of these verbs. The first item in each column has been done for you.

cerrar (e:ie)	dormir (o:ue)	repetir (e: i)
1. Uds. __cierran__	1. Mi abuela no __duerme__	1. Ellos __repiten__
2. Tú _____	2. Yo no _____	2. Teresa _____
3. Nosotras _____	3. Tú no _____	3. Tú _____
4. Mi hermano _____	4. Mis hijos no _____	4. Raúl y yo _____
5. Yo _____	5. Ud. no _____	5. Uds. _____
6. Ud. _____	6. Nosotros no _____	6. Yo _____
7. Los chicos _____	7. Él no _____	7. Ana y Simón _____
8. Ella _____	8. Uds. no _____	8. Ud. _____

Práctica

1

Preferencias With a partner, take turns asking and answering questions about what these people want to do, using the cues provided.

> **modelo**
>
> Guillermo: estudiar / pasear en bicicleta.
> **Estudiante 1:** ¿Quiere estudiar Guillermo?
> **Estudiante 2:** No, prefiere pasear en bicicleta.

1. tú: trabajar / dormir

2. Uds.: mirar la televisión / ir al cine

3. tus amigos: ir de excursión / descansar

4. tú: comer en la cafetería / ir a un restaurante

5. Elisa: ver una película / leer una revista

6. María y su hermana: tomar el sol / practicar el esquí acuático

2

Completar Complete this conversation with the appropriate forms of the verbs. Then act it out with a partner.

PABLO Óscar, voy al centro ahora.

ÓSCAR ¿A qué hora _____ (pensar) volver? El partido de fútbol _____ (empezar) a las dos.

PABLO _____ (Volver) a la una. _____ (querer) ver el partido.

ÓSCAR ¿_____ (Pensar) que (*that*) nuestro equipo _____ (poder) ganar?

PABLO No, _____ (pensar) que va a _____ (perder). Los jugadores de Guadalajara son salvajes (*wild*) cuando _____ (jugar).

3

Describir Use a verb from the list to describe what these people are doing.

cerrar	dormir	mostrar	conseguir

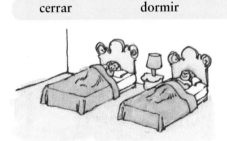

1. Las niñas

2. Yo

3. Tú

4. Pedro

Comunicación

4 **Encuesta** Your instructor will give you a worksheet. Walk around the room and ask your classmates if they play these sports. If someone plays a sport, ask where, when, and with whom he or she plays it. Note his or her name on your worksheet. Be prepared to report your findings to the class.

CONSÚLTALO

Lectura Are your classmates' preferences in sports like those of people in Spanish-speaking countries? To find out, see pp. 116-117.

Deportes	Nombres	Lugares	Día(s) y hora(s)	Otros jugadores
1. el baloncesto				
2. el béisbol				
3. el fútbol				
4. el fútbol americano				
5. el golf				
6. el hockey				
7. el tenis				
8. el vóleibol				

5 **En la televisión** Read the sports listing that will be televised this weekend and choose the programs you want to watch. Compare your choices with those of a classmate and explain why you made them. Then agree on one program you will watch together on each day.

sábado

13:30 NATACIÓN
1   Copa Mundial *(World Cup)* de Natación
15:00 TENIS
8   Abierto *(Open)* Mexicano de Tenis
     Alejandro Hernández (México)
     vs. Jacobo Díaz (España)
     Semifinales
16:00 FÚTBOL NACIONAL
3   Chivas vs. Monterrey

CABLE
16:30 FÚTBOL AMERICANO
     PROFESIONAL
21   los Vaqueros de Dallas
     vs. los Leones de Detroit
20:00 BALONCESTO PROFESIONAL
16   los Knicks de Nueva York
     vs. los Toros de Chicago

domingo

13:00 GOLF
40   Audi Senior Classic
14:30 VÓLEIBOL
1   Campeonato *(Championship)*
     Nacional de México
16:00 BALONCESTO
3   Campeonato de Cimeba
     los Correcaminos de Tampico
     vs. los Santos de San Luis
     Final

CABLE
15:00 ESQUÍ ALPINO
19   Eslálom
18:30 FÚTBOL INTERNACIONAL
30   Copa América: México vs. Argentina
     Ronda final
20:00 PATINAJE ARTÍSTICO
16   Exhibición mundial

Síntesis

6 **Situación** Work in groups of three to role-play this situation. One of you is a tour guide in a city you know well. The other two are tourists. Using some of the verbs, nouns, and other expressions you have learned, come up with a plan for your tour of the city.

4.3 Verbs with irregular **yo** forms

ANTE TODO In Spanish, several commonly used verbs have **yo** forms that are irregular in the present tense. The other forms are generally regular.

	Verbs with irregular *yo* forms						
	hacer *(to do;* *to make)*	**poner** *(to put;* *to place)*	**salir** *(to leave)*	**suponer** *(to suppose)*	**traer** *(to bring)*	**oír** *(to hear)*	**ver** *(to see)*
SINGULAR FORMS	**hago**	**pongo**	**salgo**	**supongo**	**traigo**	**oigo**	**veo**
	haces	pones	sales	supones	traes	oyes	ves
	hace	pone	sale	supone	trae	oye	ve
PLURAL FORMS	hacemos	ponemos	salimos	suponemos	traemos	oímos	vemos
	hacéis	ponéis	salís	suponéis	traéis	oís	veis
	hacen	ponen	salen	suponen	traen	oyen	ven

► Note that the **yo** forms of **hacer, poner, salir, suponer, traer,** and **oír** end in **–go:** **hago, pongo, salgo, supongo, traigo,** and **oigo.**

¡ATENCIÓN!

Salir de (*to leave from*) is used when someone is leaving a place:
Hoy sale del hospital.

• • •

To indicate someone's destination, you use **salir para** (*to leave for*):
Hoy sale para México.

• • •

Salir con means to *leave with someone, to leave with something* or *to date someone:*
Juan sale con su papá.
Yo salgo con mi mochila.
Anita sale con Miguel.

Nunca salgo a correr, no hago ejercicio, pero sí tengo energía... ¡para leer el periódico y tomar un café!

► The verb **oír** is irregular in all forms except **vosotros.** Note that the **nosotros** form has an accent mark.

► **Poner** can mean *to turn on* when referring to household appliances.

Voy a **poner** la televisión.   Álex **pone** la radio.
I'm going to turn on the television.   *Álex turns on the radio.*

¡INTÉNTALO! Provide the appropriate forms of these verbs. The first item has been done for you.

1. salir	Isabel ___*sale*___	Nosotros _____	Yo _____
2. ver	Yo _____	Uds. _____	Tú _____
3. poner	Rita y yo _____	Yo _____	Los niños _____
4. hacer	Yo _____	Tú _____	Ud. _____
5. oír	Él _____	Nosotros _____	Yo _____
6. traer	Ellas _____	Yo _____	Tú _____
7. suponer	Yo _____	Mi amigo _____	Nosotras _____

Práctica

1 **Completar** Complete this conversation with the appropriate forms of the verbs. Then act it out with a partner.

ERNESTO David, ¿qué _____ (hacer) hoy?

DAVID Ahora estudio biología, pero esta noche _____ (salir) con Luisa. Vamos al cine. Queremos _____ (ver) la nueva (*new*) película de Almodóvar.

ERNESTO ¿Y Diana? ¿Qué _____ (hacer) ella?

DAVID _____ (Salir) a comer con sus padres.

ERNESTO ¿Qué _____ (hacer) Andrés y Javier?

DAVID Tienen que _____ (hacer) las maletas. _____ (Salir) para Monterrey mañana.

ERNESTO Pues, ¿qué _____ (hacer) yo?

DAVID _____ (Suponer) que puedes estudiar o _____ (ver) la televisión.

ERNESTO No quiero estudiar. Mejor _____ (poner) el televisor. Mi programa favorito empieza en unos minutos.

2 **Oraciones** Form complete sentences using the cues provided and verbs you learned on page 109.

> **modelo**
>
> Tú / ? / libros / debajo de / escritorio
> Tú pones los libros debajo del escritorio.

1. Nosotros / ? / mucha / tarea
2. ¿Tú / ? / la radio?
3. Yo / no / ? / problema
4. Marta / ? / grabadora / clase
5. señores Marín / ? / su casa / siete
6. Yo / ? / que (*that*) / tú / ir / cine / ¿no?

3 **Describir** Use a verb from page 109 to describe what these people are doing.

1. Fernán

2. Los aficionados

3. Yo

4. Nosotros

5. La señora Vargas

6. El estudiante

Comunicación

4

Preguntas Get together with a classmate and ask each other these questions.

1. ¿Qué traes a clase?
2. ¿Quiénes traen un diccionario a clase? ¿Por qué traen un diccionario?
3. ¿A qué hora sales de tu residencia o de tu casa por la mañana? ¿A qué hora sale tu compañero/a de cuarto o tu esposo/a?
4. ¿Dónde pones tus libros cuando regresas de clase? ¿Siempre (*Always*) pones tus cosas en su lugar?
5. ¿Pones fotos de tu familia en tu casa? ¿De quiénes son?
6. ¿Oyes la radio cuando estudias?
7. ¿Qué vas a hacer esta noche?
8. ¿Haces mucha tarea los fines de semana?
9. ¿Sales con los amigos los fines de semana? ¿Qué hacen?
10. ¿Te gusta ver deportes en la televisión o prefieres ver otros programas? ¿Cuáles?

5

Charadas In groups, play a game of charades. Each person should think of two phrases using the verbs **hacer, poner, salir, suponer, oír, traer,** or **ver**. The first person to guess correctly acts out the next charade.

6

Entrevista You are doing a market research report on lifestyles. Interview a classmate to find out when he or she goes out with the following people and what they do for entertainment.

- los amigos
- el/la novio/a
- el/la esposo/a
- la familia

Síntesis

7

Situación Ask a classmate if he or she wants to go out. He or she will accept. Then find out what activities your classmate prefers so you can decide where you want to go. Finally, negotiate the place, the day, and the time for your date with your classmate.

4.4 Weather expressions

ANTE TODO In English, the verb *to be* is used to describe weather conditions: for example, *It's sunny.* Spanish, however, does not use **ser** or **estar** to express most weather conditions. Instead, it uses the verb **hacer**. To ask what the weather is like, use the question **¿Qué tiempo hace?**

—¿Qué tiempo **hace** hoy?
What's the weather like today?

—**Hace** buen/mal tiempo.
The weather is good/bad.

Expressions with hacer

Hace (mucho) sol.
It's (very) sunny.

Hace (mucho) calor.
It's (very) hot.

Hace (mucho) viento.
It's (very) windy.

Hace (mucho) frío.
It's (very) cold.

Hace fresco.
It's cool.

▶ Weather expressions are frequently used with **mucho/a**, not **muy**.

▶ **Llover (o:ue)** (*to rain*) and **nevar (e:ie)** (*to snow*) are usually used in the third person singular form: **llueve** (*it's raining*), **nieva** (*it's snowing*).

Hoy no vamos al parque porque **llueve**.
We're not going to the park today because it's raining.

Si **nieva** hoy, voy a esquiar mañana.
If it snows today, I'm going skiing tomorrow.

Other weather expressions

Está (muy) nublado.
It's (very) cloudy.

Está despejado.
It's clear.

Nieva.
It's snowing.

Llueve.
It's raining.

Hay (mucha) niebla.
It's (very) foggy.

Hay (mucha) contaminación.
It's (very) smoggy.

COMPARE & CONTRAST

Calor and **frío** are conditions that can apply to both weather and people.

El niño **tiene** calor.	**Hace** calor.
The child is hot.	*It's hot.*
Tenemos frío.	**Hace** frío.
We are cold.	*It's cold.*

English uses the verb *to be* when describing either people or the weather as *hot* or *cold.* Spanish, however, uses **tener calor/frío** to refer to people and **hacer calor/frío** to refer to weather.

¡INTÉNTALO! Complete these sentences. The first item has been done for you.

1. ¿Qué tiempo _____*hace*_____ hoy?
2. _____ fresco.
3. _____ mucha contaminación hoy.
4. Carlos _____ mucho frío.
5. _____ mal tiempo.
6. _____ despejado hoy.
7. _____ mucho frío.
8. En abril _____ mucho.
9. _____ mucho viento.
10. Julia y Ana _____ calor.
11. _____ mucho sol.
12. _____ niebla.
13. _____ muy nublado.
14. _____ calor.
15. Vamos a esquiar si _____.
16. _____ buen tiempo.

Práctica

1   **Seleccionar** Choose the word or phrase that completes each sentence logically.

1. (Hace sol, Nieva) en Cancún.
2. Durante (*During*) un tornado, (hace mucho sol, hace mucho viento).
3. Mis amigos van a esquiar si (nieva, llueve).
4. Tomo el sol cuando (hace calor, hay niebla).
5. Vamos a ver una película si hace (buen, mal) tiempo.
6. Daniel prefiere correr cuando (hay contaminación, hace fresco).
7. Ana y José van de excursión si hace (buen, mal) tiempo.
8. No queremos jugar al golf si (está despejado, llueve).

2   **El clima** With a partner, take turns asking and answering questions about the weather and temperatures in these cities.

> **modelo**
>
> **Estudiante 1:** ¿Qué tiempo hace hoy en Nueva York?
> **Estudiante 2:** Hace frío y hace viento.
> **Estudiante 1:** ¿Cuál es la temperatura máxima?
> **Estudiante 2:** Treinta y un grados (*degrees*).
> **Estudiante 1:** ¿Y la temperatura mínima?
> **Estudiante 2:** Diez grados.

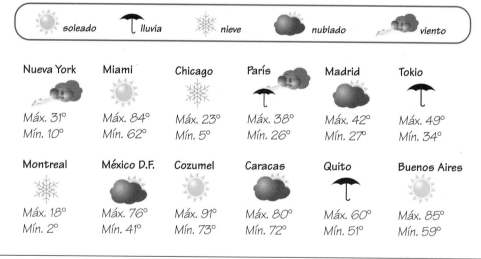

soleado   lluvia   nieve   nublado   viento

Nueva York	Miami	Chicago	París	Madrid	Tokio
Máx. 31°	Máx. 84°	Máx. 23°	Máx. 38°	Máx. 42°	Máx. 49°
Mín. 10°	Mín. 62°	Mín. 5°	Mín. 26°	Mín. 27°	Mín. 34°

Montreal	México D.F.	Cozumel	Caracas	Quito	Buenos Aires
Máx. 18°	Máx. 76°	Máx. 91°	Máx. 80°	Máx. 60°	Máx. 85°
Mín. 2°	Mín. 41°	Mín. 73°	Mín. 72°	Mín. 51°	Mín. 59°

3   **Completar** Complete these sentences with your own ideas.

1. Cuando hace sol, yo…
2. Cuando llueve, mis amigos y yo…
3. Cuando hace calor, mi familia…
4. Cuando hay contaminación, la gente…
5. Cuando hace frío, yo…
6. Cuando hace mal tiempo, mis amigos…
7. Cuando nieva, muchas personas…
8. Cuando está nublado, mis amigos y yo…
9. Cuando hace fresco, mis padres…
10. Cuando está despejado, yo…

Comunicación

4

Preguntas Get together with a classmate and ask each other the following questions.

1. ¿Hace buen tiempo o mal tiempo hoy?
2. ¿Qué tiempo va a hacer mañana?
3. ¿Nieva mucho en tu ciudad/pueblo?
4. ¿Dónde nieva mucho?
5. ¿Llueve mucho en tu ciudad/pueblo?
6. ¿Dónde llueve mucho?
7. ¿Hay mucha contaminación donde vives?
8. ¿Dónde hay mucha contaminación?
9. ¿Hay mucha niebla donde vives?
10. ¿Dónde hay mucha niebla?

5

Encuesta Your instructor will give you a worksheet. How does the weather affect what you do? Walk around the class and ask your classmates what they prefer or like to do in the following weather conditions. Note their responses on your worksheet. Make sure to personalize your survey by adding a few original questions of your own to the list. Be prepared to report your findings to the class.

Tiempo	Actividades
1. Hace mucho calor.	
2. Nieva.	
3. Hace buen tiempo.	
4. Hace fresco.	
5. Llueve.	
6. Hay mucha contaminación.	
7. Hace mucho frío.	

Síntesis

6

Situación Act out this situation with a classmate. You are going to visit a friend who lives in another part of the country for the weekend. You call your friend to tell him or her what day and time you are planning to arrive. Then you ask about the weather so that you will know how to pack for your trip. Your friend tells you about the weather forecast, and then the two of you plan some activities for the weekend based on the weather conditions.

recursos

R	WB pp. 37-46	LM p. 215-220	LCASS./CD Cass. 4/CD4	ICD-ROM Lección 4

Lectura
Antes de leer

Estrategia
Predicting content from visuals

When you are reading in Spanish, be sure to look for visual clues that will orient you as to the content and purpose of what you are reading. Photos and illustrations, for example, will often give you a good idea of the main points that the reading covers. You may also encounter very helpful visuals that are used to summarize large amounts of data in a way that is easy to comprehend; these include bar graphs, pie charts, flow charts, lists of percentages, and other sorts of diagrams.

Examinar el texto

Take a quick look at the visual elements of the magazine article in order to generate a list of ideas about its content. Then compare your list with a classmate's. Are your lists the same or are they different? Discuss your lists and make any changes needed to produce a final list of ideas.

Contestar

Read the list of ideas you wrote in **Examinar el texto,** and look again at the visual elements of the magazine article. Then answer these questions:

1. Who is the woman in the photo, and what is her role?
2. What is the article about?
3. How was the data collected?
4. What is the subject of the pie chart?
5. What is the subject of the bar graph?

---

por Pamela Aranda

¿Cuál es el deporte más popular?

El fútbol es el deporte más popular en los países de habla hispana. Mucha gente practica este deporte y tiene un equipo de fútbol favorito. Los aficionados miran los partidos en la televisión y, a veces, van al estadio. Los jóvenes juegan al fútbol con sus amigos en parques y gimnasios. A muchos jóvenes les gusta practicar este deporte y vivir la emoción de hacer un gol con su equipo.

Según una encuesta realizada entre jóvenes universitarios de países de habla hispana, los deportes más populares son:

Deportes más populares

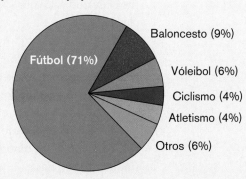

Fútbol (71%)
Baloncesto (9%)
Vóleibol (6%)
Ciclismo (4%)
Atletismo (4%)
Otros (6%)

Según *According to* **una encuesta** *survey* **atletismo** *track and field*

Después de leer

Evaluación y predicción

Which of the following sports events would be most popular among the college students surveyed? Rate them from one (most popular) to five (least popular). Which would be the most popular at your college or university?

_____ 1. La Copa Mundial de Fútbol

_____ 2. Los Juegos Olímpicos

_____ 3. El torneo de tenis de Wimbledon

_____ 4. La Serie Mundial de Béisbol

_____ 5. El Tour de Francia

Deportes en el mundo hispano

El fútbol es un deporte importante y muy popular en América, Europa, Asia y África. Cada cuatro años se realiza la Copa Mundial de Fútbol. Argentina y Uruguay han ganado este campeonato más de una vez.

Países hispanos en campeonatos mundiales de fútbol (1938-1998)

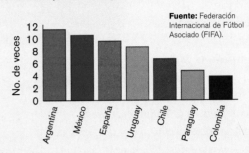

Fuente: Federación Internacional de Fútbol Asociado (FIFA).

¿Cuántas veces juegas al fútbol cada semana?

15%	3 o 4 veces	40%	1 vez
25%	2 veces	20%	0 veces

¿Cuántos partidos de fútbol ves por TV al mes?

66%	más de 4 partidos	8%	1 partido
24%	2 partidos	2%	0 partidos

¿Cuál es tu lugar favorito para ver el fútbol?

39%	el estadio
25%	la casa
17%	el restaurante/bar
12%	el club deportivo
5%	la cafetería de la universidad
2%	no especifica

el mundo *world*   se realiza *occurs*   campeonato *championship*   más de una vez *more than one time*   veces *times*

Completar

Complete the following statements with information from the article.

1. _____ is the least popular gathering place to watch soccer matches.
2. Both _____ and _____ soccer are popular pastimes in the Spanish-speaking world.
3. The second most popular sport in the Spanish-speaking countries surveyed is _____.
4. _____ and _____ have won the World Cup more than once.
5. According to the graph, the country that has participated in the most World Cups is _____.

Preguntas

Answer these questions in Spanish.

1. ¿Te gusta el fútbol? ¿Por qué?
2. ¿Miras la Copa Mundial en la televisión?
3. ¿Qué deportes miras en la televisión?
4. En tu opinión, ¿cuáles son los tres deportes más populares en tu universidad? ¿en tu comunidad? ¿en los Estados Unidos?

México

El país en cifras

▶ **Área**: 1.972.550 km^2 (761.603 millas^2), casi tres veces el área de Texas.

La situación geográfica de México, al sur de los Estados Unidos, ha influido en la economía y la sociedad de los dos países. Una de las consecuencias es la emigración de la población mexicana al país vecino. Hoy día, más de 20 millones de personas de descendencia mexicana viven en los Estados Unidos.

▶ **Población**: 101.851.000

▶ **Capital**: México, D.F.—18.372.000

▶ **Ciudades principales**: Guadalajara—4.017.000, Monterrey—3.514.000, Puebla—2.025.000, Cancún—1.325.000, Ciudad Juárez—1.226.000

SOURCE: Population Division, UN Secretariat

▶ **Moneda**: peso mexicano

▶ **Idiomas**: español (oficial), náhuatl, idiomas mayas

La bandera de México

Mexicanos célebres

▶ Benito Juárez, héroe nacional (1806-1872)

▶ Octavio Paz, poeta (1914-1998)

▶ Elena Poniatowska, periodista y escritora (1933-)

▶ Julio César Chávez, boxeador (1962-)

casi *almost* veces *times* sur *south* ha influido en *has influenced*
vecino *neighboring* vecindario *neighborhood* cortas *short*
nunca *never*

Un delfín en Baja California

ESTADOS UNIDOS

Ciudad Juárez

El castillo de Tulum cerca de Cancún

Golfo de California

Baja California

Río Grande

Río Bravo del Norte

Sierra Madre Oriental

Sierra Madre Occidental

ESTADOS UNIDOS

MÉXICO

OCÉANO ATLÁNTICO

OCÉANO PACÍFICO

AMÉRICA DEL SUR

Monterrey

Océano Pacífico

Puerto Vallarta

Ciudad de México

Guadalajara

Puebla

Acapulco

Ruinas aztecas en México D.F.

Saltador en Acapulco

recursos

R

WB
pp. 47-48

vistasonline.com

ICD-ROM
Lección 4

¡Increíble pero cierto!

En la ciudad de México cada vecindario nombra sus calles en honor a un tema especial. Un vecindario ha elegido la literatura, y tiene calles llamadas *Dickens*, *Dante* y *Shakespeare*. En otro están las calles del *Atún* y del *Cilantro*. Irónicamente, las calles del *Amor* y la *Felicidad* son cortas, mientras que la calle del *Trabajo* nunca termina.

Ciudades • **México D.F.**

La ciudad de México, fundada en 1525, también se llama el D.F. o Distrito Federal. La ciudad atrae a miles de inmigrantes y turistas por ser el centro cultural y económico del país. El crecimiento de la población es de los más altos del mundo. El D.F. tiene una población mayor que la de Nueva York o cualquier capital europea.

Artes • **Diego Rivera y Frida Kahlo**

Los pintores Diego Rivera y Frida Kahlo, casados en 1929, fueron muy importantes en la vida política de su país. Rivera, muralista, trató temas sociales e históricos. Kahlo, conocida por sus autorretratos, pintó cuadros más personales y psicológicos. Los dos se interesaron por la vida y el arte de la gente sencilla.

Historia • **Los aztecas**

Los aztecas dominaron en México desde el siglo XIV hasta el siglo XVI. Construyeron canales, puentes y pirámides con templos religiosos. Aunque el imperio azteca terminó cuando llegaron los conquistadores en 1519, todavía se siente su presencia. La ciudad de México está construida en el sitio de la capital azteca, Tenochtitlán, y muchos turistas visitan sus ruinas.

Costumbres • **Día de los muertos**

Algunos mexicanos creen que los espíritus de los muertos regresan a la tierra el dos de noviembre para visitar a los vivos. Muchas personas van al cementerio en el Día de los muertos, y algunas pasan la noche allí. También es costumbre preparar ofrendas y comer pan y dulces en forma de calaveras y de esqueletos.

Golfo de México

Península de Yucatán

Mérida

Cancún

Bahía de Campeche

racruz

Istmo de Tehuantepec

BELICE

GUATEMALA

¿Qué aprendiste? Responde a las preguntas (*questions*) con una frase completa.

1. ¿Qué lenguas hablan los mexicanos?

2. ¿Cómo es la población del D.F. en comparación a otras ciudades?

3. ¿En qué son diferentes las obras de Kahlo y Rivera?

4. ¿Qué construyeron los aztecas?

5. ¿En qué sitio está construida la capital de México?

6. ¿Cuándo celebran los mexicanos el Día de los muertos?

Conexión Internet Investiga estos temas en el sitio **www.vistasonline.com**.

1. Busca información sobre dos lugares de México. ¿Te gustaría (*Would you like*) vivir allí? ¿Por qué?
2. Busca información sobre dos artistas mexicanos. ¿Cómo se llaman sus obras (*works*) más famosas?

atrae a *attracts* **miles** *thousands* **por ser** *due to being* **crecimiento** *growth* **más altos** *highest* **cualquier** *any other* **pintores** *painters* **casados** *married* **fueron** *were* **vida** *life* **trató** *treated* **e** *and* **conocida** *known* **autorretratos** *self-portraits* **pintó** *painted* **cuadros** *paintings* **se interesaron por** *were interested in* **la vida** *life* **sencilla** *common* **dominaron** *dominated* **desde** *from* **el siglo** *century* **Contruyeron** *They built* **puentes** *bridges* **Aunque** *Although* **imperio** *empire* **terminó** *ended* **llegaron** *arrived* **todavía se siente** *is still felt* **construida** *constructed* **muertos** *dead* **Algunos** *Some* **la tierra** *Earth* **vivos** *living* **allí** *there* **ofrendas** *offerings* **pan** *bread* **dulces** *sweets* **calaveras** *skulls*

Pasatiempos

bucear	to scuba dive
escalar montañas (f. pl.)	to climb mountains
escribir una carta	to write a letter
escribir un mensaje electrónico	to write an e-mail message
escribir una (tarjeta) postal	to write a postcard
esquiar	to ski
ganar	to win
ir de excursión (a las montañas)	to go for a hike (in the mountains)
leer correo electrónico	to read e-mail
leer un periódico	to read a newspaper
leer una revista	to read a magazine
nadar	to swim
pasar tiempo	to spend time
pasear	to take a walk; to stroll
pasear en bicicleta	to ride a bicycle
pasear por la ciudad/el pueblo	to walk around the city/the town
patinar (en línea)	to skate (in-line)
practicar deportes (m. pl.)	to play sports
ser aficionado/a (a)	to be a fan (of)
tomar el sol	to sunbathe
ver películas (f. pl.)	to see movies
visitar monumentos (m. pl.)	to visit monuments
la diversión	fun activity; entertainment; recreation
el/la excursionista	hiker
el fin de semana	weekend
el pasatiempo	pastime
los ratos libres	spare (free) time
el tiempo libre	free time

Deportes

el baloncesto	basketball
el béisbol	baseball
el ciclismo	cycling
el equipo	team
el esquí (acuático)	(water) skiing
el fútbol	soccer
el fútbol americano	football
el golf	golf
el hockey	hockey
el/la jugador(a)	player
la natación	swimming
el partido	game; match
la pelota	ball
el tenis	tennis
el vóleibol	volleyball

Verbos

cerrar (e:ie)	to close
comenzar (e:ie)	to begin
conseguir (e:i)	to get; to obtain
dormir (o:ue)	to sleep
empezar (e:ie)	to begin
encontrar (o:ue)	to find
entender (e:ie)	to understand
hacer	to do; to make
ir	to go
jugar (u:ue)	to play
mostrar (o:ue)	to show
oír	to hear
pedir (e:i)	to ask for; to request
pensar (e:ie)	to think
pensar + inf.	to intend
pensar en	to think about
perder (e:ie)	to lose
poder (o:ue)	to be able to; can
poner	to put; to place
preferir (e:ie)	to prefer
querer (e:ie)	to want; to love
recordar (o:ue)	to remember
repetir (e:i)	to repeat
salir	to leave
seguir (e:i)	to follow; to continue
suponer	to suppose
traer	to bring
ver	to see
volver (o:ue)	to return

Adjetivos

deportivo/a	sports-related
favorito/a	favorite

¿Qué tiempo hace?

¿Qué tiempo hace?	How's the weather?; What's the weather like?
Está despejado.	It's clear.
Está (muy) nublado.	It's (very) cloudy.
Hace buen (mal) tiempo.	It's nice (bad) weather.
Hace (mucho) calor.	It's (very) hot.
Hace fresco.	It's cool.
Hace (mucho) frío.	It's (very) cold.
Hace (mucho) sol.	It's (very) sunny.
Hace (mucho) viento.	It's (very) windy.
Hay (mucha) contaminación.	It's (very) smoggy.
Hay (mucha) niebla.	It's (very) foggy.
llover	to rain
Llueve.	It's raining.
nevar	to snow
Nieva.	It's snowing.

Lugares

el café	café
la casa	house
el centro	downtown
el cine	movie theater
el gimnasio	gymnasium
la iglesia	church
el lugar	place
el museo	museum
el parque (municipal)	(municipal) park
la piscina	swimming pool
el restaurante	restaurant

Expresiones útiles	See page 99.

recursos

R	LCASS./CD Cass. 4/CD4	LM p. 220

Las vacaciones

5

Communicative Goals

You will learn how to:
- Discuss and plan a vacation
- Describe a hotel
- Talk about how you feel
- Talk about the seasons and the weather

Las vacaciones

Más vocabulario

la cabaña	cabin
la cama	bed
el campo	countryside
el equipaje	luggage
la estación de autobuses, del metro, de tren	bus, subway, train station
la habitación individual, doble	single, double room
la llegada	arrival
el paisaje	landscape
el pasaje (de ida y vuelta)	(round-trip) ticket
la pensión	boarding house
el piso	floor (of a building)
la planta baja	ground floor
la salida	departure; exit
la tienda de campaña	tent
acampar	to go camping
estar de vacaciones	to be on vacation
hacer las maletas	to pack (one's suitcases)
hacer una excursión	to go on a hike, tour
hacer turismo (m.)	to go sightseeing
hacer un viaje	to take a trip
ir de compras	to go shopping
ir de vacaciones	to go on vacation
ir en autobús (m.), auto(móvil) (m.), avión (m.), motocicleta (f.), taxi (m.)	to go by bus, car, plane, motorcycle, taxi
recorrer	to tour an area
turístico/a	tourist-related

Variación léxica

automóvil ←→ coche (*Esp.*), carro (*Amér. L.*)
autobús ←→ camión (*Méx.*), guagua (*P. Rico*)
motocicleta ←→ moto (*coloquial*)

la agente de viajes

el pasaporte

Confirma una reservación. (confirmar)

En la agencia de viajes

la habitación

el ascensor

el botones

el empleado

la llave

la huésped

el huésped

En el hotel

recursos

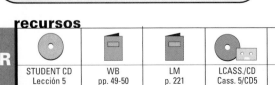

| R | STUDENT CD Lección 5 | WB pp. 49-50 | LM p. 221 | LCASS./CD Cass. 5/CD5 | ICD-ROM Lección 5 |

En el aeropuerto

En la playa

Práctica

1 **Escuchar** Indicate who would probably make each statement you hear. Each answer is used twice.

a. el agente de viajes
b. la inspectora de aduanas
c. un empleado del hotel

1. _____   3. _____   5. _____
2. _____   4. _____   6. _____

2 **Escoger** Choose the best answer for each sentence.

1. Un huésped es una persona que _____.
   a. hace una excursión
   b. está en un hotel
   c. pesca en el mar
2. Abrimos la puerta con _____.
   a. una llave
   b. una cabaña
   c. una llegada
3. Enrique tiene _____ en las montañas.
   a. un pasaporte
   b. una cabaña
   c. un pasaje
4. Antes de (*Before*) ir de vacaciones hay que _____.
   a. pescar
   b. ir en tren
   c. hacer las maletas
5. A veces (*Sometimes*) es necesario _____ en un aeropuerto internacional.
   a. hacer turismo
   b. pasar por la aduana
   c. pescar
6. Me gusta mucho ir al campo. _____ es increíble.
   a. El paisaje
   b. El pasaje
   c. El equipaje

3 **Analogías** Complete the analogies using the words below.

pasaporte	auto	mar	avión
huésped	botones	sacar	llegada

1. acampar → campo ⊜ pescar →
2. aduana → inspector ⊜ hotel →
3. llave → habitación ⊜ pasaje →
4. estudiante → libro ⊜ turista →
5. aeropuerto → viajero ⊜ hotel →
6. maleta → hacer ⊜ foto →

Las estaciones y los meses del año

el invierno: **diciembre, enero, febrero**

la primavera: **marzo, abril, mayo**

el verano: **junio, julio, agosto**

el otoño: **septiembre, octubre, noviembre**

4 **El Hotel Regis** Label the floors of the hotel.

a. _____ piso
b. _____ piso
c. _____ piso
d. _____ piso
e. _____ piso
f. _____ piso
g. _____ piso
h. _____ baja

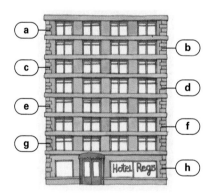

Números ordinales	
primer, primero/a	*first*
segundo/a	*second*
tercer, tercero/a	*third*
cuarto/a	*fourth*
quinto/a	*fifth*
sexto/a	*sixth*
séptimo/a	*seventh*
octavo/a	*eighth*
noveno/a	*ninth*
décimo/a	*tenth*

5 **Contestar** Look at the illustration of the months and seasons on this page. Then, with a classmate, answer these questions.

> **modelo**
>
> **Estudiante 1:** ¿Cuál es el primer mes de la primavera?
> **Estudiante 2:** marzo

1. ¿Cuál es el primer mes del invierno?
2. ¿Cuál es el segundo mes de la primavera?
3. ¿Cuál es el tercer mes del otoño?
4. ¿Cuál es el primer mes del año?
5. ¿Cuál es el quinto mes del año?
6. ¿Cuál es el octavo mes del año?
7. ¿Cuál es el décimo mes del año?
8. ¿Cuál es el segundo mes del verano?
9. ¿Cuál es el tercer mes del invierno?
10. ¿Cuál es la cuarta estación del año?

Comunicación

6

Preguntas personales With a classmate, answer the following questions.

1. ¿Cuál es la fecha de hoy? ¿Qué estación es? ¿Te gusta esta (*this*) estación? ¿Por qué? ¿Qué estación prefieres? ¿Por qué?
2. ¿Prefieres el mar o las montañas? ¿La playa o el campo? ¿Por qué?
3. Cuando estás de vacaciones, ¿qué haces? Cuando haces turismo, ¿qué te gusta hacer y ver?
4. ¿Piensas ir de vacaciones este verano? ¿Adónde quieres ir? ¿Por qué? ¿Qué deseas ver y visitar allí (*there*)? ¿Cómo vas a ir... en avión, en motocicleta...?

7

Encuesta Your instructor will give you a worksheet. Turn the phrases in the first column into yes/no questions, then use them to survey your classmates. Try to find at least one person who does each activity and note his or her name on your worksheet. Be prepared to share the results of your survey with the class.

Actividades	Nombres
1. Jugar bien a las cartas	_____
2. Acampar en las montañas o en el desierto	_____
3. Pescar en el mar	_____
4. Tener miedo de viajar en avión	_____
5. Viajar mucho en barco	_____
6. Comer mucho en restaurantes	_____
7. Hacer turismo en Puerto Rico	_____
8. Montar a caballo	_____
9. Llevar mucho equipaje en tus viajes	_____
10. Ir en motocicleta al campo	_____

8

Mis vacaciones Write a paragraph describing how you prepare for vacation and what you like to do on vacation. While brainstorming ideas for your paragraph, you might want to consider the following questions:

- During what month of the year or season do you like to travel?
- What resources do you use to help you plan your trip (travel agents, books, the Internet, etc.)?
- Do you spend your vacations with family? With friends?
- Do you plan vacations on the beach? In the mountains? In a favorite city or country?
- What activities do you enjoy when you're on vacation?

When you have finished writing, share your paragraph with the class.

9

Minidrama With two or three classmates, prepare and act out a skit about people who are on vacation or are planning a vacation. The skit should take place in one of the areas mentioned below.

1. Una agencia de viajes
2. Una casa
3. Un aeropuerto, una estación de tren o una estación de autobuses
4. Un hotel
5. El campo o la playa

Tenemos una reservación.

Don Francisco y los estudiantes llegan al hotel.

PERSONAJES

MAITE

INÉS

DON
FRANCISCO

ÁLEX

JAVIER

EMPLEADA

BOTONES

EMPLEADA ¿En qué puedo servirles?

DON FRANCISCO Mire, yo soy Francisco Castillo Moreno y tenemos una reservación a mi nombre.

EMPLEADA Mmm… no veo su nombre aquí. No está.

DON FRANCISCO ¿Está segura, señorita? Quizás la reservación está a nombre de la agencia de viajes, Ecuatur.

EMPLEADA Pues sí, aquí está… dos habitaciones dobles y una individual, de la ciento uno a la ciento tres,… todas en las primeras cabañas.

DON FRANCISCO Gracias, señorita. Muy amable.

BOTONES Bueno, la habitación ciento dos… Por favor.

INÉS Oigan, yo estoy aburrida. ¿Quieren hacer algo?

JAVIER ¿Por qué no vamos a explorar la ciudad un poco más?

INÉS ¡Excelente idea! ¡Vamos!

MAITE No, yo no voy. Estoy cansada y quiero descansar un poco porque a las seis voy a correr con Álex.

ÁLEX Y yo quiero escribir un mensaje electrónico antes de ir a correr.

JAVIER Pues nosotros estamos listos, ¿verdad, Inés?

INÉS Sí, vamos.

MAITE Adiós.

INÉS & JAVIER ¡Chau!

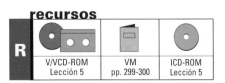

recursos

R | V/VCD-ROM Lección 5 | VM pp. 299-300 | ICD-ROM Lección 5

4

ÁLEX Hola, chicas. ¿Qué están haciendo?

MAITE Estamos descansando.

5

JAVIER Oigan, no están nada mal las cabañas, ¿verdad?

INÉS Y todo está muy limpio y ordenado.

ÁLEX Sí, es excelente.

MAITE Y las camas son tan cómodas.

9

ÁLEX Bueno, nos vemos a las seis.

MAITE Sí, hasta luego.

ÁLEX Adiós.

10

MAITE ¿Inés y Javier? Juntos otra vez.

Enfoque cultural El alojamiento

There are many different types of lodging **(alojamiento)** for travelers in Hispanic countries. In major cities there are traditional hotels, but a more economical choice is a youth hostel, or **albergue juvenil,** where people can stay in a large, barracks-type room for a very low fee. Another option is an inn, or **hostal,** usually a privately owned residence. A unique type of lodging in Spain is a **parador,** which is usually a converted castle, palace, or villa that has been preserved and emphasizes the culture and cuisine of the region.

Reacciona a la fotonovela

1 **Completar** Complete these sentences with the correct term from the word bank.

descansar	habitaciones individuales	las maletas
hacer las maletas	cansada	aburrida
las camas	la agencia de viajes	habitaciones dobles

1. La reservación para el hotel está a nombre de _____.
2. Los estudiantes tienen dos _____.
3. Maite va a _____ porque está _____.
4. El botones lleva _____ a las habitaciones.
5. Las habitaciones son buenas y _____ son cómodas.

2 **Identificar** Identify the person who would make each statement.

1. Antes de correr voy a trabajar en la computadora un poco.
2. Estoy aburrido. Tengo ganas de explorar la ciudad. ¿Vienes tú también?
3. Lo siento mucho, señor, pero su nombre no está en la lista.
4. Creo que la reservación está a mi nombre, señorita.
5. Oye, el hotel es maravilloso, ¿no? Las habitaciones están muy limpias.

EMPLEADA   **ÁLEX**   **DON FRANCISCO**   **JAVIER**   **INÉS**

¡ATENCIÓN!

The meaning of some adjectives, such as **aburrido**, changes depending on whether they are used with **ser** or **estar**. See pp.136-137.

3 **Ordenar** Place these events in correct order.

a. Las chicas descansan en su habitación. _____
b. Javier e Inés deciden ir a explorar la ciudad. _____
c. Don Francisco habla con la empleada del hotel. _____
d. Javier, Maite, Inés y Álex hablan en la habitación de las chicas. _____
e. El botones pone (*puts*) las maletas en la cama. _____

4 **Conversar** With a partner use these cues to create a conversation between a bellhop and a hotel guest.

Huésped

Ask the bellhop to carry your suitcases to your room.

Comment that the hotel is excellent and that everything is very clean.

Ask if the bellhop is sure. You think you have room 520.

Tell the bellhop to put them on the bed and thank him or her.

Botones

Say "yes, sir/ma'am/miss."

Agree, then point out the guest's room, a single room on the sixth floor.

Confirm that the guest has room 620. Ask where you should put the suitcases.

Say "you're welcome" and "goodbye."

Pronunciación

Spanish b and v

bueno	**vó**leibol	**b**iblioteca	**v**ivir

There is no difference in pronunciation between the Spanish letters **b** and **v**. However, each letter can be pronounced two different ways, depending on which letters appear next to them.

bonito   **v**iajar   tam**b**ien   in**v**estigar

B and **v** are pronounced like the English hard *b* when they appear either as the first letter of a word, at the beginning of a phrase, or after **m** or **n**.

de**b**er   no**v**io   a**b**ril   cer**v**eza

In all other positions, **b** and **v** have a softer pronunciation, which has no equivalent in English. Unlike the hard **b**, which is produced by tightly closing the lips and stopping the flow of air, the soft **b** is produced by keeping the lips slightly open.

bola   **v**ela   Cari**b**e   decli**v**e

In both pronunciations, there is no difference in sound between **b** and **v**. The English *v* sound, produced by friction between the upper teeth and lower lip, does not exist in Spanish. Instead, the soft **b** comes from friction between the two lips.

Verónica y su esposo cantan boleros.

When **b** or **v** begins a word, its pronunciation depends on the previous word. At the beginning of a phrase or after a word that ends in **m** or **n**, it is pronounced as a hard **b**.

Benito es de Boquerón pero vive en Victoria.

Words that begin with **b** or **v** are pronounced with a soft **b** if they appear immediately after a word that ends in a vowel or any consonant other than **m** or **n**.

Práctica Read these words aloud to practice the **b** and the **v**.

1. hablamos	4. van	7. doble	10. cabaña
2. trabajar	5. contabilidad	8. novia	11. llave
3. botones	6. bien	9. béisbol	12. invierno

Oraciones Read these sentences aloud to practice the **b** and the **v**.

1. Vamos a Guaynabo en autobús.
2. Voy de vacaciones a la Isla Culebra.
3. Tengo una habitación individual en el octavo piso.
4. Víctor y Eva van en avión al Caribe.
5. La planta baja es bonita también.
6. ¿Qué vamos a ver en Bayamón?
7. Beatriz, la novia de Víctor, es de Arecibo, Puerto Rico.

Refranes Read these sayings aloud to practice the **b** and the **v**.

No hay mal que por bien no venga.[1]

Hombre prevenido vale por dos.[2]

2 *An ounce of prevention equals a pound of cure.*

1 *Every cloud has a silver lining.*

recursos

R	STUDENT CD Lección 5	LM p. 222	LCASS./CD Cass. 5/CD5	ICD-ROM Lección 5

5.1 **Estar** with conditions and emotions

ANTE TODO As you learned in Lessons 1 and 2, the verb **estar** is used to talk about how you feel and to say where people, places, and things are located. **Estar** is also used with adjectives to talk about certain emotional and physical conditions.

CONSÚLTALO

The present tense of *ser* To review **ser**, see Lesson 1, p.18.

• • •

The present tense of *estar* To review **estar**, see Lesson 2, pp. 49-50.

▶ **Estar** is used with adjectives to describe the physical condition of places and things.

La habitación **está** sucia.
The room is dirty.

La puerta **está** cerrada.
The door is closed.

▶ **Estar** is also used with adjectives to describe how people feel, both mentally and physically.

Estoy aburrida. ¿Quieren hacer algo?

No, estoy cansada.

Adjectives that describe emotions and conditions

abierto/a	open	**contento/a**	happy; content	**nervioso/a**	nervous
aburrido/a	bored; boring			**ocupado/a**	busy
alegre	happy; joyful	**desordenado/a**	disorderly	**ordenado/a**	orderly
avergonzado/a	embarrassed	**enamorado/a (de)**	in love (with)	**preocupado/a (por)**	worried (about)
cansado/a	tired	**enojado/a**	mad, angry	**seguro/a**	sure
cerrado/a	closed	**equivocado/a**	wrong	**sucio/a**	dirty
cómodo/a	comfortable	**feliz**	happy	**triste**	sad
		limpio/a	clean		

¡INTÉNTALO! Provide the present tense forms of the verb **estar**. The first item has been done for you.

1. La biblioteca ___*está*___ cerrada los domingos por la noche.
2. Nosotros _____ muy ocupados todos los lunes.
3. Ellas _____ alegres porque tienen tiempo libre.
4. Javier _____ enamorado de Maribel.
5. Diana _____ enojada con su novio.
6. Yo _____ nerviosa en el avión.
7. La habitación _____ ordenada cuando vienen sus padres.
8. Uds. _____ equivocados.
9. Marina y yo _____ preocupadas por el examen.
10. Ud. _____ muy cansado los lunes por la mañana.

Práctica

1

¿Cómo están? Complete Martín's statements about how he and other people are feeling. In the first blank, fill in the correct form of **estar**. In the second blank, fill in the adjective that best fits the context.

1. Yo _____ un poco _____ porque tengo un examen mañana.
2. Mi hermana Patricia _____ muy _____ porque mañana va a hacer una excursión al campo.
3. Mis hermanos Juan y José salen de la casa a las cinco de la mañana. Por la noche, siempre _____ muy _____.
4. Mi amigo Ramiro _____ _____; su novia se llama Adela.
5. Mi papá y sus colegas _____ muy _____ hoy. ¡Hay mucho trabajo!
6. Patricia y yo _____ un poco _____ por ellos porque trabajan mucho.
7. Mi amiga Mónica _____ un poco _____ porque su novio no puede salir esta noche.
8. Nuestras clases no son muy interesantes hoy. ¿Tú _____ _____ también?

2

Describir Describe the following people and places.

1. Anabela

2. Juan y Luisa

3. la habitación de Teresa

4. la habitación de César

3

Situaciones With a partner, talk about how you feel in these situations.

1. Cuando hace sol
2. Cuando tomas un examen
3. Cuando estás de vacaciones
4. Cuando tienes mucho trabajo
5. Cuando viajas en avión
6. Cuando estás con la familia
7. Cuando estás en la clase de español
8. Cuando ves una película con tu actor favorito

5.2 The present progressive

ANTE TODO   Both Spanish and English have a present progressive tense. In both languages, it consists of the present tense of the verb *to be* and the present participle (the *-ing* form of the verb in English).

Estoy escuchando.	Carlos **está corriendo**.	Ella **está escribiendo** una carta.
I am listening.	*Carlos is running.*	*She is writing a letter.*

Hola, chicas. ¿Qué están haciendo?

Estamos descansando.

▶ The present progressive is formed with the present tense of **estar** and the present participle of the main verb.

FORM OF **ESTAR** + PRESENT PARTICIPLE		FORM OF **ESTAR** + PRESENT PARTICIPLE	
Estoy	**trabajando.**	**Estamos**	**comiendo.**
I am	*working.*	*We are*	*eating.*

▶ The present participle of regular **–ar**, **–er**, and **–ir** verbs is formed as follows:

INFINITIVE	STEM	ENDING	PRESENT PARTICIPLE
hablar	habl	**-ando**	habl**ando**
cantar	cant	**-ando**	cant**ando**
comer	com	**-iendo**	com**iendo**
escribir	escrib	**-iendo**	escrib**iendo**

> **¡ATENCIÓN!**
>
> When the stem of an **–er** or **–ir** verb ends in a vowel, the present participle ends in **–yendo**.
>
> **leer** → **le** → **leyendo**
> **oír** → **o** → **oyendo**
> **traer** → **tra** → **trayendo**

▶ **Ir**, **poder**, and **venir** have irregular present participles (**yendo, pudiendo, viniendo**), but these verbs are rarely used in the present progressive. Several other verbs have irregular present participles that you will need to learn.

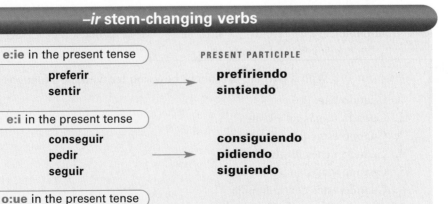

–*ir* stem-changing verbs

e:ie in the present tense	PRESENT PARTICIPLE
preferir	**prefiriendo**
sentir	**sintiendo**

e:i in the present tense	
conseguir	**consiguiendo**
pedir	**pidiendo**
seguir	**siguiendo**

o:ue in the present tense	
dormir	**durmiendo**

The use of the present progressive is much more restricted in Spanish than in English. In Spanish, the present progressive is simply used to emphasize that an action is in progress at the time of speaking.

Inés **está escuchando** música latina ahora mismo.
Inés is listening to Latin music right now.

Álex y su amigo ecuatoriano todavía **están jugando** al fútbol.
Álex and his Ecuadorian friend are still playing soccer.

In English, the present progressive is often used to talk about situations and actions that occur over an extended period of time or in the future. In Spanish, the simple present tense is used instead.

Javier **estudia** computación este semestre.
Javier is studying computer science this semester.

Inés y Maite **salen** mañana para los Estados Unidos.
Inés and Maite are leaving tomorrow for the United States.

Estamos pensando en lo mismo:

su **F**uturo

Su asesor para ganar

FIDUCOLOMBIA
Sociedad Fiduciaria S.A.

¡INTÉNTALO! Create complete sentences by putting the verbs in the present progressive. The first item has been done for you.

1. Mis amigos / descansar en la playa Mis amigos están descansando en la playa.
2. Nosotros / practicar deportes
3. Carmen / comer en casa
4. Nuestro equipo / ganar el partido
5. Yo / leer el periódico
6. Él / pensar en comprar una bicicleta
7. Uds. / explicar la lección
8. José y Francisco / dormir
9. Marisa / leer correo electrónico
10. Yo / preparar sándwiches
11. Carlos / tomar fotos
12. ¿dormir / tú?

Práctica

1 **Completar** Alfredo's Spanish class is preparing to travel to Puerto Rico. Use the present progressive of the verb in parentheses to complete Alfredo's description of what everyone is doing.

1. Yo _____ (investigar) el estado político de la isla (*island*).
2. La esposa del profesor _____ (hacer) las maletas.
3. Marta y José Luis _____ (buscar) información sobre San Juan en el Internet.
4. Enrique y yo _____ (leer) un correo electrónico de nuestro amigo puertorriqueño.
5. Javier _____ (aprender) mucho sobre la cultura puertorriqueña.
6. Y tú _____ (practicar) tu español, ¿verdad?

2 **¿Qué están haciendo?** María and her friends are vacationing at a resort in San Juan, Puerto Rico. Complete her description of what everyone is doing right now.

1. Yo

2. Javier

3. Alejandro y Rebeca

4. Celia y yo

5. Samuel

6. Lorenzo

3 **Personajes famosos** Say what these celebrities are doing right now, using the cues provided.

> **modelo**
> Serena Williams está jugando al tenis ahora mismo.

John Grisham	Mikhail Baryshnikov	bailar	hablar
Celine Dion	Picabo Street	cantar	hacer
Steven Spielberg	Regis Philbin	correr	jugar
Venus Williams	??	escribir	??
Tiger Woods	??	esquiar	??

AYUDA

John Grisham - **novelas**
Celine Dion - **canciones**
Steven Spielberg - **cine**
Venus Williams - **tenis**
Tiger Woods - **golf**
Mikhail Baryshnikov - **ballet**
Picabo Street - **esquí**
Regis Philbin - **televisión**

Comunicación

4

Un amigo preguntón You have a friend who calls you at all hours to see what you're doing. What do you tell him/her if he/she calls you at the following times?

> **modelo**
>
> 8:00 a.m.
> Estoy desayunando.

1. 5:00 a.m.	2. 9:30 a.m.	3. 11:00 a.m.	4. 12:00 p.m.
5. 2:00 p.m.	6. 5:00 p.m.	7. 9:00 p.m.	8. 2:30 a.m.

¡LENGUA VIVA!
In Spain and Latin America, time is often given based on the 24-hour clock. For example, 3:00 p.m. is said **15:00h**.

5

Describir Work with a partner and use the present progressive to describe what's going on in this beach scene.

6

Conversar Imagine that you and a classmate are each babysitting a group of children. One of you has great kids; the other's kids are mischievous. You're on the phone, telling each other what the children are doing at this very moment. Be creative, and be prepared to share some of your sentences with the class.

Síntesis

7

¿Qué están haciendo? With two other classmates, create at least three sentences about what these people are doing right now in these places. Also, say how they feel and what they are going to do.

> **modelo**
>
> Uds. están en la clase de español.
> Estamos hablando con los otros estudiantes.
> Estamos practicando los verbos.
> No estamos aburridos/as.
> Vamos a tener un examen mañana.

1. Tres amigas están de vacaciones.
2. Un padre y su hijo están en el parque.
3. Tú y tus compañeros/as están en la playa.
4. Una familia está en el centro.
5. El/la profesor(a) está en la biblioteca.
6. Unos jóvenes están en un estadio.

5.3 Comparing **ser** and **estar**

ANTE TODO You have already learned that **ser** and **estar** both mean *to be* but are used for different purposes. The following charts summarize the key differences in usage between **ser** and **estar**.

Uses of *ser*

Nationality and place of origin	Martín **es** argentino. **Es** de Buenos Aires.
Profession or occupation	Adela **es** ingeniera. Francisco **es** médico.
Characteristics of people and things	José y Clara **son** simpáticos. El clima de Puerto Rico **es** agradable.
Generalizations	¡**Es** fabuloso viajar! **Es** difícil estudiar a la una de la mañana.
Possession	**Es** la pluma de Maite. **Son** las llaves de don Francisco.
What something is made of	La bicicleta **es** de metal. Los libros **son** de papel.
Time and date	Hoy **es** martes. **Son** las dos. Hoy **es** el primero de julio.
Where or when an event takes place	El partido **es** en el estadio Santa Fe. La conferencia **es** a las siete.

Soy Francisco Castillo Moreno. Yo soy de la agencia Ecuatur.

Su nombre no está en mi lista.

Uses of *estar*

Location or spatial relationships	El aeropuerto **está** lejos de la ciudad. Tu habitación **está** en el tercer piso.
Health	¿Cómo **estás**? **Estoy** bien, gracias.
Physical states and conditions	El profesor **está** ocupado. Las ventanas **están** abiertas.
Emotional states	Marisa **está** feliz hoy. **Estoy** muy enojado con Javier.
Certain weather expressions	**Está** lloviendo. **Está** nublado.
Ongoing actions (progressive tenses)	**Estamos** estudiando para un examen. Ana **está** leyendo una novela.

Ser and *estar* with adjectives

▶ With many descriptive adjectives, **ser** and **estar** can both be used.

Juan **es** delgado.
Juan is thin.

Juan **está** más delgado hoy.
Juan is thinner today.

Ana **es** feliz siempre.
Ana is always happy.

Ana **está** feliz en la fiesta.
Ana is happy at the party.

▶ In the examples above, the sentences with **ser** have a different meaning than the sentences with **estar**. The statements with **ser** are general observations about the inherent, permanent qualities of Juan and Ana. The statements with **estar** describe conditions that are temporary and changeable.

▶ Some adjectives change in meaning when used with **ser** and **estar**.

With *ser*	With *estar*

El chico **es listo**.
The boy is smart.

La profesora **es mala**.
The professor is bad.

Jaime **es aburrido**.
Jaime is boring.

Las peras **son verdes**.
The pears are green.

El gato **es muy vivo**.
The cat is very lively.

El puente **es seguro**.
The bridge is safe.

El chico **está listo**.
The boy is ready.

La profesora **está mala**.
The professor is sick.

Jaime **está aburrido**.
Jaime is bored.

Las peras **están verdes**.
The pears are not ripe.

El gato **está vivo**.
The cat is alive.

Él no **está seguro**.
He's not sure.

¡INTÉNTALO!   Form complete sentences by using the correct form of **ser** or **estar**, the correct form of each adjective, and any other necessary words. The first item has been done for you.

1. Alejandra / cansado

   Alejandra está cansada.

2. Ellos / guapo
   _____

3. Carmen / alto
   _____

4. Yo / la clase de español
   _____

5. Película / a las once
   _____

6. Hoy / viernes
   _____

7. Nosotras / enojado
   _____

8. Antonio / médico
   _____

9. Romeo y Julieta / enamorado
   _____

10. Libros / de Ana
    _____

11. Marisa y Juan / estudiando
    _____

12. Partido de baloncesto / gimnasio
    _____

Práctica

1 **¿Ser o estar?** They say that opposites attract. Complete the statements about Andrés and Andrea using **ser** or **estar** and any other necessary words.

> **modelo**
>
> Andrés ___es___ bajo pero Andrea ___es alta___.

1. Andrés _____ un poco gordo pero Andrea _____.
2. La habitación de Andrea siempre (*always*) _____ sucia pero la habitación de Andrés _____.
3. Andrés siempre _____ contento pero Andrea siempre _____.
4. Andrea _____ rubia pero Andrés _____.
5. Andrés _____ perezoso (*lazy*) pero Andrea _____.
6. Andrea _____ muy seria pero Andrés _____.
7. A pesar de todo (*in spite of everything*), Andrés y Andrea _____ enamorados.

2 **Completar** Complete this conversation with the appropriate forms of **ser** and **estar**.

EDUARDO ¡Hola, Ceci! ¿Cómo _____?

CECILIA Hola, Eduardo. Bien, gracias. ¡Qué guapo _____ hoy!

EDUARDO Gracias. _____ muy amable. Oye, ¿qué _____ haciendo? ¿_____ ocupada?

CECILIA No, sólo _____ escribiendo una carta a mi prima Pilar.

EDUARDO ¿De dónde _____ ella?

CECILIA Pilar _____ del Ecuador. Su papá _____ médico en Quito. Pero ahora Pilar y su familia _____ de vacaciones en Ponce, Puerto Rico.

EDUARDO Y… ¿cómo _____ Pilar?

CECILIA _____ muy lista. Y también _____ alta, rubia y muy bonita.

3 **En el aeropuerto** In small groups, take turns using **ser** and **estar** to describe the following scene. Say as many things as you can.

NOTA CULTURAL

Luis Muñoz Marín International Airport in San Juan, Puerto Rico, is a major transportation hub of the Caribbean. The airport connects the region with the rest of the world via flights that depart daily for the mainland U.S. and various Caribbean nations.

Comunicación

4

Describir With a classmate, take turns describing the following people. First mention where each person is from. Then describe what each person is like, how each person is feeling, and what he or she is doing right now.

> **modelo**
>
> tu compañero/a de cuarto
>
> *Mi compañera de cuarto es de San Juan, Puerto Rico. Es muy inteligente. Está cansada pero está estudiando en la biblioteca.*

1. tu mejor (*best*) amigo/a
2. tus padres
3. tu profesor(a) favorito/a

4. tu novio/a o esposo/a
5. tu primo/a favorito/a
6. tus abuelos

5

Adivinar Get together with a partner and describe a few of your classmates to him or her using these questions as a guide. Don't mention the classmates' names. Can your partner guess which classmates you are describing?

1. ¿Cómo es?
2. ¿Cómo está?
3. ¿De dónde es?

4. ¿Dónde está?
5. ¿Qué está haciendo?

6

Dibujo Use **ser** and **estar** to describe what you see in the drawing.

Síntesis

7

Conversación Get together with a classmate you don't know very well and ask each other questions using **ser**, **estar**, and other verbs. Be sure to ask about these topics:

▶ las clases
▶ la familia

▶ los amigos
▶ los pasatiempos

5.4 Direct object nouns and pronouns

SUBJECT	VERB	DIRECT OBJECT NOUN
Álex y Javier	están tomando	fotos.
Álex and Javier	*are taking*	*photos.*

▶ A direct object noun receives the action of the verb directly and generally follows the verb. In the example above, the direct object noun answers the question *What are Javier and Álex taking?*

▶ When a direct object noun in Spanish is a person or a pet, it is preceded by the word **a**. This is called the personal **a**; there is no English equivalent for this construction.

Don Francisco visita **a** la señora Ramos.
Don Francisco is visiting Mrs. Ramos.

Don Francisco visita el Hotel Prado.
Don Francisco is visiting the Hotel Prado.

In the first sentence above, the personal **a** is required because the direct object is a person. In the second sentence, the personal **a** is not required because the direct object is a place, not a person.

¿Dónde pongo las maletas?

Puede ponerlas encima de la cama.

Hay muchos lugares interesantes por aquí. ¿Quieren ir a verlos?

Direct object pronouns

SINGULAR		PLURAL	
me	*me*	**nos**	*us*
te	*you* (fam.)	**os**	*you* (fam.)
lo	*you* (m., form.)	**los**	*you* (m., form.)
	him; it (m.)		*them* (m.)
la	*you* (f., form.)	**las**	*you* (f., form.)
	her; it (f.)		*them* (f.)

▶ Direct object pronouns are words that replace direct object nouns. Like English, Spanish sometimes uses a direct object pronoun to avoid repeating a noun that has already been mentioned.

	DIRECT OBJECT		DIRECT OBJECT PRONOUN
Maribel hace	las maletas.	Maribel	**las** hace.
Felipe compra	el sombrero.	Felipe	**lo** compra.
Vicky tiene	la llave.	Vicky	**la** tiene.

¡ATENCIÓN!

In Spain and parts of Latin America, **le** and **les** are used instead of the pronouns **lo, la, los,** and **las** when referring to people:

No le veo.
I don't see him/her.

▶ In affirmative sentences, direct object pronouns generally appear before the conjugated verb. In negative sentences, the pronoun is placed between the word **no** and the verb.

Adela practica **el tenis**.	Adela no tiene **las llaves**.
Adela **lo** practica.	Adela **no las** tiene.
Carmen compra **los pasajes**.	Diego no hace **las maletas**.
Carmen **los** compra	Diego **no las** hace.

▶ When the verb is an infinitive construction, such as **ir a** + [*infinitive*], the direct object pronoun can be placed before the conjugated form or attached to the infinitive.

Ellos van a escribir **unas postales**.	Ellos **las** van a escribir.
	Ellos van a escribir**las**.
Lidia quiere ver **una película**.	Lidia **la** quiere ver.
	Lidia quiere ver**la**.

▶ When the verb is in the present progressive, the direct object pronoun can be placed before the conjugated form or attached to the present participle.

¡ATENCIÓN!
When a direct object pronoun is attached to the present participle, an accent mark is added to maintain the proper stress. To learn more about accents, see Lesson 4, **Pronunciación,** p. 101, Lesson 10, **Ortografía**, p. 275, and Lesson 11, **Ortografía**, p. 303.

Gerardo está leyendo **la lección**.	Gerardo **la** está leyendo.
	Gerardo está leyéndo**la**.
Toni está mirando el **partido**.	Toni **lo** está mirando.
	Toni está mirándo**lo**.

¡INTÉNTALO! Change the direct object nouns into direct object pronouns and make any other necessary changes. The first item in each column has been done for you.

1. Juan tiene el pasaporte.
   Juan lo tiene.

2. Confirman la reservación.
   _____

3. Leemos la lección.
   _____

4. Estudio el vocabulario.
   _____

5. Aprendemos las palabras.
   _____

6. Escucho al profesor.
   _____

7. Escribe los párrafos.
   _____

8. Tengo los pasajes
   _____

9. Quiero un avión.
   _____

10. Van a ver la película.
    Van a verla./La van a ver.

11. Quiero ver los monumentos.
    _____

12. Vamos a tomar el examen mañana.
    _____

13. ¿Cuándo vas a hacer la tarea?
    _____

14. Están explorando el pueblo.
    _____

15. Miguel está comprando los libros.
    _____

16. Estoy leyendo las cartas de Sonia.
    _____

17. ¡Están estudiando los verbos!
    _____

18. No queremos escalar esa montaña.
    _____

Práctica

1 **Seleccionar** Choose the correct response to each question.

1. ¿Tienes el libro de español?
   a. Sí, la tengo. b. No, no los tengo. c. Sí, lo tengo.
2. ¿Me puedes llevar al partido de baloncesto?
   a. Sí, los puedo llevar. b. Sí, te puedo llevar. c. No, no las puedo llevar.
3. El artista quiere dibujarte con tu mamá, ¿no?
   a. Sí, quiere dibujarlos mañana. b. Sí, nos quiere dibujar mañana.
   c. Sí, quiere dibujarte mañana.
4. ¿Quién tiene las llaves de nuestra habitación?
   a. Yo no las tengo. b. Amalia los tiene, ¿no? c. Yo la tengo.
5. ¿Quién te lleva al aeropuerto?
   a. Yo te llevo al aeropuerto. b. Rita los lleva al aeropuerto.
   c. Mónica me lleva al aeropuerto a las seis.
6. ¿Puedes oírme?
   a. Sí, te puedo oír bien. b. No, no los oigo. c. Sí, las oigo bien.

2 **¿Quién?** The Garza family is preparing to go on a vacation to Puerto Rico. Based on the clues, answer the questions about their preparations. Be sure to use direct object pronouns in your answers.

> **modelo**
>
> ¿Quién hace las reservaciones para el hotel? (El Sr. Garza)
> El Sr. Garza las hace.

1. ¿Quién compra los pasajes para el vuelo (*flight*)? (La Sra. Garza)
2. ¿Quién tiene que hacer las maletas de los niños? (María)
3. ¿Quiénes buscan los pasaportes? (Antonio y María)
4. ¿Quién va a confirmar las reservaciones para el hotel? (La Sra. Garza)
5. ¿Quién busca la cámara? (María)
6. ¿Quién compra un mapa de Puerto Rico? (Antonio)

NOTA CULTURAL

The Garza family needs passports to travel to Puerto Rico if they are coming from a foreign country. When traveling from the U.S. mainland, however, passports are not required, since Puerto Rico is a U.S. territory.

3 **Preguntas** Imagine that you and a classmate are chatting on your cell phones, trying to find out what each of you is doing to prepare for tomorrow's trip. Follow the model.

> **modelo**
>
> buscar tu pasaporte
> **Estudiante 1:** ¿Estás buscando tu pasaporte?
> **Estudiante 2:** No, no estoy buscándolo.
> **Estudiante 1:** ¿Cuándo lo vas a buscar?
> **Estudiante 2:** Voy a buscarlo mañana (el lunes, a las dos, etc.).

1. hacer tus maletas
2. buscar tu pasaje
3. confirmar tus reservaciones
4. comprar una cámara
5. preparar los documentos de viaje
6. leer el folleto (*brochure*) del hotel

¡LENGUA VIVA!

There are many Spanish words that correspond to *ticket*. **Boleto, billete,** and **pasaje** usually refer to a ticket used for travel, such as an airplane ticket. **Entrada** and **boleto** refer to a ticket to an event, such as a concert or a movie.

Comunicación

4

Entrevista Interview a classmate using these questions. Be sure to use direct object pronouns in your responses.

1. ¿Tienes tus llaves?
2. ¿Traes tu libro a la clase de español? ¿Y tu cuaderno?
3. ¿Estudias español todos los días?
4. ¿Visitas mucho a tus abuelos?
5. ¿Quién prepara la comida (*food*) en tu casa?
6. ¿Cuándo vas a hacer la tarea de la clase de español?
7. ¿Cuándo ves a tus amigos/as?
8. ¿Ves mucho la televisión? ¿Cuándo vas a ver tu programa favorito?

5

En el centro Get together with a partner and take turns asking each other questions about the drawing. Use direct object pronouns whenever possible.

> **modelo**
>
> **Estudiante 1:** ¿Quién está leyendo el periódico?
> **Estudiante 2:** El Sr. López está leyéndolo.

Síntesis

6

Adivinanzas Play a guessing game in which you describe a person, place, or thing and your partner guesses who or what it is. Then switch roles. Each of you should give at least five descriptions.

> **modelo**
>
> **Estudiante 1:** Lo uso para (*I use it to*) escribir en mi cuaderno.
>   Es amarillo y no es muy grande. ¿Qué es?
> **Estudiante 2:** ¿Es un lápiz?
> **Estudiante 1:** ¡Sí!

5.5 Numbers 101 and higher

Numbers 101 and higher

101	ciento uno	**1.000**	mil
200	doscientos/as	**1.100**	mil cien
300	trescientos/as	**2.000**	dos mil
400	cuatrocientos/as	**5.000**	cinco mil
500	quinientos/as	**100.000**	cien mil
600	seiscientos/as	**200.000**	doscientos mil
700	setecientos/as	**550.000**	quinientos cincuenta mil
800	ochocientos/as	**1.000.000**	un millón (de)
900	novecientos/as	**8.000.000**	ocho millones (de)

▶ As shown in the preceding chart, Spanish uses a period to indicate thousands and millions, rather than a comma as used in English.

▶ The numbers 200 through 999 agree in gender with the nouns they modify.

324 maletas
trescientas veinticuatro maletas

605 pasajeros
seiscientos cinco pasajeros

Aquí está la reservación... dos habitaciones dobles y una individual, de la ciento uno a la ciento tres.

▶ The word **mil**, which can mean *a thousand* and *one thousand*, is not usually used in the plural form. **Un millón** (*a million* or *one million*), however, has the plural form **millones** in which the accent is dropped.

1.000 aviones
mil aviones

2.000.000 de turistas
dos millones de turistas

¡INTÉNTALO! Give the Spanish equivalent of each number. The first item has been done for you.

1. **102** _____ciento dos_____
2. **935** _____
3. **5.000.000** _____
4. **2001** _____
5. **1776** _____
6. **345** _____
7. **550.300** _____
8. **235** _____
9. **1999** _____
10. **113** _____
11. **205** _____
12. **2105** _____
13. **17.123** _____
14. **497** _____

¡LENGUA VIVA!

In Spanish, years are not expressed as pairs of 2-digit numbers as they are in English (1979, *nineteen seventy-nine*):

1776, mil setecientos setenta y seis

1945, mil novecientos cuarenta y cinco

2001, dos mil uno

¡ATENCIÓN!

When **millón** or **millones** is used before a noun, the word **de** is placed between the two:

1.000.000 de hombres = un millón de hombres

12.000.000 de aviones = doce millones de aviones

• • •

See Lesson 2, p. 53 to review the difference between **cien** and **ciento**:

100.000 = cien mil

2.101 = dos mil ciento uno

Práctica

1

Resolver Read the math problems aloud and solve them.

modelo

200 + 300 =

Doscientos más trescientos son quinientos.

| + más |
| − menos |
| = son/es |

1. 1000 + 753 =
2. 1.000.000 − 30.000 =
3. 10.000 + 555 =
4. 150 + 150 =
5. 100.000 + 205.000 =
6. 29.000 − 10.000 =

2

¿Cuándo? Look at the timeline and tell when each of these events occurs.

1776	1861-1865	1914-1918	1939-1945	1963	1969	1997
Independencia de los EE.UU.	Guerra Civil de los EE.UU.	Primera Guerra Mundial	Segunda Guerra Mundial	El presidente Kennedy es asesinado	El hombre llega a la Luna	El *Pathfinder* llega al planeta Marte

1. La Primera Guerra Mundial termina.
2. El *Pathfinder* llega al planeta Marte.
3. La Segunda Guerra Mundial termina.
4. La Primera Guerra Mundial comienza.
5. El hombre llega a la Luna (*Moon*).
6. La Segunda Guerra Mundial comienza.

Comunicación

3

Entrevista Work together with a classmate and use these questions to interview each other. Be prepared to report the results of your interview to the class.

1. ¿Cuántas personas hay en la clase de español?
2. ¿Cuántas personas hay en la universidad?
3. ¿Cuántas personas hay en tu ciudad?
4. ¿Cuántas personas hay en tu estado?
5. ¿Cuántas personas hay en los Estados Unidos? ¿Y cuántos hispanohablantes?
6. ¿Cuántas personas hay en el mundo (*world*)? ¿Y cuántos hispanohablantes?

¡ATENCIÓN!

Note this difference between Spanish and English:

mil millones
a billion (1,000,000,000)

un billón
a trillion
(1,000,000,000,000)

recursos

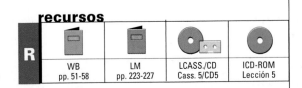

| R | WB pp. 51-58 | LM pp. 223-227 | LCASS./CD Cass. 5/CD5 | ICD-ROM Lección 5 |

Lectura
Antes de leer

Estrategia
Scanning

Scanning involves glancing over a document in search of specific information. For example, you can scan a document to identify its format, to find cognates, to locate visual clues about the document's content, or to find specific facts. Scanning allows you to learn a great deal about a text without having to read it word for word.

Examinar el texto

Scan the reading selection for cognates and write a few of them down.

1. _____
2. _____
3. _____
4. _____
5. _____

Based on the cognates you found, what do you think this document is about?

_____
_____

Preguntas

Read the following questions. Then scan the document again to look for answers to the questions.

1. What is the format of the reading selection?
   _____

2. What country is the document about?
   _____

3. What are some of the visual cues this document provides? What do they tell you about the content of the document?
   _____
   _____

4. Who produced the document, and what do you think the document is for?
   _____
   _____

Turismo ecológico en Puerto Rico

Hotel La Cabaña
~ Lajas, Puerto Rico ~

Habitaciones

- 40 individuales
- 15 dobles
- Teléfono / TV / Cable
- Aire acondicionado
- Restaurante (Bar)
- Piscina
- Área de juegos
- Cajero automático

El hotel está situado en Playa Grande, un pequeño pueblo de pescadores del mar Caribe. Es el lugar perfecto para el viajero que viene de vacaciones. Las playas son seguras y limpias, ideales para tomar el sol, descansar, tomar fotografías y nadar. Está abierto los 365 días del año. Hay una rebaja especial para estudiantes.

DIRECCIÓN: Playa Grande 406, Lajas, PR 00667, cerca del Parque Nacional Foresta.

Cajero automático *ATM* rebaja *discount*

Atracciones cercanas

Playa Grande ¿Busca la playa perfecta? Playa Grande es la playa que está buscando. Usted puede ir de pesca, sacar fotos, nadar y pasear en bicicleta. Playa Grande es un paraíso para el turista que quiere practicar deportes acuáticos. El lugar es bonito e interesante y usted tiene muchas oportunidades para descansar y disfrutar en familia.

Valle Niebla Ir de excursión, tomar café, montar a caballo, caminar, acampar, hacer picnic. Más de 100 lugares para acampar.

Bahía Fosforescente Sacar fotos, pescar, salidas de noche, excursión en barco. Una maravillosa experiencia con peces fosforescentes.

Arrecifes de Coral Sacar fotos, bucear, explorar. Es un lugar único en el Caribe.

Playa Vieja Tomar el sol, pasear en bicicleta, jugar a las cartas, escuchar música. Ideal para la familia.

Parque Nacional Foresta Sacar fotos, visitar el Museo de Arte Nativo. Reserva Mundial de la Biosfera.

Santuario de las Aves Sacar fotos, observar aves, seguir rutas de excursión.

peces *fish* **aves** *birds*

Después de leer

Listas
Which of the amenities of the Hotel La Cabaña would most interest these potential guests? Explain your choices.

1. Dos padres con un hijo de seis años y una hija de ocho años

   _____

2. Un hombre y una mujer en su luna de miel (*honeymoon*)

   _____

3. Una persona en un viaje de negocios (*business trip*)

   _____

Conversaciones
With a partner, take turns asking each other the following questions.

1. ¿Quieres visitar el Hotel La Cabaña? ¿Por qué?
2. Tienes tiempo de visitar sólo tres de las atracciones turísticas que están cerca del hotel. ¿Cuáles vas a visitar? ¿Por qué?
3. ¿Qué prefieres hacer en Valle Niebla? ¿En Playa Vieja? ¿En el Parque Nacional Foresta?

Situaciones
You have just arrived at the Hotel La Cabaña. Your classmate is the concierge. Use the phrases below to express your interests and ask him or her for suggestions about where to go.

1. montar a caballo
2. bucear
3. pasear en bicicleta
4. pescar
5. observar aves

Contestar
Answer the following questions.

1. ¿Quieres visitar el Hotel La Cabaña? Explica tu respuesta.

   _____

2. ¿Adónde quieres ir de vacaciones el verano que viene? Explica tu respuesta.

   _____

Puerto Rico

El país en cifras

▶ **Área:** 8.959 km² (3.459 millas²)
menor que el área de Connecticut

▶ **Población:** 3.930.000
*Puerto Rico es una de las islas más
densamente pobladas del mundo. Cerca
de la mitad de la población vive en San Juan,
la capital.*

▶ **Capital:** San Juan—1.410.000

SOURCE: Population Division, UN Secretariat

▶ **Ciudades principales:** Arecibo—100.000,
Bayamón—222.815, Fajardo—40.000,
Mayagüez—100.371, Ponce—187.749

▶ **Moneda:** dólar estadounidense

▶ **Idiomas:** español (oficial); inglés (oficial)
*Aproximadamente la cuarta parte de la población
puertorriqueña habla inglés. Sin embargo, en las
zonas turísticas este porcentaje es mucho más
alto. El uso del inglés es obligatorio para documentos federales.*

Bandera
de Puerto Rico

Puertorriqueños célebres

▶ **Luis Muñoz Rivera,** poeta,
periodista y político (1859-1916)

▶ **Roberto Clemente,** beisbolista
(1934-1972)

▶ **Luis Rafael Sánchez,** escritor (1936-)

▶ **Ricky Martin,** cantante y actor (1971-)

mitad *half*   subterráneo *underground*   sistema de cuevas *cave system*
bóveda *underground chamber*   caber *fit*

recursos

R | WB pp. 59-60 | vistasonline.com | ICD-ROM Lección 5

¡Increíble pero cierto!

El río *Camuy* es el tercer río subterráneo más
largo del mundo y tiene el sistema de cuevas
más grande en el hemisferio oeste. La *Cueva de
los Tres Pueblos* es una gigantesca bóveda, tan
grande que toda la fortaleza del Morro podría
caber en su interior.

Plaza de Arecibo

Hoteles en El Condado,
San Juan

Océano Atlántico

Arecibo

San Juan ★

Bayamón

Río Grande de Añasco

Mayagüez

Cordillera Central

Ponce

Sierra de Cayey

Mar Caribe

Parque de Bombas,
Ponce

Pescadores en Mayagüez

OCÉANO
ATLÁNTICO

PUERTO RICO

OCÉANO
PACÍFICO

Lugares • **El Morro**

El Morro es una fortaleza que custodiaba la bahía de San Juan entre los años 1500 y 1900. Hoy día El Morro es un museo que atrae a miles de turistas cada año. De hecho, es el sitio más fotografiado de Puerto Rico. La arquitectura de la fortaleza es impresionante. Tiene misteriosos túneles, oscuras mazmorras y vistas fabulosas de la bahía.

Artes • **Salsa**

La música salsa, viva y rítmica, está hecha para bailar. Este estilo musical nació en la ciudad de Nueva York de raíces puertorriqueñas y cubanas. Su nombre significa que la música es la "salsa" de las fiestas. Dos de sus músicos más famosos son Tito Puente y Willie Colón, los dos de Nueva York. Sus estrellas puertorriqueñas son Felipe Rodríguez y Héctor Lavoe. Hoy día, Puerto Rico es el centro mundial de la salsa; de hecho, el Gran Combo de Puerto Rico es una de las orquestas más famosas.

Fajardo

Isla de Culebra

Isla de Vieques

Ciencias • **El Observatorio de Arecibo**

El Observatorio de Arecibo tiene el radiotelescopio más grande del mundo. Gracias al telescopio los científicos pueden estudiar la atmósfera de la Tierra y la Luna, además de fenómenos celestiales como quásares y púlsares. Los científicos también escuchan emisiones de radio de otras galaxias, buscando indicios de inteligencia extraterrestre.

Historia • **Relación con los Estados Unidos**

Puerto Rico pasó a ser parte de los Estados Unidos después de la Guerra de 1898 y se hizo un estado libre asociado en 1952. Los puertorriqueños, ciudadanos estadounidenses desde 1917, tienen representación en el Congreso pero no votan en las elecciones presidenciales y no pagan impuestos federales. Hay un debate entre los puertorriqueños: ¿debe la isla seguir como estado libre asociado, hacerse un estado como los demás o hacerse independiente?

¿Qué aprendiste? Responde a las preguntas con una frase completa.

1. ¿Cuál es la moneda de Puerto Rico?
2. ¿Qué idiomas se hablan (*are spoken*) en Puerto Rico?
3. ¿Cuál es el sitio más fotografiado de Puerto Rico?
4. ¿Cómo es la música salsa?
5. ¿Qué hacen los científicos en el Observatorio de Arecibo?

Conexión Internet Investiga estos temas en el sitio **www.vistasonline.com**.

1. Describe a dos puertorriqueños famosos. ¿Cómo son? ¿Qué hacen? ¿Dónde viven? ¿Por qué son célebres?
2. Busca información sobre lugares buenos para el ecoturismo en Puerto Rico. Luego presenta un informe a la clase.

custodiaba *guarded* bahía *bay* Hoy día *Nowadays* atrae *attracts* cada *each* de hecho *in fact* mazmorras *dungeons* viva *lively* estilo *style* nació *was born* raíces *roots* salsa *sauce* estrellas *stars* mundial *worldwide* científicos *scientists* Tierra *Earth* Luna *Moon* además *as well as* indicios *evidence* pasó a ser *became* después de *after* la Guerra *War* se hizo *became* ciudadanos *citizens* desde *since* impuestos *taxes* demás *the rest*

Los viajes y las vacaciones

acampar	to camp
confirmar una reservación	to confirm a reservation
estar de vacaciones (*f. pl.*)	to be on vacation
hacer las maletas	to pack (one's suitcases)
hacer turismo (*m.*)	to go sightseeing
hacer un viaje	to take a trip
hacer una excursión	to go on a hike; to go on a tour
ir de compras (*f. pl.*)	to go shopping
ir de pesca (*f.*)	to go fishing
ir de vacaciones	to go on vacation
ir en autobús (*m.*), auto(móvil)(*m.*), avión (*m.*), barco (*m.*), motocicleta (*f.*), taxi (*m.*),	to go by bus, car, plane, boat, motorcycle, taxi
jugar a las cartas	to play cards
montar a caballo (*m.*)	to ride a horse
pasar por la aduana	to go through customs
pescar	to fish
recorrer	to tour an area
sacar/tomar fotos (*f. pl.*)	to take photos

el/la agente de viajes	travel agent
el/la huésped	guest
el/la inspector(a) de aduanas	customs inspector
el/la viajero/a	traveler

el aeropuerto	airport
la agencia de viajes	travel agency
la cabaña	cabin
el campo	countryside
el equipaje	luggage
la estación de autobuses, del metro, de tren	bus, subway, train station
la llegada	arrival
el mar	sea; ocean
el océano	ocean; sea
el paisaje	landscape; countryside
el pasaje (de ida y vuelta)	(round-trip) ticket
el pasaporte	passport

la pensión	boarding house
la playa	beach
la salida	departure; exit
la tienda de campaña	tent
turístico/a	touristic

El hotel

el ascensor	elevator
el/la botones	bellhop
la cama	bed
el/la empleado/a	employee
la habitación individual, doble	single, double room
el hotel	hotel
la llave	key
el piso	floor (of a building)
la planta baja	ground floor

Adjetivos

abierto/a	open
aburrido/a	bored; boring
agradable	pleasant
alegre	happy; joyful
amable	nice; friendly
avergonzado/a	embarrassed
cansado/a	tired
cerrado/a	closed
cómodo/a	comfortable
contento/a	happy; content
desordenado/a	disorderly
enamorado/a de	in love (with)
enojado/a	mad, angry
equivocado/a	wrong
feliz	happy
limpio/a	clean
listo/a	ready; smart
nervioso/a	nervous
ocupado/a	busy
ordenado/a	orderly
preocupado/a (por)	worried (about)
seguro/a	sure
sucio/a	dirty
triste	sad

Los números ordinales

primer, primero/a	first
segundo/a	second
tercer, tercero/a	third
cuarto/a	fourth
quinto/a	fifth
sexto/a	sixth
séptimo/a	seventh
octavo/a	eighth
noveno/a	ninth
décimo/a	tenth

Palabras adicionales

ahora mismo	right now
el año	year
¿Cuál es la fecha (de hoy)?	What is the date (today)?
la estación	season
el mes	month
todavía	yet; still

Seasons and months	See page 124.
Direct object pronouns	See page 140.
Numbers 101 and higher	See page 144.
Expresiones útiles	See page 127.

recursos

R	LCASS./CD Cass. 5/CD5
	LM p. 227

¡De compras!

6

Communicative Goals

You will learn how to:

- Talk about and describe clothing
- Express preferences in a store
- Negotiate and pay for items you buy

¡De compras!

Más vocabulario

el abrigo	coat
el almacén	department store
los calcetines	socks
el centro comercial	shopping mall
el cinturón	belt
las gafas (de sol), las gafas (oscuras)	(sun)glasses
los guantes	gloves
el impermeable	raincoat
los lentes de contacto	contact lenses
los lentes de sol	sunglasses
el mercado (al aire libre)	(open-air) market
el precio (fijo)	(fixed; set) price
la rebaja	sale
la ropa	clothing; clothes
la ropa interior	underwear
las sandalias	sandals
la tienda	shop; store
el vestido	dress
los zapatos de tenis	tennis shoes; sneakers
costar (o:ue)	to cost
gastar	to spend (money)
hacer juego (con)	to match
llevar	to wear; to take
regatear	to bargain
usar	to wear; to use
vender	to sell

Variación léxica

calcetines	⟷	medias (Amér. L.)
cinturón	⟷	correa (Col., Venez.)
gafas/lentes de sol	⟷	gafas/lentes oscuras/os, gafas/lentes negras/os
zapatos de tenis	⟷	zapatillas de deporte (Esp.), zapatillas (Arg., Perú)

los pantalones cortos

el traje de baño

los pantalones

la camiseta

el dependiente

la camisa

la clienta

el traje

el dinero

la blusa

la bolsa

el suéter

la falda

las medias

recursos

Práctica

el sombrero

Caballeros

el par

los zapatos

la chaqueta

la caja

la cartera

la vendedora

la corbata

la tarjeta de crédito

los bluejeans

la bota

1 **Escuchar** 🎧 Listen to Juanita and Vicente talk about what they're packing for their vacations. Indicate who is packing each item. If both are packing an item, write both names. If neither is packing an item, write an X.

1. abrigo _____
2. zapatos de tenis _____
3. impermeable _____
4. chaqueta _____
5. sandalias _____
6. bluejeans _____
7. gafas de sol _____
8. camisetas _____
9. traje de baño _____
10. botas _____
11. pantalones cortos _____
12. suéter _____

2 **Completar** Anita is talking about going shopping. Complete each sentence with the correct word(s), adding definite or indefinite articles when necessary.

caja	dependientas	tarjeta de crédito
vendedores	medias	centro comercial
traje de baño	par	ropa

1. Hoy voy a ir de compras al nuevo _____.
2. Voy a ir a la tienda de ropa para mujeres. Siempre hay muchas rebajas y las _____ son muy simpáticas.
3. Necesito comprarme _____ de zapatos.
4. Y tengo que comprarme _____ nuevo porque el sábado voy a la playa con mis amigos.
5. También voy a comprar unas _____ para mi mamá.
6. Voy a pagar todo (*everything*) en _____.
7. Pero hoy no llevo dinero. Voy a tener que usar mi _____.
8. Mañana voy al mercado al aire libre. Me gusta regatear con los _____.

3 **Escoger** Choose the item in each group that does not belong.

1. gafas • ropa interior • gafas de sol • lentes de contacto
2. camisa • camiseta • blusa • botas
3. bluejeans • bolsa • falda • pantalones
4. abrigo • suéter • corbata • chaqueta
5. mercado • tienda • almacén • cartera
6. usar • costar • gastar • regatear
7. botas • sandalias • zapatos • traje
8. vender • regatear • ropa interior • gastar

Los colores

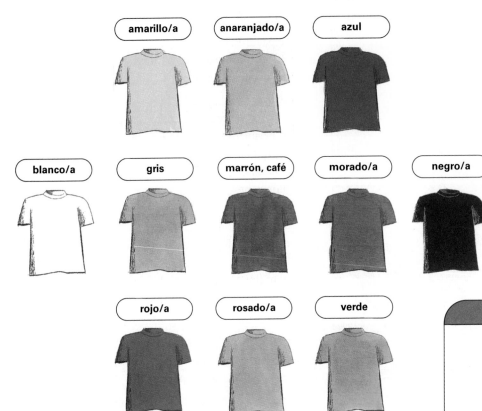

amarillo/a · anaranjado/a · azul

blanco/a · gris · marrón, café · morado/a · negro/a

rojo/a · rosado/a · verde

¡LENGUA VIVA!

The names of colors vary throughout the Spanish-speaking world. For example, **anaranjado/a** may be referred to as **naranja**, **morado/a** as **púrpura**, and **rojo/a** as **colorado**.

Other terms that will prove helpful include **claro** (*light*) and **oscuro** (*dark*): **azul claro, azul oscuro**

Adjetivos

barato/a	*cheap*
bueno/a	*good*
cada	*each*
caro/a	*expensive*
corto/a	*short (in length)*
elegante	*elegant*
hermoso/a	*beautiful*
largo/a	*long (in length)*
loco/a	*crazy*
nuevo/a	*new*
otro/a	*other; another*
pobre	*poor*
rico/a	*rich*

4 **Contrastes** Complete each phrase with the opposite of the underlined word.

1. una corbata <u>barata</u> • unas camisas…
2. unas sandalias <u>malas</u> • unos zapatos de tenis…
3. un vestido <u>corto</u> • una falda…
4. un hombre muy <u>pobre</u> • una mujer muy…
5. una cartera <u>nueva</u> • un cinturón…
6. unos trajes <u>hermosos</u> • unos bluejeans…
7. un chico que <u>compra</u> ropa • una chica que… ropa
8. unos lentes de contacto <u>limpios</u> • unas gafas…
9. un impermeable <u>grande</u> • unos suéteres…
10. unos calcetines <u>blancos</u> • unas medias…

5 **Preguntas** Answer these questions with a classmate.

1. ¿De qué color es la rosa de Texas?
2. ¿De qué colores es la bandera (*flag*) de los EE.UU.?
3. ¿De qué color es la casa donde vive el presidente de los EE.UU.?
4. ¿De qué color es el océano Atlántico?
5. ¿De qué color es la nieve?
6. ¿De qué color es el café?
7. ¿De qué colores es el dólar de los EE.UU.?
8. ¿De qué colores es una cebra (*zebra*)?

Comunicación

6 **Las maletas** With a classmate, answer these questions about the drawings.

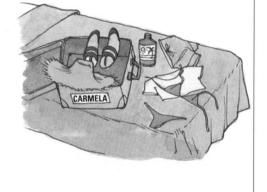

1. ¿Qué hay al lado de la maleta de Carmela?

2. ¿Qué hay en la maleta?

3. ¿De qué color son las sandalias?

4. ¿Adónde va Carmela?

5. ¿Qué tiempo va a hacer?

6. ¿Qué hay al lado de la maleta de Pepe?

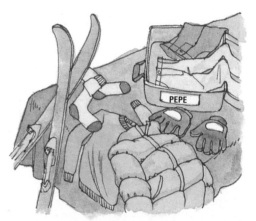

7. ¿Qué hay en la maleta?

8. ¿De qué color es el suéter?

9. ¿Qué va a hacer Pepe?

10. ¿Qué tiempo va a hacer?

CONSÚLTALO

Weather expressions
To review weather, see Lesson 4, pp. 112-113.

7 **¿Adónde van?** Imagine that you are going on a vacation with two classmates. Get together with your classmates and decide where you're going. Then draw three suitcases and write in each one what clothing each person is taking. Present your drawings to the rest of the class, answering these questions.

- ¿Adónde van?
- ¿Qué tiempo va a hacer allí (*there*)?
- ¿Qué van a hacer allí?
- ¿Qué hay en sus maletas?
- ¿De qué color es la ropa en sus maletas?

8 **Preferencias** Use these questions to interview a classmate. Then switch roles.

1. ¿Adónde vas para (*in order to*) comprar ropa? ¿Por qué?
2. ¿Qué tipo de ropa prefieres? ¿Por qué?
3. ¿Cuáles son tus colores favoritos?
4. En tu opinión, ¿es importante comprar ropa nueva frecuentemente? ¿Por qué?
5. ¿Cuánto dinero gastas en ropa cada mes? ¿Buscas rebajas?
6. ¿Regateas cuando compras ropa? ¿Usas una tarjeta de crédito?

¡Qué ropa más bonita!

Javier e Inés van de compras al mercado.

INÉS

JAVIER

EL VENDEDOR

INÉS Javier, ¡qué ropa más bonita! A mí me gusta esa camisa blanca y azul. Debe ser de algodón. ¿Te gusta?

JAVIER Yo prefiero la camisa de la izquierda... la gris con rayas rojas. Hace juego con mis botas marrones.

INÉS Está bien, Javier. Mira, necesito comprarle un regalo a mi hermana Graciela. Acaba de empezar un nuevo trabajo...

JAVIER ¿Tal vez una bolsa?

VENDEDOR Esas bolsas son típicas de las montañas. ¿Le gusta?

INÉS Sí. Quiero comprarle una a mi hermana.

VENDEDOR Buenas tardes, joven. ¿Le puedo servir en algo?

JAVIER Sí. Voy a ir de excursión a las montañas y necesito un buen suéter.

VENDEDOR ¿Qué talla usa Ud.?

JAVIER Uso talla grande.

VENDEDOR Éstos son de talla grande.

JAVIER ¿Qué precio tiene ése?

VENDEDOR ¿Le gusta este suéter? Le cuesta ciento cincuenta mil sucres.

JAVIER Quiero comprarlo. Pero, señor, no soy rico. ¿Ciento veinte mil sucres?

VENDEDOR Bueno, para usted... sólo ciento treinta mil sucres.

JAVIER Está bien, señor.

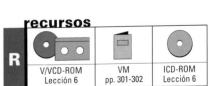

INÉS Me gusta aquélla. ¿Cuánto cuesta?

VENDEDOR Ésa cuesta ciento sesenta mil sucres. ¡Es de muy buena calidad!

INÉS Uy, demasiado cara. Quizás otro día.

JAVIER Acabo de comprarme un suéter. Y tú, ¿qué compraste?

INÉS Compré esta bolsa para mi hermana.

INÉS También compré una camisa y un sombrero. ¿Qué tal me veo?

JAVIER ¡Guapa, muy guapa!

Enfoque cultural Mercados al aire libre

Open-air markets, or **mercados al aire libre,** are an important part of the commerce and culture of many Hispanic countries. Fresh fruits and vegetables, tapestries, clothing, pottery and crafts are commonly seen among the vendors' wares. One of the most famous is the market in Otavalo, Ecuador, which has taken place every Saturday since pre-Incan times. Another popular market is **El Rastro** in Madrid, held every Sunday, where tourists can buy antiques and many other goods.

Expresiones útiles

Talking about clothing

▶ **¡Qué ropa más bonita!**
What pretty clothes!

▶ **Me gusta esta/esa camisa blanca de rayas negras.**
I like this/that white shirt with black stripes.

▶ **Está de moda.**
It's in fashion.

▶ **Debe ser de algodón/lana/seda.**
It must be cotton/wool/silk.

▶ **Es de cuadros/lunares/rayas.**
It's plaid/polka-dotted/striped.

▶ **Me gusta este/ese suéter.**
I like this/that sweater.

▶ **Es de muy buena calidad.**
It's very good quality.

▶ **¿Qué talla lleva/usa Ud.?**
What size do you wear?

▷ **Llevo/Uso talla grande.**
I wear a large.

▶ **¿Qué número calza Ud.?**
What (shoe) size do you wear?

▷ **Calzo el treinta y seis.**
I wear a size six.

Talking about how much things cost

▶ **¿Cuánto cuesta?**
How much does it cost?

▷ **Sólo cuesta noventa mil sucres.**
It only costs ninety thousand sucres.

▷ **Demasiado caro/a.**
Too expensive.

▷ **Es una ganga.**
It's a bargain.

Saying what you bought

▶ **¿Qué compró Ud./él/ella?**
What did you (form.)/he/she buy?

▷ **Compré esta bolsa para mi hermana.**
I bought this purse for my sister.

▶ **¿Qué compraste?**
What did you buy?

▷ **Acabo de comprarme un sombrero.**
I have just bought myself a hat.

Reacciona a la fotonovela

1   ¿Cierto o falso? Indicate whether each sentence is **cierto** or **falso**. Correct the false statements.

	Cierto	Falso
1. A Inés le gusta la camisa verde y amarilla.	O	O
2. Javier necesita comprarle un regalo a su hermana.	O	O
3. Las bolsas en el mercado son típicas de las montañas.	O	O
4. Javier busca un traje de baño.	O	O
5. Inés compró un sombrero, un suéter y una bolsa.	O	O
6. Javier regatea con el vendedor.	O	O

2   Identificar Provide the name of the person who would make each statement. The names may be used more than once.

1. ¿Te gusta el sombrero que compré? _____
2. Estos suéteres son de talla grande. ¿Qué talla usa Ud.? _____
3. ¿Por qué no compras una bolsa para Graciela? _____
4. Creo que mis botas hacen juego con la camisa. _____
5. Estas bolsas son excelentes, de muy buena calidad. _____
6. Creo que las blusas aquí son de algodón. _____

INÉS

JAVIER

EL VENDEDOR

CONSEJOS

When discussing prices, it's important to keep in mind singular and plural forms of verbs. Look carefully for the subject of the sentence:

La camisa **cuesta** diez dólares.

Las botas **cuestan** sesenta dólares.

El precio de las botas **es** sesenta dólares.

Los precios de la ropa **son** altos.

3   Contestar Answer the questions using the information in the **Fotonovela**.

1. Inés quiere comprarle un regalo a su hermana. ¿Por qué?
2. ¿Cuánto cuesta la bolsa típica de las montañas?
3. ¿Por qué necesita Javier un buen suéter?
4. ¿Cuál es el precio final del suéter?
5. ¿Qué compra Inés en el mercado?
6. ¿Qué talla usa Javier?

4   Conversar With a classmate, role-play a conversation in which the salesperson greets a customer in an open-air market and offers assistance. The customer is looking for a particular item of clothing. The salesperson and the customer discuss colors and sizes and negotiate a price.

AYUDA

¿Qué desea?
What would you like?

Estoy buscando...
I'm looking for...

Prefiero el/la rojo/a.
I prefer the red one.

¿Cuánto cuesta?
How much does it cost?

Es demasiado.
It's too much.

Pronunciación

The consonants **d** and **t**

¿**D**ón**d**e?   ven**d**er   na**d**ar   ver**d**a**d**

Like **b** and **v**, the Spanish **d** can also have a hard sound or a soft sound, depending on which letters appear next to it.

Don   **d**inero   tien**d**a   fal**d**a

At the beginning of a phrase and after **n** or **l**, the letter **d** is pronounced with a hard sound. This sound is similar to the English *d* in *dog*, but a little softer and duller. The tongue should touch the back of the upper teeth, not the roof of the mouth.

---

me**d**ias   ver**d**e   vesti**d**o   hués**p**e**d**

In all other positions, **d** has a soft sound. It is similar to the English *th* in *there*, but a little softer.

Don **D**iego no tiene el **d**iccionario.

When **d** begins a word, its pronunciation depends on the previous word. At the beginning of a phrase or after a word that ends in **n** or **l**, it is pronounced as a hard **d**.

Doña **D**olores es **d**e la capital.

Words that begin with **d** are pronounced with a soft **d** if they appear immediately after a word that ends in a vowel or any consonant other than **n** or **l**.

---

traje   pan**t**alones   **t**arje**t**a   **t**ien**d**a

When pronouncing the Spanish **t**, the tongue should touch the back of the upper teeth, not the roof of the mouth. Unlike the English *t*, no air is expelled from the mouth.

Práctica Read these phrases aloud to practice the **d** and the **t**.

1. Hasta pronto.
2. De nada.
3. Mucho gusto.
4. Lo siento.
5. No hay de qué.
6. ¿De dónde es usted?
7. ¡Todos a bordo!
8. No puedo.
9. Es estupendo.
10. No tengo computadora.
11. ¿Cuándo vienen?
12. Son las tres y media.

En la variedad está el gusto.[1]

Refranes Read these sayings aloud to practice the **d** and the **t**.

Aunque la mona se vista de seda, mona se queda.[2]

recursos

| R | STUDENT CD Lección 6 | LM p. 230 | LCASS./CD Cass. 6/CD6 | ICD-ROM Lección 6 |

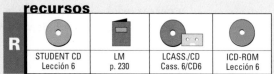

6.1 The preterite tense of regular verbs

ANTE TODO In order to talk about events in the past, Spanish uses two simple tenses: the preterite and the imperfect. In this lesson, you will learn how to form the preterite tense, which is used to express actions or states completed in the past.

Preterite of regular –ar, –er, and –ir verbs			
	–ar verbs **comprar**	**–er verbs** **vender**	**–ir verbs** **escribir**
SINGULAR FORMS			
yo	compr**é** *I bought*	vend**í** *I sold*	escrib**í** *I wrote*
tú	compr**aste**	vend**iste**	escrib**iste**
Ud./él/ella	compr**ó**	vend**ió**	escrib**ió**
PLURAL FORMS			
nosotros/as	compr**amos**	vend**imos**	escrib**imos**
vosotros/as	compr**asteis**	vend**isteis**	escrib**isteis**
Uds./ellos/ellas	compr**aron**	vend**ieron**	escrib**ieron**

> **¡ATENCIÓN!**
> The **yo** and **Ud./él/ella** forms of all three conjugations have written accents on the last syllable to show that it is stressed.

▶ As the preceding chart shows, the endings for regular **–er** and **–ir** verbs are identical in the preterite.

¿Qué compraste?

Compré esta bolsa.

▶ Note that the **nosotros/as** forms of regular **–ar** and **–ir** verbs in the preterite are identical to the present tense forms. Context will help you determine which tense is being used.

En invierno **compramos** la ropa en la tienda de la universidad.
In the wintertime, we buy clothing at the university store.

Anoche **compramos** unos zapatos de tenis y unas sandalias.
Last night we bought a pair of tennis shoes and a pair of sandals.

▶ **–Ar** and **–er** verbs that have a stem change in the present tense are regular in the preterite. They do *not* have a stem change.

	PRESENT	PRETERITE
cerrar (e:ie)	Ana **cierra** la puerta.	Ana **cerró** la puerta.
volver (o:ue)	Carlitos **vuelve** a las dos.	Carlitos **volvió** a las dos.

> **¡ATENCIÓN!**
> **Preterite of stem-changing verbs**
> -ir verbs that have a stem change in the present tense also have a stem change in the preterite. See Lesson 8, p. 218.

▶ Verbs that end in **–car**, **–gar**, and **–zar** have a spelling change in the first person singular (**yo** form) in the preterite.

bus**car**	busc-	qu-	yo bus**qu**é
lle**gar**	lleg-	gu-	yo lle**gu**é
empe**zar**	empez-	c-	yo empe**c**é

▶ Except for the **yo** form, all other forms of **–car**, **–gar**, and **–zar** verbs are regular in the preterite.

bus**qu**é, buscaste, buscó, buscamos, buscasteis, buscaron
lle**gu**é, llegaste, llegó, llegamos, llegasteis, llegaron
empe**c**é, empezaste, empezó, empezamos, empezasteis, empezaron

▶ Three other verbs —**creer**, **leer**, and **oír** — have spelling changes in the preterite. The **i** of the verb endings of **creer**, **leer**, and **oír** carries an accent in the **yo**, **tú**, **nosotros/as**, and **vosotros/as** forms, and changes to **y** in the **Ud./él/ella** and **Uds./ellos/ellas** forms.

creer	cre-	cre**í**, cre**í**ste, cre**y**ó, cre**í**mos, cre**í**steis, cre**y**eron
leer	le-	le**í**, le**í**ste, le**y**ó, le**í**mos, le**í**steis, le**y**eron
oír	o-	o**í**, o**í**ste, o**y**ó, o**í**mos, o**í**steis, o**y**eron
ver	v-	vi, viste, vio, vimos, visteis, vieron

Words commonly used with the preterite

anoche	*last night*		**pasado/a** (adj.)	*last; past*
anteayer	*the day before yesterday*		**el año pasado**	*last year*
			la semana pasada	*last week*
ayer	*yesterday*		**una vez**	*once; one time*
de repente	*suddenly*		**dos veces**	*twice; two times*
desde... hasta...	*from... until...*		**ya**	*already*

Ayer llegué a París.
Yesterday I arrived in Paris.

Anoche oí un ruido extraño.
Last night I heard a strange noise.

¡INTÉNTALO! Provide the appropriate preterite forms of the verbs. The first item in each column has been done for you.

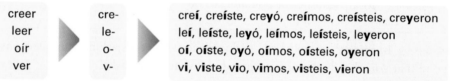

celebrar
1. Elena celebró.
2. Yo _____.
3. Los chicos _____.
4. Emilio y yo _____.
5. Tú _____.
6. Ellos _____.
7. Ud. _____.

comer
1. Los niños comieron.
2. Tú _____.
3. Ud. _____.
4. Nosotros _____.
5. Yo _____.
6. Uds. _____.
7. Carlota _____.

salir
1. Tú y yo salimos.
2. Ella _____.
3. Pablo y Elena _____.
4. Nosotros _____.
5. Yo _____.
6. Ud. _____.
7. Tú _____.

comenzar
1. Uds. comenzaron.
2. Nosotras _____.
3. Yo _____.
4. Marcos _____.
5. Tú _____.
6. Los clientes _____.
7. La vendedora _____.

Práctica

1 **Completar** Andrea is talking about what happened last weekend. Complete each sentence by choosing the correct verb and putting it in the preterite.

1. El sábado a las diez de la mañana, la profesora Mora _____ (asistir, costar, usar) a una reunión (*meeting*) de profesores.
2. A la una, yo _____ (llegar, bucear, llevar) a la tienda con mis amigos.
3. Mis amigos y yo _____ (comprar, regatear, gastar) dos o tres cosas.
4. Yo _____ (costar, comprar, escribir) unos pantalones negros y mi amigo Mateo _____ (gastar, pasear, comprar) una camisa azul.
5. A las siete, mis amigos y yo _____ (llevar, vivir, comer) en un café.
6. A las nueve, Pepe _____ (hablar, pasear, nadar) con su novia por teléfono.
7. La tarde del sábado, mi mamá les _____ (escribir, beber, vivir) una carta a nuestros parientes en Cuba.
8. La mañana del domingo mi tía Manuela _____ (decidir, salir, escribir) vender su auto y su bicicleta.
9. A las cuatro de la tarde, mi tía _____ (beber, salir, vender) su auto a la profesora Mora y su bicicleta a su amiga Loli.

2 **Preguntas** Imagine that you have a pesky friend who keeps asking you questions. Respond that you already did or have just done what he/she asks.

> **modelo**
> leer la lección
> **Estudiante 1:** ¿Leíste la lección? **Estudiante 2:** Sí, ya la leí.

1. escribir el correo electrónico
2. lavar (*to wash*) la ropa
3. oír las noticias (*news*)
4. comer el sándwich
5. practicar los verbos
6. pagar la cuenta (*bill*)
7. empezar la composición
8. ver la película *Titanic*

¡ATENCIÓN!

To say that you have just done something, use the construction **acabar** + **de** + [*infinitive*]. Note that **acabar** is used in the present tense even though the action expressed has already taken place.

José acaba de llegar.
José has just arrived.

Acabo de comprar un suéter.
I have just bought a sweater.

3 **Combinar** Combine words and phrases from each column to talk about things you and others did. Be sure to use the correct form of each verb.

> **modelo**
> Mis amigos y yo llegamos tarde a clase una vez.

yo	ver televisión	anoche
mi compañero/a de cuarto	hablar con un(a)	anteayer
mis amigos y yo	chico/a guapo/a	ayer
mi mejor (*best*) amigo/a	estudiar español	la semana pasada
mis padres	comprar ropa nueva	el año pasado
el/la profesor(a) de español	leer un buen libro	una vez
el presidente de los	llegar tarde a clase	dos veces
Estados Unidos	visitar Europa	
	escribir una carta	

AYUDA

pasado mañana
the day after tomorrow
próximo/a *next*
la semana que viene
next week
último/a *last (in a series)*
penúltimo/a
next to last

Comunicación

4 **Encuesta** Your instructor will give you **una hoja de actividades** (*a worksheet*). Walk around the room and ask people if they did each activity listed. Try to find at least two people for each activity, and note their names on your worksheet. Be prepared to report the results of your survey to the class.

> **modelo**
>
> comprar ropa nueva la semana pasada
> **Estudiante 1:** ¿Compraste ropa nueva la semana pasada?
> **Estudiante 2:** Sí, compré ropa nueva el jueves pasado.

Actividades	Nombres
1. Comprar ropa interior ayer	
2. Viajar a Europa el año pasado	
3. Ver a una persona famosa el año pasado	
4. Ver tres programas de televisión anoche	
5. Tomar tres exámenes la semana pasada	
6. Recibir un mensaje electrónico ayer	
7. Visitar otro país el verano pasado	
8. Jugar a las cartas anoche	

5 **Las vacaciones** Imagine that you took these photos on a vacation with friends. Get together with a partner and use the pictures to tell him or her about your trip.

Síntesis

6 **Conversación** Get together with a partner and have a conversation about what you did last week. Don't forget to include school activities, shopping, and pastimes.

6.2 Indirect object pronouns

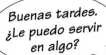

In Lesson 5, you learned that a direct object is the noun or pronoun that receives the action of the verb directly. In contrast, indirect objects are nouns or pronouns that receive the action of the verb indirectly. Note the following example:

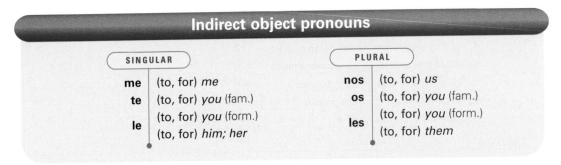

SUBJECT	I.O. PRONOUN	VERB	DIRECT OBJECT	INDIRECT OBJECT
Roberto	**le**	prestó	cien pesos	**a Luisa.**
Roberto		*loaned*	*100 pesos*	*to Luisa.*

An indirect object is the noun or pronoun that answers the question *to whom* or *for whom* an action is done. In the preceding example, the indirect object answers this question: **¿A quién le prestó Roberto cien pesos?** *To whom did Roberto loan 100 pesos?*

Indirect object pronouns

SINGULAR		PLURAL	
me	(to, for) *me*	**nos**	(to, for) *us*
te	(to, for) *you* (fam.)	**os**	(to, for) *you* (fam.)
le	(to, for) *you* (form.)	**les**	(to, for) *you* (form.)
	(to, for) *him; her*		(to, for) *them*

Buenas tardes. ¿Le puedo servir en algo?

Sí, necesito comprarme un buen suéter.

Using indirect object pronouns

▶ Spanish speakers commonly use both an indirect object pronoun and the indirect object noun to which it refers in the same sentence. This is done to emphasize and clarify to whom the pronoun refers.

I.O. PRONOUN	INDIRECT OBJECT	I.O. PRONOUN	INDIRECT OBJECT

Ella **le** vendió la ropa a **Elena.**   **Les** prestamos el dinero a **Inés y Álex.**

▶ Indirect object pronouns are also used without the indirect object noun when the person for whom the action is being done is known.

Ana **le** prestó la falda **a Elena.**   También **le** prestó unos bluejeans.
Ana loaned her skirt to Elena.   *She also loaned her a pair of blue jeans.*

▶ Indirect object pronouns are usually placed before the conjugated form of the verb. In negative sentences the pronoun is placed between **no** and the conjugated verb.

Martín **me** compró un regalo.
Martín bought me a gift.

Eva **no me** escribió una carta.
Eva didn't write a letter to me.

▶ When a conjugated verb is followed by an infinitive or the present progressive, the indirect object pronoun may be placed before the conjugated verb or attached to the infinitive or present participle.

Él quiere **hablarte** en inglés.
He wants to talk to you in English.

Él está **escribiéndole** una postal a ella.
He is writing a postcard to her.

Él **te** quiere hablar en inglés.
He wants to talk to you in English.

Él **le** está escribiendo una postal a ella.
He is writing a postcard to her.

▶ Because the indirect object pronouns **le** and **les** have multiple meanings, Spanish-speakers often clarify to whom the pronouns refer with the preposition **a** + [*pronoun*] or **a** + [*noun*].

UNCLEAR STATEMENT	CLARIFIED STATEMENTS
Yo **le** compré un abrigo.	Yo **le** compré un abrigo **a él/ella/Ud.**
Ella **le** dio *(gave)* un libro.	Ella **le** dio un libro **a Juan.**

UNCLEAR STATEMENT	CLARIFIED STATEMENTS
Él **les** vendió unos sombreros.	Él **les** vendió unos sombreros **a ellos/ellas/Uds.**
Ellos **les** hablaron muy claro.	Ellos **les** hablaron muy claro **a los turistas.**

¡ATENCIÓN!
When an indirect object pronoun is attached to a present participle, an accent mark is added to maintain the proper stress. For more information on accents, see **Pronunciación**, p. 101, **Ortografía**, p. 275 and p. 303.

¡INTÉNTALO! Use the cues in parentheses to provide the indirect object pronoun for the sentence. The first item has been done for you.

1. Juan ___le___ escribió ayer. (*to Elena*)
2. María _____ habló también. (*to us*)
3. Beatriz y Felipe _____ escribieron desde Cuba. (*to me*)
4. Marta y yo _____ compramos unos guantes. (*for them*)
5. Los vendedores _____ vendieron ropa. (*to you, fam.*)
6. La maestra _____ enseñó los verbos. (*to us*)
7. Yo _____ canté en español. (*to her*)
8. Nosotros _____ compramos dos vestidos. (*for them*)
9. Ella _____ escribió todos los días. (*to me*)

Rewrite the following sentences, attaching the indirect object pronoun to the end of the infinitive or present participle. Remember to add accent marks when necessary.

1. Susana te está escribiendo una carta. *Susana está escribiéndote una carta.*
2. Le tienes que pedir un lápiz al profesor.
3. Mi novia me va a comprar una camisa.
4. Mi novio me está preparando unos tacos.
5. La mamá le va a leer un libro al niño.

Práctica

1   **Completar** Fill in the correct pronouns to complete Mónica's description of her family's holiday shopping.

1. Juan y yo _____ compramos una blusa a nuestra hermana Gisela.
2. Mi tía _____ compró a nosotros una mesa para la casa.
3. Gisela _____ compró dos corbatas a su novio.
4. A mi mamá yo _____ compré un par de guantes negros.
5. A mi profesora _____ compré dos novelas de García Márquez.
6. Juan _____ compró un regalo a mis padres.
7. Mis padres _____ compraron a mí un traje nuevo.
8. Y a ti, yo _____ compré una sorpresa también. ¿Quieres verla?

2   **Minidiálogos** Supply the missing words in the minidialogues.

1. **NIÑOS** Mamá, ¿vas a leernos una historia (*story*)?
   MAMÁ Sí, _____ Blanca Nieves (*Snow White*).
   Creo que les va a gustar.
2. **JUAN** ¿Vas a comprarles un regalo a Héctor y a Linda?
   MONA Sí, _____ un viaje a Europa.
3. **ESTUDIANTES** Profesora, ¿_____ en español todos
   los días (*every day*)?
   PROFESORA ¡Claro que (*of course*) voy a hablarles a Uds. en español!
   Es importante hablar en español todos los días.
4. **SARA** ¿_____ una carta a Maripili?
   LAURA No, estoy escribiéndoles una carta a Alicia y Orlando. ¿Por qué?
5. **ALFREDO** Ramón, ¿_____ puedes prestar tu bicicleta hoy?
   RAMÓN No, no te puedo prestar mi bicicleta. Lo siento, es que tienes muchos
   accidentes.
6. **ESPOSO** ¿Qué me vas a comprar en el centro comercial? ¿Una camisa?
   ¿Una corbata?
   ESPOSA ¡No _____ nada!

3   **Describir** Describe what's happening in these photos based on the cues provided.

1. escribir / mensaje electrónico

2. mostrar / fotos

3. pedir / llaves

4. vender / suéter

Comunicación

4   **Entrevista** Take turns with a classmate asking and answering questions using the word bank.

> **modelo**
>
> escribir mensajes electrónicos
> **Estudiante 1:** ¿A quién le escribes mensajes electrónicos?
> **Estudiante 2:** Le escribo mensajes electrónicos a mi hermano.

comprar ropa	prestar dinero
escribir tarjetas postales	cantar canciones de amor (*love songs*)
escribir mensajes electrónicos	preparar comida (*food*) mexicana
pedir dinero	pedir ayuda con tus clases

5   **Entrevista** Use these questions to interview a classmate.

1. ¿Te gusta escribir tarjetas postales?
2. ¿Te gusta ir de compras? ¿Adónde te gusta ir?
3. ¿Les compras regalos a tus amigos/as cuando hay rebajas?
4. ¿Me compraste un regalo de Navidad el año pasado?
5. ¿Les prestas dinero a tus amigos/as? ¿Por qué?
6. ¿Me prestas cien dólares?

6   **Situación** Money is no object, so the entire Spanish class is going on a shopping spree. In groups of three, interview each other to find out what everyone is going to buy for family and friends. Be prepared to share your findings with the rest of the class.

Síntesis

7   **Minidrama** With two classmates, take turns playing the roles of two shoppers and a clerk in a clothing store. The shoppers should take turns talking about the articles of clothing they are looking for, for whom they are buying the clothes, and what they bought for the same people last year. The clerk should recommend several items, based on the shoppers' descriptions.

AYUDA

Other phrases (in addition to those given on page 157) that you can use are:

Me queda grande/pequeño.
It's big/small on me.

¿Tiene otro color?
Do you have another color?

¿Está en rebaja?
Is it on sale?

6.3 Demonstrative adjectives and pronouns

Demonstrative adjectives

ANTE TODO In Spanish, as in English, demonstrative adjectives are words that "demonstrate" or "point out" nouns. Demonstrative adjectives precede the nouns they modify and, like other Spanish adjectives you have studied, agree with them in gender and number. Observe the following examples, then study the following chart.

esta camisa	**ese** vendedor	**aquellos** zapatos
this shirt	*that salesman*	*those shoes (over there)*

Demonstrative adjectives

Singular		Plural		
MASCULINE	FEMININE	MASCULINE	FEMININE	
este	**esta**	**estos**	**estas**	*this; these*
ese	**esa**	**esos**	**esas**	*that; those*
aquel	**aquella**	**aquellos**	**aquellas**	*that; those (over there)*

▶ There are three sets of demonstrative adjectives. To determine which one to use, you must establish the relationship between the speaker and the noun(s) being pointed out.

▶ The demonstrative adjectives **este, esta, estos,** and **estas** are used to point out nouns that are close in space and time to the speaker and the listener.

Me gusta este suéter.

▶ The demonstrative adjectives **ese, esa, esos,** and **esas** are used to point out nouns that are not close in space and time to the speaker. They may, however, be close to the listener.

Me gustan esos zapatos.

▶ The demonstrative adjectives **aquel, aquella, aquellos,** and **aquellas** are used to point out nouns that are far away in space and time from the speaker and the listener.

> Aquellos chicos son mis amigos.

Demonstrative pronouns

▶ Demonstrative pronouns are identical to their corresponding demonstrative adjectives, except that they carry an accent mark on the stressed vowel.

—¿Quieres comprar **este suéter**?
Do you want to buy this sweater?

—No, no quiero **éste**. Quiero **ése**.
No, I don't want this one. I want that one.

—¿Vas a leer **estas revistas**?
Are you going to read these magazines?

—Sí, voy a leer **éstas**. También voy a leer **aquéllas**.
Yes, I'm going to read these. I'll also read those.

Demonstrative pronouns

Singular		Plural		
MASCULINE	FEMININE	MASCULINE	FEMININE	NEUTER	
éste	**ésta**	**éstos**	**éstas**	**esto**	*this (one); these*
ése	**ésa**	**ésos**	**ésas**	**eso**	*that (one); those*
aquél	**aquélla**	**aquéllos**	**aquéllas**	**aquello**	*that (one); those (over there)*

▶ Each of the three sets of demonstrative pronouns has a neuter form: **esto, eso,** and **aquello.** These forms refer to unidentified or unspecified nouns, situations, ideas, and concepts.

—¿Qué es **esto**?
What's this?

—Es una cartera.
It's a wallet.

—¿Qué es **eso**?
What's that?

—¡**Aquello** es bonito!
That's pretty!

¡INTÉNTALO! Provide the correct form of the demonstrative adjective and demonstrative pronoun for these nouns. The first item has been done for you.

1. la falda / este _____*esta falda, ésta*_____
2. los estudiantes / este _____
3. los países / aquel _____
4. la ventana / ese _____
5. los periodistas / ese _____
6. las empleadas / ese _____
7. el chico / aquel _____
8. las sandalias / este _____
9. el autobús / ese _____
10. las chicas / aquel _____

Lectura
Antes de leer

Estrategia
Skimming

Skimming involves quickly reading through a document to absorb its general meaning. This allows you to understand the main ideas without having to read word for word. When you skim a text, you might want to look at its title and subtitles. You might also want to read the first sentence of each paragraph.

Examinar el texto

Look at the format of the reading selection. How is it organized? What does the organization of the document tell you about its content?

Buscar cognados

Scan the reading selection to locate cognates and write a few of them down. Based on the cognates, what is the reading selection about?

1. _____
2. _____
3. _____
4. _____
5. _____
6. The reading selection is about _____.

Impresiones generales

Now skim the reading selection to understand its general meaning. Jot down your impressions. What new information did you learn about the document by skimming it? Based on all the information you now have, answer these questions.

1. Who produced this document?
2. What is its purpose?
3. Who is its intended audience?

¡Corona tiene las ofertas más locas del verano!

30% 40% 50%

La tienda más elegante de la ciudad con precios increíbles y con la tarjeta de crédito más conveniente del mercado.

JÓVENES

Bluejeans chicos y chicas
PACOS
Americanos. Tradicional
Ahora: $9.000 el par

30% de rebaja

Suéteres
CARAMELO
Algodón y lana.
Colores blanco, gris y negro
Antes: $10.500

Ahora: $6.825

Lentes de contacto
VISIÓN
Americanos. Colores azul, verde y morado
Antes: $15.000 el par

Ahora $10.000

Trajes de baño chicos y chicas
SUBMARINO
Microfibra. Todas las tallas
Ahora: $12.500

50% de rebaja

Gafas de sol
VISIÓN
Origen canadiense
Antes: $23.000

Ahora: $14.950

NIÑOS

Vestido de niña
GIRASOL
Tallas de la 2 a la 12.
De cuadros y rayas
Ahora: $8.625

30% de rebaja

Pantalón deportivo de niño
MILÁN
Tallas de la 4 a la 16
Ahora: $13.500

30% de rebaja

Zapatos de tenis
ACUARIO
Números del 20 al 25
Ahora: $15.000 el par

30% de rebaja

Pantalones cortos
MACARENA
Talla mediana
Ahora: $15.000

30% de rebaja

Camisetas de algodón
POLO
Antes: $15.000
Ahora: $7.500

50% de rebaja

Por la compra de $40.000, puede llevar un regalo gratis.
- Un hermoso cinturón de señora
- Un par de calcetines
- Una corbata de seda
- Una bolsa para la playa
- Una mochila
- Unas medias

real *royal* liquidación *clearance sale* antes *before* regalos *gifts*

Después de leer

Completar
Complete this paragraph about the reading selection with the correct forms of words from the word bank.

falda	rebaja
dinero	verano
increíble	zapato
hacer juego	pantalón
almacén	tarjeta de crédito

En este anuncio de periódico el _____ Corona anuncia la liquidación de _____ con grandes _____ en todos los departamentos. Con muy poco _____ Ud. puede equipar a toda su familia. Si no tiene dinero en efectivo (*cash*), puede utilizar su _____ y pagar luego. Para el caballero con gustos refinados, hay _____ importados de París y Roma. La señora elegante puede encontrar blusas de seda que _____ con todo tipo de _____ o _____. Los precios de esta liquidación son realmente _____.

¿Cierto o falso?
Indicate whether each statement is **cierto** or **falso**. Correct the false statements.

1. Hay ropa de algodón para jóvenes.
2. La ropa interior tiene una rebaja del 30%.
3. El almacén Corona tiene un departamento de zapatos.
4. Normalmente las sandalias cuestan $22.000 el par.

Preguntas
Contesta las preguntas en español.

1. Imagina que vas a ir a la tienda Corona. ¿Qué departamentos vas a visitar? ¿el departamento de ropa para señoras, el departamento de ropa para caballeros...?
2. ¿Qué vas a buscar en Corona?
3. ¿Hay tiendas similares a la tienda Corona en tu pueblo o ciudad? ¿Cómo se llaman? ¿Tienen muchas gangas?

Escritura

Estrategia

Brainstorming

How do you find ideas to write about? In the early stages of writing, brainstorming can help you generate ideas about a specific topic. Before writing your first draft, you should spend ten to fifteen minutes brainstorming and jotting down any ideas about the topic that occur to you. Whenever possible, write down your ideas in Spanish. Express your ideas in single words or phrases, and jot them down in any order. While brainstorming, don't worry about whether your ideas are good or bad. Selecting and organizing ideas should be the second stage of your writing. Remember that the more ideas you write down while you're brainstorming, the more options you'll have to choose from later when you start to organize your ideas.

Preparing interview questions

Before conducting an interview, you may find it helpful to brainstorm a list of interview questions, remembering to include the five W's (*who, what, when, where, why*) and the H (*how*). For example:

▶ ¿Cuándo vas de compras?

▶ ¿Con quién(es) vas de compras?

▶ ¿Adónde vas de compras?

▶ ¿Por qué te gusta ir de compras a ese almacén?

▶ ¿Cómo pagas? ¿Con un cheque, con una tarjeta de crédito...?

▶ ¿Cuáles son tus colores favoritos? ¿Compras mucha ropa de esos colores?

Tema

Escribe un informe

Write a report for the school newspaper about an interview you conducted with a student about his or her shopping habits and clothing preferences. First, brainstorm a list of interview questions. Then conduct the interview using the questions below as a guide, but feel free to ask other questions as they occur to you.

Examples of questions:

▶ ¿Qué tiendas, almacenes o centros comerciales prefieres?

▶ ¿Compras ropa de catálogos o por el Internet?

▶ ¿Prefieres comprar ropa cara o barata? ¿Por qué? ¿Te gusta buscar gangas?

▶ ¿Qué ropa llevas cuando vas a clase?

▶ ¿Qué ropa llevas cuando sales a bailar?

▶ ¿Qué ropa llevas cuando practicas un deporte?

▶ ¿Compras ropa para tu familia o para tus amigos/as?

Escuchar
Preparación

Based on the photograph below, what do you think Marisol has recently done? What do you think Marisol and Alicia are talking about? What else can you guess about their conversation from the visual clues in the photograph?

Estrategia
Listening for linguistic cues

You can enhance your listening comprehension by listening for specific information, such as linguistic cues. For example, if you listen for the endings of conjugated verbs, or for familiar constructions, such as **acabar de** + [*infinitive*] or **ir a** + [*infinitive*], you can find out whether an event already took place, is taking place now, or will take place in the future. Verb endings also give clues about who is participating in the action. To practice listening for linguistic cues, you will now listen to four sentences. As you listen, note whether each sentence refers to a past, present, or future action. Also jot down the subject of each sentence.

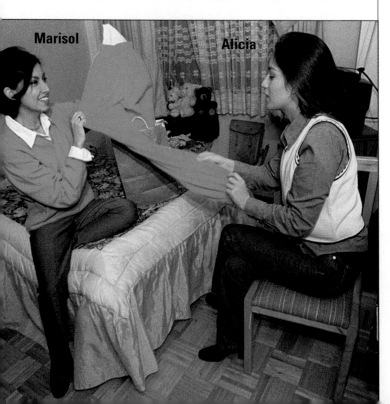

Marisol   Alicia

🎧 Ahora escucha

Now you are going to hear Marisol and Alicia's conversation. Make a list of the clothing items that each person mentions. Then put a check mark after the item if the person actually purchased it.

Marisol	Alicia
1. _____	1. _____
2. _____	2. _____
3. _____	3. _____
4. _____	4. _____

Comprensión

¿Cierto o falso?

Indicate whether each statement is **cierto** or **falso**. Then correct the false statements.

1. Marisol y Alicia acaban de ir de compras juntas (*together*).
2. Marisol va a comprar unos pantalones y una blusa mañana.
3. Marisol compró una blusa de cuadros.
4. Alicia compró unos zapatos nuevos hoy.
5. Alicia y Marisol van a ir al café.
6. Marisol gastó todo su dinero para la semana en ropa nueva.

Preguntas

Discuss the following questions with a classmate. Be sure to explain your answers.

1. ¿Crees que Alicia y Marisol son buenas amigas? ¿Por qué?
2. ¿Cuál de las dos estudiantes parece (*seems*) ser más ahorradora (*frugal*)? ¿Por qué?
3. ¿Crees que a Alicia le gusta la ropa que Marisol compró?
4. ¿Crees que la moda es importante para Alicia? ¿Para Marisol? ¿Por qué?
5. ¿Es importante para ti estar a la moda? ¿Por qué?

recursos

R STUDENT CD
Lección 6

Cuba

El país en cifras

- **Área:** 110.860 km² (42.803 millas²),
  aproximadamente el área de Pensilvania
- **Población:** 11.275.000
- **Capital:** La Habana—2.278.000

La Habana Vieja fue declarada Patrimonio Cultural de la Humanidad por la UNESCO en 1982. Este distrito es uno de los lugares más fascinantes de Cuba. En La Plaza de Armas, se puede visitar el majestuoso Palacio de Capitanes Generales, que ahora es un museo. En la calle Obispo, frecuentada por el autor Ernest Hemingway, hay hermosos cafés, clubes nocturnos y tiendas elegantes.

- **Ciudades principales:**
  Santiago de Cuba—446.000;
  Camagüey—294.000; Holguín—242.000;
  Guantánamo—208.000
  SOURCE: Population Division, UN Secretariat
- **Moneda:** peso cubano
- **Idiomas:** español (oficial)

Bandera de Cuba

Cubanos célebres

- Carlos Finlay, doctor y científico (1833-1915)
- José Martí, político y poeta (1853-1895)
- Fidel Castro, primer ministro, jefe de las fuerzas armadas (1926-)
- Zoe Valdés, escritora (1959-)

fue declarada *was declared* Patrimonio *Heritage* calle *street*
liviano *light* tira de chicle *stick of gum* colibrí *hummingbird*
abeja *bee* sino *but* ave *bird* miden *measure* apenas *just*

Fortaleza El Morro

Golfo de México

ESTADOS UNIDOS

Playa en Santiago de Cuba

Océano Atlántico

Famoso cabaret el club Tropicana de la Habana

La Habana

Cordillera de los Órganos

ESTADOS UNIDOS

CUBA

OCÉANO ATLÁNTICO

OCÉANO PACÍFICO

AMÉRICA DEL SUR

Isla de la Juventud

Mar Caribe

Camagüey

Vista aérea de campos de caña de azúcar

recursos

R	WB pp. 69-70	WB Repaso 4-6 pp. 71-72	vistasonline.com	ICD-ROM Lección 6

¡Increíble pero cierto!

Más corto y liviano que una tira de chicle, el colibrí abeja de Cuba no es sólo la más pequeña de las 320 especies de colibrí, sino también el ave más pequeña del mundo. Menores que muchos insectos, estas aves minúsculas miden apenas 5 centímetros y pesan sólo 1,95 gramos.

Baile • **Ballet Nacional de Cuba**

La bailarina Alicia Alonso fundó el Ballet Nacional de Cuba en 1948, después de convertirse en una estrella internacional en el Ballet de Nueva York y en Broadway. El Ballet Nacional de Cuba es famoso en todo el mundo por su creatividad y perfección técnica.

Economía • **La caña de azúcar y el tabaco**

La caña de azúcar es el producto agrícola más cultivado de la isla y su exportación es muy importante para la economía del país. El tabaco, que se usa para fabricar los famosos cigarros cubanos, es otro cultivo de mucha importancia.

Historia • **Los taínos**

Los taínos eran una de las tres tribus indígenas que vivían en la isla cuando llegaron los españoles en el siglo XV. Los taínos también vivían en Puerto Rico, la República Dominicana, Haití, Trinidad, Jamaica y partes de las Bahamas y la Florida. Muchos taínos huyeron a las montañas para escaparse de los españoles; sus descendientes todavía viven en la región.

Música • **Celia Cruz**

La cantante Celia Cruz es considerada la reina de la música salsa. Su carrera empezó en Cuba en los años cincuenta. Aunque Celia Cruz salió de Cuba en 1960, prefiere cantar en español. Su forma personal de cantar atrae a oyentes de todo el mundo. Ganó un *Grammy* en 1990.

Holguín

Santiago de Cuba

Guantánamo

Sierra Maestra

¿Qué aprendiste? Responde a las preguntas con una frase completa.

1. ¿Quién es el líder del gobierno de Cuba?
2. ¿Dónde está la calle Obispo?
3. ¿Qué autor está asociado con la Habana Vieja?
4. ¿Por qué es famoso el Ballet Nacional de Cuba?
5. ¿Cuáles son los dos cultivos más importantes para la economía cubana?
6. ¿Qué fabrican los cubanos con el tabaco?
7. ¿Cuándo empezó Celia Cruz su carrera musical?

Conexión Internet Investiga estos temas en el sitio **www.vistasonline.com**.

1. Busca información sobre un(a) cubano/a célebre. ¿Por qué es célebre? ¿Qué hace? ¿Todavía vive en Cuba?
2. Busca información sobre una de las ciudades principales de Cuba. ¿Qué atracciones hay en esta ciudad?

estrella *star* en todo el mundo *throughout the world* caña de azúcar *sugar cane* cultivado *grown* se usa *is used* cigarros *cigars*
eran *were* vivían *lived* huyeron *fled* reina *queen* Aunque *Although* atrae a oyentes *attracts listeners*

La ropa

el abrigo	coat
los bluejeans	jeans
la blusa	blouse
la bolsa	purse; bag
la bota	boot
el calcetín	sock
la camisa	shirt
la camiseta	t-shirt
la cartera	wallet
la chaqueta	jacket
el cinturón	belt
la corbata	tie
la falda	skirt
las gafas (de sol), las gafas (oscuras)	(sun)glasses
los guantes	gloves
el impermeable	raincoat
los lentes de contacto	contact lenses
los lentes (de sol)	(sun)glasses
las medias	pantyhose; stockings
los pantalones	pants
los pantalones cortos	shorts
la ropa	clothing; clothes
la ropa interior	underwear
la sandalia	sandal
el sombrero	hat
el suéter	sweater
el traje	suit
el traje (de baño)	(bathing) suit
el vestido	dress
los zapatos de tenis	(tennis) shoes, sneakers

Los colores

el color	color
amarillo/a	yellow
anaranjado/a	orange
azul	blue
blanco/a	white
gris	gray
marrón, café	brown
morado/a	purple
negro/a	black
rojo/a	red
rosado/a	pink
verde	green

Adjetivos

barato/a	cheap
bueno/a	good
cada	each
caro/a	expensive
corto/a	short (in length)
elegante	elegant
hermoso/a	beautiful
largo/a	long (in length)
loco/a	crazy
nuevo/a	new
otro/a	other; another
pobre	poor
rico/a	rich

Ir de compras

el almacén	department store
la caja	cash register
el centro comercial	shopping mall
el/la cliente/a	customer
el/la dependiente/a	clerk
el dinero	money
el mercado (al aire libre)	(open-air) market
el par	pair
el precio (fijo)	(fixed; set) price
la rebaja	sale
el regalo	gift
la tarjeta de crédito	credit card
la tienda	shop; store
el/la vendedor(a)	salesperson
costar (o:ue)	to cost
gastar	to spend (money)
hacer juego (con)	to match (with)
llevar	to wear
regatear	to bargain
usar	to wear; to use
vender	to sell

Palabras adicionales

acabar de (+ inf.)	to have just done something
anoche	last night
anteayer	the day before yesterday
ayer	yesterday
de repente	suddenly
desde	from; since
dos veces	twice; two times
pasado/a (*adj.*)	last; past
el año pasado	last year
prestar	to lend; to loan
una vez	once; one time
ya	already

Indirect object pronouns	See page 164.
Demonstrative adjectives and pronouns	See page 168.
Expresiones útiles	See page 157.

recursos

| R | LCASS./CD Cass. 6/CD 6 | LM p. 233 |

La rutina diaria

7

La rutina diaria

Más vocabulario

el baño, el cuarto de baño	bathroom
el champú	shampoo
el despertador	alarm clock
el jabón	soap
el maquillaje	makeup
la rutina diaria	daily routine
bañarse	to bathe; to take a bath
cepillarse el pelo	to brush one's hair
dormirse	to go to sleep; to fall asleep
lavarse la cara	to wash one's face
levantarse	to get up
maquillarse	to put on makeup
antes (de)	before
después	afterwards; then
después de	after
durante	during
entonces	then
luego	then
más tarde	later
por la mañana	in the morning
por la noche	at night
por la tarde	in the afternoon; in the evening
por último	finally

Variación léxica

afeitarse ⟷ rasurarse (Méx., Amér. C.)

ducha ⟷ regadera (Col., Méx., Venez.)

ducharse ⟷ bañarse (Amér. L.)

En la habitación por la mañana

Por la mañana

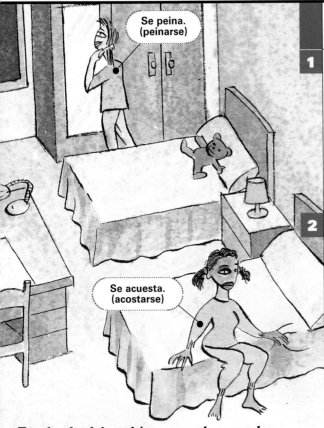

Se peina.
(peinarse)

Se acuesta.
(acostarse)

En la habitación por la noche

Se lava las manos.
(lavarse las manos)

Se cepilla los dientes.
(cepillarse los dientes)

la toalla

Por la noche

Práctica

1 **Escuchar** 🎧 Escucha las frases e indica si cada frase es **cierta** o **falsa,** según el dibujo.

1. _____   6. _____
2. _____   7. _____
3. _____   8. _____
4. _____   9. _____
5. _____   10. _____

2 **Seleccionar** Selecciona las palabras que no están relacionadas con su grupo.

1. lavabo • toalla • despertador • jabón _____
2. manos • antes de • después de • por último _____
3. acostarse • jabón • despertarse • dormirse _____
4. espejo • lavabo • despertador • entonces _____
5. dormirse • toalla • vestirse • levantarse _____
6. pelo • cara • manos • durante _____
7. espejo • champú • jabón _____
8. maquillarse • vestirse • peinarse • dientes _____
9. baño • dormirse • despertador • acostarse _____
10. ducharse • crema de afeitar • bañarse _____

3 **Identificar** Con un(a) compañero/a, identifica las cosas que cada persona necesita. Sigue el modelo.

> **modelo**
> Jorge / lavarse la cara
> **Estudiante 1:** ¿Qué necesita Jorge para lavarse la cara?
> **Estudiante 2:** Necesita jabón y una toalla.

1. Mariana /maquillarse
2. Gerardo / despertarse
3. Celia / bañarse
4. Gabriel / ducharse
5. Roberto / afeitarse
6. Sonia / lavarse el pelo
7. Vanesa / lavarse las manos
8. Manuel / vestirse
9. Simón / acostarse
10. Daniela / lavarse la cara

4 **Ordenar** Pon (*Put*) esta historia (*story*) en orden.

a. Se afeita después de cepillarse los dientes. _____

b. Se acuesta a las once y media de la noche. _____

c. Por último se duerme. _____

d. Después de afeitarse, sale para las clases. _____

e. Asiste a todas sus clases y vuelve a su casa. _____

f. Andrés se despierta a las seis y media de la mañana. _____

g. Después de volver a casa, come un poco. Luego estudia en su habitación. _____

h. Se viste y entonces se cepilla los dientes. _____

i. Se cepilla los dientes antes de acostarse. _____

j. Se ducha antes de vestirse. _____

NOTA CULTURAL

In some Spanish-speaking countries, it is common to return home around 2 p.m. for lunch, the largest meal of the day. The workday often ends between 6 and 8 p.m.

5 **La rutina diaria** Con un(a) compañero/a, mira los dibujos y describe lo que hacen Ángel y Lupe.

1.

2.

3.

4.

5.

6.

7.

8.

Comunicación

6 **Tu mejor (*best*) amigo/a** Contesta estas preguntas sobre la rutina diaria de tu mejor amigo/a.

1. ¿A qué hora se levanta durante la semana?
2. ¿A qué hora se levanta los fines de semana?
3. ¿Prefiere levantarse tarde o temprano?
4. ¿Se ducha por la mañana, por la tarde o por la noche?
5. ¿Se afeita todos los días (*every day*)? ¿Tiene barba (*beard*) o bigote (*moustache*)?
6. ¿Se maquilla todos los días?
7. ¿Se cepilla el pelo antes de acostarse?
8. ¿Se lava las manos antes de comer?
9. ¿Se acuesta tarde o temprano durante la semana?
10. ¿A qué hora se acuesta los fines de semana?

7 **Rutinas diarias** Trabajen en parejas (*pairs*) para describir la rutina diaria de dos o tres de estas personas. Pueden usar palabras de la lista.

primero	antes de	temprano
luego	después	después de
entonces	tarde	por último
durante el día		

1. un(a) profesor(a) de la universidad
2. un(a) turista
3. un hombre o una mujer de negocios (*businessman/woman*)
4. un vigilante (*night watchman*)
5. un(a) jubilado/a (*retired person*)
6. el presidente de los Estados Unidos
7. un niño de cuatro años
8. la reina (*queen*) Sofía de España

NOTA CULTURAL

Queen Sofía of Spain, wife of King Juan Carlos, was born in Greece and is related to the oldest royal families of Europe —the Czars of Russia and Queen Victoria of England.

8 **Compañeros de cuarto** En grupos, comparen las rutinas diarias de sus compañeros/as de cuarto o de los miembros de sus familias.

modelo

Estudiante 1: Mi compañera de cuarto, Sofía, se despierta muy temprano, ¡a las cinco de la mañana! Sale a correr y después se ducha. ¿Y sus compañeros de cuarto?

Estudiante 2: Yo vivo con mi hermano, Miguel, y él también se despierta muy temprano, pero lo hace para estudiar antes de ir a sus clases.

Estudiante 3: Javier, mi esposo, se despierta a las diez y cuarto. Se viste rápidamente (*quickly*) y no se ducha hasta la tarde, porque tiene clase a las once. Se acuesta muy tarde. ¿A qué hora se acuesta Sofía? ¿Y Miguel?

¡Jamás me levanto temprano!

Álex y Javier hablan de sus rutinas diarias.

PERSONAJES

DON FRANCISCO

ÁLEX

JAVIER

1

JAVIER Hola, Álex. ¿Qué estás haciendo?

ÁLEX Nada... sólo estoy leyendo mi correo electrónico. ¿Adónde fueron?

2

JAVIER Inés y yo fuimos a un mercado. Fue muy divertido. Mira, compré este suéter. Me encanta. No fue barato pero es chévere, ¿no?

ÁLEX Sí, es ideal para las montañas.

3

JAVIER ¡Qué interesantes son los mercados al aire libre! Me gustaría volver pero ya es tarde. Oye, Álex, sabes que mañana tenemos que levantarnos temprano.

ÁLEX Ningún problema.

6

JAVIER ¡Increíble! ¡Álex, el superhombre!

ÁLEX Oye, Javier, ¿por qué no puedes levantarte temprano?

JAVIER Es que por la noche no quiero dormir, sino dibujar y escuchar música. Por eso es difícil despertarme por la mañana.

7

JAVIER El autobús no sale hasta las ocho y media. ¿Vas a levantarte mañana a las seis también?

ÁLEX No, pero tengo que levantarme a las siete menos cuarto porque voy a correr.

8

JAVIER Ah, ya... ¿Puedes despertarme después de correr?

ÁLEX Éste es el plan para mañana. Me levanto a las siete menos cuarto y corro por treinta minutos. Vuelvo, me ducho, me visto y a las siete y media te despierto. ¿De acuerdo?

JAVIER ¡Absolutamente ninguna objeción!

recursos

| **R** | V/VCD-ROM Lección 7 | VM pp. 303-304 | ICD-ROM Lección 7 |

JAVIER ¿Seguro? Pues yo jamás me levanto temprano. Nunca oigo el despertador cuando estoy en casa y mi mamá se enoja mucho.

ÁLEX Tranquilo, Javier. Yo tengo una solución.

ÁLEX Cuando estoy en casa en la ciudad de México, siempre me despierto a las seis en punto. Me ducho en cinco minutos y luego me cepillo los dientes. Después me afeito, me visto y ¡listo! ¡Me voy!

DON FRANCISCO Hola, chicos. Mañana salimos temprano, a las ocho y media... ni un minuto antes ni un minuto después.

ÁLEX No se preocupe, don Francisco. Todo está bajo control.

DON FRANCISCO Bueno, pues, hasta mañana.

DON FRANCISCO ¡Ay, los estudiantes! Siempre se acuestan tarde. ¡Qué vida!

Enfoque cultural El horario de la vida diaria

En muchos países hispanos, el horario de la vida diaria es muy diferente al de EE.UU. En estos países, muchas personas trabajan de las ocho de la mañana a las dos de la tarde. A las dos salen del trabajo para ir a almorzar (*eat lunch*). Vuelven a las cuatro y salen a las seis de la tarde. Muchos utilizan esas dos horas para almorzar en casa con sus familias y, a veces (*sometimes*), dormir una siesta. También es común que la gente cene (*eats dinner*) más tarde que en los EE.UU.

Expresiones útiles

Telling where you went

▶ **¿Adónde fuiste/fue Ud.?**
Where did you go?
▷ **Fui a un mercado.**
I went to a market.
▶ **¿Adónde fueron Uds.?**
Where did you go?
▷ **Fuimos a un mercado.**
Fue muy divertido.
We went to a market.
It was a lot of fun.

Talking about morning routine

▶ **(Jamás) me levanto temprano/tarde.**
I (never) get up early/late.
▶ **Nunca oigo el despertador.**
I never hear the alarm clock.
▶ **Es difícil/fácil despertarme.**
It's hard/easy to wake up.
▶ **Cuando estoy en casa, siempre me despierto a las seis en punto.**
When I'm home, I always wake up at six on the dot.
▶ **Me ducho y luego me cepillo los dientes.**
I take a shower and then I brush my teeth.
▶ **Después me afeito y me visto.**
Afterwards, I shave and get dressed.

Reassuring someone

▶ **Ningún problema.**
No problem.
▶ **No te preocupes.** *(fam.)/*
No se preocupe. *(form.)*
Don't worry.
▶ **Todo está bajo control.**
Everything is under control.
▶ **Tranquilo.**
Stay calm.; Be cool. (lit. Quiet.)

Additional vocabulary

▶ **sino**
but (rather)

Reacciona a la fotonovela

1 **¿Cierto o falso?** Indica si las siguientes oraciones (*sentences*) son **ciertas** o **falsas**. Corrige (*Correct*) las frases falsas.

1. Álex está mirando la televisión.

2. El suéter que Javier acaba de comprar es caro pero es muy bonito.

3. Javier cree que el mercado es aburrido y no quiere volver.

4. El autobús va a salir mañana a las siete y media en punto.

5. A Javier le gusta mucho dibujar y escuchar música por la noche.

¡LENGUA VIVA!

Remember that **en punto** means *on the dot*. If the group were instead leaving at *around seven thirty*, you would say **a eso de las siete y media**.

2 **Identificar** Identifica quién puede decir las siguientes frases. Puedes usar cada nombre más de una vez.

1. ¡Ay, los estudiantes nunca se acuestan temprano!
   _____

2. ¿El despertador? ¡Jamás lo oigo por la mañana!
   _____

3. Es fácil despertarme temprano. Y sólo necesito cinco minutos para ducharme. _____

4. Mañana vamos a salir a las ocho y media.
   _____

5. Acabo de ir a un mercado fabuloso. _____

6. No se preocupe. Tenemos todo bajo control para mañana. _____

DON FRANCISCO

JAVIER

ÁLEX

3 **Ordenar** Ordena correctamente los planes que tiene Álex para mañana.

a. Voy a vestirme. _____
b. Voy a correr por media hora. _____
c. Voy a despertar a Javier a las siete y media. _____
d. Voy a volver a la habitación. _____
e. Voy a levantarme a las siete menos cuarto. _____
f. Voy a ducharme. _____

4 **Mi rutina** En parejas (*pairs*), preparen una conversación hablando de sus rutinas en la mañana y en la noche. Indiquen a qué horas hacen las actividades más importantes.

CONSÚLTALO

Telling time To review telling time in Spanish, see Lesson 1, pp. 22-23.

modelo

Estudiante 1: ¿Prefieres levantarte temprano o tarde?
Estudiante 2: Prefiero levantarme tarde... muy tarde.

Estudiante 1: ¿A qué hora te levantas durante la semana?
Estudiante 2: A las once. ¿Y tú?

Pronunciación 🎧

The consonants r and rr

ropa	**r**utina	**r**ico	**R**amón

In Spanish, **r** has a strong trilled sound at the beginning of a word. No English words have a trill, but English speakers often produce a trill when they imitate the sound of a motor.

gusta**r**	du**r**ante	p**r**imero	c**r**ema

In any other position, **r** has a weak sound similar to the English *tt* in *better* or the English *dd* in *ladder*. In contrast to English, the tongue touches the roof of the mouth behind the teeth.

piza**rr**a	co**rr**o	ma**rr**ón	abu**rr**ido

The letter **rr**, which only appears between vowels, always has a strong trilled sound.

ca**r**o	ca**rr**o	pe**r**o	pe**rr**o

Between vowels, the difference between the strong trilled **rr** and the weak **r** is very important, as a mispronunciation could lead to confusion between two different words.

Práctica Lee las palabras en voz alta, prestando (*paying*) atención a la pronunciación de la **r** y la **rr**.

1. Perú	4. madre	7. rubio	10. tarde
2. Rosa	5. comprar	8. reloj	11. cerrar
3. borrador	6. favor	9. Arequipa	12. despertador

Oraciones Lee las oraciones en voz alta, prestando atención a la pronunciación de la **r** y la **rr**.

1. Ramón Robles Ruiz es programador. Su esposa Rosaura es artista.
2. A Rosaura Robles le encanta regatear en el mercado.
3. Ramón nunca regatea… le aburre regatear.
4. Rosaura siempre compra cosas baratas.
5. Ramón no es rico pero prefiere comprar cosas muy caras.
6. ¡El martes Ramón compró un carro nuevo!

Refranes Lee en voz alta los refranes, prestando atención a la **r** y a la **rr**.

Perro que ladra no muerde.[1]

No se ganó Zamora en una hora.[2]

1 A dog's bark is worse than its bite.
2 Rome wasn't built in a day.

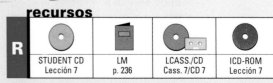

recursos

| **R** | STUDENT CD Lección 7 | LM p. 236 | LCASS./CD Cass. 7/CD 7 | ICD-ROM Lección 7 |

7.1 Reflexive verbs

ANTE TODO A reflexive verb is used to indicate that the subject does something to or for himself or herself. In other words, it "reflects" the action of the verb back to the subject. Reflexive verbs always use reflexive pronouns.

SUBJECT   REFLEXIVE VERB

Joaquín   se **ducha** por la mañana.

> **¡ATENCIÓN!**
>
> Except for **se**, reflexive pronouns have the same forms as direct and indirect object pronouns.
>
> • • •
>
> **Se** is used for both singular and plural subjects —there is no individual plural form.
>
> • • •
>
> Reflexive pronouns always agree with the subject of the verb, not the object:
> **Me lavo las manos.**

Reflexive verbs

lavarse *(to wash oneself)*

SINGULAR FORMS		
yo	**me lavo**	*I wash (myself)*
tú	**te lavas**	*you wash (yourself)*
Ud.	**se lava**	*you wash (yourself)*
él / ella	**se lava**	*he/she/washes (himself/herself)*
PLURAL FORMS		
nosotros/as	**nos lavamos**	*we wash (ourselves)*
vosotros/as	**os laváis**	*you wash (yourselves)*
Uds.	**se lavan**	*you wash (yourselves)*
ellos/ellas	**se lavan**	*they wash (themselves)*

▶ The pronoun **se** attached to an infinitive identifies it as a reflexive verb, as in **lavarse** and **levantarse**. Reflexive verbs can be used in any tense.

INFINITIVE   PRESENT TENSE   PRETERITE
levantarse   **me levanto**   **me levanté**

> **¡ATENCIÓN!**
>
> When a reflexive pronoun is attached to a present participle, an accent mark is added to maintain the original stress:
> bañando → bañán**dose**
> afeitando → afeitán**dose**
>
> • • •
>
> Parts of the body or clothing are generally not referred to with possessives, but with the definite article.
> La niña se quitó **los** zapatos.
>
> Necesito cepillarme **los** dientes.

Me ducho, me cepillo los dientes, me visto y ¡listo!

¡Ay, los estudiantes! Siempre se acuestan tarde.

▶ Reflexive pronouns follow the same rules for placement as object pronouns. They generally appear before a conjugated verb. With infinitives and present participles, they may be placed before the verb or attached to the infinitive or present participle.

Ellos **se** van a vestir.
Ellos van a vestir**se**.
They are going to get dressed.

Nos estamos lavando las manos.
Estamos laván**donos** las manos.
We are washing our hands.

Common reflexive verbs

acordarse (de) (o:ue)	*to remember*	**levantarse**	*to get up*
acostarse (o:ue)	*to go to bed*	**llamarse**	*to be called / named*
afeitarse	*to shave*	**maquillarse**	*to put on one's makeup*
bañarse	*to bathe; to take a bath*	**peinarse**	*to comb one's hair*
cepillarse	*to brush*	**ponerse**	*to put on*
despedirse (de) (e:i)	*to say good-bye (to)*	**ponerse** + *adj.*	*to become* + adj.
despertarse (e:ie)	*to wake up*	**preocuparse (por)**	*to worry (about)*
dormirse (o:ue)	*to go to sleep*	**probarse** (o:ue)	*to try on*
ducharse	*to shower*	**quedarse**	*to stay; to remain*
enojarse (con)	*to get angry (with)*	**quitarse**	*to take off*
irse	*to go away; to leave*	**sentarse** (e:ie)	*to sit down*
lavarse	*to wash (oneself)*	**sentirse** (e:ie)	*to feel*
		vestirse (e:i)	*to get dressed*

¡ATENCIÓN!

You have already learned several adjectives that can be used with **ponerse** when it means *to become*: **alegre, cómodo/a, contento/a, elegante, guapo/a, nervioso/a, rojo/a,** and **triste.**

COMPARE & CONTRAST

Unlike English, most verbs in Spanish can be reflexive or non-reflexive. If the verb acts upon the subject, the reflexive form is used. If the verb acts upon something other than the subject, the non-reflexive form is used. Compare these sentences.

Lola **lava** los platos.

Lola **se lava** la cara.

As the preceding sentences show, reflexive verbs sometimes have different meanings than their non-reflexive counterparts. For example, **lavar** means *to wash*, while **lavarse** means *to wash oneself, to wash up*.

¡INTÉNTALO! Indica el presente de los verbos reflexivos que siguen. El primero de cada columna ya está conjugado.

despertarse

1. Mis hermanos *se despiertan* tarde.
2. Tú _____ tarde.
3. Nosotros _____ tarde.
4. Benito _____ tarde.
5. Yo _____ tarde.
6. Uds. _____ tarde.
7. Ella _____ tarde.
8. Adriana y yo _____ tarde.
9. Ellos _____ tarde.

ponerse

1. Él *se pone* una chaqueta.
2. Yo _____ una chaqueta.
3. Ud. _____ una chaqueta.
4. Nosotras _____ una chaqueta.
5. Las niñas _____ una chaqueta.
6. Tú _____ una chaqueta.
7. El botones _____ una chaqueta.
8. Beatriz y Gil _____ una chaqueta.
9. Uds. _____ una chaqueta.

Práctica

1 **Nuestra rutina** La familia de Blanca sigue la misma rutina todos los días. Según (*According to*) Blanca, ¿qué hacen ellos?

> **modelo**
>
> mamá / despertarse a las 5:00
> *Mamá se despierta a las cinco.*

1. Roberto y yo / levantarse a las 7:00
2. papá / ducharse primero y / luego afeitarse
3. yo / lavarse la cara y / vestirse antes de tomar café
4. mamá / peinarse y / luego maquillarse
5. todos / sentarse a la mesa para comer
6. Roberto / cepillarse los dientes después de comer
7. yo / ponerse el abrigo antes de salir
8. nosotros / despedirse de mamá

NOTA CULTURAL

Having coffee with breakfast is as common in Spanish-speaking countries as it is in the U.S. In fact, it is not unusual for children to have a cup of **café con leche** (*coffee with milk*) with their breakfasts before heading off to school. Coffee served in Spanish-speaking countries is generally stronger than in North America, and decaffeinated coffee is not as common.

2 **Completar** Selecciona el verbo apropiado y completa la frase con la forma correcta.

1. Tú _____ (lavar / lavarse) el auto ayer, ¿no?
2. Nosotros no _____ (acordar / acordarse) de comprar champú y jabón.
3. Anoche ellos _____ (acostar / acostarse) a los niños a las ocho.
4. Yo no _____ (sentir / sentirse) bien hoy.
5. Mis amigos siempre _____ (vestir / vestirse) con ropa muy cara.
6. ¿_____ (probar / probarse) Uds. la ropa antes de comprarla?
7. Ud. _____ (preocupar / preocuparse) mucho por su hijo, ¿no?
8. En general _____ (afeitar / afeitarse) yo mismo, pero hoy el barbero (*barber*) me _____ (afeitar / afeitarse).

¡LENGUA VIVA!

In Spain a car is called a **coche** while in many parts of Latin America it is known as a **carro**. Although you'll be understood using any of these terms, using **auto (automóvil)** will surely get you where you want to go.

3 **Describir** Mira los dibujos y describe lo que estas personas hacen.

1. El joven

2. Carmen

3. Juan

4. Ellos

5. Estrella

6. Toni

Comunicación

4

Encuesta Tu profesor(a) va a darte (*to give you*) una hoja de actividades. Camina por la clase y pregúntales a tus compañeros cuándo sienten las emociones que se mencionan en la lista. Entrevista por los menos (*at least*) a dos personas y anota sus respuestas. Tienes que estar preparado/a para informar a la clase de los resultados de tu encuesta.

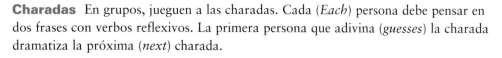

Emociones	Nombres	Ocasiones
1. Sentirse aburrido/a		
2. Sentirse avergonzado/a		
3. Sentirse cansado/a		
4. Enojarse		
5. Sentirse feliz		
6. Ponerse nervioso/a		
7. Preocuparse		
8. Sentirse triste		

5

Charadas En grupos, jueguen a las charadas. Cada (*Each*) persona debe pensar en dos frases con verbos reflexivos. La primera persona que adivina (*guesses*) la charada dramatiza la próxima (*next*) charada.

6

Debate En grupos, discutan (*discuss*) este tema (*topic*): ¿Quiénes necesitan más tiempo para arreglarse (*to get ready*) antes de salir, los hombres o las mujeres? Hagan una lista de las razones (*reasons*) que tienen para defender sus ideas e informen a la clase.

Síntesis

7

Entrevista Tu profesor(a) va a darte (*to give you*) una hoja de actividades. Completa el horario de la hoja con las actividades que hiciste (*you did*) anoche. Después de completar el horario, trabajen en parejas, comparen las actividades que hicieron y tomen apuntes de lo que (*what*) hizo el/la compañero/a.

7.2 Indefinite and negative words

ANTE TODO Indefinite words refer to people and things that are not specific, for example, *someone* or *something*. Negative words deny the existence of people and things or contradict statements, for instance, *no one* or *nothing*. As the following chart shows, Spanish indefinite words have corresponding negative words, which are opposite in meaning.

Indefinite and negative words

Indefinite words		Negative words	
algo	something; anything	**nada**	nothing; not anything
alguien	someone; somebody; anyone	**nadie**	no one; nobody; not anyone
alguno/a(s), algún	some; any	**ninguno/a, ningún**	no; none; not any
o… o	either… or	**ni… ni**	neither… nor
siempre	always	**nunca, jamás**	never
también	also; too	**tampoco**	neither; not either

▶ There are two ways to form negative sentences in Spanish. You can place the negative word before the verb, or you can place **no** before the verb and the negative word after the verb.

Nadie se levantó temprano.	**No se levantó nadie** temprano.
No one got up early.	*No one got up early.*
Ellos **nunca se enojan**.	Ellos **no se enojan nunca**.
They never get angry.	*They never get angry.*

¡ATENCIÓN!

Before a masculine, singular noun, **alguno** and **ninguno** are shortened to **algún** and **ningún**.

—¿Tienen Uds. algún amigo peruano?
—No, no tenemos ningún amigo peruano.

• • •

Alguno/a, algunos/as are not used in the same way English uses *some* or *any*. Often, **algún** is used where *a* would be used in English. Also, in negative sentences, **ninguno** always replaces **alguno**.

Yo siempre me despierto a las seis en punto. ¿Y tú?

Pues yo jamás me levanto temprano. Nunca oigo el despertador.

▶ Because they refer to people, **alguien** and **nadie** are often used with the personal **a**. The personal **a** is also used before **alguno/a, algunos/as,** and **ninguno/a** when these words refer to people and they are the direct object of the verb.

—Perdón, señor, ¿busca Ud. **a alguien**?	—Tomás, ¿buscas **a alguno** de tus hermanos?
—No, gracias, señorita, no busco **a nadie**.	—No, mamá, no busco **a ninguno**.

COMPARE & CONTRAST

In English, it is incorrect to use more than one negative word in a sentence. It is correct, however, to use indefinite words with negative words, because indefinite words are considered affirmative. In Spanish, however, sentences frequently contain two or more negative words. Compare the following Spanish and English sentences.

Nunca le escribo a **nadie**.   **No** me preocupo por **nada nunca**.
*I **never** write to **anyone**.*   *I do **not ever** worry about **anything**.*

As the preceding sentences show, once an English sentence contains one negative word (for example, *not* or *never*), no other negative word may be used. Instead, indefinite (or affirmative) words are used. In Spanish, however, once a sentence is negative, no other affirmative (that is, indefinite) word may be used. Instead, all indefinite ideas must be expressed in the negative.

▶ Although in Spanish **pero** and **sino** both mean *but*, they are not interchangeable. **Sino** is used when the first part of a sentence is negative and the second part contradicts it. In this context, **sino** means *but rather* or *on the contrary*. In all other cases, **pero** is used to mean *but*.

Los estudiantes no se acuestan
  temprano **sino** tarde.
*The students don't go to bed
  early, **but rather** late.*

Las toallas son caras,
  pero bonitas.
*The towels are expensive,
  but beautiful.*

María no habla francés
  sino español.
*Maria doesn't speak French,
  but rather Spanish.*

José es inteligente, **pero**
  no saca buenas notas.
*José is intelligent, **but**
  doesn't get good grades.*

¡INTÉNTALO! Cambia las siguientes frases para que sean negativas. La primera frase se da *(is given)* como ejemplo.

1. Siempre se viste bien.
   __Nunca__ se viste bien.
   __No__ se viste bien __nunca__.
2. Alguien se ducha.
   _____ se ducha.
   _____ se ducha _____.
3. Ellas van también.
   Ellas _____ van.
   Ellas _____ van _____.
4. Alguien se pone nervioso.
   _____ se pone nervioso.
   _____ se pone nervioso _____.
5. Tú siempre te lavas las manos.
   Tú _____ te lavas las manos.
   Tú ___ te lavas las manos _____.
6. Juan se afeita también.
   Juan _____ se afeita.
   Juan _____ se afeita _____.
7. Voy a traer algo.
   _____ voy a traer _____.
8. Mis amigos viven en una residencia o en casa.
   Mis amigos _____ viven _____ en una residencia _____ en casa.
9. La profesora hace algo en su escritorio.
   La profesora _____ hace _____ en su escritorio.
10. Tú y yo vamos al mercado.
   _____ tú _____ yo vamos al mercado.
11. Tienen un espejo en su casa.
   _____ tienen _____ espejo en su casa.
12. Algunos niños se ponen el abrigo.
   _____ niño se pone el abrigo.

Práctica

1

¿Pero o sino? Forma frases usando **pero** o **sino**.

> **modelo**
>
> el examen no es hoy / mañana
> *El examen no es hoy sino mañana.*

1. el niño no se despertó temprano / llegó puntual

2. Armando y yo no vamos a la playa / al campo

3. Alfonso es inteligente / algunas veces es antipático

4. esos señores no son ecuatorianos / peruanos

5. no nos acordamos de comprar champú / compramos jabón

6. Emilia no es morena / rubia

7. no quiero levantarme / tengo que ir a clase

8. no se acostaron tarde / temprano

2

Completar Completa esta conversación. Usa expresiones negativas en tus respuestas. Luego, dramatiza la conversación con un(a) compañero/a.

AURELIO   Ana María, ¿encontraste algún regalo para Eliana?

ANA MARÍA _____

AURELIO   ¿Viste a algunas amigas en el centro comercial?

ANA MARÍA _____

AURELIO   ¿Me llamó alguien?

ANA MARÍA _____

AURELIO   ¿Quieres ir al teatro o al cine esta noche?

ANA MARÍA _____

AURELIO   ¿No quieres salir a comer?

ANA MARÍA _____

AURELIO   ¿Hay algo interesante en la televisión esta noche?

ANA MARÍA _____

AURELIO   ¿Tienes algún problema?

ANA MARÍA _____

Comunicación

3

Opiniones Completa estas frases de una manera lógica. Luego, compara tus respuestas con las respuestas de un(a) compañero/a.

1. Mi habitación es _____ pero _____.
2. Mis padres no son _____ sino _____.
3. Mi compañero/a no es _____ pero _____.
4. Por la noche no me gusta _____ pero _____.
5. Un(a) profesor(a) ideal no es _____ sino _____.
6. Mis amigos no son _____ pero _____.

4

Quejas (Complaints) Con un(a) compañero/a, haz (*make*) una lista de cinco quejas comunes (*common*) que tienen los estudiantes. Usa expresiones negativas.

> **modelo**
> Nadie me entiende.

Ahora hagan (*make*) una lista de cinco quejas que los padres tienen de sus hijos.

> **modelo**
> Nunca limpian sus habitaciones.

5

Anuncios (Ads) Con un(a) compañero/a, mira estos anuncios. Luego, preparen su propio (*own*) anuncio usando expresiones afirmativas o negativas. La clase va a votar para decidir cuál es el anuncio más original o creativo.

¿Por qué no le regalas algo inolvidable?

Para alguien especial...

Síntesis

6

Encuesta Tu profesor(a) te va a dar (*to give*) una hoja de actividades para hacer una encuesta. Circula por la clase y pídeles a tus compañeros que comparen las actividades que hacen durante los días de la semana con las que hacen durante los fines de semana. Toma nota de las respuestas.

7.3 Preterite of **ser** and **ir**

ANTE TODO   In Lesson 6, you learned how to form the preterite tense of regular **–ar**, **–er** and **–ir** verbs. The following chart contains the preterite forms of **ir** (*to go*) and **ser** (*to be*). Since the forms are irregular, you will need to memorize them.

Preterite of *ser* and *ir*		
	ser *(to be)*	**ir** *(to go)*
SINGULAR FORMS		
yo	**fui**	**fui**
tú	**fuiste**	**fuiste**
Ud./él/ella	**fue**	**fue**
PLURAL FORMS		
nosotros/as	**fuimos**	**fuimos**
vosotros/as	**fuisteis**	**fuisteis**
Uds./ellos/ellas	**fueron**	**fueron**

¡ATENCIÓN!

Note that, whereas regular **–er** and **–ir** verbs have accent marks in the **yo** and **Ud.** forms of the preterite, **ser** and **ir** do not.

▶ Since the preterite forms of **ser** and **ir** are identical, context clarifies which of the two verbs is being used.

Él **fue** a comprar champú y jabón.
He went to buy shampoo and soap.

—¿Cómo **fue** la película anoche?
How was the movie last night?

¿Adónde fueron Uds.?

Inés y yo fuimos a un mercado. Fue muy divertido.

¡INTÉNTALO!   Completa las siguientes frases usando el pretérito de **ir** y **ser**. La primera frase de cada columna se da (*is given*) como ejemplo.

ir	ser
1. Los viajeros __fueron__ a Perú.	1. Ud. __fue__ muy amable.
2. Patricia _____ a Cuzco.	2. Yo _____ muy cordial.
3. Tú _____ a Iquitos.	3. Ellos _____ muy simpáticos.
4. Gregorio y yo _____ a Lima.	4. Nosotros _____ muy desagradables.
5. Yo _____ a Trujillo.	5. Ella _____ muy antipática.
6. Uds. _____ a Arequipa.	6. Tú _____ muy chistoso.
7. Mi padre _____ a Lima.	7. Uds. _____ muy cordiales.
8. Nosotras _____ a Cuzco.	8. La gente _____ muy agradable.
9. Él _____ a Machu Picchu.	9. Tomás y yo _____ muy corteses.
10. Ud. _____ a Nazca.	10. Los profesores _____ muy buenos.

Práctica

1

Completar Completa estas conversaciones con la forma correcta del pretérito de **ser** o **ir**. Indica el infinitivo de cada forma verbal.

Conversación 1

RAÚL ¿Adónde _____ Uds. de vacaciones?
PILAR _____ al Perú.
RAÚL ¿Cómo _____ el viaje?
PILAR ¡_____ estupendo! Machu Picchu y el Museo de Oro son increíbles.
RAÚL ¿_____ caro el viaje?
PILAR No, el precio _____ muy bajo, sólo costó tres mil dólares.

Conversación 2

ISABEL Tina y Vicente _____ novios, ¿no?
LUCÍA Sí, pero ahora no salen. Anoche Tina _____ a comer con Gregorio
y la semana pasada ellos _____ al partido de fútbol.
ISABEL ¿Ah sí? Javier y yo_____ al partido y no los vimos.

2

Descripciones Forma frases con los siguientes elementos. Usa el pretérito.

A	B	C
yo	(no) ir	a un restaurante
tú	(no) ser	en autobús
mi compañero/a		estudiante
nosotros		a casa
mis amigos		a la playa
Uds.		dependiente/a en una tienda
		en avión

Comunicación

3

Preguntas En parejas, túrnense (*take turns*) para hacerse estas preguntas.

1. ¿Adónde fuiste de vacaciones este año? ¿Con quién fuiste?
2. ¿Cómo fueron tus vacaciones?
3. ¿Fuiste de compras esta semana? ¿Adónde? ¿Qué compraste?
4. ¿Fuiste al cine la semana pasada? ¿Fueron tus amigos también?
5. ¿Qué película viste? ¿Cómo fue?
6. ¿Fuiste a la cafetería hoy? ¿A qué hora?
7. ¿Adónde fuiste durante el fin de semana? ¿Por qué?
8. ¿Quién fue tu profesor(a) favorito/a el semestre pasado? ¿Por qué?

4

Personas famosas En grupos pequeños, cada estudiante debe pensar en una persona famosa del pasado. Luego, los otros miembros del grupo tienen que hacer preguntas usando el pretérito hasta que adivinen (*they guess*) la identidad de la persona. Por ejemplo, pueden hacer preguntas acerca de (*about*) su profesión, su nacionalidad, su personalidad o su apariencia (*appearance*) física.

7.4 **Gustar** and verbs like **gustar**

ANTE TODO In Lesson 2, you learned that the expressions **me gusta(n)** and **te gusta(n)** express the English concepts of *I like* and *you like*. You will now learn more about the verb **gustar** and other similar verbs. Observe the following examples.

Me gusta ese champú.

> ENGLISH EQUIVALENT
> *I like that shampoo.*
>
> LITERAL MEANING
> *That shampoo is pleasing to me.*

¿**Te gustaron** las clases?

> ENGLISH EQUIVALENT
> *Did you like the classes?*
>
> LITERAL MEANING
> *Were the classes pleasing to you?*

▶ As the examples show, the construction **me gusta(n)** does not have a direct equivalent in English. The literal meaning of this construction is *to be pleasing to (someone)*, and it requires the use of an indirect object pronoun.

INDIRECT OBJECT PRONOUN		SUBJECT	SUBJECT		DIRECT OBJECT
Me	**gusta**	ese champú.	*I*	*like*	*that shampoo.*

▶ In the diagram above, observe how in the Spanish sentence the object being liked (**ese champú**) is really the subject of the sentence. The person who likes the object, in turn, is an indirect object because it answers the question: *To whom is the shampoo pleasing?*

¿No te gustan las computadoras?

Me gustan mucho los parques.

▶ The forms most commonly used with **gustar** and similar verbs are the third person (singular and plural). When the object or person being liked is singular, the singular form (**gusta**) is used. When two or more objects or persons are being liked, the plural form (**gustan**) is used. Observe the following diagram:

SINGULAR	me, te, le	▶	gusta gustó	▶	la película el concierto
PLURAL	nos, os, les		gustan gustaron		las papas fritas los helados

▶ To express what someone likes or does not like to do, **gustar** is followed by an infinitive. The singular form of **gustar** is used even if there is more than one infinitive.

No **nos gusta comer** a las nueve.   **Les gusta cantar** y **bailar** en las fiestas.
We don't like to eat at nine o'clock.   *They like to sing and dance at parties.*

▶ The construction **a** + [*pronoun*] (**a mí, a ti, a Ud., a él,** etc.) is used to clarify or to emphasize the person(s) who are pleased.

A ella le gustan las toallas verdes, pero **a él** no le gustan.
She likes green towels, but he doesn't like them.

A ti te gusta quedarte en casa, pero **a mí** no me gusta.
You like to stay at home, but I don't like to.

▶ The construction **a** + [*noun*] can also be used before the indirect object pronoun to clarify or to emphasize who is pleased.

A los turistas les gustó mucho Machu Picchu.
The tourists liked Machu Picchu a lot.

A Juanita le gustaron mucho los mercados al aire libre.
Juanita liked the open-air markets a lot.

▶ Other verbs in Spanish are used in the same way as **gustar**. Here is a list of the most common ones.

Verbs like *gustar*

aburrir	*to bore*	**importar**	*to be important to; to matter*
encantar	*to like very much; to love* (inanimate objects)	**interesar**	*to be interesting to; to interest*
faltar	*to lack; to need*	**molestar**	*to bother; to annoy*
fascinar	*to fascinate*	**quedar**	*to be left over; to fit* (clothing)

¡INTÉNTALO! Indica el pronombre de objeto indirecto y la forma del tiempo presente adecuados en cada frase. La primera frase de cada columna se da (*is given*) como ejemplo.

gustar

1. A él _le gusta_ viajar.
2. A mí _____ bailar.
3. A nosotras _____ cantar.
4. A Uds. _____ leer.
5. A ti _____ correr.
6. A Elena _____ gritar.
7. A mis padres _____ beber.
8. A Ud. _____ jugar tenis.
9. A mi esposo y a mí _____ dormir.
10. A Pinto _____ dibujar.
11. A todos _____ opinar.
12. A Pili no _____ pensar.

encantar

1. A ellos _les encantan_ los deportes.
2. A ti _____ las películas.
3. A Ud. _____ los viajes.
4. A mí _____ las revistas.
5. A Jorge y a Luis _____ los perros.
6. A nosotros _____ las vacaciones.
7. A Uds. _____ las fiestas.
8. A Marcela _____ los libros.
9. A mis amigos _____ los museos.
10. A ella _____ el ciclismo.
11. A Pedro _____ el limón.
12. A ti y a mí _____ el baile.

Práctica

1 **Describir** Mira los dibujos y describe lo que está pasando. Usa los siguientes verbos.

aburrir	faltar	molestar
encantar	interesar	quedar

1. A Ramón

2. A nosotros

3. A ti

4. A Sara

2 **Completar** Completa las frases con la forma correcta del verbo entre paréntesis.

1. A Adela _____ (gustar) las canciones (*songs*) de Enrique Iglesias.
2. A mí _____ (gustar) más Ricky Martin.
3. A mis amigos _____ (encantar) la música de Gloria Estefan.
4. A nosotros _____ (fascinar) los grupos de pop latino.
5. Creo que a Elena _____ (interesar) más la música clásica.
6. A mí _____ (aburrir) esa música.
7. ¿A ti _____ (faltar) dinero para el concierto de Carlos Santana?
8. Sí. Sólo_____ (quedar) cinco dólares.

3 **Gustos** Pregúntale a un(a) compañero/a si le gustaría hacer las siguientes actividades esta tarde.

> **modelo**
>
> ir al cine
>
> **Estudiante 1:** *¿Te gustaría ir al cine esta tarde?*
> **Estudiante 2:** *Sí, me gustaría ir al cine esta tarde./*
>   *No, no me gustaría ir al cine esta tarde.*

1. ir al centro comercial
2. ir a la piscina
3. jugar a las cartas
4. jugar al tenis
5. montar a caballo
6. pasear en bicicleta
7. ver una película
8. tomar algo en un café

Comunicación

4

Preguntas En parejas, túrnense para hacer y contestar estas preguntas.

1. ¿Te gusta levantarte temprano o tarde? ¿Por qué? ¿Y tu compañero/a de cuarto?
2. ¿Te gusta acostarte temprano o tarde? ¿Y tu compañero/a de cuarto?
3. ¿Te gusta bañarte o ducharte?
4. ¿Te gusta acampar o prefieres quedarte en un hotel cuando estás de vacaciones?
5. ¿Qué te gustaría hacer este verano?
6. ¿Qué te gusta más de esta universidad? ¿Qué te molesta?
7. ¿Te interesan más las ciencias o las humanidades? ¿Por qué?
8. ¿Qué cosas te molestan?

5

Encuesta Tu profesor(a) va a darte una hoja de actividades. Camina por la clase y pregúntales a tus compañeros qué cosas o actividades les encantan, les aburren, les importan y les interesan. Entrevista por los menos a tres personas. Toma notas de sus respuestas. Tienes que estar preparado/a para informar a la clase sobre los resultados de tu encuesta.

Nombre	Le encanta(n)	Le aburre(n)	Le importa(n)	Le interesa(n)

Síntesis

6

Situación En grupos de tres, trabajen con la hoja de actividades que les va a dar (*to give*) su profesor(a). Una persona es el/la dependiente/a en una tienda. Las otras dos personas son los clientes que quieren comprar ropa y/o zapatos.

recursos

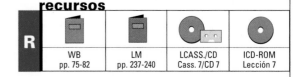

R	WB pp. 75-82	LM pp. 237-240	LCASS./CD Cass. 7/CD 7	ICD-ROM Lección 7

Lectura
Antes de leer

Estrategia
Predicting content from the title

Prediction is an invaluable strategy in reading for comprehension. We can usually predict the content of a newspaper article in English from its headline, for example. More often than not, we decide whether or not to read the article based on its headline. Predicting content from the title will help you increase your reading comprehension in Spanish.

Examinar el texto
Lee el título de la lectura y haz tres predicciones sobre el contenido. Escribe tus predicciones en una hoja de papel.

Compartir
Comparte tus ideas con un(a) compañero/a de clase.

Cognados
Haz una lista de seis cognados que encuentres en la lectura.

1. _____.
2. _____.
3. _____.
4. _____.
5. _____.
6. _____.

¿Qué te dicen los cognados sobre el tema de la lectura?

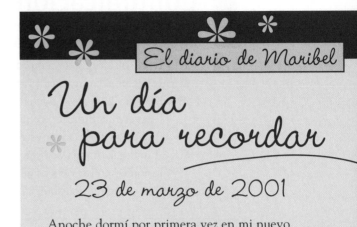

El diario de Maribel

Un día para recordar

23 de marzo de 2001

Anoche dormí por primera vez en mi nuevo apartamento. Pero dormí poco porque me despertó el radio-despertador del vecino de arriba a las 4 de la mañana. No pude volver a dormirme porque él tiene el sueño muy pesado y el despertador siguió y siguió sonando más de media hora.

Me levanté a las 4:30 con los ojos rojos y sin saber qué hacer a esas horas de la mañana en un apartamento sin muebles y lleno de cajas sin abrir. Busqué mis cosas para el baño, pero no las encontré. Intenté ducharme sin jabón, tuve que cepillarme los dientes sin cepillo de dientes y me peiné con las manos. Tampoco encontré la ropa y me tuve que poner la misma ropa que usé ayer.

Maravilloso, el día se presentaba maravilloso. A las 5:00 de la mañana empecé a ordenar el apartamento. Abrí todas las cajas y entonces me di cuenta de que el televisor y la computadora se rompieron durante la mudanza. ¡Estupendo!

A las 6:00 de la mañana empecé a oír un ruido muy extraño del piso de arriba. Intenté

identificar el ruido: ¿una cafetera exprés, algún instrumento musical desconocido para mí, el radio? Decidida, abrí la puerta, subí las escaleras y toqué la puerta, una, dos, tres veces. Miré mi reloj: las 6:30. Me enojé tanto que estuve media hora tocando la puerta.

Al fin el vecino abrió la puerta. ¿Qué puedo decir? ¿Cómo puedo describir lo que pasó entonces? Nunca en mi vida vi a un joven tan... tan, en una palabra: guapo. —Buenos días —me dijo. Yo no dije nada. —¿Quieres algo? —me preguntó. Yo no dije nada. Él sonrió y yo, en ese momento, me acordé de mi aspecto: sin lavarme, sin peinarme, sin maquillarme... —Me equivoqué de puerta —le dije y salí corriendo para mi apartamento. Con las prisas me caí y me rompí el brazo.

vecino de arriba *upstairs neighbor*
él tiene el sueño muy pesado *he's a heavy sleeper*
siguió sonando *kept on ringing* ojos *eyes* sin saber *without knowing*
muebles *furniture* lleno de cajas *full of boxes* me di cuenta *I realized*
se rompieron *broke* mudanza *move* ruido *noise*
cafetera exprés *expresso machine* desconocido *unknown* toqué *I knocked* sonrió *smiled* aspecto *appearance* Me equivoqué de *I knocked on the wrong* Con las prisas *In the rush* me caí *I fell* el brazo *arm*

Después de leer

Seleccionar
Selecciona la respuesta (*answer*) correcta.

1. ¿Quién es el/la narrador(a)? _____.
   a. la mamá de Maribel
   b. el vecino de arriba
   c. Maribel
2. ¿Qué hace por primera vez la narradora? _____.
   a. tiene un sueño muy pesado
   b. duerme en su nuevo apartamento
   c. duerme con los ojos rojos
3. ¿Por qué se levanta la narradora a las 4:30? _____.
   a. porque le duelen (*hurt*) los ojos
   b. porque tiene que limpiar (*clean*) el apartamento
   c. porque el despertador del vecino de arriba no para (*doesn't stop*) de sonar
4. ¿Qué decide hacer la narradora a las seis de la mañana? ¿Por qué? _____.
   a. lavarse los dientes / porque están sucios
   b. dar un paseo porque no puede dormir
   c. escuchar música / porque quiere molestar a los vecinos
   d. hacer una visita a su vecino / porque su vecino es muy ruidoso (*noisy*)
5. La lectura se titula *Un día para recordar* porque la narradora _____.
   a. se enoja con su nuevo vecino
   b. tiene un día horrible
   c. conoce (*meets*) a un chico muy guapo

Ordenar
Ordena los sucesos de la narración. Utiliza los números del 1 al 9.

El radio-despertador del vecino de arriba sigue sonando. ____

Se da cuenta de que el televisor y la computadora están rotos (*broken*). ____

Toca la puerta de su vecino por media hora. ____

Se va corriendo, se cae y se rompe el brazo. ____

Oye un ruido muy extraño que no puede identificar. ____

Se viste con la misma ropa de ayer. ____

La narradora no puede dormir en su nuevo apartamento. ____

Le dice a su vecino que se equivocó de puerta. ____

Se levanta y busca sus cosas para el baño, pero no las encuentra. ____

Perú

El país en cifras

- **Área:** 1.285.220 km² (496.224 millas²),
  un poco menos que el área de Alaska
- **Población:** 26.523.000
- **Capital:** Lima—7.745.000
- **Ciudades principales:** Arequipa—764.000,
  Trujillo—643.000, Chiclayo—527.000,
  Callao—442.000, Iquitos—348.000

SOURCE: Population Division, UN Secretariat

*Iquitos es un puerto muy importante en el río
Amazonas. Desde Iquitos se envían muchos
productos a otros lugares, incluyendo
goma, nueces, madera, arroz, café
y tabaco. Iquitos es también un
destino popular para los
ecoturistas que visitan la selva.*

- **Moneda:** nuevo sol
- **Idiomas:** español (oficial),
  quechua (oficial), aymará

Bandera del Perú

Peruanos célebres

- Clorinda Matto de Turner, escritora (1854-1901)
- César Vallejo, poeta (1892-1938)
- Javier Pérez de Cuellar, diplomático (1920-)
- Mario Vargas Llosa, novelista (1936-)

Mario Vargas Llosa

se envían *are shipped*   goma *rubber*   nueces *nuts*   madera *timber*
arroz *rice*   selva *jungle*   grabó *engraved*   tamaño *size*

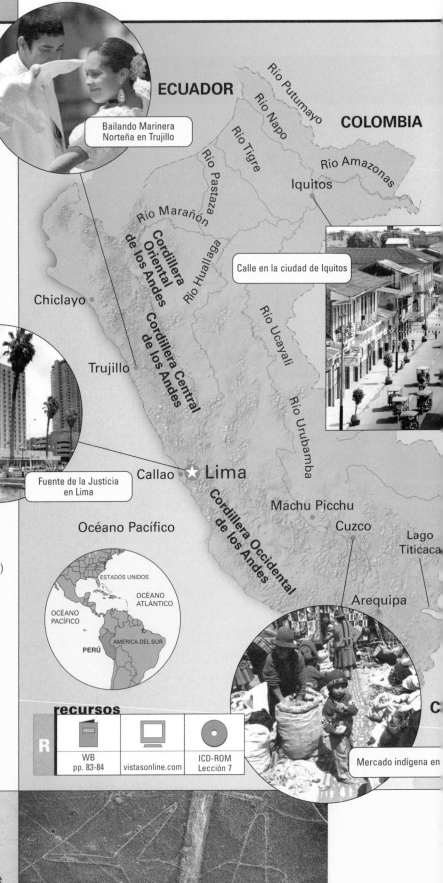

ECUADOR

COLOMBIA

Río Putumayo

Río Napo

Río Tigre

Río Amazonas

Río Pastaza

Iquitos

Bailando Marinera
Norteña en Trujillo

Río Marañón

Cordillera
Oriental
de los Andes

Río Huallaga

Calle en la ciudad de Iquitos

Chiclayo

Cordillera Central
de los Andes

Río Ucayali

Río Urubamba

Trujillo

Fuente de la Justicia
en Lima

Callao   ★ Lima

Cordillera Occidental
de los Andes

Machu Picchu

Cuzco

Lago
Titicaca

Océano Pacífico

ESTADOS UNIDOS

OCÉANO
ATLÁNTICO

OCÉANO
PACÍFICO

PERÚ

AMÉRICA DEL SUR

Arequipa

recursos

R

WB
pp. 83-84

vistasonline.com

ICD-ROM
Lección 7

Mercado indígena en

¡Increíble pero cierto!

Hace más de dos mil años la civilización nazca
de Perú grabó más de 2.000 km de líneas en el
desierto. Los dibujos sólo son descifrables desde
el aire. Uno de ellos es un cóndor del tamaño de
un estadio. Las Líneas de Nazca son aún uno de
los grandes misterios de la humanidad.

Lugares • Lima

Lima es una ciudad moderna y antigua a la vez. La hermosa Iglesia de San Francisco es notable por la influencia de la arquitectura árabe. También son fascinantes las exhibiciones sobre los incas en el Museo del Oro del Perú y en el Museo Nacional de Antropología y Arqueología. Barranco, el barrio bohemio de la ciudad, es famoso por su gran ambiente cultural y sus bares y restaurantes.

RASIL

Lugares • Machu Picchu

A 80 km (50 millas) al noroeste de Cuzco están las ruinas de Machu Picchu, una ciudad antigua del imperio inca. Esta ciudad está a una altitud de 2.350 metros (7.710 pies), entre dos cimas altísimas de los Andes. Cuando los conquistadores españoles llegaron a Perú nunca encontraron la ciudad de Machu Picchu. Sus ruinas quedaron escondidas hasta 1911, cuando el arqueólogo norteamericano Hiram Bingham las descubrió. Todavía no se sabe ni cómo se construyó una ciudad a tanta altura, ni por qué los incas abandonaron el lugar.

Economía • Llamas y alpacas

El Perú se conoce por sus llamas, alpacas, guanacos y vicuñas, todos animales mamíferos parientes del camello. Estos animales todavía son de enorme importancia para la economía del país. Dan lana para ropa, mantas, bolsas y artículos turísticos. La llama se usa también para la carga y el transporte.

Historia • Los incas

Antes del siglo XVI, los incas desarrollaron sistemas avanzados de comunicaciones y de contabilidad y construyeron acueductos, calles y templos. El 24 de junio, día del solsticio de invierno, los descendientes de los incas se reúnen en Cuzco para darle la bienvenida al sol en un festival espectacular, el Inti Raymi.

OLIVIA

¿Qué aprendiste? Responde a las preguntas con una frase completa.
1. ¿Qué productos envía Iquitos a otros lugares?
2. ¿Cuáles son las lenguas oficiales del Perú?
3. ¿Por qué es notable la Iglesia de San Francisco en Lima?
4. ¿Por qué los conquistadores españoles no encontraron la ciudad de Machu Picchu?
5. ¿Qué hacen los peruanos con la lana de sus llamas y alpacas?
6. ¿Quiénes celebran el Inti Raymi?

Conexión Internet Investiga estos temas en el sitio **www.vistasonline.com**.
1. Investiga la cultura incaica. ¿Cuáles son algunos de los aspectos interesantes de su cultura?
2. Busca información sobre dos artistas, escritores o músicos peruanos, y presenta un breve informe a tu clase.

---

antigua *old*   a la vez *at the same time*   cimas *summits*   escondidas *hidden*   no se sabe *is not known*   se conoce *is known*
mamíferos *mammalian*   mantas *blankets*   desarrollaron *developed*   construyeron *built*   calles *roads*   bienvenida *welcome*

Los verbos reflexivos

acordarse (de) (o:ue)	to remember
acostarse (o:ue)	to go to bed
afeitarse	to shave
bañarse	to bathe; take a bath
cepillarse el pelo	to brush one's hair
cepillarse los dientes	to brush one's teeth
despedirse (de) (e:i)	to say good-bye (to)
despertarse (e:ie)	to wake up
dormirse (o:ue)	to go to sleep; to fall asleep
ducharse	to shower; to take a shower
enojarse (con)	to get angry (with)
irse	to go away; to leave
lavarse la cara	to wash one's face
lavarse las manos	to wash one's hands
levantarse	to get up
llamarse	to be called; to be named
maquillarse	to put on one's makeup
peinarse	to comb one's hair
ponerse	to put on
ponerse + *adj.*	to become + adj.
preocuparse (por)	to worry (about)
probarse (o:ue)	to try on
quedarse	to stay; to remain
quitarse	to take off
sentarse (e:ie)	to sit down
sentirse (e:ie)	to feel
vestirse (e:i)	to get dressed

En el baño

el baño, el cuarto de baño	bathroom
el champú	shampoo
la crema de afeitar	shaving cream
el despertador	alarm clock
la ducha	shower
el espejo	mirror
el jabón	soap
el lavabo	sink
el maquillaje	make-up
la toalla	towel

Palabras de secuencia

antes (de)	before
después	afterwards; then
después de	after
durante	during
entonces	then
luego	afterwards; then
más tarde	later
por último	finally

Palabras afirmativas y negativas

algo	something; anything
alguien	someone; somebody; anyone
alguno/a, algún, algunos/as	some; any
jamás	never; not ever
nada	nothing; not anything
nadie	no one; nobody; not anyone
ni… ni	neither… nor
ninguno/a, ningún	no; none; not any
nunca	never; not ever
o… o	either… or
siempre	always
también	also; too
tampoco	neither; not either

Gustar y verbos similares

aburrir	to bore
encantar	to like very much; to love (inanimate things)
faltar	to lack; to need
fascinar	to fascinate
gustar	to be pleasing to; to like
importar	to be important to; to matter
interesar	to be interesting to; to interest
me gustaría(n) …	I would like…
molestar	to bother; to annoy
quedar	to be left over; to fit (clothing)

Palabras adicionales

llamar (por teléfono)	to call (on the phone)
por la mañana	in the morning
por la noche	at night
por la tarde	in the afternoon; in the evening
la rutina diaria	daily routine

Expresiones útiles	*See page 185.*

La comida

8

Communicative Goals

You will learn how to:
- Order food in a restaurant
- Talk about and describe food

La comida

Más vocabulario

el/la camarero/a	waiter
la comida	food; meal
el/la dueño/a	owner; landlord
los entremeses	hors d'oeuvres
el menú	menu
el plato (principal)	(main) dish
la sección de (no) fumar	(non) smoking section
el aceite	oil
el agua (mineral)	(mineral) water
el ajo	garlic
las arvejas	peas
el azúcar	sugar
la bebida	drink
los cereales	cereal; grain
la cerveza	beer
los frijoles	beans
la leche	milk
la margarina	margarine
la mayonesa	mayonnaise
el melocotón	peach
la papa	potato
el pollo (asado)	(roast) chicken
el queso	cheese
el refresco	soft drink
el sándwich	sandwich
el vinagre	vinegar
el yogur	yogurt
delicioso/a	delicious
rico/a	tasty; delicious
sabroso/a	tasty; delicious

Variación léxica

camarones ←→ gambas

camarero ←→ mesero (*Amér. L.*), mesonero (*Ven.*), mozo (*Arg., Chile, Urug., Perú*)

refresco ←→ gaseosa (*Amér. C., Amér. S.*)

sándwich ←→ bocadillo (*Esp.*)

Las frutas

la pera

la banana

las uvas

la naranja

el limón

Las verduras

el maíz

la cebolla

la lechuga

el champiñón

la zanahoria

el tomate

recursos

STUDENT CD Lección 8	WB pp. 85-86	LM p. 241	LCASS./CD Cass. 8/CD8	ICD-ROM Lección 8

R

Práctica

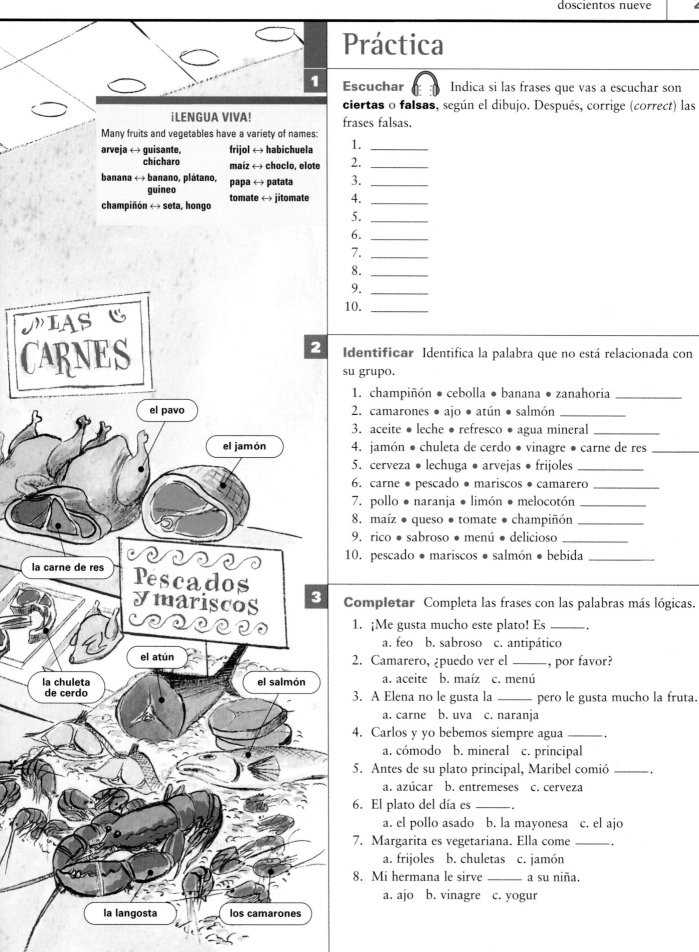

¡LENGUA VIVA!

Many fruits and vegetables have a variety of names:

arveja ↔ guisante, chícharo

banana ↔ banano, plátano, guineo

champiñón ↔ seta, hongo

frijol ↔ habichuela

maíz ↔ choclo, elote

papa ↔ patata

tomate ↔ jitomate

LAS CARNES

- el pavo
- el jamón
- la carne de res
- la chuleta de cerdo

Pescados y mariscos

- el atún
- el salmón
- la langosta
- los camarones

1 **Escuchar** 🎧 Indica si las frases que vas a escuchar son **ciertas** o **falsas**, según el dibujo. Después, corrige (*correct*) las frases falsas.

1. _____
2. _____
3. _____
4. _____
5. _____
6. _____
7. _____
8. _____
9. _____
10. _____

2 **Identificar** Identifica la palabra que no está relacionada con su grupo.

1. champiñón • cebolla • banana • zanahoria _____
2. camarones • ajo • atún • salmón _____
3. aceite • leche • refresco • agua mineral _____
4. jamón • chuleta de cerdo • vinagre • carne de res _____
5. cerveza • lechuga • arvejas • frijoles _____
6. carne • pescado • mariscos • camarero _____
7. pollo • naranja • limón • melocotón _____
8. maíz • queso • tomate • champiñón _____
9. rico • sabroso • menú • delicioso _____
10. pescado • mariscos • salmón • bebida _____

3 **Completar** Completa las frases con las palabras más lógicas.

1. ¡Me gusta mucho este plato! Es _____.
   a. feo   b. sabroso   c. antipático
2. Camarero, ¿puedo ver el _____, por favor?
   a. aceite   b. maíz   c. menú
3. A Elena no le gusta la _____ pero le gusta mucho la fruta.
   a. carne   b. uva   c. naranja
4. Carlos y yo bebemos siempre agua _____.
   a. cómodo   b. mineral   c. principal
5. Antes de su plato principal, Maribel comió _____.
   a. azúcar   b. entremeses   c. cerveza
6. El plato del día es _____.
   a. el pollo asado   b. la mayonesa   c. el ajo
7. Margarita es vegetariana. Ella come _____.
   a. frijoles   b. chuletas   c. jamón
8. Mi hermana le sirve _____ a su niña.
   a. ajo   b. vinagre   c. yogur

el desayuno

el jugo de naranja

el café

el pan tostado

la mantequilla

la salchicha

el huevo

el almuerzo

el té helado

la manzana

la hamburguesa

el pan

las papas fritas

la cena

la sal

la pimienta

la sopa

el vino tinto

el arroz

la ensalada

los espárragos

el bistec

NOTA CULTURAL

In Guatemala, a typical breakfast might include **huevos**, **frijoles**, **fruta**, **tortillas**, **jugo**, and **café**.

Other popular breakfast foods are:

madalenas (*muffins*) Spain

pan dulce (*sweet roll*) México

champurradas (*sugar cookies*) Guatemala

gallopinto (*fried rice and beans*) Costa Rica

perico (*scrambled eggs with peppers and onions*) Venezuela

Más vocabulario

almorzar (o:ue)	*to have lunch*
cenar	*to have dinner*
desayunar	*to have breakfast*
pedir (e:i)	*to order (food)*
probar (o:ue)	*to taste; to try*
recomendar (e:ie)	*to recommend*
servir (e:i)	*to serve*

4

Completar Trabaja con un(a) compañero/a de clase para relacionar cada producto con el grupo alimenticio (*food group*) correcto.

modelo

___La carne___ es del grupo uno.

el aceite	la carne	las bananas	los espárragos
el azúcar	los cereales	la leche	el arroz
el café	los frijoles	el pescado	

1. _____ y el queso son del grupo cuatro.
2. _____ son del grupo ocho.
3. _____ y el pollo son del grupo tres.
4. _____ es del grupo cinco.
5. _____ es del grupo dos.
6. Las manzanas y _____ son del grupo siete.
7. _____ es del grupo seis.
8. _____ son del grupo diez.
9. _____ y los tomates son del grupo nueve.
10. El pan y _____ son del grupo diez.

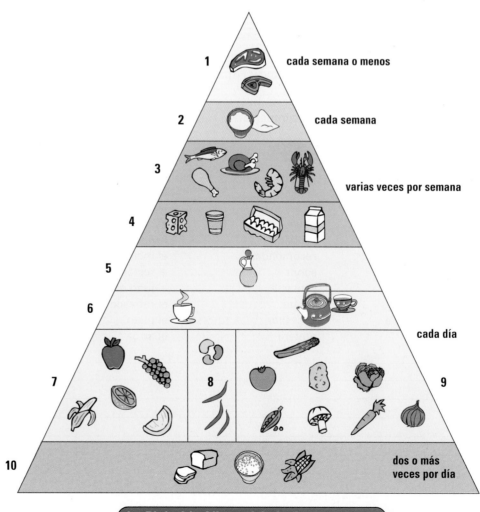

1 — cada semana o menos
2 — cada semana
3 — varias veces por semana
4
5
6 — cada día
7   8   9
10 — dos o más veces por día

La Pirámide Alimenticia Latinoamericana

5 **¿Cierto o falso?** Consulta la Pirámide Alimenticia Latinoamericana de la página 211 e indica si las frases son **ciertas** o **falsas**. Corrige las frases falsas.

> **modelo**
> El queso está en el grupo diez.
> *Falso. En ese grupo están el maíz, el pan y el arroz.*

1. La manzana, la banana, el limón y las arvejas están en el grupo siete.
2. En el grupo cuatro están los huevos, la leche y el aceite.
3. El azúcar está en el grupo dos.
4. En el grupo diez están el pan, el arroz y el maíz.
5. El pollo está en el grupo uno.
6. En el grupo nueve están la lechuga, el tomate, las arvejas, la naranja, la papa, los espárragos y la cebolla.
7. En el grupo seis están el café y el té.
8. En el grupo cinco está el arroz.
9. En el grupo tres están el pescado, el yogur y el bistec.
10. En el grupo ocho está la cerveza.

6 **Combinar** Combina palabras de cada columna, en cualquier (*any*) orden, para formar diez frases lógicas sobre las comidas. Añade otras palabras si es necesario.

> **modelo**
> La camarera nos sirve el almuerzo.

A	B	C
El/La camarero/a	almorzar	el almuerzo
El/La dueño/a	cenar	la sección de no fumar
Mi familia	desayunar	la cena
Mi novio/a	pedir	el desayuno
Mis amigos y yo	probar	la ensalada
Tía Ana	recomendar	el melocotón
Miguel	servir	el restaurante
Teresa y Pablo	sentarse	el jugo de naranja
Mi hermano/a	gustar	el refresco
El/La médico/a	necesitar	el plato
Yo	preferir	el arroz

1. _____
2. _____
3. _____
4. _____
5. _____
6. _____
7. _____
8. _____
9. _____
10. _____

NOTA CULTURAL

Rice is a staple of Caribbean, Central American, and Mexican cuisine. It often accompanies main dishes and is served with beans, as in Guatemala's **arroz con frijoles**. It's also frequently the main dish, as in **arroz con pollo** (*chicken and rice casserole*).

Comunicación

7

Un menú Con un(a) compañero/a de clase, usa la Pirámide Alimenticia Latinoamericana de la página 211 para crear un menú para una cena especial. Incluye alimentos de los diez grupos para los entremeses, los platos principales y las bebidas. Luego presenta el menú a la clase.

8

Conversación En grupos, contesten las siguientes preguntas.

1. ¿A qué hora, dónde y con quién cenas?
2. ¿Qué comidas te gustan más para la cena?
3. ¿A qué hora, dónde y con quién almuerzas?
4. ¿Cuáles son las comidas más (*most*) típicas de tu almuerzo?
5. ¿Desayunas? ¿Qué comes y bebes por la mañana?
6. ¿Qué comida deseas probar?
7. ¿Comes cada día comidas de los diferentes grupos de la pirámide alimenticia? ¿Cuáles son las comidas y bebidas más frecuentes en tu dieta?
8. ¿Qué comida recomiendas a tus amigos? ¿Por qué?
9. ¿Eres vegetariano/a? ¿Crees que ser vegetariano/a es una buena idea? ¿Por qué?
10. ¿Te gusta cocinar (*cook*)? ¿Qué comidas preparas para tus amigos? ¿Para tu familia?

> **¡LENGUA VIVA!**
>
> In addition to **beber**, the verb **tomar** is often used to express *to drink*.

9

Describir Con dos compañeros/as de clase, describe las dos fotos, contestando las siguientes preguntas.

▶ ¿Quiénes están en las fotos?

▶ ¿Dónde están?

▶ ¿Qué hora es?

▶ ¿Qué comen y qué beben?

¿Qué tal la comida?

Don Francisco y los estudiantes van al restaurante El Cráter.

PERSONAJES

MAITE

INÉS

DON FRANCISCO

ÁLEX

JAVIER

DOÑA RITA

CAMARERO

JAVIER ¿Sabes dónde estamos?

INÉS Mmm, no sé. Oiga, don Francisco, ¿sabe Ud. dónde estamos?

DON FRANCISCO Estamos cerca de Cotacachi.

ÁLEX ¿Dónde vamos a almorzar, don Francisco? ¿Conoce un buen restaurante en Cotacachi?

DON FRANCISCO Pues, conozco a doña Rita Perales, la dueña del mejor restaurante de la ciudad, el restaurante El Cráter.

DOÑA RITA Hombre, don Paco, ¿Ud. por aquí?

DON FRANCISCO Sí, doña Rita... y hoy le traigo clientes. Le presento a Maite, Inés, Álex y Javier. Los llevo a las montañas para ir de excursión.

MAITE Voy a tomar un caldo de patas y un lomo a la plancha.

JAVIER Para mí las tortillas de maíz y el ceviche de camarón.

ÁLEX Yo también quisiera las tortillas de maíz y el ceviche.

INÉS Voy a pedir caldo de patas y lomo a la plancha.

DON FRANCISCO Yo quiero tortillas de maíz y una fuente de fritada, por favor.

DOÑA RITA Y de tomar, les recomiendo el jugo de piña, frutilla y mora. ¿Se lo traigo a todos?

TODOS Sí, perfecto.

CAMARERO ¿Qué plato pidió Ud.?

MAITE Un caldo de patas y lomo a la plancha.

recursos

R

| V/VCD-ROM Lección 8 | VM pp. 305-306 | ICD-ROM Lección 8 |

DOÑA RITA ¡Bienvenidos al restaurante El Cráter! Están en muy buenas manos... don Francisco es el mejor conductor del país. Y no hay nada más bonito que nuestras montañas. Pero si van a ir de excursión deben comer bien. Vengan chicos, por aquí.

JAVIER ¿Qué nos recomienda Ud.?

DOÑA RITA Bueno, las tortillas de maíz son riquísimas. La especialidad de la casa es el caldo de patas... ¡tienen que probarlo! El lomo a la plancha es un poquito más caro que el caldo pero es sabrosísimo. También les recomiendo el ceviche y la fuente de fritada.

DOÑA RITA ¿Qué tal la comida? ¿Rica?

JAVIER Rica, no. ¡Riquísima!

ÁLEX Sí, y nos la sirvieron tan rápidamente.

MAITE Una comida deliciosa, gracias.

DON FRANCISCO Hoy es el cumpleaños de Maite...

DOÑA RITA ¡Ah! Tenemos unos pasteles que están como para chuparse los dedos...

Enfoque cultural La comida hispana

La cocina (*cuisine*) hispana es una combinación de comidas e ingredientes de varias regiones. La carne de res, la papa, el maíz y el chile, por ejemplo, son característicos de los países andinos. Los frijoles, el arroz, la caña de azúcar y la banana son productos típicos de los países del Caribe. La cocina española incorpora pescados y carnes cocinados (*cooked*) con condimentos como el ajo y la cebolla. La comida típica de Centroamérica es similar a la mexicana y consta de (*consists of*) carne, pescados, chile, tortillas y salsas.

Expresiones útiles

Finding out where you are
▶ **¿Sabe Ud./Sabes dónde estamos?**
Do you know where we are?
▷ **Estamos cerca de Cotacachi.**
We're near Cotacachi.

Talking about people and places you're familiar with
▶ **¿Conoce Ud./Conoces un buen restaurante en Cotacachi?**
Do you know a good restaurant in Cotacachi?
▷ **Sí, conozco varios.**
Yes, I know several.
▶ **¿Conoce/Conoces a doña Rita?**
Do you know doña Rita?

Ordering food
▶ **¿Qué le puedo traer?**
What can I bring you?
▷ **Voy a tomar/pedir un caldo de patas y un lomo a la plancha.**
I am going to have/to order the beef soup and grilled flank steak.
▷ **Para mí las tortillas de maíz y el ceviche de camarón, por favor.**
Corn tortillas and lemon-marinated shrimp for me, please.
▷ **Yo también quisiera...**
I also would like...
▷ **Y de tomar, el jugo de piña, frutilla y mora.**
And pineapple/strawberry/blackberry juice to drink.
▶ **¿Qué plato pidió Ud.?**
What did you order?
▷ **Yo pedí un caldo de patas.**
I ordered the beef soup.

Talking about the food at a restaurant
▶ **¿Qué tal la comida?**
How is the food?
▷ **Muy rica, gracias.**
Very tasty, thanks.
▷ **¡Riquísima!**
Extremely delicious!

Reacciona a la fotonovela

1 **Escoger** Escoge la respuesta (*answer*) que completa mejor (*best*) cada oración.

1. Don Francisco lleva a los estudiantes a _____ al restaurante de una amiga.
   a. cenar   b. desayunar   c. almorzar
2. Doña Rita es _____.
   a. la hermana de don Francisco   b. la dueña del restaurante
   c. una camarera que trabaja en El Cráter
3. Doña Rita les recomienda a los viajeros _____.
   a. el caldo de patas y el lomo a la plancha
   b. el bistec, las verduras frescas y el vino tinto   c. unos pasteles (*cakes*)
4. Inés va a pedir _____.
   a. las tortillas de maíz y una fuente de fritada (*mixed grill*)
   b. el ceviche de camarón y el caldo de patas
   c. el caldo de patas y el lomo a la plancha

NOTA CULTURAL

Ceviche is a typical South American dish made with raw fish, shrimp or shellfish, onions, and hot peppers. The ingredients are marinated in lime juice and salt for several hours before serving.

2 **Identificar** Indica quién puede decir las siguientes frases.

1. No me gusta esperar en los restaurantes.
   ¡Qué bueno que nos sirvieron rápidamente!
2. Les recomiendo la especialidad de la casa.
3. ¡Maite y yo pedimos los mismos platos!
4. Disculpe, señora... ¿qué platos recomienda Ud.?
5. Yo conozco a una señora que tiene un restaurante
   excelente. Les va a gustar mucho.
6. Hoy es mi cumpleaños (*birthday*).

INÉS   **ÁLEX**   **DOÑA RITA**

MAITE   **DON FRANCISCO**   **JAVIER**

3 **Preguntas** Contesta las siguientes preguntas sobre la **Fotonovela**.

1. ¿Dónde comieron don Francisco y los estudiantes?
2. ¿Cuál es la especialidad de El Cráter?
3. ¿Qué pidió Inés? ¿Y Álex? ¿Qué tomaron todos?
4. ¿Qué tal los pasteles en El Cráter?

4 **En el restaurante**

1. Prepara con un(a) compañero/a una conversación en la que le preguntas si conoce algún buen restaurante en tu comunidad. Tu compañero/a responde que él/ella sí conoce un restaurante que sirve una comida deliciosa. Lo/La invitas a cenar y tu compañero/a acepta. Determinan la hora para verse en el restaurante y se despiden (*say goodbye*).
2. Trabaja con un(a) compañero/a para representar los papeles (*roles*) de un(a) cliente/a y un(a) camarero/a en un restaurante. El/La camarero/a te pregunta qué te puede servir y tú preguntas cuál es la especialidad de la casa. El/La camarero/a te dice cuál es la especialidad y te recomienda algunos platos del menú. Tú pides entremeses, un plato principal y una bebida. El/La camarero/a te da las gracias y luego te sirve la comida.

CONSÚLTATO

Indefinite and negative words
To review indefinite words like **algún**, see Lesson 7, pp.192-193.

Pronunciación 🎧

ll, ñ, c, and z

pollo	**llave**	**ella**	**cebolla**

Most Spanish speakers pronounce the letter **ll** like the *y* in *yes*.

mañana	**señor**	**baño**	**niña**

The letter *ñ* is pronounced much like the *ny* in *canyon*.

café	**colombiano**	**cuando**	**rico**

Before **a**, **o**, or **u**, the Spanish **c** is pronounced like the *c* in *car*.

cereales	**delicioso**	**conducir**	**conocer**

Before **e** or **i**, the Spanish **c** is pronounced like the *s* in *sit*. (In parts of Spain, **c** before **e** or **i** is pronounced like the *th* in *think*.)

zeta	**zanahoria**	**almuerzo**	**cerveza**

The Spanish **z** is pronounced like the *s* in *sit*. (In parts of Spain, **z** before a vowel is pronounced like the *th* in *think*.)

Práctica Lee las palabras en voz alta.

1. mantequilla
2. cuñado
3. aceite
4. manzana
5. español
6. cepillo
7. zapato
8. azúcar
9. quince
10. compañera
11. almorzar
12. calle

Oraciones Lee las oraciones en voz alta.

1. Mi compañero de cuarto se llama Toño Núñez. Su familia es de la ciudad de Guatemala y de Quetzaltenango.
2. Dice que la comida de su mamá es deliciosa, especialmente su pollo al champiñón y sus tortillas de maíz.
3. Creo que Toño tiene razón porque hoy cené en su casa y quiero volver mañana para cenar allí otra vez.

Refranes Lee los refranes en voz alta.

Las apariencias engañan.[1]

Panza llena, corazón contento.[2]

1 Looks can be deceiving.
2 A full belly makes a happy heart.

recursos

R			
STUDENT CD Lección 8	LM p. 242	LCASS./CD Cass. 8/CD 8	ICD-ROM Lección 8

8.1 Preterite of stem-changing verbs

ANTE TODO As you learned in Lesson 6, **–ar** and **–er** stem-changing verbs have no stem change in the preterite. **–Ir** stem-changing verbs, however, do have a stem change. Study the following charts and observe where the stem changes occur.

Preterite of –ir stem-changing verbs		
	servir (to serve)	**dormir** (to sleep)
SINGULAR FORMS yo	serví	dormí
tú	serviste	dormiste
Ud./él/ella	si**r**vió	du**r**mió
PLURAL FORMS nosotros/as	servimos	dormimos
vosotros/as	servisteis	dormisteis
Uds./ellos/ellas	si**r**vieron	du**r**mieron

▶ Stem-changing **–ir** verbs, in the preterite only, have a stem change in the third-person singular and plural forms. The stem change consists of either **e** to **i** or **o** to **u**.

(e ➙ i) pedir: **p**idió, **p**idieron   (o ➙ u) morir: **m**urió, **m**urieron (to die)

Perdón, ¿quiénes pidieron las tortillas de maíz?

¿Y qué plato pidió usted?

¡INTÉNTALO! Cambia los infinitivos al pretérito.

1. Yo ___serví___. (servir, dormir, pedir, preferir, repetir, seguir)

2. Ud. _____. (morir, conseguir, pedir, sentirse, despedirse, vestirse)

3. Tú _____. (conseguir, servir, morir, pedir, dormir, repetir)

4. Ellas _____. (repetir, dormir, seguir, preferir, morir, servir)

5. Nosotros _____. (seguir, preferir, servir, vestirse, despedirse, dormirse)

6. Uds. _____. (sentirse, vestirse, conseguir, pedir, despedirse, dormirse)

7. Él _____. (dormir, morir, preferir, repetir, seguir, pedir)

Práctica

1 **Completar** Completa las siguientes frases para describir lo que pasó anoche en el restaurante El Famoso.

1. Paula y Humberto Suárez llegaron al restaurante El Famoso a las ocho y _____ (seguir) al camarero a una mesa en la sección de no fumar.
2. El Sr. Suárez _____ (pedir) una chuleta de cerdo. La Sra. Suárez decidió probar los camarones.
3. Para tomar, los dos _____ (pedir) vino tinto.
4. El camarero _____ (repetir) el pedido (*the order*) para confirmarlo.
5. La comida tardó mucho (*took a long time*) en llegar y los Srs. Suárez _____ (dormirse) esperando la comida.
6. A las nueve el camarero les _____ (servir) la comida.
7. Después de comer la chuleta de cerdo, el Sr. Suárez _____ (sentirse) muy mal.
8. De repente, el Sr. Suárez se _____ (morir).
9. Pobre Sr. Suárez... ¿por qué no _____ (pedir) los camarones?

2 **El camarero loco** En el restaurante La Hermosa trabaja un camarero muy loco que siempre comete muchos errores. Indica lo que los clientes pidieron y lo que el camarero les sirvió.

> **modelo**
> Armando / papas fritas
> Armando pidió papas fritas pero el camarero le sirvió maíz.

1. Nosotros / jugo de naranja
2. Beatriz / queso
3. Tú / arroz

4. Elena y Alejandro /atún
5. Ud. / agua mineral
6. Yo / hamburguesa

Comunicación

3 **Oraciones** Completa las oraciones de una manera lógica.

> **modelo**
>
> Yo jugué al baloncesto pero Tomás y Paco...
> Yo jugué al baloncesto pero Tomás y Paco jugaron al tenis.

1. Mi compañero/a de cuarto se despertó tarde pero yo...
2. Yo pedí ensalada de frutas pero mis amigos...
3. Lorena me recomendó el bistec pero Sofía y Carolina...
4. Esteban almorzó al mediodía pero yo...
5. Yo serví la carne pero Alonso...
6. Yo me dormí temprano pero ellos...
7. Nosotros preferimos los mariscos pero Sandra...
8. Celia se sintió enferma pero nosotros...
9. Nosotros repetimos el postre pero ustedes...
10. Yo seguí todas las instrucciones del profesor pero Manuela...

4 **Entrevista** Trabajen en parejas y túrnense para entrevistar a su compañero/a.

1. ¿Te acostaste tarde o temprano anoche? ¿A qué hora te dormiste? ¿Dormiste bien?
2. ¿A qué hora te despertaste esta mañana? Y ¿a qué hora te levantaste?
3. ¿A qué hora vas a acostarte esta noche?
4. ¿Llegaste a tiempo (*on time*) a la clase de español?
5. ¿Cuándo empezaste a estudiar español?
6. ¿Quién preparó la cena en tu casa anoche? Y ¿quién la sirvió?
7. ¿Quién va a preparar y servir la cena en tu casa esta noche?
8. ¿Se durmió alguien en alguna de tus clases la semana pasada? ¿En qué clase?

Síntesis

5 **Describir** En grupos, estudien la foto y las preguntas que siguen. Luego, describan la cena romántica de Eduardo y Rosa.

▶ ¿Adónde salieron a cenar?

▶ ¿Qué pidieron?

▶ ¿Les sirvieron la comida rápidamente?

▶ ¿Les gustó la comida?

▶ ¿Cuánto costó?

▶ ¿Van a volver a este restaurante en el futuro?

CONSÚLTALO

Words commonly used with the preterite
To review time expressions such as **anoche**, see Lesson 6, p. 161.

8.2 Double object pronouns

ANTE TODO In Lessons 5 and 6, you learned that direct and indirect object pronouns replace nouns and that they often refer to nouns that have already been referenced. You will now learn how to use direct and indirect object pronouns together. Observe the following diagram.

Indirect Object Pronouns			**Direct Object Pronouns**	
me	nos		lo	los
te	os	**+**	la	las
le (se)	les (se)			

▶ When direct and indirect object pronouns are used together, the indirect object pronoun always precedes the direct object pronoun.

I.O.   D.O.
El camarero **me** muestra **el menú.**   ⟶   **DOUBLE OBJECT PRONOUNS** El camarero **me lo** muestra.
The waiter shows me the menu.   *The waiter shows it to me.*

I.O.   D.O.
Nos sirven **los platos.**   ⟶   **DOUBLE OBJECT PRONOUNS** **Nos los** sirven.
They serve us the dishes.   *They serve them to us.*

I.O.   D.O.
Maribel **te** pidió **una hamburguesa.**   ⟶   **DOUBLE OBJECT PRONOUNS** Maribel **te la** pidió.
Maribel ordered a hamburger for you.   *Maribel ordered it for you.*

Y de tomar, les recomiendo el jugo de piña... ¿Se lo traigo a todos?

Sí, perfecto.

▶ In Spanish, two pronouns that begin with the letter **l** cannot be used together. Therefore, the indirect object pronouns **le** and **les** always change to **se** when they are used with **lo, los, la,** and **las.**

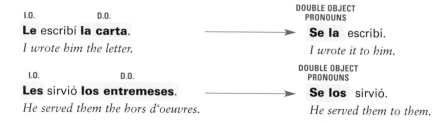

I.O.   D.O.
Le escribí **la carta.**   ⟶   **DOUBLE OBJECT PRONOUNS** **Se la** escribí.
I wrote him the letter.   *I wrote it to him.*

I.O.   D.O.
Les sirvió **los entremeses.**   ⟶   **DOUBLE OBJECT PRONOUNS** **Se los** sirvió.
He served them the hors d'oeuvres.   *He served them to them.*

▶ Because **se** has multiple meanings, Spanish speakers often clarify to whom the pronoun refers by adding **a Ud., a él, a ella, a Uds., a ellos,** or **a ellas.**

¿El sombrero? Carlos **se** lo vendió
a ella.
The hat? Carlos sold it to her.

¿Las verduras? Ellos **se** las compran
a Ud.
The vegetables? They buy them for you.

▶ Double object pronouns follow the same rules for placement as single object pronouns. They are placed before a conjugated verb, and, with infinitives and present participles, they may be placed before the conjugated verb or attached to the end of the infinitive or present participle.

<table>
<tr><td align="center">DOUBLE OBJECT
PRONOUNS
Te lo voy a mostrar.</td><td align="center">DOUBLE OBJECT
PRONOUNS
Voy a mostrár**telo.**</td></tr>
<tr><td align="center">DOUBLE OBJECT
PRONOUNS
Nos las están sirviendo.</td><td align="center">DOUBLE OBJECT
PRONOUNS
Están sirviéndo**noslas.**</td></tr>
</table>

¡ATENCIÓN!

When pronouns are attached to an infinitive or a present participle, an accent mark is added to maintain the original stress. You will learn more about accents in **Ortografía,** p. 275.

mostrar →   **mostrártelo**
sirviendo →   **sirviéndonoslas**

Qué tal la comida, ¿rica?

Sí, y nos la sirvieron tan rápidamente.

   Escribe el pronombre de objeto directo o indirecto que falta en cada frase.

Objeto directo

1. ¿La ensalada? El camarero nos ___la___ sirvió.
2. ¿El salmón? La dueña me _____ recomienda.
3. ¿La comida? Voy a preparárte _____.
4. ¿Las bebidas? Estamos pidiéndose _____.
5. ¿Los refrescos? Te _____ puedo traer ahora.
6. ¿Los platos de arroz? Van a servírnos _____ después.

Objeto indirecto

1. ¿Puedes traerme tu plato? No, no ___te___ lo puedo traer.
2. ¿Quieres mostrarle la carta? Sí, voy a mostrár _____ la ahora.
3. ¿Les serviste la carne? No, no _____ la serví.
4. ¿Vas a leerle el menú? No, no _____ lo voy a leer.
5. ¿Me recomiendas la langosta? Sí, _____ la recomiendo.
6. ¿Cuándo vas a prepararnos la cena? _____ la voy a preparar en una hora.

Práctica

AYUDA

Here are some other useful expressions:

ahora mismo
right now

inmediatamente
immediately

¡A la orden!
At your service.

¡Ya voy!
I'm on my way.

1

Responder Imagínate que trabajas de camarero/a en un restaurante. Responde a las órdenes de estos clientes usando pronombres.

> **modelo**
>
> Sra. Gómez: Una ensalada, por favor.
> Sí, señora. Enseguida *(Right away)* se la traigo.

1. Sr. López: La mantequilla, por favor.
2. Srta. Rivas: Los camarones, por favor.
3. Sra. Lugones: El pollo asado, por favor.
4. Tus compañeros/as de cuarto: Un café, por favor.
5. Tu profesor(a) de español: Papas fritas, por favor.
6. Dra. González: La chuleta de cerdo, por favor.
7. Tus padres: Los champiñones, por favor.
8. Dr. Torres: La cuenta *(check)*, por favor.

2

¿Quién? La Sra. Cevallos está hablando sola de los planes para una cena con su familia y amigos. Cambia los sustantivos *(nouns)* subrayados por pronombres de objeto directo y haz los otros cambios necesarios.

> **modelo**
>
> ¡No tengo carne! ¿Quién va a traerme la carne del supermercado? (Mi esposo)
> Mi esposo va a traérmela./Mi esposo me la va a traer.

1. ¡Las invitaciones! ¿Quién les mandó las invitaciones a los invitados *(guests)*? (Mi hija)
2. No tengo tiempo de ir a la panadería *(bakery)*. ¿Quién me puede comprar el pan? (Mi hijo)
3. ¡Ay! No tengo suficientes platos. ¿Quién puede prestarme los platos que necesito? (Mi mamá)
4. Nos falta mantequilla. ¿Quién nos trae la mantequilla? (Mi cuñada)
5. ¡Los postres *(desserts)*! ¿Quién está preparándonos los postres? (Silvia y Renata)
6. No hay suficientes sillas. ¿Quiénes nos traen las sillas que faltan? (Héctor y Lorena)
7. No tengo tiempo de pedirle el azúcar a Mónica. ¿Quién puede pedirle el azúcar? (Mi hijo)
8. ¿Quién va a servirles la cena a los invitados? (Mis hijos)

Comunicación

3

Contestar Trabajen en parejas y háganse preguntas usando las palabras interrogativas **¿Quién?** o **¿Cuándo?** Sigan el modelo.

> **modelo**
>
> nos enseña español
>
> **Estudiante 1:** ¿Quién nos enseña español?
> **Estudiante 2:** La profesora Camacho nos lo enseña.

1. te puede explicar (*explain*) la tarea cuando no la entiendes
2. les vende los libros de texto a los estudiantes
3. te escribe mensajes electrónicos
4. te prepara la comida
5. te compró esa blusa
6. le enseñó español al/a la profesor(a)
7. vas a comprarme boletos (*tickets*) para un concierto
8. me vas a prestar tu computadora
9. nos va a recomendar el menú de la cafetería
10. me vas a mostrar tu casa o apartamento

4

Preguntas Hazle estas preguntas a un(a) compañero/a.

1. ¿Me prestas tu coche (*car*)? ¿Ya le prestaste tu coche a otro/a amigo/a?
2. ¿Me puedes comprar un coche nuevo?
3. ¿Quién te presta dinero cuando lo necesitas?
4. ¿Les prestas dinero a tus amigos/as? ¿Por qué?
5. ¿Les prestas tu casa a tus amigos/as? ¿Por qué?
6. ¿Nos compras el almuerzo a mí y a los otros compañeros de clase?
7. ¿Me describes tu casa?
8. ¿Quién te va a preparar la cena esta noche?
9. ¿Quién te va a preparar el desayuno mañana?
10. ¿Vas a leerles la historia de Blanca Nieves (*Snow White*) a tus nietos/as? ¿Qué otras historias les vas a leer?

Síntesis

5

Regalos de Navidad Tu profesor(a) va a darte (*to give you*) una hoja de actividades. En parejas, cada uno/a de Uds. tiene parte de la lista de los regalos de Navidad (*Christmas gifts*) que Berta pidió y los regalos que sus parientes le compraron. Conversen entre Uds. para completar sus listas.

> **modelo**
>
> **Estudiante 1:** ¿Qué le pidió Berta a su mamá?
> **Estudiante 2:** Le pidió una computadora.
> **Estudiante 1:** ¿Se la compró?
> **Estudiante 2:** Sí, se la compró.

8.3 Saber and conocer

ANTE TODO Spanish has two verbs that mean *to know*, **saber** and **conocer**, which cannot be used interchangeably. Note that all forms of **saber** and **conocer** are regular in the present tense except their **yo** forms.

		Saber and *conocer*	
		saber *(to know)*	**conocer** *(to know)*
SINGULAR FORMS	yo	**sé**	**conozco**
	tú	**sabes**	**conoces**
	Ud./él/ella	**sabe**	**conoce**
PLURAL FORMS	nosotros/as	**sabemos**	**conocemos**
	vosotros/as	**sabéis**	**conocéis**
	Uds./ellos/ellas	**saben**	**conocen**

¡ATENCIÓN!

The following verbs are also conjugated like **conocer:**

conducir *to drive*
ofrecer *to offer*
parecer *to seem*
traducir *to translate*

▶ **Saber** means *to know a fact or piece(s) of information* or *to know how to do something.*

No **sé** tu número de teléfono.
I don't know your telephone number.

Mi hermana **sabe** hablar francés.
My sister knows how to speak French.

▶ **Conocer** means *to know* or *be familiar/acquainted* with a person, place, or thing.

¿**Conoces** la ciudad de Nueva York?
Do you know New York City?

No **conozco** a tu amigo Esteban.
I don't know your friend Esteban.

▶ When the direct object of **conocer** is a person or pet, the personal **a** is used.

¿Conoces los restaurantes de Tegucigalpa?   *but*   ¿Conoces **a** Rigoberta Menchú?

¡INTÉNTALO! Escribe las formas apropiadas de los siguientes verbos.

saber

1. José no ___*sabe*___ la hora.
2. Sara y yo _____ jugar al tenis.
3. ¿Por qué no _____ tú estos verbos?
4. Mis padres _____ hablar japonés.
5. Yo _____ a qué hora es la clase.
6. Ud. no _____ dónde vivo.
7. Mi hermano no _____ nadar.
8. Nosotros _____ muchas cosas.
9. Carlos nunca _____ qué hora es.
10. Yo _____ dónde comer bien.

verbos como conocer

1. Ud. y yo ___*conocemos*___ (conocer) bien Miami.
2. Mi compañero _____ (conducir) muy mal.
3. Esta clase _____ (parecer) muy buena.
4. Ellos siempre me _____ (ofrecer) ayuda.
5. Yo _____ (traducir) del chino al inglés.
6. Ana, ¿_____ (conocer) los poemas de Mistral?
7. Luis, ¡_____ (parecer) triste!
8. Uds. _____ (conducir) con cuidado.
9. Yo siempre _____ (ofrecer) café a mis amigos.
10. Nadie me _____ (conocer) bien.

Práctica

1 **Completar** Completa las frases con la forma apropiada de **saber** o **conocer**.

1. Mi hermana mayor _____ conducir, pero yo no_____.
2. —¿_____ a Carla, mi sobrina? —No, no la _____.
3. —¿_____ Uds. el número de Marta? —Nosotras no lo _____.
4. —Nosotros no _____ Guatemala. —Ah, ¿no? Yo _____ bien las ciudades de Escuintla, Mazatenango, Quetzaltenango y Antigua.
5. —Todavía no _____ a tu novio. —Sí, ya lo _____. Mañana te lo presento.
6. Yo _____ esquiar, pero Tino y Luis son pequeños y no _____.
7. Roberto _____ bien el Popol Vuh, el libro sagrado de los mayas, y también _____ leer los jeroglíficos de los templos mayas.

CONSÚLTALO

Panorama Locate the Guatemalan cities mentioned here, on p. 238.

2 **Emparejar** Empareja (*match*) las oraciones de la columna A con las oraciones de la columna B y escribe la forma correcta de los verbos en la columna B.

A

1. María del Carmen tiene mucha sed.
2. ¿Puedes traducir la carta del Sr. Jiménez?
3. ¿Sabes cuándo es el concierto de Shakira?
4. Gloria, tú no tienes automóvil, ¿verdad?
5. Ése es el hijastro de mi cuñada María José.
6. ¿A qué hora vuelve el ingeniero?

B

a. ¿Ah, sí? Pues no lo _____ (conocer). ¡Qué guapo!
b. Con gusto le _____ (ofrecer) una bebida.
c. No _____ (saber). No me acuerdo.
d. En este instante no puedo, pero más tarde se la _____ (traducir).
e. No lo sé, pero si _____ (conseguir) la información te llamo.
f. No, pero _____ (conducir) el de mis padres.

3 **Combinar** Combina las columnas A, B y C para hacer oraciones completas.

modelo
No conozco a Stephen King. / Stephen King conoce a Meg Ryan.

A	B	C
Connie Chung	(no) conocer	Meg Ryan
Bill Gates	(no) saber	cantar
Gloria Estefan		el lago de Atitlán
y Ricky Martin		en Guatemala
Billy Crystal		hablar dos lenguas extranjeras
Stephen King		hacer reír (*laugh*) a la gente
Whoopie Goldberg		la fecha de hoy
yo		escribir novelas de horror
tú		programar computadoras
tu compañero/a		Steve Jobs
tu profesor(a)		muchas personas importantes

Comunicación

4

Entrevista Pregúntale a un(a) compañero/a qué deportes practica y por qué.

> **modelo**
>
> **Estudiante 1:** ¿Sabes esquiar? (bucear, nadar, patinar, escalar
> montañas, jugar vóleibol, etc.)
> **Estudiante 2:** Sí, sé esquiar porque aprendí de niño/a./
> Sí, sé esquiar porque me gusta mucho la nieve./
> No, no sé esquiar, pero me gustaría saber.

5

Encuesta Tu profesor(a) va a darte (*to give you*) una hoja de actividades. Camina por la clase y pregúntales por lo menos (*at least*) a dos compañeros qué ciudades de la lista conocen y por qué. Toma nota de sus respuestas y luego informa a la clase de los resultados.

Austin	Cincinnati	Los Angeles	New Orleans	St. Louis
Boston	Denver	Memphis	New York	San Francisco
Chicago	Kansas City	Miami	Phoenix	Seattle

6

Preguntas Con un(a) compañero/a, háganse las siguientes preguntas.

1. ¿Qué restaurantes buenos conoces? ¿Vas mucho a comer a los restaurantes?
2. En tu familia, ¿quién sabe cantar mejor (*best*)? ¿Tu opinión es objetiva?
3. ¿Conoces a algún artista hispano?
4. ¿Sabes usar bien el Internet? ¿Te parecen fáciles o difíciles las computadoras?
5. ¿Sabes escuchar cuando alguien te habla de sus problemas?
6. ¿Conoces a algún (alguna) chef famoso/a? ¿Qué tipo de comida prepara?
7. ¿Conoces a algún (alguna) escritor(a) famoso/a?
8. ¿Sabes si ofrecen cursos de administración de empresas en la universidad?

Síntesis

7

Conversar En parejas, túrnense para hacerse preguntas usando las frases de la lista. Luego informen a la clase de los resultados.

> **modelo**
>
> conocer el estado de Utah
> **Estudiante 1:** ¿Conoces el estado de Utah?
> **Estudiante 2:** Sí, conozco el estado de Utah./
> Yo no, pero mi novio sí lo conoce.

AYUDA

Whereas in English we make contrasts by using *do/does*, in Spanish it is common to use **sí/no**.

Yo no lo conozco, pero mi novio **sí lo conoce**.

*I don't know it, but my boyfriend **does**.*

traducir bien	saber afeitarse con sólo una mano
conducir muy mal	saber maquillarse muy bien
estudiar mucho	conocer a alguien famoso
preocupar(se) demasiado	saber quedarse en silencio
creer que siempre tiene razón	conocer el Gran Cañón
peinar(se) de una manera elegante	saber seleccionar platos del menú

8.4 Comparisons and superlatives

ANTE TODO Spanish and English use comparisons to indicate which of two people or things has a lesser, equal, or greater degree of a quality. Both languages also use superlatives to express the highest or lowest degree of a quality.

> ### Comparisons
>
> menos interesante | más rápido | tan sabroso como
> *less interesting* | *quicker* | *as delicious as*
>
> ### Superlatives
>
> el mejor | el peor | el más rápido
> *the best* | *the worst* | *the fastest*

Comparisons of inequality

▶ Comparisons of inequality are formed by placing **más** (*more*) or **menos** (*less*) before adjectives, adverbs, and nouns and **que** (*than*) after them.

$$\text{más/menos} + \begin{bmatrix} \textit{adjective} \\ \textit{adverb} \\ \textit{noun} \end{bmatrix} + \text{que}$$

> ### adjectives
>
> Los bistecs son **más caros que** el pollo. | Estas uvas son **menos sabrosas que** esa pera.
> *Steaks are more expensive than chicken.* | *These grapes are less tasty than that pear.*
>
> ### adverbs
>
> Me acuesto **más tarde que** tú. | Mi hermano corre **menos rápido que** Alfredo.
> *I go to bed later than you (do).* | *My brother runs less quickly than Alfredo.*
>
> ### nouns
>
> Juan prepara **más platos que** José. | Susana come **menos carne que** Enrique.
> *Juan prepares more dishes than José.* | *Susana eats less meat than Enrique.*

> **¡ATENCIÓN!**
>
> Note that while English has a comparative form for short adjectives (*faster*), such forms do not exist in Spanish (**más** rápido).
>
> • • •
>
> When the comparison involves a numerical expression, **de** is used before the number instead of **que**.
>
> Hay más **de** cincuenta naranjas.
>
> Llego en menos **de** diez minutos.

Tengo más hambre que un elefante.

El lomo a la plancha es un poquito más caro pero es sabrosísimo.

▶ With verbs, the following construction is used to make comparisons of inequality:

$$\begin{bmatrix} \textit{verb} \end{bmatrix} + \text{más/menos que}$$

Mis hermanos **comen más que** yo. | Arturo **duerme menos que** su padre.
My brothers eat more than I (do). | *Arturo sleeps less than his father (does).*

Comparisons of equality

The following construction is used to make comparisons of equality.

$$\textbf{tan} + \begin{bmatrix} \textit{adjective} \\ \textit{adverb} \end{bmatrix} + \textbf{como}$$

$$\textbf{tanto/a(s)} + \begin{bmatrix} \textit{singular noun} \\ \textit{plural noun} \end{bmatrix} + \textbf{como}$$

Yo comí **tanta comida como** tú.
I ate as much food as you (did).

Uds. probaron **tantos platos como** ellos.
You tried as many dishes as they did.

▶ Comparisons of equality with verbs are formed by placing **tanto como** after the verb. Note that in this construction **tanto** does not change in number or gender.

$$\begin{bmatrix} \textit{verb} \end{bmatrix} + \textbf{tanto como}$$

No **duermo tanto como** mi tía.
I don't sleep as much as my aunt.

Estudiamos tanto como ustedes.
We study as much as you (do).

Superlatives

▶ The following construction is used to form superlatives. Note that the noun is always preceded by a definite article and that **de** is equivalent to the English *in* or *of*.

$$\textbf{el/la/los/las} + \begin{bmatrix} \textit{noun} \end{bmatrix} + \textbf{más/menos} + \begin{bmatrix} \textit{adjective} \end{bmatrix} + \textbf{de}$$

Es **el café más rico del** país.
It's the most delicious coffee in the country.

Es el menú **menos caro de** todos éstos.
It is the least expensive menu of all of these.

▶ The noun in a superlative construction can be omitted if it is clear who is the person, place, or thing being referred to.

¿El restaurante El Cráter?
  Es **el más elegante** de la ciudad.
The El Cráter restaurant?
  It's the most elegant (one) in the city.

Recomiendo el pollo asado.
  Es **el más sabroso** del menú.
I recommend the roast chicken.
  It's the most delicious on the menu.

Irregular comparisons and superlatives

Irregular comparative and superlative forms

Adjective		Comparative form		Superlative form	
bueno/a	good	**mejor**	better	**el/la mejor**	(the) best
malo/a	bad	**peor**	worse	**el/la peor**	(the) worst
grande	big	**mayor**	bigger	**el/la mayor**	(the) biggest
pequeño/a	small	**menor**	smaller	**el/la menor**	(the) smallest
joven	young	**menor**	younger	**el/la menor**	(the) youngest
viejo/a	old	**mayor**	older	**el/la mayor**	(the) oldest

Inés, ¿tienes hermanos?

Sí, tengo un hermano mayor.

¿Adónde vamos a almorzar, don F?

Pues, conozco el mejor restaurante de la ciudad, el restaurante El Cráter.

▶ When **grande** and **pequeño/a** refer to age, the irregular comparative and superlative forms, **mayor** and **menor**, are used. However, when these adjectives refer to size, the regular forms, **más grande** and **más pequeño/a**, are used.

CONSÚLTALO

Descriptive adjectives
To review how **bueno**, **malo**, and **grande** shorten before nouns, see Lesson 3, p.72.

Isabel es **la mayor** de su familia.
Isabel is the oldest in her family.

Tu ensalada es **más grande** que ésa.
Your salad is bigger than that one.

Yo soy **menor** que tú.
I'm younger than you.

Pedí **el plato más pequeño** del menú.
I ordered the smallest dish on the menu.

▶ The adverbs **bien** and **mal** have the same irregular comparative forms as the adjectives **bueno/a** and **malo/a**.

Julio nada **mejor** que los otros chicos.
Julio swims better than the other boys.

Ellas cantan **peor** que las otras chicas.
They sing worse than the other girls.

Absolute Superlatives

▶ In Spanish the absolute superlative is equivalent to *extremely, exceptionally, super,* or *very* before an adjective or adverb. You encountered an absolute superlative when you learned how to say **Me gusta(n) muchísimo...**

▶ To form the absolute superlative of most adjectives and adverbs, drop the final vowel and add **-ísimo.**

malo → mal- → malísimo

¡El bistec está **malísimo**!
The steak is very bad!

mucho → much- → muchísimo

Comes **muchísimo**.
You eat a lot (very, very much).

difícil + -ísimo → dificilísimo

Esta prueba es **dificilísima**.
This quiz is exceptionally difficult.

fácil + ísimo → facilísimo

Los exámenes son **facilísimos**.
The tests are extremely easy.

▶ Adjectives and adverbs whose stem ends in **c, g,** or **z** change spelling to **qu**, **gu**, and **c** in the absolute superlative.

rico → riquísimo   **largo → larguísimo**   **feliz → felicísimo**

▶ Adjectives that end in **–n** or **–r** normally form the absolute superlative by adding **-císimo.**

joven + -císimo → jovencísimo   **trabajador + -císimo → trabajadorcísimo**

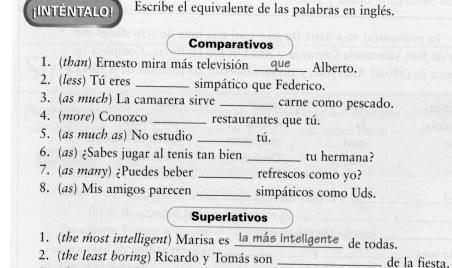

¡INTÉNTALO!   Escribe el equivalente de las palabras en inglés.

Comparativos

1. (*than*) Ernesto mira más televisión ___que___ Alberto.
2. (*less*) Tú eres _____ simpático que Federico.
3. (*as much*) La camarera sirve _____ carne como pescado.
4. (*more*) Conozco _____ restaurantes que tú.
5. (*as much as*) No estudio _____ tú.
6. (*as*) ¿Sabes jugar al tenis tan bien _____ tu hermana?
7. (*as many*) ¿Puedes beber _____ refrescos como yo?
8. (*as*) Mis amigos parecen _____ simpáticos como Uds.

Superlativos

1. (*the most intelligent*) Marisa es _la más inteligente_ de todas.
2. (*the least boring*) Ricardo y Tomás son _____ de la fiesta.
3. (*the worst*) Miguel y Antonio son _____ estudiantes de la clase.
4. (*the oldest*) Mi profesor de biología es _____ de la universidad.
5. (*extremely delicious*) El pollo de esta tienda es _____.
6. (*the youngest*) Carlos es _____ de mis hermanos.
7. (*the best*) Este plato es _____ del restaurante.
8. (*extremely tall*) Sara es _____.

Lectura
Antes de leer

Estrategia
Reading for the main idea

As you know, you can learn a great deal about a reading selection by looking for cognates, titles and subtitles, and formatting. You can skim to get the gist of the reading selection and scan it for specific information. Reading for the main idea is another useful strategy; it involves locating the topic sentences of each paragraph in order to determine the author's purpose for writing a particular piece. Topic sentences can provide clues about the content of each paragraph, as well as the general organization of the reading. Your choice of which reading strategies to use will depend on the style and format of each reading selection.

Examinar el texto

En esta sección tenemos dos textos diferentes. ¿Qué estrategias puedes usar para leer la crítica culinaria? ¿Cuáles son las apropiadas para familiarizarte con el menú? Utiliza las estrategias más eficaces para cada texto. ¿Qué tienen en común? ¿Qué tipo de comida sirven en el restaurante?

Identificar la idea principal

Lee la primera frase de cada párrafo de la crítica culinaria del restaurante **La feria del maíz**. Apunta el tema principal de cada párrafo. Luego lee todo el primer párrafo. ¿Crees que el restaurante le gustó al/a la autor(a) de la crítica culinaria? ¿Por qué? Ahora lee la crítica entera. En tu opinión, ¿cuál es la idea principal de la crítica? ¿Por qué la escribió el/la autor(a)? Compara tus opiniones con las de un(a) compañero/a.

MENÚ

Entremeses
Tortilla servida con
- Ajiaceite (chile, aceite)   • Ajicomino (chile, comino)

Pan tostado servido con
- Queso frito a la pimienta   • Salsa de ajo y mayonesa

Sopas
- Tomate   • Cebolla   • Verduras   • Pollo y huevo
- Carne de res   • Mariscos

Entradas
Tomaticán
(tomate, papas, maíz, chile, guisantes, zanahorias y verduras)

Tamales
(maíz, azúcar, ajo, cebolla)

Frijoles enchilados
(frijoles negros, carne de cerdo o de res, arroz, chile)

Chilaquil
(tortilla de maíz, queso, hierbas y chile)

Tacos
(tortillas, pollo, verduras y mole)

Cóctel de mariscos
(camarones, langostas, vinagre, sal, pimienta, aceite)

Postres
- Plátanos caribeños   • Cóctel de frutas al ron
- Uvate (uvas, azúcar de caña y ron)   • Flan napolitano
- Helado de piña y naranja   • Pastel de yogur

Después de leer

Preguntas

En parejas, contesten las siguientes preguntas sobre la crítica culinaria de **La feria del maíz.**

1. ¿Quién es el dueño y chef de **La feria del maíz**?

2. ¿Qué tipo de comida se sirve en el restaurante?

3. ¿Cuál es el problema con el servicio?

4. ¿Cómo es el ambiente del restaurante?

5. ¿Qué comidas probó el autor de la crítica culinaria?

6. ¿Quieren probar Uds. el restaurante **La feria del maíz**? ¿Por qué?

23F

Gastronomía

Cuatro estrellas para La feria del maíz

Sobresaliente. En el nuevo restaurante **La feria del maíz** Ud. va a encontrar la perfecta combinación entre la comida tradicional y el encanto de la vieja Antigua. Ernesto Sandoval, antiguo jefe de cocina del famoso restaurante **El fogón**, ha conseguido superarse en su nueva aventura culinaria.

El gerente, el experimentado José Sierra, controla a la perfección la calidad del servicio. El mesero que me

La feria del maíz
13 calle 4-41 Zona 1
La Antigua, Guatemala
2329912

lunes a sábado
10:30am-11:30pm
domingo 10:00am-10:00pm

Comida ♦♦♦♦♦

Servicio ♦♦♦

Ambiente ♦♦♦♦

Precio ♦♦♦

atendió esa noche fue muy amable en todo momento. Sólo hay que comentar que, debido al éxito inmediato de **La feria del maíz**, se necesitan más meseros para atender a los clientes de una

forma más eficaz. En esta ocasión, el mesero tardó unos veinte minutos en traerme la bebida.

Afortunadamente, no me importó mucho la espera entre plato y plato, pues el ambiente es tan agradable que me sentí como en casa. Por fuera, la fachada del restaurante mantiene el estilo colonial de Antigua. Por dentro, el estilo es elegante y rústico a la vez. Cuando el tiempo lo permite, se puede comer también en el patio, lleno de flores.

El servicio de meseros y el ambiente agradable del local pasan a un segundo plano cuando llega la comida, de una calidad y consistencia

extraordinarias. Las tortillas están hechas en casa, y se sirven con un ajiaceite delicioso. La sopa de mariscos es excelente, y los tamales, pues, tengo que confesar que son mejores que los de mi abuelita. También recomiendo los tacos de pollo, servidos con un mole muy rico. De postre, don Ernesto me preparó su especialidad, un flan napolitano sabrosísimo.

Los precios pueden parecer altos para una comida tradicional, sin embargo, la calidad de los productos con que se cocinan los platos y el ambiente acogedor de **La feria del maíz** hacen que la experiencia valga la pena.

Bebidas

• Cerveza negra • Chilate (bebida de maíz, chile y cacao)
• Jugos de fruta • Agua mineral • Té helado
• Vino tinto/blanco • Ron

Sobresaliente *Outstanding* **ha conseguido superarse** *has outdone himself*
gerente *manager* **altos** *high* **hacen...pena** *make the experience well worthwhile*

Un(a) guía turístico/a

Tú eres un(a) guía turístico/a en Guatemala. Estás en el restaurante **La feria del maíz** con un grupo de turistas americanos. Ellos no hablan español y quieren comer, pero necesitan tu ayuda. ¿Qué error comete cada turista?

1. La Sra. Johnson es diabética y no puede comer azúcar. Pide sopa de verdura y tamales. No pide nada de postre.

2. Los señores Petit son vegeterianos y piden sopa de tomate, frijoles enchilados y plátanos caribeños.

3. El Sr. Smith, que es alérgico al chocolate, pide tortilla servida con ajiaceite, chilaquil y chilate para beber.

4. La adorable hija del Sr. Smith tiene sólo cuatro años y le gustan mucho las verduras y las frutas naturales. Su papá le pide tomiticán y un cóctel de frutas.

5. La Srta. Jackson está a dieta y pide uvate, flan napolitano y helado.

Guatemala

El país en cifras

- ▶ **Área:** 108.890 km² (42.042 millas²),
  un poco más pequeño que Tennessee
- ▶ **Población:** 11.995.000
- ▶ **Capital:** la ciudad de Guatemala—3.491.000
- ▶ **Ciudades principales:**
  Quezaltenango—101.000, Escuintla—68.000,
  Mazatenango—42.000, Puerto Barrios—39.000

SOURCE: Population Division, UN Secretariat

- ▶ **Moneda:** quetzal
- ▶ **Idiomas:** español (oficial),
  lenguas mayas

El español es la lengua de un 60 por ciento de la población, mientras que el otro 40 por ciento tiene una de las lenguas mayas (cakchiquel, quiché, y kekchícomo entre otras) como materna. Una palabra que las lenguas mayas tienen en común es ixim, que significa maíz, un cultivo de mucha importancia en estas culturas.

Bandera de Guatemala

Guatemaltecos célebres

- ▶ **Carlos Mérida,** pintor (1891-1984)
- ▶ **Miguel Ángel Asturias,** escritor (1899-1974)
- ▶ **Margarita Carrera,** poeta y ensayista (1929-)
- ▶ **Rigoberta Menchú Tum,** activista (1959-)

por ciento *percent*   mientras que *while*   cultivo *crop*   telas *fabrics*
tinte *dye*   zancudos *mosquitos*   aplastados *crushed*
hace... destiñan *keeps the colors from running*   agradecidos *grateful*
hayan tejido *have woven*

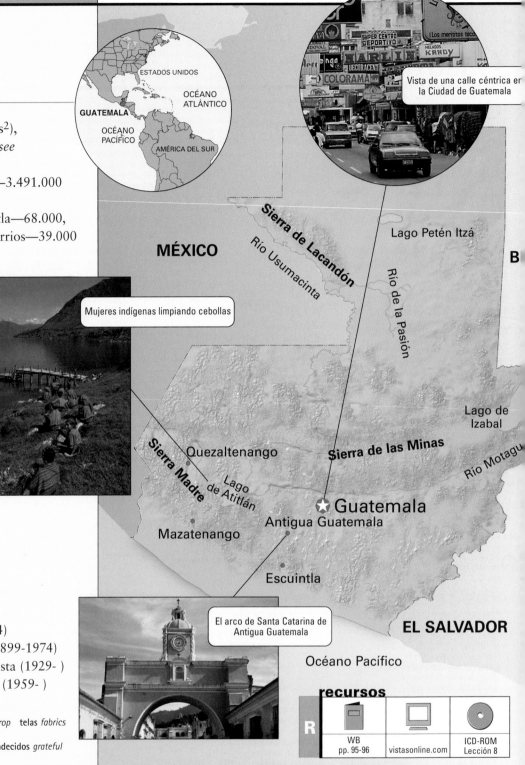

Vista de una calle céntrica en la Ciudad de Guatemala

Mujeres indígenas limpiando cebollas

El arco de Santa Catarina de Antigua Guatemala

ESTADOS UNIDOS
OCÉANO ATLÁNTICO
GUATEMALA
OCÉANO PACÍFICO
AMÉRICA DEL SUR

MÉXICO

Sierra de Lacandón
Río Usumacinta
Lago Petén Itzá
Río de la Pasión
B

Lago de Izabal

Quezaltenango
Sierra Madre
Lago de Atitlán
Sierra de las Minas
Río Motagu

★ Guatemala
Antigua Guatemala

Mazatenango

Escuintla

EL SALVADOR

Océano Pacífico

recursos

R	WB pp. 95-96	vistasonline.com	ICD-ROM Lección 8

¡Increíble pero cierto!

¿Qué ingrediente secreto se encuentra en las telas tradicionales de Guatemala? ¡El mosquito! El excepcional tinte es producto de una mezcla de flores y de zancudos aplastados. El insecto hace que los colores no se destiñan. Quizás ésta es la razón por la que los artesanos, agradecidos, han tejido la figura del zancudo en muchos *huipiles.*

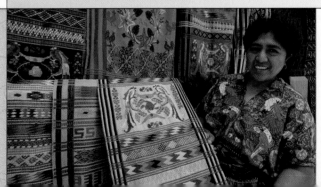

Ciudades • **La Antigua Guatemala**

La Antigua Guatemala fue fundada en 1543. Fue una capital de gran importancia hasta 1773, cuando un terremoto la destruyó. La Antigua Guatemala ha conservado el carácter original de su arquitectura y hoy día se ha convertido en uno de los centros turísticos del país. Su celebración de la Semana Santa es, para muchas personas, la más importante del hemisferio.

Naturaleza • **El quetzal**

El quetzal simbolizaba la libertad para los antiguos mayas porque creían que este pájaro no podía vivir en cautividad. En la actualidad el quetzal es el símbolo nacional. El pájaro da su nombre a la moneda nacional y aparece en los billetes del país. Desafortunadamente, está en peligro de extinción. Para protegerlo, el gobierno mantiene una reserva biológica especial.

Historia • **Los mayas**

Desde 1500 a.C. hasta 900 d.C. los mayas habitaron gran parte de lo que ahora es Guatemala. Su civilización era muy avanzada. Construyeron pirámides, templos y observatorios; descubrieron y usaron el cero antes que los europeos, y desarrollaron un calendario complejo y preciso.

Artesanía • **La ropa tradicional**

La ropa tradicional de los guatemaltecos refleja el sentido del orden y el amor a la naturaleza de la cultura maya. Es de colores vivos y tiene formas geométricas en los diseños. Además, el diseño y los colores de cada *huipil* indican el pueblo de origen y a veces el sexo y la edad de la persona que lo lleva.

¿Qué aprendiste? Responde a las preguntas con una frase completa.

1. ¿Qué significa la palabra *ixim*?
2. ¿Quién es Rigoberta Menchú?
3. ¿Qué pájaro representa a Guatemala?
4. ¿Qué simbolizaba el quetzal para los mayas?
5. ¿Cuál es la moneda nacional de Guatemala?
6. ¿Qué celebración de la Antigua Guatemala es la más importante del hemisferio para muchas personas?
7. ¿Qué construyeron los mayas?
8. ¿Qué descubrieron los mayas antes que los europeos?
9. ¿Qué refleja la ropa tradicional de los guatemaltecos?
10. ¿Qué indica un *huipil* con su diseño y sus colores?

Conexión Internet Investiga estos temas en el sitio **www.vistasonline.com**.

1. Busca información sobre Rigoberta Menchú. ¿De dónde es? ¿Qué libros ha publicado (*has she published*)? ¿Por qué es famosa?
2. Estudia un sitio arqueológico en Guatemala para aprender más sobre los mayas, y prepara un breve informe para tu clase.

terremoto *earthquake* **destruyó** *destroyed* **ha conservado** *has preserved* **se ha convertido** *has turned into* **Semana Santa** *Holy Week*
simbolizaba *symbolized* **antiguos** *ancient* **pájaro** *bird* **cautividad** *captivity* **billetes** *paper money* **peligro** *danger* **protegerlo** *protect it*
Construyeron *They constructed* **descubrieron** *discovered* **desarrollaron** *developed* **complejo** *complex* **sentido del orden** *sense of order*
vivos *bright* **diseños** *designs*

Mar caribe

Golfo de Honduras

uerto ríos

NDURAS

Comidas

el/la camarero/a	waiter
la comida	food; meal
el/la dueño/a	owner; landlord
el menú	menu
la sección de (no) fumar	(non) smoking section
el almuerzo	lunch
la cena	dinner
el desayuno	breakfast
los entremeses	hors d'oeuvres
el plato (principal)	(main) dish
delicioso/a	delicious
rico/a	tasty; delicious
sabroso/a	tasty; delicious
almorzar (o:ue)	to have lunch
cenar	to have dinner
desayunar	to have breakfast
pedir (e:i)	to order (food)
probar (o:ue)	to taste; to try
recomendar (e:ie)	to recommend
servir (e:i)	to serve

Las frutas

la banana	banana
las frutas	fruits
el limón	lemon
la manzana	apple
el melocotón	peach
la naranja	orange
la pera	pear
la uva	grape

Las verduras

el arroz	rice
la cebolla	onion
el champiñón	mushroom
la ensalada	salad
los espárragos	asparagus
los frijoles	beans
las arvejas	peas
la lechuga	lettuce
el maíz	corn
las papas/patatas (fritas)	(fried) potatoes; French fries
el tomate	tomato
las verduras	vegetables
la zanahoria	carrot

La carne y el pescado

el atún	tuna
el bistec	steak
los camarones	shrimp
la carne	meat
la carne de res	beef
la chuleta (de cerdo)	(pork) chop
la hamburguesa	hamburger
el jamón	ham
la langosta	lobster
los mariscos	shellfish
el pavo	turkey
el pescado	fish
el pollo (asado)	(roast) chicken
la salchicha	sausage
el salmón	salmon

Otras comidas

el aceite	oil
el azúcar	sugar
el ajo	garlic
los cereales	cereal; grains
el huevo	egg
la mantequilla	butter
la margarina	margarine
la mayonesa	mayonnaise
el pan (tostado)	(toasted) bread
la pimienta	black pepper
el queso	cheese
la sal	salt
el sándwich	sandwich
la sopa	soup
el vinagre	vinegar
el yogur	yogurt

Bebidas

el agua (mineral)	(mineral) water
la bebida	drink
el café	coffee
la cerveza	beer
el jugo (de fruta)	(fruit) juice
la leche	milk
el refresco	soft drink
el té (helado)	(iced) tea
el vino (blanco/tinto)	(white/red) wine

Verbos

conducir	to drive
conocer	to know; to be acquainted with
ofrecer	to offer
parecer	to seem; to appear
saber	to know; to know how
traducir	to translate
morir (o:ue)	to die

Las comparaciones

como	like; as
más de (+ number)	more than
más… que	more … than
menos de (+ number)	less than
menos… que	less … than
tan… como	as … as
tantos/as… como	as many… as
tanto… como	as much… as
el/la mayor	the oldest
el/la mejor	the best
el/la menor	the youngest
el/la peor	the worst
mejor	better
peor	worse

Palabras adicionales

conmigo	with me
contigo	with you (fam.)
despacio	slowly
rápido/a	quickly; fast

Pronouns after prepositions	See page 234.
Expresiones útiles	See page 215.

recursos

R | LCASS./CD Cass. 8/CD8 | LM p. 247

Las fiestas

9

Communicative Goals

You will learn how to:
- Express congratulations
- Express gratitude
- Ask for and pay the bill at a restaurant

Las fiestas

Más vocabulario

la amistad	friendship
el amor	love
el aniversario de bodas	wedding anniversary
la boda	wedding
el cumpleaños	birthday
el día de fiesta	holiday
el divorcio	divorce
el matrimonio	marriage
la Navidad	Christmas
el/la recién casado/a	newlywed
la quinceañera	young woman's fifteenth birthday celebration
la sorpresa	surprise
cambiar (de)	to change
celebrar	to celebrate
cumplir años	to have a birthday
dejar una propina	to leave a tip
divertirse (e:ie)	to have fun
graduarse (en)	to graduate (from)
invitar	to invite
jubilarse	to retire (from work)
nacer	to be born
odiar	to hate
pagar la cuenta	to pay the bill
pasarlo bien/mal	to have a good/bad time
reírse (e:i)	to laugh
relajarse	to relax
sorprender	to surprise
sonreír (e:i)	to smile
juntos/as	together

Variación léxica

pastel ⟷ torta (*Arg., Venez.*)

comprometerse ⟷ prometerse (*Esp.*)

la pareja

el pastel de chocolate

la botella de vino

el flan de caramelo

las galletas

los postres

el champán

los dulces

 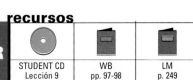

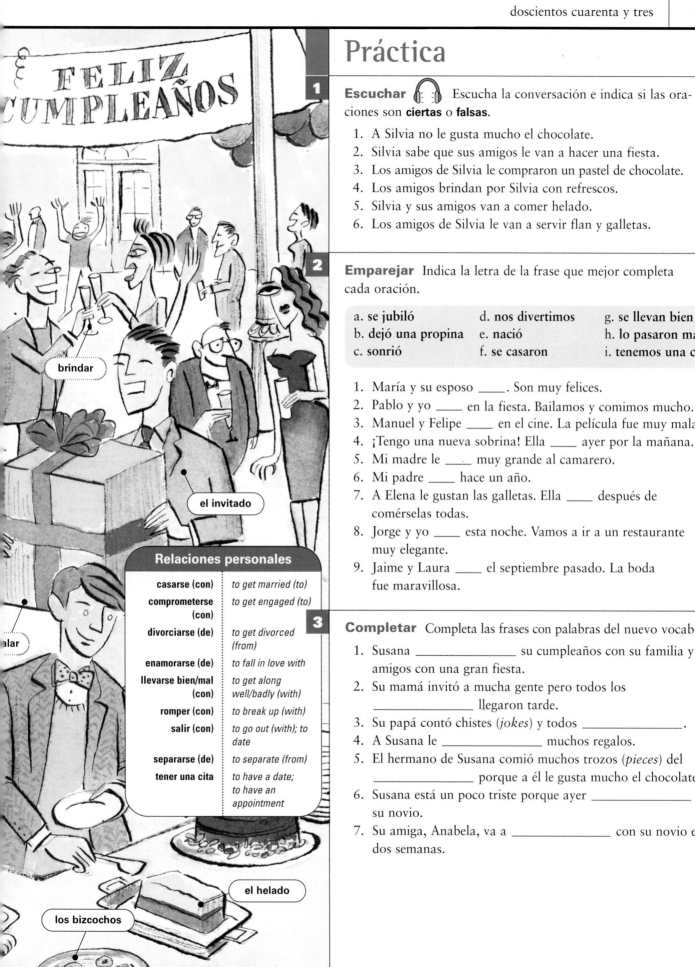

FELIZ CUMPLEAÑOS

brindar

el invitado

Relaciones personales

casarse (con)	*to get married (to)*
comprometerse (con)	*to get engaged (to)*
divorciarse (de)	*to get divorced (from)*
enamorarse (de)	*to fall in love with*
llevarse bien/mal (con)	*to get along well/badly (with)*
romper (con)	*to break up (with)*
salir (con)	*to go out (with); to date*
separarse (de)	*to separate (from)*
tener una cita	*to have a date; to have an appointment*

el helado

los bizcochos

Práctica

1 **Escuchar** Escucha la conversación e indica si las oraciones son **ciertas** o **falsas**.

1. A Silvia no le gusta mucho el chocolate.
2. Silvia sabe que sus amigos le van a hacer una fiesta.
3. Los amigos de Silvia le compraron un pastel de chocolate.
4. Los amigos brindan por Silvia con refrescos.
5. Silvia y sus amigos van a comer helado.
6. Los amigos de Silvia le van a servir flan y galletas.

2 **Emparejar** Indica la letra de la frase que mejor completa cada oración.

a. **se jubiló**	d. **nos divertimos**	g. **se llevan bien**
b. **dejó una propina**	e. **nació**	h. **lo pasaron mal**
c. **sonrió**	f. **se casaron**	i. **tenemos una cita**

1. María y su esposo ____. Son muy felices.
2. Pablo y yo ____ en la fiesta. Bailamos y comimos mucho.
3. Manuel y Felipe ____ en el cine. La película fue muy mala.
4. ¡Tengo una nueva sobrina! Ella ____ ayer por la mañana.
5. Mi madre le ____ muy grande al camarero.
6. Mi padre ____ hace un año.
7. A Elena le gustan las galletas. Ella ____ después de comérselas todas.
8. Jorge y yo ____ esta noche. Vamos a ir a un restaurante muy elegante.
9. Jaime y Laura ____ el septiembre pasado. La boda fue maravillosa.

3 **Completar** Completa las frases con palabras del nuevo vocabulario.

1. Susana _____ su cumpleaños con su familia y sus amigos con una gran fiesta.
2. Su mamá invitó a mucha gente pero todos los _____ llegaron tarde.
3. Su papá contó chistes (*jokes*) y todos _____.
4. A Susana le _____ muchos regalos.
5. El hermano de Susana comió muchos trozos (*pieces*) del _____ porque a él le gusta mucho el chocolate.
6. Susana está un poco triste porque ayer _____ su novio.
7. Su amiga, Anabela, va a _____ con su novio en dos semanas.

Las etapas de la vida de Sergio

el nacimiento

la niñez

la adolescencia

la juventud

la madurez

la vejez

Más vocabulario	
las etapas de la vida	*the stages of life*
la muerte	*death*
el estado civil	*marital status*
casado/a	*married*
divorciado/a	*divorced*
soltero/a	*single*
separado/a	*separated*
viudo/a	*widower/widow*

4

Las etapas de la vida Identifica las etapas de la vida que se describen (*are described*) en las siguientes (*following*) frases.

1. Mi abuela se jubiló y se mudó (*moved*) a Viña del Mar.
2. Mi padre trabaja para una compañía grande en Santiago.
3. ¿Viste a mi nuevo sobrino en el hospital? Es precioso y ¡tan pequeño!
4. Mi abuelo murió este año.
5. Mi hermana se enamoró de un chico nuevo en la escuela.
6. ¿Mi hermano? Tiene 22 años y le encantan los juegos de video.
7. Mi hermana pequeña juega con muñecas (*dolls*).

NOTA CULTURAL

Viña del Mar is a seaside town west of Santiago, Chile. In addition to its wonderful beaches, hotels, casinos, and restaurants, an international song festival takes place there every year.

5

Opuestos Túrnate (*Take turns*) con un(a) compañero/a para decir que sus afirmaciones son falsas y corrígelas usando los opuestos de las expresiones subrayadas.

> **modelo**
>
> **Estudiante 1:** Nuestros amigos <u>lo pasaron mal</u> en la playa.
> **Estudiante 2:** No, te equivocas (*you're wrong*). Ellos lo pasaron bien.

1. Fernando <u>odia</u> a Merche.
2. Rafael <u>se comprometió</u> con Alicia.
3. Nadia <u>se separó</u> de Eduardo, ¿no?
4. La <u>juventud</u> es la etapa de la vida cuando nos jubilamos.
5. El <u>nacimiento</u> es el fin de la vida.
6. A los sesenta y cinco años muchas personas <u>comienzan a trabajar</u>.
7. Julián y Pepi <u>se divorcian</u> mañana.

AYUDA

Other ways to contradict someone:

No es verdad.
It's not true.

Creo que no.
I don't think so.

¡Claro que no!
Of course not!

¡Que va!
¡Go on!

Comunicación

6

Una fiesta Trabaja con dos compañeros/as para planear una fiesta. Recuerda incluir la siguiente información.

1. ¿Qué tipo de fiesta es? ¿Dónde va a ser? ¿Cuándo va a ser?
2. ¿A quiénes van a invitar?
3. ¿Qué van a comer? ¿Quiénes van a llevar o a preparar la comida?
4. ¿Qué van a beber? ¿Quiénes van a llevar las bebidas?
5. ¿Qué van a hacer todos durante la fiesta?

7

Encuesta Tu profesor(a) va a darte (*to give you*) una hoja de actividades. Haz las preguntas de la hoja a dos o tres compañeros/as de clase para saber qué actitudes tienen en sus relaciones personales. Luego comparte los resultados de la encuesta (*survey*) con la clase y comenta tus conclusiones.

¡LENGUA VIVA!

While **a buen/a amigo/a** is a *good friend*, the term **amigo/a íntimo/a** refers to a *close friend*, or a very good friend, without any sexual overtones.

Preguntas	Nombres	Actitudes
1. ¿Te importa la amistad? ¿Por qué?		
2. ¿Es mejor tener un buen amigo/a o muchos amigos/as?		
3. ¿Cuáles son las características que buscas en tus amigos/as?		
4. ¿Tienes novio/a? ¿A qué edad (*age*) es posible enamorarse?		
5. ¿Deben las parejas hacer todas las cosas juntos? ¿Deben tener las mismas opiniones? ¿Por qué?		

8

Una fiesta memorable Cuenta (*Tell*) la historia de una fiesta memorable. La historia debe incluir la siguiente información.

- ¿Qué?
- ¿Dónde?
- ¿Cómo?
- ¿Por qué?
- ¿Cuándo?
- ¿Quién?
- ¿Cuántos?

9

Minidrama En parejas, consulten la ilustración de la página 244, y luego preparen un minidrama para representar (*to act out*) las etapas de la vida de una persona real o imaginaria.

¡Feliz cumpleaños, Maite!

Don Francisco y los estudiantes celebran el cumpleaños de Maite en el restaurante El Cráter.

PERSONAJES

MAITE

INÉS

DON
FRANCISCO

ÁLEX

JAVIER

DOÑA RITA

CAMARERO

INÉS A mí me encantan los dulces. Maite, ¿tú qué vas a pedir?

MAITE Ay, no sé. Todo parece tan delicioso. Quizás el pastel de chocolate.

JAVIER Para mí el pastel de chocolate con helado. Me encanta el chocolate. Y tú Álex, ¿qué vas a pedir?

ÁLEX Generalmente prefiero la fruta, pero hoy creo que voy a probar el pastel de chocolate.

DON FRANCISCO Yo siempre tomo un flan y un café.

DOÑA RITA & CAMARERO ¡Feliz cumpleaños, Maite!

INÉS ¿Hoy es tu cumpleaños, Maite?

MAITE Sí, el 22 de junio. Y parece que vamos a celebrarlo.

TODOS MENOS MAITE ¡Felicidades!

ÁLEX Yo también acabo de cumplir los veintitrés años.

MAITE ¿Cuándo?

ÁLEX El cuatro de mayo.

DOÑA RITA Aquí tienen un flan, pastel de chocolate con helado... y una botella de vino para dar alegría.

MAITE ¡Qué sorpresa! ¡No sé qué decir! Muchísimas gracias.

DON FRANCISCO El conductor no puede tomar vino. Doña Rita, gracias por todo. ¿Puede traernos la cuenta?

DOÑA RITA Enseguida, Paco.

recursos

R

V/VCD-ROM
Lección 9

VM
pp. 307-308

ICD-ROM
Lección 9

MAITE ¡Gracias! Pero, ¿quién le dijo que es mi cumpleaños?

DOÑA RITA Lo supe por don Francisco.

ÁLEX Ayer te lo pregunté, ¡y no quisiste decírmelo! ¿Eh? ¡Qué mala eres!

JAVIER ¿Cuántos años cumples?

MAITE Veintitrés.

INÉS Creo que debemos dejar una buena propina. ¿Qué les parece?

MAITE Sí, vamos a darle una buena propina a la Sra. Perales. Es simpatiquísima.

DON FRANCISCO Gracias una vez más. Siempre lo paso muy bien aquí.

MAITE Muchísimas gracias, Sra. Perales. Por la comida, por la sorpresa y por ser tan amable con nosotros.

Enfoque cultural Las celebraciones hispanas

Las celebraciones de la independencia, los carnavales y la Semana Santa son fiestas importantísimas en los países hispanos. Las fechas de Navidad y Noche Vieja (*New Year's Eve*) son, quizás, las más festejadas (*celebrated*). Otra celebración importante es el santo. Cada día del año tiene un santo asignado, y algunas personas que se llaman igual que el santo del día (*who have the same name as the day's saint*) lo celebran. El 19 de marzo, por ejemplo, los que se llaman José o Josefa celebran el día de San José.

Expresiones útiles

Celebrating a birthday party

▶ **¡Feliz cumpleaños!**
  Happy birthday!
▶ **¡Felicidades!**
  Congratulations! (for an event such as a birthday or anniversary)
▶ **¡Felicitaciones!**
  Congratulations! (for an event such as an engagement or a good grade on a test)

▶ **¿Quién le dijo que es mi cumpleaños?**
  Who told you that it's my birthday?
▷ **Lo supe por don Francisco.**
  I found it out through don Francisco.

▶ **¿Cuántos años cumples/cumple Ud.?**
  How old are you now?
▷ **Veintitrés.**
  Twenty-three.

Asking for and getting the bill

▶ **¿Puede traernos la cuenta?**
  Can you bring us the bill?
▶ **La cuenta, por favor.**
  The bill, please.
▷ **Enseguida, señor/señora/señorita.**
  Right away, sir/ma'am/miss.

Expressing gratitude

▶ **¡(Muchas) gracias!**
  Thank you (very much)!
▶ **Muchísimas gracias.**
  Thank you very, very much.
▶ **Gracias por todo.**
  Thanks for everything.
▶ **Gracias una vez más.**
  Thanks again. (lit. Thanks one more time.)

Leaving a tip

▶ **Creo que debemos dejar una buena propina. ¿Qué les parece?**
  I think we should leave a good tip. What do you guys think?
▷ **Sí, vamos a darle una buena propina.**
  Yes, let's give her a good tip.

Reacciona a la fotonovela

1

Completar Completa las frases con la información correcta, según la fotonovela.

1. De postre, don Francisco siempre pide _____.
2. A Javier le encanta _____.
3. Álex cumplió los _____ años _____.
4. Hoy Álex quiere tomar algo diferente. De postre, quiere pedir _____.
5. Los estudiantes van a dejar _____ a doña Rita.

2

Identificar Identifica quién puede decir las siguientes frases.

1. Gracias, doña Rita, pero no puedo tomar vino.
2. ¡Qué simpática es doña Rita! Fue tan amable conmigo.
3. A mí me encantan los dulces y los pasteles, ¡especialmente si son de chocolate!
4. Mi amigo acaba de informarme que hoy es el cumpleaños de Maite.
5. ¿Tienen algún postre de fruta? Los postres de fruta son los mejores.
6. Me parece una buena idea dejarle una buena propina a la dueña. ¿Qué piensan Uds.?

JAVIER   **ÁLEX**

INÉS   MAITE

DON FRANCISCO   DOÑA RITA

NOTA CULTURAL

Tipping in Latin America and Spain is not as customary as it is in the United States. Since the waitstaff isn't as dependent on tips, only small tips are left. However, it's generally a good idea to tip well when large parties are served or the service is exceptional.

3

Completar Selecciona algunas de las opciones de la lista para completar las frases.

pedir	una botella de vino	la cuenta	el amor
la quinceañera	la galleta	una sorpresa	¡Qué sorpresa!
celebrar	un postre	el divorcio	día de fiesta

1. Maite no sabe que van a celebrar su cumpleaños porque es _____.
2. Cuando una pareja celebra su aniversario y quiere tomar algo especial, compra _____.
3. Después de una cena o un almuerzo, es normal pedir _____.
4. De postre, Inés y Maite no saben exactamente lo que van a _____.
5. Después de comer en un restaurante, tienes que pagar _____.
6. Una pareja de enamorados nunca piensa en _____.
7. Hoy no trabajamos porque es un _____.

CONSÚLTALO

The Latin American version of the debutante party is the **quinceañera**. A party for a girl turning fifteen, it is the moment when she is "presented" to society. To read more, see p. 261.

4

Fiesta sorpresa Trabajen en grupos para representar una conversación en la que uno/a de Uds. está celebrando su cumpleaños en un restaurante. Un(a) amigo/a le desea feliz cumpleaños a su compañero/a y le pregunta cuántos años cumple. Luego, cada uno/a le pide al/a la camarero/a un postre y algo para beber. Después de comerse los postres, un(a) amigo/a pide la cuenta y otro/a habla de dejar una propina. Los dos que no cumplen años dicen que quieren pagar la cuenta y el/la que cumple años les da las gracias por todo.

Pronunciación 🎧

The letters **h**, **j**, and **g**

helado   **hombre**   **hola**   **hermosa**

The Spanish **h** is always silent.

José   **jubilarse**   **dejar**   **pareja**

The letter **j** is pronounced much like the English *h* in *his*.

---

agencia   **general**   **Gil**   **Gisela**

The letter **g** can be pronounced three different ways. Before **e** or **i**, the letter **g** is pronounced much like the English *h*.

Gustavo, gracias por llamar el domingo.

At the beginning of a phrase or after the letter **n**, the Spanish **g** is pronounced like the English *g* in *girl*.

Me gradué en agosto.

In any other position, the Spanish **g** has a somewhat softer sound.

Guerra   **conseguir**   **guantes**   **agua**

In the combinations **gue** and **gui**, the **g** has a hard sound and the **u** is silent. In the combination **gua**, the **g** has a hard sound and the **u** is pronounced like the English *w*.

Práctica   Lee las palabras en voz alta, prestando atención a la **h**, la **j** y la **g**.

1. hamburguesa	5. geografía	9. seguir	13. Jorge
2. jugar	6. magnífico	10. gracias	14. tengo
3. oreja	7. espejo	11. hijo	15. ahora
4. guapa	8. hago	12. galleta	16. guantes

Oraciones   Lee las oraciones en voz alta, prestando atención a la **h**, la **j** y la **g**.

1. Hola. Me llamo Gustavo Hinojosa Lugones y vivo en Santiago de Chile.
2. Tengo una familia grande; somos tres hermanos y tres hermanas.
3. Voy a graduarme en mayo.
4. Para celebrar mi graduación mis padres van a regalarme un viaje a Egipto.
5. ¡Qué generosos son!

Refranes   Lee los refranes en voz alta, prestando atención a la **h**, la **j** y la **g**.

A la larga, lo más dulce amarga.[1]

El hábito no hace al monje.[2]

1 Too much of a good thing.   2 The clothes don't make the man.

recursos

R	STUDENT CD Lección 9	LM p. 250	LCASS./CD Cass. 9/CD 9	ICD-ROM Lección 9

9.1 Dar and decir

		dar *(to give)*	**decir** *(to say; to tell)*
SINGULAR FORMS	yo	**doy**	**digo**
	tú	das	dices
	Ud./él/ella	da	dice
PLURAL FORMS	nosotros/as	damos	decimos
	vosotros/as	dais	decís
	Uds./ellos/ellas	dan	dicen
	present participle	**dando**	**diciendo**

▶ **Dar** and **decir** are both irregular in the first person singular of the present tense. The other forms of **dar** are regular, and those of **decir** follow the pattern of **-ir** stem-changing verbs **(e:i)**.

▶ Both **dar** and **decir** are frequently used with indirect object pronouns, as well as with double object pronouns.

Mis padres **me dan** muchos regalos. ⟶ Mis padres **me los dan**.
My parents give me a lot of gifts. *My parents give them to me.*

Te digo la respuesta. ⟶ **Te la digo.**
I am telling you the answer. *I am telling it to you.*

¡INTÉNTALO! Completa las frases con las formas correctas de los verbos indicados.

dar

1. Mis amigos me __*dan*__ consejos.
2. Graciela y yo le _____ regalos a Miguel.
3. Yo te _____ este libro.
4. Tú les _____ tu dirección electrónica a tus amigos.
5. Mi padre nos _____ dulces.
6. Mis hijos me _____ mucha alegría.

decir

1. Yo siempre te __*digo*__ la verdad.
2. Elena y yo les _____ nuestra dirección.
3. Isabel no nos _____ mentiras.
4. Mis hermanos me _____ todo.
5. Tú les _____ tu número de teléfono.
6. Uds. me _____ la fecha del examen.

Práctica

1

Completar Completa estas conversaciones con la forma correcta de **dar** o **decir**.

HIJO   Papá, ¿me _____ (dar) diez pesos para ir al cine?

PADRE   ¿Qué _____ (decir)? Te _____ (dar) dinero todas las semanas.

         ¿Por qué no se lo pides a tu mamá?

HIJO   Mamá _____ (decir) que no tiene dinero.

SUSANA   Oye, Armando, ¿oíste que Adela _____ (dar) una fiesta de fin de año?

ARMANDO No... ¿a qué hora empieza?

SUSANA   A las ocho. Todos _____ (decir) que va a ser estupenda.

2

Combinar Combina elementos de las tres columnas y agrega (*add*) todas las palabras necesarias para formar frases completas.

> Mis amigos y yo siempre les damos regalos a nuestros profesores.

yo	siempre	dar consejos
tú	nunca	decir la verdad
mi compañero/a		dar fiestas
mi mejor amigo/a		dar alegría
Mis amigos y yo		decir mentiras
Mis padres		dar regalos

Comunicación

3

Preguntas En parejas, túrnense para hacerse estas preguntas.

1. ¿Te dan tus profesores mucha tarea? ¿Qué dices cuando te la dan?
2. ¿Les dan los profesores muchos exámenes a los estudiantes?
3. ¿Das una fiesta este fin de semana? ¿Sabes quiénes dan una fiesta?
4. ¿Te gusta dar fiestas? ¿Por qué sí o no?
5. ¿Les das regalos a todos tus amigos? ¿Cuándo les das regalos y por qué?
6. ¿Qué dices cuando alguien te da un regalo?
7. ¿Tus padres te dan muchos consejos? ¿Qué te dicen? ¿Siempres sigues sus consejos?
8. ¿Qué otras personas te dan consejos? ¿Te dan consejos buenos o malos?
9. ¿A quiénes das consejos?
10. ¿Quiénes te dan dinero? ¿Por qué te lo dan?
11. ¿Les das dinero a tus amigos? ¿Por qué sí o por qué no?
12. ¿Siempre les dices la verdad a tus amigos? ¿Y a tus profesores?

4

Debate En grupos, comenten estos temas (*topics*). Hagan una lista de las razones (*reasons*) que tienen para defender sus opiniones en cada caso e informen a la clase.

▶ ¿Es mejor decir siempre la verdad?

▶ ¿Es mejor dar regalos o recibirlos?

9.2 Irregular preterites

ANTE TODO   You already know that the verbs **ir** and **ser** are irregular in the preterite. You will now learn other verbs whose preterite forms are also irregular.

Preterite of *tener, venir* and *decir*

		tener (e → u)	**venir** (e → i)	**decir** (e → i)
SINGULAR FORMS	yo	tuv**e**	vin**e**	dij**e**
	tú	tuv**iste**	vin**iste**	dij**iste**
	Ud./él/ella	tuv**o**	vin**o**	dij**o**
PLURAL FORMS	nosotros/as	tuv**imos**	vin**imos**	dij**imos**
	vosotros/as	tuv**isteis**	vin**isteis**	dij**isteis**
	Uds./ellos/ellas	tuv**ieron**	vin**ieron**	dij**eron**

▶ In the chart above, observe how the conjugations of these verbs show a stem change. The **e** in **tener** changes to **u**, the **e** in **venir** and **decir** changes to **i**, and the **c** in **decir** changes to **j**.

▶ The following verbs observe similar stem-changes to **tener, venir** and **decir**.

INFINITIVE	U-STEM	PRETERITE FORMS
poder	pud-	pude, pudiste, pudo, pudimos, pudisteis, pudieron
poner	pus-	puse, pusiste, puso, pusimos, pusisteis, pusieron
saber	sup-	supe, supiste, supo, supimos, supisteis, supieron
estar	estuv-	estuve, estuviste, estuvo, estuvimos, estuvisteis, estuvieron

INFINITIVE	I-STEM	PRETERITE FORMS
querer	quis-	quise, quisiste, quiso, quisimos, quisisteis, quisieron
hacer	hic-	hice, hiciste, hizo, hicimos, hicisteis, hicieron

INFINITIVE	J-STEM	PRETERITE FORMS
traer	traj-	traje, trajiste, trajo, trajimos, trajisteis, trajeron
conducir	conduj-	conduje, condujiste, condujo, condujimos, condujisteis, condujeron
traducir	traduj-	traduje, tradujiste, tradujo, tradujimos, tradujisteis, tradujeron

¡ATENCIÓN!

The endings of these verbs are the regular preterite endings of **–er/–ir** verbs, except for the **yo** and **Ud.** forms. Note that these two endings are unaccented.

• • •

The verbs with **j**-stems omit the letter **i** in the **Uds.** form. For example, **tener → tuvieron**, but **decir → dijeron**. Most verbs that end in **–cir** are **j**-stem verbs in the preterite. For example, **producir → produje, produjiste,** etc.

¿**Dijiste** larga distancia?

En tarjetas prepagadas ninguna te da más minutos para hablar

The preterite of *dar*

yo	d**i**		nosotros/as	d**imos**
tú	d**iste**		vosotros/as	d**isteis**
Ud./él/ella	d**io**		Uds./ellos/ellas	d**ieron**

SINGULAR FORMS — PLURAL FORMS

▶ The endings for **dar** are the same as the regular preterite endings for **–er** and **–ir** verbs, except that there are no accent marks.

La camarera me **dio** el menú.
The waiter gave me the menu.

Le **di** a Juan algunos consejos.
I gave Juan some advice.

Los invitados le **dieron** un regalo.
The guests gave him/her a gift.

Nosotros **dimos** una gran fiesta.
We gave a great party.

▶ The preterite of **hay** (*inf.* **haber**) is **hubo** *(there was; there were)*.

CONSÚLTALO

Note that there are other ways to say *there was* or *there were* in Spanish. See Lesson 10, pp. 276-277.

Doña Rita les dio una botella de vino a los viajeros.

Hubo una fiesta en el restaurante El Cráter.

¡INTÉNTALO! Escribe en cada espacio en blanco la forma correcta en pretérito del verbo que está entre paréntesis.

1. (querer) tú _quisiste_
2. (decir) Ud. _____
3. (hacer) nosotras _____
4. (traer) yo _____
5. (conducir) ellas _____
6. (estar) ella _____
7. (tener) tú _____
8. (dar) ella y yo _____
9. (traducir) yo _____
10. (haber) ayer _____
11. (saber) Ud. _____
12. (poner) ellos _____

13. (venir) yo _vine_
14. (poder) tú _____
15. (querer) Uds. _____
16. (estar) nosotras _____
17. (decir) tú _____
18. (saber) ellos _____
19. (hacer) él _____
20. (poner) yo _____
21. (traer) nosotras _____
22. (tener) yo _____
23. (dar) tú _____
24. (poder) Uds. _____

Práctica

1

Completar Completa estas frases con el pretérito de los verbos entre paréntesis.

1. El sábado _____ (haber) una fiesta sorpresa para Elsa en mi casa.
2. Sofía _____ (hacer) un pastel para la fiesta y Miguel _____ (traer) un flan.
3. Los amigos y parientes de Elsa _____ (venir) y _____ (traer) regalos.
4. El hermano de Elsa no _____ (venir) porque _____ (tener) que trabajar.
5. Su tía María Dolores tampoco _____ (poder) venir.
6. Cuando Elsa abrió la puerta, todos gritaron (*shouted*): "¡Feliz cumpleaños!" y su esposo le _____ (dar) un beso.
7. Al final de la fiesta, todos _____ (decir) que se divirtieron mucho.
8. La fiesta le _____ (dar) a Elsa tanta alegría que no _____ (poder) dormir esa noche.

NOTA CULTURAL

A very popular dessert in Spanish-speaking countries, **flan** is a gelatinous custard made with eggs and topped with a caramel sauce. Delicious variations exist made with fruit or cheese.

2

Describir Usa los verbos apropiados para describir lo que estas personas hicieron.

dar	hacer	venir	traducir
estar	poner	tener	traer

1. El Sr. López

2. Norma

3. Anoche nosotros

4. Roberto y Elena

Comunicación

3

Preguntas En parejas, túrnense para hacerse estas preguntas.

1. ¿Qué hiciste anoche?
2. Y tu compañero/a, ¿qué hizo?
3. ¿Quiénes no estuvieron en clase la semana pasada?
4. ¿Qué trajiste a clase hoy?
5. ¿Hiciste la tarea para esta clase? ¿Cuándo la hiciste? ¿Se la diste al/a la profesor(a)?
6. ¿Hubo una fiesta en tu casa o residencia el sábado pasado?
7. ¿Alguien te dio una fiesta de cumpleaños el año pasado? ¿Quién?
8. ¿Cuándo fue la última (*last*) vez que tus parientes vinieron a visitarte? ¿Te trajeron algo? ¿Qué te trajeron?
9. ¿Les diste a tus padres un regalo para su aniversario? ¿Qué les regalaste?
10. ¿Le dijiste una mentira (*lie*) a tu novio/a o esposo/a la semana pasada?

4

Encuesta Tu profesor(a) va a darte una hoja de actividades. Circula por la clase y haz preguntas hasta que encuentres a alguien que corresponda a cada descripción de la lista. Luego informa a la clase de los resultados de tu encuesta.

Descripciones	Nombres
1. Tuvo un examen ayer.	
2. Trajo dulces a clase.	
3. Condujo su carro a clase.	
4. Estuvo en la biblioteca ayer.	
5. Dio consejos a alguien ayer.	
6. No pudo levantarse esta mañana.	
7. Hizo un viaje a un país hispano en el verano.	
8. Tuvo una cita anoche.	
9. Fue a una fiesta el fin de semana pasado.	
10. Tuvo que trabajar el sábado pasado.	

Síntesis

5

Conversación Trabaja con un(a) compañero/a para comparar cómo celebraron Uds. el Día de Acción de Gracias (*Thanksgiving Day*) en casa el año pasado. Incluyan la siguiente información en la conversación.

▶ Cuál fue el menú

▶ Quiénes vinieron a la comida y quiénes no pudieron venir

▶ Quiénes prepararon la comida o trajeron algo

▶ Si Uds. tuvieron que preparar algo

▶ Lo que la gente hizo antes y después de comer

9.3 Verbs that change meaning in the preterite

 **ANTE TODO**   The verbs **conocer, saber, poder,** and **querer** change meanings when used in the preterite. Because of this, each of them corresponds to more than one verb in English.

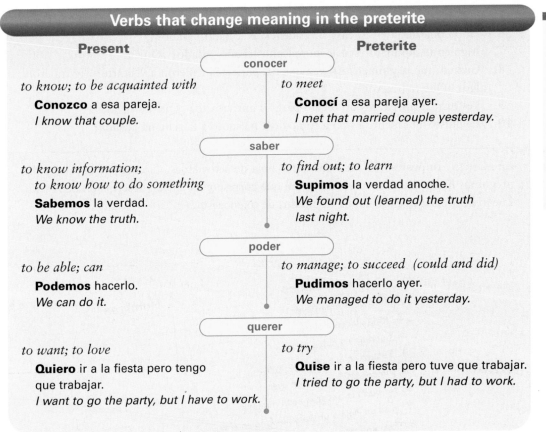

Verbs that change meaning in the preterite

Present   **Preterite**

conocer

to know; to be acquainted with   *to meet*

Conozco a esa pareja.   **Conocí** a esa pareja ayer.
I know that couple.   *I met that married couple yesterday.*

saber

to know information;   *to find out; to learn*
to know how to do something

Sabemos la verdad.   **Supimos** la verdad anoche.
We know the truth.   *We found out (learned) the truth last night.*

poder

to be able; can   *to manage; to succeed (could and did)*

Podemos hacerlo.   **Pudimos** hacerlo ayer.
We can do it.   *We managed to do it yesterday.*

querer

to want; to love   *to try*

Quiero ir a la fiesta pero tengo   **Quise** ir a la fiesta pero tuve que trabajar.
que trabajar.   *I tried to go the party, but I had to work.*
I want to go the party, but I have to work.

> **¡ATENCIÓN!**
>
> In the preterite, the verbs **poder** and **querer** have different meanings, depending on whether they are used in affirmative or negative sentences.
>
> **pude** *I was able (to)*
> **no pude** *I failed (to)*
> **quise** *I tried (to)*
> **no quise** *I refused (to)*

¡INTÉNTALO!   Cambia los verbos del presente al pretérito.

1. No quiero hacerlo.
   No <u>quise</u> hacerlo.

2. ¿Sabes la respuesta?
   ¿ _____ la respuesta?

3. Las chicas pueden divertirse.
   Las chicas _____ divertirse.

4. ¿Conoces a los recién casados?
   ¿ _____ a los recién casados?

5. No puedo encontrar a Patricia.
   No _____ encontrar a Patricia.

6. Josefina quiere relajarse.
   Josefina _____ relajarse.

7. Conocemos a Julio.
   _____ a Julio hoy.

8. Ella no puede venir a la fiesta.
   Ella no _____ venir a la fiesta.

9. Queremos pasarlo bien.
   _____ pasarlo bien.

10. Uds. saben del problema, ¿no?
    Uds. _____ del problema, ¿no?

11. No queremos ir a la fiesta.
    No _____ ir a la fiesta.

12. Puedes venir conmigo
    _____ venir conmigo.

Práctica

NOTA CULTURAL

Easter Island, or **Isla de Pascua,** is a remote Chilean territory located in the South Pacific. The immense statues found there are one of the world's greatest mysteries: no one knows how or why they were built. To learn more, see p. 265.

1

Oraciones Forma frases con los siguientes elementos. Usa el pretérito.

1. Anoche / nosotros / saber / que / Carlos y Eva / divorciarse

2. Tú / conocer / Nora / clase / historia / ¿no?

3. ¿Poder / Uds. / visitar / Isla de Pascua?

4. Ayer / yo / saber / que / Paco / querer / romper / Olivia

5. El señor Navarro / querer / jubilarse / pero / no poder

6. Gustavo y Elena / conocer / mi esposo / quinceañera

7. Yolanda / no poder / dormir / anoche

8. Irma / saber / que / nosotros / comer / galletas

Comunicación

2

Completar Completa estas frases de una manera lógica.

1. Ayer mi compañero/a de cuarto supo…
2. Esta mañana no pude…
3. Conocí a mi mejor amigo/a en…
4. Mis padres no quisieron…
5. Mi mejor amigo/a no pudo…
6. Mi novio/a y yo nos conocimos en…
7. La semana pasada supe…
8. Ayer mis amigos quisieron…

3

Telenovela *(Soap opera)* En parejas, escriban el diálogo para una escena de una telenovela. La escena trata de *(is about)* una situación amorosa entre tres personas: Mirta, Daniel y Raúl. Usen el pretérito de **conocer, poder, querer** y **saber** en su diálogo.

Síntesis

4

Conversación En una hoja de papel, escribe dos listas: las cosas que hiciste durante el fin de semana y las cosas que quisiste hacer pero no pudiste. Luego, tu un(a) compañero/a, comparen sus listas y expliquen por qué no pudieron hacer esas cosas.

9.4 ¿Qué? and ¿cuál?

ANTE TODO You've already learned how to use interrogative words and phrases. As you know, **¿qué?** and **¿cuál?** or **¿cuáles?** mean *what?* or *which?* However, they are not interchangeable.

▶ **¿Qué?** is used to ask for a definition or an explanation.

¿Qué es el flan?
What is flan?

¿Qué estudias?
What do you study?

▶ **¿Cuál(es)?** is used when there is a choice among several possibilities.

¿Cuál quieres, el más corto
o el más largo?
*Which (one) do you want,
the shortest or the longest?*

¿Cuáles son tus medias,
las negras o las blancas?
*Which ones are your socks,
the black ones or the white ones?*

▶ **¿Cuál?** cannot be used before a noun; in this case, **¿qué?** is used.

¿Cuál es tu color favorito?
What is your favorite color?

¿Qué colores te gustan?
What colors do you like?

▶ **¿Qué?** used before a noun has the same meaning as **¿cuál?**

¿Qué regalo te gusta?
What (Which) gift do you like?

¿Qué dulces quieren Uds.?
What (Which) sweets do you want?

Interrogative words and phrases

¿a qué hora?	*at what time?*	**¿cuánto/a?**	*how much?*
¿adónde?	*(to) where?*	**¿cuántos/as?**	*how many?*
¿cómo?	*how?*	**¿de dónde?**	*from where?*
¿cuál(es)?	*what?; which?*	**¿dónde?**	*where?*
¿cuándo?	*when?*	**¿qué?**	*what?; which?*
		¿quién(es)?	*who?*

¡INTÉNTALO! Completa las preguntas con **¿qué?** o **¿cuál(es)?**, según el contexto.

1. ¿ _____Cuál_____ de los dos te gusta más?
2. ¿ _____ es tu teléfono?
3. ¿ _____ tipo de pastel pediste?
4. ¿ _____ es una quinceañera?
5. ¿ _____ haces ahora?
6. ¿ _____ son tus platos favoritos?
7. ¿ _____ bebidas te gustan más?
8. ¿ _____ es esto?
9. ¿ _____ es el mejor?
10. ¿ _____ es tu opinión?

11. ¿ _____ fiestas celebras tú?
12. ¿ _____ vino prefieres?
13. ¿ _____ es tu clase favorita?
14. ¿ _____ pones en la mesa?
15. ¿ _____ restaurante prefieres?
16. ¿ _____ estudiantes estudian más?
17. ¿ _____ quieres comer esta noche?
18. ¿ _____ es la tarea para mañana?
19. ¿ _____ color prefieres?
20. ¿ _____ opinas?

Práctica

1

Completar Completa estas frases con una palabra interrogativa. Luego, túrnate con un(a) compañero/a para hacer y contestar las preguntas. **¡Ojo!** A veces se puede usar más de una palabra interrogativa.

1. ¿En _____ país nacieron tus padres?
2. ¿_____ es la fecha de tu cumpleaños?
3. ¿_____ naciste?
4. ¿_____ es tu estado civil?
5. ¿_____ te relajas?
6. ¿_____ son tus programas favoritos de la televisión?
7. ¿_____ es tu mejor amigo?
8. ¿_____ van tus amigos para divertirse?
9. ¿_____ postres te gustan? ¿_____ te gusta más?
10. ¿_____ problemas tuviste el primer día de clase?

Comunicación

2

Una invitación En parejas, lean esta invitación. Luego, túrnense para hacerse preguntas basadas en la información de la invitación.

Fernando Sandoval Valera   Lorenzo Vásquez Amaral
Isabel Arzipe de Sandoval   Elena Soto de Vásquez
tienen el agrado de invitarlos
a la boda de sus hijos
María Luisa y José Antonio
La ceremonia religiosa tendrá lugar
el sábado 10 de junio a las dos de la tarde
en el Templo de Santo Domingo
(Calle Santo Domingo, 961).
Después de la ceremonia sírvase pasar a la recepción en el salón
de baile del Hotel Metrópoli (Sotero del Río, 465).

3

Situación Trabaja con un(a) compañero/a. Una persona va a ser el/la director(a) de banquetes del Hotel Metrópoli. La otra persona es el padre o la madre de María Luisa, quien quiere hacer los arreglos (*plans*) para una recepción después de la boda de su hija. Su profesor(a) va a darles hojas de actividades para la situación.

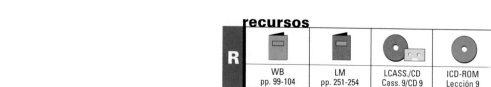

recursos			
R	WB pp. 99-104	LM pp. 251-254	LCASS./CD Cass. 9/CD 9	ICD-ROM Lección 9

Lectura

Antes de leer

Estrategia
Recognizing word families

Recognizing root words can help you guess the meaning of words in context, ensuring better comprehension of a reading selection. Using this strategy will enrich your Spanish vocabulary as well.

Examinar el texto

Familiarízate con el texto usando las estrategias de lectura más efectivas para ti. ¿Qué tipo de documento es? ¿De qué tratan las cuatro secciones del documento? Explica tus respuestas.

Raíces

Completa el siguiente cuadro para ampliar tu vocabulario. Usa palabras de la lectura de esta lección y el vocabulario de las lecciones anteriores. ¿Qué significan las palabras que escribiste en el cuadro?

modelo

Verbo	Sustantivos	Otras formas
agradecer	agradecimiento/ gracias	agradecido

1. estudiar	———	———
2. ———		celebrado
3. ———	baile	———
4. bautizar	———	———

¿De qué tratan...? *What are they about?* Raíces *Roots* cuadro *chart*

Vida social

Matrimonio
Espinoza Álvarez-Reyes Salazar

El día sábado 30 de octubre de 2000 a las 19 horas, se celebró el matrimonio de Silvia Reyes y Carlos Espinoza en la Catedral de Santiago. La ceremonia fue oficiada por el pastor Federico Salas y participaron los padres de los novios, el señor Jorge Espinoza y señora, y el señor José Alfredo Reyes y señora.

Después de la ceremonia, los padres de los recién casados ofrecieron una fiesta con baile en el restaurante Doña Mercedes.

Bautismo

José María recibió el bautismo el 30 de septiembre de 2000.

Sus padres, don Roberto Lagos Moreno y doña María Angélica Sánchez, compartieron la alegría de la fiesta con todos sus parientes y amigos. La ceremonia religiosa se realizó en la Catedral de Aguas Blancas. Después de la ceremonia, padres, parientes y amigos celebraron una fiesta en la residencia de la familia Lagos.

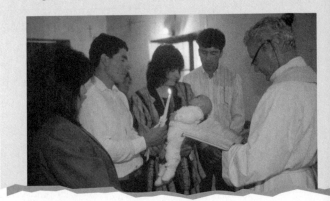

Fiesta quinceañera

32B

El médico don Amador Larenas Fernández y la señora Felisa Vera de Larenas celebraron los quince años de su hija Ana Ester junto a sus parientes y amigos. La quinceañera tiene su residencia en la ciudad de La Paz y es estudiante del Colegio Francés. La fiesta de presentación en sociedad de la señorita Ana Ester fue el día viernes 24 de mayo a las 19 horas en el Club Español. Entre los invitados especiales se encontraron el alcalde de la ciudad, don Pedro Castedo y su esposa. La música estuvo a cargo de la Orquesta Americana. ¡Feliz cumpleaños! le deseamos a la señorita Ana Ester en su fiesta bailable.

Expresión de Gracias
Carmen Godoy Tapia

Agradecemos sinceramente a todas las personas que nos acompañaron en el último adiós de nuestra apreciada esposa, madre, abuela y tía, la señora Carmen Godoy Tapia. El funeral tuvo lugar el día 28 de abril de 2000 en la ciudad de Capri. La vida de Carmen Godoy fue un ejemplo de trabajo, amistad, alegría y amor para todos nosotros. La familia agradece de todo corazón a todos los parientes y amigos su asistencia al funeral.
Su esposo, hijos y familia.

será *will be* **ofrecerán** *will throw* **alcalde** *mayor* **tuvo lugar** *took place* **agradecemos** *we thank* **de todo corazón** *sincerely* **asistencia** *attendance*

Después de leer

Corregir
Escribe estos comentarios otra vez para corregir la información errónea.

1. El alcalde y su esposa asistieron a la boda de Silvia y Carlos.

2. Todos los anuncios tratan de eventos felices.

3. Ana Ester Larenas cumple dieciséis años.

4. Amador Larenas y Felisa Vera son hermanos.

5. Carmen Godoy Tapia agradeció a las personas que asistieron al funeral.

Identificar
Escribe el nombre de la(s) persona(s) descrita(s).

1. Dejó viudo a su esposo en la primavera de 2000.

2. Sus padres y todos los invitados brindaron por él, pero él no entendió por qué.

3. El Club Español les presentó una cuenta considerable para pagar.

4. Unió a los novios en santo matrimonio.

5. La celebración de su cumpleaños marcó el principio de su vida adulta.

Un anuncio
Trabaja con dos o tres compañeros/as de clase e inventen un anuncio breve sobre una celebración importante. Esta celebración puede ser una graduación, un matrimonio o una gran fiesta en la que Uds. participan. Incluyan la siguiente información.

1. Nombres de los participantes
2. La fecha, la hora y la dirección
3. Otros detalles de interés

anuncios *announcements* **tratan de** *have to do with* **agradeció** *thanked* **descritas** *described* **Unió** *He united* **principio** *beginning*

Escritura

Estrategia
Using a dictionary

A common mistake made by beginning language learners is to embrace the dictionary as the ultimate resource for reading, writing, and speaking. While it is true that the dictionary is a useful tool that can provide valuable information about vocabulary, using the dictionary correctly requires that you understand the elements of each entry.

If you glance at a Spanish-English dictionary, you will notice that its format is similar to that of an English dictionary. The word is listed first, usually followed by its pronunciation. Then come the definitions, organized by parts of speech. Sometimes the most frequently used definitions are listed first.

To find the best word for your needs, you should refer to the abbreviations and the explanatory notes that appear next to the entries. For example, imagine that you are writing about your pastimes. You want to write, "I want to buy a new racket for my match tomorrow," but you don't know the Spanish word for "racket." In the dictionary, you may find an entry like this:

> **racket** s 1. alboroto; 2. raqueta (*dep.*)

The abbreviation key at the front of the dictionary says that *s* corresponds to **sustantivo** (*noun*). Then, the first word you see is **alboroto**. The definition of **alboroto** is *noise* or *racket*, so **alboroto** is probably not the word you're looking for. The second word is **raqueta,** followed by the abbreviation *dep.*, which stands for **deportes**. This indicates that the word **raqueta** is the best choice for your needs.

Tema

Escribir una composición

Compara una celebración familiar (como una boda o una fiesta de cumpleaños o una graduación) a la que tú asististe recientemente con otro tipo de celebración. Utiliza palabras y expresiones de la siguiente lista.

Para expresar similitudes

además, también	*also*
al igual que	*the same as*
como	*as; like*
de la misma manera	*in the same manner (way)*
del mismo modo	*in the same manner (way)*
tan + *adjetivo* + como	*as + adjective + as*
tanto/a(s) + *sustantivo* + como	*as many (much) + noun + as*

Para expresar diferencias

a diferencia de	*unlike*
a pesar de	*in spite of*
aunque	*although*
en cambio	*on the other hand*
más/menos... que	*more/less ... than*
no obstante	*nevertheless; however*
por otro lado	*on the other hand*
por el contrario	*on the other hand*
sin embargo	*nevertheless; however*

Escuchar
Preparación

Lee la invitación. ¿De qué crees que van a hablar Rosa y Josefina?

Estrategia

Guessing the meaning of words through context

When you hear an unfamiliar word, you can often guess its meaning by listening to the words and phrases around it. To practice this strategy, you will now listen to a paragraph. Jot down the unfamiliar words that you hear. Then listen to the paragraph again and jot down the word or words that are the most useful clues to the meaning of each unfamiliar word.

Margarita Robles de García
y Roberto García Olmos

Piden su presencia en la celebración
del segundo aniversario de bodas
el día 13 de marzo de 2001
con una misa en la Iglesia Virgen del Coromoto
a las 6:30

seguida por cena y baile
en el restaurante El Campanero,
Calle Principal, Las Mercedes
a las 8:30

 ## Ahora escucha

Ahora escucha la conversación entre Josefina y Rosa. Cuando oigas una de las palabras de la columna A, usa el contexto para identificar el sinónimo o la definición en la columna B.

A

____ **festejar**
____ **dicha**
____ **bien parecido**
____ **finge (fingir)**
____ **soporta (soportar)**
____ **yo lo disfruté (disfrutar)**

B

a. conmemoración religiosa de una muerte
b. tolera
c. suerte
d. celebrar
e. me divertí
f. horror
g. crea una ficción
h. guapo

Comprensión

¿Cierto o falso?

Lee cada frase e indica si lo que dice es **cierto** o **falso**. Corrige las frases falsas.

1. A la fiesta de Margarita y Roberto no fueron tantos invitados porque Margarita y Roberto no conocen a mucha gente.

2. Algunos fueron a la fiesta con una pareja y otros fueron sin compañero/a.

3. Margarita y Roberto decidieron celebrar el segundo aniversario porque no celebraron el matrimonio con una fiesta.

4. A Rosa y a Josefina les parece interesante Rafael.

5. Josefina se divirtió mucho en la fiesta porque bailó toda la noche con Rafael.

Preguntas

1. ¿Son solteras Rosa y Josefina? ¿Cómo lo sabes?

2. ¿Tienen las chicas una amistad de mucho tiempo con la pareja que celebra su aniversario? ¿Cómo lo sabes?

recursos

R | STUDENT CD Lección 9

Chile

El país en cifras

- **Área:** 756.950 km^2 (292.259 millas^2), *dos veces el área de Montana*
- **Población:** 15.589.000 *Aproximadamente el 80 por ciento de la población es urbana, y la tercera parte de los chilenos vive en la capital.*
- **Capital:** Santiago de Chile—5.720.000
- **Ciudades principales:** Concepción—356.000, Viña del Mar—326.000, Valparaíso—283.000, Temuco—246.000

SOURCE: Population Division, UN Secretariat

- **Moneda:** peso chileno
- **Idiomas:** español (oficial), mapuche

Bandera de Chile

Chilenos célebres

- Bernardo O'Higgins, militar y héroe nacional (1778-1842)
- Gabriela Mistral, poeta y diplomática (1889-1957)
- Pablo Neruda, poeta (1904-1973)
- Isabel Allende, novelista (1942-)

Pablo Neruda

la tercera parte *a third*   militar *soldier*   el terremoto *earthquake*
heridas *wounded*   hogar *home*

Pescadores de Valparaíso

PERÚ

Pampa del Tamarugal

Cordillera de los Andes

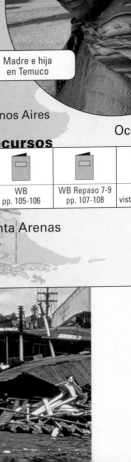
Palacio de la Moneda en Santiago

BOLIVIA

Una calle de Santiago

Océano Pacífico

Valparaíso   Viña del Mar

★ Santiago de Chile   ARGENTINA

Río Maipo

Vista de la costa de Viña del Mar

Concepción

Temuco

Madre e hija en Temuco

Lago Buenos Aires

Océano Atlántico

recursos

R

| WB pp. 105-106 | WB Repaso 7-9 pp. 107-108 | vistasonline.com | ICD-RO Lección |

Estrecho de Magallanes

Punta Arenas

Isla Grande de Tierra del Fuego

¡Increíble pero cierto!

El terremoto más grande de la historia tuvo lugar en Chile el 22 de mayo de 1960. Registró la intensidad récord de 9.5 en la escala de Richter. 2.000 personas murieron, 3.000 resultaron heridas, 2.000.000 perdieron su hogar y la geografía del país se modificó notablemente.

Lugares • **La Isla de Pascua**

La Isla de Pascua recibió ese nombre porque los exploradores holandeses llegaron a la isla por primera vez el día de Pascua de 1722. Ahora es parte del territorio de Chile. La Isla de Pascua es famosa por los *moai*, estatuas enormes que representan personas con rasgos muy exagerados. Estas estatuas las construyeron los *rapa nui*, los antiguos habitantes de la zona. En la actualidad no se sabe mucho sobre los *rapa nui* ni tampoco se sabe por qué decidieron abandonar la isla.

Deportes • **Los deportes de invierno**

Hay muchos lugares para practicar los deportes de invierno en Chile porque las montañas nevadas de los Andes ocupan gran parte del país. El Parque Nacional de Villarrica, por ejemplo, situado al pie de un volcán y junto a un lago, es un sitio popular para el esquí y el *snowboard*. Para los que prefieren deportes más extremos, el centro de esquí Valle Nevado ofrece el heli-esquí.

Ciencias • **Astronomía**

Los observatorios chilenos, situados en los Andes, son lugares excelentes para las observaciones astronómicas. Científicos de todo el mundo van a Chile para estudiar las estrellas y otros fenómenos de la galaxia. Hoy día Chile está construyendo observatorios y telescopios nuevos que darán imágenes aún más nítidas del universo.

Economía • **El vino**

La producción de vino comenzó en Chile en el siglo XVI. Ahora la industria del vino constituye una parte importante de la actividad agrícola del país y la exportación de sus productos ha subido mucho en los últimos años. Los vinos chilenos reciben el aprecio internacional por su gran variedad, sus ricos y complejos sabores y su precio moderado. Los más conocidos internacionalmente son los vinos de Aconcagua, de Santiago y de Huasco.

¿Qué aprendiste? Responde a las preguntas con una frase completa.

1. ¿Qué porcentaje (*percentage*) de la población chilena es urbana?

2. ¿Qué son los *moai*? ¿Dónde están?

3. ¿Qué deporte extremo se practica (*is practiced*) en el centro de esquí Valle Nevado?

4. ¿Por qué van a Chile científicos de todo el mundo?

5. ¿Cuándo comenzó la producción de vino en Chile?

6. ¿Por qué reciben los vinos chilenos el aprecio internacional?

Conexión Internet Investiga estos temas en el sitio **www.vistasonline.com**.

1. Busca información sobre Pablo Neruda e Isabel Allende. ¿Dónde y cuándo nacieron? ¿Cuáles son algunas de sus obras (*works*)? ¿Cuáles son algunos de los temas de sus obras?

2. Busca información sobre sitios donde los chilenos y los turistas practican deportes de invierno en Chile. Selecciona un sitio y descríbelo a tu clase.

La Isla de Pascua *Easter Island*   **holandeses** *Dutch*   **rasgos** *features*   **no se sabe mucho** *not much is known*   **junto a** *beside*   **lago** *lake*
los que *those who*   **Científicos** *Scientists*   **estrellas** *stars*   **Hoy día** *Currently*   **darán imágenes aún más nítidas** *will yield even clearer images*
siglo *century*   **ha subido** *has gone up*   **últimos años** *recent years*   **complejos sabores** *complex flavors*

Celebraciones

el aniversario (de bodas)	(wedding) anniversary
la boda	wedding
el cumpleaños	birthday
el día de fiesta	holiday
la fiesta	party
el/la invitado/a	guest
la Navidad	Christmas
la quinceañera	young woman's fifteenth birthday celebration
la sorpresa	surprise
brindar	to toast (drink)
celebrar	to celebrate
cumplir años	to have a birthday
dejar una propina	to leave a tip
divertirse (e:ie)	to have fun
invitar	to invite
pagar la cuenta	to pay the bill
pasarlo bien (mal)	to have a good (bad) time
regalar	to give (as a gift)
reírse (e:i)	to laugh
relajarse	to relax
sonreír (e:i)	to smile
sorprender	to surprise

Postres y otras comidas

el bizcocho	biscuit
la botella (de vino)	bottle (of wine)
el champán	champagne
los dulces	sweets; candy
el flan (de caramelo)	baked (caramel) custard
la galleta	cookie
el helado	ice cream
el pastel (de chocolate)	(chocolate) cake; pie
el pastel de cumpleaños	birthday cake
el postre	dessert

Relaciones personales

la amistad	friendship
el amor	love
el divorcio	divorce
el estado civil	marital status
el matrimonio	marriage
la pareja	(married) couple; partner
el/la recién casado/a	newlywed
el/la viudo/a	widower/widow
casarse (con)	to get married (to)
comprometerse (con)	to get engaged (to)
divorciarse (de)	to get divorced (from)
enamorarse (de)	to fall in love (with)
llevarse bien/mal (con)	to get along well/ badly (with)
odiar	to hate
romper (con)	to break up (with)
salir (con)	to go out (with); to date
separarse (de)	to separate (from)
tener una cita	to have a date; to have an appointment
casado/a	married
divorciado/a	divorced
juntos/as	together
separado/a	separated
soltero/a	single; unmarried

Palabras adicionales

la alegría	joy
el apellido	last name
el beso	kiss
el consejo	(a piece of) advice
la mentira	lie
la respuesta	answer
la verdad	truth

Las etapas de la vida

la adolescencia	adolescence
la etapa	stage; step
la juventud	youth
la madurez	maturity; middle age
la muerte	death
el nacimiento	birth
la niñez	childhood
la vejez	old age
la vida	life
cambiar (de)	to change
graduarse (en)	to graduate (from)
jubilarse	to retire (from work)
nacer	to be born

Verbos

dar	to give
decir (que)	to say (that); to tell (that)

Expresiones útiles	See page 247.

recursos

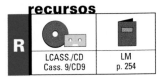

R	LCASS./CD Cass. 9/CD9	LM p. 254

En el consultorio

10

En el consultorio

el corazón

el paciente

el ojo

la nariz

la doctora

la cabeza

la oreja

el cuello

la boca

la garganta

el estómago

el dedo

la rodilla

la pierna

SALIDA

Más vocabulario

el accidente	accident
la clínica	clinic
el consultorio	doctor's office
el cuerpo	body
el/la dentista	dentist
el examen médico	physical exam
la farmacia	pharmacy
el hospital	hospital
el oído	(sense of) hearing
la operación	operation
la sala de emergencia(s)	emergency room
la salud	health
el síntoma	symptom
caerse	to fall (down)
darse con	to bump into; to run into
doler (o:ue)	to hurt
enfermarse, estar	to get sick; to be sick
enfermo/a	sick
lastimarse (el pie)	to injure one's (foot)
poner una inyección	to give an injection
recetar	to prescribe
romperse (la pierna)	to break (one's leg)
sacar(se) una muela	to have a tooth removed
sufrir una enfermedad	to suffer an illness
torcerse (o:ue) (el tobillo)	to sprain (one's ankle)
toser	to cough

Variación léxica

resfriado ⟷ resfrío (Cono Sur), catarro

sala de ⟷ sala de urgencias
emergencia(s)   (Amér. L.)

romperse ⟷ quebrarse (Amér. L.)

síntomas y condiciones médicas

el dolor (de cabeza)	(head)ache; pain
la gripe	flu
la infección	infection
el resfriado	cold
la tos	cough
congestionado/a	congested; stuffed up
embarazada	pregnant
grave	grave; serious
mareado/a	dizzy; nauseated
médico/a	medical
saludable	healthy
sano/a	healthy
ser alérgico/a (a)	to be allergic (to)
tener dolor (m.)	to have pain
tener fiebre	to have a fever

recursos

R	STUDENT CD Lección 10	WB pp. 109–110	LM p. 255	LCASS./CD Cass. 10/CD10	ICD-ROM Lección 10

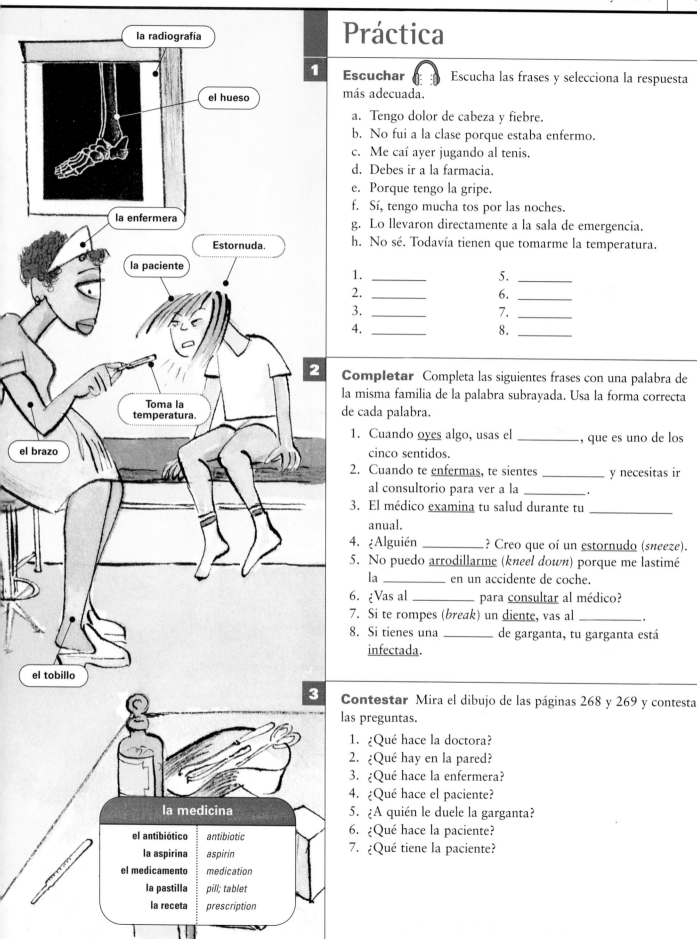

la radiografía

el hueso

la enfermera

la paciente

Estornuda.

Toma la temperatura.

el brazo

el tobillo

la medicina

el antibiótico	*antibiotic*
la aspirina	*aspirin*
el medicamento	*medication*
la pastilla	*pill; tablet*
la receta	*prescription*

Práctica

1 **Escuchar** 🎧 Escucha las frases y selecciona la respuesta más adecuada.

a. Tengo dolor de cabeza y fiebre.
b. No fui a la clase porque estaba enfermo.
c. Me caí ayer jugando al tenis.
d. Debes ir a la farmacia.
e. Porque tengo la gripe.
f. Sí, tengo mucha tos por las noches.
g. Lo llevaron directamente a la sala de emergencia.
h. No sé. Todavía tienen que tomarme la temperatura.

1. _____   5. _____
2. _____   6. _____
3. _____   7. _____
4. _____   8. _____

2 **Completar** Completa las siguientes frases con una palabra de la misma familia de la palabra subrayada. Usa la forma correcta de cada palabra.

1. Cuando <u>oyes</u> algo, usas el _____, que es uno de los cinco sentidos.
2. Cuando te <u>enfermas</u>, te sientes _____ y necesitas ir al consultorio para ver a la _____.
3. El médico <u>examina</u> tu salud durante tu _____ anual.
4. ¿Alguién _____? Creo que oí un <u>estornudo</u> (*sneeze*).
5. No puedo <u>arrodillarme</u> (*kneel down*) porque me lastimé la _____ en un accidente de coche.
6. ¿Vas al _____ para <u>consultar</u> al médico?
7. Si te rompes (*break*) un <u>diente</u>, vas al _____.
8. Si tienes una _____ de garganta, tu garganta está <u>infectada</u>.

3 **Contestar** Mira el dibujo de las páginas 268 y 269 y contesta las preguntas.

1. ¿Qué hace la doctora?
2. ¿Qué hay en la pared?
3. ¿Qué hace la enfermera?
4. ¿Qué hace el paciente?
5. ¿A quién le duele la garganta?
6. ¿Qué hace la paciente?
7. ¿Qué tiene la paciente?

4

Asociaciones Trabajen en parejas para identificar las partes del cuerpo que Uds. asocian con las siguientes actividades. Sigan el modelo.

> **modelo**
>
> nadar
>
> **Estudiante 1:** Usamos los brazos para nadar.
>
> **Estudiante 2:** Usamos las piernas también.

1. hablar por teléfono
2. tocar el piano
3. correr en el parque
4. escuchar música
5. ver una película

6. toser
7. llevar zapatos
8. comprar perfume
9. estudiar biología
10. comer lomo a la plancha

5

Cuestionario Contesta el cuestionario seleccionando las respuestas que reflejen mejor tus experiencias. Suma (*Add*) los puntos de cada respuesta y anota el resultado. Después, con el resto de la clase, compara y analiza los resultados del cuestionario y comenta lo que dicen de la salud y de los hábitos de todo el grupo.

¿Tienes buena salud?

27-30 puntos	Salud y hábitos excelentes
23-26 puntos	Salud y hábitos buenos
22 puntos o menos	Salud y hábitos problemáticos

1. ¿Con qué frecuencia te enfermas? (resfriados, gripe, etc.)
Cuatro veces por año o más. (1 punto)
Dos o tres veces por año. (2 puntos)
Casi nunca. (3 puntos)

2. ¿Con qué frecuencia tienes dolores de estómago o problemas digestivos?
Con mucha frecuencia. (1 punto)
A veces. (2 puntos)
Casi nunca. (3 puntos)

3. ¿Con qué frecuencia sufres de dolores de cabeza?
Frecuentemente. (1 punto)
A veces. (2 puntos)
Casi nunca. (3 puntos)

4. ¿Comes verduras y frutas?
No, casi nunca como verduras ni frutas. (1 punto)
Sí, a veces. (2 puntos)
Sí, todos los días. (3 puntos)

5. ¿Eres alérgico/a a algo?
Sí, a muchas cosas. (1 punto)
Sí, a algunas cosas. (2 puntos)
No. (3 puntos)

6. ¿Haces ejercicios aeróbicos?
No, casi nunca hago ejercicios aeróbicos. (1 punto)
Sí, a veces. (2 puntos)
Sí, con frecuencia. (3 puntos)

7. ¿Con qué frecuencia te haces un examen médico?
Nunca o casi nunca. (1 punto)
Cada dos años. (2 puntos)
Cada año y/o antes de practicar un deporte. (3 puntos)

8. ¿Con qué frecuencia vas al dentista?
Nunca voy al dentista. (1 punto)
Sólo cuando me duele una muela. (2 puntos)
Por lo menos una vez por año. (3 puntos)

9. ¿Qué comes normalmente por la mañana?
No como nada por la mañana. (1 punto)
Tomo una bebida dietética. (2 puntos)
Como cereal y fruta. (3 puntos)

10. ¿Con qué frecuencia te sientes mareado/a?
Frecuentemente. (1 punto)
A veces. (2 puntos)
Casi nunca. (3 puntos)

Comunicación

6 **En el consultorio** Trabajen en parejas y túrnense para representar los papeles (*roles*) de un(a) médico/a y su paciente. Sigan el modelo.

> **modelo**
>
> **Estudiante 1:** Me duele la garganta y toso.
> **Estudiante 2:** Creo que Ud. tiene una infección de la garganta. Voy a recetarle un antibiótico.

7 **¿Qué le pasó?** Trabajen en un grupo de dos o tres personas. Hablen de lo que les pasó y de cómo se sienten las personas que aparecen en los dibujos.

8 **Un accidente** Cuéntale (*Tell*) a la clase un accidente o una enfermedad que tuviste. Incluye información que conteste las siguientes preguntas.

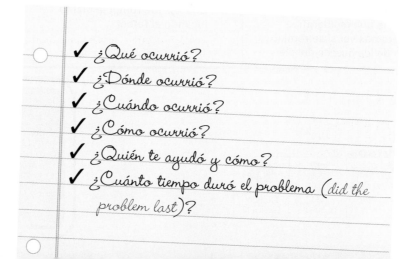

✔ ¿Qué ocurrió?
✔ ¿Dónde ocurrió?
✔ ¿Cuándo ocurrió?
✔ ¿Cómo ocurrió?
✔ ¿Quién te ayudó y cómo?
✔ ¿Cuánto tiempo duró el problema (*did the problem last*)?

¡Uf! ¡Qué dolor!

Don Francisco y Javier van a la clínica de la doctora Márquez.

1

JAVIER Estoy aburrido... tengo ganas de dibujar. Con permiso.

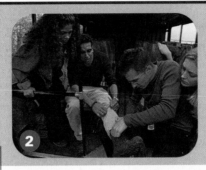

2

INÉS ¡Javier! ¿Qué te pasó?

JAVIER ¡Ay! ¡Uf! ¡Qué dolor! ¡Creo que me rompí el tobillo!

3

DON FRANCISCO No te preocupes, Javier. Estamos cerca de la clínica donde trabaja la doctora Márquez, mi amiga.

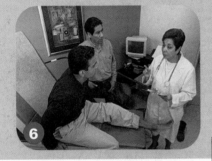

6

DRA. MÁRQUEZ ¿Cuánto tiempo hace que se cayó?

JAVIER Ya se me olvidó... déjeme ver... este... eran más o menos las dos o dos y media cuando me caí... o sea hace más de una hora. ¡Me duele mucho!

DRA. MÁRQUEZ Bueno, vamos a sacarle una radiografía. Queremos ver si se rompió uno de los huesos del pie.

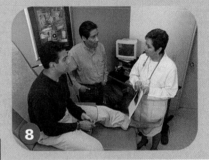

7

DON FRANCISCO Sabes, Javier, cuando era chico yo les tenía mucho miedo a los médicos. Visitaba mucho al doctor porque me enfermaba con mucha frecuencia... tenía muchas infecciones de la garganta. No me gustaban las inyecciones ni las pastillas. Una vez me rompí la pierna jugando al fútbol...

8

JAVIER ¡Doctora! ¿Qué dice? ¿Está roto el tobillo?

DRA. MÁRQUEZ Tranquilo, le tengo buenas noticias, Javier. No está roto el tobillo. Apenas está torcido.

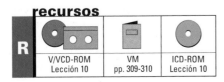

JAVIER ¿Tengo dolor? Sí, mucho. ¿Dónde? En el tobillo. ¿Tengo fiebre? No lo creo. ¿Estoy mareado? Un poco. ¿Soy alérgico a algún medicamento? No. ¿Embarazada? Definitivamente NO.

DRA. MÁRQUEZ ¿Cómo se lastimó el pie?

JAVIER Me caí cuando estaba en el autobús.

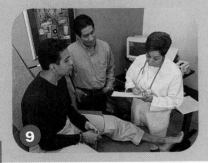

JAVIER Pero, ¿voy a poder ir de excursión con mis amigos?

DRA. MÁRQUEZ Creo que sí. Pero debe descansar y no caminar mucho durante un par de días. Le receto unas pastillas para el dolor.

DRA. MÁRQUEZ Adiós, Francisco. Adiós, Javier. ¡Cuidado! ¡Buena suerte en las montañas!

Enfoque cultural La medicina en los países hispanos

Varios factores económicos y culturales hacen que el sistema de sanidad de los países hispanos sea diferente del sistema estadounidense. En las farmacias, muchas veces las personas consultan sus síntomas con el farmacéutico y él mismo (*he himself*) les da el medicamento, sin necesidad de recetas médicas. La influencia de las culturas indígenas se refleja en la importancia que tienen los curanderos (*folk medicine practitioners*) en muchas regiones. Éstos combinan hierbas medicinales y elementos religiosos para curar las enfermedades.

Expresiones útiles

Discussing medical conditions

▶ **¡Ay, qué dolor!**
Oh, what pain!
▶ **Creo que me rompí el tobillo.**
I think I broke my ankle.

▶ **¿Cómo se lastimó el pie?**
How did you hurt your foot?
▷ **Me caí en el autobús.**
I fell when I was on the bus.

▶ **¿Te duele el tobillo?**
Does your ankle hurt? (fam.)
▶ **¿Le duele el tobillo?**
Does your ankle hurt? (form.)
▷ **Sí, (me duele) mucho.**
Yes, (it hurts) a lot.

▶ **¿Es Ud. alérgico/a a algún medicamento?**
Are you allergic to any medication?
▷ **Sí, soy alérgico/a a la penicilina.**
Yes, I'm allergic to penicillin.

▶ **¿Está roto el tobillo?**
Is the ankle broken?
▷ **No está roto. Apenas está torcido.**
It's not broken. It's just twisted.
▶ **Le receto unas pastillas para el dolor.**
I'll prescribe some pills for the pain.

Talking about childhood medical problems

▶ **¿Te enfermabas frecuentemente?**
Did you get sick frequently? (fam.)
▷ **Sí, me enfermaba frecuentemente.**
Yes, I used to get sick frequently.

▶ **Tenía muchas infecciones.**
I used to get a lot of infections.
▶ **No me gustaban las inyecciones ni las pastillas.**
I didn't like injections or pills.

Reacciona a la fotonovela

1 **¿Cierto o falso?** Decide si lo que dicen las siguientes frases sobre Javier es **cierto** o **falso**. Corrige las frases falsas.

	Cierto	Falso
1. Está aburrido y tiene ganas de hacer algo creativo.	○	○
2. Cree que se rompió la rodilla.	○	○
3. Se lastimó cuando se cayó en el autobús.	○	○
4. Es alérgico a dos medicamentos.	○	○
5. No está mareado pero sí tiene un poco de fiebre.	○	○

2 **Identificar** Identifica quién puede decir las siguientes frases.

1. Hace años me rompí la pierna cuando estaba jugando al fútbol.
2. Hace más de una hora que me rompí la pierna. Me duele muchísimo.
3. Tengo que sacarle una radiografía. No sé si se rompió uno de los huesos del pie.
4. No hay problema, vamos a ver a mi amiga la doctora.
5. Bueno, parece que el tobillo no está roto. Qué bueno, ¿no?
6. No sé si voy a poder ir de excursión con el grupo.

DRA. MÁRQUEZ

DON FRANCISCO

JAVIER

NOTA CULTURAL
Besides Costa Rica (see **Panorama**, p.290), Spain, Mexico, and Argentina offer medical care free. In Spain, for example, medical care is subsidized with public funds.

3 **Ordenar** Pon los siguientes eventos en el orden correcto.

a. La doctora le saca una radiografía. _____
b. La doctora le receta unas pastillas para el dolor. _____
c. Javier se lastima el tobillo en el autobús. _____
d. Don Francisco le habla a Javier de cuando era chico. _____
e. Javier quiere dibujar un rato (*a while*). _____
f. Don Francisco lo lleva a una clínica. _____

4 **En el consultorio** Trabajen en parejas para representar los papeles (*roles*) de un(a) médico/a y su paciente. El/La paciente se cayó en su casa y piensa que se rompió un dedo. Preparen una conversación en la que el/la médico/a le pregunta al/a la paciente si le duele y cuánto tiempo hace que se cayó. El/La paciente describe su dolor. Finalmente, el/la médico/a le recomienda un tratamiento (*treatment*). Usen las siguientes preguntas y frases en su conversación.

¿Cómo se lastimó...?	Estoy...
¿Le duele...?	¿Es usted alérgico/a a algún medicamento?
¿Cuánto tiempo hace que...?	
Tengo...	Usted debe...

Ortografía

El acento y las sílabas fuertes

In Spanish, written accent marks are used on many words. Here is a review of some of the principles governing word stress and the use of written accents.

as-pi-ri-na gri-pe   to-man   an-tes

In Spanish, when a word ends in a vowel, **-n**, or **-s**, the spoken stress usually falls on the next-to-last syllable. Words of this type are very common and do not need a written accent.

a-**sí**   in-glés   in-fec-**ción**   hé-ro-e

When a word ends in a vowel, **-n**, or **-s**, and the spoken stress does *not* fall on the next-to-last syllable, then a written accent is needed.

hos-pi-tal   **na-**riz   re-ce-**tar**   to-**ser**

When a word ends in any consonant *other* than **-n** or **-s**, the spoken stress usually falls on the last syllable. Words of this type are very common and do not need a written accent.

lá-**piz**   fút-**bol**   hués-**ped**   sué-**ter**

When a word ends in any consonant *other* than **-n** or **-s** and the spoken stress does *not* fall on the last syllable, then a written accent is needed.

far-ma-**cia**   bio-lo-**gí-**a   su-**cio**   frí-o

Diphthongs (two weak vowels or a strong and weak vowel together) are normally pronounced as a single syllable. A written accent is needed when a diphthong is broken into two syllables.

sol   pan   mar   tos

Spanish words of only one syllable do not usually carry a written accent.

Práctica Busca las palabras que necesitan acento y escribe su forma correcta.

1. sal-mon
2. ins-pec-tor
3. nu-me-ro
4. fa-cil
5. ju-go
6. a-bri-go
7. ra-pi-do
8. sa-ba-do
9. vez
10. me-nu
11. o-pe-ra-cion
12. im-per-me-a-ble
13. a-de-mas
14. re-ga-te-ar
15. an-ti-pa-ti-co
16. far-ma-cia
17. es-qui
18. pen-sion
19. pa-is
20. per-don

El ahorcado (*Hangman*) Juega al ahorcado para adivinar las palabras.

1. _ l _ _ _ _ _ a   Vas allí cuando estás enfermo.
2. _ _ _ _ e _ c _ _ n   Se usa para poner una vacuna (*vaccination*).
3. _ _ d _ o _ _ _ _ _ _ a Ves los huesos.
4. _ _ _ _ i _ o   Trabaja en un hospital.
5. a _ _ _ b _ _ _ _ _ _ _ Es una medicina.

10.1 The imperfect tense

ANTE TODO In Lesson 8 you learned how to form and use the preterite tense. You will now learn the imperfect tense, which you can use to describe past activities in a different way.

		cantar	beber	escribir
The imperfect of regular verbs				
SINGULAR FORMS	yo	cant**aba**	beb**ía**	escrib**ía**
	tú	cant**abas**	beb**ías**	escrib**ías**
	Ud./él/ella	cant**aba**	beb**ía**	escrib**ía**
PLURAL FORMS	nosotros/as	cant**ábamos**	beb**íamos**	escrib**íamos**
	vosotros/as	cant**abais**	beb**íais**	escrib**íais**
	Uds./ellos/ellas	cant**aban**	beb**ían**	escrib**ían**

¡ATENCIÓN!
Note that the imperfect endings of –er and –ir verbs are the same. Also note that the **nosotros** form of –ar verbs always carries an accent mark on the first **a** of the ending. All forms of –er and –ir verbs carry an accent on the first **i** of the ending.

Sabes, Javier, cuando era chico yo les tenía mucho miedo a los médicos.

De niño tenía que ir mucho a una clínica en San Juan. ¡No me gustaban nada las inyecciones!

▶ Although many verbs have stem changes in the present and preterite tenses, these same verbs do not have stem changes in the imperfect.

entender (e: ie)	**Entendíamos** japonés.
servir (e:i, i)	El camarero les **servía** el café.
doler (o:ue)	A Javier le **dolía** el tobillo.
jugar (u:ue)	Yo **jugaba** al tenis con mi compañero de cuarto.

▶ The imperfect form of **hay** is **había** (*there was; there were; there used to be*).

Había un solo médico en la sala.
There was only one doctor in the room.

Había dos pacientes allí.
There were two patients there.

		ir	ser	ver
Irregular verbs in the imperfect				
SINGULAR FORMS	yo	**iba**	**era**	**veía**
	tú	**ibas**	**eras**	**veías**
	Ud./él/ella	**iba**	**era**	**veía**
PLURAL FORMS	nosotros/as	**íbamos**	**éramos**	**veíamos**
	vosotros/as	**ibais**	**erais**	**veíais**
	Uds./ellos/ellas	**iban**	**eran**	**veían**

¡ATENCIÓN!
Ir, **ser**, and **ver** are the only verbs in Spanish that are irregular in the imperfect.

Uses of the imperfect

CONSÚLTALO

You will learn more about the contrast between the preterite and the imperfect in Lesson 11, 304–305.

▶ The imperfect is used to describe past events in a different way than the preterite. As a general rule, the imperfect is used to describe actions which are seen by the speaker as incomplete or "continuing," while the preterite is used to describe actions which have been completed. The imperfect expresses what was happening at a certain time or how things used to be. The preterite, in contrast, expresses a completed action.

—¿Qué te **pasó**?
What happened to you?

—¿Dónde **vivías** de niño?
Where did you live as a child?

—Me **torcí** el tobillo.
I sprained my ankle.

—**Vivía** en San José.
I lived in San José.

▶ The following words and expressions are often used with the imperfect because they express habitual or repeated actions: **de niño/a** (*as a child*), **todos los días** (*every day*), **mientras** (*while*).

Uses of the imperfect

Habitual or repeated actions	**Íbamos** al parque los domingos. *We used to go to the park on Sundays.*
Events or actions that were in progress	Yo **leía** mientras él **estudiaba**. *I was reading while he was studying.*
Physical characteristics	**Era** alto y guapo. *He was tall and handsome.*
Mental or emotional states	**Quería** mucho a su familia. *He loved his family very much.*
Time-telling	**Eran** las tres y media. *It was 3:30.*
Age	Los niños **tenían** seis años. *The children were six years old.*

¡INTÉNTALO! Indica la forma correcta de cada verbo en el imperfecto.

1. Yo ___hablaba___ (hablar, bailar, descansar, correr, comer, decidir, vivir)

2. Tú _____ (nadar, encontrar, comprender, venir, ir, ser, ver)

3. Ud. _____ (hacer, regatear, asistir, ser, pasear, poder, ir)

4. Nosotras _____ (ser, tomar, ir, poner, seguir, ver, pensar)

5. Ellos _____ (salir, viajar, ir, querer, ser, pedir, empezar)

6. Yo _____ (ver, estornudar, sufrir, ir, dar, ser, toser)

Práctica

1 Completar Primero, completa las frases con la forma correcta de los verbos. Luego, pon las oraciones en un orden lógico y compara tus respuestas con las de un(a) compañero/a.

1. El doctor dijo que no _____ (ser) nada grave.
2. El doctor _____ (querer) ver la nariz del niño.
3. Su mamá _____ (estar) dibujando cuando Miguelito entró llorando.
4. Miguelito _____ (tener) miedo. Fueron a la sala de emergencias.
5. Miguelito no _____ (ir) a jugar más. Ahora quería ir a casa a descansar.
6. Los niños _____ (jugar) al béisbol en el patio.
7. _____ (ser) las dos de la tarde.
8. El niño le dijo a la enfermera que _____ (dolerle) la nariz.

2 Transformar Forma oraciones completas. Usa las formas correctas del imperfecto y añade todas las palabras necesarias.

1. Julieta y César / ser / paramédicos

2. trabajar / juntos y / llevarse / bien

3. cuando / haber / accidente, / siempre / analizar / situación / con cuidado

4. preocuparse / mucho / por / pacientes

5. si / paciente / tener / mucho / dolor, / ponerle / inyección

3 En el hospital Completa las frases con las formas correctas del imperfecto de los verbos de la lista. Algunos verbos se usan más de una vez.

doler	mirar	querer	enfermarse
esperar	estar	poder	sentirse
estornudar	toser	tener	caerse

1. Después de correr 10 kilómetros, a Dora le _____ muchísimo los pies.
2. Ema _____ el termómetro; con tanta fiebre no _____ leerlo.
3. Arturo _____ porque la enfermera _____ muy ocupada.
4. Carolina y Juan _____ mucho y _____ muy congestionados porque _____ la gripe.
5. Lorenzo _____ dolor de muelas pero no _____ ir al dentista.
6. Paco y Luis _____ dolor de estómago y _____ unas pastillas para el dolor.
7. A Juan le _____ la cabeza y _____ mareado.
8. Luisa _____ mucho porque es alérgica al polen.
9. Antes de la operación le _____ todo el cuerpo.
10. De niño, nunca _____ ir al médico.
11. Mi hermana _____ con mucha frecuencia cuando era pequeña.
12. Juan Carlos siempre _____ de la bicicleta.

Comunicación

4

Entrevista Trabajen en parejas. Un(a) estudiante usa estas preguntas para entrevistar a su compañero/a. Luego compartan los resultados de la entrevista con la clase.

1. Cuando eras estudiante de primaria, ¿te gustaban tus profesores/as?
2. ¿Veías mucha televisión cuando eras niño?
3. Cuando tenías diez años, ¿cuál era tu programa de televisión favorito?
4. Cuando eras niño/a, ¿qué hacía tu familia durante las vacaciones?
5. ¿Cuántos años tenías en 1993?
6. Cuando eras estudiante de secundaria, ¿qué hacías con tus amigos/as?
7. Cuando tenías quince años, ¿cuál era tu grupo musical favorito?
8. Antes de tomar esta clase, ¿sabías hablar español?

5

Describir En parejas, túrnense para describir lo que hacían durante algunos momentos de su vida. Pueden usar las sugerencias de la lista u otras ideas. Luego informen a la clase sobre la vida del/de la compañero/a.

> **modelo**
>
> De niña, mi familia y yo siempre íbamos a Puntarenas. Tomábamos el tren. Salíamos a las 6 de la mañana. Todos los días nadábamos. En Navidad mis papás siempre hacían una gran fiesta. Mi mamá y mis tías preparaban un montón de comida. Toda la familia venía.

- Las vacaciones cuando eras niño/a
- Ocasiones especiales
- Qué hacías durante el verano
- Celebraciones con tus amigos/as
- Celebraciones con tu familia
- Cómo era tu escuela
- Cómo eran tus amigos/as
- Los viajes que hacías
- A qué jugabas
- Cuándo te sentías enfermo/a

Síntesis

6

En el consultorio Tu profesor(a) va a darte una hoja de actividades. La hoja contiene una lista de las personas que fueron al consultorio del Dr. Donoso ayer. En parejas indiquen a qué hora llegaron las personas al consultorio y cuáles eran sus problemas.

10.2 Constructions with **se**

ANTE TODO In Lesson 7 you learned how to use **se** as the third person reflexive pronoun (**Él se despierta. Ellos se visten. Ella se baña.**). **Se** can also be used to form constructions in which the person performing the action is not expressed or is de-emphasized.

Impersonal constructions with *se*

▶ In Spanish, verbs that are not reflexive can be used with **se** to form impersonal constructions. These are statements in which the person performing the action is not expressed or defined. In English, the passive voice or indefinite subjects *(you, they, one)* are used.

> **Se habla** español en Costa Rica.
> *Spanish is spoken in Costa Rica.*

> **Se hacen** operaciones aquí.
> *They perform operations here.*

> **Se puede leer** en la sala de espera.
> *You can read in the waiting room.*

> **Se necesitan** medicinas enseguida.
> *They need medicines right away.*

> **¡ATENCIÓN!**
>
> Note that the third person singular verb form is used with singular nouns and the third person plural form is used with plural nouns:
>
> **Se vende ropa.**
>
> **Se venden camisas.**

▶ You often see the impersonal **se** in signs, advertisements, and directions.

SE PROHÍBE NADAR

Se necesitan programadores
GRUPO TECNO
Tel. 778-34-34

ENTRADA
←
Se entra por la izquierda

Se for unplanned events

¿Cuánto tiempo hace que se cayó?

Ya se me olvidó.

Bueno, vamos a sacarle una radiografía para ver si se le rompió el hueso.

▶ **Se** is also used to form statements that describe accidental or unplanned events. In this construction, the person who performs the action is de-emphasized, so as to imply that the accident or unplanned event is not his or her direct responsibility. These statements are constructed using the following pattern.

se + [INDIRECT OBJECT PRONOUN] + [VERB] + [SUBJECT]

Se   me   cayó   la pluma.

▶ In this type of construction, what would normally be the direct object of the sentence becomes the subject, and it agrees with the verb, not with the indirect object pronoun.

I.O. PRONOUN	VERB	SUBJECT
me	perdieron	las llaves.
te	cayó	la taza.
Se le	dañó	el radio.
nos	rompieron	las botellas.
os	olvidaron	las pastillas.
les		

▶ The following verbs are the ones most frequently used with **se** to describe unplanned events. Note also that while Spanish has a verb for *fall* (**caer**), there is no exact translation for *drop*; **dejar caer** (*let fall*) is often used to mean *to drop*.

caer	*to fall; to drop*	**perder (e:ie)**	*to lose*
dañar	*to damage; to break down*	**quedar**	*to be left behind*
olvidar	*to forget*	**romper**	*to break*

CONSÚLTALO

See Lesson 8, page 234 for an explanation of prepositional pronouns.

▶ To clarify or emphasize who is the person involved in the action, this construction commonly begins with the preposition **a** + [*noun*] or **a** + [*prepositional pronoun*].

Al estudiante se le perdió la tarea.
The student lost his homework.

A mí se me cayeron los cuadernos.
I dropped the notebooks.

A Diana se le olvidó ir a clase ayer.
Diana forgot to go to class yesterday.

A Uds. se les quedaron los libros en casa.
You left the books at home.

 Completa las frases de la columna A con **se** impersonal y los verbos correspondientes en presente. Completa las frases de la columna B con **se** para sucesos imprevistos y los verbos en pretérito.

A

1. _Se enseñan_ (enseñar) cinco lenguas en esta universidad.
2. _____ (comer) muy bien en El Cráter.
3. _____ (vender) muchas camisetas allí.
4. _____ (servir) platos exquisitos cada noche.
5. _____ (necesitar) mucho dinero.
6. _____ (buscar) secretaria.

B

1. _Se me rompieron_ (*I broke*) las gafas.
2. _____ (*You* (fam.) *dropped*) las pastillas.
3. _____ (*They lost*) la receta.
4. _____ (*You* (form.) *left*) aquí la radiografía.
5. _____ (*We forgot*) pagar la medicina.
6. _____ (*They left*) los cuadernos en casa.

Práctica

1 **¿Cierto o falso?** Lee estas oraciones sobre la vida en 1901. Indica si lo que dice cada oración es cierto o falso. Luego corrige las oraciones falsas.

1. Se veía mucha televisión.
2. Se escribían muchos libros.
3. Se viajaba mucho en tren.
4. Se montaba a caballo.
5. Se mandaba mucho correo electrónico.
6. Se preparaban muchas comidas en casa.
7. Se llevaban minifaldas.
8. Se pasaba mucho tiempo con la familia.

2 **Traducir** Traduce estos letreros (*signs*) y anuncios (*ads*) al español.

1. Engineers needed
2. Eating and drinking prohibited
3. Programmers sought
4. We speak English
5. Computers sold
6. No talking
7. Teacher needed
8. Books sold
9. Do not enter
10. Spanish spoken

3 **¿Qué pasó?** Mira los dibujos e indica lo que pasó en cada uno.

1. camarero / pastel

2. Sr. Álvarez / espejo

3. Arturo / tarea

4. Sra. Domínguez / llaves

5. Carla y Lupe / botellas de vino

6. Juana / platos

Comunicación

4

Preguntas Trabajen en parejas y usen estas preguntas para entrevistarse.

1. ¿Qué comidas se sirven en tu restaurante favorito?
2. ¿Se te olvidó invitar a alguien a tu última fiesta o comida?
3. ¿A qué hora se abre la cafetería de tu universidad?
4. ¿Alguna vez se te quedó algo importante en la casa?
5. ¿Alguna vez se te perdió algo importante durante un viaje?
6. ¿Qué se vende en la librería de la universidad?
7. ¿Sabes si en la librería se aceptan cheques?
8. ¿Alguna vez se te rompió un plato o un vaso (*glass*)?
9. ¿Alguna vez se te cayó una botella de vino?

5

Minidiálogos En parejas, preparen los siguientes minidiálogos. Luego preséntenlos a la clase.

1. A Spanish professor asks for a student's workbook. The student explains why he or she doesn't have it.
2. A tourist asks the bellhop where the best food in the city is served, and the bellhop gives several suggestions.
3. A patient tells the doctor that he or she can't walk. The doctor examines the patient and explains what's wrong.
4. A parent asks a child how the plates got broken. The child apologizes profusely and explains what happened.

Síntesis

6

Anuncios En grupos, preparen dos anuncios de televisión para presentar a la clase. Usen el imperfecto y por lo menos dos construcciones con **se** en cada uno.

> **modelo**
>
> Se me cayeron unos libros en el pie y me dolía mucho. Pero ahora no, gracias a SuperAspirina 500. ¡Dos pastillas y se me fue el dolor! Se puede comprar SuperAspirina 500 en todas las farmacias Recetamax.

10.3 Adverbs

ANTE TODO   Adverbs are words that describe how, when, and where actions take place. They can modify verbs, adjectives, and even other adverbs. In previous lessons, you have already learned many Spanish adverbs. Study the adverbs in the list below and see if you can determine what they mean.

bien	nunca	temprano
mal	hoy	ayer
muy	siempre	aquí

▶ The most common adverbs are those which end in **–mente.** These are equivalent to the English adverbs which end in *-ly*.

lentamente *slowly*   **generalmente** *generally*
verdaderamente *truly, really*   **simplemente** *simply*

▶ To form adverbs which end in **–mente,** add **–mente** to the feminine form of the adjective. If the adjective does not have a special feminine form, just add **–mente** to the standard form.

ADJECTIVE	FEMININE FORM	SUFFIX	ADVERB
lento	lenta	-mente	lentamente
fabuloso	fabulosa	-mente	fabulosamente
enorme		-mente	enormemente
feliz		-mente	felizmente

▶ Adverbs that end in **–mente** generally follow the verb, while adverbs that modify an adjective or another adverb precede the word they modify.

Javier dibuja **maravillosamente.**   Inés está **casi siempre** ocupada.
Javier draws wonderfully.   *Inés is almost always busy.*

Common adverbs and adverbial expressions

a menudo	*often*	**así**	*like this; so*	**menos**	*less*
a tiempo	*on time*	**bastante**	*enough; rather*	**muchas**	*a lot; many*
a veces	*sometimes*	**casi**	*almost*	**veces**	*times*
además (de)	*furthermore; besides*	**con frecuencia**	*frequently*	**poco**	*little*
		de vez en	*from time to*	**por lo menos**	*at least*
apenas	*hardly; scarcely*	**cuando**	*time*	**pronto**	*soon*

¡INTÉNTALO!   Transforma los siguientes adjetivos en adverbios.

1. alegre   *alegremente*   5. real _____   9. maravilloso _____

2. constante _____   6. frecuente _____   10. normal _____

3. gradual _____   7. tranquilo _____   11. básico _____

4. perfecto _____   8. regular _____   12. afortunado _____

Práctica

1 **Escoger** Completa las oraciones con los adverbios adecuados.

1. La cita era para las dos pero llegamos _____. (aquí, nunca, tarde)
2. El problema fue que _____ se nos descompuso el despertador. (aquí, ayer, así)
3. La recepcionista no se enojó porque sabe que normalmente llego _____. (a veces, a tiempo, poco)
4. _____ el doctor estaba listo. (por lo menos, mal, casi)
5. _____ tuvimos que esperar cinco minutos. (así, además, apenas)
6. El doctor dijo que nuestra hija Irene necesitaba una operación _____. (temprano, menos, inmediatamente)
7. Cuando salió de la operación, le preguntamos _____ al doctor cómo estaba Irene. (con frecuencia, nerviosamente, muchas veces)
8. _____ nos contestó que Irene estaba bien. (por lo menos, afortunadamente, a menudo)

Comunicación

2 **¿Con qué frecuencia?** Tu profesor(a) va a darte una hoja de actividades. Circula por la clase y pregúntales a tus compañeros/as con qué frecuencia ellos/ellas y sus amigos/as hacen las cosas que se mencionan en la lista. Anota sus respuestas y luego comparte la información con la clase.

Actividades	con mucha frecuencia	de vez en cuando	casi nunca	nunca
1. Nadar				
2. Jugar al tenis				
3. Hacer la tarea				
4. Salir a bailar				
5. Mirar la televisión				
6. Dormir en clase				
7. Perder las gafas				
8. Tomar medicina				
9. Ir al dentista				

10.4 Time expressions with **hacer**

▶ Spanish and English use different constructions to tell how long something has been going on.

Hace dos años que vivo aquí.
I've lived here for two years.

Hace un mes que está aquí.
He's been here for a month.

English uses the present perfect (*I've lived*) or the present perfect progressive (*I've been living*) plus the preposition *since* or *for*. Spanish, in contrast, uses the present tense (**vivo**) plus the expression **hace... que...** (literally, *it makes... that...*).

Hace + [*period of time*] + **que** + [*present tense*]

Hace un mes que trabaja aquí.
He's worked (or been working) here for a month.

Hace tres años que estudian.
They've studied (or been studying) for three years.

▶ The question form **¿Cuánto tiempo hace que...?** is used with the present tense to ask how long something has been going on.

—**¿Cuánto tiempo hace que hablas** español?
(For) how long have you been speaking Spanish?

—**¿Cuánto tiempo hace que tose** su hija?
How long has your daughter been coughing?

—**Hace tres años que hablo** español.
I've been speaking Spanish for three years.

—**Hace dos días que tose.**
She's been coughing for two days.

▶ If the preterite is used instead of the present tense, it tells how long ago something happened. In this case, the **hacer** expression can either precede or follow the rest of the sentence. If it follows, the **que** is not needed.

Hace + [*period of time*] + **que** + [*preterite tense*]
or
[*Preterite tense*] + **hace** + [*period of time*]

—**¿Cuánto tiempo hace que** Ud. **se lastimó** el pie?
How long ago did you hurt your foot?

—**Hace** un mes **que me lastimé** el pie. *or*
—**Me lastimé** el pie **hace un mes.**
I hurt my foot a month ago.

 **¡INTÉNTALO!**   Completa las oraciones utilizando expresiones de tiempo con **hacer**. Usa el tiempo presente en las oraciones 1 a 3 y el pretérito en las oraciones 4 a 6.

1. Ana / estudiar / veinte minutos   <u>Hace veinte minutos que Ana estudia.</u>

2. Nosotros / estar enfermos / una semana

3. Tú / tener fiebre / tres días

4. Alberto / llegar / dos horas

5. Yo / hacer la tarea / una hora

6. Ellas / jugar al fútbol / dos horas

Práctica

1 **Minidiálogos** Completa los minidiálogos con las palabras adecuadas.

1. **JUAN** ¿_____ tiempo hace que vives en esta ciudad?
   DORA Mmm… _____ dos años que _____ aquí.

2. **SARA** ¿Cuánto _____ hace que ustedes llegaron?
   LUPE _____ hace una hora.

3. **SILVIA** ¿Cuánto tiempo _____ que sales con Julia?
   CARLOS Hace _____ año.

4. **ROSA** ¿Cuánto tiempo hace que _____ el pie?
   PACO _____ el pie hace _____ mes.

5. **ALINA** ¿_____ años hace que _____ alemán?
   MARTA _____ cinco años que lo estudio.

6. **ARMANDO** Tú y Laura _____ hace dos años, ¿no?
   ALBERTO No, hace tres _____ que nos casamos.

Comunicación

2 **Lectura** Trabajen en parejas. Lean la información sobre Costa Rica. Luego, háganse preguntas basadas en la información.

modelo

¿Cuánto tiempo hace que Óscar Arias ganó el Premio Nobel de la Paz? Hace más de diez años.

¡En breve!

COSTA RICA

- En 1502 Cristóbal Colón llegó al área que ahora se conoce como Puerto Limón.
- La Universidad de Costa Rica se fundó en 1940.
- El periódico La Nación se fundó en 1946.
- Se abolió el ejército en 1948.

- La Guerra Civil tuvo lugar en 1948.
- En 1970 se estableció un extenso sistema de parques nacionales.
- Óscar Arias, presidente de 1986 a 1990, ganó el Premio Nobel de la Paz en 1987.

recursos

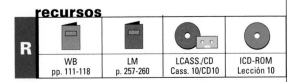

| R | WB pp. 111-118 | LM p. 257-260 | LCASS./CD Cass. 10/CD10 | ICD-ROM Lección 10 |

Lectura

Antes de leer

Estrategia

Activating background knowledge

Using what you already know about a particular subject will often help you better understand a reading selection. For example, if you read an article about a recent medical discovery, you might think about what you already know about health in order to understand unfamiliar words or concepts.

Examinar el texto

Utiliza las estrategias de lectura que tú consideras las más efectivas para hacer unas observaciones preliminares acerca del texto. Después trabajen en parejas para comparar sus observaciones acerca del texto. Luego contesten las siguientes preguntas:

- Analiza el formato del texto. ¿Qué tipo de texto es? ¿Dónde crees que se publicó este artículo?
- ¿Quiénes son Carla Baron y Tomás Monterrey?
- Mira la foto del libro. ¿Qué sugiere el título del libro sobre su contenido?

Conocimiento previo

Ahora comparen su conocimiento previo sobre el cuidado de la salud en los viajes. Consideren las siguientes preguntas:

- ¿Viajaste alguna vez a otro estado o a otro país?
- ¿Tuviste algunos problemas durante tus viajes a causa del agua, de la comida o del clima del país?
- ¿Olvidaste poner en tu maleta algún medicamento u otro producto que despúes necesitaste para prevenir o curar un problema de salud?
- ¿Qué más información tienes sobre el tema a través de las historias de otras personas o de lo que has leído?
- Imagina que un(a) amigo/a tuyo/a se va de viaje. Dile por lo menos cinco cosas que debe hacer para prevenir cualquier problema de salud.

Conocimiento previo *Background knowledge* a causa de *due to*
prevenir *prevent* a través de *through* lo...leído *what you have read* tuyo *of yours*

Libro de la semana

Cómo hacer un viaje saludable y feliz

Carla Baron

Después de leer

Correspondencias Busca las correspondencias entre los Problemas y las Recomendaciones.

Problemas

1. el agua _____
2. el sol _____
3. la comida _____
4. la identificación _____
5. el clima _____

Recomendaciones

a. Hay que adaptarse a los ingredientes no familiares.
b. Toma sólo productos purificados (*purified*).
c. Es importante llevar ropa adecuada cuando viajas.
d. Lleva loción o crema con alta protección solar.
e. Lleva tu pasaporte.

Entrevista a Carla Baron
por Tomás Monterrey

Tomás: ¿Por qué escribió su libro *Cómo hacer un viaje saludable y feliz?*

Carla: Me encanta viajar, conocer otras culturas y escribir. Mi primer viaje lo hice cuando era estudiante universitaria. Todavía recuerdo el día en que llegamos a San Juan, Puerto Rico.

Era el panorama ideal para unas vacaciones maravillosas, pero al llegar a la habitación del hotel, bebí mucha agua de la llave y luego pedí un jugo de frutas con mucho hielo. El clima en San Juan es tropical y yo tenía mucha sed y calor. Las consecuencias llegaron en menos de media hora: pasé dos días con dolor abdominal y corriendo hacia el cuarto de baño cada 10 minutos. Desde entonces, siempre que viajo sólo bebo agua mineral y llevo un pequeño bolso con medicinas necesarias como pastillas para el dolor y también bloqueador solar, una crema repelente de mosquitos y un desinfectante.

Tomás: ¿Son reales las situaciones que se narran en su libro?

Carla: Sí, son reales y son mis propias historias. A menudo los autores crean caricaturas divertidas de un turista en dificultades. ¡En mi libro la turista en dificultades soy yo!

Tomás: ¿Qué recomendaciones puede hallar el lector en su libro?

Carla: Bueno, mi libro es anecdótico y humorístico, pero el tema de la salud se trata de manera seria. En general, se dan recomendaciones sobre ropa adecuada para cada sitio, consejos para protegerse del sol, y comidas y bebidas adecuadas para el turista que viaja a cualquier país del Caribe o de la América del Sur.

Tomás: ¿Tiene algún consejo para las personas que se enferman en sus viajes?

Carla: Muchos turistas toman el avión sin saber nada acerca del país que van a visitar. Ponen toda su ropa en la maleta, toman el pasaporte, la cámara fotográfica y ¡a volar! Es necesario tomar precauciones porque nuestro cuerpo necesita adaptarse al clima, al sol, a la humedad, al agua y a la comida. Se trata de viajar, disfrutar de las maravillas del mundo y regresar a casa con hermosos recuerdos. En resumen, la clave es "prevenir en vez de curar".

llave *faucet* hielo *ice* hacia *toward* reales *true* propias *own* historias *stories* hallar *to find* se trata *is treated* cualquier *any* sin *without* acerca del *about* volar *to fly* Se trata de *It's a question of* disfrutar de *to enjoy* clave *key* en vez de *instead of*

Seleccionar Selecciona la respuesta correcta.

1. El tema principal de este libro es _____.
   a. Puerto Rico b. la salud y el agua c. otras culturas
   d. el cuidado de la salud en los viajes

2. Las situaciones narradas en el libro son _____.
   a. autobiográficas b. inventadas c. ficticias

3. ¿Qué recomendaciones no vas a encontrar en este libro? _____
   a. cómo vestirse adecuadamente
   b. cómo prevenir las quemaduras solares
   c. consejos sobre la comida y la bebida
   d. cómo dar propina en los **países** del Caribe o de América del Sur

4. En opinión de la Srta. Baron, _____.
   a. es bueno tomar agua de la llave y beber jugo de frutas con mucho hielo
   b. es mejor tomar solamente agua embotellada (*bottled*)
   c. los minerales son buenos para el dolor abdominal
   d. es importante visitar el cuarto de baño cada 10 minutos

5. ¿Cuál de los siguientes productos no usa la autora cuando viaja a otros países? _____
   a. desinfectante
   b. cremas preventivas
   c. un libro anecdótico y humorístico
   d. pastillas medicinales

Costa Rica

NATIONAL connections cultures STANDARDS

El país en cifras

- **Área:** 51.100 km² (19.730 millas²), *aproximadamente el área de Virginia Occidental*
- **Población:** 4.200.000
  Costa Rica es el país de Centroamérica con la población más homogénea. El 98% de sus habitantes es blanco y mestizo. Más del 50% de la población es de descendencia española y un alto porcentaje tiene sus raíces en otros países europeos.
- **Capital:** San José —1.037.000
- **Ciudades principales:**
  Alajuela —173.000, Cartago —119.000, Puntarenas —102.000, Heredia —73.000

SOURCE: Population Division, UN Secretariat

- **Moneda:** colón costarricense
- **Idiomas:** español (oficial)

Bandera de Costa Rica

Costarricenses célebres

- Carmen Lyra, escritora (1888–1949)
- Chavela Vargas, cantante (1919-)
- Óscar Arias Sánchez, político (1949-)
- Claudia Poll, nadadora olímpica (1972-)

Óscar Arias recibió el Premio Nobel de la Paz en 1987.

homogénea *homogenous*   mestizo *of indigenous and white parentage*
descendencia *descent*   raíces *roots*   nadadora *swimmer*

¡Increíble pero cierto!

Costa Rica es el único país latinoamericano que no tiene ejército. Sin gastos militares, el gobierno ha podido invertir más en la educación y las artes. En la foto aparece el Museo Nacional de Costa Rica, antiguo cuartel del ejército.

Celebración del Viernes Santo

Cráter del Volcán Poás

NICARAGUA

Río Tempisque

Cordillera de Guanacaste

Río San Juan

Volcán Poás

Cordillera Central

Cordillera de Tilarán

Alajuela

Puntarenas

Heredia

Río Grande de Tárcoles

Volcán Irazú

Cartago

San José

Cordille

Océano Pacífico

El Gran Hotel en San José

Iglesia en Cartago

ESTADOS UNIDOS

OCÉANO ATLÁNTICO

COSTA RICA

OCÉANO PACÍFICO

AMÉRICA DEL SUR

recursos

| R | WB pp. 119-120 | vistasonline.com | ICD-ROM Lección 10 |

Lugares • **Los parques nacionales**

Establecido para proteger los delicados ecosistemas de la región y su biodiversidad, el sistema de parques nacionales cubre el 12% del territorio de Costa Rica. En los parques, los ecoturistas pueden ver hermosas cataratas, montañas y cuevas, además de una multitud de plantas exóticas. Algunos parques ofrecen también la oportunidad de ver quetzales, monos, jaguares, armadillos, osos perezosos y elegantes mariposas en su hábitat natural.

Economía • **Las plantaciones de café**

Costa Rica fue el primer país centroamericano en desarrollar la industria cafetera. En el siglo XIX los costarricenses empezaron a exportar su café, de rico aroma y sabor, a Inglaterra, lo cual contribuyó mucho a la prosperidad de la nación. Hoy día más de 50.000 costarricenses trabajan cultivando el café, que representa alrededor del 15% de las exportaciones anuales del país.

Sociedad • **Una nación progresista**

Un modelo de democracia y de estabilidad, Costa Rica es también uno de los países más progresistas del mundo. Provee servicios médicos gratuitos a todos sus ciudadanos y también a los turistas. En 1870 Costa Rica eliminó la pena de muerte y en 1948 eliminó el ejército e hizo obligatoria y gratuita la educación para todos los costarricenses.

¿Qué aprendiste? Responde a las preguntas con una frase completa.

PANAMÁ

1. ¿Cómo se llama la capital de Costa Rica?

2. ¿Quién es Claudia Poll?

3. ¿Qué porcentaje del territorio de Costa Rica cubren los parques nacionales?

4. ¿Qué protegen los parques nacionales?

5. ¿Qué pueden ver los turistas en los parques nacionales?

6. ¿Cuántos costarricenses trabajan en las plantaciones de café hoy día?

7. ¿Cuándo eliminó Costa Rica la pena de muerte?

Bañistas en Limón

Conexión Internet Investiga estos temas en el sitio **www.vistasonline.com**.

1. Busca información sobre Óscar Arias Sánchez. ¿Quién es? ¿Por qué se le considera (*is he considered*) un costarricense célebre?

2. Busca información sobre los artistas de Costa Rica. ¿Qué artista, escritor o cantante te interesa más? ¿Por qué?

Establecido *Established* **proteger** *protect* **cubre** *covers* **cataratas** *waterfalls* **cuevas** *caves* **además de** *in addition to* **monos** *monkeys* **osos perezosos** *sloths* **mariposas** *butterflies* **desarrollar** *develop* **cafetera** *coffee (adj.)* **siglo** *century* **sabor** *flavor* **Inglaterra** *England* **Hoy día** *Nowadays* **alrededor del** *around* **mundo** *world* **Provee** *It provides* **gratuitos** *free* **ciudadanos** *citizens* **pena de muerte** *death penalty* **ejército** *army*

Nicaragua

El país en cifras

▶ **Área:** 129.494 km² (49.998 millas²), *aproximadamente el área de Nueva York*

Nicaragua es el país más grande de América Central. Su terreno es muy variado e incluye bosques tropicales, montañas, sabanas y marismas, además de unos cuarenta volcanes.

▶ **Población:** 5.359.000

▶ **Capital:** Managua—1.020.000

Managua está en una región de gran inestabilidad geográfica, con muchos volcanes y terremotos. Hace unos años los nicaragüenses decidieron no construir más rascacielos porque no resisten los terremotos.

▶ **Ciudades principales:** León—249.000, Masaya—149.000, Granada—113.000

SOURCE: Population Division, UN Secretariat

▶ **Moneda:** córdoba

▶ **Idiomas:** español (oficial), misquito, inglés

Bandera de Nicaragua

Nicaragüenses célebres

▶ Rubén Darío, poeta (1867-1916)
▶ Violeta Barrios de Chamorro, política y ex-presidenta (1930-)
▶ Daniel Ortega, político y ex-presidente (1945-)
▶ Gioconda Belli, poeta (1948-)

bosques *forests*   sabanas *grasslands*   marismas *marshes*
terremotos *earthquakes*   rascacielos *skyscrapers*   tiburón *shark*
agua dulce *freshwater*   bahía *bay*   científicos *scientists*
fue cercada *was closed off*

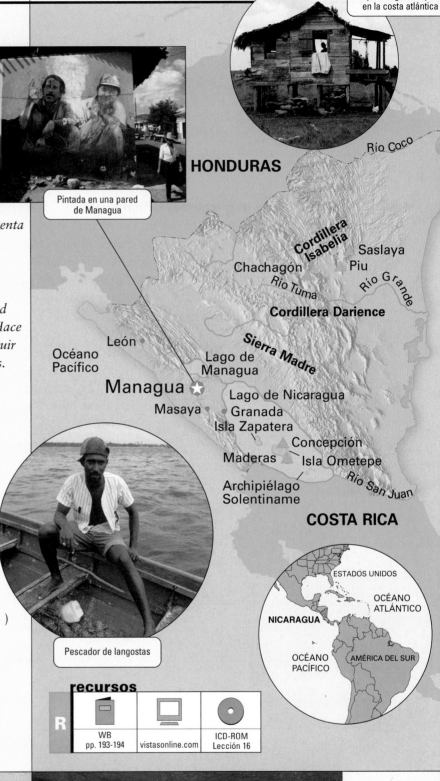

Típico hogar misquito en la costa atlántica

Pintada en una pared de Managua

HONDURAS

Río Coco

Cordillera Isabelia

Saslaya
Piu

Chachagón

Río Tuma

Río Grande

Cordillera Darience

León

Océano Pacífico

Sierra Madre

Lago de Managua

Managua ★

Masaya

Lago de Nicaragua

Granada

Isla Zapatera

Concepción

Maderas

Isla Ometepe

Archipiélago Solentiname

Río San Juan

COSTA RICA

Pescador de langostas

ESTADOS UNIDOS

OCÉANO ATLÁNTICO

NICARAGUA

OCÉANO PACÍFICO

AMÉRICA DEL SUR

recursos

R

WB
pp. 193-194

vistasonline.com

ICD-ROM
Lección 16

¡Increíble pero cierto!

En el lago Nicaragua está la única especie de tiburón de agua dulce del mundo. Los científicos creen que el lago fue antes una enorme bahía que luego fue cercada por erupciones volcánicas. Esta teoría explicaría la presencia de tiburones, atunes y otras especies de peces que sólo viven en mares y océanos.

Historia • Las huellas de Acahualinca

Managua tiene un gran número de sitios prehistóricos. Las huellas de Acahualinca son uno de los restos más famosos y antiguos, pues tienen más de 6000 años. Están a orillas del Lago de Managua y las huellas, que son tanto de humanos como de animales, se dirigen hacia una misma dirección. Este hecho hace que hoy día se piense que éstos corrían hacia el lago para escapar de una erupción volcánica.

Artes • Ernesto Cardenal (1925-)

Ernesto Cardenal, poeta y sacerdote católico, es uno de los escritores más famosos de Nicaragua, país conocido por sus grandes poetas. Autor de más de 35 libros, ya desde joven creía que la poesía podía cambiar la sociedad, y trabajó para establecer la igualdad y la justicia en su país. En los años 60, Cardenal creó la comunidad artística del Archipiélago Solentiname en el Lago Nicaragua. Fue ministro de cultura del país desde 1979 hasta 1988 y también vicepresidente de Casa de los Tres Mundos, una organización dedicada al intercambio cultural.

Naturaleza • El Lago Nicaragua

El Lago Nicaragua, con un área de más de 8000 km^2 (3100 millas^2), es el más grande de América Central. En sus aguas viven muchos peces exóticos y hay más de 370 islas que se formaron por las erupciones del volcán Mombacho. La isla más importante del archipiélago es la Isla Zapatera, que antiguamente fue un cementerio indígena y donde todavía se encuentran estatuas prehistóricas.

¿Qué aprendiste? Responde a las preguntas con una frase completa.

1. ¿Por qué no hay muchos rascacielos en Managua?

2. Nombra dos ex-presidentes de Nicaragua.

3. ¿Qué especie única vive en el Lago Nicaragua?

4. ¿Cómo se piensa que se formaron las huellas de Acahualinca?

5. ¿Por qué es famoso el Archipiélago Solentiname?

6. ¿Qué cree Ernesto Cardenal acerca de la poesía?

7. ¿Cómo se formaron las islas del Lago Nicaragua?

8. ¿Qué hay de interés en la Isla Zapatera?

Conexión Internet Investiga estos temas en el sitio **www.vistasonline.com**.

1. ¿Dónde se habla inglés en Nicaragua y por qué?

2. ¿Qué información hay ahora sobre la economía y/o los derechos humanos en Nicaragua?

huellas *footprints* restos *remains* antiguos *ancient* orillas *shores* se dirigen *are headed* hecho *fact* hacia *toward* sacerdote *priest* poesía *poetry* igualdad *equality* intercambio *exchange* peces *fish* estatuas *statues*

El cuerpo

la boca	mouth
el brazo	arm
la cabeza	head
el corazón	heart
el cuello	neck
el cuerpo	body
el dedo	finger
el estómago	stomach
la garganta	throat
el hueso	bone
la nariz	nose
el oído	(sense of) hearing; inner ear
el ojo	eye
la oreja	(outer) ear
el pie	foot
la pierna	leg
la rodilla	knee
el tobillo	ankle

La salud

el accidente	accident
el antibiótico	antibiotic
la aspirina	aspirin
la clínica	clinic
el consultorio	doctor's office
el/la dentista	dentist
el dolor (de cabeza)	(head)ache; pain
el/la enfermero/a	nurse
el examen médico	physical exam
la farmacia	pharmacy
la gripe	flu
el hospital	hospital
la infección	infection
el medicamento	medication
la medicina	medicine
la operación	operation
el/la paciente	patient
la pastilla	pill; tablet
la radiografía	X-ray
la receta	prescription
el resfriado	cold (illness)
la sala de emergencia(s)	emergency room
la salud	health
el síntoma	symptom
la tos	cough

Verbos

caerse	to fall (down)
dañar	to damage; to break down
darse con	to bump into; to run into
doler (o:ue)	to hurt
enfermarse	to get sick
estar enfermo/a	to be sick
estornudar	to sneeze
lastimarse (el pie)	to hurt one's (foot); to injure one's (foot)
olvidar	to forget
poner una inyección	to give an injection
prohibir	to prohibit
quedar	to be left behind
recetar	to prescribe
romper	to break
romperse (la pierna)	to break (one's leg)
sacar(se) una muela	to have a tooth removed
ser alérgico/a (a)	to be allergic (to)
sufrir una enfermedad	to suffer an illness
tener dolor (m.) de (rodilla)	to have a pain in one's (knee)
tener fiebre (f.)	to have a fever
tomar la temperatura	to take someone's temperature
torcerse (o:ue) (el tobillo)	to sprain (one's ankle)
toser	to cough

Adjetivos

congestionado/a	congested; stuffed-up
embarazada	pregnant
grave	grave; serious
mareado/a	dizzy; nauseated
médico/a	medical
saludable	healthy
sano/a	healthy

Adverbios

a menudo	often
a tiempo	on time
a veces	sometimes
además (de)	furthermore; besides
apenas	hardly; scarcely
así	like this; so
bastante	enough; rather
casi	almost
con frecuencia	frequently
de niño/a	as a child
de vez en cuando	from time to time
menos	less
mientras	while
muchas veces	a lot; many times
poco	little
por lo menos	at least
pronto	soon
todos los días	every day

Otras palabras y expresiones

Hace + time + que + verb in the preterite	to have done something in the past (ago)
Hace + time + que + verb in the present	to have been doing something for a period of time

Expresiones útiles	See page 273.

recursos

R	LCASS./CD Cass. 10/CD10	LM p. 260

La tecnología

Communicative Goals

You will learn how to:

- Talk about using technology and electronic products
- Use common expressions on the telephone
- Talk about car trouble

La tecnología

Más vocabulario

la autopista, la carretera	highway
la avenida	avenue
el bulevar	boulevard
la calle	street
el camino	road
la circulación, el tráfico	traffic
los frenos	brakes
el garaje, el taller (mecánico)	(mechanic's) garage; repair shop
el kilómetro	kilometer
la licencia de conducir	driver's license
el/la mecánico/a	mechanic
la milla	mile
el motor	motor
la mujer policía	police officer (f.)
la multa	fine
la policía	police (force)
la velocidad máxima	speed limit
arrancar	to start
arreglar	to fix; to arrange
bajar	to go down
bajar(se) de	to get off of/out of (a vehicle)
chocar (con)	to run into; to crash
conducir, manejar	to drive
estacionar	to park
parar	to stop
subir	to go up
subir(se) a	to get on/into (a vehicle)
lento/a	slow
lleno/a	full

Variación léxica

baúl ⟷ cajuela (*Méx.*); maletera (*Perú*)

gasolinera ⟷ bencinera (*Chile*)

la gasolinera

REPSOL

HOTEL

el semáforo

CORRIENTES

Revisa el aceite. (revisar)

el capó

el parabrisas

el policía

el walkman

el teléfono celular

el radio

el volante

la llanta

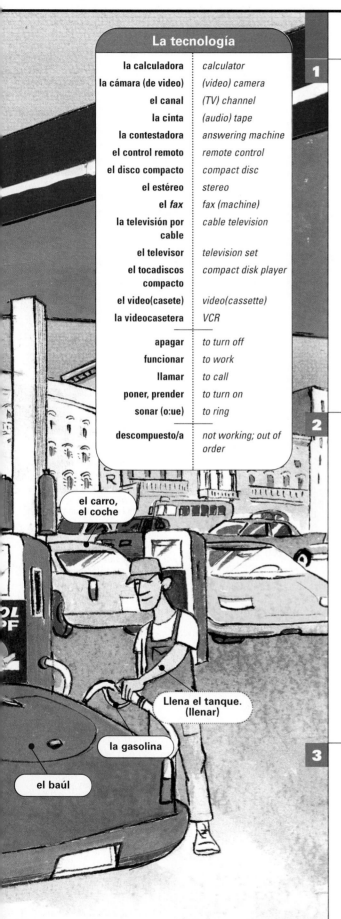

La tecnología	
la calculadora	calculator
la cámara (de video)	(video) camera
el canal	(TV) channel
la cinta	(audio) tape
la contestadora	answering machine
el control remoto	remote control
el disco compacto	compact disc
el estéreo	stereo
el fax	fax (machine)
la televisión por cable	cable television
el televisor	television set
el tocadiscos compacto	compact disk player
el video(casete)	video(cassette)
la videocasetera	VCR
apagar	to turn off
funcionar	to work
llamar	to call
poner, prender	to turn on
sonar (o:ue)	to ring
descompuesto/a	not working; out of order

el carro, el coche

Llena el tanque. (llenar)

la gasolina

el baúl

Práctica

1 Escuchar 🎧 Escucha la conversación entre un joven y el empleado de una gasolinera. Después completa las oraciones.

1. El empleado de la gasolinera llena el tanque, revisa el aceite y _____.
   a. estaciona   b. limpia el parabrisas   c. maneja
2. La próxima semana el joven tiene que _____.
   a. manejar hasta Córdoba   b. manejar hasta la gasolinera
   c. revisar las llantas
3. El joven va a volver mañana porque el empleado _____.
   a. va a llenar el tanque   b. va a revisar los frenos
   c. va a darle una multa
4. Para revisar los frenos, el empleado necesita _____.
   a. un par de minutos   b. un par de días
   c. un par de horas
5. Hoy el joven va _____.
   a. a Córdoba   b. a las montañas   c. a la playa
6. La gasolina cuesta _____.
   a. 22 pesos   b. 32 pesos   c. 24 pesos

2 Oraciones Escribe oraciones usando los elementos siguientes. Usa el pretérito y agrega (add) las palabras necesarias.

1. Marisa / poner / su / maletas / baúl
2. Yo / apagar / radio / diez / noche
3. ¿Quién / poner / videocasetera?
4. Daniel y su esposa / comprar / coche / nuevo / ayer
5. Sara y yo / ir / gasolinera / para / llenar / tanque
6. Jaime / decidir / comprar / calculadora / nuevo
7. Sandra / perder / control remoto
8. David / poner / contestadora / y / acostarse
9. teléfono / sonar / pero / yo / no contestar
10. Yo / comprar / llanta / nuevo / para / coche

3 Completar Completa las siguientes frases con las palabras correctas.

1. Para poder conducir legalmente necesitas…
2. Para parar tu coche necesitas usar…
3. Si tu carro no funciona debes llevarlo a…
4. Para llenar el tanque de tu coche necesitas ir a…
5. Para que (In order that) funcione bien el motor, es importante revisar…
6. Otra palabra para autopista es…
7. Si manejas demasiado rápido, la policía te puede dar…
8. Otra palabra para coche es…

La computadora	
el archivo	*file*
el Internet	*Internet*
el módem	*modem*
la página principal	*home page*
el programa de computación	*software*
la red	*network; Internet*
el sitio Web	*website*
guardar	*to save*
imprimir	*to print*
navegar (en)	*to surf (the Internet)*

4   **Diálogo**   Completa el diálogo con las formas correctas de las siguientes palabras.

arreglar	funcionar	llamar	prender
descompuesto	la impresora	navegar	la red
el disco	imprimir	la pantalla	el teléfono celular

JUAN CARLOS   Mariana, la computadora portátil no _____. Ven a ver, no veo nada en _____.

MARIANA   Pues, ¿la _____?

JUAN CARLOS   Claro que sí, ¡no soy tonto! ¿Piensas que tiene un virus?

MARIANA   Espero que no. Vamos a ver... Ay, Juan Carlos, te olvidaste de poner la batería.

JUAN CARLOS   Ah sí, tienes razón... Mariana, ahora no puedo conectarme a _____. Parece que el módem está _____. ¿Sabes cómo lo puedo _____?

MARIANA   ¡Ay, mi amor! No es eso. Es que estoy hablando por teléfono con Sara. Si quieres, la puedo _____ por _____.

JUAN CARLOS   Sí, gracias... bueno, ahora sí estoy conectado. Voy a _____ un rato, y después voy a _____ el trabajo para mi clase de historia... pero, Mariana, ¿dónde está _____?

MARIANA   Lo siento, ésa sí está descompuesta. Pablo la está arreglando. No sé cómo vas a imprimir tu trabajo ahora.

JUAN CARLOS   No te preocupes. Puedo llevar _____ a la universidad.

MARIANA   ¡Qué buena idea! ¡Eres tan inteligente, mi amor!

NOTA CULTURAL

Cellular phones have become very popular in Latin America. In Chile, for example, where their use in automobiles is restricted by law, they have become such a status symbol that police have stopped motorists for using cell phones only to find that the phones were fake!

Comunicación

5

Preguntas Trabajen en grupos para contestar las siguientes preguntas. Después compartan sus respuestas con la clase.

CONSÚLTALO

Time expressions with hacer To review expressions like **hace…que**, see Lesson 10, p. 286.

1. a. ¿Tienes licencia de conducir?
   b. ¿Cuánto tiempo hace que la recibiste?
   c. ¿Tienes carro?
2. a. ¿Siempre paras cuando ves la luz amarilla del semáforo?
   b. ¿Manejas muy rápido? ¿Sobrepasas (*Do you exceed*) la velocidad máxima?
   c. ¿Recibes muchas multas de la policía de tráfico?
   d. ¿Chocaste con otro coche el año pasado?
3. ¿Cuáles de las siguientes actividades haces tú normalmente: llenar el tanque, limpiar el parabrisas, lavar (*wash*) el coche, revisar el aceite, cambiar el aceite, revisar las llantas, llenar las llantas de aire, arreglar el carro?
4. ¿Qué se puede hacer para hacer más seguras las calles, las avenidas y los bulevares de tu ciudad?
5. a. ¿Miras la televisión con frecuencia?
   b. ¿Qué programas ves?
   c. ¿Tienes televisión por cable?
   d. ¿Tienes una videocasetera? ¿Un DVD? ¿Un DVD en la computadora?
   e. ¿Cómo escuchas música: por radio, estéreo, *walkman,* tocadiscos compacto o computadora?
6. a. ¿Tienes un teléfono celular? ¿Un buscapersonas (*pager*)?
   b. Para comunicarte con tus amigos/as, ¿qué utilizas más: el teléfono, el teléfono por Internet o el correo electrónico?
   c. En tu opinión, ¿cuáles son las ventajas (*advantages*) y desventajas de los diferentes modos de comunicación?
7. a. ¿Con qué frecuencia usas la computadora?
   b. ¿Tienes una computadora personal?
   c. ¿Qué programas de computación tienes?
   d. ¿Tienes tu propia página principal? ¿Cómo es?
8. ¿Cómo usas la tecnología para divertirte? ¿y para comunicarte? ¿y para trabajar?

6

Situación Con un(a) compañero/a de clase, prepara una conversación entre el/la director(a) de ventas (*sales*) de una tienda de computadoras y uno de los clientes siguientes. El/La director(a) de ventas debe hacer preguntas para saber lo que el cliente desea hacer con la computadora y mostrarle la computadora que debe comprar.

1. el padre o la madre de un niño de seis años
2. una jubilada (*female retiree*) que quiere aprender cosas nuevas
3. una mujer que va a crear una empresa (*business*) nueva en su casa
4. un estudiante que va a ir a la universidad y no sabe nada de computadoras
5. un hombre de negocios (*businessman*) que viaja mucho

7

El taller En parejas, escriban un diálogo entre un(a) mecánico/a y un(a) cliente/a cuyo (*whose*) coche se dañó (*was damaged*) en un accidente. El/La cliente/a le dice al/a la mecánico/a qué ocurrió en el accidente y los dos hablan de las partes dañadas (*damaged*).

Tecnohombre, ¡mi héroe!

El autobús se daña.

PERSONAJES

MAITE

INÉS

DON FRANCISCO

ÁLEX

JAVIER

SR. FONSECA

ÁLEX ¿Bueno? ... Con él habla... Ah, ¿cómo estás? ... Aquí, yo muy bien. Vamos para Ibarra. ¿Sabes lo que pasó? Esta tarde íbamos para Ibarra cuando Javier tuvo un accidente en el autobús. Se cayó y tuvimos que llevarlo a una clínica.

JAVIER Episodio veintiuno: Tecnohombre y los superamigos suyos salvan el mundo una vez más.

INÉS Oh, Tecnohombre, ¡mi héroe!

MAITE ¡Qué cómicos! Un día de éstos, ya van a ver...

ÁLEX Van a ver quién es realmente Tecnohombre. Mis superamigos y yo nos hablamos todos los días por el teléfono Internet, trabajando para salvar el mundo. Pero ahora, con su permiso, quiero escribirle un mensaje electrónico a mi mamá y navegar en la red un ratito.

INÉS Pues... no sé... creo que es el alternador. A ver... sí... Mire, don Francisco... está quemado el alternador.

DON FRANCISCO Ah, sí. Pero aquí no podemos arreglarlo. Conozco a un mecánico pero está en Ibarra, a veinte kilómetros de aquí.

ÁLEX ¡Tecnohombre, a sus órdenes!

DON FRANCISCO ¡Eres la salvación, Álex! Llama al Sr. Fonseca al cinco, treinta y dos, cuarenta y siete, noventa y uno. Nos conocemos muy bien. Seguro que nos ayuda.

ÁLEX Buenas tardes. ¿Con el Sr. Fonseca por favor? ... Soy Álex Morales, cliente de Ecuatur. Le hablo de parte del señor Francisco Castillo... Es que íbamos para Ibarra y se nos dañó el autobús. ... Pensamos que es el... el alternador... Estamos a veinte kilómetros de la ciudad...

recursos

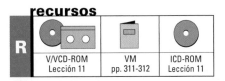

| R | V/VCD-ROM Lección 11 | VM pp. 311-312 | ICD-ROM Lección 11 |

DON FRANCISCO Chicos, creo que tenemos un problema con el autobús. ¿Por qué no se bajan?

DON FRANCISCO Mmm, no veo el problema.

INÉS Cuando estaba en la escuela secundaria, trabajé en el taller de mi tío. Me enseñó mucho sobre mecánica. Por suerte, arreglé unos autobuses como éste.

DON FRANCISCO ¡No me digas! Bueno, ¿qué piensas?

SR. FONSECA Creo que va a ser mejor arreglar el autobús allí mismo. Tranquilo, enseguida salgo.

ÁLEX Buenas noticias. El Sr. Fonseca viene enseguida. Piensa que puede arreglar el autobús aquí mismo.

MAITE ¡La Mujer Mecánica y Tecnohombre, mis héroes!

DON FRANCISCO ¡Y los míos también!

Enfoque cultural El transporte en la ciudad

En las ciudades hispanas suele haber (*there is usually*) más transporte público que en las estadounidenses y sus habitantes dependen menos de los carros. En los países hispanos también es más frecuente el uso de carros pequeños y de motocicletas que gastan poca gasolina. En las ciudades españolas, por ejemplo, la gasolina es muy cara y también hay poco espacio para el estacionamiento (*parking*); por eso es tan frecuente el uso de vehículos pequeños y económicos.

Expresiones útiles

Talking on the telephone

▶ **Aló./¿Bueno?/Diga.**
Hello.

▶ **¿Quién habla?**
Who is speaking?

▶ **¿De parte de quién?**
Who is calling?

▷ **Con él/ella habla.**
This is he/she.

▷ **Le hablo de parte de Francisco Castillo.**
I'm speaking to you on behalf of Francisco Castillo.

▶ **¿Puedo dejar un recado?**
May I leave a message?

▶ **Está bien. Llamo más tarde.**
That's fine. I'll call later.

Talking about bus or car problems

▶ **¿Qué pasó?**
What happened?

▷ **Se nos dañó el autobús.**
The bus broke down.

▷ **Se nos pinchó una llanta.**
We had a flat tire.

▷ **Está quemado el alternador.**
The alternator is burned out.

Saying how far away things are

▶ **Está a veinte kilómetros de aquí.**
It's twenty kilometers from here.

▶ **Estamos a veinte kilómetros de la ciudad.**
We're twenty kilometers from the city.

Expressing surprise

▶ **¡No me digas!**
You don't say! (fam.)

▶ **¡No me diga!**
You don't say! (form.)

Offering assistance

▶ **A sus órdenes.**
At your service.

Additional vocabulary

▶ **aquí mismo**
right here

Reacciona a la fotonovela

1 **Seleccionar** Selecciona las respuestas que completan correctamente las siguientes frases.

1. Álex quiere _____.
   a. llamar a su mamá por teléfono celular   b. escribirle a su mamá y navegar en la red
   c. hablar por teléfono Internet y navegar en la red
2. Se les dañó el autobús. Inés dice que _____.
   a. el alternador está quemado   b. se les pinchó una llanta
   c. el taller está quemado
3. Álex llama al mecánico, el señor _____.
   a. Castillo   b. Ibarra   c. Fonseca
4. Maite llama a Inés la "Mujer Mecánica" porque antes _____.
   a. trabajaba en el taller de su tío   b. arreglaba computadoras
   c. conocía a muchos mecánicos
5. El grupo está a _____ de la ciudad.
   a. veinte millas   b. veinte grados centígrados   c. veinte kilómetros

NOTA CULTURAL

In the U.S., Internet addresses typically end with *.com*, *.net*, or *.edu*. Other countries each have their own unique domain code. Here are the codes for some Spanish-speaking countries:

Argentina	ar
Colombia	co
Mexico	mx
Spain	es
Venezuela	ve

2 **Identificar** Identifica quién puede decir las siguientes frases.

1. Gracias a mi tío tengo un poco de experiencia arreglando autobuses.
2. Sé manejar un autobús pero no sé arreglarlo. ¿Por qué no llamamos a mi amigo?
3. Sabes, admiro mucho a la Mujer Mecánica y a Tecnohombre.
4. Aló... Sí, ¿de parte de quién?
5. El nombre de Tecnohombre fue idea mía. ¡Qué cómico!, ¿no?

JAVIER   ÁLEX

MAITE

INÉS   DON FRANCISCO

3 **Completar** Completa las siguientes frases con palabras de la lista.

computadora portátil	lleno	descompuesto
un parabrisas	"Diga"	"No me diga"
un teclado	el volante	el capó

1. La computadora de Álex tiene una pantalla, un monitor y _____.
2. Si tu coche no arranca, debes levantar _____ y ver cuál es el problema.
3. Se les dañó el autobús en la carretera. Ahora está _____.
4. Cuando Álex le escribe una carta a su mamá lo hace en su _____.
5. Cuando contestas el teléfono, debes decir: _____.

¡LENGUA VIVA!

There are various ways to say that a car is broken down. Synonyms for **descompuesto** include **averiado**, **roto**, **varado**, and **en pana**. You can also say **se rompió** or simply **no funciona**.

•••

While **rueda** means *wheel* everywhere, *tires* are variously called **llantas**, **neumáticos**, **gomas**, and **cauchos**.

4 **Situaciones** Trabaja con un(a) compañero/a para representar los papeles de un(a) mecánico/a y un(a) conductor(a). El/La conductor(a) llama al/a la mecánico/a por teléfono y explica cuál es el problema del coche. Después indica dónde está en relación con el taller. El/La mecánico/a dice que puede ir enseguida. Usen estas preguntas y frases en su conversación:

- Aló./¿Bueno?/Diga.
- ¿Quién habla?
- Con él/ella habla.
- ¿Qué pasó?
- Se me dañó el coche.
- Estoy a... kilómetros de...

Ortografía

La acentuación de palabras similares

Although accent marks usually indicate which syllable in a word is stressed, they are also used to distinguish between words that have the same or similar spellings.

Él maneja **el** coche.   **Sí, voy si** quieres.

Although one-syllable words do not usually carry written accents, some *do* have accent marks to distinguish them from words that have the same spelling but different meanings.

Sé cocinar.   **Se** baña.   ¿Tomas **té**?   **Te** duermes.

Sé (*I know*) and **té** (*tea*) have accent marks to distinguish them from the pronouns **se** and **te**.

---

para **mí**   **mi** cámara   **Tú** lees.   **tu** estéreo

Mí (*me*) and **tú** (*you*) have accent marks to distinguish them from the possessive adjectives **mi** and **tu**.

¿Por qué vas?   Voy **porque** quiero.

Several words of more than one syllable also have accent marks to distinguish them from words that have the same or similar spellings.

Éste es rápido.   **Este** módem es rápido.

Demonstrative pronouns have accent marks to distinguish them from demonstrative adjectives.

¿Cuándo fuiste?   Fui **cuando** me llamó.

¿Dónde trabajas?   Voy al taller **donde** trabajo.

Adverbs have accent marks when they are used to convey a question.

Práctica Marca los acentos en las palabras que los necesitan.

ANA   Alo, soy Ana. ¿Que tal?

JUAN   Hola, pero... ¿por que me llamas tan tarde?

ANA   Porque mañana tienes que llevarme a la universidad. Mi auto esta dañado.

JUAN   ¿Como se daño?

ANA   Se daño el sabado. Un vecino (*neighbor*) choco con el.

Crucigrama Utiliza las siguientes pistas (*clues*) para completar el crucigrama. ¡Ojo con los acentos!

Horizontales

1. Él _____ levanta.
4. No voy _____ no puedo.
7. Tú _____ acuestas.
9. ¿ _____ es el examen?
10. Quiero este video y _____.

Verticales

2. ¿Cómo _____ Ud.?
3. Eres _____ mi hermano.
5. ¿_____ tal?
6. Me gusta _____ suéter.
8. Navego _____ la red.

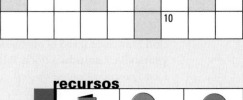

11.1 The preterite and the imperfect

ANTE TODO Now that you have learned the forms of the preterite and imperfect, you will learn more about how they are used. The preterite and the imperfect are not interchangeable. In Spanish, the choice between these two tenses depends on the context and on the point of view of the speaker.

Por suerte, arreglé unos autobuses como éste.

Íbamos para Ibarra y se nos dañó el autobús.

COMPARE & CONTRAST

Uses of the preterite	**Uses of the imperfect**

▶ To express actions that are viewed by the speaker as completed

Don Francisco **estacionó** el autobús.
Don Francisco parked the bus.

Fueron a Buenos Aires ayer.
They went to Buenos Aires yesterday.

▶ To express the beginning or end of a past action

La película **empezó** a las nueve.
The movie began at nine o'clock.

Ayer **terminé** el proyecto para la clase de química.
Yesterday I finished the project for chemistry class.

▶ To narrate a series of past actions or events

Prendí la computadora, **leí** mi correo electrónico y luego le **escribí** un mensaje a Inés.
I turned on the computer, read my e-mail, and then wrote Inés a message.

Don Francisco **paró** el autobús, **abrió** la ventanilla y **saludó** a doña Rita.
Don Francisco stopped the bus, opened the window, and greeted doña Rita.

▶ To describe an ongoing past action with no reference to its beginning or end

Maite **conducía** muy rápido en Madrid.
Maite was driving very fast in Madrid.

Javier **esperaba** en el garaje.
Javier was waiting in the garage.

▶ To express habitual past actions and events

Cuando **era** joven, jugaba al tenis.
When I was young, I used to play tennis.

Álex siempre **revisaba** su correo electrónico a las tres.
Álex always checked his e-mail messages at three o'clock.

▶ To describe mental, physical, and emotional states or conditions

La chica **quería** descansar. **Se sentía** mal y **tenía** dolor de cabeza.
The girl wanted to rest. She felt ill and had a headache.

Ellos **eran** altos y **tenían** ojos verdes.
They were tall and had green eyes.

Estábamos felices de ver a la familia.
We were happy to see the family.

▶ The preterite and the imperfect often appear in the same sentence. In such cases the imperfect describes what *was happening*, while the preterite describes the action that "interrupted" the ongoing activity.

Navegaba en la red cuando **sonó** el teléfono.
I was surfing the web when the phone rang.

Maite **leía** el periódico cuando llegó Álex.
Maite was reading the newspaper when Álex arrived.

▶ You will also see the preterite and the imperfect used together in lengthy narratives such as fiction stories, news stories, and retelling of events. In these cases the imperfect provides all of the background information, such as the time, the weather, and the location, while the preterite indicates the specific events that occurred.

Eran las dos de la mañana y el detective ya no **podía** mantenerse despierto. **Se bajó** lentamente del coche, **estiró** las piernas y **levantó** los brazos hacia el cielo oscuro.
It was two in the morning, and the detective could no longer stay awake. He slowly stepped out of the car, stretched his legs, and raised his arms towards the darkened skies.

La luna **estaba** llena y no **había** en el cielo ni una sola nube. De repente, el detective **escuchó** un grito espeluznante proveniente del parque.
The moon was full and there wasn't a single cloud in the sky. Suddenly, the detective heard a piercing scream coming from the park.

NASA • La sonda se estrelló antes de orbitar

Mars cayó en Marte

La agencia espacial estadounidense perdió la comunicación con la sonda Mars Climate Orbiter, justo en el momento en que se ponía en órbita alrededor de Marte. La nave se estrelló por un error de navegación importante. Se habían invertido USD 25 millones y sería la primera estación meteorológica interplanetaria. PASE A LA A6

¡INTÉNTALO! Completa estas historias (*stories*) con el pretérito o el imperfecto y explica por qué se usa ese tiempo verbal en cada ocasión.

El pretérito

1. (ir) Tomás y yo ___fuimos___ al parque ayer.
2. (nadar) _____ por la tarde.
3. (tomar) Después _____ el sol.
4. (regresar) _____ a casa a las cinco.
5. (leer) Tomás preparó la cena. Yo _____ el periódico.
6. (dormirse) Mientras Tomás veía una película, yo _____.

El imperfecto

1. (ser) _____ las doce.
2. (haber) _____ mucha gente en la calle.
3. (estar) Los novios _____ en el café.
4. (almorzar) Todos los días _____ juntos.
5. (servir) El camarero les _____ ensaladas.
6. (llover) Cuando los novios salieron del café, _____.

Práctica

1 **Seleccionar** Utiliza el tiempo verbal adecuado, según (*according to*) el contexto.

1. Arturo _____ (manejar) por la autopista cuando de repente _____ (ver) que le _____ (seguir) dos policías. Él _____ (parar) el coche, y los policías _____ (aproximarse) (*approached*) al coche y le _____ (pedir) la licencia de conducir.

2. Tú _____ (aprender) a manejar cuando _____ (tener) quince años, ¿no?

3. Esta mañana se me _____ (pinchar) una llanta. _____(Ir) a buscar la llanta de repuesto (*spare*) en el baúl, pero cuando la _____ (encontrar), también _____ (estar) desinflada (*flat*).

4. El lunes mi papá _____ (llevar) el carro al taller mecánico porque los frenos _____ (hacer) un ruido extraño (*strange noise*). El mecánico los _____ (revisar) pero no _____ (poder) encontrar ningún problema.

5. De niño, mi hijo siempre _____ (decir) que _____ (querer) ser mecánico porque le _____(fascinar) los motores de los carros.

6. Nosotros _____ (estacionar) el carro y después _____ (ir) a ver las cataratas (*waterfalls*) de Iguazú. _____ (Ser) un viaje magnífico.

CONSÚLTALO

The **Cataratas de Iguazú** are a chain of nearly 300 waterfalls that make up one of the most magnificent sights in South America. To learn more, see **Panorama** p. 321.

2 **Completar** Completa esta noticia con la forma correcta del pretérito o el imperfecto.

Un accidente trágico

Ayer temprano por la mañana _____ (haber) un trágico accidente en la calle Ayacucho en el centro de Buenos Aires cuando un autobús _____(chocar) con un carro. La mujer que _____ (manejar) el carro _____ (morir) al instante y los paramédicos _____ (tener) que llevar a su pasajero al hospital porque _____ (sufrir) varias fracturas y una conmoción (*concussion*) cerebral. Su estado de salud es todavía muy grave. El conductor del autobús _____ (decir) que no _____ (ver) el carro hasta el último (*last*) momento porque _____ (haber) mucha niebla y _____ (estar) lloviendo. Él _____ (intentar) (*to attempt*) dar un viraje brusco (*to swerve*), pero _____ (perder) el control del autobús y no _____ (poder) evitar (*to avoid*) el choque. Según nos informaron, no _____ (lastimarse) ningún pasajero.

CONSEJOS

Reading Spanish-language newspapers is a good way to practice verb tenses. You will find that both the imperfect and the preterite occur with great regularity. Many newsstands carry international papers, and many Spanish-language newspapers (such as Spain's *El País*, Mexico's *Reforma*, and Argentina's *Clarín*) are now on the Web.

3 **Completar** Completa las frases de una manera lógica. Usa el pretérito o el imperfecto. En parejas, comparen sus respuestas.

1. De niño/a, yo...
2. Yo manejaba el coche mientras...
3. Anoche mi novio/a...
4. Ayer el/la profesor(a)...
5. La semana pasada un(a) amigo/a...
6. A menudo mi madre...
7. Esta mañana en la cafetería...
8. Navegábamos en la red cuando...

Comunicación

4 **Entrevista** Usa estas preguntas para entrevistar a un(a) compañero/a acerca de su primer(a) novio/a. Si quieres, puedes añadir (*to add*) otras preguntas.

1. ¿Quién fue tu primer(a) novio/a?
2. ¿Cuántos años tenían Uds. cuando se conocieron?
3. ¿Cómo era él/ella?
4. ¿Qué le gustaba hacer? ¿Le interesaban los deportes?
5. ¿Por cuánto tiempo salieron Uds.?
6. ¿Qué hacían Uds. cuando salían?
7. ¿Pensaban casarse?
8. ¿Cuándo y por qué rompieron Uds.?

5 **Encuesta** Tu profesor(a) va a darte una hoja de actividades. Circula por la clase y pregúntales a tus compañeros/as con qué frecuencia hicieron las actividades de la lista en el pasado. Informa a la clase de los resultados de tu encuesta.

Actividades	Nombres	Frecuencia
1. Cambiar una llanta pinchada		
2. Ir al taller mecánico		
3. Revisar el aceite del carro		
4. Chocar con otro carro		
5. Comprar discos compactos		
6. Usar una cámara de video		
7. Crear un sitio Web		
8. Usar un teléfono celular		

6 **Situación** Anoche alguien robó (*stole*) el examen de la Lección 11 de la oficina de tu profesor(a) y tú tienes que averiguar (*to find out*) quién lo hizo. Pregúntales a tres compañeros dónde estaban, con quién estaban y qué hicieron entre las ocho y las doce de la noche.

Síntesis

7 **Escribir** Escribe una composición breve sobre la primera vez que manejaste un carro o el día en que fuiste al Departamento de Tráfico para conseguir tu licencia de conducir. Incluye los siguientes puntos en tu composición: una descripción del día, la hora y el tiempo, tu edad (*age*), qué pasó y cómo te sentías.

11.2 Por and para

ANTE TODO Unlike English, Spanish has two words that mean *for*: **por** and **para**. These two prepositions are not interchangeable. Study the following charts to see how they are used.

Es para usted. Es un cliente de don Paco.

Álex habla por teléfono.

Por is used to indicate...	
▶ **Motion or a general location** *(around, through, along, by)*	La excursión nos llevó **por** el centro. *The tour took us through downtown.* Pasamos **por** el parque y **por** el río. *We passed by the park and along the river.*
▶ **Duration of an action** *(for, during, in)*	Estuve en la Patagonia **por** un mes. *I was in Patagonia for a month.* Miguel estudió **por** la noche. *Miguel studied during the night.*
▶ **Reason or motive for an action** *(because of, on account of, on behalf of)*	Lo hizo **por** su familia. *She did it on behalf of her family.* Papá llegó a casa tarde **por** el tráfico. *Dad arrived home late because of the traffic.*
▶ **Object of a search** *(for, in search of)*	Vengo **por** ti a las ocho. *I'm coming for you at eight.* Maite fue **por** su cámara. *Maite went in search of her camera.*
▶ **Means by which something is done** *(by, by way of, by means of)*	Ellos viajan **por** la autopista. *They travel by (by way of) the highway.* ¿Hablaste con la policía **por** teléfono? *Did you talk to the police by (on the) phone?*
▶ **Exchange or substitution** *(for, in exchange for)*	Le di dinero **por** la videocasetera. *I gave him money for the VCR.* Muchas gracias **por** el video. *Thank you very much for the video.*
▶ **Unit of measure** *(per, by)*	José manejaba a 120 kilómetros **por** hora. *José was driving 120 kilometers per hour.*

¡ATENCIÓN!

Por is also used in several idiomatic expressions, including:
por aquí *around here*
por ejemplo *for example*
por eso *that's why; therefore*
por fin *finally*

¡ATENCIÓN!

Remember that when giving an exact time, **de** is used instead of **por** before **la mañana**, **la tarde**, etc.

La clase empieza a las nueve **de** la mañana.

• • •

In addition to **por**, **durante** is also commonly used to mean *for* when referring to time.

Esperé al médico **durante** cincuenta minutos.

Para is used to indicate...

▶ **Destination**
(*toward, in the direction of*)

Salimos **para** Córdoba el sábado.
We are leaving for Córdoba on Saturday.

▶ **Deadline or a specific time in the future**
(*by, for*)

Él va a arreglar el carro **para** el viernes.
He will fix the car by Friday.

▶ **Purpose or goal** + *infinitive*
(*in order to*)

Juan estudia **para** (ser) mecánico.
Juan is studying to be a mechanic.

▶ **Purpose** + *noun*
(*for, used for*)

Es una llanta **para** el carro.
It's a tire for the car.

▶ **The recipient of something**
(*for*)

Compré una calculadora **para** mi hijo.
I bought a calculator for my son.

▶ **Comparison with others or an opinion**
(*for, considering*)

Para un joven, es demasiado serio.
For a young person, he is too serious.

Para mí, esta lección no es difícil.
For me, this lesson isn't difficult.

▶ **In the employ of**
(*for*)

Sara trabaja **para** Telecom Argentina.
Sara works for Telecom Argentina.

▶ In many cases it is grammatically correct to use either **por** or **para** in a sentence. The meaning of the sentence is different, however, depending on which preposition is used.

Caminé **por** el parque.
I walked through the park.

Caminé **para** el parque.
I walked to (toward) the park.

Trabajó **por** su padre.
He worked for (in place of) his father.

Trabajó **para** su padre.
He worked for his father('s company).

¡INTÉNTALO!   Completa estas frases con las preposiciones **por** o **para.**

1. Jugamos al fútbol __por__ la mañana.
2. Necesitas un módem _____ navegar en la red.
3. Entraron _____ la puerta.
4. Quiero un pasaje _____ Buenos Aires.
5. _____ arrancar el carro, necesito la llave.
6. Arreglé el televisor _____ mi amigo.
7. Estuvieron nerviosos _____ el examen.
8. ¿No hay una gasolinera _____ aquí?

9. Esta computadora es _____ Ud.
10. Juan está enfermo. Tengo que trabajar _____ él.
11. Estuvimos en Cancún _____ dos meses.
12. _____ mí, el español es difícil.
13. Tengo que estudiar la lección _____ el lunes.
14. Voy a ir _____ el camino más corto.
15. Compré dulces _____ mi novia.
16. Compramos el auto _____ un buen precio.

Práctica

1 **Completar** Completa este párrafo con las preposiciones **por** o **para.**

El mes pasado mi esposo y yo hicimos un viaje a Buenos Aires y sólo pagamos dos mil dólares _____ los pasajes. Estuvimos en Buenos Aires _____ una semana y recorrimos toda la ciudad. Durante el día caminamos _____ la plaza San Martín, el microcentro y el barrio de La Boca, donde viven muchos artistas. _____ la noche fuimos a una tanguería, que es una especie de teatro _____ mirar a la gente bailar tango. Dos días después decidimos hacer una excursión _____ las pampas _____ ver el paisaje y un rodeo con gauchos. _____ eso, alquilamos (*we rented*) un carro y pasamos unos días muy agradables. El último (*last*) día que estuvimos en Buenos Aires fuimos a Galerías Pacíficas _____ comprar recuerdos (*souvenirs*) _____ nuestros hijos y nietos. Compramos tantos regalos que tuvimos que pagar impuestos (*duties*) cuando pasamos _____ la aduana al regresar.

2 **Oraciones** Añade (*Add*) **por** o **para** y forma frases con los siguientes elementos.

A	B	C	D
▸ (no) fui	▸ al mercado	▸ comprar frutas	▸ coche
▸ (no) fuimos	▸ a las montañas	▸ tres días	▸ esquiar
	▸ a Mar del Plata	▸ razones económicas	▸ mi madre
		▸ tomar el sol	▸ nadar

3 **Describir** Usa **por** o **para** y el tiempo presente para describir estos dibujos.

1. _____   2. _____   3. _____

4. _____   5. _____   6. _____

CONSÚLTALO

To learn more about Buenos Aires, Argentina's capital, see **Panorama**, p. 320.

NOTA CULTURAL

The **pampa** or **pampas** is a vast region of flat grasslands which covers the majority of Argentina's interior, ranging from prairies to desert. The **pampas** are the home of the **gauchos**, nomadic cowboys known for their skill at riding horses and using a lasso and bolas.

NOTA CULTURAL

Mar del Plata is a resort city on the coast of Argentina. Known as "the Pearl of the Atlantic," the city is visited by large numbers of vacationers for its beaches and casinos.

Comunicación

4

Descripciones Usa **por** o **para** y completa estas frases de una manera (*manner*) lógica. Luego, compara tus respuestas con las de un(a) compañero/a.

1. En casa, hablo con mis amigos…
2. Mi padre/madre trabaja…
3. Ayer fui al taller…
4. Los miércoles tengo clases…
5. A veces voy a la biblioteca…
6. Esta noche tengo que estudiar…
7. Necesito… dólares…
8. Compré un regalo…
9. Mi mejor amigo/a estudia…
10. Necesito hacer la tarea…

5

Encuesta Tu profesor(a) va a darte una hoja de actividades. Camina por la clase y haz preguntas hasta que encuentres a alguien que responda a cada descripción que se menciona en la lista. Luego presenta los resultados a la clase.

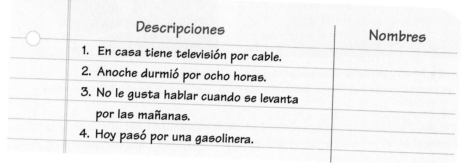

Descripciones	Nombres
1. En casa tiene televisión por cable.	
2. Anoche durmió por ocho horas.	
3. No le gusta hablar cuando se levanta por las mañanas.	
4. Hoy pasó por una gasolinera.	

6

Situación Dramatiza esta situación con un(a) compañero/a. Uno de Uds. quiere comprar un carro y necesita que su padre/madre le preste dinero. Para convencerlo/la, el/la hijo/a menciona varias razones por las cuales (*which*) necesita el carro.

Síntesis

7

Una subasta (*auction*) Trabajen en grupos. Cada estudiante debe traer un objeto o una foto del objeto para vender a la clase. Luego, un(a) estudiante es el/la vendedor(a) y los otros son los postores (*bidders*). Para empezar la subasta, el/la vendedor(a) tiene que describir el objeto y explicar para qué se usa y por qué alguien debe comprarlo.

modelo

Vendedor(a)   Aquí tengo una videocasetera Sony. Pueden usar esta videocasetera para ver películas en su casa o para grabar (*to record*) sus programas favoritos. Sólo hace un año que la compré y todavía funciona perfectamente. ¿Quién ofrece $150.00 para empezar?

Postor(a) 1   Te doy $50.00.

Vendedor(a)   ¿Quién me ofrece $60.00 por la videocasetera? Es una ganga a este precio. Yo pagué $200.00 por ella.

Postor(a) 2   Te doy $60.00 por la videocasetera.

11.3 Reciprocal reflexives

ANTE TODO   In Lesson 7, you learned that reflexive pronouns indicate that the subject of a sentence does the action to itself. Reciprocal pronouns, on the other hand, express a shared or reciprocal action between two or more people or things. In this context, the reflexive pronoun means *(to) each other* or *(to) one another*.

Luis y Marta **se** miran en el espejo.   Luis y Marta **se** miran.
Luis and Marta look at themselves in the mirror.   *Luis and Marta look at each other.*

▶ Only the plural forms of the reflexive pronouns **(nos, os, se)** are used to express reciprocal actions because the action must involve more than one person or thing.

Cuando **nos vimos** en la calle,   **Nos ayudamos** cuando usamos
    nos abrazamos.   la computadora.
When we saw each other on the   *We help each other when we use*
    street, we hugged one another.   *the computer.*

Uds. **se** van a **encontrar** en el   Las amigas **se saludaron** y
    Café Tortoni, ¿no?   **se besaron**.
You are meeting each other at   *The friends greeted each other*
    the Café Tortoni, right?   *and kissed one another.*

¡INTÉNTALO!   Indica el reflexivo recíproco adecuado y el presente o el pretérito de estos verbos.

El presente

1. (escribir) Los novios *se escriben* .
    Nosotros _____.
    Ana y Ernesto _____.
2. (escuchar) Mis tíos _____.
    Nosotros _____.
    Ellos _____.
3. (ver) Nosotros _____.
    Fernando y Tomás _____.
    Uds. _____.
4. (llamar) Ellas _____.
    Mis hermanos _____.
    Pepa y yo _____.

El pretérito

1. (saludar) Nicolás y tú *se saludaron* .
    Nuestros vecinos _____.
    Nosotros _____.
2. (hablar) Los amigos _____.
    Elena y yo _____.
    Nosotras _____.
3. (conocer) Alberto y yo _____.
    Uds. _____.
    Ellos _____.
4. (odiar) Ana y Javier _____.
    Los primos _____.
    Mi hermana y yo _____.

Práctica

1 **Un amor recíproco** Describe a Laura y a Elián usando los verbos recíprocos.

modelo

Laura veía a Elián todos los días. Elián veía a Laura todos los días.
Laura y Elián se veían todos los días.

1. Laura conocía bien a Elián. Elián conocía bien a Laura.

2. Laura miraba a Elián con amor. Elián la miraba con amor también.

3. Laura entendía bien a Elián. Elián entendía bien a Laura.

4. Laura hablaba con Elián todas las noches por teléfono. Elián hablaba con Laura todas las noches por teléfono.

5. Laura ayudaba a Elián con los problemas. Elián la ayudaba también con los problemas.

2 **Describir** Mira los dibujos y describe lo que estas personas hicieron.

1. Las hermanas _____.   2. Ellos _____.

3. Gilberto y Mercedes _____ /
_____ / _____.

4. Tú y yo _____ /
_____.

Comunicación

3 **Preguntas** En parejas, túrnense para hacerse estas preguntas.

1. ¿Se vieron tú y tu mejor amigo/a ayer? ¿Cuándo se ven Uds. normalmente?
2. ¿Dónde se encuentran tú y tus amigos?
3. ¿Se ayudan tú y tu mejor amigo/a con sus problemas?
4. ¿Se entienden bien tú y tu novio/a?
5. ¿Dónde se conocieron tú y tu novio/a? ¿Cuánto tiempo hace que se conocen Uds.?
6. ¿Cuándo se dan regalos tú y tu novio/a?
7. ¿Se escriben tú y tus amigos por correo electrónico o prefieren llamarse por teléfono?
8. ¿Siempre se llevan bien tú y tu compañero/a de cuarto? Explica.

11.4 Stressed possessive adjectives and pronouns

ANTE TODO In contrast to English, Spanish has two types of possessive adjectives: the unstressed (or short) forms you learned in Lesson 3 and the stressed (or long) forms. The stressed possessive adjectives are used for emphasis or to express the English phrases *of mine, of yours, of his,* and so on.

Stressed possessive adjectives

Masculine	Feminine	Masculine	Feminine	
mío	**mía**	**míos**	**mías**	*my; (of) mine*
tuyo	**tuya**	**tuyos**	**tuyas**	*your; (of) yours* (fam.)
suyo	**suya**	**suyos**	**suyas**	*your; (of) yours* (form.); *his;* *(of) his; her; (of) hers; its*
nuestro	**nuestra**	**nuestros**	**nuestras**	*our; (of) ours*
vuestro	**vuestra**	**vuestros**	**vuestras**	*your; (of) yours* (fam.)
suyo	**suya**	**suyos**	**suyas**	*your; (of) yours* (form.); *their; (of) theirs*

> **¡ATENCIÓN!**
>
> Used with **un/una**, these possessives are similar in meaning to the English expression *of mine/yours/etc.*
>
> **Juancho es un amigo mío.**
> *Juancho is a friend of mine.*

▶ Stressed possessive adjectives must agree in gender and number with the nouns they modify.

su impresora → la impresora **suya**
her printer *her printer*

nuestros televisores → los televisores **nuestros**
our television sets *our television sets*

▶ Stressed possessive adjectives are placed after the noun they modify, while unstressed possessive adjectives are placed before the noun.

Son **mis** llaves. Son las llaves **mías**.
They are my keys. *They are my keys.*

▶ A definite article, an indefinite article, or a demonstrative adjective usually precedes a noun modified by a stressed possessive adjective.

Me encantan { **unos** discos compactos **tuyos**. *I love some compact discs of yours.*
los discos compactos **tuyos**. *I love your compact discs.*
estos discos compactos **tuyos**. *I love these compact discs of yours.*

▶ Since **suyo, suya, suyos,** and **suyas** have more than one meaning, you can avoid confusion by using the construction: [*article*] + [*noun*] + **de** + [*subject pronoun*].

el teclado **suyo** { el teclado **de él/ella** *his/her keyboard*
el teclado **de Ud.** *your keyboard*
el teclado **de ellos/ellas** *their keyboard*
el teclado **de Uds.** *your keyboard*

> **CONSÚLTALO**
>
> **Possessive adjectives** Note that this is the same construction you learned in Lesson 3 for clarifying **su** and **sus**. To review unstressed possessive adjectives, see Lesson 3, p. 75.

Possessive pronouns

▶ Possessive pronouns are used to replace a noun + [*possessive adjective*]. In Spanish, the possessive pronouns have the same forms as the stressed possessive adjectives, and they are preceded by a definite article.

la calculadora **nuestra**   **la nuestra**
el *fax* **tuyo**   **el tuyo**
los archivos **suyos**   **los suyos**

▶ A possessive pronoun agrees in number and gender with the noun it replaces.

—Aquí está **mi coche**. ¿Dónde está **el tuyo**?
Here's my car. Where is yours?

—¿Tienes **las cintas** de Carlos?
Do you have Carlos' tapes?

—**El mío** está en el taller de mi hermano.
Mine is at my brother's garage.

—No, pero tengo **las nuestras.**
No, but I have ours.

¡LENGUA VIVA!

The definite article (**el/la**) is usually omitted when a stressed possessive follows the verb **ser**.

Perdone, ¿pero **es suya** esta cámara?

No, no **es mía**.

Episodio veintiuno: Tecnohombre y los superamigos suyos salvan el mundo una vez más.

La Mujer Mecánica y Tecnohombre, ¡mis héroes!

¡Y los míos también!

¡INTÉNTALO! Indica las formas tónicas (*stressed*) de estos adjetivos posesivos y los pronombres posesivos correspondientes.

	adjetivos	**pronombres**
1. su videocasetera	la videocasetera suya	la suya
2. mi televisor	_____	_____
3. nuestros discos	_____	_____
4. tus cintas	_____	_____
5. su módem	_____	_____
6. mis videos	_____	_____
7. nuestra impresora	_____	_____
8. tu estéreo	_____	_____
9. nuestro carro	_____	_____
10. mi computadora	_____	_____

Práctica

1 **Frases** Forma frases con las siguientes palabras. Usa el presente.

1. Un / amiga / suyo / vivir / Córdoba
2. ¿Me / prestar / calculadora / tuyo?
3. El / coche / suyo / nunca / funcionar / bien
4. No / nos / interesar / problemas / suyo
5. Yo / querer / cámara / mío / ahora mismo
6. Un / amigos / nuestro / manejar / como / loco

2 **¿Es suyo?** Un policía ha capturado al hombre que robó (*robbed*) en tu casa. Ahora quieren saber qué cosas son tuyas. Túrnate con un(a) compañero/a para hacer el papel del policía y usa las pistas (*clues*) para contestar las preguntas.

> **modelo**
>
> No/viejo
> **Policía:** Esta calculadora, ¿es suya?
> **Estudiante:** No, no es mía. La mía era más vieja.

1. Sí   2. Sí   3. Sí

4. No/grande   5. No/pequeño   6. No/de Shakira

3 **Conversaciones** Completa estas conversaciones con las formas adecuadas de los pronombres posesivos.

1. —La casa de los Ortiz estaba en la avenida 9 de Julio. ¿Dónde estaba la casa de Uds.?
   —_____ estaba en la calle Bolívar.
2. —A Carmen le encanta su monitor nuevo.
   —¿Sí? A José no le gusta _____.
3. —Puse mis discos aquí. ¿Dónde pusiste _____, Alfonso?
   —Puse _____ en el escritorio.
4. —Se me olvidó traer mis cintas. ¿Trajeron Uds. _____?
   —No, dejamos _____ en casa.
5. —Yo compré una computadora de Gateway y Marta compró _____ de Dell. ¿De qué marca (*brand*) es _____?
   —_____ es de IBM.

Comunicación

4

Comparar Trabajen en parejas. Intenta (*Try to*) convencer a tu compañero/a de que algo que tú tienes es mejor que el que él/ella tiene. Pueden hablar de sus carros, estéreos, discos compactos, clases, horarios o trabajos.

> **modelo**
>
> **Estudiante 1:** Mi computadora tiene una pantalla de
>   quince pulgadas (inches). ¿Y la tuya?
> **Estudiante 2:** La mía es mejor porque tiene una pantalla
>   de diecisiete pulgadas.
> **Estudiante 1:** Pues la mía…

Síntesis

5

Anuncios Lee este anuncio (*ad*) con un(a) compañero/a. Luego, preparen su propio (*own*) anuncio usando los adjetivos o los pronombres posesivos. Presenten el anuncio a la clase.

Esta computadora y esta impresora pueden ser suyas por sólo $899

Características de la computadora
• Procesador: Intel Pentium III a 1000 Mhz
• 256Mb de memoria
• Disco duro de 24 Gb
• Módem: 56 Kbps
• Sistema operativo: Windows 2000

Características de la impresora
• Velocidad 5 páginas por minuto en blanco y negro
• Resolución de 600 x 600
El precio incluye un año de servicio de Internet gratis.
Para más información, llame al 362-1990 o visite nuestro sitio Web www.fiera.com.

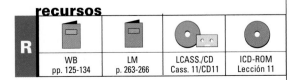

Lectura
Antes de leer

Estrategia
Recognizing borrowed words

One way languages grow is by borrowing words from each other. English words that relate to technology are often borrowed by Spanish and other languages throughout the world. Sometimes the words are modified slightly to fit the sounds of the languages that borrow them. When reading in Spanish, you can often increase your understanding by looking for words borrowed from English or other languages you know.

Examinar el texto

Mira brevemente la selección. ¿De qué trata? ¿Cómo lo sabes?

Buscar

Esta lectura contiene varias palabras tomadas del inglés. Trabaja con un(a) compañero/a para encontrarlas.

Predecir

Trabaja con un(a) compañero/a para contestar las siguientes preguntas.

1. Examina el título, las tablas y el vocabulario. ¿Qué te dicen sobre el contenido del texto?
2. Usa tu experiencia personal para predecir los tipos de tecnologías incluidas en el artículo:
   - ¿Qué tipos de tecnologías se han desarrollado desde que tú naciste?
   - ¿Y en la década pasada?
   - ¿Y en el pasado año?
3. ¿Cómo han afectado las nuevas tecnologías
   - a los empresarios?
   - a los estudiantes?
   - a las familias?

brevemente *briefly*   **¿De qué trata?** *What is it about?*   **tomadas** *taken*
empresarios *business owners*

La tecnología

Los argentinos atrapados en la Red

En el primer año del nuevo milenio, el número de usuarios de Internet superó el millón en la Argentina. Así lo indica un informe con datos recopilados por el gerente de Marketing de Telecom, José Pagés. Asimismo, la conexión al Internet desde los hogares creció un 60 por ciento en el último año.

Como demuestran estas cifras, es sin duda el Internet la novedad tecnológica que está teniendo un mayor impacto social, especialmente entre los jóvenes. En el año 2000 ya existían en el país más de dos millones de computadoras personales—una computadora por cada 15 habitantes. Unas 900.000 máquinas, el 40% del total, están en las viviendas particulares. Los argentinos que instalan una PC en su hogar la utilizan principalmente, al igual que ocurre en los Estados Unidos y en otros países, para recibir y enviar correo electrónico, navegar en la Red en busca de noticias e información, como procesadores de textos y para jugar.

Este apabullante auge en el uso de la Red refleja la aceptación de las novedades tecnológicas en todos los sectores de la sociedad. Las escuelas incorporan la computación como curso oficial desde el año 1990 y las empresas ya trabajan con sofisticadas redes de comunicaciones. Las computadoras y el *fax* no faltan en casi ningún negocio y los niños

La tecnología en la Argentina

1990 Argentina se conectó a la Red junto con Austria, Bélgica, Brasil, Chile, Grecia, India, Irlanda, Corea, España y Suiza.

1995 965 personas de cada 100.000 tenían un teléfono celular.

Después de leer

Completar

Completa las siguientes frases según el texto.

1. En el año 2000 el número de usuarios superó _____.

2. Según el artículo, el sector de la población argentina más afectado por los avances tecnológicos es _____.

3. Los argentinos utilizan las PC en casa para _____.

4. La computación como curso oficial se estableció en el año _____.

5. Los aficionados argentinos al fútbol ven partidos internacionales en _____.

Interpretar las estadísticas

Responde a las siguientes preguntas utilizando la "Proyección de usuarios del Internet en la Argentina".

1. ¿Entre qué años se proyecta el mayor aumento en el número de usuarios?

2. ¿Para qué año se piensa que casi cinco millones y medio de argentinos van a estar conectados al Internet?

3. Según la proyección, ¿qué porcentaje de la población argentina va a usar el Internet en el año 2002?

4. Según la proyección, ¿qué porcentaje de la población argentina va a tener acceso al Internet en el año 2005?

Conversar

Con dos o tres compañeros/as, hablen de los siguientes temas.

1. De todas las nuevas tecnologías que se describen en el artículo, ¿cuáles usan ustedes?

2. ¿Cómo afectan la vida de las personas las tecnologías descritas? ¿Qué aspectos de la vida se simplifican? ¿Qué problemas plantea el desarrollo de nuevas tecnologías?

3. ¿Qué cambios se predicen tanto en los Estados Unidos como en la Argentina debido al creciente (*due to the growing*) número de usuarios del Internet?

24D

aprenden con programas de computación educativos. Los gauchos usan teléfono celular y los aficionados al fútbol siguen los partidos internacionales en la televisión por cable.

En este ambiente tecnológico favorable, los servicios de la Red se multiplican. En marzo del año 2000, 52.400 argentinos compraron por Internet y gastaron cerca de 3 millones de pesos. El 98% de los que compraron productos por la Red volvería a hacerlo y el 61% de los que jamás compraron vía Internet está dispuesto a hacerlo este año.

En medio de este gran abanico de posibilidades tecnológicas no hay que olvidar a los jóvenes fanáticos del mundo digital que ya están armando su propia empresa de Internet. El futuro es ya una realidad en la vida de los argentinos, que han descubierto que el mundo tan sólo está a un clic de distancia.

Proyección de usuarios del Internet en la Argentina

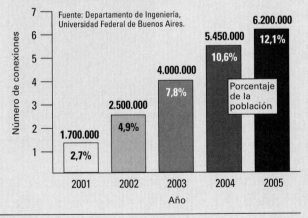

Fuente: Departamento de Ingeniería, Universidad Federal de Buenos Aires.

Número de conexiones / Año

- 2001: 1.700.000 — 2,7%
- 2002: 2.500.000 — 4,9%
- 2003: 4.000.000 — 7,8%
- 2004: 5.450.000 — 10,6%
- 2005: 6.200.000 — 12,1%

Porcentaje de la población

1998 Argentina tenía casi 3.500.000 de abonados a la televisión por cable.

2000 El número de usuarios del Internet superó el millón.

1999 La página web de la Universidad de Buenos Aires (UBA) recibió cerca de 25.000 mensajes de correo electrónico.

---

superó *exceeded* **recopilados** *compiled* **Asimismo** *Likewise*
hogares *homes* **mayor** *greater* **apabullante auge** *overwhelming increase*
gauchos *Argentine cowboys* **abanico** *range*
están armando *are putting together* **abonados** *subscribers*

Argentina

El país en cifras

▸ **Área:** 2.780.400 km^2 (1.074.000 millas^2)
*Argentina es el país de habla española más
grande del mundo. Su territorio es dos veces
el tamaño de Alaska.*

▸ **Población:** 37.944.000

▸ **Capital:** Buenos Aires —12.830.000
*En Buenos Aires vive cerca del
cuarenta por ciento de la población
total del país. La ciudad es conocida
como el "París de Sudamérica" por
el estilo parisino de muchas de sus
calles y edificios.*

Buenos Aires

▸ **Ciudades principales:**
Córdoba —1.482.000, Rosario —
1.314.000, Mendoza —982.000

SOURCE: Population Division, UN Secretariat

▸ **Moneda:** peso argentino

▸ **Idiomas:** español (oficial), guaraní

Bandera de Argentina

Argentinos célebres

▸ Jorge Luis Borges, escritor (1899–1986)
▸ María Eva Duarte de Perón ("Evita"),
  primera dama (1919–1952)
▸ Mercedes Sosa, cantante (1935–)
▸ Gato Barbieri, saxofonista (1935–)

tamaño *size* conocida *known* parisino *Parisian* primera dama *First Lady*
ancha *wide* lado *side* mide *it measures* campo *field*

Gauchos de la provincia
de Córdoba

BOLIVIA

PARAGUAY

Las catar
de Igua

ESTADOS UNIDOS

OCÉANO
ATLÁNTICO

OCÉANO
PACÍFICO

AMÉRICA DEL SUR

ARGENTINA

San Miguel
De Tucumán

La Cordillera
de los Andes

Córdoba

Aconcagua

Rosario

Río Paraná

URUGUA

Mendoza

CHILE

Buenos Aires

San Carlos
de Bariloche

Océano
Atlántico

Montañas de Patagonia

Patagonia

Vista de San Carlos
de Bariloche

Tierra del Fuego

recursos

R	WB pp. 133-134	vistasonline.com	ICD-ROM Lección 11

¡Increíble pero cierto!

La Avenida 9 de Julio en Buenos Aires es
la calle más ancha del mundo. De lado a
lado mide cerca de 140 metros, lo que es
equivalente a un campo y medio de fútbol.
Su nombre conmemora el día de la independencia de Argentina.

BRASIL

Historia • Inmigración europea

Se dice que la Argentina es el país más "europeo" de toda la América Latina. Esto se debe a que, después del año 1880, una gran cantidad de inmigrantes dejó Europa para establecerse en este país. Las diferentes culturas de estos inmigrantes, que venían principalmente de Italia, Alemania, España e Inglaterra, han dejado una profunda huella en la música, el cine, el arte y la arquitectura de la Argentina.

Artes • El tango

El tango, un baile cuyos sonidos y ritmos tienen raíces africanas, italianas y españolas, es uno de los símbolos culturales más importantes de la Argentina. Se originó entre los porteños, muchos de ellos inmigrantes, en la década de 1880. Se hizo popular en París y luego entre la clase alta de Argentina. En un principio, el tango era un baile provocativo y violento, pero se hizo más romántico durante los años 30. Hoy día es popular en todo el mundo.

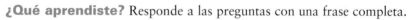

Lugares • Las cataratas de Iguazú

Entre las fronteras de la Argentina, el Paraguay y el Brasil, al norte de Buenos Aires y cerca de la confluencia de los ríos Iguazú y Paraná, están las famosas cataratas de Iguazú. Estas extensas e imponentes cataratas tienen unos 70 m (230 pies) de altura y, en época de lluvias, llegan a medir 4 km (2.5 mi) de ancho. Situadas en el Parque Nacional de Iguazú, las cataratas son uno de los sitios turísticos más visitados de la América del Sur.

¿Qué aprendiste? Responde a las preguntas con una frase completa.

1. ¿Qué porcentaje de la población de la Argentina vive en la capital?

2. ¿Quién es Mercedes Sosa?

3. Se dice que la Argentina es el país más europeo de América Latina. ¿Por qué?

4. ¿Qué tipo de baile es uno de los símbolos culturales más importantes de la Argentina?

5. ¿Dónde y cuándo se originó el tango?

6. ¿Cómo era el tango en un principio?

7. ¿En qué parque nacional están las cataratas de Iguazú?

Ceramista en
Buenos Aires

Conexión Internet Investiga estos temas en el sitio **www.vistasonline.com**.

1. Busca información sobre el tango. ¿Te gustan los ritmos y sonidos del tango? ¿Por qué? ¿Se baila el tango en tu comunidad?

2. ¿Quiénes fueron Juan y Eva Perón y qué importancia tienen en la historia de la Argentina?

Esto se debe a que *This is due to the fact that* **principalmente** *mainly* **han dejado una profunda huella** *have left a deep mark* **cuyos** *whose* **raíces** *roots* **porteños** *people of Buenos Aires* **En un principio** *At first* **Hoy día** *Nowadays* **mundo** *world* **cataratas** *waterfalls* **confluencia** *junction* **imponentes** *imposing* **altura** *height*

Uruguay

El país en cifras

▶ **Área:** 176.220 km² (68.039 millas²)
el tamaño del estado de Washington

▶ **Población:** 3.385.000

▶ **Capital:** Montevideo—1.238.000

Casi la mitad de los habitantes de Uruguay vive en Montevideo. Situada en el estuario del famoso Río de la Plata, esta ciudad cosmopolita e intelectual es también un destino popular para las vacaciones, gracias a sus hermosas playas de arena blanca que llegan hasta la ciudad de Punta del Este.

▶ **Ciudades principales:** Salto—77.000,
Paysandú—75.000, Las Piedras—61.000,
Rivera—55.000

SOURCE: Population Division, UN Secretariat

▶ **Moneda:** peso uruguayo

▶ **Idiomas:** español (oficial)

Bandera de Uruguay

Uruguayos célebres

▶ Horacio Quiroga, escritor (1878-1937)

▶ Juana de Ibarbourou, escritora (1895-1979)

▶ Mario Benedetti, escritor (1920-)

▶ Cristina Peri Rossi, escritora y profesora (1941-)

la mitad *half*   arena *sand*   récord mundial *world record*   vaca *cow*

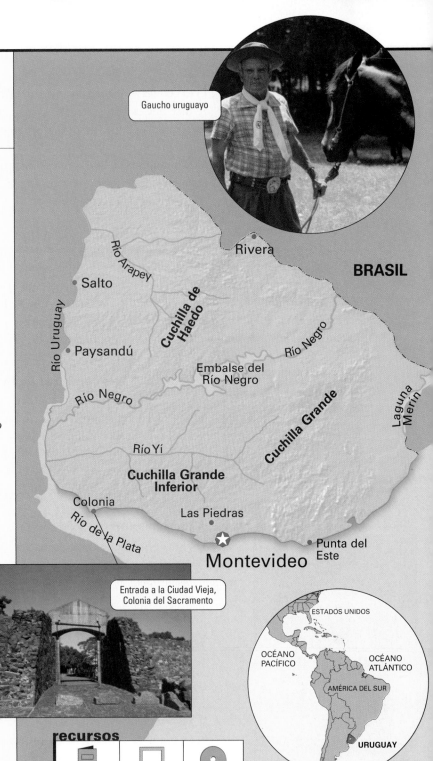

Gaucho uruguayo

Entrada a la Ciudad Vieja,
Colonia del Sacramento

recursos

R | WB pp. 137-138 | vistasonline.com | ICD-ROM Lección 18

¡Increíble pero cierto!

¡Uruguay es el país más carnívoro del planeta! Los uruguayos tienen el récord mundial de consumo de carne de res per cápita. Cada año, cada uruguayo consume 80 kilogramos de carne de res o, lo que es lo mismo, ¡¡MEDIA VACA!!

Costumbres • **La carne y el mate**

La gran importancia de la ganadería en las economías de Uruguay y Argentina se refleja en sus hábitos culinarios. Para los uruguayos, como para los argentinos, la carne de res es esencial en la dieta diaria. Algunos platos típicos son el asado, la parrillada y el chivito. El mate, una infusión similar al té, es también muy típico de esta región. Es una bebida de origen indígena que está muy presente en la vida social y familiar de estos países aunque, curiosamente, no se puede consumir en bares o restaurantes.

Deportes • **El fútbol**

El fútbol es, sin duda, el deporte nacional del Uruguay. La práctica de este deporte empezó muy pronto en Uruguay. Ya en 1891 se formó el primer equipo de fútbol uruguayo y, en 1930, se celebró en el país la primera Copa Mundial. A partir de los años treinta empezó el fútbol profesional uruguayo. Los grandes éxitos no le faltan a la selección nacional: ganó los campeonatos olímpicos del 1923 y del 1928, y los campeonatos mundiales del 1930 y del 1950. Los uruguayos ya están trabajando para que la Copa Mundial de 2030 se celebre en su país.

Costumbres • **El Carnaval**

El Carnaval de Montevideo es el más largo del mundo y uno de los mejores de Sudamérica. Dura unos cuarenta días y en él participan casi todos los habitantes de la ciudad. Durante el Carnaval, los uruguayos disfrutan de desfiles, bailes y música en las calles de su capital. La celebración más popular es el Desfile de las Llamadas, en el que se desfila al ritmo del candombe, un atractivo baile de tradición africana.

¿Qué aprendiste? Responde a las preguntas con una frase completa.
1. ¿Qué tienen en común los uruguayos célebres mencionados en la página 322?
2. ¿Qué comida es esencial en la dieta uruguaya?
3. ¿En qué países es importante la ganadería?
4. ¿Qué es el mate?
5. ¿Cuándo se formó el primer equipo uruguayo de fútbol?
6. ¿Cuándo se celebró la primera Copa Mundial de fútbol?
7. ¿Cuál es la celebración más popular del Carnaval de Montevideo?
8. ¿Cuántos días dura el Carnaval de Montevideo?

Edificio del Parlamento en Montevideo

Conexión Internet Investiga estos temas en el sitio **www.vistasonline.com**.
1. Uruguay es célebre por ser un país de muchos escritores. Busca información sobre uno de ellos y escribe una biografía.
2. Investiga cuáles son las comidas y bebidas favoritas de los uruguayos. Descríbelas e indica cuáles te gustaría probar y por qué.

---

ganadería *cattle raising* asado *barbecue* parrillada *beef platter* chivito *goat* éxitos *successes* selección *team* mundiales *world (adj.)* Dura *It lasts* disfrutan de *enjoy* desfiles *parades*

La tecnología

la calculadora	calculator
la cámara (de video)	(video) camera
el canal	(TV) channel
la cinta	(audio)tape
la contestadora	answering machine
el control remoto	remote control
el disco compacto	compact disk
el estéreo	stereo
el *fax*	fax (machine)
el radio	radio (set)
el teléfono (celular)	(cell) telephone
la televisión por cable	cable television
el televisor	televison set
el tocadiscos compacto	compact disk player
el video(casete)	video(cassette)
la videocasetera	VCR
el *walkman*	walkman
apagar	to turn off
funcionar	to work
llamar	to call
poner, prender	to turn on
sonar (o:ue)	to ring
descompuesto/a	not working; out of order

La computadora

el archivo	file
la computadora portátil	portable computer; laptop
el disco	(computer) disk
la impresora	printer
el Internet	Internet
el módem	modem
el monitor	(computer) monitor
la página principal	home page
la pantalla	screen
el programa de computación	software
el ratón	mouse
la red	network; Internet
el sitio Web	Web site
el teclado	keyboard
guardar	to save
imprimir	to print
navegar (en)	to surf (the Internet)

El carro

la autopista, la carretera	highway
la avenida	avenue
el baúl	trunk
el bulevar	boulevard
la calle	street
el camino	road
el capó	hood
el carro, el coche	car
la circulación, el tráfico	traffic
los frenos	brakes
el garaje, el taller (mecánico)	garage; (mechanic's) repair shop
la gasolina	gasoline
la gasolinera	gas station
el kilómetro	kilometer
la licencia de conducir	driver's license
la llanta	tire
el/la mecánico/a	mechanic
la milla	mile
el motor	motor
la multa	fine
el parabrisas	windshield
el policía/la mujer policía	police officer
la policía	police (force)
el semáforo	traffic light
la velocidad máxima	speed limit
el volante	steering wheel
arrancar	to start
arreglar	to fix; to arrange
bajar	to go down
bajar(se) de	to get off of/out of (a vehicle)
chocar (con)	to run into
conducir, manejar	to drive
estacionar	to park
llenar (el tanque)	to fill (the tank)
parar	to stop
revisar (el aceite)	to check (the oil)
subir	to go up
subir(se) a	to get on/into (a vehicle)
lento/a	slow
lleno/a	full

Verbos

abrazar(se)	to hug; to embrace (each other)
ayudar(se)	to help (each other)
besar(se)	to kiss (each other)
encontrar(se) (o:ue)	to meet (each other); to find (each other)
saludar(se)	to greet (each other)

Otras palabras y expresiones

para	for; in order to
por	for; by; by means of; through; along; during; in; because of; due to; in exchange for; for the sake of; on behalf of
por aquí	around here
por ejemplo	for example
por eso	that's why; therefore
por fin	finally

Stressed possessive adjectives and pronouns	See page 314.
Expresiones útiles	See page 301.

recursos

| R | LCASS./CD Cass. 11/CD11 | LM p. 266 |

La vivienda

Communicative Goals

You will learn how to:

• Welcome people to your home
• Describe your house or apartment
• Talk about household chores
• Give instructions

La vivienda

Más vocabulario

las afueras	*suburbs; outskirts*
el alquiler	*rent (payment)*
el ama (m., f.) de casa	*housekeeper; caretaker*
el balcón	*balcony*
el barrio	*neighborhood*
la cafetera	*coffee maker*
el cartel	*poster*
el edificio de apartamentos	*apartment building*
el electrodoméstico	*electrical appliance*
la entrada	*entrance*
la escalera	*stairs; stairway*
el garaje	*garage*
el (horno de) microondas	*microwave (oven)*
el jardín	*garden; yard*
la lavadora	*washing machine*
la luz	*light, electricity*
la mesita de noche	*night stand*
los muebles	*furniture*
el pasillo	*hallway*
el patio	*patio; yard*
la pintura	*painting; picture*
la secadora	*clothes dryer*
el sótano	*basement; cellar*
la tostadora	*toaster*
el/la vecino/a	*neighbor*
la vivienda	*housing*
alquilar	*to rent*
mudarse	*to move (from one house to another)*

Variación léxica

alcoba, dormitorio ⟷	aposento *(Rep. Dom.)*; recámara *(Méx.)*
apartamento ⟷	departamento *(Amér. L.)*; piso *(Esp.)*
lavar los platos ⟷	lavar/fregar los trastes *(Amér. C., Rep. Dom.)*

el altillo

la alcoba, el dormitorio

la cómoda

el armario

el cuadro

Hace la cama. (hacer)

la almohada

la manta

Los quehaceres domésticos

arreglar	*to neaten; to straighten up*
barrer el suelo	*to sweep the floor*
cocinar	*to cook*
ensuciar	*to get (something) dirty*
hacer quehaceres domésticos	*to do household chores*
lavar (el suelo, los platos)	*to wash (the floor, the dishes)*
limpiar la casa	*to clean the house*
planchar la ropa	*to iron the clothes*
quitar la mesa	*to clear the table*

la sala

las cortinas

la lámpara

la mesita

el sofá

Pasa la aspiradora. (pasar)

la alfombra

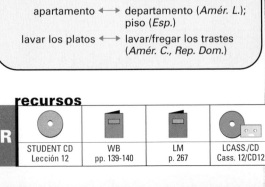

la oficina

el sillón

la pared

el estante

Sacude los muebles.
(sacudir)

la cocina

el refrigerador

el congelador

la cocina, la estufa

el horno

el lavaplatos

Saca la basura.
(sacar)

Práctica

1 **Escuchar** 🎧 Escucha la conversación y completa las frases.

1. Pedro va a limpiar primero _____.
2. Paula va a comenzar en _____.
3. Pedro le recuerda (*reminds*) a Paula que debe
   _____ en la alcoba de huéspedes.
4. Pedro va a _____ en el sótano.
5. Pedro también va a limpiar _____.
6. Ellos están limpiando la casa porque
   _____.

2 **Escoger** Escoge la letra de la respuesta correcta.

1. Cuando quieres salir al aire libre y estás en el tercer piso,
   vas _____.
   a. al pasillo   b. al balcón   c. al sótano
2. Cuando quieres tener una lámpara y un despertador cerca
   de tu cama, puedes ponerlos en _____.
   a. el barrio   b. el cuadro   c. la mesita de noche
3. Si no quieres vivir en el centro de la ciudad, puedes
   mudarte _____.
   a. al alquiler   b. a las afueras   c. a la vivienda
4. Guardamos (*We keep*) los pantalones, las camisas y los
   zapatos en _____.
   a. la secadora   b. el armario   c. el patio
5. Para subir de la planta baja al primer piso, usamos _____.
   a. las entradas   b. los carteles   c. las escaleras
6. Ponemos cuadros y pinturas en _____.
   a. las paredes   b. los quehaceres   c. los jardines

3 **Definiciones** En parejas, identifiquen cada cosa que se describe.
Luego inventen sus propias descripciones de algunas palabras
y expresiones de las páginas 326 y 327.

> **modelo**
> **Estudiante 1:** Si vives en un apartamento, lo tienes
>   que pagar cada mes.
> **Estudiante 2:** el alquiler

1. Es donde pones la cabeza cuando duermes.
2. Es el quehacer doméstico que haces después de
   comer.
3. Cubren (*They cover*) las ventanas y decoran la sala
   a la vez (*at the same time*).
4. Algunos ejemplos son las cómodas, las mesitas y
   los sillones.
5. Son las personas que viven en tu barrio.

¡Les va a encantar la casa!

Don Francisco y los estudiantes llegan a Ibarra.

PERSONAJES

INÉS

DON FRANCISCO

ÁLEX

JAVIER

SRA. VIVES

1

SRA. VIVES ¡Hola, bienvenidos!

DON FRANCISCO Sra. Vives, le presento a los chicos. Chicos, ésta es la Sra. Vives, el ama de casa.

2

SRA. VIVES Encantada. Síganme que quiero mostrarles la casa. ¡Les va a encantar!

3

SRA. VIVES Esta alcoba es para los chicos. Tienen dos camas, una mesita de noche, una cómoda… En el armario hay más mantas y almohadas por si las necesitan.

6

SRA. VIVES Ésta es la sala. El sofá y los sillones son muy cómodos. Pero, por favor, ¡no los ensucien!

7

SRA. VIVES Allí están la cocina y el comedor. Al fondo del pasillo hay un baño.

8

DON FRANCISCO Chicos, a ver… ¡atención! La Sra. Vives les va a preparar las comidas. Pero quiero que Uds. la ayuden con los quehaceres domésticos. Quiero que arreglen sus alcobas, que hagan las camas, que pongan la mesa… ¿entendido?

JAVIER No se preocupe… la vamos a ayudar en todo lo posible.

ÁLEX Sí, cuente con nosotros.

recursos

R | V/VCD-ROM Lección 12 | VM pp. 313-314 | ICD-ROM Lección 12

SRA. VIVES Javier, no ponga las maletas en la cama. Póngalas en el piso, por favor.

SRA. VIVES Tomen Uds. esta alcoba, chicas.

INÉS Insistimos en que nos deje ayudarla a preparar la comida.

SRA. VIVES No, chicos, no es para tanto, pero gracias por la oferta. Descansen un rato que seguramente están cansados.

ÁLEX Gracias. A mí me gustaría pasear por la ciudad.

INÉS Perdone, don Francisco, ¿a qué hora viene el guía mañana?

DON FRANCISCO ¿Martín? Viene temprano, a las siete de la mañana. Les aconsejo que se acuesten temprano esta noche. ¡Nada de televisión ni de conversaciones largas!

ESTUDIANTES ¡Ay, don Francisco!

Enfoque cultural Las viviendas

Del mismo modo que en los países hispanos era típico construir las ciudades en torno a una plaza central, también era frecuente construir las casas alrededor de un patio abierto central. Aunque esta arquitectura tradicional ya no es muy común, la importancia del patio sigue intacta en la cultura hispana. No es extraño ver crecer árboles de mangos y de aguacates en los patios de las casas de los países tropicales de América Latina. En el sur de España, los geranios y otras flores alegran los balcones y terrazas de las viviendas.

Expresiones útiles

Welcoming people

▶ **¡Bienvenido(s)/a(s)!**
Welcome!

Showing people around the house

▶ **Síganme... que quiero mostrarles la casa.**
Follow me... I want to show you the house.
▶ **Esta alcoba es para los chicos.**
This bedroom is for the guys.
▶ **Ésta es la sala.**
This is the living room.
▶ **Allí están la cocina y el comedor.**
The kitchen and dining room are over there.
▶ **Al fondo del pasillo hay un baño.**
At the end of the hall there is a bathroom.

Telling people what to do

▶ **Quiero que la ayude(n) con los quehaceres domésticos.**
I want you to help her with the household chores.
▶ **Quiero que arregle(n) su(s) alcoba(s).**
I want you to straighten your room(s).
▶ **Quiero que haga(n) las camas.**
I want you to make the beds.
▶ **Quiero que ponga(n) la mesa.**
I want you to set the table.
▶ **Cuente con nosotros.**
You can count on us.
▶ **Insistimos en que nos deje ayudarla a preparar la comida.**
We insist that you let us help you make the food.
▶ **Le (Les) aconsejo que se acueste(n) temprano.**
I recommend that you go to bed early.

Other expressions

▶ **No es para tanto.**
It's not a big deal.
▶ **Gracias por la oferta.**
Thanks for the offer.

Reacciona a la fotonovela

1 **¿Cierto o falso?** Indica si lo que dicen las siguientes frases es **cierto** o **falso**. Corrige las frases falsas.

	Cierto	Falso
1. Las alcobas de los estudiantes tienen dos camas, dos mesitas de noche y una cómoda.	○	○
2. La señora Vives no quiere que Javier ponga las maletas en la cama.	○	○
3. El sofá y los sillones están en la sala.	○	○
4. Los estudiantes tienen que sacudir los muebles y sacar la basura.	○	○
5. Los estudiantes van a preparar las comidas.	○	○

2 **Identificar** Identifica quién puede decir las siguientes frases.

1. Nos gustaría preparar la comida esta noche. ¿Le parece bien a Ud.?
2. Miren, si quieren otra almohada o manta, hay más en el armario.
3. Tranquilo, tranquilo, que nosotros vamos a ayudarla muchísimo.
4. Tengo ganas de caminar un poco por la ciudad.
5. No quiero que nadie mire la televisión esta noche. ¡Tenemos que levantarnos temprano mañana!

ÁLEX   JAVIER

INÉS

DON FRANCISCO   SRA. VIVES

3 **Completar** Completa las frases con la palabra correcta de la siguiente lista.

el garaje	la cocina	la sala
la alcoba	la oficina	el sótano

1. ¿Tienes hambre? Ahora mismo voy a preparar la cena en _____.
2. ¡Qué cansada estoy! Creo que voy a dormir un rato en _____.
3. ¿Quieres conversar un rato o mirar la televisión? ¿Por qué no vamos a _____?
4. Oye, quiero mirar la televisión contigo pero primero tengo que escribir un mensaje electrónico en _____.
5. El coche está descompuesto y no lo podemos usar. Ahora está en _____.

4 **Mi casa** Dibuja el plano (*floor plan*) de una casa o de un apartamento. Puede ser el plano de la casa o del apartamento donde vives o de donde te gustaría vivir. Después, trabajen en parejas y describan lo que se hace en cuatro de las habitaciones. Para terminar, pídanse (*ask for*) ayuda para hacer dos quehaceres domésticos. Pueden usar estas frases en su conversación.

Quiero mostrarte...	Al fondo hay...
Ésta es (la cocina).	Quiero que me ayudes a (sacar la basura).
Allí yo (preparo la comida).	

Ortografía

Las mayúsculas y las minúsculas

Here are some of the rules that govern the use of capital letters (**mayúsculas**) and lowercase letters (**minúsculas**) in Spanish.

Los estudiantes llegaron al aeropuerto a las dos. Luego fueron al hotel.

In both Spanish and English, the first letter of every sentence is capitalized.

Rubén Blades **Panamá** **Colón** **los Andes**

The first letter of all proper nouns (names of people, countries, cities, geographical features, etc.) is capitalized.

Cien años de soledad *Don Quijote de la Mancha*
El País *Muy Interesante*

The first letter of the first word in titles of books, films, and works of art is generally capitalized, as well as the first letter of any proper names. In newspaper and magazine titles, as well as other short titles, the initial letter of each word is often capitalized.

la señora Ramos **don Francisco**
el presidente **Sra. Vives**

Titles associated with people are *not* capitalized unless they appear as the first word in a sentence. Note, however, that the first letter of an abbreviated title is capitalized.

Último **Álex** **MENÚ** **PERDÓN**

Accent marks should be retained on capital letters. In practice, however, this rule is often ignored.

lunes **viernes** **marzo** **primavera**

The first letter of days, months, and seasons are <u>not</u> capitalized.

español **estadounidense** **japonés** **panameños**

The first letter of nationalities and languages is <u>not</u> capitalized.

Práctica Corrige las mayúsculas y minúsculas incorrectas.

1. soy lourdes romero. Soy Colombiana.
2. éste Es mi Hermano álex.
3. somos De panamá.
4. ¿es ud. La sra. benavides?
5. ud. Llegó el Lunes, ¿no?

recursos

R ICD-ROM
Lección 12

Palabras desordenadas Lee el diálogo de las serpientes. Ordena las letras para saber de qué palabras se trata. Después escribe las letras indicadas para descubrir por qué llora Pepito.

Profesor Herrera, ¿es cierto que somos venenosas?

Sí, Pepito. ¿Por qué lloras?

m n a a P á ⬭_ _ _ _ _ _
s t e m r a ⬭_ _ _ _ _ _
i g s l é n _ _ _⬭_ _ _
y a U r u g u _ _ _⬭_ _ _ _
r o ñ e s a _ _ _ _ _⬭_

¡ _orque __e acabo de morder la __en _u_ !

venenosas *venomous*
morder *to bite*

12.1 Relative pronouns

ANTE TODO In both English and Spanish, relative pronouns are used to combine two sentences or clauses that share a common element, such as a noun or pronoun. Study the following diagram.

Éste es **el cuarto** de Manuela.
This is Manuela's room.

Ella usa **el cuarto** para estudiar.
She uses the room to study.

Éste es el cuarto **que** Manuela usa para estudiar.
This is the bedroom that Manuela uses to study.

Lourdes es muy inteligente.
Lourdes is very intelligent.

Lourdes estudia español.
Lourdes is studying Spanish.

Lourdes, **quien** estudia español, es muy inteligente.
Lourdes, who studies Spanish, is very intelligent.

Pueden usar las almohadas que están en el armario.

Chicos, ésta es la Sra. Vives, quien les va a mostrar la casa.

▶ Spanish has three frequently-used relative pronouns, as shown in the following list.

que	*that; which; who*
quien(es)	*who; whom; that*
lo que	*that which; what*

¡ATENCIÓN!

Interrogative words (**qué**, **quién**, etc.) always carry an accent. Relative pronouns, however never carry a written accent.

▶ **Que** is the most frequently used relative pronoun. It can refer to things or to people. Unlike its English counterpart, *that*, **que** is never omitted.

¿Dónde está la cafetera **que** compré?
Where is the coffee maker (that) I bought?

El hombre **que** limpia es Pedro.
The man who is cleaning is Pedro.

▶ The relative pronoun **quien** refers only to people and is often used after a preposition or the personal **a**. Note that **quien** has only two forms: **quien** (singular) and **quienes** (plural).

¿Son las chicas **de quienes** me hablaste la semana pasada?
Are they the girls you told me about last week?

Eva, **a quien** conocí anoche, es mi nueva vecina.
Eva, whom I met last night, is my new neighbor.

▶ **Quien(es)** is occasionally used instead of **que** in clauses set off by commas.

> Lola, **quien** es cubana, es médica.
> *Lola, who is Cuban, is a doctor.*

> Su tía, **que** es alemana, ya llegó.
> *His aunt, who is German, already arrived.*

▶ Unlike **que** and **quien(es)**, **lo que** doesn't refer to a specific noun. It refers to an idea, a situation, or a past event and means *what, that which,* or *the thing that.*

Este mercado tiene todo lo que Inés necesita.

A la Sra. Vives no le gustó lo que hizo Javier.

Este mercado tiene todo **lo que**
Inés necesita.
This market has everything that Inés needs.

Lo que me molesta es el calor.
What bothers me is the heat.

A la Sra. Vives no le gustó **lo que**
hizo Javier con sus maletas.
Mrs. Vives didn't like what Javier did with his suitcases.

Lo que quiero es una casa.
What I want is a house.

¡INTÉNTALO! Completa las siguientes oraciones con pronombres relativos.

1. Voy a utilizar los platos ____*que*____ me regaló mi abuela.
2. Ana comparte una casa con la chica a _____ conocimos en la fiesta de Jorge.
3. Este apartamento tiene todo _____ necesitamos.
4. Puedes estudiar en la alcoba _____ está a la derecha de la cocina.
5. Los señores _____ viven en esa casa acaban de llegar de Centroamérica.
6. Los niños a _____ viste en nuestro jardín son mis sobrinos.
7. La piscina _____ ves desde la ventana es la piscina de mis vecinos.
8. Fue Úrsula _____ ayudó a mamá con los quehaceres.
9. Ya te dije que es mi padre _____ alquiló el apartamento.
10. _____ te dijo Pablo no es cierto.
11. Tengo que sacudir los muebles _____ están en el altillo una vez al mes.
12. No entiendo por qué no lavaste los platos _____ te dije.
13. La mujer a _____ saludaste vive en las afueras.
14. ¿Sabes _____ necesita esta alcoba?
15. ¡No quiero volver a hacer _____ hice ayer.
16. No me gusta vivir con personas a _____ no conozco.

Práctica

1 **Combinar** Combina elementos de la columna A y la columna B para formar oraciones lógicas.

A

1. Ése es el hombre _____.
2. La mujer _____.
3. No traje _____.
4. ¿Te gusta el regalo _____?
5. ¿Cómo se llama el programa _____?
6. El profesor Montero, _____.

B

a. con quien bailaba Fernando se llama Isabel
b. que te compró Cecilia
c. quien enseña biología en la universidad, es de Panamá
d. que arregló mi auto
e. lo que necesito para la clase de matemáticas
f. que comiste en el restaurante
g. que viste en la televisión anoche

2 **Completar** Completa la historia sobre la casa que Jaime y Tina quieren comprar, usando los pronombres relativos **que, quien, quienes** o **lo que**.

1. Jaime y Tina son los chicos a _____ conocí la semana pasada.
2. Quieren comprar una casa _____ está en las afueras de la ciudad.
3. Es una casa _____ era de una artista famosa.
4. La artista, a _____ yo conocía, murió el año pasado y no tenía hijos.
5. Ahora se vende la casa con todos los muebles _____ ella tenía.
6. La sala tiene una alfombra persa _____ trajo de Kuwait.
7. Los armarios de toda la casa tienen mucho espacio, _____ a Tina le encanta.

3 **Combinar** Javier y Ana acaban de casarse y han comprado una casa y muchas otras cosas. Combina sus declaraciones para formar una sola oración con los pronombres relativos **que, quien(es)** y **lo que**.

> **modelo**
>
> Vamos a usar los cubiertos nuevos mañana. Los pusimos en el comedor.
> Mañana vamos a usar los cubiertos nuevos que pusimos en el comedor.

1. Tenemos una cafetera nueva. Mi prima nos la regaló.

2. Tenemos una cómoda nueva. Es bueno porque no hay espacio en el armario.

3. Esos platos no nos costaron mucho. Están encima del horno.

4. Esas copas me las regaló mi amiga Amalia. Ella viene a visitarme mañana.

5. La lavadora está casi nueva. Nos la regalaron mis suegros.

6. La vecina nos dio una manta de lana. Ella la compró en México.

Comunicación

4

Entrevista En parejas, túrnense para hacerse las siguientes preguntas.

1. ¿Quién era la persona que más quehaceres domésticos hacía en tu casa cuando eras niño/a? ¿Quién era la persona que trabajaba más tiempo fuera de la casa?
2. ¿Cómo se llama el producto que usas para limpiar el piso?
3. ¿Dónde compras los productos que usas para limpiar la casa?
4. Cuando eras niño/a, ¿siempre hacías todo lo que te decían tus padres?
5. ¿Quiénes son las personas con quienes más sales los fines de semana? ¿Quién es la persona a quien más llamas por teléfono?
6. ¿Cuál es el deporte que más te gusta? ¿Cuál es el que menos te gusta?
7. ¿Cuál es el barrio de tu ciudad que más te gusta y por qué?
8. ¿Quién es la persona a quien más llamas cuando tienes problemas?
9. ¿Quién es la persona a quien más admiras? ¿Por qué?
10. ¿Qué es lo que más te gusta de tu casa?
11. ¿Qué es lo que más te molesta de tus amigos?
12. ¿Qué es lo que menos te gusta de tu barrio?

5

Diálogo En grupos, preparen un diálogo para presentar a la clase. Una persona hace el papel del/de la cliente/a que quiere comprar una casa; la otra es el/la agente. Utilicen pronombres relativos.

> **modelo**
>
> **Cliente:** Me interesa comprar la casa que está enfrente del mar. ¿Cuántas alcobas tiene?
> **Agente:** Tiene dos, pero la alcoba que tiene balcón es muy grande.
> **Cliente:** Bueno, lo que quiero es una casa con tres alcobas. La persona con quien hablé ayer me dijo que la casa tenía tres alcobas.

Síntesis

6

Definir En parejas, definan las palabras. Usen los pronombres **que, quien(es)** y **lo que.** Luego compartan sus definiciones con la clase.

> **modelo**
>
> lavadora Es lo que se usa para lavar la ropa.
> pastel Es un postre que comes en tu cumpleaños.

las afueras	enfermera	manta	tenedor
alquiler	flan	patio	termómetro
amigos	guantes	postre	vaso
aspiradora	jabón	sillón	vecino

12.2 Formal (**Ud.** and **Uds.**) commands

ANTE TODO   In Spanish, the command forms are used to give orders or advice. Formal commands are used with people you address as **Ud.** or **Uds.** Observe the following examples, then study the chart.

CONSEJOS

Learning these command forms will be very helpful since the same forms are used for the subjunctive, which you will begin learning in **Estructura 12.3.**

Hable con ellos, don Francisco.
Talk with them, don Francisco.

Laven los platos ahora mismo.
Wash the dishes right now.

Coma frutas y verduras.
Eat fruits and vegetables.

Beban menos té y café.
Drink less tea and coffee.

Formal commands (*Ud.* and *Uds.*)

Infinitive	Present tense *yo* form	*Ud.* command	*Uds.* command
limpiar	limpi**o**	limpi**e**	limpi**en**
barrer	barr**o**	barr**a**	barr**an**
sacudir	sacud**o**	sacud**a**	sacud**an**
decir	dig**o**	dig**a**	dig**an**
salir	salg**o**	salg**a**	salg**an**
venir	veng**o**	veng**a**	veng**an**
volver (o:ue)	vuelv**o**	vuelv**a**	vuelv**an**
servir (e:i)	sirv**o**	sirv**a**	sirv**an**

▶ The **Ud.** and **Uds.** commands are formed by dropping the final **–o** of the **yo** form of the present tense. For **–ar** verbs, add **–e** or **–en**. For **–er** and **–ir** verbs, add **–a** or **–an**.

No se preocupe... La vamos a ayudar en todo lo posible.

Sí, cuente con nosotros.

▶ Verbs with irregular **yo** forms maintain the same irregularity in their formal commands. These verbs include **conducir, conocer, decir, hacer, ofrecer, oír, poner, salir, tener, traducir, traer, venir,** and **ver.**

Oiga, don Francisco...
Listen, don Francisco...

Ponga la mesa, por favor.
Set the table, please.

¡Salga inmediatamente!
Leave immediately!

Hagan la cama antes de salir.
Make the bed before leaving.

▶ Note also that stem-changing verbs maintain their stem-changes in **Ud.** and **Uds.** commands.

e:ie	o:ue	e:i
No **pierda** la llave.	**Vuelva** temprano, joven.	**Sirva** la sopa, por favor.
Cierren la puerta.	**Duerman** bien, chicos.	**Repitan** las frases.

▶ Verbs ending in **-car, -gar,** and **-zar** have a spelling change in the command forms.

sa**car**	**c** → **qu**	sa**qu**e, sa**qu**en
ju**gar**	**g** → **gu**	jue**gu**e, jue**gu**en
almor**zar**	**z** → **c**	almuer**c**e, almuer**c**en

The following verbs have irregular formal commands.

Infinitive	Ud. command	Uds. command
dar	**dé**	**den**
estar	**esté**	**estén**
ir	**vaya**	**vayan**
saber	**sepa**	**sepan**
ser	**sea**	**sean**

▶ To make a formal command negative, simply place **no** before the verb.

No ponga las maletas en la cama.
Don't put the suitcases on the bed.

No ensucien los sillones.
Don't dirty the armchairs.

▶ In affirmative commands, reflexive, indirect and direct object pronouns are always attached to the end of the verb.

Siénten**se**, por favor
Síga**me**, Laura.

Acuésten**se** ahora.
Póngan**las** en el suelo, por favor.

In negative commands, these pronouns always precede the verb.

No **se** preocupe.
No **me** lo dé.

No **los** ensucien.
No **nos las** traigan.

▶ **Ud.** and **Uds.** can be used with the command forms to strike a more formal tone. In such instances they follow the command form.

Muéstrele Ud. la foto a su amigo.
Show the photo to your friend.

Tomen Uds. esta alcoba.
Take this bedroom.

¡INTÉNTALO! Indica cuáles son los mandatos (*commands*) afirmativos y negativos correspondientes para cada ocasión.

Escúchelo   *No lo escuche*

1. escucharlo (Ud.) _____ . _____ .

2. decírmelo (Uds.) _____ . _____ .

3. salir (Ud.) _____ . _____ .

4. servírnoslo (Uds.) _____ . _____ .

5. barrerla (Ud.) _____ . _____ .

6. hacerlo (Ud.) _____ . _____ .

7. ir (Uds.) _____ . _____ .

8. sentarse (Uds.) _____ . _____ .

Práctica

1 **Completar** La Sra. González quiere mudarse de casa. Ayúdala a organizarse. Indica el mandato (*command*) formal de cada verbo.

1. _____ los anuncios (*ads*) del periódico y _____. (leer, guardar)
2. _____ personalmente y _____ las casas Ud. misma. (ir, ver)
3. El día de la mudanza (*On moving day*) _____ tranquila. _____ y haga las camas temprano para poder descansar bien en la noche. (estar, almorzar)
4. _____ tiempo para hacer las maletas tranquilamente. No _____ las maletas a los niños más grandes. (sacar, hacerles)
5. Primero, _____ a todos en casa que Ud. va a estar ocupada. No _____ que Ud. va a hacerlo todo. (decirles, decirles)
6. Decida qué casa quiere y _____ al agente. _____ un contrato de alquiler. (llamar, pedirle)
7. No _____. _____ que todo va a salir bien. (preocuparse, saber)
8. _____ un camión (*truck*) para ese día y _____ la hora exacta de llegada. (contratar, preguntarles)

2 **¿Qué dicen?** Mira los dibujos y escribe un mandato lógico para cada uno. Usa palabras que aprendiste en las páginas 326 y 327.

1. _____

2. _____

3. _____

4. _____

5. _____

6. _____

Comunicación

3 **Solucionar** Trabajen en parejas para presentar los siguientes problemas. Un(a) estudiante presenta los problemas de la columna A y el/la otro/a los de la columna B. Usen mandatos y túrnense para ofrecer soluciones.

> *modelo*
>
> **Estudiante 1:** Vilma se torció un tobillo jugando al tenis. Es la tercera vez.
> **Estudiante 2:** No juegue más al tenis. / Vaya a ver a un especialista.

A	**B**
1. Se me perdió el libro de español con todas mis notas.	1. Mis hijas no se levantan temprano. Siempre llegan tarde a la escuela.
2. A Vicente se le cayó la botella de vino para la cena.	2. A mi hermana le robaron las maletas. Era su primer día de vacaciones.
3. ¿Cómo? ¿Se te olvidó traer el traje de baño a la playa?	3. Nuestra casa es demasiado pequeña para nuestra familia.
4. Se nos quedaron los boletos en la casa. El avión sale en una hora.	4. Me preocupo constantemente por Roberto. Trabaja demasiado.

4 **Diálogos** En parejas, escojan dos situaciones y preparen diálogos para presentar a la clase. Usen mandatos formales.

CONSÚLTALO

Did you know that on December 31, 1999, the United States ceded control of the Panama Canal to the government of Panama, ending nearly 100 years of administration by the U.S.? To learn more, see **Panorama**, pp. 354-355.

> *modelo*
>
> **Lupita:** Sr. Ramírez, siento mucho llegar tan tarde. Mi niño se enfermó. ¿Qué debo hacer?
> **Sr. Ramírez:** No se preocupe. Siéntese y descanse un poco.

SITUACIÓN 1 Profesor Rosado, no vine la semana pasada porque el equipo jugaba en Boquete. ¿Qué debo hacer para ponerme al día (*catch up*)?

SITUACIÓN 2 Los invitados de la boda llegan a las cuatro de la tarde, la mesa está sin poner y el champán sin servir. Los camareros apenas están llegando. ¿Qué deben hacer los camareros?

SITUACIÓN 3 Mi novio es un poco aburrido. No le gustan ni el cine, ni los deportes, ni salir a comer. Tampoco habla mucho. ¿Qué puedo hacer o qué le puedo decir?

SITUACIÓN 4 Tengo que preparar una presentación para mañana sobre el Canal de Panamá. ¿Por dónde comienzo?

Síntesis

5 **Presentar** En grupos, preparen un anuncio (*ad*) de televisión para presentar a la clase. El anuncio debe tratar de (*be about*) un detergente, un electrodoméstico, una agencia inmobiliaria o un gimnasio. Usen mandatos, los pronombres relativos (**que, quien(es)** o **lo que**) y el **se** impersonal.

> *modelo*
>
> Compre el lavaplatos Siglo XXI. Tiene todo lo que Ud. desea. Es el lavaplatos que mejor funciona. Venga a verlo ahora mismo... No pierda ni un minuto más. Se aceptan tarjetas de crédito.

12.3 The present subjunctive

ANTE TODO With the exception of formal commands, all of the verb forms you have been using have been in the indicative mood. The indicative is used to state facts and to express actions or states that the speaker considers to be real and definite. In contrast, the subjunctive mood expresses the speaker's attitudes toward events, as well as actions or states the speaker views as uncertain or hypothetical.

Quiero que ustedes ayuden con los quehaceres domésticos.

Insistimos en que nos deje ayudarla a preparar la comida.

		hablar	comer	escribir
SINGULAR FORMS	yo	habl**e**	com**a**	escrib**a**
	tú	habl**es**	com**as**	escrib**as**
	Ud./él/ella	habl**e**	com**a**	escrib**a**
PLURAL FORMS	nosotros/as	habl**emos**	com**amos**	escrib**amos**
	vosotros/as	habl**éis**	com**áis**	escrib**áis**
	Uds./ellos/ellas	habl**en**	com**an**	escrib**an**

Present subjunctive of regular verbs

¡LENGUA VIVA!
You may think that English has no subjunctive, but it does! It used to be very common but now survives mostly in set expressions such as *if I were you* and *be that as it may.*

▶ The present subjunctive is formed very much like **Ud.** and **Uds.** commands. From the **yo** form of the present indicative, drop the **-o** ending, and replace it with the subjunctive endings.

INFINITIVE	PRESENT INDICATIVE	VERB STEM	PRESENT SUBJUNCTIVE
hablar	**hablo**	habl-	**hable**
comer	**como**	com-	**coma**
escribir	**escribo**	escrib-	**escriba**

▶ The present subjunctive endings are:

–ar verbs

–e	**–emos**
–es	**–éis**
–e	**–en**

–er and –ir verbs

–a	**–amos**
–as	**–áis**
–a	**–an**

CONSEJOS
Note that, in the present subjunctive, –**ar** verbs use endings normally associated with present tense –**er** and –**ir** verbs. Likewise, –**er** and –**ir** verbs in the present subjunctive use endings normally associated with –**ar** verbs in the present tense. Note also that, in the present subjunctive, the **yo** form is the same as the **Ud./él/ella** form.

▶ Verbs with irregular **yo** forms show the same irregularity in the present subjunctive.

Infinitive	Present indicative	Verb stem	Present subjunctive
conducir	conduzco	**conduzc-**	**conduzca**
conocer	conozco	**conozc-**	**conozca**
decir	digo	**dig-**	**diga**
hacer	hago	**hag-**	**haga**
ofrecer	ofrezco	**ofrezc-**	**ofrezca**
oír	oigo	**oig-**	**oiga**
parecer	parezco	**parezc-**	**parezca**
poner	pongo	**pong-**	**ponga**
tener	tengo	**teng-**	**tenga**
traducir	traduzco	**traduzc-**	**traduzca**
traer	traigo	**traig-**	**traiga**
venir	vengo	**veng-**	**venga**
ver	veo	**ve-**	**vea**

▶ To maintain the **-c, -g,** and **-z** sounds, verbs ending in **-car, -gar,** and **-zar** have a spelling change in all forms of the present subjunctive.

sacar: saque, saques, saque, saquemos, saquéis, saquen

jugar: juegue, juegues, juegue, juguemos, juguéis, jueguen

almorzar: almuerce, almuerces, almuerce, almorcemos, almorcéis, almuercen

Present subjunctive of stem-changing verbs

▶ **-Ar** and **-er** stem-changing verbs have the same stem changes in the subjunctive as they do in the present indicative.

pensar (e:ie): piense, pienses, piense, pensemos, penséis, piensen

mostrar (o:ue): muestre, muestres, muestre, mostremos, mostréis, muestren

entender (e:ie): entienda, entiendas, entienda, entendamos, entendáis, entiendan

volver (o:ue): vuelva, vuelvas, vuelva, volvamos, volváis, vuelvan

▶ **–Ir** stem-changing verbs have the same stem changes in the subjunctive as they do in the present indicative, but in addition, the **nosotros/as** and **vosotros/as** forms undergo a stem change. The unstressed **e** changes to **i,** while the unstressed **o** changes to **u.**

pedir (e:i): pida, pidas, pida, pidamos, pidáis, pidan

sentir (e:ie): sienta, sientas, sienta, sintamos, sintáis, sientan

dormir (o:ue): duerma, duermas, duerma, durmamos, durmáis, duerman

Irregular verbs in the present subjunctive

▶ The following five verbs are irregular in the present subjunctive.

Irregular verbs in the present subjunctive

		dar	estar	ir	saber	ser
SINGULAR FORMS	yo	dé	esté	vaya	sepa	sea
	tú	des	estés	vayas	sepas	seas
	Ud./él/ella	dé	esté	vaya	sepa	sea
PLURAL FORMS	nosotros/as	demos	estemos	vayamos	sepamos	seamos
	vosotros/as	deis	estéis	vayáis	sepáis	seáis
	Uds./ellos/ellas	den	estén	vayan	sepan	sean

General uses of the subjunctive

▶ The subjunctive is mainly used to express: 1) will and influence, 2) emotion, 3) doubt, disbelief, and denial, and 4) indefiniteness and nonexistence.

▶ The subjunctive is most often used in complex sentences that consist of a main clause and a subordinate clause. The main clause contains a verb or expression that triggers the use of the subjunctive. The conjunction **que** connects the subordinate clause to the main clause.

Es muy importante   que   **vayas** al hotel ahora mismo.

▶ Some expressions are always followed by clauses in the subjunctive. These include:

Es bueno que...	**Es mejor que...**	**Es malo que...**
It's good that...	*It's better that...*	*It's bad that...*
Es importante que...	**Es necesario que...**	**Es urgente que...**
It's important that...	*It's necessary that...*	*It's urgent that...*

¡INTÉNTALO!   Indica el presente de subjuntivo de los siguientes verbos.

1. (alquilar, beber, vivir)   yo _alquile, beba, viva_
2. (estudiar, aprender, asistir)   tú _____
3. (encontrar, poder, dormir)   él _____
4. (hacer, tener, venir)   nosotras _____
5. (dar, hablar, escribir)   ellos _____
6. (pagar, empezar, buscar)   Uds. _____
7. (ser, ir, saber)   yo _____
8. (estar, dar, oír)   tú _____
9. (arreglar, leer, abrir)   nosotros _____
10. (cantar, leer, vivir)   ellas _____

Práctica

1 **Completar** Completa las oraciones conjugando los verbos entre paréntesis. Luego empareja las oraciones del primer grupo con las del segundo grupo.

1. Es mejor que _____ en casa. (nosotros, cenar)
2. Es importante que _____ algo para calmar el dolor. (yo, tomar)
3. Señora, es urgente que le _____ la muela. Parece que tiene una infección. (yo, sacar)
4. Es malo que Ana les _____ tantos dulces a los niños. (dar)
5. Es necesario que _____ a la una de la tarde. (Uds., llegar)
6. Es importante que _____ temprano. (nosotros, acostarse)

a. Es importante que _____ más verduras. (ellos, comer)
b. No, es mejor que _____ a comer. (nosotros, salir)
c. Y yo creo que es urgente que _____ al doctor. (tú, llamar)
d. En mi opinión, no es necesario que _____ tanto. (nosotros, dormir)
e. ¿Ah, sí? ¿Es necesario que me _____ un antibiótico también? (yo, tomar)
f. Para llegar a tiempo, es necesario que _____ temprano. (nosotros, almorzar)

Comunicación

2 **Minidiálogos** En parejas, completen los minidiálogos de una manera lógica.

> **modelo**
> **Miguelito:**   Mamá, no quiero arreglar mi cuarto.
> **Sra. Casas:** Es necesario que lo arregles. Y es importante que sacudas los muebles también.

1. **MIGUELITO** Mamá, no quiero estudiar. Quiero salir a jugar con mis amigos.
   SRA. CASAS _____

2. **MIGUELITO** Mamá, es que no me gustan las verduras. Prefiero comer pasteles.
   SRA. CASAS _____

3. **MIGUELITO** ¿Tengo que poner la mesa, mamá?
   SRA. CASAS _____

4. **MIGUELITO** No me siento bien, mamá. Me duele todo el cuerpo y tengo fiebre.
   SRA. CASAS _____

3 **Entrevista** Trabajen en parejas. Entrevístense usando estas preguntas. Expliquen sus respuestas.

1. ¿Es importante que los niños ayuden con los quehaceres domésticos?
2. ¿Es urgente que los norteamericanos aprendan otras lenguas?
3. Si un(a) norteamericano/a quiere aprender francés, ¿es mejor que lo aprenda en Francia?
4. En su universidad, ¿es necesario que los estudiantes vivan en residencias estudiantiles?
5. ¿Es bueno que todos los estudiantes participen en algún deporte?
6. ¿Es importante que todos los estudiantes asistan a la universidad?

12.4 Subjunctive with verbs of will and influence

 You will now learn how to use the subjunctive with verbs and expressions of will and influence.

Quiero que tengas dientes más blancos.

▶ Verbs of will and influence are often used when someone wants to affect the actions or behavior of other people.

Enrique **quiere** que salgamos a cenar.
Enrique wants us to go out for dinner.

Paola **prefiere** que cenemos en casa.
Paola prefers that we have dinner at home.

▶ Here is a list of widely used verbs of will and influence.

Verbs of will and influence			
aconsejar	to advise	**pedir** (e:i)	to ask (for)
desear	to wish; to desire	**preferir** (e:ie)	to prefer
importar	to be important; to matter	**prohibir**	to prohibit
insistir (en)	to insist (on)	**querer** (e:ie)	to want
mandar	to order	**recomendar** (e:ie)	to recommend
necesitar	to need	**rogar** (o:ue)	to beg; to plead
		sugerir (e:ie)	to suggest

▶ Some impersonal expressions, such as **es necesario que, es importante que, es mejor que** and **es urgente que,** are considered expressions of will or influence.

▶ When the main clause contains an expression of will or influence, the subjunctive is required in the subordinate clause, provided that the two clauses have different subjects.

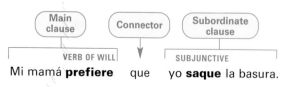

Main clause	Connector	Subordinate clause
VERB OF WILL		SUBJUNCTIVE
Mi mamá **prefiere**	que	yo **saque** la basura.

Quiero que arreglen sus alcobas, que hagan las camas, que pongan la mesa...

...y les aconsejo que se acuesten temprano esta noche.

▶ Indirect object pronouns are often used with the verbs **aconsejar, importar, mandar, pedir, prohibir, recomendar, rogar,** and **sugerir.**

Te aconsejo que estudies.
I advise you to study.

Le sugiero que vaya a casa.
I suggest that he go home.

Les recomiendo que barran el suelo.
I recommend that you sweep the floor.

Le ruego que no venga.
I beg him not to come.

▶ Note that all the forms of **prohibir** in the present tense carry a written accent, except for the **nosotros** form: **prohíbo, prohíbes, prohíbe, prohibimos, prohibís, prohíben.**

Ella les **prohíbe** que miren la televisión.
She prohibits them from watching television.

Nos **prohíben** que nademos en la piscina.
They prohibit that we swim in the swimming pool.

▶ The infinitive is used with words or expressions of will and influence if there is no change of subject in the sentence.

No quiero **sacudir** los muebles.
I don't want to dust the furniture.

Paco prefiere **descansar.**
Paco prefers to rest.

Es importante **sacar** la basura.
It's important to take out the trash.

No es necesario **quitar** la mesa.
It's not necessary to clear the table.

¡INTÉNTALO!   Completa cada oración con la forma correcta del verbo entre paréntesis.

1. Te sugiero que ____vayas____ (ir) con ella al supermercado.
2. Él necesita que yo le _____ (prestar) dinero.
3. No queremos que tú _____ (hacer) nada especial para nosotros.
4. Mis papás quieren que yo _____ (limpiar) mi cuarto.
5. Nos piden que la _____ (ayudar) a preparar la comida.
6. Quieren que tú _____ (sacar) la basura todos los días.
7. Quiero _____ (descansar) esta noche.
8. Es importante que Uds. _____ (limpiar) la casa.
9. Su tía les manda que _____ (poner) la mesa.
10. Te aconsejo que no _____ (salir) con él.
11. Mi tío insiste en que mi prima _____ (hacer) la cama.
12. Prefiero _____ (ir) al cine.
13. Es necesario _____ (estudiar).
14. Recomiendo que ustedes _____ (pasar) la aspiradora.

Práctica

1 **Completar** Completa el diálogo con palabras de la lista.

ponga	sea	saber	haga
prohíbe	quiere	comas	diga
cocina	sé	ser	vaya

IRENE Tengo problemas con Vilma. Sé que debo hablar con ella. ¿Qué me recomiendas que le _____?

JULIA Pues, necesito _____ más antes de darte consejos.

IRENE Bueno, para empezar me _____ que traiga dulces a la casa.

JULIA Pero chica, tiene razón. Es mejor que tú no _____ cosas dulces.

IRENE Sí, ya lo sé. Pero quiero que _____ más flexible. Además, insiste en que yo _____ todo en la casa.

JULIA Yo _____ que Vilma _____ y hace los quehaceres todos los días.

IRENE Sí, pero siempre que hay fiesta me pide que _____ los cubiertos y las copas en la mesa y que _____ al sótano por las servilletas y los platos. ¡Es lo que más odio: ir al sótano!

JULIA Mujer, ¡Vilma sólo _____ que ayudes en la casa!

2 **Aconsejar** En parejas, lean lo que dice cada persona. Luego den consejos lógicos usando verbos como **aconsejar, recomendar** y **prohibir**. Sus consejos deben ser diferentes de lo que la persona quiere hacer.

modelo

Isabel: Quiero conseguir un comedor con los muebles más caros del mundo.

Consejo: Te aconsejamos que consigas unos muebles menos caros.

1. **DAVID** Pienso poner el congelador en el sótano.
2. **SARA** Voy a ir a la gasolinera para comprar unas copas de cristal elegantes.
3. **SR. ALARCÓN** Insisto en comenzar a arreglar el jardín en marzo.
4. **SRA. VILLA** Quiero ver las tazas y los platos de la tienda El Ama de Casa Feliz.
5. **DOLORES** Voy a poner servilletas de tela (cloth) para los cuarenta invitados.
6. **SR. PARDO** Pienso poner todos mis muebles nuevos en el altillo.
7. **SRA. GONZÁLEZ** Hay una fiesta en mi casa esta noche pero no quiero arreglar la casa.
8. **CARLITOS** Hoy no tengo ganas de hacer las camas ni de quitar la mesa.

3 **Preguntas** En parejas, túrnense para contestar las preguntas. Usen el subjuntivo.

1. ¿Te dan consejos tus amigos? ¿Qué te aconsejan? ¿Aceptas sus consejos? ¿Por qué?
2. ¿Qué te sugieren tus profesores que hagas antes de terminar los cursos que llevas?
3. ¿Insisten tus amigos en que salgas mucho con ellos?
4. ¿Qué quieres que te regalen tu familia y tus amigos/as en tu cumpleaños?
5. ¿Qué le recomiendas tú a un(a) amigo/a que no quiere salir los sábados con su novio/a?
6. ¿Qué les aconsejas a los nuevos estudiantes de tu universidad?

Comunicación

4 **Inventar** En parejas, preparen una lista de seis personas famosas. Un(a) estudiante da el nombre de una persona famosa y el/la otro/a le da un consejo.

> *modelo*
>
> **Estudiante 1:** Judge Judy.
> **Estudiante 2:** Le recomiendo que sea más simpática con la gente.
> **Estudiante 2:** Leonardo DiCaprio.
> **Estudiante 1:** Le aconsejo que haga más películas.

5 **Hablar** En parejas, miren la ilustración y denle consejos a Gerardo sobre cómo arreglar su casa. Usen expresiones impersonales y verbos como **aconsejar, sugerir** y **recomendar.**

> *modelo*
>
> Es mejor que arregles el apartamento más a menudo.
> Te aconsejo que no dejes para mañana lo que puedes hacer hoy.

recursos

| R | WB pp. 141-148 | LM p. 269-272 | LCASS./CD Cass. 12/CD12 | ICD-ROM Lección 12 |

Lectura

Antes de leer

Estrategia

Locating the main parts of a sentence

Did you know that a text written in Spanish is an average of 15% longer than the same text written in English? Because the Spanish language tends to use more words to express ideas, you will often encounter long sentences when reading in Spanish. Of course, the length of sentences varies with genre and with authors' individual styles. To help you understand long sentences, identify the main parts of the sentence before trying to read it in its entirety. First locate the main verb of the sentence, along with its subject, ignoring any words or phrases set off by commas. Then reread the sentence, adding details like direct and indirect objects, transitional words, and prepositional phrases.

Examinar el texto

Mira el formato de la lectura. ¿Qué tipo de documento es? ¿Qué cognados encuentras en la lectura? ¿Qué te dicen sobre el tema de la selección?

¿Probable o improbable?

Mira brevemente el texto e indica si las siguientes frases son probables o improbables.

1. Este folleto es de interés turístico.
2. El folleto describe un lugar histórico cubano.
3. El folleto incluye algunas explicaciones de arquitectura.
4. Esperan atraer visitantes al lugar.

Frases largas

Mira el texto y busca algunas frases largas. Con un(a) compañero/a, identifiquen las partes principales de la frase y después examinen las descripciones adicionales. ¿Qué significan las frases?

folleto *brochure*   atraer *to attract*   épocas *time periods*   herencia *heritage*

Bienvenidos al Palacio de Las Garzas

El palacio está abierto de martes a domingo. Para más información, llame al teléfono 507-226-7000. También puede solicitar un folleto a la casilla 3467, Ciudad de Panamá, Panamá.

Después de leer

Ordenar

Pon los siguientes eventos en el orden cronológico adecuado.

_____ El palacio se convirtió en residencia presidencial.

_____ Durante diferentes épocas, maestros, médicos y banqueros practicaron su profesión en el palacio.

_____ El Dr. Belisario Porras ocupó el palacio por primera vez.

_____ Los colonizadores construyeron el palacio.

_____ Se renovó el palacio.

_____ Los turistas pueden visitar el palacio de martes a domingo.

El Palacio de Las Garzas es la residencia oficial del Presidente de Panamá desde 1903. Fue construido en 1673 para ser la casa de un gobernador español. Con el paso de los años fue almacén, escuela, hospital, aduana, banco y por último, palacio presidencial.

En la actualidad el edificio tiene tres pisos, pero los planos originales muestran una construcción de un piso con un gran patio en el centro. La restauración del palacio comenzó en el año 1922 y los trabajos fueron realizados por el arquitecto Villanueva-Myers y el pintor Roberto Lewis. El palacio, un monumento al estilo colonial, todavía conserva su elegancia y buen gusto, y es una de las principales atracciones turísticas del barrio Casco Viejo.

Planta baja
El patio de las Garzas

Una antigua puerta de hierro recibe a los visitantes. El patio interior todavía conserva los elementos originales de la construcción: piso de mármol, columnas de perla gris y una magnífica fuente de agua en el centro. Aquí están las nueve garzas que dan el nombre al palacio y que representan las nueve provincias de Panamá.

Primer piso
El salón Amarillo

Aquí el turista puede visitar una galería de cuarenta y un retratos de gobernadores y personajes ilustres de Panamá. La principal atracción de este salón es el sillón presidencial, que se usa especialmente cuando hay cambio de presidente. Otros atractivos de esta área son el comedor de Los Tamarindos, que se destaca por la elegancia de sus muebles y sus lámparas de cristal, y el patio andaluz, con sus coloridos mosaicos que representan la unión de la cultura indígena y la española.

El salón Dr. Belisario Porras

Este elegante y majestuoso salón es uno de los lugares más importantes del Palacio de Las Garzas. Lleva su nombre en honor al Dr. Belisario Porras, quien fue tres veces presidente de Panamá (1912-1916, 1918-1920 y 1920-1924).

Segundo piso

Es el área residencial del palacio y el visitante no tiene acceso a ella. Los armarios, las cómodas y los espejos de la alcoba fueron comprados en Italia y Francia por el presidente Porras, mientras que las alfombras, cortinas y frazadas son originarias de España.

Garzas *Herons* **solicitar** *request* **casilla** *post office box*
Casco Viejo *Old Quarter* **hierro** *iron* **mármol** *marble* **retratos** *portraits*
se destaca *stands out* **frazadas** *blankets*

Preguntas

Contesta las preguntas.

1. ¿Qué sala es notable por sus muebles elegantes y sus lámparas de cristal?
2. ¿En qué parte del palacio se encuentra la residencia del presidente?
3. ¿Dónde empiezan los turistas su visita al palacio?
4. ¿En qué lugar se representa artísticamente la rica herencia cultural de Panamá?
5. ¿Qué salón honra la memoria de un gran panameño?
6. ¿Qué partes del palacio te gustaría más visitar? ¿Por qué? Explica tu respuesta.

Conversación

En grupos de tres o cuatro estudiantes, hablen sobre lo siguiente:

1. ¿Qué tiene en común el Palacio de las Garzas con otras residencias presidenciales u otras casas muy grandes?
2. ¿Te gustaría vivir en el Palacio de las Garzas? ¿Por qué?
3. Imagina que puedes diseñar tu palacio ideal. Describe los planos para cada piso del palacio.

Escritura

Estrategia

Using idea maps

How do you organize your ideas for a first draft? Often, the organization of ideas represents the most challenging part of the writing process. Idea maps are useful for organizing pertinent information. Imagine that you are writing a description of your family. Here is an example of an idea map you might use, changing the facts to fit your own situation.

MAPA DE IDEAS

- 45 años
- 43 años
- moreno trabajador inteligente alto
- **Simón** *padre*
- **Rosa** *madre*
- trabajadora simpática bonita
- **Mi familia**
- **José** *hermano*
- moreno alto escucha música rock
- 15 años

Tema

Escribir un contrato de arrendamiento

Eres el/la administrador(a) de un edificio de apartamentos. Prepara un contrato de arrendamiento para los nuevos inquilinos. El contrato debe incluir los siguientes detalles:

▶ La dirección del apartamento y del/de la administrador(a)

▶ Las fechas del contrato

▶ El precio del alquiler y el día que se debe pagar

▶ El precio del depósito

▶ Información y reglas acerca de:
  • la basura
  • el correo
  • los animales domésticos
  • el ruido
  • los servicios de electricidad y agua
  • el uso de electrodomésticos

▶ Otros aspectos importantes de la vida comunitaria

contrato de arrendamiento *lease*   administrador(a) *manager*   inquilinos *tenants*
dirección *address*   reglas *rules*   ruido *noise*   servicios *utilities*

Escuchar

Preparación

Mira el dibujo. ¿Qué pistas te da para comprender la conversación que vas a escuchar? ¿Qué significa *bienes raíces*?

Estrategia

Using visual cues

Visual cues like illustrations and headings provide useful clues about what you will hear. To practice this strategy, you will listen to a passage related to the following photo. Jot down the clues the photo gives you as you listen.

🎧 Ahora escucha

Mira los anuncios de esta página y escucha la conversación entre el Sr. Núñez, Adriana y Felipe. Luego indica si cada descripción se refiere a la casa ideal de Adriana y Felipe, a la casa del anuncio o al apartamento del anuncio.

Frases	La casa ideal	La casa del anuncio	El apartamento del anuncio
Es barato.	____	____	____
Tiene cuatro alcobas.	____	____	____
Tiene una oficina.	____	____	____
Tiene un balcón.	____	____	____
Tiene una cocina moderna.	____	____	____
Tiene un jardín muy grande.	____	____	____
Tiene un patio.	____	____	____

18G

Bienes raíces

Se vende.
4 alcobas, 3 baños, cocina moderna, jardín con árboles frutales.
B/. 225.000

Se alquila.
2 alcobas, 1 baño. Balcón. Urbanización Las Brisas. 525

Comprensión

Preguntas

1. ¿Cuál es la relación entre el Sr. Núñez, Adriana y Felipe? ¿Cómo lo sabes?
2. ¿Qué diferencia de opinión hay entre Adriana y Felipe sobre dónde quieren vivir?
3. Usa la información de los dibujos y la conversación para entender lo que dice Adriana al final. ¿Qué significa "todo a su debido tiempo"?

Conversación

1. ¿Qué tienen en común el apartamento y la casa del anuncio con el lugar donde tú vives?
2. ¿Qué piensas de la recomendación del Sr. Núñez?
3. ¿Qué tipo de sugerencias te da tu familia sobre dónde vivir?
4. ¿Dónde prefieres vivir tú? ¿en un apartamento o en una casa? Explica por qué.

recursos

STUDENT CD
Lección 12

pistas *clues*   anuncio *advertisement*

Panamá

El país en cifras

- **Área:** 78.200 km^2 (30.193 millas^2), *aproximadamente el área de Carolina del Sur*
- **Población:** 2.942.000
- **Capital:** La ciudad de Panamá — 1.228.000
- **Ciudades principales:** Colón — 138.000, David — 125.000

SOURCE: Population Division, UN Secretariat

- **Moneda:** balboa; Es equivalente al dólar estadounidense.

En Panamá circulan los billetes de dólar estadounidense. El país centroamericano, sin embargo, acuña sus propias monedas. "El peso" es una moneda grande equivalente a cincuenta centavos. La moneda de cinco centavos es llamada frecuentemente "real".

- **Idiomas:** español (oficial), chibcha, inglés

La mayoría de los panameños son bilingües. La lengua materna del 14% de los panameños es el inglés.

Bandera de Panamá

Panameños célebres

- Manuel Antonio Noriega, militar y dictador (1934-)
- Rod Carew, beisbolista (1945-)
- Mireya Moscoso, política (1947-)
- Rubén Blades, músico y político (1948-)

Mujer cuna lavando una mola

Un turista disfruta del bosque tropical colgado de un cable

COSTA RICA

Lago Gatún

Canal de Panamá

Islas Sar Blas

Cordillera de San Bla

Río Chepo

Bocas del Toro

Mar Caribe

Colón

ESTADOS UNIDOS

OCÉANO ATLÁNTICO

PANAMÁ

AMÉRICA DEL SUR

Serranía de Tabasaraí

Ciudad de Panamá

David

Río Cobre

Océano Pacífico

Isla del Rey

Isla de Coiba

Golfo de Panamá

Ruinas de un fuerte panameño

recursos

R			
	WB pp. 149-150	vistasonline.com	ICD-ROM Lección 12

acuñar *to mint* moneda *coin* centavos *cents*
actualmente *currently* peaje *toll* promedio *average*

¡Increíble pero cierto!

¿Conocías estos datos sobre el Canal de Panamá?

- El viaje en barco de Nueva York a Tokio a través del Canal de Panamá es 3.000 millas más corto.
- Su construcción costó 639 millones de dólares.
- Actualmante lo usan 38 barcos al día.
- El peaje promedio cuesta 40.000 dólares.

Tokio

Nueva York

PANAMÁ

Lugares • **El Canal de Panamá**

El Canal de Panamá une los océanos Pacífico y Atlántico. Se empezó a construir en 1903 y se terminó diez años después. Es la fuente principal de ingresos del país, gracias al dinero que se recauda de los más de 12.000 buques que pasan anualmente por el canal.

Artes • **La mola**

La mola es una forma de arte textil de los cunas, una tribu indígena que vive en las islas San Blas en Panamá. Las molas se hacen con capas y fragmentos de tela de colores vivos. Sus diseños son muchas veces abstractos, inspirados en las formas del coral. Las molas tradicionales son las más apreciadas y sus diseños son completamente geométricos. Antes sólo se usaban como ropa, pero hoy día también se usan para decorar las casas.

Deportes • **El buceo**

Panamá, cuyo nombre significa "lugar de muchos peces", es un sitio excelente para los amantes del buceo, el buceo con esnórkel y la pesca. Las playas en los dos lados del istmo, el mar Caribe a un lado y el océano Pacífico al otro, son muy variadas. Unas están destinadas al turismo y otras poseen un gran valor ecológico, por la riqueza y diversidad de su vida marina, abundante en arrecifes de coral. En la playa Bluff, por ejemplo, se pueden observar cuatro especies de tortugas en peligro de extinción.

COLOMBIA

¿Qué aprendiste? Responde a las preguntas con una frase completa.

1. ¿Cuál es la lengua materna del catorce por ciento de los panameños?

2. ¿A qué unidad monetaria (*monetary unit*) es equivalente el balboa?

3. ¿Qué océanos une el Canal de Panamá?

4. ¿Quién es Rubén Blades?

5. ¿Qué son las molas?

6. ¿Cómo son los diseños de las molas?

7. ¿Para qué se usaban las molas antes?

8. ¿Cómo son las playas de Panamá?

9. ¿Qué significa "Panamá"?

Vista de la Ciudad de Panamá

Conexión Internet Investiga estos temas en el sitio **www.vistasonline.com**.

1. Investiga la historia de las relaciones entre Panamá y los Estados Unidos y la decisión de devolver (*give back*) el Canal a Panamá. ¿Estás de acuerdo con la decisión? Explica tu opinión.

2. Investiga los cunas u otro grupo indígena de Panamá. ¿En qué partes del país viven? ¿Qué lenguas hablan? ¿Cómo es su cultura?

une *connects*   fuente *source*   ingresos *income*   se recauda *is collected*   buques *ships*   capas *layers*   tela *fabric*   vivos *bright*
apreciadas *valued*   hoy día *nowadays*   cuyo *whose*   peces *fish*   amantes *lovers*   buceo *diving*   istmo *isthmus*   poseen *possess*
valor *value*   riqueza *richness*   arrecifes *reefs*   tortugas *tortoises*   peligro *danger*

El Salvador

El país en cifras

▶ **Área:** 21.040 km² (8.124 millas²),
el tamaño de Massachusetts

▶ **Población:** 6.519.000

*El Salvador es el país centroamericano más
pequeño y también el que tiene más habitantes.
Su población, como la de Honduras, es muy
homogénea: casi el 95 por ciento es mestiza.*

▶ **Capital:** San Salvador—1.490.000

▶ **Ciudades principales:** Soyapango—252.000,
Santa Ana—202.000, San Miguel—183.000,
Mejicanos—145.000

SOURCE: Population Division, UN Secretariat

▶ **Moneda:** colón

▶ **Idiomas:** español (oficial), náhuatl, lenca

Bandera de El Salvador

Salvadoreños célebres

▶ **Óscar Romero,** arzobispo y activista por los
derechos humanos (1917-1980)

▶ **Claribel Alegría,**
poeta, novelista y
cuentista (1924-)

▶ **Roque Dalton,** poeta,
ensayista y novelista
(1935-1975)

▶ **María Eugenia Brizuela,**
política (1956-)

Óscar Romero

mestiza *of indigenous and white parentage*   **arzobispo** *archbishop*
derechos humanos *human rights*   **cuentista** *story writer*   **estalló** *exploded*
guerra *war*   **duró** *lasted*

Ruinas de Tazumal

Salvadoreña muestra huevos
de pato en El Jocotal.

GUATEMALA

Lago de
Guija

Río de la Paz

Volcán
de Colón

Santa Ana

Río Lempa

Mejicanos   Ilobasco

HONDURAS

San Salvador

Soyapango

Río Torola

San Miguel

Río Goascorán

Volcán de San   Vicente

Río Lempa

Volcán de
San Miguel

Océano
Pacífico

La Libertad

Golfo
de Fonseca

Aeropuerto Ilopango
en San Salvador

ESTADOS UNIDOS

OCÉANO
ATLÁNTICO

EL SALVADOR

OCÉANO
PACÍFICO

AMÉRICA DEL SUR

recursos

R	WB pp. 151-152	WB Repaso 10-12 pp. 153-154	vistasonline.com	ICD-ROM Lección 17

¡Increíble pero cierto!

En 1969, cuando El Salvador perdió contra
Honduras en un partido de clasificación para la
Copa Mundial de Fútbol, estalló una terrible guerra
entre los dos países. Aunque la famosa "Guerra del
Fútbol" duró sólo 100 días, las relaciones entre los
dos países fueron tensas durante casi una década.

Deportes • El *surfing*

El Salvador, con unos 300 kilómetros de costa en el Océano Pacífico, es un gran centro de *surfing* por la gran calidad de sus olas. La Libertad es la playa que está más cerca de la capital, y allí las condiciones son perfectas para el *surfing*. Por eso van surfistas de todo el mundo a este pequeño pueblo salvadoreño. Los fines de semana hay muchísima gente en La Libertad y entonces los surfistas van para el oeste, por la Costa del Bálsamo, donde las olas también son buenas.

Naturaleza • El Parque Nacional Montecristo

El bosque nuboso Montecristo, al norte del país, es el punto donde se unen Guatemala, Honduras y El Salvador. Este bosque, que está a una altitud de 2.400 metros (7.900 pies), recibe 200 centímetros (80 pulgadas) de lluvia al año y con frecuencia tiene una humedad relativa de 100 por ciento. Viven en este bosque muchas especies interesantes de plantas y animales, como orquídeas, pumas y tucanes y sus árboles son tan altos y espesos que ocultan la luz del sol.

Artes • La artesanía de Ilobasco

Ilobasco es un pueblo de grandes artesanos. Sus objetos de arcilla y de cerámica tienen tanta fama que se organizan excursiones para ver cómo se hacen paso a paso. Los productos más tradicionales de Ilobasco son los juguetes, los adornos y los utensilios de cocina. Las "sorpresas" de Ilobasco, pequeñas piezas de cerámica que representan escenas de la vida diaria, son especialmente populares.

¿Qué aprendiste? Responde a las preguntas con una frase completa.

1. ¿Qué es el náhuatl?

2. ¿Quién es María Eugenia Brizuela?

3. ¿Por qué es El Salvador un buen lugar para practicar el *surfing*?

4. ¿A qué altitud está el bosque nuboso?

5. ¿Cuáles son algunos de los animales y las plantas que viven en el bosque nuboso?

6. ¿Qué países se unen en el bosque nuboso Montecristo?

7. ¿Por qué es famoso el pueblo de Ilobasco?

8. ¿Qué se puede ver en una excursión en Ilobasco?

9. ¿Qué son las "sorpresas" de Ilobasco?

Conexión Internet Investiga estos temas en el sitio **www.vistasonline.com**.

1. El Parque Nacional Montecristo es una reserva natural; busca información sobre otros parques o zonas protegidas en El Salvador. ¿Cómo son estos lugares? ¿Qué tipos de plantas y animales se encuentran allí?

2. Busca información sobre museos u otros lugares turísticos en San Salvador (u otra ciudad de El Salvador).

olas *waves*   **surfistas** *surfers*   **mundo** *world*   **El bosque nuboso** *Cloud forest*   **se unen** *come together*   **pulgadas** *inches*   **humedad** *humidity*   **orquídeas** *orchids*   **árboles** *trees*   **espesos** *thick*   **ocultan** *hide*   **arcilla** *clay*   **paso a paso** *step by step*   **juguetes** *toys*   **adornos** *ornaments*   **piezas** *pieces*

Viviendas

las afueras	suburbs; outskirts
el alquiler	rent
el ama (*m., f.*) de casa	housekeeper; caretaker
el barrio	neighborhood
el edificio de apartamentos	apartment building
el/la vecino/a	neighbor
la vivienda	housing
alquilar	to rent
mudarse	to move (from one house to another)

Cuartos y otros lugares

la alcoba, el dormitorio	bedroom
el altillo	attic
el balcón	balcony
la cocina	kitchen
el comedor	dining room
la entrada	entrance
la escalera	stairs; stairway
el garaje	garage
el jardín	garden; yard
la oficina	office
el pasillo	hallway
el patio	patio; yard
la sala	living room
el sótano	basement; cellar

Muebles y otras cosas

la alfombra	carpet; rug
la almohada	pillow
el armario	closet
el cartel	poster
la cómoda	chest of drawers
las cortinas	curtains
el cuadro	picture
el estante	bookcase; bookshelves
la lámpara	lamp
la luz	light; electricity
la manta	blanket
la mesita	end table
la mesita de noche	night stand
los muebles	furniture
la pared	wall
la pintura	painting; picture
el sillón	armchair
el sofá	couch; sofa

Electrodomésticos

la cafetera	coffee maker
la cocina, la estufa	stove
el congelador	freezer
el electrodoméstico	electric appliance
el horno (de microondas)	(microwave) oven
la lavadora	washing machine
el lavaplatos	dishwasher
el refrigerador	refrigerator
la secadora	clothes dryer
la tostadora	toaster

Para poner la mesa

la copa	wineglass; goblet
la cuchara	(table or large) spoon
el cuchillo	knife
el plato	plate
la servilleta	napkin
la taza	cup
el tenedor	fork
el vaso	glass
poner la mesa	to set the table
quitar la mesa	to clear the table

Quehaceres domésticos

arreglar	to neaten; to straighten up
barrer el suelo	to sweep the floor
cocinar	to cook
ensuciar	to get (something) dirty
hacer la cama	to make the bed
hacer quehaceres domésticos	to do household chores
lavar	to wash
limpiar la casa	to clean the house
pasar la aspiradora	to vacuum
planchar la ropa	to iron the clothes
sacar la basura	to take out the trash
sacudir los muebles	to dust the furniture

Verbos y expresiones verbales

aconsejar	to advise
insistir (en)	to insist (on)
mandar	to order
recomendar (e:ie)	to recommend
rogar (o:ue)	to beg; to plead
sugerir (e:ie)	to suggest
Es bueno que…	It's good that…
Es importante que…	It's important that…
Es malo que…	It's bad that…
Es mejor que…	It's better that…
Es necesario que…	It's necessary that…
Es urgente que…	It's urgent that…

Relative pronouns	See page 334.
Expresiones útiles	See page 331.

recursos

R	LCASS./CD Cass. 12/CD12	LM p. 272

La naturaleza

13

La naturaleza

el ave, el pájaro

el cráter

el volcán

el pez

la vaca

el árbol

el césped, la hierba

el perro

el gato

Más vocabulario

el animal	animal
el bosque (tropical)	(tropical; rain) forest
el cielo	sky
el desierto	desert
la estrella	star
la luna	moon
el mundo	world
la naturaleza	nature
la planta	plant
la región	region; area
la selva, la jungla	jungle
la tierra	land; soil
la conservación	conservation
la contaminación (del aire; del agua)	(air; water) pollution
la deforestación	deforestation
la ecología	ecology
el ecoturismo	ecotourism
la energía (nuclear; solar)	(nuclear; solar) energy
la extinción	extinction
el gobierno	government
la ley	law
la lluvia (ácida)	(acid) rain
el medio ambiente	environment
el peligro	danger
la población	population
el recurso natural	natural resource
la solución	solution
puro/a	pure

Variación léxica

césped ←→ pasto (*Perú*); grama (*Venez.*); zacate (*Méx.*)

recursos

la nube

el sol

el valle

el sendero

el lago

la piedra

el río

la flor

Práctica

1 **Escuchar** 🎧 Mientras escuchas las frases, anota los sustantivos (*nouns*) que se refieren a las plantas, los animales, la tierra y el cielo.

Plantas	Animales	Tierra	Cielo
_____	_____	_____	_____
_____	_____	_____	_____

2 **Seleccionar** Selecciona la palabra que no está relacionada con cada grupo.

1. estrella • gobierno • luna • sol
2. gatos • peces • perros • hierba
3. contaminación • extinción • ecoturismo • deforestación
4. lago • río • mar • peligro •
5. vaca • gato • pájaro • población
6. conservación • lluvia ácida • ecología • recurso natural
7. cielo • cráter • aire • nube
8. desierto • solución • selva • bosque
9. nube • cielo • lluvia • piedra
10. flor • hierba • sendero • árbol

3 **Definir** Trabaja con un(a) compañero/a para definir o describir cada palabra. Sigue el modelo.

> **modelo**
> **Estudiante 1:** ¿Qué es el cielo?
> **Estudiante 2:** El cielo está sobre la tierra y tiene nubes.

1. la población
2. un valle
3. la lluvia
4. la naturaleza
5. un desierto
6. la extinción
7. la ecología
8. un sendero

4 **Describir** Trabajen en parejas para describir las siguientes fotos.

El reciclaje

Recicla la lata
de aluminio.
(reciclar)

el envase
de plástico

Recoge la
botella de vidrio.
(recoger)

La conservación

conservar	to conserve
contaminar	to pollute
controlar	to control
cuidar	to take care of
dejar de (+ *inf.*)	to stop (doing something)
desarrollar	to develop
descubrir	to discover
destruir	to destroy
estar afectado/a (por)	to be affected (by)
estar contaminado/a	to be polluted
evitar	to avoid
mejorar	to improve
proteger	to protect
reducir	to reduce
resolver (o:ue)	to resolve; to solve
respirar	to breathe

5 **Completar** Selecciona la palabra o la expresión adecuada para completar cada frase.

contaminar	se desarrollaron	resolver
controlan	descubrir	recoger
destruyen	están afectadas	cuidan
reciclamos	proteger	mejoramos

1. Si vemos basura en las calles, la debemos _____.
2. Los científicos trabajan para _____ nuevas soluciones.
3. Es necesario que todos trabajemos juntos para _____ los problemas del medio ambiente.
4. Debemos _____ el medio ambiente porque hoy día está en peligro.
5. Muchas leyes nuevas _____ el número de árboles que se puede cortar (*cut down*).
6. Las primeras civilizaciones _____ cerca de los ríos y los mares.
7. Todas las personas del mundo _____ por la contaminación.
8. Los turistas deben tener cuidado de no _____ las regiones que visitan.
9. Podemos conservar los recursos si _____ el aluminio, el vidrio y el plástico.
10. La lluvia ácida, la contaminación y la deforestación _____ el medio ambiente.

Comunicación

6

Encuesta Tu profesor(a) te va a dar una hoja de actividades. Haz una encuesta a tus compañeros/as para saber el grado de importancia que les dan a los problemas que se mencionan en la lista y anota sus respuestas. Después dibuja una gráfica de barras (*bar graph*) para mostrar los resultados.

> **modelo**
>
> **Estudiante 1:** ¿Qué importancia tiene la deforestación?
> **Estudiante 2:** Pienso que el problema de la deforestación es importantísimo.

Escala (el grado de importancia)	Problemas	Nombres
importantísimo	1. la deforestación	
muy importante	2. la población	
importante	3. la contaminación del aire	
poco importante	4. la contaminación del agua	
no es importante	5. la reducción de los recursos naturales	

Ahora contesta estas preguntas.

1. ¿Qué problema consideras tú el más grave? ¿Por qué?
2. ¿Qué problema escogieron tus compañeros/as de clase como el más grave? ¿Estás de acuerdo (*Do you agree*) con ellos? ¿Por qué?
3. ¿Cómo se puede evitar o resolver el problema más importante?
4. ¿Es necesario resolver el problema menos importante? ¿Por qué?

7

Situaciones Trabajen en grupos pequeños para representar las siguientes situaciones.

1. Un(a) representante de una agencia ambiental (*environmental*) habla con el/la presidente/a de una compañía industrial que está contaminando un río o el aire.
2. Un(a) guía de ecoturismo habla con un grupo sobre cómo disfrutar (*enjoy*) y conservar el medio ambiente.
3. Un(a) representante de la universidad habla con un grupo de nuevos estudiantes sobre la campaña (*campaign*) ambiental de la universidad y trata de reclutar (*tries to recruit*) miembros para un club que trabaja para la protección del medio ambiente.

8

Escribir una carta Trabajen en parejas para escribir una carta a una empresa real o imaginaria que esté contaminando el medio ambiente. Expliquen las consecuencias que sus acciones van a tener para el medio ambiente. Sugiéranle algunas ideas para que solucionen el problema. Utilicen por lo menos diez palabras de las páginas 360–362.

¡Qué paisaje más hermoso!

Martín y los estudiantes visitan el sendero en las montañas.

PERSONAJES

MAITE

INÉS

DON
FRANCISCO

ÁLEX

JAVIER

MARTÍN

1

DON FRANCISCO Chicos, les
presento a Martín Dávalos, el
guía de la excursión. Martín,
nuestros pasajeros—Maite,
Javier, Inés y Álex.

2

MARTÍN Mucho gusto. Voy a lle-
varlos al área donde vamos a
ir de excursión mañana. ¿Qué
les parece?

ESTUDIANTES ¡Sí! ¡Vamos!

3

MAITE ¡Qué paisaje más
hermoso!

INÉS No creo que haya lugares
más bonitos en el mundo.

6

JAVIER Entiendo que mañana
vamos a cruzar un río. ¿Está
contaminado?

MARTÍN En las montañas el río
no parece estar afectado por
la contaminación. Cerca de las
ciudades, sin embargo, el río
tiene bastante contaminación.

7

ÁLEX ¡Qué aire tan puro se
respira aquí! No es como
en la ciudad de México...
Tenemos un problema
gravísimo de contaminación.

MARTÍN A menos que resuelvan
ese problema, los habitantes
van a sufrir muchas
enfermedades en el futuro.

8

INÉS Creo que todos debemos
hacer algo para proteger el
medio ambiente.

MAITE Yo creo que todos los
países deben establecer leyes
que controlen el uso de
automóviles.

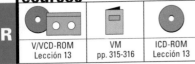

MARTÍN Esperamos que Uds. se diviertan mucho, pero es necesario que cuiden la naturaleza.

JAVIER Se pueden tomar fotos, ¿verdad?

MARTÍN Sí, con tal de que no toques las flores o las plantas.

ÁLEX ¿Hay problemas de contaminación en esta región?

MARTÍN La contaminación es un problema en todo el mundo. Pero aquí tenemos un programa de reciclaje. Si ves por el sendero botellas, papeles o latas, recógelos.

JAVIER Pero Maite, ¿tú vas a dejar de usar tu carro en Madrid?

MAITE Pues voy a tener que usar el metro... Pero tú sabes que mi coche es tan pequeñito... casi no contamina nada.

INÉS ¡Ven, Javier!

JAVIER ¡¡Ya voy!!

Enfoque cultural El ecoturismo

La contaminación es un problema en todo el mundo, incluyendo los países hispanohablantes. Sin embargo (*However*), el ecoturismo enseña a los turistas y a los habitantes de las regiones turísticas la importancia de cuidar el medio ambiente. El ecoturismo es muy popular en los bosques tropicales de países como Costa Rica y Perú, donde hay animales y plantas que están en peligro de extinción. Gracias al ecoturismo, los turistas visitan las tiendas propias de los habitantes de la zona y así se evita que el turismo altere estas regiones.

Expresiones útiles

Talking about the environment

▶ **¿Hay problemas de contaminación en esta región?**
Are there problems with pollution in this region/area?

▷ **La contaminación es un problema en todo el mundo.**
Pollution is a problem throughout the world.

▶ **¿Está contaminado el río?**
Is the river polluted?

▷ **En las montañas el río no parece estar afectado por la contaminación.**
In the mountains, the river does not seem to be affected by pollution.

▷ **Cerca de las ciudades el río tiene bastante contaminación.**
Near the cities, the river is pretty polluted.

▶ **¡Qué aire tan puro se respira aquí!**
The air you breathe here is so pure!

▶ **Es necesario que cuiden la naturaleza.**
It's necessary that you take care of nature.

▶ **Tenemos un problema gravísimo de contaminación.**
We have an extremely serious problem with pollution.

▶ **Creo que todos debemos hacer algo para proteger el medio ambiente.**
I think we should all do something to protect the environment.

▶ **No toques las flores o las plantas.**
Don't touch the flowers or the plants.

▶ **Tenemos un programa de reciclaje.**
We have a recycling program.

▶ **Si ves por el sendero botellas, papeles o latas, recógelos.**
If you see bottles, papers, or cans along the trail, pick them up.

Reacciona a la fotonovela

1 **Seleccionar** Selecciona la respuesta más lógica para cada frase.

1. Martín va a llevar a los estudiantes al lugar donde van a _____.
   a. contaminar el río b. bailar c. ir de excursión

2. El río está más afectado por la contaminación _____.
   a. cerca de los bosques b. en las ciudades c. en las montañas

3. Martín quiere que los estudiantes _____.
   a. limpien los senderos b. descubran nuevos senderos c. no usen sus autos

4. La naturaleza está formada por _____.
   a. los ríos, las montañas y las leyes b. los animales, las latas y los ríos
   c. los lagos, los animales y las plantas

5. La contaminación del aire puede producir _____.
   a. problemas del estómago b. enfermedades respiratorias c. enfermedades mentales

2 **Identificar** Identifica quién puede decir las siguientes frases. Puedes usar cada nombre más de una vez.

ÁLEX INÉS

MAITE

MARTÍN JAVIER

1. Es necesario que hagamos algo por el medio ambiente, ¿pero qué?
2. En mi ciudad es imposible respirar aire limpio. ¡Está muy contaminado!
3. En el futuro, a causa del problema de la contaminación, las personas van a tener problemas de salud.
4. El metro es una excelente alternativa al coche.
5. ¿Está limpio o contaminado el río?
6. Puedes usar tu cámara pero sin tocar las plantas, por favor.
7. De todos los lugares del mundo, me parece que éste es el mejor.
8. Como todo el mundo usa automóviles, debemos establecer leyes para controlar cómo y cuándo usarlos.

3 **Preguntas** Responde a las siguientes preguntas usando la información de **Fotonovela**.

1. Según Martín, ¿qué es necesario que hagan los estudiantes? ¿Qué no pueden hacer?

2. ¿Qué problemas del medio ambiente mencionan Martín y los estudiantes?

3. ¿Qué cree Maite que deben hacer los países?

4. ¿Qué cosas se pueden reciclar? Menciona tres.

5. ¿Qué otro medio de transporte importante dice Maite que hay en Madrid?

4 **El medio ambiente** En parejas, discutan algunos problemas ambientales y sus posibles soluciones. Usen las siguientes preguntas y frases en su conversación.

- ¿Hay problemas de contaminación donde vives?
- Tenemos un problema muy grave de contaminación de...
- ¿Cómo podemos resolver los problemas de la contaminación?

Ortografía

Los signos de puntuación

In Spanish, as in English, punctuation marks are important because they help you express your ideas in a clear, organized way.

No podía ver las llaves. Las buscó por los estantes, las mesas, las sillas, el suelo; minutos después, decidió mirar por la ventana. Allí estaban…

The **punto y coma (;)**, the **tres puntos (…)**, and the **punto (.)** are used in very similar ways in Spanish and English.

Argentina, Brasil, Paraguay y Uruguay son miembros de Mercosur.

In Spanish, the **coma (,)** is not used before **y** or **o** in a series.

| 13,5% | 29,2° | 3.000.000 | $2.999,99 |

In numbers, Spanish uses a **coma** where English uses a decimal point and a **punto** where English uses a comma.

 **Cómo te llamas** **¿Dónde está? ¡Ven aquí! Hola**

Questions in Spanish are preceded and followed by **signos de interrogación (¿ ?)**, and exclamations are preceded and followed by **signos de exclamación (¡ !)**.

Práctica Lee el párrafo e indica los signos de puntuación necesarios.

Ayer recibí la invitación de boda de Marta mi amiga colombiana inmediatamente empecé a pensar en un posible regalo fui al almacén donde Marta y su novio tenían una lista de regalos había de todo copas cafeteras tostadoras finalmente decidí regalarles un perro ya sé que es un regalo extraño pero espero que les guste a los dos

¿Palabras de amor? El siguiente diálogo tiene diferentes significados (*meanings*) dependiendo de los signos de puntuación que utilices y el lugar donde los pongas. Intenta encontrar los diferentes significados.

JULIÁN	me quieres
MARISOL	no puedo vivir sin ti
JULIÁN	me quieres dejar
MARISOL	no me parece mala idea
JULIÁN	no eres feliz conmigo
MARISOL	no soy feliz

recursos

R	LM p. 274	LCASS./CD Cass. 13/CD 13	ICD-ROM Lección 13

13.1 The subjunctive with verbs of emotion

ANTE TODO In the previous lesson, you learned how to use the subjunctive with expressions of will and influence. You will now learn how to use the subjunctive with verbs and expressions of emotion.

Marta **espera** (que) yo **vaya** al lago este fin de semana.

▶ When the verb in the main clause of a sentence expresses an emotion or feeling such as hope, fear, joy, pity, surprise, etc., the subjunctive is required in the subordinate clause.

Nos alegramos de que te **gusten** las flores.
We are happy that you like the flowers.

Siento que tú no **puedas** venir mañana.
I'm sorry that you can't come tomorrow.

Temo que Ana no **pueda** ir mañana con nosotros.
I'm afraid that Ana won't be able to go with us tomorrow.

Le **sorprende** que Juan **sea** tan joven.
It surprises him that Juan is so young.

Esperamos que Uds. se diviertan mucho en la excursión.

Es triste que tengamos un problema grave de contaminación en la ciudad de México.

Common verbs and expressions of emotion

alegrarse (de)	*to be happy*	**tener miedo (de)**	*to be afraid (of)*
esperar	*to hope; to wish*	**es extraño**	*it's strange*
gustar	*to be pleasing; to like*	**es una lástima**	*it's a shame*
molestar	*to bother*	**es ridículo**	*it's ridiculous*
sentir (e:ie)	*to be sorry; to regret*	**es terrible**	*it's terrible*
sorprender	*to surprise*	**es triste**	*it's sad*
temer	*to be afraid; to fear*	**ojalá (que)**	*I hope (that); I wish (that)*

Me molesta que la gente no **recicle** el plástico.
It bothers me that people don't recycle plastic.

Es triste que tengamos problemas con la deforestación.
It's sad that we have problems with deforestation.

▶ As with expressions of will and influence, the infinitive, not the subjunctive, is used after an expression of emotion when there is no change of subject from the main clause to the subordinate clause. Compare these sentences.

Temo **llegar** tarde.
I'm afraid I'll arrive late.

Temo que mi novio **llegue** tarde.
I'm afraid my boyfriend will arrive late.

▶ The expression **ojalá (que)** means *I hope* or *I wish*, and it is always followed by the subjunctive. Note that the use of **que** with this expression is optional.

Ojalá (que) se conserven nuestros recursos naturales.
I hope (that) our natural resources will be conserved.

Ojalá (que) recojan la basura hoy.
I hope (that) they collect the garbage today.

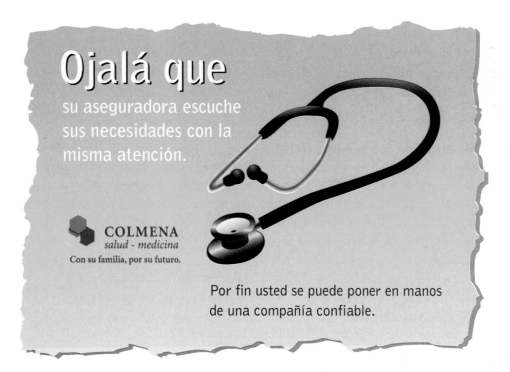

¡INTÉNTALO! Completa las oraciones con las formas correctas de los verbos.

1. Ojalá que ellos <u>descubran</u> (descubrir) nuevas formas de energía.
2. Espero que Ana nos _____ (ayudar) a recoger la basura en la carretera.
3. Es una lástima que la gente no _____ (reciclar) más.
4. Esperamos _____ (proteger) el aire de nuestra comunidad.
5. Me alegro de que mis amigos _____ (querer) conservar la naturaleza.
6. A mis padres les gusta que nosotros _____ (participar) en programas de conservación.
7. Es ridículo _____ (contaminar) el medio ambiente.
8. Espero que tú _____ (venir) a la reunión (*meeting*) del Club de Ecología.
9. Siento que nuestras ciudades _____ (estar) afectadas por la contaminación.
10. Ojalá que yo _____ (poder) hacer algo para reducir la contaminación.

Práctica

1

Completar Completa el diálogo con palabras de la lista. Compara tus respuestas con las de un(a) compañero/a.

Bogotá, Colombia

alegro	salga	puedan
encuentren	lleguen	tengo miedo de
reduzcan	molesta	vayan
estén	ojalá	visitar

OLGA Me alegro de que Adriana y Raquel _____ a Colombia. ¿Van a estudiar?

SARA Sí. Es una lástima que _____ una semana tarde. Ojalá que la universidad las ayude a buscar casa. _____ que no consigan dónde vivir.

OLGA Me _____ que seas tan pesimista, pero sí, yo también espero que _____ gente simpática y que hablen mucho español.

SARA Sí, ojalá. Van a hacer un estudio sobre la deforestación en las costas. Es triste que en tantos países los recursos naturales _____ en peligro.

OLGA Pues, me _____ de que no se queden mucho en la capital por la contaminación, pero _____ tengan tiempo de viajar por el país.

SARA Sí, espero que _____ por lo menos ir al Museo del Oro. Sé que también esperan _____ la catedral de sal de Zipaquirá.

2

Transformar Transforma los siguientes elementos en frases completas para formar un diálogo entre Juan y la madre de Raquel. Añade palabras si es necesario. Luego, con un(a) compañero/a, presenta el diálogo a la clase.

1. Juan, / esperar / (tú) escribirle / Raquel. / Ser / tu / novia. / Ojalá / no / sentirse / sola

2. molestarme / (Ud.) decirme / lo que / tener / hacer. / Ahora / mismo / estarle / escribiendo

3. alegrarme / oírte / decir / eso. / Ser / terrible / estar / lejos / cuando / nadie / recordarte

4. señora, / ¡yo / tener / miedo / (ella) no recordarme / mí! / Ser / triste / estar / sin / novia

5. ser / ridículo / (tú) sentirte / así. / Tú / saber / ella / querer / casarse / contigo

6. ridículo / o / no, / sorprenderme / (todos) preocuparse / ella / y / (nadie) acordarse / mí

Comunicación

3

Comentar En parejas, túrnense para formar oraciones sobre su ciudad, sus clases, su gobierno o algún otro tema, usando expresiones como **me alegro de que, temo que** y **es extraño que.** Luego reaccionen a los comentarios de su compañero/a.

> **modelo**
>
> **Estudiante 1:** Me alegro de que vayan a limpiar el río.
> **Estudiante 2:** Yo también. Me preocupa que el agua del río esté tan sucia.

4

Contestar Lee el mensaje electrónico que Raquel le escribió a su novio Juan. Luego, en parejas, contesten el mensaje usando expresiones como **me sorprende que, me molesta que** y **es una lástima que.**

AYUDA

Echar de menos (a alguien) and **extrañar (a alguien)**, are two ways of saying *to miss (someone).*

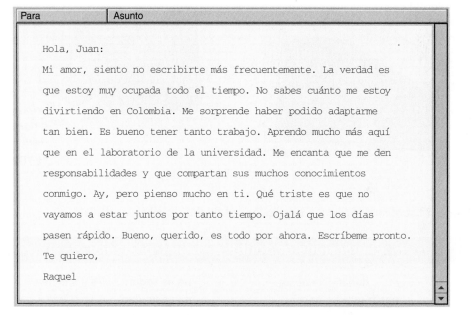

Para	Asunto

Hola, Juan:

Mi amor, siento no escribirte más frecuentemente. La verdad es que estoy muy ocupada todo el tiempo. No sabes cuánto me estoy divirtiendo en Colombia. Me sorprende haber podido adaptarme tan bien. Es bueno tener tanto trabajo. Aprendo mucho más aquí que en el laboratorio de la universidad. Me encanta que me den responsabilidades y que compartan sus muchos conocimientos conmigo. Ay, pero pienso mucho en ti. Qué triste es que no vayamos a estar juntos por tanto tiempo. Ojalá que los días pasen rápido. Bueno, querido, es todo por ahora. Escríbeme pronto.

Te quiero,

Raquel

Síntesis

5

Problemas Tu profesor(a) te va a dar una hoja de actividades. Escribe tres problemas ecológicos que te preocupen. Luego, circula por la clase y describe cada problema a un(a) compañero/a. Escribe las soluciones que te ofrece. Después, comparte la información con la clase.

> **modelo**
>
> **Estudiante 1:** Me molesta que mi país no evite la deforestación.
> **Estudiante 2:** Ojalá que el gobierno haga más para proteger los bosques.

13.2 The subjunctive with doubt, disbelief, and denial

 Just as the subjunctive is required with expressions of emotion, influence, and will, it is also used with expressions of doubt, disbelief, and denial.

Main clause		Subordinate clause
Dudan	(que)	su hijo les **diga** la verdad.

▶ The subjunctive is always used in a subordinate clause when there is a change of subject and the expression in the main clause implies negation or uncertainty.

¡No creo que haya lugares más bonitos en el mundo!

Dudo que el río esté contaminado aquí en las montañas.

▶ Here is a list of some common expressions of doubt, disbelief, or denial.

Expressions of doubt, disbelief, or denial

dudar	to doubt	**no es seguro**	it's not certain
negar (e:ie)	to deny	**no es verdad**	it's not true
no creer	not to believe	**es imposible**	it's impossible
no estar seguro/a (de)	not to be sure	**es improbable**	it's improbable
no es cierto	it's not true; it's not certain	**(no) es posible**	it's (not) possible
		(no) es probable	it's (not) probable

El gobierno **niega** que el agua **esté** contaminada.
The government denies that the water is contaminated.

Dudo que el gobierno **resuelva** el problema.
I doubt that the government will solve the problem.

Es probable que **haya** menos bosques y selvas en el futuro.
It's probable that there will be fewer forests and jungles in the future.

No es verdad que mi hermano **estudie** ecología.
It's not true that my brother studies ecology.

¡LENGUA VIVA!

In English, the expression *it is probable* indicates a fairly high degree of certainty. In Spanish, however, **es probable** implies uncertainty and therefore triggers the subjunctive in the subordinate clause:
Es muy probable que venga Elena.

▶ The indicative is used in a subordinate clause when there is no doubt or uncertainty in the main clause. Here is a list of some expressions of certainty.

Expressions of certainty

no dudar	*not to doubt*	**estar seguro/a (de)**	*to be sure*
no cabe duda de	*there is no doubt*	**es cierto**	*it's true; it's certain*
no hay duda de	*there is no doubt*	**es seguro**	*it's certain*
no negar (e:ie)	*not to deny*	**es verdad**	*it's true*
		es obvio	*it's obvious*

No negamos que **hay** demasiados carros en las carreteras.
We don't deny that there are too many cars on the highways.

Es verdad que Colombia **es** un país bonito.
It's true that Colombia is a beautiful country.

No hay duda de que el Amazonas **es** uno de los ríos más largos.
There is no doubt that the Amazon is one of the longest rivers.

Es obvio que los tigres **están** en peligro de extinción.
It's obvious that tigers are in danger of extinction.

▶ In affirmative sentences, the verb **creer** expresses belief or certainty, so it is followed by the indicative. In negative sentences, however, when doubt is implied, **creer** is followed by the subjunctive.

No creo que **haya** vida en el planeta Marte.
I don't believe that there is life on the planet Mars.

Creo que **debemos** usar exclusivamente la energía solar.
I believe we should exclusively use solar energy.

▶ The expressions **quizás** and **tal vez** are usually followed by the subjunctive because they imply doubt about something.

Quizás haga sol mañana.
Perhaps it will be sunny tomorrow.

Tal vez veamos la luna esta noche.
Perhaps we will see the moon tonight.

¡INTÉNTALO!   Completa estas frases con la forma correcta del verbo.

1. Dudo que ellos ___trabajen___ (trabajar).
2. Es cierto que él _____ (comer) mucho.
3. Es imposible que ellos _____ (salir).
4. Es probable que Uds. _____ (ganar).
5. No creo que ella _____ (volver).
6. Es posible que nosotros _____ (ir).
7. Dudamos que tú _____ (reciclar).
8. Creo que ellos _____ (jugar) al fútbol.
9. No niego que Uds. _____ (estudiar).
10. Es posible que ella no _____ (venir) a casa.
11. Es probable que ellos _____ (dormir).
12. Es posible que Marta _____ (llamar).
13. Tal vez Juan no nos _____ (oír).
14. No es cierto que ellos nos _____ (ayudar).
15. Es obvio que Luis _____ (aburrirse).
16. Creo que Juana _____ (ir) a casarse.

Práctica

1 **Dudas** Carolina es una chica que siempre miente. Expresa tus dudas sobre lo que Carolina está diciendo ahora. Usa las expresiones entre paréntesis para tus respuestas.

> **modelo**
>
> El próximo año mi familia y yo vamos de vacaciones por diez meses. (dudar)
>
> *¡Ja! Dudo que vayan de vacaciones por ese tiempo. ¡Uds. no son ricos!*

1. Estoy escribiendo una novela en español. (no creer)
2. Mi tía es la directora del *Sierra Club*. (no ser verdad)
3. Dos profesores míos juegan para los Osos *(Bears)* de Chicago. (ser imposible)
4. Mi mejor amiga conoce al chef Emeril. (no ser cierto)
5. Mi padre es dueño del Centro Rockefeller. (no ser posible)
6. Yo ya tengo un doctorado *(doctorate)* en lenguas. (ser improbable)

AYUDA

Some useful expressions to express that you don't believe someone:

¡Qué va!
¡Imposible!
¡No te lo creo!
¡Es mentira!

2 **Escoger** Escoge las respuestas correctas para completar el diálogo. Luego dramatiza el diálogo con un(a) compañero/a.

RAÚL Uds. dudan que yo realmente _____ (estudio/estudie). No niego que a veces me _____ (divierto/divierta) demasiado, pero no cabe duda de que _____ (tomo/tome) mis estudios en serio. Estoy seguro de que cuando me vean graduarme van a pensar de manera diferente. Creo que no _____ (tienen/tengan) razón con sus críticas.

PAPÁ Es posible que tu mamá y yo no _____ (tenemos/tengamos) razón. Es cierto que a veces _____ (dudamos/dudemos) de ti. Pero no hay duda de que te _____ (pasas/pases) toda la noche en el Internet y oyendo música. No es nada seguro que _____ (estás/estés) estudiando.

RAÚL Es verdad que _____ (uso/use) mucho el Internet pero, ¡piensen! ¿No es posible que _____ (es/sea) para buscar información para mis clases? ¡No hay duda de que el Internet _____ (es/sea) el mejor recurso del mundo! Es obvio que Uds. _____ (piensan/piensen) que no hago nada, pero no es cierto.

PAPÁ No dudo que esta conversación nos _____ (va/vaya) a ayudar. Pero tal vez esta noche _____ (puedes/puedas) trabajar sin música. ¿Está bien?

¡LENGUA VIVA!

Some useful Internet terms in Spanish:

dirección de Internet → *web address*
el sitio → *website*
la página → *page*
el enlace → *link*
navegar → *surf, browse*
hacer clic en → *click on*
bajar → *download*
conectarse → *log on*
desconectarse → *log off*

Comunicación

3

Diálogo En parejas, miren la ilustración y desarrollen un diálogo interesante entre un(a) conservacionista y un(a) burócrata (*bureaucrat*) del gobierno.

> **modelo**
>
> **Conservacionista:** Queremos reducir la contaminación del aire. Pero dudo que el gobierno nos vaya a ayudar.
>
> **Burócrata:** Es obvio que el gobierno está haciendo muchas cosas para reducir la contaminación del aire.

4

Adivinar Escribe cinco oraciones sobre tu vida presente y futura. Cuatro deben ser falsas y sólo una debe ser cierta. Presenta tus oraciones al grupo. El grupo adivina (*guesses*) cuál es la oración cierta y expresa sus dudas sobre las falsas.

> **modelo**
>
> **Estudiante 1:** Quiero irme un año a la selva a trabajar.
>
> **Estudiante 2:** Dudo que te guste vivir en la selva.
>
> **Estudiante 3:** En cinco años voy a ser presidente de los Estados Unidos.
>
> **Estudiante 2:** No creo que seas presidente de los Estados Unidos en cinco años. ¡Tal vez en treinta!

AYUDA

Some verbs for talking about plans:

esperar → *to hope to*

querer → *to want to*

pretender → *to intend*

pensar → *to plan to*

Síntesis

5

Intercambiar En grupos, escriban un párrafo sobre los problemas del medio ambiente en su estado o en su comunidad. Compartan su párrafo con otro grupo, que va a ofrecer opiniones y soluciones. Luego presenten su párrafo, con las opiniones y soluciones del otro grupo, a la clase.

13.3 Conjunctions that require the subjunctive

ANTE TODO   In both Spanish and English, conjunctions are words or phrases that connect other words and clauses in sentences. Certain conjunctions commonly introduce adverbial clauses, which describe *how, why, when,* and *where* an action takes place.

Main clause	Conjunction	Adverbial clause
Vamos a visitar a Carlos	**antes de que**	**regrese** a California.

▶ In Spanish, the subjunctive is used in an adverbial clause when it expresses a hypothetical situation, uncertainty as to whether an action or event will take place, or a condition that may or may not be fulfilled.

Voy a dejar un recado **en caso de que** Gustavo me llame.
I'm going to leave a message in case Gustavo calls me.

Voy al supermercado **para que** tengas algo de comer.
I'm going to the store so that you'll have something to eat.

CONSÚLTALO

Since much of the future (if not all!) is uncertain, the subjunctive is very commonly used when a subordinate clause expresses a future action. You will learn more about this in Lesson 14, p. 404.

▶ Here is a list of the conjunctions that always require the subjunctive.

Conjunctions that require the subjunctive

a menos que	*unless*	**en caso (de) que**	*in case (that)*
antes (de) que	*before*	**para que**	*so that*
con tal (de) que	*provided that*	**sin que**	*without*

Algunos animales van a morir **a menos que** haya leyes para protegerlos.
Some animals are going to die unless there are laws to protect them.

Voy a salir **sin que** mis hermanos me vean.
I'm going to leave without my brothers seeing me.

Ellos nos llevan a la selva **para que** veamos las plantas tropicales.
They are taking us to the jungle so that we may see the tropical plants.

Voy a tomar esa clase **con tal de que** tú la tomes también.
I'm going to take that class provided that you take it too.

¡ATENCIÓN!

The expression **sin que** works differently than *without*. Whereas English speakers say: *We do it without them (their) asking us,* in Spanish the second verb is conjugated; it is not a gerund:
Lo hacemos sin que nos lo pidan.

COMPARE & CONTRAST

You have learned that expressions of emotion, doubt, and will are followed by an infinitive when there is no change of subject from the main clause to the subordinate clause. An infinitive is also used after the prepositions **antes de, para,** and **sin** when there is no change of subject. Compare these sentences.

Te llamamos mañana **antes de que salgas** para Cartagena.

We will call you tomorrow before you leave for Cartagena.

Te llamamos mañana **antes de salir** para Cartagena.

We will call you tomorrow before leaving for Cartagena.

Tus padres trabajan mucho **para que tú puedas** vivir bien.

Your parents work a lot so that you are able to live well.

Tus padres trabajan muchísimo **para vivir** bien.

Your parents work very hard in order to live well.

In contrast, the subjunctive is always used after **a menos que, con tal (de) que,** and **en caso (de) que** even when there is no change of subject from the main clause to the subordinate clause.

Puedes ir al río esta tarde **con tal (de) que** vuelvas pronto.

You can go to the river this afternoon provided that you come back right away.

Vamos de excursión mañana **a menos que estemos** enfermos.

We'll go hiking tomorrow unless we're feeling sick.

¡INTÉNTALO!   Completa las oraciones con la forma correcta de los verbos entre paréntesis.

1. Voy a establecer un club de ecología para que mis amigos y yo _podamos_ (poder) aprender más sobre el medio ambiente.
2. Siempre reciclo los envases de plástico para _____ (reducir) la contaminación del medio ambiente.
3. No podemos evitar la lluvia ácida a menos que el gobierno y la gente _____ (trabajar) juntos para controlar la contaminación del aire.
4. El gobierno va a establecer parques nacionales para _____ (proteger) las selvas y los bosques.
5. Elisa quiere hablar con el presidente del club de ecología antes de que _____ (comenzar) la reunión *(meeting)*.
6. No podemos conducir nuestros carros sin _____ (contaminar) el aire.
7. Debemos recoger la basura en las calles y en las carreteras sin que nadie nos lo _____ (pedir).
8. Debemos crear parques para proteger las aves y los otros animales en caso de que la gente _____ (destruir) sus hábitats naturales.
9. No voy de excursión a menos que _____ (ir) también un guía.
10. Antes de _____ (nadar) en algún río pregunto si el agua está contaminada.

Práctica

1   **Completar**   La Sra. Montero habla de una excursión que quiere hacer con su familia. Completa las oraciones con la forma correcta de cada verbo.

1. Voy a llevar a mis hijos al parque para que _____ (aprender) sobre la naturaleza.
2. Voy a pasar todo el día allí con tal de que todos nosotros _____ (tener) tiempo.
3. En bicicleta podemos explorar el parque sin _____ (caminar) demasiado.
4. Vamos a bajar al cráter a menos que se _____ (prohibir).
5. Vamos a llevar al perro para que _____ (protegernos).
6. No pensamos ir muy lejos en caso de que _____ (llover).
7. Queremos cenar a la orilla (*shore*) del río a menos que no _____ (haber) suficiente luz.
8. Mis hijos van a ver muchas cosas interesantes antes de _____ (salir) del parque.

2   **Oraciones**   Completa las siguientes oraciones de una manera lógica.

1. No podemos controlar la contaminación del aire a menos que...
2. Voy a reciclar los productos de papel y de vidrio para que...
3. Con tal de que se ponga fin a (*put to an end to*) la deforestación...
4. Debemos proteger los animales en peligro de extinción para que...
5. Mis amigos y yo vamos a recoger la basura de la universidad para...
6. No podemos desarrollar nuevas fuentes (*sources*) de energía sin...
7. Tenemos que eliminar la contaminación del agua para...
8. No podemos proteger la naturaleza sin que...

3   **Organizaciones**   En parejas, lean las descripciones de las organizaciones de conservación. Luego expresa en tus propias (*own*) palabras las opiniones de cada organización.

Organización:
Fundación Río Orinoco
Problema:
La destrucción de los ríos
Solución: Programa para limpiar las orillas de los ríos y reducir la erosión y así proteger los ríos

Organización: Oficina de Turismo Internacional

Problema: Necesidad de mejorar la imagen del país en el mercado turístico internacional
Solución: Plan para promover el ecoturismo en los 33 parques nacionales usando agencias de publicidad e implementando un plan agresivo de conservación

Organización: Asociación Nabusimake-Pico Colón
Problema: Un lugar turístico popular en Sierra Nevada, Santa Marta, que necesita mejor mantenimiento

Solución: Programa de voluntarios para limpiar y mejorar los senderos

Comunicación

4 **Preguntas** En parejas, túrnense para hacerse las siguientes preguntas.

1. ¿Qué haces cada noche antes de acostarte?
2. ¿Qué haces en la clase cada día antes de que llegue el/la profesor(a)?
3. ¿Qué hacen tus padres para que puedas asistir a la universidad?
4. ¿Qué puedes hacer para mejorar tu español?
5. ¿Qué quieres hacer mañana a menos que haga mal tiempo?
6. ¿Qué haces en tus clases sin que los profesores lo sepan?

5 **Comparar** En parejas, comparen su rutina diaria con algo que van a hacer en el futuro. Usen palabras de la lista.

antes de	con tal de que	para	sin
antes de que	en caso de que	para que	sin que

modelo

Estudiante 1: Siempre leo antes de acostarme pero hoy quiero estudiar para mi examen.

Estudiante 2: Todos los sábados llevo a mi primo al parque para que juegue. Pero el sábado que viene, con tal de que no llueva, lo voy a llevar a las montañas.

Síntesis

6 **Tic-Tac-Toe** En grupos de cuatro, formen dos equipos. Una persona comienza una frase y otra persona de su equipo la termina usando palabras de la gráfica (*chart*). El primer equipo que forme tres oraciones seguidas (*in a row*) gana el *tic-tac-toe*. ¡Ojo! Hay que usar la conjunción o la preposición y el verbo correctamente. Si no, ¡no cuenta!

NOTA CULTURAL

Tic-tac-toe has various names in the Spanish-speaking world, including **tres en raya, tres en línea, ta-te-ti, gato, la vieja,** and **triqui-triqui.**

modelo

Equipo 1

Estudiante 1: Dudo que podamos eliminar la deforestación...

Estudiante 2: sin que nos ayude el gobierno.

Equipo 2

Estudiante 1: Creo que podemos conservar nuestros recursos naturales...

Estudiante 2: con tal de que todos hagamos algo para ayudar.

a menos que	con tal de que	para que
antes de que	para	sin que
sin	en caso de que	antes de

13.4 Familiar (tú) commands

ANTE TODO In Lesson 12, you learned how to use formal commands. You will now learn familiar (**tú**) commands. **Tú** commands are used when you want to give advice to or instruct someone you normally address with the familiar **tú**.

Negative *tú* commands

Infinitive	Present subjunctive	Negative *tú* command
cuidar	tú cuides	**no cuides** (tú)
tocar	tú toques	**no toques** (tú)
temer	tú temas	**no temas** (tú)
volver	tú vuelvas	**no vuelvas** (tú)
insistir	tú insistas	**no insistas** (tú)
pedir	tú pidas	**no pidas** (tú)

No toques las plantas, no salgas del sendero…

…pero si ves por el sendero botellas, papeles o latas, recógelos.

▶ Like **Ud.** and **Uds.** commands, negative **tú** commands have the same form as the **tú** form of the present subjunctive. Note that the pronoun **tú** is not used with familiar commands, except for emphasis.

> Julia, no **molestes** a los animales.
> *Julia, don't annoy the animals.*

> Carlos, no **comas** esa planta.
> *Carlos, don't eat that plant.*

¡ATENCIÓN!

As in other forms of the subjunctive, the negative familiar commands keep the same stem changes as the indicative. See Lesson 12, pp. 342-343.

Affirmative *tú* commands

Infinitive	Present indicative	Affirmative *tú* command
cuidar	cuida	**cuida** (tú)
tocar	toca	**toca** (tú)
temer	teme	**teme** (tú)
volver	vuelve	**vuelve** (tú)
insistir	insiste	**insiste** (tú)
pedir	pide	**pide** (tú)

▶ Unlike other command forms, affirmative **tú** commands do not resemble the forms of the present subjunctive. Instead, they usually have the same form as the third person singular of the present indicative.

> **Recicla** el papel.
> *Recycle paper.*

> **Protege** nuestro medio ambiente.
> *Protect our environment.*

¡LENGUA VIVA!

To form affirmative **vosotros** commands, drop the –r from the infinitive and add –d:

evitar → **evitad**
poner → **poned**
salir → **salid**

Negative **vosotros** commands have the same form as the **vosotros** forms of the present subjunctive:

no evitéis
no pongáis
no salgáis

▶ There are eight irregular affirmative **tú** commands.

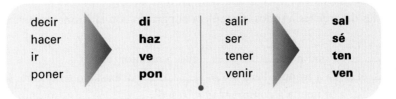

decir	**di**	salir	**sal**
hacer	**haz**	ser	**sé**
ir	**ve**	tener	**ten**
poner	**pon**	venir	**ven**

¡**Ten** cuidado con el perro!
Be careful with the dog!

¡**Sal** de aquí ahora mismo!
Leave here at once!

Pon las latas en la basura.
Put the cans in the trash.

Haz los ejercicios.
Do the exercises.

▶ Since **ir** and **ver** have the same **tú** command (**ve**), context will determine the meaning.

Ve al supermercado con José.
Go to the supermarket with José.

Ve ese programa... es muy interesante.
See that program... it's very interesting.

COMPARE & CONTRAST

The placement of reflexive and object pronouns in **tú** commands follows the same rules as in formal commands. Note that when a pronoun is attached to a command of more than two syllables, a written accent is used to maintain the original stress pattern. Compare the following examples.

¡Alégra**te**!
Be happy!

No **te** sientas triste.
Don't feel sad.

Di**me**.
Tell me.

No **me lo** digas.
Don't tell me (it).

¡Alégren**se**!
Be happy!

No **se** sientan tristes.
Don't feel sad.

Díga**me**.
Tell me.

No **me lo** diga.
Don't tell me (it).

¡LENGUA VIVA!

Reflexive **vosotros** commands drop the **–d** and attach **os**:

sentaos
levantaos

The negative forms follow the normal pattern:

no os sentéis
no os levantéis

¡INTÉNTALO! Indica los mandatos (*commands*) familiares de estos verbos.

	Mandato afirmativo	**Mandato negativo**
1. cambiar	_Cambia_ el aceite.	No _cambies_ el aceite.
2. correr	_____ más rápido.	No _____ más rápido.
3. salir	_____ ahora.	No _____ ahora.
4. tocar	_____ las flores.	No _____ las flores.
5. venir	_____ aquí.	No _____ aquí.
6. levantarse	_____ temprano.	No _____ temprano.
7. volver	_____ pronto.	No _____ pronto.
8. hacerlo	_____ ya.	No _____ ahora.

Práctica

1 **Completar** Unos amigos van a tener una cena en casa de Olga. Ella es la coordinadora y les da órdenes a todos. Completa el párrafo con la forma correcta de cada verbo.

1. No _____ en una hora. _____ ahora mismo. (venir)
2. _____ el arroz a tiempo. Pero no lo _____ demasiado temprano. (hacer)
3. No _____ a la tienda a comprar los refrescos. _____ al sótano. (ir)
4. _____ que no quieres preparar la cebolla, pero no _____ que no quieres ayudar. (decirme)
5. No _____ tan antipático con Katia. _____ amable que es muy niña. (ser)
6. _____ cuidado con el cuchillo, pero no _____ miedo de usarlo. (tener)
7. _____ al balcón, pero no _____ al patio. Ayer llovió mucho. (salir)

2 **Cambiar** Pedro y Marina no pueden ponerse de acuerdo (*agree*) cuando le dan órdenes a su hijo Miguel. Lee las órdenes que Pedro le da a Miguel. Después, usa la información entre paréntesis para formar las órdenes que le da Marina. Sigue el modelo.

> **modelo**
> Recoge la basura. (poner la mesa)
> No recojas la basura, Miguel. Pon la mesa.

1. Barre el suelo. (pasar la aspiradora)
2. Plancha la ropa. (hacer las camas)
3. Saca la basura. (quitar la mesa)
4. Ve al supermercado. (quedarte aquí)
5. Pon el radio. (poner la televisión)
6. Dale los libros a Katia. (dárselos a Juan)
7. Prepara la cena. (limpiar el carro)
8. Corta el césped. (bañar al gato)

3 **Desastres** La Sra. Valenzuela está pasando un mal día. Su casa está muy desordenada y le da órdenes a su esposo y a sus hijos/as para que ordenen todo. Forma los mandatos que ella le da a su familia.

> **modelo**
> Hay mucha basura en la cocina. (Pilar)
> Pilar, saca la basura de la cocina.

1. Las ventanas están abiertas. (Martín)
2. El perro ladra (*barks*) porque tiene hambre. (Lola)
3. La alfombra está sucia. (Pedro)
4. El gato se ha subido al televisor. (Pilar)
5. Juanito está tirando los papeles del escritorio del Sr. Valenzuela. (Lola)
6. Pilar está escuchando música a todo volumen. (Martín)
7. Los muebles de la sala están llenos de polvo. (Pedro)
8. Las flores del jardín necesitan agua. (Lola)

¡LENGUA VIVA!

While in English one says that the music is *loud* or *soft,* in Spanish one says **está alta** or **está baja**. The corresponding verbs are **subir** (*turn up*) and **bajar** (*turn down*)

Comunicación

4

Diálogo En parejas, preparen un diálogo entre Ramón y Luisa Aguilera. Ellos se dan órdenes negativas y positivas sobre lo que tienen que hacer para llegar a tiempo a una fiesta. Usen mandatos afirmativos y negativos. Luego presenten el diálogo a la clase.

> **modelo**
>
> **Luisa:** ¡Sal del cuarto de baño ya!
> **Ramón:** ¡No me des órdenes!
> **Luisa:** Pero tengo que maquillarme.
> **Ramón:** Y yo tengo que ducharme. Oye, ¿qué hora es?
> **Luisa:** Son las siete menos veinte.
> **Ramón:** ¡Ay! ¡Tráeme una toalla!

5

Órdenes Circula por la clase e intercambia órdenes con tus compañeros/as. Debes seguir las órdenes que ellos te dan o reaccionar apropiadamente.

> **modelo**
>
> **Estudiante 1:** Dame todo tu dinero.
> **Estudiante 2:** No, no quiero dártelo. Muéstrame tu cuaderno.
> **Estudiante 1:** Aquí está.
> **Estudiante 3:** Ve a la pizarra y escribe tu nombre.
> **Estudiante 4:** No quiero. Hazlo tú.

Síntesis

6

Anuncios Miren estos anuncios (*ads*). Luego, en grupos pequeños, preparen tres anuncios para asociaciones conservacionistas. Los anuncios pueden ser para un periódico, una revista, etc.

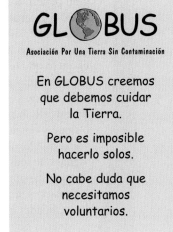

GLOBUS
Asociación Por Una Tierra Sin Contaminación

En GLOBUS creemos
que debemos cuidar
la Tierra.

Pero es imposible
hacerlo solos.

No cabe duda que
necesitamos
voluntarios.

¡ATENCIÓN!

Esta reserva
ecológica es
de todos los
colombianos.

Cuídala. Recoge la basura.

Protégela. No toques las plantas.

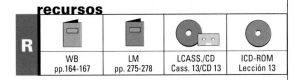

recursos

R	WB pp.164-167	LM pp. 275-278	LCASS./CD Cass. 13/CD 13	ICD-ROM Lección 13

Lectura
Antes de leer

Estrategia
Recognizing the purpose of a text

When you are faced with an unfamiliar text, it is important to determine the writer's purpose. If you are reading an editorial in a newspaper, for example, you know that the journalist's objective is to persuade you of his or her point of view. Identifying the purpose of a text will help you better comprehend its meaning.

Examinar el texto

Utiliza las estrategias de lectura para familiarizarte con el texto. Después contesta las siguientes preguntas y compara tus respuestas con las de un(a) compañero/a.

- ¿De qué trata la lectura?
- ¿Es una fábula, un poema, un artículo de periódico…?
- ¿Cómo lo sabes?

Predicciones

Lee estas predicciones sobre la lectura e indica si estás de acuerdo con ellas. Después compara tus opiniones con las de un(a) compañero/a.

1. La lectura es un género de ficción.
2. Los personajes son animales.
3. La acción tiene lugar en un zoológico.
4. Hay una moraleja.

Determinar el propósito

Con un(a) compañero/a, hablen de los posibles propósitos del texto. Consideren las siguientes preguntas.

- ¿Qué te dice el género del texto sobre los posibles propósitos del texto?
- ¿Piensas que el texto puede tener más de un propósito? ¿Por qué?

¿De qué trata la lectura? *What is the reading about?* fábula *fable* estás de acuerdo *you agree* género *type* personajes *characters* moraleja *moral* propósito *purpose*

De lo que le ocurrió a un zorro con un cuervo que tenía un pedazo de queso en el pico

(un fragmento adaptado de El conde Lucanor)

Don Juan Manuel

El noble español don Juan Manuel (1282–1348) es uno de los escritores más importantes de la literatura medieval. Sus historias inspiraron a autores tan célebres como Shakespeare y Cervantes. Su obra más conocida, El conde Lucanor, *es una colección de fábulas y cuentos didácticos populares cuyo objetivo era enseñar a través de la diversión. En esta ocasión presentamos la famosa fábula del zorro y el cuervo que siglos más tarde adaptó La Fontaine.*

Hubo una vez un cuervo que encontró un gran pedazo de queso. Lo tomó con el pico y se subió a un árbol para poder comérselo más tranquilamente, sin que nadie le molestara. Pasó en ese momento un zorro por el pie del árbol y al ver el queso que tenía el cuervo, comenzó a pensar en la manera de quitárselo. Y entonces le dijo:

—Don Cuervo, hace mucho tiempo que oí hablar de Ud., de su prudencia y de su nobleza. Lo busqué y hoy la fortuna hace que lo encuentre y, ahora que lo veo, entiendo que tiene más virtudes de las que todos me decían. Y para que vea que no lo digo por adular, ahora mismo voy a hablar de las virtudes que yo encuentro en Ud. y de las cualidades que la gente le critica. Toda la gente piensa que el color de sus plumas, de sus ojos, del pico, de las patas y de las uñas es de un color demasiado oscuro y por esa causa

piensan que es menos bello. La gente no se da cuenta de su error, pues tan negras y tan brillantes son sus alas que parecen de color añil, al igual que las plumas del pavo real, que es el ave más hermosa del mundo. De la misma forma, sus ojos son negros, que es el color de los ojos más bello, pues los ojos son para ver y todas las cosas negras son las que más confortan la visión. Los ojos negros son, pues, los mejores y por eso los ojos más alabados son los de la gacela, que tiene los ojos más oscuros de entre todos los animales. También hay que decir que sus patas y uñas son más fuertes que las de ninguna ave del mismo tamaño, y que su vuelo es el de mayor ligereza, que no le preocupa volar en contra del viento por fuerte que sea, cosa que ninguna otra ave puede hacer con tanta agilidad como Ud. Y pienso yo, que como Dios hace todas las cosas con razón, estoy seguro de que no le negó otra virtud, pues no va a permitir que otra ave cante mejor que Ud. Y como Dios le ha hecho tan perfecto y sé que tiene más virtudes de las que yo oí antes de conocerle, le pido oír su canto que siempre estaré muy agradecido.

La intención del zorro era engañar al cuervo, pues todos sus razonamientos eran ciertos menos este último. Y cuando el cuervo vio cómo el zorro le alababa, y cómo le decía la verdad en todas las ocasiones, creyó que le decía la verdad en todo y que era su amigo. No sospechó que lo hacía para quitarle el queso que tenía en el pico, y entonces, abrió el pico para cantar. Al abrirlo cayó el queso a la tierra y el zorro lo tomó y se fue. Así engañó el zorro al cuervo, haciéndole creer que tenía más virtudes de las que tenía en realidad.

pedazo *piece* pico *beak*
didácticos *intended to instruct*
cuyo *whose* a través de *through* zorro *fox*
cuervo *crow* siglos *centuries* adular *to flatter*
patas *feet* uñas *claws* se da cuenta de *realizes*
añil *indigo* pavo real *peacock* alabados *praised*
gacela *gazelle* tamaño *size* vuelo *flight*
ligereza *agility* volar *to fly*
en contra de *against* Dios *God*
agradecido *grateful* engañar *to deceive*
alababa *praised*

Después de leer

Corregir

Escribe los siguientes comentarios otra vez, corrigiendo la información errónea.

1. Los personajes son un pavo real y una gacela.

2. La narración tiene lugar en un zoológico.

3. El zorro adula al cuervo porque quiere ser su amigo.

4. El cuervo engañó al zorro.

5. La modestia no era una virtud del zorro.

Contestar

Contesta estas preguntas.

1. ¿Cuál es la moraleja de la fábula?
2. En tu opinión, ¿qué adjetivos describen mejor al zorro y al cuervo? Explica tu respuesta.
3. ¿Te gustaría ser amigo/a del zorro? ¿Y del cuervo? ¿Por qué?
4. ¿Qué otras fábulas o leyendas conoces? ¿Qué características tienen en común con esta fábula? ¿En qué son diferentes?
5. ¿Cuál fue el propósito de don Juan Manuel cuando escribió esta fábula?

Diálogos

En pequeños grupos, escojan una fábula que todos conozcan. Escriban un pequeño diálogo en el que cada uno interprete el papel de un personaje principal. No olviden incluir el papel del narrador, que será el que comparta la moraleja con el público al final de la representación. Consideren las siguientes ideas como punto de partida.

- La zorra y las uvas (*the fox and the grapes*)
- El lobo disfrazado de cordero (*the wolf in sheep's clothing*)
- La gallina de los huevos de oro (*the goose who laid the golden eggs*)
- La liebre y la tortuga (*the hare and the tortoise*)

escojan *choose* papel *role* punto de partida *point of departure*

Colombia

El país en cifras

▶ **Área:** 1,138.910 km² (439.734 millas²),
tres veces el área de Montana

▶ **Población:** 43.821.000

De todos los países de habla hispana, sólo México tiene más habitantes que Colombia. Casi toda la población colombiana vive en las áreas montañosas y la costa occidental del país. Aproximadamente el 55% de la superficie del país está sin poblar.

▶ **Capital:** Santa Fé de Bogotá—6.547.000

▶ **Ciudades principales:** Cali—2.893.000,
Medellín—3.070.000, Barranquilla—1.853.000,
Cartagena—768.000

SOURCE: Population Division, UN Secretariat

Medellín

▶ **Moneda:** peso colombiano

▶ **Idiomas:** español (oficial), chibcha, araucano

Bandera de Colombia

Colombianos célebres

▶ Edgar Negret, escultor, pintor (1920-)

▶ Gabriel García Márquez, escritor (1928-)

▶ Juan Pablo Montoya, automovilista (1975-)

▶ Shakira, cantante (1977-)

habitantes *inhabitants* occidental *western* superficie *surface*
sin poblar *unpopulated* arrojaban *threw* oro *gold*
cacique *chief* dioses *gods* llevó *led*

Plaza Bolívar, Bogotá

Baile típico de Barranquilla

Barranquilla
Cartagena

Mar Caribe

PANAMÁ

Sierra Nevada de Santa Marta

VENEZUELA

ESTADOS UNIDOS

OCÉANO ATLÁNTICO

COLOMBIA

OCÉANO PACÍFICO

AMÉRICA DEL SUR

Cordillera Occidental de los Andes

Río Magdalena

Medellín

Cordillera Central de los Andes

Río Meta

Cali

Volcán Nevado del Huíla

Bogotá

Cordillera Oriental de los Andes

Océano Pacífico

Cultivo de caña de azúcar cerca de Cali

ECUADOR

recursos

PERÚ

R | WB pp. 159-160 | vistasonline.com | ICD-ROM Lección 13

¡Increíble pero cierto!

Laguna de Guatavita

En el siglo XVI los exploradores españoles oyeron la leyenda de El Dorado. Esta leyenda cuenta que los indios, como parte de un ritual, arrojaban oro al lago Guatavita y el cacique se sumergía cubierto de oro en honor a los dioses. Aunque esto era cierto, muy pronto la exageración llevó al mito de una ciudad de oro.

Lugares • **El Museo del Oro**

El famoso Museo del Oro del Banco de la República fue fundado en Bogotá en 1939 para preservar las piezas de orfebrería de la época precolombina. En el museo, que tiene más de 30.000 piezas de oro, se pueden ver joyas, ornamentos sagrados y figuras que sirvieron de ídolos. El cuidado con el que están hechos los objetos de oro refleja la creencia de las tribus indígenas de que el oro era la expresión física de la energía creadora de los dioses.

Literatura • **Gabriel García Márquez (1928-)**

Gabriel García Márquez, ganador del Premio Nobel de Literatura en 1982, es uno de los escritores contemporáneos más importantes del mundo. García Márquez publicó su primer cuento en 1947, cuando era estudiante universitario. Su obra más conocida, *Cien años de soledad,* está escrita en el estilo literario llamado "realismo mágico", un estilo que mezcla la realidad con lo irreal y lo mítico.

Historia • **Cartagena de Indias**

Los españoles fundaron la ciudad de Cartagena de Indias en 1533 y construyeron a su lado la fortaleza más grande de las Américas, el Castillo de San Felipe de Barajas. En la ciudad de Cartagena se conservan muchos edificios de la época colonial, como iglesias, monasterios, palacios y mansiones. Cartagena es conocida también por el Festival de Música del Caribe y su prestigioso Festival Internacional de Cine.

¿Qué aprendiste? Responde a las preguntas con una frase completa.

1. ¿Qué idiomas se hablan en Colombia?

2. ¿Qué país de habla hispana tiene más habitantes que Colombia?

3. ¿Quién es Edgar Negret?

4. ¿Para qué fue fundado el Museo del Oro?

5. ¿Qué tipos de objetos hay en el Museo del Oro?

6. ¿Quién ganó el Premio Nobel de Literatura en 1982?

7. ¿Cuál es la obra más famosa de García Márquez?

8. ¿Qué es el "realismo mágico"?

9. ¿Qué construyeron los españoles al lado de la ciudad de Cartagena de Indias?

10. ¿Qué festivales internacionales se celebran en Cartagena?

BRASIL

Conexión Internet Investiga estos temas en el sitio **www.vistasonline.com.**

1. Busca información sobre las ciudades más grandes de Colombia. ¿Qué lugares de interés hay en estas ciudades? ¿Qué puede hacer el turista en estas ciudades?

2. Busca información sobre pintores y escultores colombianos como Edgar Negret, Débora Arango o Fernando Botero. ¿Cuáles son algunas de sus obras más conocidas? ¿Cuáles son sus temas?

Oro *Gold* fundado *founded* orfebrería *goldsmithing* joyas *jewels* sagrados *sacred* están hechos *are made* creencia *belief* creadora *creative* dioses *gods* ganador *winner* cuento *story* obra *work* más conocida *best-known* estilo *style* mezcla *mixes* mítico *mythical* fortaleza *fortress* se conservan *are preserved*

Honduras

El país en cifras

▶ **Área:** 112.492 km² (43.870 millas²),
un poco más grande que Tennessee

▶ **Población:** 6.828.000

*Cerca del 90 por ciento de la población de
Honduras es mestiza. Todavía hay pequeños
grupos indígenas como los jicaque, los miskito
y los paya que mantienen su cultura sin
influencias exteriores y no hablan español.*

▶ **Capital:** Tegucigalpa—1.016.000

Tegucigalpa

▶ **Ciudades principales:**
San Pedro Sula—470.000, El Progreso—81.000,
La Ceiba—72.000

SOURCE: Population Division, UN Secretariat

▶ **Moneda:** lempira

▶ **Idiomas:** español (oficial), miskito, garífuna

Bandera de Honduras

Hondureños célebres

▶ José Antonio Velásquez, pintor (1906-1983)
▶ Argentina Díaz Lozano, escritora (1909-)
▶ Carlos Roberto Reina, juez y presidente
del país (1926-)
▶ Roberto Sosa, escritor (1930-)

mestiza *of indigenous and white parentage*   juez *judge*
presos *prisoners*   madera *wood*

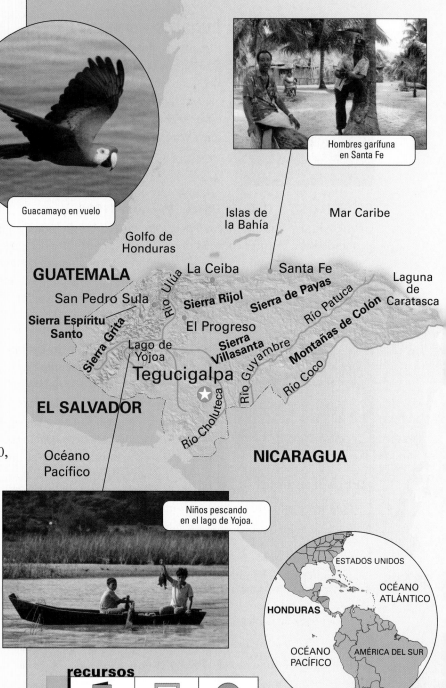
Guacamayo en vuelo

Hombres garífuna en Santa Fe

Niños pescando en el lago de Yojoa.

recursos

R | WB pp. 203-204 | vistasonline.com | ICD-ROM Lección 17

¡Increíble pero cierto!

Los presos de la Penitenciaría Central de
Tegucigalpa hacen objetos de madera, hamacas
y hasta instrumentos musicales. Sus artesanías
son tan populares que hay una pequeña tienda
en la prisión donde los turistas pueden regatear
con este especial grupo de artesanos.

Lugares • Copán

Copán es el sitio arqueológico más importante de Honduras, y para los que estudian la cultura maya es uno de los más fascinantes de la región. Aproximadamente en 400 d.C., la ciudad era muy grande, con más de 150 edificios y plazas, patios y canchas para el juego de pelota. Los restos más interesantes de Copán son las esculturas pintadas que adornan los edificios, los cetros ceremoniales de piedra y el templo llamado Rosalila.

Economía • Las plantaciones de bananas

La exportación de bananas es muy importante para la economía hondureña. Su comercialización empezó en 1889, cuando la Standard Fruit Company envió bananas a Nueva Orleans. La fruta se hizo muy popular y rápidamente empezó a dar grandes beneficios a dos compañías norteamericanas, la Standard Fruit y la United Fruit Company. Debido al enorme poder económico que tenían en el país, estas compañías intervinieron muchas veces en la política hondureña.

Artes • José Antonio Velásquez, (1906-1983)

José Antonio Velásquez fue uno de los pintores primitivistas más famosos de su tiempo. Se le compara a pintores europeos del mismo movimiento artístico, como Paul Gauguin o Emil Nolde, por su estilo y por la importancia que Velásquez le daba a las escenas de la vida diaria. En sus pinturas no hay perspectiva y los colores de los paisajes son puros.

¿Qué aprendiste? Responde a las preguntas con una frase completa.

1. ¿Qué es la lempira?

2. ¿Qué es Copán?

3. ¿Dónde está el templo Rosalila?

4. ¿Qué exportación es importante para la economía de Honduras?

5. ¿Cuándo empezó la comercialización de bananas?

6. ¿Qué movimiento artístico seguía José Antonio Velásquez?

7. ¿A qué daba Velásquez importancia en su pintura?

Conexión Internet Investiga estos temas en el sitio **www.vistasonline.com**.

1. ¿Cuáles son algunas de las exportaciones principales de Honduras, además de las bananas? ¿A qué países exporta Honduras sus productos?

2. Busca información sobre Copán u otro sitio arqueológico en Honduras. En tu opinión, ¿cuáles son los aspectos más interesantes del sitio?

canchas *ball courts*   restos *remains*   cetros *thrones*   envió *sent*   beneficios *profits*   Debido al *Due to*   poder *power*   intervinieron *intervened*
primitivistas *primitivists*   escenas *scenes*   pinturas *paintings*

La naturaleza

el árbol	tree
el bosque (tropical)	(tropical; rain) forest
el césped, la hierba	grass
el cielo	sky
el cráter	crater
el desierto	desert
la estrella	star
la flor	flower
el lago	lake
la luna	moon
el mundo	world
la naturaleza	nature
la nube	cloud
la piedra	stone
la planta	plant
la región	region; area
el río	river
la selva, la jungla	jungle
el sendero	trail; trailhead
el sol	sun
la tierra	land; soil
el valle	valley
el volcán	volcano

Animales

el animal	animal
el ave, el pájaro	bird
el gato	cat
el perro	dog
el pez	fish
la vaca	cow

recursos

R	LCASS./CD Cass. 13/CD 13	LM p. 278

El medio ambiente

la conservación	conservation
la contaminación (del aire; del agua)	(air; water) pollution
la deforestación	deforestation
la ecología	ecology
el ecoturismo	ecotourism
la energía (nuclear, solar)	(nuclear, solar) energy
el envase	container
la extinción	extinction
el gobierno	government
la lata	(tin) can
la ley	law
la lluvia (ácida)	(acid) rain
el medio ambiente	environment
el peligro	danger
la población	population
el reciclaje	recycling
el recurso natural	natural resource
la solución	solution
conservar	to conserve
contaminar	to pollute
controlar	to control
cuidar	to take care of
dejar de (+ *inf.*)	to stop (doing something)
desarrollar	to develop
descubrir	to discover
destruir	to destroy
estar afectado/a (por)	to be affected (by)
estar contaminado/a	to be polluted
evitar	to avoid
mejorar	to improve
proteger	to protect
reciclar	to recycle
recoger	to pick up
reducir	to reduce
resolver (o:ue)	to resolve; to solve
respirar	to breathe
de aluminio	(made) of aluminum
de plástico	(made) of plastic
de vidrio	(made) of glass
puro/a	pure

Emociones

alegrarse (de)	to be happy
esperar	to hope; to wish
sentir (e:ie)	to be sorry; to regret
temer	to fear
es extraño	it's strange
es una lástima	it's a shame
es ridículo	it's ridiculous
es terrible	it's terrible
es triste	it's sad
ojalá (que)	I hope (that); I wish (that)

Dudas y certezas

(no) dudar	(not) to doubt
(no) negar (e:ie)	(not) to deny
(no) creer	(not) to believe
es imposible	it's impossible
es improbable	it's improbable
es obvio	it's obvious
No cabe duda (de) que…	There is no doubt that…
No hay duda (de) que…	There is no doubt that…
(no) es posible	it's (not) possible
(no) es probable	it's (not) probable
(no) es cierto	it's (not) certain
(no) es verdad	it's (not) true
(no) es seguro	it's (not) certain

Conjunciones

a menos que	unless
antes (de) que	before
con tal (de) que	provided (that)
en caso (de) que	in case (that)
para que	so that
sin que	without

Expresiones útiles	See page 365.

En la ciudad

Communicative Goals

You will learn how to:
- Give advice to others
- Give and receive directions
- Discuss daily chores

En la ciudad

Más vocabulario

la frutería	*fruit store*
la heladería	*ice cream shop*
la pastelería	*pastry shop*
la pescadería	*fish market*
la cuadra	*(city) block*
la dirección	*address*
la esquina	*corner*
derecho	*straight (ahead)*
enfrente de	*opposite; facing*
hacia	*toward*
cruzar	*to cross*
doblar	*to turn*
hacer diligencias	*to run errands*
quedar	*to be located*
el cheque (de viajero)	*(traveler's) check*
la cuenta corriente	*checking account*
la cuenta de ahorros	*savings account*
ahorrar	*to save (money)*
cobrar	*to cash (a check)*
depositar	*to deposit*
firmar	*to sign*
llenar (un formulario)	*to fill out (a form)*
pagar a plazos	*to pay in installments*
pagar al contado, en efectivo	*to pay in cash*
pedir prestado	*to borrow*
pedir un préstamo	*to apply for a loan*
ser gratis	*to be free of charge*

Variación léxica

cheque de viajero ←→ cheque de viaje (*Esp.*)

cuadra ←→ manzana (*Esp.*)

direcciones ←→ indicaciones (*Esp.*)

doblar ←→ girar; virar; voltear

hacer diligencias ←→ hacer mandados (*Amér. L.*)

la peluquería, el salón de belleza

el banco

el supermercado

la panadería

la joyería

el cajero automático

Da direcciones. (dar)

Está perdida. (estar)

recursos

Práctica

el letrero

la carnicería

la zapatería

la lavandería

1 **Escuchar** 🎧 Mira el dibujo de las páginas 392 y 393. Luego escucha las frases e indica si lo que dice cada una es **cierto** o **falso.**

	Cierto	Falso		Cierto	Falso
1.	○	○	6.	○	○
2.	○	○	7.	○	○
3.	○	○	8.	○	○
4.	○	○	9.	○	○
5.	○	○	10.	○	○

2 **Seleccionar** Selecciona los lugares de la lista en los que haces las siguientes diligencias.

banco	frutería	pescadería
carnicería	joyería	salón de belleza
pastelería	lavandería	zapatería

1. comprar galletas
2. comprar manzanas
3. comprar un collar (*necklace*)
4. cortarte (*to cut*) el pelo
5. lavar la ropa
6. comprar pescado
7. comprar pollo
8. comprar sandalias

3 **Completar** Llena los espacios en blanco con las palabras más adecuadas.

1. El banco me regaló un reloj. Fue _____.
2. Me gusta _____ dinero, pero no me molesta gastarlo.
3. La cajera me dijo que tenía que _____ el cheque en el dorso (*on the back*) para cobrarlo.
4. Para pagar con un cheque, necesito tener dinero en mi _____.
5. Mi madre va a un _____ para obtener dinero en efectivo cuando el banco está cerrado.
6. Cada viernes, Julio lleva su cheque al banco y lo _____ para tener dinero en efectivo.
7. Cada viernes Ana lleva su cheque al banco y lo _____ en su cuenta de ahorros.
8. Anoche en el restaurante, Marco _____ en vez de usar una tarjeta de crédito.
9. Cuando viajas, es buena idea llevar cheques _____.
10. Para pedir un préstamo, Miguel y Susana tuvieron que _____ cuatro formularios.

En el correo

4   **Diálogo**   Completa el diálogo entre Juanita y el cartero con las palabras más adecuadas.

CARTERO   Buenas tardes, ¿es Ud. la señorita Ramírez? Le traigo un _____.

JUANITA   Sí, soy yo. ¿Quién lo envía?

CARTERO   La Sra. Ramírez. Y también tiene Ud. dos _____.

JUANITA   Ay, pero ¡ninguna es de mi novio! ¿No llegó nada de Manuel Fuentes?

CARTERO   Sí, pero él echó la carta al _____ sin poner un _____ en el sobre.

JUANITA   Entonces, ¿qué recomienda Ud. que haga?

CARTERO   Sugiero que vaya al _____. Con tal de que pague el costo del sello, se le puede dar la carta sin ningún problema.

JUANITA   Uy, otra diligencia, y no tengo mucho tiempo esta tarde para _____ cola en el correo, pero voy enseguida. ¡Ojalá que sea una carta de amor!

5   **En el banco**   Trabajen en grupos para representar estas situaciones.

Un(a) empleado/a de un banco ayuda a...

1. un(a) estudiante universitario/a que quiere abrir una cuenta corriente.
2. una pareja de recién casados que quiere pedir un préstamo al banco para comprar una casa.
3. una persona que quiere información de los servicios que ofrece el banco.
4. un(a) estudiante que va a ir a estudiar al extranjero (*abroad*) y quiere saber qué tiene que hacer para llevar su dinero de una forma segura.

¡LENGUA VIVA!

In Spanish, **Soy yo** means *That's me* or *It's me.* **¿Eres tú?/ ¿Es Ud.?** means *Is that you?*

6

Diligencias Trabajen en parejas para repartirse (*divide up*) las siguientes diligencias. Primero decidan quién va a hacer cada diligencia y después cuál es la manera más rápida de llegar a los diferentes sitios (*places*) desde el campus.

¡ATENCIÓN!

Note these different meanings:

quedar *to be located; to be left over; to fit*

quedarse *to stay, to remain*

> **modelo**
>
> Cobrar unos cheques
> **Estudiante 1:** *Yo voy a cobrar unos cheques. ¿Cómo llego al banco?*
> **Estudiante 2:** *Conduce hacia el norte hasta cruzar la calle Oak.*
> *El banco queda en la esquina a la izquierda.*

1. Enviar un paquete
2. Comprar botas nuevas
3. Comprar un pastel de cumpleaños
4. Lavar unas camisas
5. Pedir un préstamo
6. Comprar helado
7. Cortarte (*to cut*) el pelo
8. Comprar langosta

7

El Hatillo Trabajen en parejas para representar los papeles (*roles*) de un(a) turista que está perdido/a en El Hatillo y de un(a) residente de la ciudad que quiere ayudarle.

NOTA CULTURAL

El Hatillo is a small town near Caracas that is a popular for its quaint architecture, restaurants, and handicrafts shops.

CONSÚLTALO

Simón Bolívar (1783-1830) is considered the liberator of much of South America. In his honor, the Venezuelan unit of currency is called the *bolívar*. To learn more, see **Panorama** p. 417.

> **modelo**
>
> Plaza Sucre, Café Primavera
> **Estudiante 1:** *Perdón, ¿por dónde queda la Plaza Sucre?*
> **Estudiante 2:** *Del Café Primavera, camine derecho por la calle Sucre hasta cruzar la calle Comercio. Doble a la izquierda y camine una cuadra. La Plaza Sucre queda a la derecha.*

1. Plaza Bolívar, farmacia
2. Casa de la Cultura, Plaza Sucre
3. banco, terminal
4. estacionamiento (este), escuela
5. Plaza Sucre, estacionamiento (oeste)
6. joyería, banco
7. farmacia, joyería
8. zapatería, iglesia

8

Direcciones En grupos, escriban un minidrama en el que unos/as turistas están preguntando cómo llegar a diferentes sitios de la comunidad en la que viven Uds. Luego preséntenlo a la clase.

Estamos perdidos.

Maite y Álex hacen diligencias en el centro.

1

2

3

MARTÍN & DON FRANCISCO
Buenas tardes.

JAVIER Hola. ¿Qué tal? Estamos conversando sobre la excursión de mañana.

DON FRANCISCO ¿Ya tienen todo lo que necesitan? A todos los excursionistas yo siempre les recomiendo llevar zapatos cómodos, una mochila, gafas oscuras y un suéter por si hace frío.

JAVIER Todo listo, don Francisco.

MARTÍN Les aconsejo que traigan algo de comer.

ÁLEX Mmm... no pensamos en eso.

MAITE ¡Deja de preocuparte tanto, Álex! Podemos comprar algo en el supermercado ahora mismo. ¿Vamos?

6

7

8

JOVEN ¡Hola! ¿Puedo ayudarte en algo?

MAITE Sí, estamos perdidos. ¿Hay un banco por aquí con cajero automático?

JOVEN Mmm... no hay ningún banco en esta calle que tenga cajero automático.

JOVEN Pero conozco uno en la calle Pedro Moncayo que sí tiene cajero automático. Cruzas esta calle y luego doblas a la izquierda. Sigues todo derecho y antes de que lleguen a la Joyería Crespo van a ver un letrero grande del Banco del Pacífico.

MAITE También buscamos un supermercado.

JOVEN Pues, allí mismo enfrente del banco hay un supermercado pequeño. Fácil, ¿no?

MAITE Creo que sí. Muchas gracias por su ayuda.

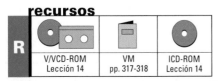

ÁLEX ¡Excelente idea! En cuanto termine mi café te acompaño.

MAITE Necesito pasar por el banco y por el correo para mandar unas cartas.

ÁLEX Está bien.

ÁLEX ¿Necesitan algo del centro?

INÉS ¡Sí! Cuando vayan al correo, ¿pueden echar estas postales al buzón? Además necesito unas estampillas.

ÁLEX Por supuesto.

MAITE Ten, guapa, tus sellos.

INÉS Gracias, Maite. ¿Qué tal les fue en el centro?

MAITE ¡Superbien! Fuimos al banco y al correo. Luego en el supermercado compramos comida para la excursión. Y antes de regresar, paramos en una heladería.

MAITE ¡Ah! Y otra cosa. Cuando llegamos al centro conocimos a un joven muy simpático que nos dio direcciones. Era muy amable... ¡y muy guapo!

Enfoque cultural Las tiendas especializadas

La popularidad de los supermercados está aumentando (*growing*) en los países hispanos, pero todavía muchas personas van a tiendas especializadas para comprar comidas como la carne, el pescado, el pan y los dulces. La pulpería, por ejemplo, es una tienda típica de las zonas rurales de algunos países de América Latina. La gente va a una pulpería para tomar una bebida o comprar productos esenciales. Otra tienda típica de algunos países hispanos es la rosticería, donde se asan (*roast*) y venden carnes para llevar (*takeout*).

Expresiones útiles

Giving advice

▷ **Les recomiendo/Hay que llevar zapatos cómodos.**
I recommend that you/It's necessary to wear comfortable shoes.

▷ **Les aconsejo que traigan algo de comer.**
I advise you to bring something to eat.

Talking about errands

▷ **Necesito pasar por el banco.**
I need to go by the bank.

▷ **En cuanto termine mi café te acompaño.**
As soon as I finish my coffee, I'll go with you.

Getting directions

▷ **Estamos perdidos.**
We're lost.

▶ **¿Hay un banco por aquí con cajero automático?**
Is there a bank around here with an ATM?

▷ **Crucen esta calle y luego doblen a la izquierda/derecha.**
Cross this street and then turn to the left/right.

▷ **Sigan todo derecho.**
Go straight ahead.

▷ **Antes de que lleguen a la joyería van a ver un letrero grande.**
Before you get to the jewelry store, you're going to see a big sign.

▶ **¿Por dónde queda el supermercado?**
Where is the supermarket?

▷ **Está a dos cuadras de aquí.**
It's two blocks from here.

▷ **Queda en la calle Flores.**
It's on Flores street.

▷ **Pues, allí mismo enfrente del banco hay un supermercado.**
Well, right in front of the bank there is a supermarket.

Reacciona a la fotonovela

1

¿Cierto o falso? Decide si lo que dicen las siguientes frases es **cierto** o **falso**.
Corrige las frases falsas.

	Cierto	Falso
1. Don Francisco insiste en que los excursionistas lleven una cámara.	○	○
2. Inés escribió unas postales y ahora necesita mandarlas por correo.	○	○
3. El joven dice que el Banco del Atlántico tiene un cajero automático.	○	○
4. Enfrente del banco hay una heladería.	○	○

CONSÚLTALO

The subjunctive with verbs of will and influence To review the use of verbs like **insistir**, see Lesson 12, pp. 346-347.

2

Identificar Identifica quién puede decir las siguientes frases.

1. Quiero ir contigo pero primero quiero terminar mi desayuno, ¿está bien?
2. Insisto en que lleven ropa apropiada para una excursión como, por ejemplo, zapatos para caminar.
3. Van a tener hambre en la excursión. ¿Por qué no traen un poco de fruta?
4. Yo también necesito algo del correo. ¿Me puedes comprar unas estampillas?
5. A ver... tengo que ir al banco, al supermercado y ¿qué más? Ah, necesito mandar unas cartas.
6. Miren, después de doblar a la izquierda, van a ver el letrero del banco.

JOVEN

MARTÍN

INÉS

ÁLEX

MAITE

DON FRANCISCO

3

Ordenar Pon los eventos de la **Fotonovela** en el orden correcto.

a. Un joven ayuda a Álex y a Maite a encontrar el banco porque están perdidos.___
b. Álex y Maite comen un helado.___
c. Inés les da unas postales a Maite y a Álex para echar al buzón.___
d. Maite y Álex van al banco y al correo.___
e. Álex termina su café.___
f. Maite y Álex van al supermercado y compran comida.___

4

Conversación Un(a) compañero/a y tú son vecinos/as. Uno/a de Uds. acaba de mudarse y necesita ayuda porque no conoce la ciudad. Los dos tienen que hacer algunas diligencias y deciden hacerlas juntos/as. Preparen una conversación breve en la que hagan planes para ir a los siguientes lugares.

▶ un banco

▶ una lavandería

▶ un supermercado

▶ una heladería

▶ una panadería

AYUDA

primero *first*

luego *then*

¿Sabes dónde queda...?
Do you know where...is?

¿Qué te parece?
What do you think?

¡Cómo no!
Why not?

Ortografía

Las abreviaturas

In Spanish, as in English, abbreviations are often used in order to save space and time while writing. Here are some of the most commonly used abbreviations in Spanish.

---

usted ➝ Ud.   **ustedes** ➝ Uds.

As you have already learned, the subject pronouns **usted** and **ustedes** are often abbreviated.

---

don ➝ D.   **doña** ➝ Dña.   **doctor(a)** ➝ Dr(a).

señor ➝ Sr.   **señora** ➝ Sra.   **señorita** ➝ Srta.

These titles are frequently abbreviated.

---

centímetro ➝ cm   **metro** ➝ m   **kilómetro** ➝ km

litro ➝ l   **gramo** ➝ g, gr   **kilogramo** ➝ kg

The abbreviations for these units of measurement are often used, but without periods.

---

por ejemplo ➝ p. ej.   **página(s)** ➝ pág(s).

These abbreviations are often seen in books.

---

derecha ➝ dcha.   **izquierda** ➝ izq., izqda.

código postal ➝ C.P.   **número** ➝ n.º

These abbreviations are often used in mailing addresses.

Banco ➝ Bco.   **Compañía** ➝ Cía.

cuenta corriente ➝ c/c.   **Sociedad Anónima (*Inc.*)** ➝ S.A.

These abbreviations are frequently used in the business world.

Práctica Escribe otra vez la siguiente información usando las abreviaturas adecuadas.

1. doña María
2. señora Pérez
3. Compañía Mexicana de Inversiones
4. usted

5. Banco de Santander
6. doctor Medina
7. Código Postal 03697
8. cuenta corriente número 20-453

Emparejar En la tabla hay 9 abreviaturas. Empareja los cuadros necesarios para formarlas.

S.	c.	C.	c	co.	U
B	c/	Sr	A.	D	dc
ta.	P.	ña.	ha.	m	d.

recursos

| R | LM p. 280 | LCASS./CD Cass. 14/CD 14 | ICD-ROM Lección 14 |

14.1 The subjunctive in adjective clauses

ANTE TODO In Lesson 13, you learned that the subjunctive is used in adverbial clauses after certain conjunctions. You will now learn how the subjunctive can be used in adjective clauses to express that the existence of someone or something is uncertain or indefinite.

¡ATENCIÓN!

Adjective clauses are subordinate clauses that modify a noun or pronoun in the main clause of a sentence. That noun or pronoun is called the *antecedent*.

¿Hay un banco por aquí que tenga cajero automático?

No hay ningún banco en esta calle que tenga cajero automático.

▶ The subjunctive is used in an adjective (or subordinate) clause that refers to a person, place, thing, or idea that either does not exist or whose existence is uncertain or indefinite. In the examples below, compare the differences in meaning between the statements using the indicative and those using the subjunctive.

Indicative	Subjunctive
Necesito **el libro** que **tiene** información sobre Venezuela.	Necesito **un libro** que **tenga** información sobre Venezuela.
I need the book that has information about Venezuela.	*I need a book that has information about Venezuela.*
Quiero vivir en **esta casa** que **tiene** jardín.	Quiero vivir en **una casa** que **tenga** jardín.
I want to live in this house that has a garden.	*I want to live in a house that has a garden.*
En mi barrio, hay **una heladería** que **vende** helado de mango.	En mi barrio no hay **ninguna heladería** que **venda** helado de mango.
In my neighborhood, there's an ice cream store that sells mango ice cream.	*In my neighborhood, there is no ice cream store that sells mango ice cream.*

▶ When the adjective clause refers to a person, place, thing, or idea that is clearly known, certain, or definite, the indicative is used.

Quiero vivir en **la casa** que **tiene** jardín.
I want to live in the house that has a garden.

Busco **al profesor** que **enseña** japonés.
I'm looking for the professor who teaches Japanese.

Conozco **a alguien** que **va** a esa peluquería.
I know someone who goes to that beauty salon.

Tengo **un amigo** que **vive** cerca de mi casa.
I have a friend who lives near my house.

▶ The personal **a** is not used with direct objects that are hypothetical people. However, as you learned in Lesson 7, **alguien** and **nadie** are always preceded by the personal **a** when they function as direct objects.

Necesitamos **un empleado** que
sepa usar computadoras.
*We need an employee who knows
how to use computers.*

Necesitamos **al empleado** que
sabe usar computadoras.
*We need the employee who knows how
to use computers.*

Buscamos **a alguien** que **pueda**
cocinar.
*We're looking for someone who
can cook.*

No conocemos **a nadie** que **pueda**
cocinar.
*We don't know anyone who can
cook.*

▶ The subjunctive is commonly used in questions with adjective clauses when the speaker is trying to find out information about which he or she is uncertain. However, if the person who responds to the question knows the information, the indicative is used.

—¿Hay un parque que **esté** cerca de
nuestro hotel?
Is there a park that's near our hotel?

—Sí, hay un parque que **está** muy
cerca del hotel.
*Yes, there's a park that's very near
the hotel.*

SECCIÓN
AMARILLA
**Busque cualquier
información que
necesite.**

¡INTÉNTALO! Escoge entre el subjuntivo o el indicativo para completar cada oración.

1. Necesito una persona que ___pueda___ (puede/pueda) cantar bien.
2. Buscamos a alguien que _____ (tiene/tenga) paciencia.
3. ¿Hay restaurantes aquí que _____ (sirven/sirvan) comida japonesa?
4. Tengo una amiga que _____ (saca/saque) fotografías muy bonitas.
5. Hay una carnicería que _____ (está/esté) cerca de aquí.
6. No vemos ningún apartamento que nos _____ (interesa/interese).
7. Conozco a un estudiante que _____ (come/coma) hamburguesas todos los días.
8. ¿Hay alguien que _____ (dice/diga) la verdad?

Práctica

1   **Completar** Completa estas frases con la forma correcta del indicativo o del subjuntivo de los verbos entre paréntesis.

1. Buscamos un hotel que _____ (tener) piscina.
2. ¿Sabe Ud. dónde _____ (quedar) el Correo Central?
3. ¿Hay algún buzón por aquí donde yo _____ (poder) echar una carta?
4. Ana quiere ir a la carnicería que _____ (estar) en la avenida Lecuna.
5. Encontramos un restaurante que _____ (servir) comida venezolana típica.
6. ¿Conoces a alguien que _____ (saber) mandar un *fax* por computadora?
7. Necesitas al empleado que _____ (entender) este nuevo programa de computación.
8. No hay nada en este mundo que _____ (ser) gratis.

2   **Oraciones** Forma frases con los siguientes elementos. Usa el presente del indicativo o del subjuntivo y luego, haz los cambios que sean necesarios.

1. mi / amigos / conocer / un / heladería / que / vender / helados / de / 51 / sabores (*flavors*)

2. ¿hay / alguien / que / saber / dirección / de / ese / heladería?

3. Marta / querer / comprarle / su / hija / un / zapatos / que / gustar

4. Ella / no / encontrar / nada / que / gustar / en / ese / zapatería

5. ¿tener / Ud. / algo / que / ser / más / barato?

6. ¿conocer / tú / alguno / banco / que / ofrecer / cuentas / corriente / gratis?

7. nosotros / no / conocer / nadie / que / firmar / un / documento / sin / leerlo / primero

8. no / hay / ninguno / cosa / que / a mí / interesar / en ese / joyería

3   **Anuncios clasificados** En parejas, lean estos anuncios y luego describan el tipo de persona u objeto que se busca.

CLASIFICADOS

VENDEDOR(A) Se necesita persona dinámica y responsable con buena presencia. Experiencia mínima de un año. Horario de trabajo flexible. Llamar a Joyería Aurora de 10 a 13h y de 16 a 18h. Tel: 263-7553

PELUQUERÍA UNISEX Se busca persona con experiencia en peluquería y maquillaje para trabajar tiempo completo. Llamar de 9 a 13, 30h. Tel: 261-3548

COMPARTIR APARTAMENTO Se necesita compañera para compartir apartamento de 2 alcobas en el Chaco. Alquiler $500 por mes. No fumar. Llamar al 951-3642 entre 19 y 22h.

CLASES DE INGLÉS Profesor de Inglaterra con diez años de experiencia ofrece clases para grupos o instrucción privada para individuos. Llamar al 933-4110 de 16:30 a 18:30.

SE BUSCA CONDOMINIO Se busca condominio en Sabana Grande con 3 alcobas, 2 baños, sala, comedor y aire acondicionado. Tel: 977-2018.

EJECUTIVO DE CUENTAS Se requiere joven profesional con al menos dos años de experiencia en el sector financiero. Se ofrecen beneficios excelentes. Enviar currículum vitae al Banco Unión, Avda. Urdaneta 263, Caracas.

Comunicación

4 **Completar** Completa estas frases de una manera lógica. Luego, compara tus respuestas con las de un(a) compañero/a.

1. Deseo un trabajo (*job*) que...
2. Algún día espero tener un apartamento (una casa) que...
3. Mis padres buscan un carro que..., pero yo quiero un carro que...
4. Tengo un(a) novio/a que...
5. Un consejero/a (*advisor*), debe ser una persona que...
6. Mi compañero/a de cuarto conoce a alguien que...
7. No conozco a nadie que...
8. Me gustaría conocer a alguien que...
9. En esta clase no hay nadie que...
10. No tengo ningún profesor que...

5 **Encuesta** Tu profesor(a) va a darte una hoja de actividades. Circula por la clase y pregúntales a tus compañeros/as si conocen a alguien que haga cada actividad que se menciona en la lista. Si dicen que conocen a una persona así, pregúntales quién es y anota sus respuestas. Luego informa a la clase de los resultados de tu encuesta.

Actividades	Nombres	Respuestas
1. Trabajar en un supermercado		
2. Querer ser cartero/a		
3. No tener tarjeta de crédito		
4. Necesitar un préstamo		
5. Saber ahorrar dinero		
6. Hablar japonés		
7. Ser venezolano/a		
8. Graduarse este año		
9. Casarse en el verano		
10. Preocuparse por su situación económica		
11. Comprender el subjuntivo		
12. Pedir prestado el carro de sus padres		

Síntesis

6 **Agencia de viajes** Tu profesor(a) va a darte una hoja de actividades con instrucciones. Trabaja con un(a) compañero/a para realizar esta actividad. Una persona va a ser un(a) agente de viajes, la otra va a ser el/la cliente.

14.2 Conjunctions followed by the subjunctive or the indicative

ANTE TODO In Lesson 13, you learned that certain conjunctions are always followed by the subjunctive. There is another set of conjunctions that can be followed by either the subjunctive or the indicative, depending on the context in which they are used.

En cuanto termine mi café, te acompaño.

Cuando vayan al correo, ¿pueden echar estas postales al buzón?

▶ All of the conjunctions in the following list refer to time and are used to connect a main clause and a subordinate clause.

cuando	*when*
después (de) que	*after*
en cuanto	*as soon as*
hasta que	*until*
tan pronto como	*as soon as*

▶ The present subjunctive is required in the subordinate clause when the main clause expresses a future action or a condition that has not yet occurred.

Voy a firmar el cheque **tan pronto como** ellos me lo **den.**
I'm going to sign the check as soon as they give it to me.

Voy a llamarte **después de que** Miguel **se vaya.**
I'm going to call you after Miguel leaves.

▶ With this use of the present subjunctive, the verb in the main clause either is a command or refers to the future. Also, note that the main clause can come either before or after the subordinate clause.

Cuando tenga tiempo, **voy a enviar** esta carta a mi hija.
When I have time, I'm going to mail this letter to my daughter.

No salgas **hasta que** tú y tu hermano **limpien** su cuarto.
Don't go out until you and your brother clean your room.

▶ If the verb in the main clause expresses a real-life action that habitually happens or that has happened in the past, the indicative, *not* the subjunctive, is used in the subordinate clause.

Habitual Actions ➝ Indicative

Siempre pago al contado **cuando tengo** dinero.
I always pay in cash when I have money.

Nunca miro la televisión **hasta que termino** de comer.
I never watch television until I finish eating.

Por las mañanas, me ducho **en cuanto me despierto.**
In the morning, I take a shower as soon as I awake.

Siempre me afeito **después de que me ducho.**
I always shave after I take a shower.

Past Actions ➝ Indicative

El sábado salí **tan pronto como pude.**
On Saturday I went out as soon as I could.

Julia no me pudo mandar el paquete **hasta que supo** mi dirección.
Julia couldn't send me the package until she found out my address.

Envié el mensaje electrónico **en cuanto** lo **terminé.**
I sent the e-mail message as soon as I finished it.

Fuimos de compras **después de que salimos** de la conferencia.
We went shopping after we left the conference.

Siempre garantizamos la energía
hasta que alguien los separa.

ISAGEN

¡INTÉNTALO! Completa las oraciones con el subjuntivo o el indicativo de los verbos.

1. Le voy a escribir tan pronto como ___tenga___ (tengo/tenga) tiempo.
2. Apaga la televisión en cuanto te lo _____ (pido/pida).
3. Mi hermana me llamó ayer en cuanto _____ (volví/vuelva) a la residencia.
4. Siempre ahorro dinero cuando _____ (como/coma) en casa.
5. Vamos a leer los documentos cuando los _____ (recibimos/recibamos).
6. De niño, siempre iba a la heladería tan pronto como _____ (tenía/tenga) dinero.
7. Vamos a salir después de que el mesero nos _____ (da/dé) la cuenta.
8. Espera aquí hasta que nosotros _____ (volvemos/volvamos).
9. Siempre llamo a mis amigos en cuanto _____ (llego/llegue) a casa.
10. Vamos a pedir la comida cuando tú _____ (tienes/tengas) hambre.

Práctica

1   **Completar** Completa las oraciones con las formas adecuadas de los verbos en el indicativo o el subjuntivo. Piensa si cada verbo trata de una acción pasada o habitual (indicativo) o de una acción futura (subjuntivo).

1. Desde que (*since*) _____ (empezar) a trabajar, siempre pago todo al contado. Pero algún día, cuando yo _____ (comprar) una casa, voy a tener que aprender a pagar a plazos.

2. Tan pronto como _____ (ir) todos a la panadería a comer pan dulce, empezó a llover. Yo le dije a Sandra: «No me muevo de aquí hasta que _____ (salir) el sol».

3. Hasta que tú _____ (echar) al buzón el cheque para la cuenta de la electricidad, no voy a estar tranquilo. Después de que tú _____ (perder) el trabajo el mes pasado, no pagamos muchas cosas a tiempo.

4. Te voy a llevar a la heladería de Macuto cuando yo _____ (tener) tiempo. Después de que yo _____ (terminar) de estudiar en la universidad, voy a tener más tiempo libre.

5. Tan pronto como Uds. _____ (perderse), ¿no pensaron en pedir direcciones? Normalmente, cuando Felipe y yo no _____ (estar) seguros, buscamos una gasolinera para preguntar.

2   **Un cuento** Completa el cuento (*story*) con la forma adecuada de los siguientes verbos.

comer	despertar	ir	preparar
poder	terminar	dar	acompañar

Lupe se levantó por la mañana tan pronto como su marido se _____ de la casa. Ella le quería _____ una sorpresa de aniversario. Salió a la calle, hablando consigo misma (*talking to herself*): «Mañana sábado, cuando Félix se _____, le voy a llevar el café a la cama, y en cuanto _____ su desayuno, le voy a pedir que me _____ a casa de mi prima para recoger unas cosas. Perfecto. Mientras todos preparan la fiesta sorpresa, nosotros vamos a ir a hacer diligencias. En cuanto _____ de preparar todo, Rosa me va a llamar al teléfono celular». Esa mañana, Lupe fue al banco, al supermercado, a la peluquería... todo tenía que estar perfecto. Volvió a su casa tan pronto como _____. Durante toda la tarde siguió pensando en todos los detalles, las invitaciones, la comida... Llegó su marido por la noche, se acostaron y a la mañana siguiente Félix no se despertó hasta que Lupe le _____ su café.

Comunicación

3

Encuesta Tu profesor(a) va a darte una hoja de actividades. Hazles las preguntas de la tabla (*chart*) a tres compañeros/as de clase. Después, anota sus respuestas en la hoja de actividades.

4

Oraciones Con un(a) compañero/a, completa las oraciones que siguen, basándote en tus propias experiencias. Puedes usar el verbo en el indicativo o en el subjuntivo.

> **modelo**
>
> Hasta que sepa / supe...
> No quiero ir a Venezuela hasta que sepa hablar el español.
> No quise invitar a mi novia a comer hasta que aprendí a cocinar.

1. Cuando compre / compré una casa...
2. En cuanto tenga / tuve que pedir prestado...
3. Tan pronto como abra / abrí una cuenta...
4. Hasta que estudie / estudié...
5. Después de que vaya / fui...
6. Cuando tenga / tuve suficiente dinero...
7. En cuanto cumpla / cumplí...
8. Cuando sea / era...

Síntesis

5

¿Dónde queda? En parejas, miren el mapa. Después, uno/a de los compañeros/as dice dónde está y adónde quiere llegar y el/la otro/a le da direcciones. Túrnense para pedir direcciones.

> **modelo**
>
> **Estudiante 1:** Estoy en el estacionamiento y quiero ir a la pescadería.
> **Estudiante 2:** Cuando salgas del estacionamiento, dobla a la derecha y camina hasta que...

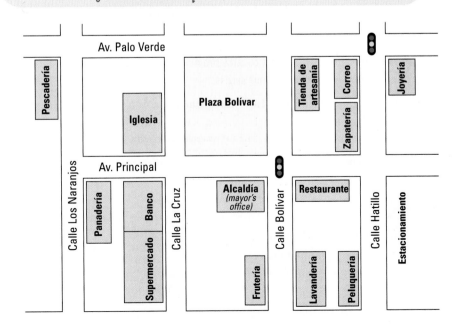

14.3 Nosotros/as commands

 **ANTE TODO** You have already learned familiar (**tú**) commands and formal (**Ud./Uds.**) commands. You will now learn **nosotros/as** commands, which are used to give orders or suggestions that include yourself and other people. **Nosotros/as** commands correspond to the English *Let's*.

Crucemos la calle.	**No crucemos** la calle.
Let's cross the street.	*Let's not cross the street.*

▶ Both affirmative and negative **nosotros/as** commands are generally formed by using the first-person plural form of the present subjunctive.

¿Quieres ir al supermercado?

¡Excelente idea! ¡Vamos!

▶ The affirmative *Let's* + [*verb*] command may also be expressed with **vamos a** + [*infinitive*]. Remember, however, that **vamos a** + [*infinitive*] can also mean *we are going to (do something)*. Context and tone of voice determine which meaning is being expressed.

Vamos a cruzar la calle.	**Vamos a trabajar** mucho.
Let's cross the street.	*We're going to work a lot.*

▶ To express the command *Let's go*, the present indicative form of **ir** (**vamos**) is used, not the present subjunctive. For the negative command, however, the present subjunctive is used.

Vamos a la pescadería.	No **vayamos** a la pescadería.
Let's go to the fish market.	*Let's not go to the fish market.*

▶ Object pronouns are always attached to affirmative **nosotros/as** commands. A written accent is added to maintain the original stress.

Firmemos el cheque. → **Firmémoslo.**   **Escribamos** a Ana y Raúl. → **Escribámosles.**

▶ Object pronouns are placed in front of negative **nosotros/as** commands.

No **les paguemos** el préstamo.   No **se lo digamos** a ellos.

¡INTÉNTALO! Indica los mandatos afirmativos y negativos de la primera persona del plural (**nosotros/as**) de los siguientes verbos.

1. estudiar ___estudiemos, no estudiemos___
2. cenar _____
3. leer _____
4. decidir _____
5. decir _____
6. cerrar _____
7. levantarse _____
8. irse _____

Práctica

1

Completar Completa esta conversación con los mandatos de **nosotros/as.** Luego, representa la conversación con un(a) compañero/a.

MARÍA Sergio, ¿quieres hacer diligencias ahora o por la tarde?

SERGIO No _____ (dejarlas) para más tarde. _____ (Hacerlas) ahora. ¿Qué tenemos que hacer?

MARÍA Necesito comprar sellos.

SERGIO Yo también. _____ (Ir) al correo.

MARÍA Pues, antes de ir al correo, necesito sacar dinero de mi cuenta corriente.

SERGIO Bueno, _____ (buscar) un cajero automático.

MARÍA ¿Tienes hambre?

SERGIO Sí. _____ (Cruzar) la calle y _____ (entrar) en ese café.

MARÍA Buena idea.

SERGIO ¿Nos sentamos aquí?

MARÍA No, no _____ (sentarse) aquí; _____ (sentarse) enfrente de la ventana.

SERGIO ¿Qué pedimos?

MARÍA _____ (Pedir) café y pan dulce.

2

Responder Responde a cada mandato según las indicaciones. Usa los mandatos de **nosotros/as** y sustituye los pronombres por los objetos directos e indirectos.

> **modelo**
>
> Vamos a vender el carro. (Sí)
> Sí, vendámoslo.

1. Vamos a levantarnos a las seis. (Sí)
2. Vamos a enviar los paquetes. (No)
3. Vamos a depositar el cheque. (Sí)
4. Vamos al supermercado. (No)
5. Vamos a mandar esta tarjeta postal a nuestros amigos. (No)
6. Vamos a limpiar la habitación. (Sí)
7. Vamos a mirar la televisión. (No)
8. Vamos a bailar. (Sí)
9. Vamos a pintar la sala. (No)
10. Vamos a comprar estampillas. (Sí)

Comunicación

3

Preguntar Tú y un(a) compañero/a están en Caracas. Túrnense para hacerse estas preguntas. Contesten las preguntas con un mandato afirmativo o negativo de **nosotros/as.**

1. ¿Nos quedamos en un hotel o en una pensión?
2. ¿Cruzamos la calle aquí o caminamos una cuadra más?
3. ¿Vamos al supermercado o comemos en un restaurante?
4. ¿Vamos al cine en taxi o en autobús?
5. ¿Salimos para el cine a las seis o las seis y media?
6. ¿Hacemos cola o buscamos otra película?
7. ¿Volvemos al hotel después de la película o tomamos algo en un café?
8. ¿Pagamos la cuenta en efectivo o con tarjeta de crédito?

4

Decisiones Trabajen en grupos pequeños. Uds. están en Caracas por dos días. Lean esta página de una guía turística sobre la ciudad y decidan qué van a hacer hoy por la mañana, por la tarde y por la noche. Usen los mandatos afirmativos o negativos de **nosotros/as.**

modelo

> Visitemos el Museo de Arte Contémporaneo Sofía Imber
> esta tarde. Quiero ver las esculturas de Jesús Rafael Soto.

Guía de Caracas

MUSEOS
- **Museo de Arte Colonial** Avenida Panteón
- **Museo de Arte Contemporáneo Sofía Imber** Parque Central Esculturas de Jesús Rafael Soto y pinturas de Miró, Chagall y Picasso.
- **Galería de Arte Nacional** Parque Central. Colección de más de 4000 obras de arte venezolano.

SITIOS DE INTERÉS
- **Plaza Bolívar**
- **Jardín Botánico** Avenida Interna UCV. De 8:00 a 5:00.
- **Parque del Este** Avenida Francisco de Miranda Parque más grande de la ciudad con serpentarium.
- **Casa Natal de Simón Bolívar** Esquina de Sociedad de la avenida Universitaria. Casa colonial donde nació El Libertador.

RESTAURANTES
- **El Barquero** Avenida Luis Roche
- **Restaurante El Coyuco** Avenida Urdaneta
- **Restaurante Sorrento** Avenida Francisco Solano
- **Café Tonino** Avenida Andrés Bello

NOTA CULTURAL

Jesús Rafael Soto (1932–) is a modern Venezuelan sculptor/painter whose "kinetic" works often involve parts that shimmer and vibrate, bringing the viewer into closer contact with the work.

Síntesis

5

Situación Tú y un(a) compañero/a viven juntos en un apartamento y tienen problemas económicos. Describan los problemas y sugieran algunas soluciones. Usen los mandatos afirmativos o negativos de **nosotros/as.**

modelo

> Es importante que reduzcamos nuestros gastos
> (*expenses*). Hagamos un presupuesto (*budget*).

14.4 Past participles used as adjectives

ANTE TODO In Lesson 5, you learned about present participles (**estudiando**). Both Spanish and English have past participles. The past participles of English verbs often end in **–ed** (*to turn* ➤ *turned*), but many are also irregular (*to buy* ➤ *bought; to drive* ➤ *driven*).

▶ In Spanish, regular **–ar** verbs form the past participle with **–ado.** Regular **–er** and **–ir** verbs form the past participle with **–ido.**

¡ATENCIÓN!

The past participles of **–er** and **–ir** verbs whose stems end in **–a**, **–e**, or **–o** carry a written accent mark on the **i** of the **–ido** ending.

caer	**caído**
creer	**creído**
leer	**leído**
oír	**oído**
reír	**reído**
sonreír	**sonreído**
traer	**traído**

INFINITIVE	STEM	PAST PARTICIPLE
bailar	bail-	**bailado**
comer	com-	**comido**
vivir	viv-	**vivido**

Irregular past participles

abrir	**abierto**	morir	**muerto**
decir	**dicho**	poner	**puesto**
describir	**descrito**	resolver	**resuelto**
descubrir	**descubierto**	romper	**roto**
escribir	**escrito**	ver	**visto**
hacer	**hecho**	volver	**vuelto**

CONSEJOS

You already know several participles used as adjectives: **aburrido, interesado, nublado, perdido,** etc.

• • •

Note that all irregular past participles except **dicho** and **hecho** end in **–to.**

▶ In Spanish, as in English, past participles can be used as adjectives. They are often used with the verb **estar** to describe a condition or state that results from an action. Like other Spanish adjectives, they must agree in gender and number with the nouns they modify.

En la entrada hay algunos letreros **escritos** en español.
In the entrance, there are some signs written in Spanish.

La joyería **está cerrada.**
The jewelry store is closed.

Tenemos la mesa **puesta** y la cena **hecha.**
We have the table set and dinner made.

El cheque ya **está firmado.**
The check is already signed.

¡INTÉNTALO! Indica la forma correcta del participio pasado de estos verbos.

1. hablar ___hablado___
2. beber _____
3. decidir _____
4. romper _____
5. escribir _____
6. cantar _____
7. oír _____
8. traer _____

9. correr _____
10. leer _____
11. ver _____
12. hacer _____
13. morir _____
14. reír _____
15. mirar _____

Práctica

1 **Completar** Completa estas frases con la forma adecuada del participio pasado del verbo que está entre paréntesis.

1. El hombre _____ (describir) en ese documento es un criminal.
2. María Conchita Alonso es una actriz y cantante muy _____ (conocer).
3. ¿Está _____ (descubrir) ya todo el petróleo de Venezuela?
4. Los libros _____ (usar) son muy baratos.
5. Los documentos están _____ (firmar).
6. Tenemos el documento _____ (firmar) desde hace una semana.

2 **Preparaciones** Tú y tu compañero/a van a hacer un viaje. Túrnense para hacerse las siguientes preguntas sobre los preparativos (*preparations*). Usen el participio pasado en sus respuestas.

> **modelo**
>
> **Estudiante 1:** ¿Firmaste el cheque de viajero?
> **Estudiante 2:** Sí, el cheque de viajero ya está firmado.

1. ¿Compraste los boletos para el avión?
2. ¿Confirmaste las reservaciones para el hotel?
3. ¿Firmaste tu pasaporte?
4. ¿Lavaste la ropa?
5. ¿Resolviste el problema con el banco?
6. ¿Pagaste todas las cuentas?
7. ¿Hiciste todas las diligencias?
8. ¿Hiciste las maletas?

3 **Describir** Tú y un(a) compañero/a son agentes de policía y tienen que investigar un crimen que ocurrió en el hotel Coliseo. Miren el dibujo y describan lo que encontraron al entrar en la suite del Sr. Villalonga. Usen el participio pasado en la descripción.

> **modelo**
>
> La puerta del baño no estaba cerrada.

AYUDA

You may want to use the past participle of these verbs to describe the illustration:

abrir *to open*
desordenar *to make untidy*
hacer *to do, to make*
poner *to turn on (a machine)*
tirar *to throw*

Comunicación

4   **Preguntas**   En parejas, túrnense para hacerse estas preguntas.

1. ¿Quiénes están aburridos en la clase?
2. ¿Hay alguien que esté dormido en la clase?
3. ¿Dejas la luz prendida en tu cuarto?
4. ¿Está ordenado tu cuarto?
5. ¿Prefieres comprar libros usados o nuevos? ¿Por qué?
6. ¿Tienes mucho dinero ahorrado?
7. ¿Necesitas pedirles dinero prestado a tus padres?
8. ¿Estás preocupado/a por el medio ambiente?
9. ¿Qué haces cuando no estás preparado/a para una clase?
10. ¿Qué haces cuando estás perdido/a en una ciudad?

5   **Encuesta**   Tu profesor(a) va a darte una hoja de actividades. Circula por la clase y haz preguntas hasta que encuentres a las personas que responden a cada descripción y anota sus respuestas. Luego informa a la clase de los resultados de tu encuesta.

AYUDA

Remember that **llevar** means *to wear* in addition to *to take* or *to bring*.

Descripciones	Nombres	Otra información
1. Tiene algo roto. ¿Qué es?		
2. Lleva algo hecho en un país hispano. ¿Qué es?		
3. Tiene algo traído de otro país. ¿Qué es?		
4. Tiene las respuestas escritas en su libro.		
5. Tiene la cama hecha.		
6. Su cuarto está desordenado. ¿Por qué?		
7. Sabe los nombres de dos venezolanos muy conocidos. ¿Quiénes son?		
8. Está interesado/a en trabajar en un banco. ¿Por qué?		

Síntesis

6   **Situación**   Tu profesor(a) va a darte una hoja de actividades. Trabaja con un(a) compañero/a. Una persona va a ser el/la recepcionista (*desk clerk*) de un hotel. La otra persona es un(a) huésped en el hotel.

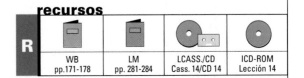

recursos

R	WB pp.171-178	LM pp. 281-284	LCASS./CD Cass. 14/CD 14	ICD-ROM Lección 14

Lectura
Antes de leer

Estrategia
Identifying point of view

You can understand a narrative more completely if you identify the point of view of the narrator. You can do this by simply asking yourself from whose perspective the story is being told. Some stories are narrated in the first person. That is, the narrator is a character in the story, and everything you read is filtered through that person's thoughts, emotions, and opinions. Other stories have an omniscient narrator who is not one of the story's characters and who reports the thoughts and actions of all the characters.

Examinar el texto

Lee brevemente el cuento. ¿De qué trata? ¿Cómo lo sabes? ¿Se narra en primera persona o tiene un narrador omnisciente? ¿Cómo lo sabes?

Seleccionar

Completa cada frase con la información adecuada.

1. Los personajes son _____.
   a. árabes b. franceses c. argentinos
2. Abderrahmán era _____.
   a. el ingeniero más sabio de los árabes
   b. un califa importante
   c. supervisor de la construcción de la ciudad
3. El cuento tiene que ver con _____.
   a. la construcción de una ciudad
   b. los problemas del califa con su esposa
   c. la burocracia en Bagdad
4. El supervisor de la construcción prometió terminar el proyecto dentro de _____.
   a. diez años b. cuatro años c. un año

GRANDEZAS DE LA BUROCRACIA

Marco Denevi

Marco Denevi nació en Buenos Aires, Argentina en 1922 y murió en la misma ciudad en 1998. Su novela Rosaura a las diez *le llevó a la fama en 1955. Escribió cuentos, novelas, obras teatrales y, a partir de 1980, se dedicó a escribir periodismo político. La obra de Denevi, candidato al Premio Nobel de Literatura, se caracteriza por su ingenio y sentido del humor.*

Denevi, Marco, *Falsificaciones*, Buenos Aires, Corregidor, 1999, pág. 52

Después de leer

Completar

Completa cada frase con la información adecuada.

1. Abderrahmán quería fundar _____.
2. Kamaru-l-Akmar prometió _____.
3. Después del primer año, Kamaru-l-Akmar pidió _____.
4. Abderrahmán se enojó porque _____.
5. Cuando Abderrahmán vio la ciudad, dijo que _____.
6. Mientras planeaban la futura ciudad, los ingenieros y arquitectos construyeron _____.

---

personajes *characters* cuento *story* tiene que ver con *has to do with* dentro de *within*

Cuentan que Abderrahmán decidió fundar la ciudad más hermosa del mundo, para lo cual mandó llamar a una multitud de ingenieros, de arquitectos y de artistas a cuya cabeza estaba Kamaru-l-Akmar, el primero y el más sabio de los ingenieros árabes.

Kamaru-l-Akmar prometió que en un año la ciudad estaría edificada, con sus alcázares, sus mezquitas y jardines más bellos que los de Susa y Ecbatana y aún que los de Bagdad. Pero solicitó al califa que le permitiera construirla con entera libertad y fantasía y según sus propias ideas, y que no se dignase verla sino una vez que estuviese concluida. Abderrahmán, sonriendo, accedió.

Al cabo del primer año Kamaru-l-Akmar pidió otro año de prórroga, que el califa gustosamente le concedió. Esto se repitió varias veces. Así transcurrieron no menos de diez años. Hasta que Abderrahmán, encolerizado, decidió ir a investigar.

Cuando llegó, una sonrisa le borró el ceño adusto. ¡Es la más hermosa ciudad que han contemplado ojos mortales! —le dijo a Kamaru-l-Akmar—. ¿Por qué no me avisaste que estaba construida?

Kamaru-l-Akmar inclinó la frente y no se atrevió a confesar al califa que lo que estaba viendo eran los palacios y jardines que los ingenieros, arquitectos y demás artistas habían levantado para sí mismos mientras estudiaban los planes de la futura ciudad.

Así fue construida Zahara, a orillas del Guadalquivir.

grandezas *grandeurs* **a partir de 1980** *from 1980 on*
ingenio *creative mind* **fundar** *to found* **sabio** *wise*
estaría edificada *would be built* **alcázares** *fortresses*
mezquitas *mosques* **aún** *even*
sino una vez que estuviese concluida *until it was finished*
Al cabo de *At the end of* **prórroga** *extension*
transcurrieron *passed* **encolerizado** *angry*
le borró el ceño adusto *wiped the stern frown off his face*
frente *forehead* **no se atrevió** *didn't dare* **a orillas de** *on the shores of*

Contestar

Contesta estas preguntas.

1. Describe al califa y a Kamaru-l-Akmar. ¿Qué tipo de personas crees que son? Explica tu respuesta.
2. ¿Por qué el ingeniero no quiere que Abderrahmán vea la ciudad antes de que termine la construcción? Explica tu respuesta.
3. ¿Qué significa la palabra **burocracia?**
4. ¿Por qué este cuento se llama *Grandezas de la burocracia?*
5. ¿Crees que el narrador de este cuento está a favor o en contra de la burocracia? Explica tu opinión.
6. ¿Cuáles son algunos ejemplos de la burocracia en tu vida?

Diálogo

Trabaja con un(a) compañero/a para preparar un diálogo en tres partes, basándose en la lectura. Después presenten el diálogo a la clase.

▶ Primera parte: El califa habla con el más sabio de los ingenieros sobre la ciudad que quiere fundar.

▶ Segunda parte: Kamaru-l-Akmar pide la séptima prórroga y explica por qué es necesaria. El califa se la concede pero no está muy contento.

▶ Tercera parte: Abderrahmán y Kamaru-l-Akmar visitan el lugar de construcción en el décimo año.

a favor de *in favor of* **en contra de** *against*

Venezuela

El país en cifras

▸ **Área:** 912.050 km^2 (352.144 millas^2),
aproximadamente dos veces el área de California

▸ **Población:** 24.170.000

▸ **Capital:** Caracas—3.198.000

▸ **Ciudades principales:** Maracaibo—2.014.000,
Valencia—2.068.000, Maracay—1.162.000,
Barquisimeto—957.000

SOURCE: Population Division, UN Secretariat

▸ **Moneda:** bolívar

▸ **Idiomas:** español (oficial), arahuaco, caribe
*El yanomami es uno de los idiomas indígenas
que se habla en Venezuela. La cultura de los
yanomami tiene su centro en el sur de Venezuela,
en el bosque tropical. Muchos antropólogos
han estudiado esta tribu por la agresividad
que utiliza para defender sus tradiciones
y costumbres.*

Bandera de Venezuela

Venezolanos célebres

▸ **Teresa Carreño,** compositora y
pianista (1853-1917)

▸ **Rómulo Gallegos,** escritor y político
(1884-1979)

▸ **Andrés Eloy Blanco,** poeta (1897-1955)

▸ **Baruj Benacerraf,** científico (1920-)
*Baruj Benacerraf, junto con dos de sus colegas,
recibió el Premio Nobel por sus investigaciones
en el campo de la inmunología y las enfermedades
autoinmunes. Nacido en Caracas, Benacerraf también
vivió en París y reside ahora en los Estados Unidos.*

campo *field*   caída *drop*   la denominan *give it the name*

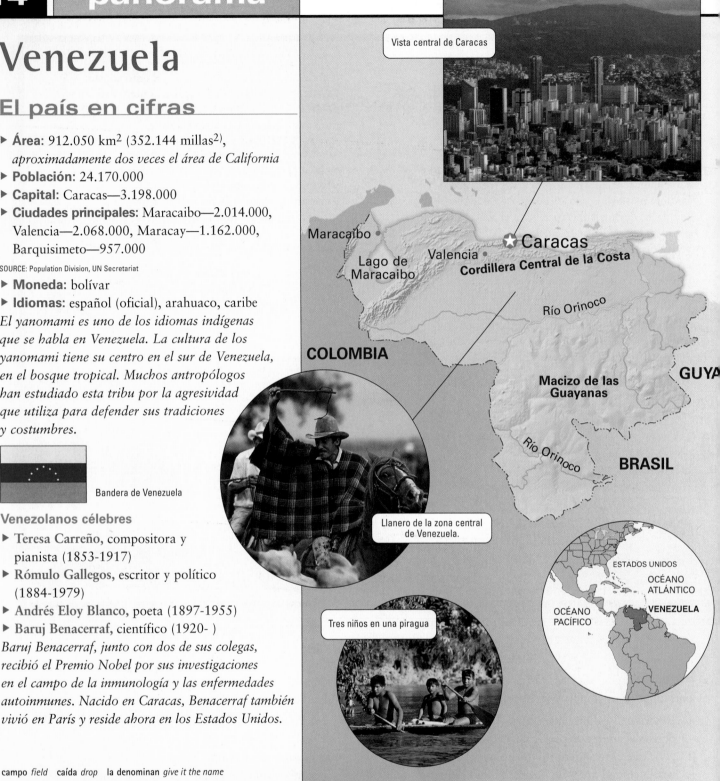

Vista central de Caracas

Maracaibo

Lago de Maracaibo

Valencia

⭐ Caracas

Cordillera Central de la Costa

COLOMBIA

Río Orinoco

Macizo de las Guayanas

GUYA

Río Orinoco

BRASIL

Llanero de la zona central de Venezuela.

Tres niños en una piragua

ESTADOS UNIDOS

OCÉANO ATLÁNTICO

VENEZUELA

OCÉANO PACÍFICO

¡Increíble pero cierto!

Con una caída de 979 m. (3,212 pies) desde
la meseta de Auyan Tepuy, Salto Ángel (*Angel
Falls*), en Venezuela, es la catarata más alta
del mundo, ¡diecisiete veces más alta que las
cataratas del Niágara! James C. Angel la
descubrió en 1937. Los indígenas de la zona
la denominan Churún Merú.

recursos

R

WB
pp. 179-180

vistasonline.com

ICD-ROM
Lección 14

Economía • **El petróleo**

La industria petrolera es muy importante para la economía venezolana. La mayor concentración de petróleo se encuentra debajo del lago Maracaibo, el lago más grande de América del Sur. En 1976 se nacionalizaron las empresas petroleras y pasaron a ser propiedad del estado con el nombre de Petróleos de Venezuela. Este producto representa más del 70% de las exportaciones del país, siendo Estados Unidos su principal comprador.

Actualidades • **Caracas**

Debido al *boom* petrolero de los años cincuenta, Caracas se ha convertido en una ciudad cosmopolita. Sus rascacielos y excelentes sistemas de transporte hacen que se cuente entre las ciudades más modernas de Latinoamérica. El metro, construido en 1983, es de los más recientes y sus extensas carreteras y autopistas conectan la ciudad con el interior del país. El corazón de la ciudad es el Parque Central, una zona de centros comerciales, tiendas, restaurantes y clubes.

Historia • **Simón Bolívar (1783-1830)**

A finales del siglo XVIII, Venezuela, al igual que otros países sudamericanos, todavía estaba bajo el dominio de la corona española. El general Simón Bolívar, nacido en Caracas, fue llamado "El Libertador" porque fue el líder del movimiento independentista sudamericano que liberó el área que hoy es Venezuela, Colombia, Ecuador, Perú y Bolivia. Con la ayuda de su lugarteniente, José Antonio Sucre, Bolívar contribuyó a formar el destino de América.

¿Qué aprendiste? Responde a las preguntas con una frase completa.

1. ¿Cuál es la moneda de Venezuela?

2. ¿Quién fue Rómulo Gallegos?

3. ¿Cuál es el lago más grande de América del Sur?

4. ¿Cuál es el producto más exportado de Venezuela?

5. ¿Qué ocurrió en 1976 con las empresas petroleras?

6. ¿Cómo se llama la capital de Venezuela?

7. ¿Qué hay en el Parque Central de Caracas?

8. ¿Por qué es conocido Simón Bolívar como "El Libertador"?

9. ¿Quién era el lugarteniente de Simón Bolívar?

Tejedor en Los Aleros, aldea en los Andes de Venezuela

Conexión Internet Investiga estos temas en el sitio **www.vistasonline.com**.

1. Busca información sobre Simón Bolívar. ¿Cuáles son algunos de los episodios más importantes de su vida? ¿Crees que Bolívar fue un estadista (*statesman*) de primera categoría? ¿Por qué?

2. Prepara un plan para un viaje de ecoturismo por el Orinoco. ¿Qué quieres ver y hacer durante la excursión? ¿Por qué?

se nacionalizaron *were nationalized* **empresas petroleras** *oil companies* **propiedad** *property* **comprador** *buyer* **Debido al** *Due to*
se ha convertido *has turned into* **rascacielos** *skyscrapers* **hacen que se cuente** *make it rank* **más recientes** *newest* **siglo** *century*
corona *crown* **nacido** *born* **lugarteniente** *chief lieutenant* **tejedor** *weaver* **aldea** *village*

La República Dominicana

El país en cifras

▸ **Área:** 48.730 km^2 (18.815 millas^2), *el área combinada de New Hampshire y Vermont*

▸ **Población:** 8.752.000

La isla La Española estuvo bajo el dominio de España hasta 1697, cuando la parte oeste de la isla pasó a ser territorio francés. Hoy día está dividida políticamente en dos países, La República Dominicana en la zona este de la isla y Haití en el oeste.

SOURCE: Population Division, UN Secretariat

▸ **Capital:** Santo Domingo—3.760.000

La mitad de la población de la República Dominicana vive en la capital.

▸ **Ciudades principales:** Santiago de los Caballeros—1.632.000, La Vega—335.000, Puerto Plata—255.000, San Pedro de Macorís—213.000

▸ **Moneda:** peso dominicano

▸ **Idiomas:** español (oficial), francés criollo

Bandera de la República Dominicana

Dominicanos célebres

▸ **Juan Pablo Duarte,** político y padre de la patria (1808-1876)

▸ **Celeste Woss y Gil,** pintora (1891-1985)

▸ **Juan Luis Guerra,** compositor y cantante de merengue (1956-)

▸ **Sammy Sosa,** beisbolista (1968-)

---

isla *island*   criollo *creole*   mitad *half*
padre de la patria *founding father*   fortaleza *fortress*
se construyó *was built*   naufragó *wrecked*
restos *remains*   enterrado *buried*

Catedral de Santa María la Menor

Hombres tocando los palos en una misa en Nochebuena

Océano Atlántico

Española

Puerto Plata

Santiago

Bahía Escocesa

Pico Duarte

Río Yuna

La Vega

HAITÍ

Cordillera Central

Río San Juan

San Pedro de Macorís

Sierra de Neiba

Santo Domingo

Sierra de Baoruco

Bahía de Ocoa

Mar Caribe

ESTADOS UNIDOS

LA REPÚBLICA DOMINICANA

OCÉANO PACÍFICO

OCÉANO ATLÁNTICO

AMÉRICA DEL SUR

Trabajadores del campo recogen la cosecha de ajos

recursos

R	WB pp. 181-182	vistasonline.com	ICD-ROM Lección 16

¡Increíble pero cierto!

La primera fortaleza del Nuevo Mundo se construyó en la República Dominicana en 1492 cuando la Santa María, uno de los tres barcos de Cristóbal Colón, naufragó allí. Aunque la fortaleza, hecha con los restos del barco, fue destruida por tribus indígenas, el amor de Colón por la isla nunca murió. Colón insistió en ser enterrado allí.

Ciudades • **Santo Domingo**

Santo Domingo, fundada en 1496, tiene algunas de las construcciones coloniales más antiguas del hemisferio. La ciudad es famosa no sólo por la belleza de su arquitectura sino también por el buen estado de los edificios gracias a las restauraciones. Los lugares más visitados son la Calle de las Damas, llamada así porque por ella paseaban las señoras de la corte del Virrey; el Alcázar de Colón, un palacio construido en 1509 por Diego Colón, hijo de Cristóbal; y la Fortaleza Ozama, la más vieja de las Américas, construida en 1503.

Deportes • **El béisbol**

El béisbol es un deporte muy practicado en el Caribe. Los primeros países hispanos que tuvieron una liga fueron Cuba y México, donde se empezó a jugar al béisbol en el siglo XIX. Hoy día este deporte es un pasatiempo nacional en la República Dominicana. Sammy Sosa, Pedro Martínez y Manny Ramírez son sólo tres de los muchísimos beisbolistas dominicanos que han conseguido enorme éxito y popularidad entre los aficionados.

Artes • **El merengue**

El merengue es una música para bailar que tiene su origen en la República Dominicana. Tradicionalmente, las canciones hablaban de los problemas sociales de los campesinos. Entre 1930 y 1960, el merengue se popularizó en las ciudades y empezó a transformar su estilo, adoptando un tono más urbano en el que se usaban grandes orquestas. Uno de los cantantes más famosos y que más ha ayudado a internacionalizar esta música es Juan Luis Guerra.

¿Qué aprendiste? Responde a las preguntas con una frase completa.

1. Aproximadamente, ¿qué porcentaje de la población vive en la capital?

2. ¿Cuándo se fundó la ciudad de Santo Domingo?

3. ¿Qué es el Alcázar de Colón?

4. Nombra tres beisbolistas famosos de la República Dominicana.

5. ¿Cuáles fueron los primeros países hispanos en tener una liga de béisbol?

6. ¿De qué hablaban las canciones de merengue tradicionales?

7. ¿Cuándo se popularizó el merengue en las ciudades?

8. ¿Qué cantante ha ayudado a internacionalizar el merengue?

Conexión Internet Investiga estos temas en el sitio **www.vistasonline.com**.

1. Busca más información sobre la isla La Española. ¿Cómo son las relaciones entre la República Dominicana y Haití?

2. Busca más información sobre la zona colonial de Santo Domingo: la Catedral de Santa María, la Casa de Bastidas o el Panteón Nacional. ¿Cómo son estos edificios? ¿Te gustan? Explica tus respuestas.

antiguas *old* **restauraciones** *restorations* **corte del Virrey** *Viceroy's court* **liga** *league* **siglo** *century* **han conseguido** *have reached*
éxito *success* **campesinos** *rural people* **orquestas** *orchestras* **cantantes** *singers* **ha ayudado** *have helped*

En la ciudad

el banco	bank
la carnicería	butcher shop
el correo	post office
la frutería	fruit store
la heladería	ice cream shop
la joyería	jewelry store
la lavandería	laundromat
la panadería	bakery
la pastelería	pastry shop
la peluquería, el salón de belleza	beauty salon
la pescadería	fish market
el supermercado	supermarket
la zapatería	shoe store
hacer cola	to stand in line
hacer diligencias	to run errands

En el banco

el cajero automático	ATM
la cuenta corriente	checking account
la cuenta de ahorros	savings account
el cheque (de viajero)	(traveler's) check
ahorrar	to save (money)
cobrar	to cash (a check)
depositar	to deposit
firmar	to sign
llenar (un formulario)	to fill out (a form)
pagar a plazos	to pay in installments
pagar al contado, en efectivo	to pay in cash
pedir prestado	to borrow
pedir un préstamo	to apply for a loan
ser gratis	to be free of charge

Direcciones

la cuadra	(city) block
la dirección	address
la esquina	corner
el letrero	sign
cruzar	to cross
dar direcciones	to give directions
doblar	to turn
estar perdido/a	to be lost
quedar	to be located
(al) este	(to the) east
(al) norte	(to the) north
(al) oeste	(to the) west
(al) sur	(to the) south
derecho	straight (ahead)
enfrente de	opposite; facing
hacia	toward

En el correo

el cartero	mail carrier
el correo	mail
el paquete	package
la estampilla, el sello	stamp
el sobre	envelope
echar (una carta) al buzón	to put (a letter) in the mailbox; to mail
enviar, mandar	to send; to mail

Conjunciones

después (de) que	after
en cuanto	as soon as
hasta que	until
tan pronto como	as soon as

Past participles used as adjectives	See page 411.
Expresiones útiles	See page 397.

recursos

| R | LCASS./CD Cass. 14/CD 14 | LM p. 284 |

El bienestar

15

Communicative Goals

You will learn how to:

- Talk about health, well being, and physical activities
- Describe an action or event in the immediate past
- Describe an action or event that occurred before another past event

El bienestar

el teleadicto

Hace ejercicios de estiramiento.
(hacer)

la clase de ejercicios aeróbicos

Suda.
(sudar)

el monitor

Hace ejercicio.
(hacer)

el músculo

Más vocabulario

adelgazar	to lose weight; to slim down
aliviar el estrés	to reduce stress
aliviar la tensión	to reduce tension
apurarse, darse prisa	to hurry; to rush
aumentar de peso, engordar	to gain weight
calentarse (e:ie)	to warm up
disfrutar (de)	to enjoy; to reap the benefits (of)
la droga	drug
el/la drogadicto/a	drug addict
entrenarse	to practice; to train
estar a dieta	to be on a diet
estar en buena forma	to be in good shape
hacer gimnasia	to work out
llevar una vida sana	to lead a healthy lifestyle
mantenerse en forma	to stay in shape
sufrir muchas presiones	to be under a lot of pressure
tratar de *(+ inf.)*	to try (to do something)
activo/a	active
débil	weak
flexible	flexible
fuerte	strong
sedentario/a	sedentary; related to sitting
tranquilo/a	calm; quiet
en exceso	in excess; too much
sin	without
el bienestar	well-being

Variación léxica

hacer ejercicios aeróbicos ⟷ hacer aerobic *(Esp.)*

recursos

No fumar.

el masaje

Hace ejercicios aeróbicos.
(hacer)

Levanta pesas.
(levantar)

Práctica

1 **Escuchar** 🎧 Mira el dibujo en las páginas 422 y 423. Luego escucha las frases e indica si lo que se dice en cada frase es **cierto** o **falso**.

	Cierto	Falso		Cierto	Falso
1.	○	○	6.	○	○
2.	○	○	7.	○	○
3.	○	○	8.	○	○
4.	○	○	9.	○	○
5.	○	○	10.	○	○

2 **Identificar** Identifica el opuesto (*opposite*) de cada palabra.

sin	mantenerse en forma
tranquilo	flexible
engordar	sedentario
fuerte	apurarse
estar enfermo	sufrir muchas presiones

1. activo
2. adelgazar
3. aliviar el estrés
4. débil
5. rígido
6. ir despacio
7. estar sano
8. con
9. nervioso
10. ser teleadicto

3 **Combinar** Combina palabras de cada columna para formar diez frases lógicas sobre el bienestar.

1. David levanta pesas
2. Estás en buena forma
3. Felipe se lastimó
4. José y Rafael
5. María y yo somos
6. Mi hermano
7. Sara hace ejercicios de
8. Mis primas están a dieta
9. Para llevar una vida sana
10. Ellos sufren muchas

a. aumentó de peso.
b. estiramiento.
c. fuertes.
d. presiones.
e. porque quieren adelgazar.
f. porque haces ejercicio.
g. sudan mucho.
h. un músculo de la pierna.
i. no se debe fumar.
j. y corre mucho.

La nutrición

- la proteína
- la grasa
- el colesterol
- los minerales
- las vitaminas

La nutrición

la bebida alcohólica	alcoholic beverage
la caloría	calorie
la merienda	snack
la nutrición	nutrition
comer una dieta equilibrada	to eat a balanced diet
consumir alcohol	to consume alcohol
merendar (e:ie)	to have a snack in the afternoon
descafeinado/a	decaffeinated

4 **Completar** Completa cada frase con la palabra adecuada.

1. Después de hacer ejercicio, como pollo o bistec porque contienen ____.
   a. drogas b. proteínas c. grasa
2. Para ____ es necesario consumir comidas de todos los grupos alimenticios.
   a. aliviar el estrés b. correr c. comer una dieta equilibrada
3. Claribel y Cecilia ____ una buena comida.
   a. disfrutan de b. tratan de c. sudan
4. Juan no come chocolate ni papas fritas porque contienen ____.
   a. dietas b. vitaminas c. mucha grasa
5. Mi padre no come mantequilla porque él necesita reducir ____.
   a. la nutrición b. el colesterol c. el bienestar
6. Miguel cuenta ____ porque está a dieta.
   a. las pesas b. los músculos c. las calorías

CONSÚLTALO

To review what you have learned about nutrition and food groups, see **Contextos** Lesson 8, pp. 208-211.

5 **La nutrición** En parejas, comenten los tipos de comida que comen y las consecuencias que tienen para su salud. Luego compartan la información con la clase.

1. ¿Cuántas comidas con mucha grasa comes regularmente? ¿Piensas que debes comer menos comidas de este tipo? ¿Por qué?
2. ¿Compras comidas con muchos minerales y vitaminas? ¿Necesitas consumir más comidas que los contienen? ¿Por qué?
3. ¿Tiene algún miembro de tu familia problemas con el colesterol? ¿Qué haces para evitar (avoid) problemas con el colesterol?
4. ¿Eres vegetariano/a? ¿Conoces a alguien que sea vegetariano/a? ¿Qué piensas de la idea de no comer carne u otros productos animales? ¿Es posible comer una dieta equilibrada sin comer carne? Explica.
5. ¿Bebes cafeína en exceso? ¿Cuáles son los productos que contienen cafeína? ¿Cuáles son algunas de las ventajas (advantages) y los problemas asociados con la cafeína?
6. ¿Crees que llevas una vida sana? ¿Y tus amigos? ¿Crees que en general los estudiantes llevan una vida sana? ¿Por qué?

AYUDA

Some useful words:
sano = saludable
en general = por lo general
estricto
normalmente
muchas veces
a veces
de vez en cuando

Comunicación

6 **Encuesta** Tu profesor(a) va a darte una hoja de actividades. Haz una encuesta en la clase para encontrar a dos personas que realicen las actividades que se mencionan en la lista. Anota sus nombres en la tabla y luego pregúntales a ellos/as por qué hacen estas cosas.

Actividades	Nombre y respuesta	Nombre y respuesta
1. Entrenarse para un deporte		
2. Hacer ejercicios aeróbicos regularmente		
3. Mantenerse en forma		
4. Consumir poco alcohol		
5. No fumar		
6. Relajarse para aliviar la tensión		
7. Comer una dieta equilibrada		
8. Tomar bebidas descafeinadas		
9. Calentarse antes de hacer gimnasia		
10. Merendar frutas y verduras		

7 **Un anuncio** En grupos de cuatro, imaginen que son dueños/as de un gimnasio con un equipo (*equipment*) moderno, monitores cualificados y un(a) nutricionista. Preparen y presenten un anuncio para la televisión que hable del gimnasio y atraiga (*attracts*) a una gran variedad de nuevos clientes. No se olviden de presentar la siguiente información:

▶ Las ventajas de estar en buena forma
▶ El equipo que tienen
▶ Los servicios y clases que ofrecen
▶ Las características únicas del gimnasio
▶ La dirección y el teléfono del gimnasio
▶ El precio para los socios (*members*) del gimnasio

8 **Recomendaciones para la salud** En parejas, imaginen que están preocupados con los malos hábitos de un(a) amigo/a suyo/a que no está bien últimamente (*lately*). Escriban y representen un diálogo en el cual hablan de lo que está pasando en la vida de su amigo/a y los cambios que necesita hacer para llevar una vida sana.

9 **El teleadicto** Con un(a) compañero/a, representen los papeles (*play the roles*) de un(a) nutricionista y un(a) teleadicto/a. La persona sedentaria habla de sus malos hábitos en las comidas y de que no hace ejercicio. También dice que toma demasiado café y que siente mucho estrés. El/La nutricionista le sugiere una dieta equilibrada y una rutina para mantenerse en buena forma. El/La teleadicto/a le da las gracias por su ayuda.

PERSONAJES

MAITE

INÉS

DON FRANCISCO

ÁLEX

JAVIER

MARTÍN

¡Qué buena excursión!

Martín y los estudiantes van de excursión a las montañas.

MARTÍN Buenos días, don Francisco.

DON FRANCISCO ¡Hola, Martín!

MARTÍN Ya veo que han traído lo que necesitan. ¡Todos han venido muy bien equipados!

MARTÍN Muy bien. ¡Atención, chicos! Primero hagamos algunos ejercicios de estiramiento…

MARTÍN Es bueno que se hayan mantenido en buena forma. Entonces, jóvenes, ¿ya están listos?

JAVIER ¡Sí, listísimos! No puedo creer que finalmente haya llegado el gran día.

DON FRANCISCO ¡Hola! ¡Qué alegría verlos! ¿Cómo les fue en la excursión?

JAVIER Increíble, don Efe. Nunca había visto un paisaje tan espectacular. Es un lugar estupendo. Saqué mil fotos y tengo montones de escenas para dibujar.

MAITE Nunca había hecho una excursión. ¡Me encantó! Cuando vuelva a España, voy a tener mucho que contarle a mi familia.

INÉS Ha sido la mejor excursión de mi vida. Amigos, Martín, don Efe, mil gracias.

recursos

| R | V/VCD-ROM Lección 15 | VM pp. 319-320 | ICD-ROM Lección 15 |

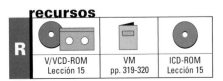

MARTÍN ¡Fabuloso! ¡En marcha, pues!

DON FRANCISCO ¡Adiós! ¡Cuídense!

Martín y los estudiantes pasan ocho horas caminando en las montañas. Hablan, sacan fotos y disfrutan del paisaje. Se divierten muchísimo.

ÁLEX Sí, gracias, Martín. Gracias por todo.

MARTÍN No hay de qué. Ha sido un placer.

DON FRANCISCO Chicos, pues, es hora de volver. Creo que la Sra. Vives nos ha preparado una cena muy especial.

Enfoque cultural Para estar en buena forma

Mientras a algunos hispanos les gusta ir al gimnasio para mantenerse en forma, otros prefieren practicar deportes. En Argentina, por ejemplo, se juega mucho al fútbol, en Venezuela se juega al béisbol y en Colombia y España hay muchos aficionados al ciclismo. Otro deporte conocido en el mundo hispano es el jai alai, que es un juego de pelota originario del País Vasco (España). Su nombre significa "día de fiesta" en vascuence y es un deporte que se practica también en México y en la Florida (EE.UU.).

Expresiones útiles

Getting ready to start a hike

▶ **Ya veo que han traído lo que necesitan.**
I see that you have brought what you need.

▶ **¡Todos han venido muy bien equipados!**
Everyone has come very well equipped!

▶ **Primero hagamos algunos ejercicios de estiramiento.**
First let's do some stretching exercises.

▶ **No puedo creer que finalmente haya llegado el gran día.**
I can't believe that the big day has finally arrived.

▶ **¿(Están) listos?**
(Are you) ready?

▷ **¡En marcha, pues!**
Let's get going, then!

Talking about an excursion

▶ **¿Cómo les fue en la excursión?**
How did the hike go?

▷ **Nunca había visto un paisaje tan espectacular.**
I had never seen such spectacular scenery.

▷ **Nunca había hecho una excursión. ¡Me encantó!**
I had never gone on a hike before. I loved it!

▷ **Ha sido la mejor excursión de mi vida.**
It's been the best hike of my life.

Courtesy expressions

▶ **Gracias por todo.**
Thanks for everything.

▶ **Ha sido un placer.**
It's been a pleasure.

▶ **¡Cuídense!**
Take care!

Reacciona a la fotonovela

1 **Seleccionar** Selecciona la respuesta que mejor completa cada frase.

1. Antes de salir, Martín les recomienda a los estudiantes que hagan _____.
   a. ejercicios de estiramiento b. ejercicios aeróbicos c. gimnasia

2. Los excursionistas hablaron, _____ en las montañas.
   a. levantaron pesas y se divirtieron b. caminaron y dibujaron
   c. sacaron fotos y disfrutaron del paisaje

3. Inés dice que ha sido la mejor excursión _____.
   a. del viaje b. del año c. de su vida

4. Cuando Maite vuelva a España, va a _____.
   a. tener montones de escenas para dibujar b. tener mucho que contarle a su familia
   c. tener muchas fotos que enseñarle a su familia

5. La señora Vives les ha preparado _____.
   a. una cena especial b. un día en las montañas muy especial
   c. una excursión espectacular

2 **Identificar** Identifica quién puede decir las siguientes frases.

1. Oye, muchísimas gracias por el mejor día de mi vida. ¡Fue divertidísimo!

2. Parece que están todos preparados, ¿no? ¡Perfecto! Bueno, ¡vamos!

3. Cuando vea a mis papás y a mis hermanos voy a tener mucho que contarles.

4. Debemos volver ahora para comer. ¡Vamos a tener una cena especial!

5. El lugar fue fenomenal, uno de los más bonitos que he visto. ¡Qué bueno que traje mi cámara!

6. ¡Gracias por todo, Martín!

JAVIER

INÉS

ÁLEX

MAITE

DON FRANCISCO

MARTÍN

3 **Completar** Selecciona algunas de las palabras que se ofrecen en la lista para completar cada frase.

grasa	aliviar el estrés	vitamina
teleadicta	un masaje	mantenerse en forma

1. A Javier le duelen los músculos después de caminar tanto. Hoy lo que necesita es _____.

2. Don Francisco a veces sufre presiones y estrés en su trabajo. Debe hacer ejercicio para _____.

3. A Inés le encanta salir con amigos o leer un buen libro. Ella nunca va a ser una _____.

4. Álex trata de comer una dieta equilibrada. Por ejemplo, trata de llevar una dieta sin mucha _____.

5. A Maite no le duelen los músculos. Cuatro veces por semana hace gimnasia para _____.

Ortografía

Las letras b y v

Since there is no difference in pronunciation between the Spanish letters **b** and **v**, spelling words that contain these letters can be tricky. Here are some tips.

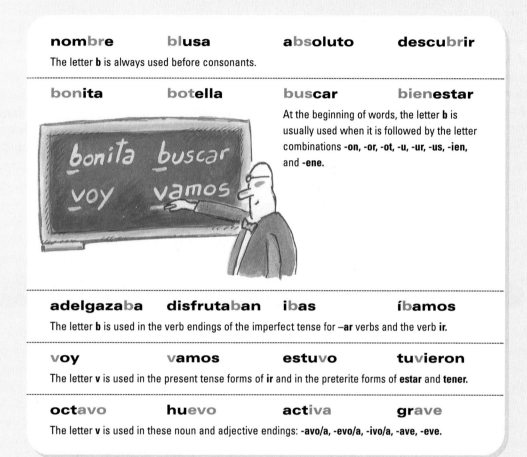

nomb**re**   **b**lusa   **a**b**soluto**   **descu**b**rir**

The letter **b** is always used before consonants.

bonita   **bot**ella   **bus**car   **bien**estar

At the beginning of words, the letter **b** is usually used when it is followed by the letter combinations **-on, -or, -ot, -u, -ur, -us, -ien,** and **-ene**.

adelgazab**a**   **disfruta**b**an**   **i**b**as**   **í**b**amos**

The letter **b** is used in the verb endings of the imperfect tense for **–ar** verbs and the verb **ir**.

voy   **v**amos   **estu**v**o**   **tu**v**ieron**

The letter **v** is used in the present tense forms of **ir** and in the preterite forms of **estar** and **tener**.

octavo   **hu**evo   **act**iva   **gr**ave

The letter **v** is used in these noun and adjective endings: **-avo/a, -evo/a, -ivo/a, -ave, -eve**.

Práctica Completa las palabras con las letras **b** o **v**.

1. Una __ez me lastimé el __razo cuando esta__a __uceando.
2. Manuela se ol__idó sus li__ros en el auto__ús.
3. Ernesto tomó el __orrador y se puso todo __lanco de tiza.
4. Para tener una __ida sana y saluda__le necesitas tomar __itaminas.
5. En mi pue__lo hay un __ule__ar que tiene muchos ár__oles.

El ahorcado (*Hangman*) Juega al ahorcado para adivinar las palabras.

1. __ _u_ __ __ _s_   Están en el cielo
2. __ _u_ __ __ _n_   Relacionado con el correo
3. __ _o_ __ _e_ __ __ _a_   Está llena de líquido
4. __ _i_ __ __ _e_   Fenómeno meteorológico
5. __ _e_ __ __ __ __ __ _s_   Los "ojos" de la casa

recursos

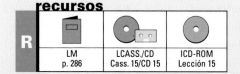

| R | LM p. 286 | LCASS./CD Cass. 15/CD 15 | ICD-ROM Lección 15 |

15.1 The present perfect

ANTE TODO In Lesson 14, you learned how to form past participles. You will now learn how to form the present perfect indicative (**el pretérito perfecto de indicativo**), a compound tense that uses the past participle. The present perfect is used to talk about what someone *has done*. In Spanish, it is formed with the present tense of the auxiliary verb **haber** and a past participle.

CONSÚLTALO

Past participles used as adjectives
To review what you have learned about participles, see Lesson 14, p. 411.

Ya veo que han traído todo lo que necesitan.

Todos han venido muy bien equipados.

Present indicative of *haber*

Singular forms		Plural forms	
yo	**he**	nosotros/as	**hemos**
tú	**has**	vosotros/as	**habéis**
Ud./él/ella	**ha**	Uds./ellos/ellas	**han**

Tú no **has cerrado** la puerta.
You haven't closed the door.

Yo ya **he leído** esos libros.
I've already read those books.

¿**Ha asistido** Juan a la clase?
Has Juan attended the class?

Hemos presentado el proyecto.
We have presented the project.

▶ The past participle does not change in form when it is part of the present perfect tense. It only changes in form when it is used as an adjective.

Clara **ha abierto** la ventana.
Clara has opened the window.

Yo **he cerrado** la puerta.
I've closed the door.

Las ventanas están **abiertas.**
The windows are open.

La puerta está **cerrada.**
The door is closed.

▶ In Spanish, the present perfect indicative is generally used just as it is used in English: to talk about what someone has done or what has occurred. It usually refers to the recent past.

He trabajado cuarenta horas esta semana.
I have worked forty hours this week.

¿Cuál es el último libro que **has leído**?
What is the last book that you have read?

¡ATENCIÓN!

Remember that to say that someone has *just done something*, **acabar de** + [*infinitive*] is used, not the present perfect.
Juan acaba de llegar.
Juan has just arrived.

¡LENGUA VIVA!

The present perfect is being used less and less in American English. In Spanish, it continues to be used widely, especially in Spain.

▶ In English, the auxiliary verb and the past participle are often separated. In Spanish, however, these two elements—**haber** and the past participle—cannot be separated by any word.

Siempre **hemos vivido** en Bolivia.
We have always lived in Bolivia.

Ud. nunca **ha venido** a mi oficina.
You have never come to my office.

Creo que la Sra. Vives nos ha preparado una cena muy especial.

Gracias, Martín.

No hay de qué. Ha sido un placer.

▶ The word **no** and any object or reflexive pronouns are placed immediately before **haber.**

Yo **no he cobrado** el cheque.
I have not cashed the check.

¿Por qué **no lo has cobrado**?
Why haven't you cashed it?

Susana ya **lo ha hecho.**
Susana has already done it.

Ellos **no la han arreglado.**
They haven't fixed it.

▶ Note that *to have* can be either a main verb or an auxiliary verb in English. As a main verb, it corresponds to **tener,** while as an auxiliary, it corresponds to **haber.**

Tengo muchos amigos.
I have a lot of friends.

He tenido mucho éxito.
I have had a lot of success.

▶ To form the present perfect of **hay,** use the third person singular of haber **(ha) + habido.**

Ha habido muchos problemas con el nuevo profesor.
There have been a lot of problems with the new professor.

Ha habido un accidente en la calle Central.
There has been an accident at Central Street.

¡INTÉNTALO! Indica el pretérito perfecto de indicativo de los siguientes verbos.

1. (disfrutar, comer, vivir) yo _he disfrutado, he comido, he vivido_
2. (traer, adelgazar, compartir) tú _____
3. (venir, estar, correr) Ud. _____
4. (leer, resolver, poner) ella _____
5. (decir, romper, hacer) ellos _____
6. (mantenerse, dormirse) nosotros _____
7. (estar, escribir, ver) yo _____
8. (vivir, correr, morir) él _____

Práctica

1 **Completar** Estas oraciones describen el bienestar o los problemas de unos estudiantes. Completa las oraciones con el pretérito perfecto de indicativo de los verbos de la lista.

adelgazar	hacer	sufrir
comer	aumentar	llevar

1. Luisa _____ muchas presiones este año.
2. Juan y Raúl _____ de peso porque no hacen ejercicio.
3. Pero María y yo _____ porque trabajamos demasiado y nos olvidamos de comer.
4. Casi toda la vida, yo _____ una vida muy sana.
5. Pero tú y yo no _____ gimnasia este semestre.

2 **¿Qué has hecho?** Indica si has hecho lo siguiente.

> **modelo**
>
> Escalar una montaña
>
> Sí, he escalado varias montañas./No, no he escalado nunca una montaña.

1. Jugar al baloncesto
2. Viajar a Bolivia
3. Conocer a una persona famosa
4. Levantar pesas
5. Comer un insecto
6. Ver el programa *Friends*
7. Aprender un idioma
8. Bailar salsa
9. Ver una película española
10. Escuchar música latina
11. Estar despierto 24 horas
12. Bucear

3 **La vida sana** Hace poco tiempo que Marisela ha decidido cambiar su estilo de vida porque quiere llevar una vida sana. Explica lo que ha hecho según el modelo. Luego explica lo que tú has hecho al respecto (*in that regard*).

> **modelo**
>
> Encontrar un gimnasio
>
> Marisela ha encontrado un buen gimnasio cerca de su casa.
> Yo no he encontrado un gimnasio pero sé que debo buscar uno.

1. Tratar de estar en forma
2. Estar a dieta los últimos dos meses
3. Dejar de tomar refrescos
4. Hacerse una prueba del colesterol
5. Entrenar cinco días a la semana
6. Cambiar de una vida sedentaria a una vida activa
7. Tomar vitaminas por las noches y por las mañanas
8. Hacer ejercicio para relajarse
9. Consumir mucha proteína
10. Dejar de fumar

Comunicación

4

Descripción En parejas, describan lo que ha(n) hecho y lo que no ha(n) hecho la(s) persona(s) en cada dibujo. Usen la imaginación.

1. Jorge y Raúl

2. Luisa

3. Jacobo

4. Natalia y Diego

5. Ricardo

6. Carmen

5

Describir En parejas, identifiquen a una persona que lleva una vida muy sana. Puede ser una persona que conocen o un personaje que aparece en una película o programa de televisión. Entre los dos, escriban una descripción de lo que la persona ha hecho para llevar una vida sana.

> **modelo**
>
> Arnold Schwarzenegger siempre ha hecho todo lo posible para mantenerse en forma. Él...

Síntesis

6

Situación El/La enfermero/a de la clínica de la universidad está conversando con un(a) estudiante que no se siente nada bien. El/La enfermero/a debe averiguar de dónde viene el problema e investigar los hábitos del/de la estudiante. El/La estudiante le explica lo que ha hecho en los últimos meses y cómo se ha sentido. Luego el/la enfermero/a le da recomendaciones al/a la estudiante de cómo llevar una vida más sana.

15.2 The past perfect

ANTE TODO   The past perfect indicative (**el pretérito pluscuamperfecto de indicativo**) is used to talk about what someone *had done* or what *had occurred* before another past action, event, or state. Like the present perfect, the past perfect uses a form of **haber**—in this case, the imperfect—plus the past participle.

Nunca había visto un paisaje tan espectacular.

Nunca había hecho una excursión.

Past perfect indicative

		cerrar	perder	asistir
SINGULAR FORMS	yo	**había** cerrado	**había** perdido	**había** asistido
	tú	**habías** cerrado	**habías** perdido	**habías** asistido
	Ud./él/ella	**había** cerrado	**había** perdido	**había** asistido
PLURAL FORMS	nosotros/as	**habíamos** cerrado	**habíamos** perdido	**habíamos** asistido
	vosotros/as	**habíais** cerrado	**habíais** perdido	**habíais** asistido
	Uds./ellos/ellas	**habían** cerrado	**habían** perdido	**habían** asistido

Antes de 2001, **había vivido** en California.
Before 2001, I had lived in California.

Cuando llegamos, Luis ya **había salido.**
When we arrived, Luis had already left.

▶ The past perfect is often used with the word **ya** (*already*) to indicate that an action, event, or state had already occurred before another. Remember that, unlike its English equivalent, **ya** cannot be placed between **haber** and the past participle.

Ella **ya había salido** cuando llamaron.
She had already left when they called.

Cuando llegué, Raúl **ya se había acostado.**
When I arrived, Raúl had already gone to bed.

¡INTÉNTALO!   Indica el pretérito pluscuamperfecto de indicativo de cada verbo.

1. Nosotros ya __habíamos cenado__ (cenar) cuando nos llamaron.
2. Antes de tomar esta clase, yo no _____ (estudiar) nunca el español.
3. Antes de ir a México, ellos nunca _____ (ir) a otro país.
4. Eduardo nunca _____ (entrenarse) antes de este año.
5. Tú siempre _____ (llevar) una vida sana antes del año pasado.
6. Antes de conocerte, yo ya te _____ (ver) muchas veces.

Práctica

1 **Completar** Completa los minidiálogos con las formas correctas del pretérito pluscuamperfecto de indicativo.

1. **SARA**   Antes de cumplir los 15 años, ¿_____ (estudiar) tú otra lengua?
   JOSÉ   Sí, _____ (tomar) clases de inglés y de italiano.

2. **DOLORES**   Antes de 2000, ¿_____ (viajar) tú y tu familia a Europa?
   TOMÁS   Sí, _____ (visitar) Europa tres veces.

3. **ANTONIO**   Antes de este año, ¿_____ (correr) Ud. en un maratón?
   SRA. VERA   No, nunca lo _____ (hacer).

4. **SOFÍA**   Antes de su enfermedad, ¿_____ (sufrir) muchas presiones tu tío?
   IRENE   Sí... y mi tío nunca _____ (mantenerse) en buena forma.

2 **Quehaceres** Indica lo que ya había hecho cada miembro de la familia antes de la llegada de la madre, la Sra. Ferrer.

3 **Tu vida** Indica si ya habías hecho las siguientes cosas antes de cumplir los 16 años.

1. Hacer un viaje en avión
2. Escalar una montaña
3. Escribir un poema
4. Leer una novela
5. Enamorarse
6. Tomar una clase de educación física
7. Montar a caballo
8. Ir de pesca
9. Manejar un carro
10. Navegar en la red

Comunicación

4

Oraciones En parejas, una persona completa las siguientes oraciones con el pretérito pluscuamperfecto de indicativo y la otra persona forma una pregunta basada en cada oración.

> **modelo**
>
> Antes de vivir aquí, yo...
> **Estudiante 1:** Antes de vivir aquí, yo había vivido en California.
> **Estudiante 2:** ¿Habías vivido en otros lugares antes de vivir aquí?

1. Cuando yo llamé a mi mejor amigo/a la semana pasada, él/ella ya...
2. Antes de este año, mis amigos y yo nunca...
3. Hasta el año pasado yo siempre...
4. Antes de cumplir los veinte años, mi mejor amigo/a...
5. Antes de cumplir los treinta años, mis padres ya...
6. Hasta que cumplí los dieciocho años, yo no...
7. Antes de este semestre, el/la profesor(a) de español no...
8. Antes de tomar esta clase, yo nunca...

5

Lo dudo Tu profesor(a) va a darte una hoja de actividades. Escribe cinco oraciones, algunas ciertas y algunas falsas, de cosas que habías hecho antes de venir a la universidad. Luego, en grupos, túrnense para leer sus oraciones. Cada miembro del grupo debe decir "es cierto" o "lo dudo" después de cada una. Escribe la reacción de cada compañero/a en la columna apropiada. ¿Quién obtuvo más respuestas correctas?

Oraciones	Miguel	Ana	Beatriz
1. Cuando tenía 10 años, ya había manejado el carro de mi papá.	Lo dudo.	Es cierto.	Lo dudo.
2.			
3.			
4.			
5.			

Síntesis

6

Entrevista En parejas, preparen una conversación en la que un(a) reportero/a de televisión está entrevistando (*interviewing*) a un actor/una actriz famoso/a que está haciendo un video de ejercicios aeróbicos. El/La reportero/a le hace preguntas para descubrir la siguiente información:

▶ Si siempre se había mantenido en forma antes de hacer este video
▶ Si había seguido una dieta especial antes de hacer este video
▶ Qué le recomienda a la gente que quiere mantenerse en forma
▶ Qué le recomienda a la gente que quiere adelgazar
▶ Qué va a hacer cuando termine este video

15.3 The present perfect subjunctive

ANTE TODO The present perfect subjunctive (**el pretérito perfecto de subjuntivo**) is equivalent to the present perfect indicative, except that it is used to talk about what *has happened* when the subjunctive tense is required in the subordinate clause. The present perfect subjunctive is formed using the present subjunctive of the auxiliary verb **haber** and a past participle.

Present perfect indicative			Present perfect subjunctive		
PRESENT INDICATIVE OF **HABER**		PAST PARTICIPLE	PRESENT SUBJUNCTIVE OF **HABER**		PAST PARTICIPLE
yo	**he**	**hablado**	**yo**	**haya**	**hablado**

Present perfect subjunctive

		cerrar	perder	asistir
SINGULAR FORMS	yo	**haya** cerrado	**haya** perdido	**haya** asistido
	tú	**hayas** cerrado	**hayas** perdido	**hayas** asistido
	Ud./él/ella	**haya** cerrado	**haya** perdido	**haya** asistido
PLURAL FORMS	nosotros/as	**hayamos** cerrado	**hayamos** perdido	**hayamos** asistido
	vosotros/as	**hayáis** cerrado	**hayáis** perdido	**hayáis** asistido
	Uds./ellos/ellas	**hayan** cerrado	**hayan** perdido	**hayan** asistido

▶ The same conditions which trigger the use of the present subjunctive apply to the present perfect subjunctive.

Present subjunctive	Present perfect subjunctive
Espero que **duermas** bien.	Espero que **hayas dormido** bien.
I hope that you sleep well.	*I hope that you have slept well.*
No creo que **aumente** de peso.	No creo que **haya aumentado** de peso.
I don't think he will gain weight.	*I don't think he has gained weight.*

▶ The action expressed by the present perfect subjunctive is seen as occurring before the action expressed in the main clause.

Me alegro que Uds. **se hayan reído** tanto esta tarde.	Dudo que ella **se haya divertido** mucho con su suegra.
I'm glad that you have laughed so much this afternoon.	*I doubt that she has enjoyed herself much with her mother-in-law.*

¡ATENCIÓN!

The perfect forms are often used with **ya** (*already*). Remember that **ya** must come either before or after **haber** and the participle, which are never separated in Spanish.

Dudo que Enrique **ya** lo **haya hecho.**

Dudo que Enrique lo **haya hecho ya.**

• • •

The present perfect subjunctive is used for a recent action even if that action would be in the past tense in English.

No creo que lo **hayas dicho** bien.
I don't think you said it right.

Espero que él **haya llegado.**
I hope he arrived.

¡INTÉNTALO! Indica el pretérito perfecto de subjuntivo de los verbos entre paréntesis.

1. Me gusta que Uds. _____hayan dicho_____ (decir) la verdad.
2. No creo que tú _____ (comer) tanto.
3. Es imposible que Ud. _____ (poder) hacer tal cosa.
4. Me alegro de que tú y yo _____ (merendar) juntas.
5. Es posible que yo _____ (adelgazar) un poco esta semana.
6. Espero que _____ (haber) suficiente comida en la celebración.

Práctica

1 **Completar** Laura está preocupada por su familia y sus amigos/as. Completa las oraciones con la forma correcta del pretérito perfecto de subjuntivo de los verbos entre paréntesis.

1. ¡Qué lástima que Julio _____ (sentirse) tan mal! Dudo que _____ (entrenarse) lo suficiente.
2. No creo que Lourdes y su amiga _____ (irse) de ese trabajo donde siempre tienen tantos problemas. Espero que Lourdes _____ (aprender) a aliviar el estrés.
3. Es triste que Nuria y yo _____ (perder) el partido. Esperamos que los monitores del gimnasio nos _____ (preparar) un buen programa para ponernos en forma.
4. No estoy segura de que Samuel _____ (llevar) una vida sana. Es bueno que él _____ (decidir) mejorar su dieta.
5. Me preocupa mucho que Ana y Rosa _____ (fumar) tanto de jóvenes (*as young people*). Es increíble que ellas no _____ (enfermarse).
6. Me alegro de que mi abuela _____ (disfrutar) de buena salud toda su vida. Es increíble que ella _____ (cumplir) noventa años.

2 **Describir** Haz dos comentarios sobre la(s) persona(s) que hay en cada dibujo usando frases como **no creo que, dudo que, es probable que, me alegro de que, espero que** y **siento que.** Usa el pretérito perfecto de subjuntivo.

CONSÚLTALO

To review verbs of will and influence, see Lesson 12, pp. 346-347. To review expressions of doubt, disbelief, and denial, see Lesson 13, pp. 372-373.

modelo
Es probable que Javier haya levantado pesas por muchos años.
Me alegro de que Javier se haya mantenido en forma.

Javier

1. Rosa y Sandra

2. Roberto

3. Mariela

4. Lorena y su amigo

5. Sra. Matos

6. Sonia y René

Comunicación

3 **¿Sí o no?** En parejas, comenten estas afirmaciones (*statements*) usando frases de la lista.

> Es imposible que...   No creo que...   Me alegro de que (no)...
> Dudo que...   Es bueno que (no)...   Espero que (no)...

modelo

Estudiante 1: Ya llegó el fin del año escolar.

Estudiante 2: Es imposible que haya llegado el fin del año escolar.

1. Recibí una A en la clase de español.
2. Tu mejor amigo aumentó de peso recientemente.
3. Madonna dio un concierto ayer con Plácido Domingo.
4. Mis padres ganaron un millón de dólares.
5. He aprendido a hablar japonés.
6. Nuestro/a profesor(a) vino aquí de Bolivia.
7. Salí anoche con...
8. El año pasado mi familia y yo fuimos de excursión a...

4 **Viaje por Bolivia** Imaginen que sus amigos, Luis y Julia, están viajando por Bolivia y que les han mandado postales a ustedes. En grupos, lean las postales y conversen de lo que les ha escrito Luis. Usen frases como **dudo que, espero que, me alegro de que, temo que, siento que** y **es posible que.**

NOTA CULTURAL

Aymara is recognized as an official language of Bolivia, along with Spanish. Over half of the population speaks indigenous languages.

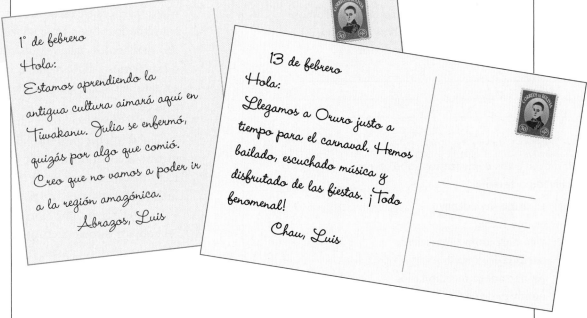

1º de febrero

Hola:

Estamos aprendiendo la antigua cultura aimará aquí en Tiwakanu. Julia se enfermó, quizás por algo que comió. Creo que no vamos a poder ir a la región amazónica.

Abrazos, Luis

13 de febrero

Hola:

Llegamos a Oruro justo a tiempo para el carnaval. Hemos bailado, escuchado música y disfrutado de las fiestas. ¡Todo fenomenal!

Chau, Luis

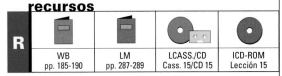

recursos

R	WB pp. 185-190	LM pp. 287-289	LCASS./CD Cass. 15/CD 15	ICD-ROM Lección 15

Lectura
Antes de leer

Estrategia
Making inferences

For dramatic effect and to achieve a smoother writing style, authors often do not explicitly supply the reader with all the details of a story. Clues in the text can help you infer those things the writer chooses not to state in a direct manner. You simply "read between the lines" to fill in the missing information and draw conclusions about the story. To practice making inferences, read the following statement:

A Liliana le encanta ir al gimnasio. Hace años que empezó a levantar pesas.

Based on this statement alone, what inferences can you draw about Liliana?

Examinar el texto

Lee el texto brevemente y haz una lista de algunos de los cognados y de otras palabras que conoces. Según esta lista, ¿de qué trata el texto?

_____   _____
_____   _____
_____   _____

¿Cierto o falso?

Indica si estos comentarios sobre el texto son **ciertos** o **falsos.**

	Cierto	Falso
1. El título del cuento es una fecha.	○	○
2. Una narradora omnisciente narra la historia.	○	○
3. La narradora menciona los nombres de varias calles.	○	○
4. La narradora dice que va a caminar todos los días.	○	○

■ Noviembre 24, 1992 ■
María Velázquez

María Velázquez nació en México, D.F. en 1945. Estudió antropología social en la Universidad Iberoamericana y trabajó en el Taller de Cuento de la revista **Punto de Partida** *de la Universidad Nacional Autónoma de México en 1978. Vivió en California, Estados Unidos, por casi diez años (1982-1991), época en la que participó en el Taller de Cuento de la Universidad de California en Irvine. El cuento que presentamos a continuación pertenece a la colección* **Aun sin saber quién eres,** *que se publicó en 1998.*

A los dos nos gusta mucho ir a caminar todas las mañanas, muy temprano, pues desde que ya no montas a caballo es un buen ejercicio. En cuanto mis hijos se van en el camión de la escuela, antes de las siete, me visto rápido y me pongo los tenis. Le coloco a Babar su correa, tomo las llaves y me voy volando para recogerte en la esquina de tu casa, donde me esperas. Todos los días nos vamos subiendo por Sierra Madre, felices de estar juntos y caminando a buen paso. A veces nos detenemos para ver las casas o esperamos a Babar que le ladra a cualquier ser viviente que se le acerca.

Generalmente hacemos el mismo recorrido, subimos hasta Reforma y bajamos por Prado Sur; luego subimos otra vez por Pirineos y volvemos a bajar por Sierra Madre. Muchas veces no hablamos, pero siempre me tomas la mano. Nos gusta ver las casas, fijarnos en cómo las han arreglado, recordando cómo eran antes, hace años, cuando nos cambiamos a este rumbo. Me preguntas por mis hijos y deseas saber cosas de ellos. Todos los días quieres verlos. Luego te callas y sigues caminando en silencio, siempre a mi lado, como cuando era niña. Yo también me quedo callada, como si no hiciera falta hablar o como si ya todo estuviese dicho.

También hoy en la mañana me vestí rápido y me puse los tenis, apuré a Babar, que parecía tener flojera, y salí corriendo rumbo a tu casa. En la esquina me detuve en seco, pues sentí que me faltaba el aire. De repente, así de sopetón, me di cuenta de que hace más de dos años habías muerto y de que nunca has ido a caminar conmigo.

cuento *short story* pertenece *belongs* correa *leash*
me voy volando *I rush off* a buen paso *at a good clip*
que le ladra a cualquier ser viviente que se le acerca *who barks at any living being who comes near him*
hacemos el mismo recorrido *we take the same route* fijar *to notice*
rumbo *area* te callas *you fall silent* callada *silent*
como si no hiciera falta hablar *as if there were no need to talk*
como si ya todo estuviese dicho *as if everything had already been said*
tener flojera *to be lazy* rumbo a *on the way to*
me detuve en seco *I stopped suddenly* de sopetón *suddenly, brusquely*

Después de leer

Resumen

Lee la selección una vez más y completa este resumen con las formas correctas de las siguientes palabras. Hay dos palabras que no son necesarias.

antiguo	pasear	vivir
recorrido	morir	montar

1. En este microcuento de la mexicana María Velázquez, la narradora sale a _____ todas las mañanas.
2. Ella dice que es un buen ejercicio para su compañero porque él ya no _____ a caballo.
3. Los protagonistas hacen generalmente el mismo _____.
4. La narradora se imagina que pasea con alguien que _____ hace dos años.

Inferencias

Contesta estas preguntas.

1. ¿Quién es la narradora?
2. ¿Quién es Babar?
3. ¿De quién habla la narradora? ¿Por qué lo extraña (*miss*) tanto la narradora?
4. ¿Qué siente la narradora?

Asociaciones

¿Cuáles de estos adjetivos asocias con la narradora? Explica tu respuesta.

contenta	preocupada
aburrida	nerviosa
triste	enamorada
cansada	amable
alegre	trabajadora
avergonzada	enojada

Preguntas

Contesta estas preguntas con un(a) compañero/a.

1. ¿Sales a pasear todos los días? ¿Adónde?
2. ¿Te gusta pasear con tus amigos/as o prefieres ir solo/a (*alone*)?
3. ¿Qué haces tú cuando extrañas (*you miss*) a alguien?

Escritura

Estrategia

Listing key words

Before beginning your first draft, you may find it helpful to prepare a list of key words that you may be able to use.

If you prepare a list of potentially useful words ahead of time, you may find it easier to avoid using the dictionary while writing your first draft. You will probably also learn a few new Spanish words while preparing your list of key words.

Listing useful vocabulary is also a valuable organizational strategy, since the act of brainstorming key words will help you to form ideas about your topic. In addition, a list of key words can help you avoid redundancies when you write.

If you were writing a description of what you do to stay fit, your list of key words would probably include terms related to nutrition, exercise, and stress management. What are a few of the words you might include?

1. _____
2. _____
3. _____
4. _____
5. _____
6. _____

Tema

Escribir un plan personal de bienestar

Desarrolla un plan personal para mejorar tu bienestar, tanto físico como emocional. Tu plan debe describir:

1. Lo que has hecho para mejorar tu bienestar y llevar una vida sana
2. Lo que no has podido hacer todavía
3. Las actividades que debes hacer en los próximos meses

Considera también la siguiente lista de preguntas.

La nutrición

▶ ¿Comes una dieta equilibrada?
▶ ¿Consumes suficientes vitaminas y minerales? ¿Consumes demasiada grasa?
▶ ¿Quieres aumentar de peso o adelgazar?
▶ ¿Qué puedes hacer para mejorar tu dieta?

El ejercicio

▶ ¿Haces ejercicio? ¿Con qué frecuencia?
▶ ¿Vas al gimnasio? ¿Qué tipo de ejercicios haces allí?
▶ ¿Practicas algún deporte?
▶ ¿Qué puedes hacer para mejorar tu bienestar físico?

El estrés

▶ ¿Sufres muchas presiones?
▶ ¿Qué actividades o problemas te causan estrés?
▶ ¿Qué haces (o debes hacer) para aliviar el estrés y sentirte más tranquilo/a?
▶ ¿Qué puedes hacer para mejorar tu bienestar emocional?

Escuchar
Preparación

Mira la foto. ¿Qué pistas te da de lo que vas a oír?

Estrategia
Listening for the gist/
Listening for cognates

Combining these two strategies is an easy way to get a good sense of what you hear. When you listen for the gist, you get the general idea of what you're hearing, which allows you to interpret cognates and other words in a meaningful context. Similarly, the cognates give you information about the details of the story that you might not have understood when listening for the gist. To practice these strategies, you will listen to a short paragraph. Write down the gist of what you hear and jot down a few cognates. Based on the gist and the cognates, what conclusions can you draw about what you heard?

🎧 Ahora escucha

Escucha lo que dice Ofelia Cortez de Bauer. Anota algunos de los cognados que escuchas y también la idea general del discurso.

_____

_____

_____

_____

Idea general: _____

Comprensión

¿Cierto o falso?

Indica si lo que dicen las siguientes frases es **cierto** o **falso**. Corrige las oraciones que son falsas.

	Cierto	Falso
1. La señora Bauer habla de la importancia de estar en buena forma y hace gimnasia con frecuencia.	○	○
2. Según ella, lo más importante es que lleves el programa sugerido por los expertos.	○	○
3. La señora Bauer participa en actividades individuales y de grupo.	○	○
4. El único objetivo del tipo de programa que ella sugiere es adelgazar.	○	○

Preguntas

1. Imagina que el programa de radio sigue. Según las pistas que ella dio, ¿qué vas a oír en la segunda parte?
2. ¿A qué tipo de público le interesa el tema del que habla la señora Bauer?
3. ¿Sigues los consejos de la señora Bauer? Explica tu respuesta.
4. ¿Qué piensas de los consejos que ella da? ¿Hay otra información que ella debía haber incluido?

pistas _clues_ discurso _speech_ género _genre_
propósito _purpose_ público _audience_
debía haber incluido _should have included_

Bolivia

El país en cifras

▶ **Área:** 1.098.580 km^2 (424.162 millas^2), *equivalente al área total de Francia y España*

▶ **Población:** 8.705.000

Los indios quechua y aimará constituyen más de la mitad de la población de Bolivia. Estos grupos indígenas han mantenido sus culturas y lenguas tradicionales. Los mestizos, personas de descendencia indígena y europea, representan la tercera parte de la población. El 15% restante es criollo, gente de ascendencia europea nacida en América Latina. Una gran mayoría de los bolivianos, más o menos el 70%, vive en el altiplano.

▶ **Capital:** La Paz, sede del gobierno, capital administrativa—1.564.000; Sucre, sede del Tribunal Supremo, capital constitucional y judicial—189.000

▶ **Ciudades principales:** Santa Cruz de la Sierra—1.115.000, Cochabamba—794.000, Oruro—202.000, Potosí—124.000

SOURCE: Population Division, UN Secretariat

▶ **Moneda:** peso boliviano

▶ **Idiomas:** español (oficial), aimará (oficial), quechua (oficial)

Bandera de Bolivia

Bolivianos célebres

▶ Jesús Lara, escritor (1898-1980)
▶ Víctor Paz Estenssoro, político y presidente (1907-)
▶ María Luisa Pacheco, pintora (1919-1982)
▶ Matilde Casazola, poeta (1942-)

mitad *half* **restante** *remaining* **altiplano** *high plateau*
sede *seat* **paraguas** *umbrella* **cascada** *waterfall*

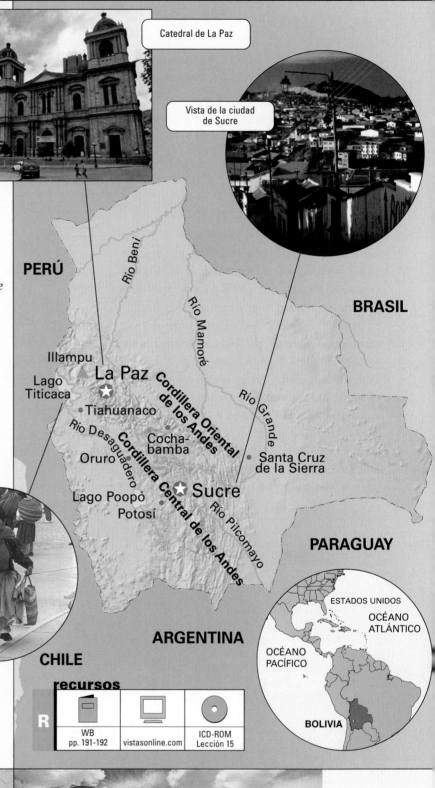

Catedral de La Paz

Vista de la ciudad de Sucre

Mujer indígena con bebé

PERÚ

BRASIL

Río Beni

Río Mamoré

Illampu

Lago Titicaca

La Paz

Cordillera Oriental de los Andes

Río Grande

Tiahuanaco

Río Desaguadero

Cochabamba

Cordillera Central de los Andes

Oruro

Santa Cruz de la Sierra

Lago Poopó

Sucre

Potosí

Río Pilcomayo

PARAGUAY

ARGENTINA

CHILE

ESTADOS UNIDOS

OCÉANO ATLÁNTICO

OCÉANO PACÍFICO

BOLIVIA

recursos

| R | WB pp. 191-192 | vistasonline.com | ICD-ROM Lección 15 |

¡Increíble pero cierto!

La Paz es la capital más alta del mundo. Su aeropuerto está situado a una altitud de 3,600 m. (12,000 pies). Ah, y si viajas en carro hasta La Paz, ¡no te olvides el paraguas! En la carretera, que cruza 9.000 metros de densa selva, te encontrarás con una cascada.

Lugares • **El Lago Titicaca**

Titicaca, situado en los Andes de Bolivia y Perú, es el lago navegable más alto del mundo y está a una altitud de 3.815 metros (12.500 pies). También es el segundo lago más grande, después del Maracaibo, de América del Sur, con un área de más de 8.000 km^2 (3.000 millas^2). La mitología inca cuenta que los hijos del Dios Sol emergieron de las profundas aguas del Lago Titicaca para fundar su imperio. Los indígenas de la zona todavía hacen botes de totora a la manera antigua y los usan para navegar las claras aguas del lago.

Artes • **La música andina**

La música andina, compartida por Bolivia, Perú, Ecuador, Chile y Argentina, es el aspecto más conocido de su folklore. Hay muchos conjuntos profesionales que dan a conocer esta música popular de origen indígena alrededor del mundo. Uno de los grupos más importantes son los Kjarkas, que llevan más de veinticinco años actuando en los escenarios internacionales. Los instrumentos típicos que se usan son la zampoña y la quena (dos tipos de flauta), el arpa, el bombo, la guitarra y el charango, que es una pequeña guitarra andina.

Historia • **Tiahuanaco**

Tiahuanaco, que significa "Ciudad de los dioses", es un sitio arqueológico de ruinas preincaicas situado cerca de La Paz y el Lago Titicaca. Se piensa que los antepasados de los indígenas aymará fundaron este centro ceremonial hace unos 15.000 años. En el año 1100 la ciudad tenía más o menos 60.000 habitantes. En este sitio se pueden ver el Templo de Kalasasaya, el Monolito Ponce, el Templete Subterráneo, la Puerta del Sol y la Puerta de la Luna. La Puerta del Sol es un impresionante monumento que tiene tres metros de alto y cuatro de ancho y que pesa aproximadamente unas 10 toneladas.

¿Qué aprendiste? Responde a las preguntas con una frase completa.

1. ¿Qué idiomas se hablan en Bolivia?

2. ¿Dónde vive la mayoría de los bolivianos?

3. ¿Cuál es la capital administrativa de Bolivia?

4. ¿Cómo se llama la moneda de Bolivia?

5. Según la mitología inca, ¿qué ocurrió en el lago Titicaca?

6. ¿Qué hacen los indios con la totora?

7. ¿Qué es la quena?

8. ¿Qué es el charango?

9. ¿Qué es la Puerta del Sol?

10. ¿Cómo se llama el sitio arqueológico situado cerca de La Paz y el Lago Titicaca?

Conexión Internet Investiga estos temas en el sitio **www.vistasonline.com**.

1. Busca información sobre un(a) boliviano/a célebre. ¿Cuáles son algunos de los episodios más importantes de su vida? ¿Qué ha hecho esta persona? ¿Por qué es célebre?

2. Busca información sobre Tiahuanaco u otro sitio arqueológico en Bolivia. ¿Qué han descubierto los arqueólogos en ese sitio?

cuenta *tells the story* **Dios** *God* **botes de totora** *reed boats* **fundar** *to found* **imperio** *empire* **manera** *way* **conjuntos** *groups*
dan a conocer *make known* **alrededor** *around* **arpa** *harp* **bombo** *drum* **antepasados** *ancestors* **ancho** *wide* **pesa** *weighs*

Paraguay

El país en cifras

▸ **Área:** 406.750 km² (157.046 millas²), *el tamaño de California*

▸ **Población:** 5.778.000

▸ **Capital:** Asunción—1.343.000

▸ **Ciudades principales:** Ciudad del Este— 134.000, San Lorenzo—133.000, Lambaré— 100.000, Fernando de la Mora—95.000

SOURCE: Population Division, UN Secretariat

▸ **Moneda:** guaraní

▸ **Idiomas:** español (oficial), guaraní (oficial)

Las tribus indígenas que vivían en la zona antes de la llegada de los españoles hablaban guaraní. Ahora el 90 por ciento de los paraguayos habla esta lengua, que se usa con frecuencia en canciones, poemas, periódicos y libros. Varias instituciones, como el Teatro Guaraní, ayudan a preservar la cultura y la lengua guaraníes.

Bandera de Paraguay

Paraguayos célebres

▸ **Agustín Barrios**, guitarrista y compositor (1885-1944)

▸ **Josefina Plá**, escritora y ceramista (1909-1999)

▸ **Augusto Roa Bastos**, escritor (1918-)

▸ **Olga Blinder**, pintora (1921-)

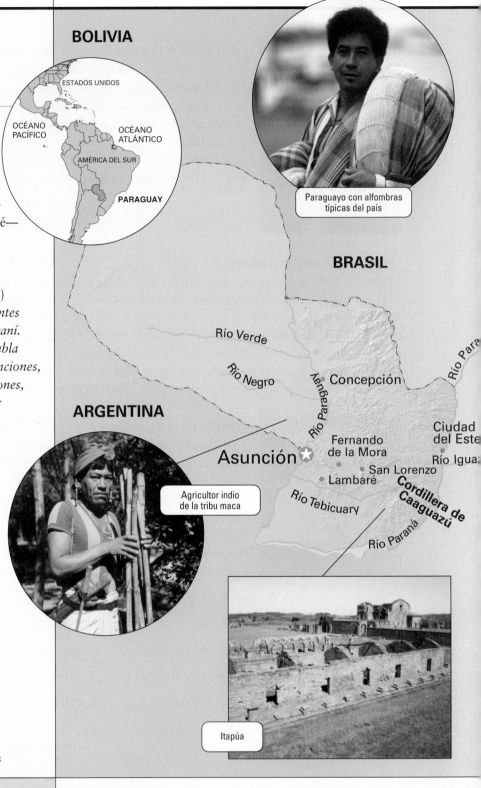

Paraguayo con alfombras típicas del país

Agricultor indio de la tribu maca

Itapúa

sin parar *nonstop* Aunque *Although* lugareños *local residents*

¡Increíble pero cierto!

En Paraguay, hay una pequeña zona cerca del río Paraná en la que llueve tanto que, según cuenta la leyenda, ha llovido sin parar por un millón de años. Aunque esto pueda ser difícil de verificar, una cosa sí es cierta: los lugareños no han visto en su vida un día sin lluvia.

recursos

R

| WB pp. 193-194 | WB Repaso 13-15 pp. 195-196 | vistasonline.com | ICD-ROM Lección 18 |

Artesanía • **El ñandutí**

El ñandutí es la creación artesanal más conocida de Paraguay. Es un fino encaje hecho a mano que generalmente tiene forma circular. En guaraní, su nombre significa telaraña y se llama así porque imita su trazado. Normalmente, estos encajes son blancos, pero también los hay de colores, y sus diseños pueden ser geométricos o florales. Aunque el ñandutí tiene su origen en Itaguá, hoy día es muy conocido en toda Sudamérica.

Ciencias • **La represa Itaipú**

La represa Itaipú, la obra hidroeléctrica más importante hasta nuestros días, está en la frontera entre Paraguay y Brasil. Su construcción empezó en 1974 y terminó once años más tarde. El proyecto dio trabajo a 100.000 paraguayos y, durante los primeros cinco años, se usó suficiente concreto como para construir un edificio de 350 pisos. Al estar cerca de las famosas Cataratas de Iguazú, muchos turistas visitan la represa para admirar lo imponente de la construcción.

Naturaleza • **Los ríos Paraguay y Paraná**

Los ríos Paraguay y Paraná sirven de frontera natural entre Paraguay y Argentina y son las principales rutas de transporte dentro de Paraguay. El río Paraná tiene unos 3.200 km navegables, y por él pasan barcos de más de 5.000 toneladas. El río Paraguay, su principal afluente, cruza todo el país, separando el Gran Chaco, una zona con muy pocos habitantes, de la meseta Paraná, donde vive la mayoría de los paraguayos.

¿Qué aprendiste? Responde a las preguntas con una frase completa.

1. ¿Quién es Augusto Roa Bastos?

2. ¿Cómo se llama la moneda de Paraguay?

3. ¿Qué es el ñandutí?

4. ¿De dónde es el ñandutí?

5. ¿Qué forma imita el ñandutí?

6. En total, ¿cuántos años tomó la construcción de la represa Itaipú?

7. ¿A cuántos paraguayos dio trabajo la construcción de la represa?

8. ¿Qué países separan los ríos Paraguay y Paraná?

9. ¿Qué distancia se puede navegar por el Paraná?

Conexión Internet Investiga estos temas en el sitio **www.vistasonline.com**.

1. Busca información sobre Alfredo Stroessner, el ex-presidente de Paraguay. ¿Por qué se le considera un dictador?

2. Busca información sobre la historia de Paraguay. En tu opinión, ¿cuáles fueron los episodios decisivos en su historia?

encaje *lace* telaraña *spiderweb* trazado *outline; design* diseños *designs* represa *dam* lo imponente *the impressiveness* meseta *plateau*

El bienestar

el bienestar	well-being
la clase de ejercicios aeróbicos	aerobics class
la droga	drug
el/la drogadicto/a	drug addict
el masaje	massage
el/la monitor(a)	trainer
el músculo	muscle
el/la teleadicto/a	couch potato
adelgazar	to lose weight; to slim down
aliviar el estrés	to reduce stress
aliviar la tensión	to reduce tension
apurarse	to hurry; to rush
aumentar de peso, engordar	to gain weight
calentarse (e:ie)	to warm up
disfrutar (de)	to enjoy; to reap the benefits (of)
entrenarse	to practice; to train
estar a dieta	to be on a diet
estar en buena forma	to be in good shape
(no) fumar	(not) to smoke
hacer ejercicio	to exercise
hacer ejercicios aeróbicos	to do aerobics
hacer ejercicios de estiramiento	to do stretching exercises
hacer gimnasia	to work out
levantar pesas	to lift weights
llevar una vida sana	to lead a healthy lifestyle
mantenerse en forma	to stay in shape
sudar	to sweat
sufrir muchas presiones	to be under a lot of pressure
tratar de (+ inf.)	to try (to do something)
activo/a	active
débil	weak
flexible	flexible
fuerte	strong
sedentario/a	sedentary; related to sitting
tranquilo/a	calm; quiet

La nutrición

la bebida alcohólica	alcoholic beverage
la caloría	calorie
el colesterol	cholesterol
la grasa	fat
la merienda	afternoon snack
el mineral	mineral
la nutrición	nutrition
la proteína	protein
la vitamina	vitamin
comer una dieta equilibrada	to eat a balanced diet
consumir alcohol	to consume alcohol
merendar (e:ie)	to have a snack in the afternoon
descafeinado/a	decaffeinated

Palabras adicionales

en exceso	in excess; too much
sin	without

Expresiones útiles	See page 427.

recursos

R	LCASS./CD Cass. 15/CD 15	LM p. 289

Apéndice A

Plan de escritura

1 **Ideas y organización**

Begin by organizing your writing materials. If you prefer to write by hand, you may want to have a few spare pens and pencils on hand, as well as an eraser or correction fluid. If you prefer to use a word-processing program, make sure you know how to use Spanish accent marks, the **tilde,** and Spanish punctuation marks. Then make a list of the resources you can consult while writing. Finally, make a list of the basic ideas you want to cover. Beside each idea, jot down a few Spanish words and phrases you may want to use while writing.

2 **Primer borrador**

Write your first draft, using the resources and ideas you gathered in **Ideas y organización.**

3 **Comentario**

Exchange papers with a classmate and comment on each other's work, using these questions as a guide. Begin by mentioning what you like about your classmate's writing.

a. How can your classmate make his or her writing clearer, more logical, or more organized?

b. What suggestions do you have for making the writing more interesting or complete?

c. Do you see any spelling or grammatical errors?

4 **Redacción**

Revise your first draft, keeping in mind your classmate's comments. Also, incorporate any new information you may have. Before handing in the final version, review your work using these guidelines:

a. Make sure each verb agrees with its subject. Then check the gender and number of each article, noun, and adjective.

b. Check your spelling and punctuation.

c. Consult your **Anotaciones para mejorar la escritura** (see description below) to avoid repetition of previous errors.

5 **Evaluación y progreso**

You may want to share what you've written with a classmate, a small group, or the entire class. After your instructor has returned your paper, review the comments and corrections. On a separate sheet of paper, write the heading **Anotaciones para mejorar** (*Notes for improving*) **la escritura** and list your most common errors. Place this list and your corrected document in your writing portfolio (**Carpeta de trabajos**) and consult it from time to time to gauge your progress.

Algunas estrategias

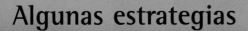

Considering audience and purpose

Before you write, think about what you are writing and the people for whom you are writing it. Try to write in a way that would appeal to and meet the needs of your audience.

Organizing information logically

There are many ways to organize your writing. You may, for example, want to organize your information chronologically (e.g., events in the history of a country), sequentially (e.g., steps in a recipe), or in order of importance. Some people prepare an outline before they write. Others jot information down on note cards and then arrange the note cards in a logical order. If you are organizing information chronologically or sequentially, you may want to use adverbs or adverbial phrases (e.g., **primero, luego, entonces, más tarde, al final**) to indicate the sequence in which events occurred.

Improving your style

You can improve your style by using complex sentences and avoiding redundancies. You can use linking words (e.g., **pero, y, o**) to connect simple sentences and create more complex ones. To avoid redundancy with verbs and nouns, consult a **diccionario de sinónimos.** You can also avoid redundancy by replacing nouns with direct object pronouns, possessive adjectives, demonstrative adjectives, and pronouns. For example: Have you seen my <u>racquet</u>? I can't seem to find it anywhere. Do you mind if I borrow <u>yours</u>?

Doing a comparative analysis

You may want to create a Venn diagram in order to organize your information visually before comparing or contrasting people, places, objects, events, or issues. To create a Venn diagram, draw two circles that overlap and label the top of each circle with the names of the people or things you are comparing. In the outer rings of the two circles, list the differences between the people or things. Then list their similarities where the two circles overlap. When you write a comparative analysis or give your opinions, be sure to express yourself clearly and support your ideas with appropriate details, facts, examples, and other forms of evidence.

Writing strong introductions and conclusions

Introductions and conclusions focus the reader's attention on your topic. The introduction previews the topic and informs your reader of the important points that will be covered. The conclusion concisely sums up the information. A compelling fact or statistic, a humorous anecdote, or a question directed to the reader are all interesting ways to begin or end your writing.

Glossary of Grammatical Terms

ADJECTIVE A word that modifies, or describes, a noun or pronoun.

muchos libros
many books

un hombre **rico**
*a **rich** man*

las mujeres **altas**
*the **tall** women*

Demonstrative adjective An adjective that specifies which noun a speaker is referring to.

esta fiesta
this party

ese chico
that boy

aquellas flores
those flowers

Possessive adjective An adjective that indicates ownership or possession.

mi mejor vestido
my best dress

Éste es **mi** hermano.
*This is **my** brother*

Stressed possessive adjective A possessive adjective that emphasizes the owner or possessor.

Es un libro **mío**.
*It's **my book**./It's a book **of mine**.*

Es amiga **tuya**; yo no la conozco.
*She's a friend **of yours**; I don't know her.*

ADVERB A word that modifies, or describes, a verb, adjective, or other adverb.

Pancho escribe **rápidamente**.
*Pancho writes **quickly**.*

Este cuadro es **muy** bonito.
*This picture is **very** pretty.*

ARTICLE A word that points out a noun in either a specific or a non-specific way.

Definite article An article that points out a noun in a specific way.

el libro
the book

la maleta
the suitcase

los diccionarios
the dictionaries

las palabras
the words

Indefinite article An article that points out a noun in a general, non-specific way.

un lápiz
a pencil

una computadora
a computer

unos pájaros
some birds

unas escuelas
some schools

CLAUSE A group of words that contains both a conjugated verb and a subject, either expressed or implied.

Main (or Independent) clause A clause that can stand alone as a complete sentence.

Pienso ir a cenar pronto.
I plan to go to dinner soon.

Subordinate (or Dependent) clause A clause that does not express a complete thought and therefore cannot stand alone as a sentence.

Entraron en la casa **sin que lo supiéramos nosotros**.
*They came into the house **without our knowing it**.*

COMPARATIVE A construction used with an adjective or adverb to express a comparison between two people, places, or things.

Este programa es **más interesante** que el otro.
*This program is **more interesting** than the other one.*

Tomás no es **tan alto como** Alberto.
*Tomás is not **as tall as** Alberto.*

CONJUGATION A set of the forms of a verb for a specific tense or mood or the process by which these verb forms are presented.

Preterite conjugation of **cantar:**

canté	cantamos
cantaste	cantasteis
cantó	cantaron

CONJUNCTION A word used to connect words, clauses, or phrases.

Susana es de Cuba **y** Pedro es de España.
*Susana is from Cuba **and** Pedro is from Spain.*

No quiero estudiar **pero** tengo que hacerlo.
*I don't want to study, **but** I have to.*

CONTRACTION The joining of two words into one. The only contractions in Spanish are **al** and **del**.

Mi hermano fue **al** concierto ayer.
*My brother went **to the** concert yesterday.*

Saqué dinero **del** banco.
*I took money **from the** bank.*

DIRECT OBJECT A noun or pronoun that directly receives the action of the verb.

Tomás lee **el libro.**   La **pagó** ayer.
*Tomás reads **the book.***   *She paid **it** yesterday.*

GENDER The grammatical categorizing of certain kinds of words, such as nouns and pronouns, as masculine, feminine, or neuter.

Masculine
articles **el, un**
pronouns **él, lo, éste, ése, aquél**
adjective **simpático, mío**

Feminine
articles **la, una**
pronouns **ella, la, ésta, ésa, aquélla**
adjective **simpática, mía**

IMPERSONAL EXPRESSION A third-person expression with no expressed or specific subject.

Es muy importante.   **Llueve** mucho.
*It's **very important.***   *It's **raining** hard.*

Aquí **se habla** español.
*Spanish **is spoken** here.*

INDIRECT OBJECT A noun or pronoun that receives the action of the verb indirectly; the object, often a living being, to or for whom an action is performed.

Eduardo **le** dio un libro **a Linda.**
*Eduardo gave a book **to Linda.***

La profesora **me** dio una C en el examen.
*The professor gave **me** a C on the test.*

INFINITIVE The basic form of a verb. Infinitives in Spanish end in **-ar, -er,** or **-ir.**

hablar   correr   abrir
to speak   *to run*   *to open*

INTERROGATIVE An adjective or pronoun used to ask a question.

¿**Quién** habla?   ¿**Cuántos** compraste?
***Who** is speaking?*   ***How many** did you buy?*

¿**Qué** piensas hacer hoy?
***What** do you plan to do today?*

INVERSION Changing the word order of a sentence, often to form a question.

Statement: Elena pagó la cuenta del restaurante.

Inversion: ¿Pagó Elena la cuenta del restaurante?

MOOD A grammatical distinction of verbs that indicates whether the verb is intended to make a statement or command or to express a doubt, emotion, or condition contrary to fact.

Imperative mood Verb forms used to make commands.

Di la verdad.   **Caminen Uds.** conmigo.
*Tell **the truth.***   *Walk **with me.***

¡**Comamos ahora!**
*Let's eat **now!***

Indicative mood Verb forms used to state facts, actions, and states considered to be real.

Sé que **tienes** el dinero.
*I **know** that **you have** the money.*

Subjunctive mood Verb forms used principally in subordinate (dependent) clauses to express wishes, desires, emotions, doubts, and certain conditions, such as contrary-to-fact situations.

Prefieren que **hables** en español.
*They prefer that **you speak** in Spanish.*

Dudo que Luis **tenga** el dinero necesario.
*I doubt that Luis **has** the necessary money.*

NOUN A word that identifies people, animals, places, things, and ideas.

hombre   gato
man   *cat*

México   casa
Mexico   *house*

libertad
freedom

Verb conjugation tables

The verb lists

The list of verbs below and the model-verb tables that start on page 590 show you how to conjugate every verb taught in **VISTAS**. Each verb in the list is followed by a model verb conjugated according to the same pattern. The number in parentheses indicates where in the tables you can find the conjugated forms of the model verb. If you want to find out how to conjugate **divertirse**, for example, look up number 33, **sentir**, the model for verbs that follow the **i:ie** stem-change pattern.

How to use the verb tables

In the tables you will find the infinitive, past and present participles, and all the simple forms of each model verb. The formation of the compound tenses of any verb can be inferred from the table of compound tenses, pages 590–597, either by combining the past participle of the verb with a conjugated form of **haber** or combining the present participle with a conjugated form of **estar**.

abrazar (z:c) like cruzar (37)

abrir like vivir (3) *except* past participle is abierto

aburrir(se) like vivir (3)

acabar de like hablar (1)

acampar like hablar (1)

acompañar like hablar (1)

aconsejar like hablar (1)

acordarse (o:ue) like contar (24)

acostarse (o:ue) like contar (24)

adelgazar (z:c) like cruzar (37)

afeitarse like hablar (1)

ahorrar like hablar (1)

alegrarse like hablar (1)

aliviar like hablar (1)

almorzar (o:ue) like contar (24) *except* (z:c)

alquilar like hablar (1)

anunciar like hablar (1)

apagar (g:gu) like llegar (41)

aplaudir like vivir (3)

apreciar like hablar (1)

aprender like comer (2)

apurarse like hablar (1)

arrancar (c:qu) like tocar (43)

arreglar like hablar (1)

asistir like vivir (3)

aumentar like hablar (1)

ayudar(se) like hablar (1)

bailar like hablar (1)

bajar(se) like hablar (1)

bañarse like hablar (1)

barrer like comer (2)

beber like comer (2)

besar(se) like hablar (1)

brindar like hablar (1)

bucear like hablar (1)

buscar (c:qu) like tocar (43)

caber (4)

caer(se) (5)

calentarse (e:ie) like pensar (30)

calzar (z:c) like cruzar (37)

cambiar like hablar (1)

caminar like hablar (1)

cantar like hablar (1)

casarse like hablar (1)

celebrar like hablar (1)

cenar like hablar (1)

cepillarse like hablar (1)

cerrar (e:ie) like pensar (30)

chocar (c:qu) like tocar (43)

cobrar like hablar (1)

cocinar like hablar (1)

comenzar (e:ie) (z:c) like empezar (26)

comer (2)

compartir like vivir (3)

comprar like hablar (1)

comprender like comer (2)

comprometerse like comer (2)

comunicarse (c:qu) like tocar (43)

conducir (c:zc) (6)

confirmar like hablar (1)

conocer (c:zc) (35)

conseguir (e:i) like seguir (32)

conservar like hablar (1)

consumir like vivir (3)

contaminar like hablar (1)

contar (o:ue) (24)

controlar like hablar (1)

correr like comer (2)

costar (o:ue) like contar (24)

creer (y) (36)

cruzar (z:c) (37)

cubrir like vivir (3) *except* past participle is cubierto

cuidar like hablar (1)

cumplir like vivir (3)

dañar like hablar (1)

dar(se) (7)

deber like comer (2)

decidir like vivir (3)

decir (e:i) (8)

declarar like hablar (1)

dejar like hablar (1)

depositar like hablar (1)

desarrollar like hablar (1)

desayunar like hablar (1)

descansar like hablar (1)

describir like vivir (3) *except* past participle is descrito

descubrir like vivir (3) *except* past participle is descubierto

desear like hablar (1)

despedirse (e:i) like pedir (29)

despertarse (e:ie) like pensar (30)

destruir (y) (38)

dibujar like hablar (1)

disfrutar like hablar (1)

divertirse (e:ie) like sentir (33)

divorciarse like hablar (1)

doblar like hablar (1)

doler (o:ue) like volver (34) *except* past participle is regular

dormir(se) (o:ue) (25)

ducharse like hablar (1)

dudar like hablar (1)

durar like hablar (1)

echar like hablar (1)

elegir (e:i) like pedir (29) *except* (g:j)

emitir like vivir (3)

empezar (e:ie) (z:c) (26)

enamorarse like hablar (1)

encantar like hablar (1)

encontrar(se) (o:ue) like contar (24)

enfermarse like hablar (1)

engordar like hablar (1)

enojarse like hablar (1)

enseñar like hablar (1)

ensuciar like hablar (1)

entender (e:ie) (27)

entrenarse like hablar (1)

entrevistar like hablar (1)

enviar (envío) (39)

escalar like hablar (1)

escribir like vivir (3) *except* past participle is escrito

escuchar like hablar (1)

esculpir like vivir (3)

esperar like hablar (1)

esquiar (esquío) like enviar (39)

establecer (c:zc) like conocer (35)

estacionar like hablar (1)

estar (9)

estornudar like hablar (1)

estudiar like hablar (1)

evitar like hablar (1)

explicar (c:qu) like tocar (43)

explorar like hablar (1)

faltar like hablar (1)

fascinar like hablar (1)

firmar like hablar (1)

fumar like hablar (1)

funcionar like hablar (1)

ganar like hablar (1)

gastar like hablar (1)

graduarse (gradúo) (40)

guardar like hablar (1)

gustar like hablar (1)

haber (hay) (10)

hablar (1)

hacer (11)

importar like hablar (1)

imprimir like vivir (3)

informar like hablar (1)

insistir like vivir (3)

interesar like hablar (1)

invertir (e:ie) like sentir (33)

invitar like hablar (1)

ir(se) (12)

jubilarse like hablar (1)

jugar (u:ue) (g:gu) (28)

lastimarse like hablar (1)

lavar(se) like hablar (1)

leer (y) like creer (36)

levantar(se) like hablar (1)

limpiar like hablar (1)

llamar(se) like hablar (1)

llegar (g:gu) (41)

llenar like hablar (1)

llevar(se) like hablar (1)

llover (o:ue) like volver (34) *except* past participle is regular

luchar like hablar (1)

mandar like hablar (1)

manejar like hablar (1)

mantener(se) (e:ie) like **tener** (20)

maquillarse like hablar (1)

mejorar like hablar (1)

merendar (e:ie) like pensar (30)

mirar like hablar (1)

molestar like hablar (1)

montar like hablar (1)

morir (o:ue) like dormir (25) *except* past participle is muerto

mostrar (o:ue) like contar (24)

mudarse like hablar (1)

nacer (c:zc) like conocer (35)

nadar like hablar (1)

navegar (g:gu) like llegar (41)

necesitar like hablar (1)

negar (e:ie) like pensar (30) *except* (g:gu)

nevar (e:ie) like pensar (30)

obedecer (c:zc) like conocer (35)

obtener (e:ie) like tener (20)

ocurrir like vivir (3)

odiar like hablar (1)

ofrecer (c:zc) like conocer (35)

oír (f3)

olvidar like hablar (1)

pagar (g:gu) like llegar (41)

parar like hablar (1)

parecer (c:zc) like conocer (35)

pasar like hablar (1)

pasear like hablar (1)

patinar like hablar (1)

pedir (e:i) (29)

peinarse like hablar (1)

pensar (e:ie) (30)

perder (e:ie) like entender (27)

pescar (c:qu) like tocar (43)

pintar like hablar (1)

planchar like hablar (1)

poder (o:ue) (14)

ponchar like hablar (1)

poner(se) (15)

practicar (c:qu) like tocar (43)

preferir (e:ie) like sentir (33)

preguntar like hablar (1)

preocuparse like hablar (1)

preparar like hablar (1)

presentar like hablar (1)

prestar like hablar (1)

probar(se) (o:ue) like contar (24)

prohibir like vivir (3)

proteger (g:j) (42)

publicar (c:qu) like tocar (43)

quedar(se) like hablar (1)

querer (e:ie) (16)

quitar(se) like hablar (1)

recetar like hablar (1)

recibir like vivir (3)

reciclar like hablar (1)

recoger (g:j) like proteger (42)

recomendar (e:ie) like pensar (30)

recordar (o:ue) like contar (24)

reducir (c:zc) like conducir (6)

regalar like hablar (1)

regatear like hablar (1)

regresar like hablar (1)

reír(se) (e:i) (31)

relajarse like hablar (1)

renunciar like hablar (1)

repetir (e:i) like pedir (29)

resolver (o:ue) like volver (34)

respirar like hablar (1)

revisar like hablar (1)

rogar (o:ue) like contar (24) *except* (g:gu)

romper(se) like comer (2) *except* past participle is roto

saber (17)

sacar (c:qu) like tocar (43)

sacudir like vivir (3)

salir (18)

saludar(se) like hablar (1)

seguir (e:i) (32)

sentarse (e:ie) like pensar (30)

sentir(se) (e:ie) (33)

separarse like hablar (1)

ser (19)

servir (e:i) like pedir (29)

solicitar like hablar (1)

sonar (o:ue) like contar (24)

sonreír (e:i) like reír(se) (31)

sorprender like comer (2)

subir like vivir (3)

sudar like hablar (1)

sufrir like vivir (3)

sugerir (e:ie) like sentir (33)

suponer like poner (15)

temer like comer (2)

tener (e:ie) (20)

terminar like hablar (1)

tocar (c:qu) (43)

tomar like hablar (1)

torcerse (o:ue) like volver (34) *except* (c:z) and past participle is regular; for ex, **yo tuerzo**

toser like comer (2)

trabajar like hablar (1)

traducir (c:zc) like conducir (6)

traer (21)

transmitir like vivir (3)

tratar like hablar (1)

usar like hablar (1)

vender like comer (2)

venir (e:ie) (22)

ver (23)

vestirse (e:i) like pedir (29)

viajar like hablar (1)

visitar like hablar (1)

vivir (3)

volver (o:ue) (34)

Regular verbs: simple tenses

1

Infinitive	INDICATIVE Present	Imperfect	Preterite	Future	Conditional	SUBJUNCTIVE Present	Past	IMPERATIVE
hablar	hablo	hablaba	hablé	hablaré	hablaría	hable	hablara	
	hablas	hablabas	hablaste	hablarás	hablarías	hables	hablaras	habla tú (no hables)
Participles:	habla	hablaba	habló	hablará	hablaría	hable	hablara	hable Ud.
hablando	hablamos	hablábamos	hablamos	hablaremos	hablaríamos	hablemos	habláramos	hablemos
hablado	habláis	hablabais	hablasteis	hablaréis	hablaríais	habléis	hablarais	hablad (no habléis)
	hablan	hablaban	hablaron	hablarán	hablarían	hablen	hablaran	hablen Uds.

2

Infinitive	INDICATIVE Present	Imperfect	Preterite	Future	Conditional	SUBJUNCTIVE Present	Past	IMPERATIVE
comer	como	comía	comí	comeré	comería	coma	comiera	
	comes	comías	comiste	comerás	comerías	comas	comieras	come tú (no comas)
Participles:	come	comía	comió	comerá	comería	coma	comiera	coma Ud.
comiendo	comemos	comíamos	comimos	comeremos	comeríamos	comamos	comiéramos	comamos
comido	coméis	comíais	comisteis	comeréis	comeríais	comáis	comierais	comed (no comáis)
	comen	comían	comieron	comerán	comerían	coman	comieran	coman Uds.

3

Infinitive	INDICATIVE Present	Imperfect	Preterite	Future	Conditional	SUBJUNCTIVE Present	Past	IMPERATIVE
vivir	vivo	vivía	viví	viviré	viviría	viva	viviera	
	vives	vivías	viviste	vivirás	vivirías	vivas	vivieras	vive tú (no vivas)
Participles:	vive	vivía	vivió	vivirá	viviría	viva	viviera	viva Ud.
viviendo	vivimos	vivíamos	vivimos	viviremos	viviríamos	vivamos	viviéramos	vivamos
vivido	vivís	vivíais	vivisteis	viviréis	viviríais	viváis	vivierais	vivid (no viváis)
	viven	vivían	vivieron	vivirán	vivirían	vivan	vivieran	vivan Uds.

All verbs: compound tenses

PERFECT TENSES

INDICATIVE

Present Perfect		Past Perfect		Future Perfect		Conditional Perfect	
he	hablado	había	hablado	habré	hablado	habría	hablado
has	comido	habías	comido	habrás	comido	habrías	comido
ha	vivido	había	vivido	habrá	vivido	habría	vivido
hemos		habíamos		habremos		habríamos	
habéis		habíais		habréis		habríais	
han		habían		habrán		habrían	

SUBJUNCTIVE

Present Perfect		Past Perfect	
haya	hablado	hubiera	hablado
hayas	comido	hubieras	comido
haya	vivido	hubiera	vivido
hayamos		hubiéramos	
hayáis		hubierais	
hayan		hubieran	

PROGRESSIVE TENSES

	INDICATIVE				SUBJUNCTIVE	
Present Progressive	Past Progressive	Future Progressive	Conditional Progressive	Present Progressive	Past Progressive
estoy	estaba	estaré	estaría	esté	estuviera
estás	estabas	estarás	estarías	estés	estuvieras
está	estaba	estará	estaría	esté	estuviera
estamos hablando	estábamos hablando	estaremos hablando	estaríamos hablando	estemos hablando	estuviéramos hablando
estáis comiendo	estabais comiendo	estaréis comiendo	estaríais comiendo	estéis comiendo	estuvierais comiendo
están viviendo	estaban viviendo	estarán viviendo	estarían viviendo	estén viviendo	estuvieran viviendo

Irregular verbs

		INDICATIVE					SUBJUNCTIVE		IMPERATIVE
Infinitive	Present	Imperfect	Preterite	Future	Conditional	Present	Past	
4 caber	quepo	cabía	cupe	cabré	cabría	quepa	cupiera	
	cabes	cabías	cupiste	cabrás	cabrías	quepas	cupieras	cabe tú (no quepas)
	cabe	cabía	cupo	cabrá	cabría	quepa	cupiera	quepa Ud.
Participles:	cabemos	cabíamos	cupimos	cabremos	cabríamos	quepamos	cupiéramos	quepamos
cabiendo	cabéis	cabíais	cupisteis	cabréis	cabríais	quepáis	cupierais	cabed (no quepáis)
cabido	caben	cabían	cupieron	cabrán	cabrían	quepan	cupieran	quepan Uds.
5 caer(se)	caigo	caía	caí	caeré	caería	caiga	cayera	
	caes	caías	caíste	caerás	caerías	caigas	cayeras	cae tú (no caigas)
	cae	caía	cayó	caerá	caería	caiga	cayera	caiga Ud. (no caiga)
Participles:	caemos	caíamos	caímos	caeremos	caeríamos	caigamos	cayéramos	caigamos
cayendo	caéis	caíais	caísteis	caeréis	caeríais	caigáis	cayerais	caed (no caigáis)
caído	caen	caían	cayeron	caerán	caerían	caigan	cayeran	caigan Uds.
6 conducir	conduzco	conducía	conduje	conduciré	conduciría	conduzca	condujera	
(c:zc)	conduces	conducías	condujiste	conducirás	conducirías	conduzcas	condujeras	conduce tú (no conduzcas)
	conduce	conducía	condujo	conducirá	conduciría	conduzca	condujera	conduzca Ud. (no conduzca)
Participles:	conducimos	conducíamos	condujimos	conduciremos	conduciríamos	conduzcamos	condujéramos	conduzcamos
conduciendo	conducís	conducíais	condujisteis	conduciréis	conduciríais	conduzcáis	condujerais	conducid (no conduzcáis)
conducido	conducen	conducían	condujeron	conducirán	conducirían	conduzcan	condujeran	conduzcan Uds.

7. dar — Participles: dando, dado

	INDICATIVE					SUBJUNCTIVE		IMPERATIVE
	Present	Imperfect	Preterite	Future	Conditional	Present	Past	
	doy	daba	di	daré	daría	dé	diera	
	das	dabas	diste	darás	darías	des	dieras	da tú (no des)
	da	daba	dio	dará	daría	dé	diera	dé Ud.
	damos	dábamos	dimos	daremos	daríamos	demos	diéramos	demos
	dais	dabais	disteis	daréis	daríais	deis	dierais	dad (no deis)
	dan	daban	dieron	darán	darían	den	dieran	den Uds.

8. decir (e:i) — Participles: diciendo, dicho

	INDICATIVE					SUBJUNCTIVE		IMPERATIVE
	Present	Imperfect	Preterite	Future	Conditional	Present	Past	
	digo	decía	dije	diré	diría	diga	dijera	
	dices	decías	dijiste	dirás	dirías	digas	dijeras	di tú (no digas)
	dice	decía	dijo	dirá	diría	diga	dijera	diga Ud.
	decimos	decíamos	dijimos	diremos	diríamos	digamos	dijéramos	digamos
	decís	decíais	dijisteis	diréis	diríais	digáis	dijerais	decid (no digáis)
	dicen	decían	dijeron	dirán	dirían	digan	dijeran	digan Uds.

9. estar — Participles: estando, estado

	INDICATIVE					SUBJUNCTIVE		IMPERATIVE
	Present	Imperfect	Preterite	Future	Conditional	Present	Past	
	estoy	estaba	estuve	estaré	estaría	esté	estuviera	
	estás	estabas	estuviste	estarás	estarías	estés	estuvieras	está tú (no estés)
	está	estaba	estuvo	estará	estaría	esté	estuviera	esté Ud.
	estamos	estábamos	estuvimos	estaremos	estaríamos	estemos	estuviéramos	estemos
	estáis	estabais	estuvisteis	estaréis	estaríais	estéis	estuvierais	estad (no estéis)
	están	estaban	estuvieron	estarán	estarían	estén	estuvieran	estén Uds.

10. haber — Participles: habiendo, habido

	INDICATIVE					SUBJUNCTIVE		IMPERATIVE
	Present	Imperfect	Preterite	Future	Conditional	Present	Past	
	he	había	hube	habré	habría	haya	hubiera	
	has	habías	hubiste	habrás	habrías	hayas	hubieras	
	ha	había	hubo	habrá	habría	haya	hubiera	
	hemos	habíamos	hubimos	habremos	habríamos	hayamos	hubiéramos	
	habéis	habíais	hubisteis	habréis	habríais	hayáis	hubierais	
	han	habían	hubieron	habrán	habrían	hayan	hubieran	

11. hacer — Participles: haciendo, hecho

	INDICATIVE					SUBJUNCTIVE		IMPERATIVE
	Present	Imperfect	Preterite	Future	Conditional	Present	Past	
	hago	hacía	hice	haré	haría	haga	hiciera	
	haces	hacías	hiciste	harás	harías	hagas	hicieras	haz tú (no hagas)
	hace	hacía	hizo	hará	haría	haga	hiciera	haga Ud.
	hacemos	hacíamos	hicimos	haremos	haríamos	hagamos	hiciéramos	hagamos
	hacéis	hacíais	hicisteis	haréis	haríais	hagáis	hicierais	haced (no hagáis)
	hacen	hacían	hicieron	harán	harían	hagan	hicieran	hagan Uds.

12. ir — Participles: yendo, ido

	INDICATIVE					SUBJUNCTIVE		IMPERATIVE
	Present	Imperfect	Preterite	Future	Conditional	Present	Past	
	voy	iba	fui	iré	iría	vaya	fuera	
	vas	ibas	fuiste	irás	irías	vayas	fueras	ve tú (no vayas)
	va	iba	fue	irá	iría	vaya	fuera	vaya Ud.
	vamos	íbamos	fuimos	iremos	iríamos	vayamos	fuéramos	vamos
	vais	ibais	fuisteis	iréis	iríais	vayáis	fuerais	id (no vayáis)
	van	iban	fueron	irán	irían	vayan	fueran	vayan Uds.

13. oír (y) — Participles: oyendo, oído

	INDICATIVE					SUBJUNCTIVE		IMPERATIVE
	Present	Imperfect	Preterite	Future	Conditional	Present	Past	
	oigo	oía	oí	oiré	oiría	oiga	oyera	
	oyes	oías	oíste	oirás	oirías	oigas	oyeras	oye tú (no oigas)
	oye	oía	oyó	oirá	oiría	oiga	oyera	oiga Ud.
	oímos	oíamos	oímos	oiremos	oiríamos	oigamos	oyéramos	oigamos
	oís	oíais	oísteis	oiréis	oiríais	oigáis	oyerais	oíd (no oigáis)
	oyen	oían	oyeron	oirán	oirían	oigan	oyeran	oigan Uds.

14 poder (o:ue)
Participles: pudiendo, podido

	INDICATIVE					SUBJUNCTIVE		IMPERATIVE
	Present	Imperfect	Preterite	Future	Conditional	Present	Past	
	puedo	podía	pude	podré	podría	pueda	pudiera	
	puedes	podías	pudiste	podrás	podrías	puedas	pudieras	puede tú (no puedas)
	puede	podía	pudo	podrá	podría	pueda	pudiera	pueda Ud.
	podemos	podíamos	pudimos	podremos	podríamos	podamos	pudiéramos	podamos
	podéis	podíais	pudisteis	podréis	podríais	podáis	pudierais	poded (no podáis)
	pueden	podían	pudieron	podrán	podrían	puedan	pudieran	puedan Uds.

15 poner
Participles: poniendo, puesto

	INDICATIVE					SUBJUNCTIVE		IMPERATIVE
	Present	Imperfect	Preterite	Future	Conditional	Present	Past	
	pongo	ponía	puse	pondré	pondría	ponga	pusiera	
	pones	ponías	pusiste	pondrás	pondrías	pongas	pusieras	pon tú (no pongas)
	pone	ponía	puso	pondrá	pondría	ponga	pusiera	ponga Ud.
	ponemos	poníamos	pusimos	pondremos	pondríamos	pongamos	pusiéramos	pongamos
	ponéis	poníais	pusisteis	pondréis	pondríais	pongáis	pusierais	poned (no pongáis)
	ponen	ponían	pusieron	pondrán	pondrían	pongan	pusieran	pongan Uds.

16 querer (e:ie)
Participles: queriendo, querido

	INDICATIVE					SUBJUNCTIVE		IMPERATIVE
	Present	Imperfect	Preterite	Future	Conditional	Present	Past	
	quiero	quería	quise	querré	querría	quiera	quisiera	
	quieres	querías	quisiste	querrás	querrías	quieras	quisieras	quiere tú (no quieras)
	quiere	quería	quiso	querrá	querría	quiera	quisiera	quiera Ud.
	queremos	queríamos	quisimos	querremos	querríamos	queramos	quisiéramos	queramos
	queréis	queríais	quisisteis	querréis	querríais	queráis	quisierais	quered (no queráis)
	quieren	querían	quisieron	querrán	querrían	quieran	quisieran	quieran Uds.

17 saber
Participles: sabiendo, sabido

	INDICATIVE					SUBJUNCTIVE		IMPERATIVE
	Present	Imperfect	Preterite	Future	Conditional	Present	Past	
	sé	sabía	supe	sabré	sabría	sepa	supiera	
	sabes	sabías	supiste	sabrás	sabrías	sepas	supieras	sabe tú (no sepas)
	sabe	sabía	supo	sabrá	sabría	sepa	supiera	sepa Ud.
	sabemos	sabíamos	supimos	sabremos	sabríamos	sepamos	supiéramos	sepamos
	sabéis	sabíais	supisteis	sabréis	sabríais	sepáis	supierais	sabed (no sepáis)
	saben	sabían	supieron	sabrán	sabrían	sepan	supieran	sepan Uds.

18 salir
Participles: saliendo, salido

	INDICATIVE					SUBJUNCTIVE		IMPERATIVE
	Present	Imperfect	Preterite	Future	Conditional	Present	Past	
	salgo	salía	salí	saldré	saldría	salga	saliera	
	sales	salías	saliste	saldrás	saldrías	salgas	salieras	sal tú (no salgas)
	sale	salía	salió	saldrá	saldría	salga	saliera	salga Ud.
	salimos	salíamos	salimos	saldremos	saldríamos	salgamos	saliéramos	salgamos
	salís	salíais	salisteis	saldréis	saldríais	salgáis	salierais	salid (no salgáis)
	salen	salían	salieron	saldrán	saldrían	salgan	salieran	salgan Uds.

19 ser
Participles: siendo, sido

	INDICATIVE					SUBJUNCTIVE		IMPERATIVE
	Present	Imperfect	Preterite	Future	Conditional	Present	Past	
	soy	era	fui	seré	sería	sea	fuera	
	eres	eras	fuiste	serás	serías	seas	fueras	sé tú (no seas)
	es	era	fue	será	sería	sea	fuera	sea Ud.
	somos	éramos	fuimos	seremos	seríamos	seamos	fuéramos	seamos
	sois	erais	fuisteis	seréis	seríais	seáis	fuerais	sed (no seáis)
	son	eran	fueron	serán	serían	sean	fueran	sean Uds.

20 tener (e:ie)
Participles: teniendo, tenido

	INDICATIVE					SUBJUNCTIVE		IMPERATIVE
	Present	Imperfect	Preterite	Future	Conditional	Present	Past	
	tengo	tenía	tuve	tendré	tendría	tenga	tuviera	
	tienes	tenías	tuviste	tendrás	tendrías	tengas	tuvieras	ten tú (no tengas)
	tiene	tenía	tuvo	tendrá	tendría	tenga	tuviera	tenga Ud.
	tenemos	teníamos	tuvimos	tendremos	tendríamos	tengamos	tuviéramos	tengamos
	tenéis	teníais	tuvisteis	tendréis	tendríais	tengáis	tuvierais	tened (no tengáis)
	tienen	tenían	tuvieron	tendrán	tendrían	tengan	tuvieran	tengan Uds.

21 traer

Infinitive	INDICATIVE					SUBJUNCTIVE		IMPERATIVE
	Present	Imperfect	Preterite	Future	Conditional	Present	Past	
traer	traigo	traía	traje	traeré	traería	traiga	trajera	
	traes	traías	trajiste	traerás	traerías	traigas	trajeras	trae tú (no traigas)
Participles:	trae	traía	trajo	traerá	traería	traiga	trajera	traiga Ud.
trayendo	traemos	traíamos	trajimos	traeremos	traeríamos	traigamos	trajéramos	traigamos
traído	traéis	traíais	trajisteis	traeréis	traeríais	traigáis	trajerais	traed (no traigáis)
	traen	traían	trajeron	traerán	traerían	traigan	trajeran	traigan Uds.

22 venir (e:ie)

Infinitive	INDICATIVE					SUBJUNCTIVE		IMPERATIVE
	Present	Imperfect	Preterite	Future	Conditional	Present	Past	
venir (e:ie)	vengo	venía	vine	vendré	vendría	venga	viniera	
	vienes	venías	viniste	vendrás	vendrías	vengas	vinieras	ven tú (no vengas)
Participles:	viene	venía	vino	vendrá	vendría	venga	viniera	venga Ud.
viniendo	venimos	veníamos	vinimos	vendremos	vendríamos	vengamos	viniéramos	vengamos
venido	venís	veníais	vinisteis	vendréis	vendríais	vengáis	vinierais	venid (no vengáis)
	vienen	venían	vinieron	vendrán	vendrían	vengan	vinieran	vengan Uds.

23 ver

Infinitive	INDICATIVE					SUBJUNCTIVE		IMPERATIVE
	Present	Imperfect	Preterite	Future	Conditional	Present	Past	
ver	veo	veía	vi	veré	vería	vea	viera	
	ves	veías	viste	verás	verías	veas	vieras	ve tú (no veas)
Participles:	ve	veía	vio	verá	vería	vea	viera	vea Ud.
viendo	vemos	veíamos	vimos	veremos	veríamos	veamos	viéramos	veamos
visto	veis	veíais	visteis	veréis	veríais	veáis	vierais	ved (no veáis)
	ven	veían	vieron	verán	verían	vean	vieran	vean Uds.

Stem changing verbs

24 contar (o:ue)

Infinitive	INDICATIVE					SUBJUNCTIVE		IMPERATIVE
	Present	Imperfect	Preterite	Future	Conditional	Present	Past	
contar (o:ue)	cuento	contaba	conté	contaré	contaría	cuente	contara	
	cuentas	contabas	contaste	contarás	contarías	cuentes	contaras	cuenta tú (no cuentes)
Participles:	cuenta	contaba	contó	contará	contaría	cuente	contara	cuente Ud.
contando	contamos	contábamos	contamos	contaremos	contaríamos	contemos	contáramos	contemos
contado	contáis	contabais	contasteis	contaréis	contaríais	contéis	contarais	contad (no contéis)
	cuentan	contaban	contaron	contarán	contarían	cuenten	contaran	cuenten Uds.

25 dormir (o:ue)

Infinitive	INDICATIVE					SUBJUNCTIVE		IMPERATIVE
	Present	Imperfect	Preterite	Future	Conditional	Present	Past	
dormir (o:ue)	duermo	dormía	dormí	dormiré	dormiría	duerma	durmiera	
	duermes	dormías	dormiste	dormirás	dormirías	duermas	durmieras	duerme tú (no duermas)
Participles:	duerme	dormía	durmió	dormirá	dormiría	duerma	durmiera	duerma Ud.
durmiendo	dormimos	dormíamos	dormimos	dormiremos	dormiríamos	durmamos	durmiéramos	durmamos
dormido	dormís	dormíais	dormisteis	dormiréis	dormiríais	durmáis	durmierais	dormid (no durmáis)
	duermen	dormían	durmieron	dormirán	dormirían	duerman	durmieran	duerman Uds.

26 empezar (e:ie) (c)

Infinitive	INDICATIVE					SUBJUNCTIVE		IMPERATIVE
	Present	Imperfect	Preterite	Future	Conditional	Present	Past	
empezar (e:ie) (c)	empiezo	empezaba	empecé	empezaré	empezaría	empiece	empezara	
	empiezas	empezabas	empezaste	empezarás	empezarías	empieces	empezaras	empieza tú (no empieces)
Participles:	empieza	empezaba	empezó	empezará	empezaría	empiece	empezara	empiece Ud.
empezando	empezamos	empezábamos	empezamos	empezaremos	empezaríamos	empecemos	empezáramos	empecemos
empezado	empezáis	empezabais	empezasteis	empezaréis	empezaríais	empecéis	empezarais	empezad (no empecéis)
	empiezan	empezaban	empezaron	empezarán	empezarían	empiecen	empezaran	empiecen Uds.

27 — entender (e:ie)
Participles: entendiendo, entendido

	INDICATIVE					SUBJUNCTIVE		IMPERATIVE
	Present	Imperfect	Preterite	Future	Conditional	Present	Past	
	entiendo	entendía	entendí	entenderé	entendería	entienda	entendiera	
	entiendes	entendías	entendiste	entenderás	entenderías	entiendas	entendieras	entiende tú (no entiendas)
	entiende	entendía	entendió	entenderá	entendería	entienda	entendiera	entienda Ud.
	entendemos	entendíamos	entendimos	entenderemos	entenderíamos	entendamos	entendiéramos	entendamos
	entendéis	entendíais	entendisteis	entenderéis	entenderíais	entendáis	entendierais	entended (no entendáis)
	entienden	entendían	entendieron	entenderán	entenderían	entiendan	entendieran	entiendan Uds.

28 — jugar (u:ue) (gu)
Participles: jugando, jugado

	INDICATIVE					SUBJUNCTIVE		IMPERATIVE
	Present	Imperfect	Preterite	Future	Conditional	Present	Past	
	juego	jugaba	jugué	jugaré	jugaría	juegue	jugara	
	juegas	jugabas	jugaste	jugarás	jugarías	juegues	jugaras	juega tú (no juegues)
	juega	jugaba	jugó	jugará	jugaría	juegue	jugara	juegue Ud.
	jugamos	jugábamos	jugamos	jugaremos	jugaríamos	juguemos	jugáramos	juguemos
	jugáis	jugabais	jugasteis	jugaréis	jugaríais	juguéis	jugarais	jugad (no juguéis)
	juegan	jugaban	jugaron	jugarán	jugarían	jueguen	jugaran	jueguen Uds.

29 — pedir (e:i)
Participles: pidiendo, pedido

	INDICATIVE					SUBJUNCTIVE		IMPERATIVE
	Present	Imperfect	Preterite	Future	Conditional	Present	Past	
	pido	pedía	pedí	pediré	pediría	pida	pidiera	
	pides	pedías	pediste	pedirás	pedirías	pidas	pidieras	pide tú (no pidas)
	pide	pedía	pidió	pedirá	pediría	pida	pidiera	pida Ud.
	pedimos	pedíamos	pedimos	pediremos	pediríamos	pidamos	pidiéramos	pidamos
	pedís	pedíais	pedisteis	pediréis	pediríais	pidáis	pidierais	pedid (no pidáis)
	piden	pedían	pidieron	pedirán	pedirían	pidan	pidieran	pidan Uds.

30 — pensar (e:ie)
Participles: pensando, pensado

	INDICATIVE					SUBJUNCTIVE		IMPERATIVE
	Present	Imperfect	Preterite	Future	Conditional	Present	Past	
	pienso	pensaba	pensé	pensaré	pensaría	piense	pensara	
	piensas	pensabas	pensaste	pensarás	pensarías	pienses	pensaras	piensa tú (no pienses)
	piensa	pensaba	pensó	pensará	pensaría	piense	pensara	piense Ud.
	pensamos	pensábamos	pensamos	pensaremos	pensaríamos	pensemos	pensáramos	pensemos
	pensáis	pensabais	pensasteis	pensaréis	pensaríais	penséis	pensarais	pensad (no penséis)
	piensan	pensaban	pensaron	pensarán	pensarían	piensen	pensaran	piensen Uds.

31 — reír(se) (e:i)
Participles: riendo, reído

	INDICATIVE					SUBJUNCTIVE		IMPERATIVE
	Present	Imperfect	Preterite	Future	Conditional	Present	Past	
	río	reía	reí	reiré	reiría	ría	riera	
	ríes	reías	reíste	reirás	reirías	rías	rieras	ríe tú (no rías)
	ríe	reía	rió	reirá	reiría	ría	riera	ría Ud.
	reímos	reíamos	reímos	reiremos	reiríamos	riamos	riéramos	riamos
	reís	reíais	reísteis	reiréis	reiríais	riáis	rierais	reíd (no riáis)
	ríen	reían	rieron	reirán	reirían	rían	rieran	rían Uds.

32 — seguir (e:i) (gu)
Participles: siguiendo, seguido

	INDICATIVE					SUBJUNCTIVE		IMPERATIVE
	Present	Imperfect	Preterite	Future	Conditional	Present	Past	
	sigo	seguía	seguí	seguiré	seguiría	siga	siguiera	
	sigues	seguías	seguiste	seguirás	seguirías	sigas	siguieras	sigue tú (no sigas)
	sigue	seguía	siguió	seguirá	seguiría	siga	siguiera	siga Ud.
	seguimos	seguíamos	seguimos	seguiremos	seguiríamos	sigamos	siguiéramos	sigamos
	seguís	seguíais	seguisteis	seguiréis	seguiríais	sigáis	siguierais	seguid (no sigáis)
	siguen	seguían	siguieron	seguirán	seguirían	sigan	siguieran	sigan Uds.

33 — sentir (e:ie)
Participles: sintiendo, sentido

	INDICATIVE					SUBJUNCTIVE		IMPERATIVE
	Present	Imperfect	Preterite	Future	Conditional	Present	Past	
	siento	sentía	sentí	sentiré	sentiría	sienta	sintiera	
	sientes	sentías	sentiste	sentirás	sentirías	sientas	sintieras	siente tú (no sientas)
	siente	sentía	sintió	sentirá	sentiría	sienta	sintiera	sienta Ud.
	sentimos	sentíamos	sentimos	sentiremos	sentiríamos	sintamos	sintiéramos	sintamos
	sentís	sentíais	sentisteis	sentiréis	sentiríais	sintáis	sintierais	sentid (no sintáis)
	sienten	sentían	sintieron	sentirán	sentirían	sientan	sintieran	sientan Uds.

34

Infinitive	INDICATIVE					SUBJUNCTIVE		IMPERATIVE
	Present	Imperfect	Preterite	Future	Conditional	Present	Past	
volver (o:ue)	**vuelvo**	volvía	volví	volveré	volvería	**vuelva**	volviera	
	vuelves	volvías	volviste	volverás	volverías	**vuelvas**	volvieras	**vuelve** tú (no **vuelvas**)
	vuelve	volvía	volvió	volverá	volvería	**vuelva**	volviera	**vuelva** Ud.
Participles:	volvemos	volvíamos	volvimos	volveremos	volveríamos	volvamos	volviéramos	volvamos
volviendo	volvéis	volvíais	volvisteis	volveréis	volveríais	volváis	volvierais	volved (no **volváis**)
vuelto	**vuelven**	volvían	volvieron	volverán	volverían	**vuelvan**	volvieran	**vuelvan** Uds.

Verbs with spelling changes only

35

Infinitive	INDICATIVE					SUBJUNCTIVE		IMPERATIVE
	Present	Imperfect	Preterite	Future	Conditional	Present	Past	
conocer (c:zc)	**conozco**	conocía	conocí	conoceré	conocería	**conozca**	conociera	
	conoces	conocías	conociste	conocerás	conocerías	**conozcas**	conocieras	conoce tú (no **conozcas**)
	conoce	conocía	conoció	conocerá	conocería	**conozca**	conociera	**conozca** Ud.
Participles:	conocemos	conocíamos	conocimos	conoceremos	conoceríamos	**conozcamos**	conociéramos	**conozcamos**
conociendo	conocéis	conocíais	conocisteis	conoceréis	conoceríais	**conozcáis**	conocierais	conoced (no **conozcáis**)
conocido	conocen	conocían	conocieron	conocerán	conocerían	**conozcan**	conocieran	**conozcan** Uds.

36

Infinitive	INDICATIVE					SUBJUNCTIVE		IMPERATIVE
	Present	Imperfect	Preterite	Future	Conditional	Present	Past	
creer (y)	creo	creía	**creí**	creeré	creería	crea	**creyera**	
	crees	creías	**creíste**	creerás	creerías	creas	**creyeras**	cree tú (no creas)
	cree	creía	**creyó**	creerá	creería	crea	**creyera**	crea Ud.
Participles:	creemos	creíamos	**creímos**	creeremos	creeríamos	creamos	**creyéramos**	creamos
creyendo	creéis	creíais	**creísteis**	creeréis	creeríais	creáis	**creyerais**	creed (no creáis)
creído	creen	creían	**creyeron**	creerán	creerían	crean	**creyeran**	crean Uds.

37

Infinitive	INDICATIVE					SUBJUNCTIVE		IMPERATIVE
	Present	Imperfect	Preterite	Future	Conditional	Present	Past	
cruzar (c)	cruzo	cruzaba	**crucé**	cruzaré	cruzaría	**cruce**	cruzara	
	cruzas	cruzabas	cruzaste	cruzarás	cruzarías	**cruces**	cruzaras	cruza tú (no **cruces**)
	cruza	cruzaba	cruzó	cruzará	cruzaría	**cruce**	cruzara	**cruce** Ud.
Participles:	cruzamos	cruzábamos	cruzamos	cruzaremos	cruzaríamos	**crucemos**	cruzáramos	**crucemos**
cruzando	cruzáis	cruzabais	cruzasteis	cruzaréis	cruzaríais	**crucéis**	cruzarais	cruzad (no **crucéis**)
cruzado	cruzan	cruzaban	cruzaron	cruzarán	cruzarían	**crucen**	cruzaran	**crucen** Uds.

38

Infinitive	INDICATIVE					SUBJUNCTIVE		IMPERATIVE
	Present	Imperfect	Preterite	Future	Conditional	Present	Past	
destruir (y)	**destruyo**	destruía	destruí	destruiré	destruiría	**destruya**	**destruyera**	
	destruyes	destruías	destruiste	destruirás	destruirías	**destruyas**	**destruyeras**	**destruye** tú (no **destruyas**)
	destruye	destruía	**destruyó**	destruirá	destruiría	**destruya**	**destruyera**	**destruya** Ud.
Participles:	destruimos	destruíamos	destruimos	destruiremos	destruiríamos	**destruyamos**	**destruyéramos**	**destruyamos**
destruyendo	destruís	destruíais	destruisteis	destruiréis	destruiríais	**destruyáis**	**destruyerais**	destruid (no **destruyáis**)
destruido	**destruyen**	destruían	**destruyeron**	destruirán	destruirían	**destruyan**	**destruyeran**	**destruyan** Uds.

39

Infinitive	INDICATIVE					SUBJUNCTIVE		IMPERATIVE
	Present	Imperfect	Preterite	Future	Conditional	Present	Past	
enviar (envío)	**envío**	enviaba	envié	enviaré	enviaría	**envíe**	enviara	
	envías	enviabas	enviaste	enviarás	enviarías	**envíes**	enviaras	**envía** tú (no **envíes**)
	envía	enviaba	envió	enviará	enviaría	**envíe**	enviara	**envíe** Ud.
Participles:	enviamos	enviábamos	enviamos	enviaremos	enviaríamos	**enviemos**	enviáramos	enviemos
enviando	enviáis	enviabais	enviasteis	enviaréis	enviaríais	**enviéis**	enviarais	enviad (no **enviéis**)
enviado	**envían**	enviaban	enviaron	enviarán	enviarían	**envíen**	enviaran	**envíen** Uds.

40 graduarse (gradúo)
Participles: graduando, graduado

	INDICATIVE					SUBJUNCTIVE		IMPERATIVE
	Present	Imperfect	Preterite	Future	Conditional	Present	Past	
	gradúo	graduaba	gradué	graduaré	graduaría	gradúe	graduara	
	gradúas	graduabas	graduaste	graduarás	graduarías	gradúes	graduaras	gradúa tú (no gradúes)
	gradúa	graduaba	graduó	graduará	graduaría	gradúe	graduara	gradúe Ud.
	graduamos	graduábamos	graduamos	graduaremos	graduaríamos	graduemos	graduáramos	graduemos
	graduáis	graduabais	graduasteis	graduaréis	graduaríais	graduéis	graduarais	graduad (no graduéis)
	gradúan	graduaban	graduaron	graduarán	graduarían	gradúen	graduaran	gradúen Uds.

41 llegar (gu)
Participles: llegando, llegado

	INDICATIVE					SUBJUNCTIVE		IMPERATIVE
	Present	Imperfect	Preterite	Future	Conditional	Present	Past	
	llego	llegaba	llegué	llegaré	llegaría	llegue	llegara	
	llegas	llegabas	llegaste	llegarás	llegarías	llegues	llegaras	llega tú (no llegues)
	llega	llegaba	llegó	llegará	llegaría	llegue	llegara	llegue Ud.
	llegamos	llegábamos	llegamos	llegaremos	llegaríamos	lleguemos	llegáramos	lleguemos
	llegáis	llegabais	llegasteis	llegaréis	llegaríais	lleguéis	llegarais	llegad (no lleguéis)
	llegan	llegaban	llegaron	llegarán	llegarían	lleguen	llegaran	lleguen Uds.

42 proteger (j)
Participles: protegiendo, protegido

	INDICATIVE					SUBJUNCTIVE		IMPERATIVE
	Present	Imperfect	Preterite	Future	Conditional	Present	Past	
	protejo	protegía	protegí	protegeré	protegería	proteja	protegiera	
	proteges	protegías	protegiste	protegerás	protegerías	protejas	protegieras	protege tú (no protejas)
	protege	protegía	protegió	protegerá	protegería	proteja	protegiera	proteja Ud.
	protegemos	protegíamos	protegimos	protegeremos	protegeríamos	protejamos	protegiéramos	protejamos
	protegéis	protegíais	protegisteis	protegeréis	protegeríais	protejáis	protegierais	proteged (no protejáis)
	protegen	protegían	protegieron	protegerán	protegerían	protejan	protegieran	protejan Uds.

43 tocar (qu)
Participles: tocando, tocado

	INDICATIVE					SUBJUNCTIVE		IMPERATIVE
	Present	Imperfect	Preterite	Future	Conditional	Present	Past	
	toco	tocaba	toqué	tocaré	tocaría	toque	tocara	
	tocas	tocabas	tocaste	tocarás	tocarías	toques	tocaras	toca tú (no toques)
	toca	tocaba	tocó	tocará	tocaría	toque	tocara	toque Ud.
	tocamos	tocábamos	tocamos	tocaremos	tocaríamos	toquemos	tocáramos	toquemos
	tocáis	tocabais	tocasteis	tocaréis	tocaríais	toquéis	tocarais	tocad (no toquéis)
	tocan	tocaban	tocaron	tocarán	tocarían	toquen	tocaran	toquen Uds.

Guide to Vocabulary

Note on alphabetization

Formerly, **ch**, **ll**, and **ñ** were considered separate letters in the Spanish alphabet, **ch** appearing after **c**, **ll** after **l**, and **ñ** after **n**. In current practice, for purposes of alphabetization, **ch** and **ll** are not treated as separate letters, but **ñ** still follows **n**. Therefore, in this glossary you will find that **año**, for example, appears after **anuncio**.

Abbreviations used in this glossary

adj.	adjective	*interj.*	interjection	*poss.*	possessive
adv.	adverb	*i.o.*	indirect object	*prep.*	preposition
conj.	conjunction	*m.*	masculine	*pron.*	pronoun
d.o.	direct object	*n.*	noun	*ref.*	reflexive
f.	feminine	*obj.*	object	*sing.*	singular
fam.	familiar	*p.p.*	past participle	*sub.*	subject
form.	formal	*pl.*	plural	*v.*	verb

Spanish-English

A

a *prep.* at; to 1
  ¿A qué hora...? At what time . . . ? 1
  a bordo aboard 1
  a dieta on a diet 15
  a la derecha to the right 2
  a la izquierda to the left 2
  a la plancha grilled 8
  a la(s) + *time* at + *time* 1
  a menos que unless 13
  a menudo often 10
  a nombre de in the name of 5
  a plazos in installments 14
  A sus órdenes. At your service. 11
  a tiempo on time 10
  a veces sometimes 10
  a ver let's see 2
¡Abajo! *adv.* Down! 15
abeja *f.* bee
abierto/a *p.p.* open 5
abogado/a *m., f.* lawyer
abrazar(se) *v.* to hug; to embrace (each other) 11
abrazo *m.* hug
abrigo *m.* coat 6
abril *m.* April 5
abrir *v.* to open 3
abuelo/a *m., f.* grandfather; grandmother 3
abuelos *pl.* grandparents 3
aburrido/a *adj.* bored; boring 5
aburrir *v.* to bore 7
aburrirse *v.* to get bored
acabar de (+ *inf.*) *v.* to have just (*done something*) 6
acampar *v.* to camp 5
accidente *m.* accident 10
acción *f.* action
aceite *m.* oil 8

ácido/a *adj.* acid 13
acompañar *v.* to go with; to accompany 14
aconsejar *v.* to advise 12
acontecimiento *m.* event
acordarse (de) (o:ue) *v.* to remember 7
acostarse (o:ue) *v.* to go to bed 7
activo/a *adj.* active 15
actor *m.* actor
actriz *f.* actor
actualidades *f., pl.* news; current events
acuático/a *adj.* aquatic 4
adelgazar *v.* to lose weight; to slim down 15
además (de) *adv.* furthermore; besides; in addition (to) 10
adicional *adj.* additional
adiós *m.* good-bye 1
adjetivo *m.* adjective
administración de empresas *f.* business administration 2
adolescencia *f.* adolescence 9
¿adónde? *adv.* where? (destination) 2
aduana *f.* customs 5
aeróbico/a *adj.*, aerobic 15
aeropuerto *m.* airport 5
afectado/a *adj.* affected 13
afeitarse *v.* to shave 7
aficionado/a *adj.* fan 4
afirmativo/a *adj.* affirmative
afueras *f., pl.* suburbs; outskirts 12
agencia de viajes *f.* travel agency 5
agente de viajes *m., f.* travel agent 5
agosto *m.* August 5
agradable *adj.* pleasant 5
agua *f.* water 8
  agua mineral mineral water 8
ahora *adv.* now 2
  ahora mismo right now 5

ahorrar *v.* to save money 14
ahorros *m.* savings 14
aire *m.* air 6
ajo *m.* garlic 8
al (*contraction of* **a + el**) 2
  al aire libre open-air 6
  al contado in cash 14
  al este to the east 14
  al fondo (de) at the end (of) 12
  al lado de beside 2
  al norte to the north 14
  al oeste to the west 14
  al sur to the south 14
alcoba *f.* bedroom 12
alcohol *m.* alcohol 15
alcohólico/a *adj.* alcoholic 15
alegrarse (de) *v.* to be happy 13
alegre *adj.* happy; joyful 5
alegría *f.* joy 9
alemán, alemana *adj.* German 3
alérgico/a *adj.* allergic 10
alfombra *f.* carpet; rug 12
algo *pron.* something; anything 7
algodón *m.* cotton 6
alguien *pron.* someone; somebody; anyone 7
algún, alguno/a(s) *adj.* any; some 7
aliviar *v.* to ease; alleviate 15
  aliviar el estrés/la tensión to reduce stress/tension 15
allí *adv.* there 5
  allí mismo right there 14
almacén *m.* department store 6
almohada *f.* pillow 12
almorzar (o:ue) *v.* to have lunch 8
almuerzo *m.* lunch 8
aló *interj.* hello (*on the telephone*) 11
alquilar *v.* to rent 12
alquiler *m.* rent 12

alternador *m.* alternator 11
altillo *m.* attic 12
alto/a *adj.* tall 3
aluminio *m.* aluminum 13
amable *adj.* nice; friendly 5
ama de casa *f.* housekeeper; caretaker; housewife 12
amarillo/a *adj.* yellow 6
amigo/a *m., f.* friend 3
amistad *f.* friendship 9
amor *m.* love 9
anaranjado/a *adj.* orange 6
animal *m.* animal 13
aniversario (de bodas) *m.* (wedding) anniversary 9
anoche *adv.* last night 6
anteayer *adv.* the day before yesterday 6
antes *adv.* before 7
    antes (de) que *conj.* before 13
    antes de *prep.* before 7
antibiótico *m.* antibiotic 10
antipático/a *adj.* unpleasant 3
anunciar *v.* to announce; to advertise
anuncio *m.* advertisement
año *m.* year 2, 5
el año pasado *last* year 6
apagar *v.* to turn off 11
aparato *m.* appliance 12
apartamento *m.* apartment 12
apellido *m.* last name 9
apenas *adv.* hardly; scarcely; just 10
aplaudir *v.* to applaud
apreciar *v.* to appreciate
aprender *v.* to learn 3
apurarse *v.* to hurry; to rush 15
aquel, aquella *adj.* that; those (over there) 6
aquél, aquélla *pron.* that; those (over there) 6
aquello *neuter, pron.* that; that thing; that fact 6
aquellos/as *pl. adj.* that; those (over there) 6
aquéllos/as *pl. pron.* those (ones) (over there) 6
aquí *adv.* here 1
    Aquí está... Here it is . . . 5
    Aquí estamos en... Here we are in . . . 2
    aquí mismo right here 11
árbol *m.* tree 13
archivo *m.* file 11
armario *m.* closet 12
arqueólogo/a *m., f.* archaeologist
arquitecto/a *m., f.* architect
arrancar *v.* to start (*a car*) 11
arreglar *v.* to fix; to arrange 11
arriba *adv.* up 15
arroz *m.* rice 8
arte *m.* art 2
artes *f., pl.* arts

artesanía *f.* craftsmanship; crafts
artículo *m.* article
artista *m., f.* artist 3
artístico/a *adj.* artistic
arveja *m.* pea 8
asado/a *adj.* roasted 8
ascenso *m.* promotion
ascensor *m.* elevator 5
así *adj.* thus; so (*in such a way*) 10
    así así so so 1
asistir (a) *v.* to attend 3
aspiradora *f.* vacuum cleaner 12
aspirante *m. f.* candidate; applicant
aspirina *f.* aspirin 10
atún *m.* tuna 8
aumentar *v.* **de peso** to gain weight 15
aumento *m.* increase
    aumento de sueldo pay raise
aunque although
autobús *m.* bus 1
automático/a *adj.* automatic 14
auto(móvil) *m.* auto(mobile) 5
autopista *f.* highway 11
ave *f.* bird 13
avenida *f.* avenue 11
aventura *f.* adventure
avergonzado/a *adj.* embarrassed 5
avión *m.* airplane 5
¡Ay! *interj.* Oh! 10
    ¡Ay, qué dolor! Oh, what pain! 10
ayer *adv.* yesterday 6
ayudar (a) *v.* to help 12
ayudarse *v.* to help each other 11
azúcar *m.* sugar 8
azul *adj. m., f.* blue 6

B

bailar *v.* to dance 2
bailarín/bailarina *m., f.* dancer
baile *m.* dance
bajar(se) *v.* to go down; to get off (of) 11
bajo/a *adj.* short (*in height*) 3
bajo control under control 7
balcón *m.* balcony 12
ballet *m.* ballet
baloncesto *m.* basketball 4
banana *f.* banana 8
banco *m.* bank 14
banda *f.* band
bandera *f.* flag
bañarse *v.* to bathe take a bath 7
baño *m.* bathroom 7
barato/a *adj.* cheap 6
barco *m.* ship 5

barrer *v.* to sweep 12
    barrer el suelo *v.* to sweep the floor 12
barrio *m.* neighborhood 12
bastante *adv.* enough; rather 10; pretty
basura *f.* trash 12
baúl *m.* trunk 11
beber *v.* to drink 3
bebida *f.* drink 8
béisbol *m.* baseball 4
bellas artes *f., pl.* fine arts
belleza *f.* beauty 14
beneficio *m.* benefit
besar(se) *v.* to kiss (each other) 11
beso *m.* kiss 9
biblioteca *f.* library 2
bicicleta *f.* bicycle 4
bien *adj.* good well 1
bienestar *m.* well-being 15
bienvenido/a *adj.* welcome 12
billete *m.* paper money 8
billón *m.* trillion 5
biología *f.* biology 2
bistec *m.* steak 8
bizcocho *m.* biscuit 9
blanco/a *adj.* white 6
bluejeans *m., pl.* jeans 6
blusa *f.* blouse 6
boca *f.* mouth 10
boda *f.* wedding 9
boleto *m.* ticket
bolsa *f.* purse, bag 6
bombero/a *m., f.* firefighter
bonito/a *adj.* pretty 3
borrador *m.* eraser 2
bosque *m.* forest 13
    bosque tropical tropical forest; rainforest 13
bota *f.* boot 6
botella *f.* bottle 9
    botella de vino bottle of wine 9
botones *m., sing.* bellhop 5
brazo *m.* arm 10
brindar *v.* to toast (*drink*) 9
bucear *v.* to (scuba) dive 4
bueno *adv.* well 2
bueno/a, buen *adj.* good 3, 6
    Buen viaje. Have a good trip. 1
    buena forma good shape (*physical*) 15
    Buena idea. Good idea. 4
    Buenas noches. Good evening; Good night. 1
    Buenas tardes. Good afternoon. 1
    buenísimo extremely good 8
    ¿Bueno? Hello. (*on telephone*) 11
    Buenos días. Good morning. 1
bulevar *m.* boulevard 11
buscar *v.* to look for 2
buzón *m.* mailbox 14

C

caballo *m.* horse 5
cabaña *f.* cabin 5
cabe: no cabe duda (de) que...
there's no doubt that ... 13
cabeza *f.* head 10
cada *adj. m., f.* each 6
caerse *v.* to fall (down) 10
café *m.* café 4; *adj. m., f.* brown
6; coffee 8
cafetera *f.* coffee maker 12
cafetería *f.* cafeteria 2
caído/a *p.p.* fallen 14
caja *f.* cash register 6
cajero/a *m., f.* cashier 14
cajero automático *m.* automatic teller machine (ATM) 14
calcetín *m.* sock 6
calculadora *f.* calculator 11
caldo *m.* soup 8
caldo de patas *m.* beef soup 8
calentarse *v.* to warm up 15
calidad *f.* quality 6
calle *m.* street 11
calor *m.* heat 4
caloría *f.* calorie 15
calzar *v.* to take size ... shoes 6
cama *f.* bed 5
cámara *f.* camera 11
cámara de video *f.* videocamera
11
camarero/a *m., f.* waiter 8
camarón *m.* shrimp 8
cambiar (de) *v.* to change 9
cambio *m.* de moneda currency
exchange 8
caminar *v.* to walk 2
camino *m.* road 11
camión *m* truck; bus
camisa *f.* shirt 6
camiseta *f.* t-shirt 6
campo *m.* countryside 5
canadiense *adj.* Canadian 3
canal *m.* channel (TV) 11
canción *f.* song
candidato/a *m., f.* candidate
cansado/a *adj.* tired 5
cantante *m., f.* singer
cantar *v.* to sing 2
capital *f.* capital (city) 1
capó *m.* hood 11
cara *f.* face 7
caramelo *m.* caramel 9
carne *f.* meat 8
carne de res *f.* beef 8
carnicería *f.* butcher shop 14
caro/a *adj.* expensive 6
carpintero/a *m., f.* carpenter
carrera *f.* career
carretera *f.* highway 11
carro *m.* car; automobile 11
carta *f.* letter 4; *(playing)* card 5
cartel *m.* poster 12

cartera *f.* wallet 6
cartero *m.* mail carrier 14
casa *f.* house; home 4
casado/a *adj.* married 9
casarse (con) *v.* to get married
(to) 9
casi *adv.* almost 10
catorce *adj.* fourteen 1
cebolla *f.* onion 8
celebrar *v.* to celebrate 9
celular *adj.* cellular 11
cena *f.* dinner 8
cenar *v.* to have dinner 8
centro *m.* downtown 4
centro comercial shopping
mall 6
cepillarse los dientes/el pelo
v. to brush one's teeth/one's
hair 7
cerámica *f.* pottery
cerca de *prep.* near 2
cerdo *m.* pork 8
cereales *m., pl.* cereal; grains 8
cero *m.* zero 1
cerrado/a *p.p.* closed 5
cerrar (e:ie) *v.* to close 4
cerveza *f.* beer 8
césped *m.* grass 13
ceviche *m.* marinated fish dish 8
ceviche de camarón *m.*
marinated shrimp 8
chaleco *m.* vest 6
champán *m.* champagne
champiñón *m.* mushroom 8
champú *m.* shampoo 7
chaqueta *f.* jacket 6
chau *fam. interj.* bye 1
cheque *m.* (bank) check 14
cheque de viajero *m.* traveler's
check 14
chévere *adj., fam.* terrific
chico/a *adj.* boy/girl 1
chino/a *adj.* Chinese 3
chocar (con) *v.* to run into 11
chocolate *m.* chocolate 9
choque *m.* collision
chuleta *f.* chop *(food)* 8
chuleta de cerdo *f.* pork
chop 8
ciclismo *m.* cycling 4
cielo *m.* sky 13
cien(to) one hundred 5
ciencia *f.* science 2
ciencia ficción *f.* science
fiction
científico/a *m., f.* scientist
cierto *m.* certain; true 13
cifra *f.* figure
cinco five 1
cincuenta fifty 2
cine *m.* movie theater 4
cinta *f.* (audio)tape 11
cinturón *m.* belt 6
circulación *f.* traffic 11

cita *f.* date; appointment 9
ciudad *f.* city 4
ciudadano/a *adj.* citizen
claro que sí *fam.* of course
clase *f.* class 2
clase de ejercicios aeróbicos
f. aerobics class 15
clásico/a *adj.* classical
cliente/a *m., f.* customer 6
clínica *f.* clinic 10
cobrar *v.* to cash a check 14
coche *m.* car; automobile 11
cocina *f.* kitchen; stove 12
cocinar *v.* to cook 12
cocinero/a *m., f.* cook, chef
cola *f.* line 14
colesterol *m.* cholesterol 15
color *m.* color 6
comedia *f.* comedy; play
comedor *m.* dining room 12
comenzar (e:ie) *v.* to begin 4
comer *v.* to eat 3
comercial *adj.* commercial;
business-related
comida *f.* food; meal 8
como like; as 8
¿cómo? what; how 1
¿Cómo es...? What's... like? 3
¿Cómo está Ud.? *form.*
How are you? 1
¿Cómo estás? *fam.* How are
you? 1
¿Cómo les fue...? *pl.* How did
. . . go for you? 15
¿Cómo se llama (Ud.)?
(form.) What's your name? 1
¿Cómo te llamas (tú)? *(fam.)*
What's your name? 1
cómoda *f.* chest of drawers 12
cómodo/a *adj.* comfortable 5
compañero/a de clase *m., f.*
classmate 2
compañero/a de cuarto *m., f.*
roommate 2
compañía *f.* company; firm
compartir *v.* to share 3
completamente *adv.* completely
compositor(a) *m., f.* composer
comprar *v.* to buy 2
compras *f., pl.* purchases 5
ir de compras go shopping
comprender *v.* to understand 3
comprobar *v.* to check
comprometerse (con) *v.* to get
engaged (to) 9
computación *f.* computer science 2
computadora *f.* computer 1
computadora portátil *f.*
portable computer; laptop 11
comunicación *f.* communication
comunicarse (con) *v.* to communicate (with)
comunidad *f.* community 1
con *prep.* with 2

Con él/ella habla. This is he/she. (*on telephone*) 11

con frecuencia *adv.* frequently 10

Con permiso. Pardon me., Excuse me. 1

con tal (de) que provided (that) 13

concierto *m.* concert

concordar *v.* to agree 8

concurso *m.* contest; game show

conducir *v.* to drive 8, 11

conductor(a) *m., f.* chauffeur; driver 1

confirmar *v.* to confirm 5

confirmar *v.* **la reservación** *f.* to confirm the reservation 5

congelador *m.* freezer 12

congestionado/a *adj.* congested; stuffed-up 10

conmigo *pron.* with me 4

conocer *v.* to know; to be acquainted with 8

conocido *adj.* known 2

conseguir (e:i) *v.* to get; to obtain 4

consejero/a *m., f.* counselor; advisor

consejo *m.* advice 9

conservación *f.* conservation 13

conservar *v.* to conserve 13

construir *v.* build 4

consultorio *m.* doctor's office 10

consumir *v.* consume 15

contabilidad *f.* accounting 2

contador(a) *m., f.* accountant

contaminación *f.* pollution; contamination 4

contaminación del aire/del agua air/water pollution 13

contaminado/a *adj.* polluted 13

contaminar *v.* to pollute 13

contar (con) *v.* to count (on) 12

contento/a *adj.* happy; content 5

contestadora *f.* answering machine 11

contestar *v.* to answer 2

contigo *fam. pron.* with you 8

contratar *v.* to hire

control *m.* control 7

control remoto remote control 11

controlar *v.* to control 13

conversación *f.* conversation 2

conversar *v.* to talk 2

copa *f.* wineglass; goblet 12

corazón *m.* heart 10

corbata *f.* tie 6

corredor(a) *m., f.* **de bolsa** stockbroker

correo *m.* post office; mail 14

correo electrónico *m.* e-mail 4

correr *v.* to run; to jog 3

cortesía *f.* courtesy 1

cortinas *f., pl.* curtains 12

corto/a *adj.* short (*in length*) 6

cosa *f.* thing 1

costar (o:ue) *f.* to cost 6

cráter *m.* crater 13

creer (en) *v.* to believe (in) 3

creído/a *p.p.* believed 14

crema de afeitar *f.* shaving cream 7

crimen *m.* crime; murder

cruzar *v.* to cross 14

cuaderno *m.* notebook 1

cuadra *f.* city block 14

¿cuál(es)? which?; which ones?; what? 2

¿Cuál es la fecha (de hoy)? What is the date (today)? 5

cuadro *m.* picture 12

cuadros *m., pl.* plaid 6

cuando when 7

¿cuándo? when? 2

¿cuánto/a(s)? how much?, how many? 1

¿Cuánto cuesta...? How much does . . . cost? 6

¿Cuántos años tienes? How old are you? 3

cuarenta forty 2

cuarto de baño *m.* bathroom 7

cuarto *m.* room 7

cuarto/a *adj.* fourth 5

menos cuarto quarter to (time)

y cuarto quarter after (time)

cuatro four 1

cuatrocientos/as *m., f.* four hundred 5

cubiertos *m., pl.* silverware

cubierto/a *p.p.* covered 14

cubrir *v.* to cover 14

cuchara *f.* tablespoon 12

cuchillo *m.* knife 12

cuello *m.* neck 10

cuenta *f.* bill 9; account 14

cuenta corriente *f.* checking account 14

cuenta de ahorros *f.* savings account 14

cuento *m.* story

cuerpo *m.* body 10

cuidado *m.* care 3

cuidar *v.* to take care of 13

cultura *f.* culture

cumpleaños *m., sing.* birthday 9

cumplir años *v.* to have a birthday 9

cuñado/a *m., f.* brother-in-law; sister-in-law 3

currículum *m.* résumé; curriculum vitae

curso *m.* course 2

D

danza *f.* dance

dañar *v.* to damage; to breakdown 11

dar *v.* to give 9

dar direcciones *v.* to give directions 14

dar un consejo *v.* to give advice 9

darse con *v.* to bump into; to run into 10

de *prep.* of; from 1

¿De dónde eres (tú)? *fam.* Where are you from? 1

¿De dónde es (Ud.)? *form.* Where are you from? 1

¿De parte de quién? Who is calling? (*on telephone*) 11

¿de quién? whose (*sing.*) 1

¿de quiénes? whose (*pl.*) 1

de algodón (made of) cotton 6

de aluminio (made of) aluminum 13

de compras shopping 5

de cuadros plaid 6

de excursión hiking 4

de hecho in fact 5

de ida y vuelta roundtrip 5

de la mañana in the morning; A.M. 1

de la noche in the evening; at night; P.M. 1

de la tarde in the afternoon; in the early evening; P.M. 1

de lana (made of) wool 6

de lunares polka-dotted 6

de mi vida of my life 15

de moda in fashion 6

De nada. You're welcome. 1

de ninguna manera no way

de niño/a as a child 10

de parte de on behalf of 11

de plástico (made of) plastic 13

de rayas striped 6

de repente suddenly 6

de seda (made of) silk 6

de vaqueros western (genre)

de vez en cuando from time to time 10

de vidrio (made of) glass 13

debajo de *prep.* below; under 2

deber (+ infin.) *v.* to have to (*do something*), should (*do something*) 3

deber *m.* responsibility; obligation

debido a due to 3

débil *adj.* weak 15

decidido/a *adj.* decided 14

decidir *v.* to decide 3

décimo/a *adj.* tenth 5

decir *v.* **(que)** to say (that); to tell (that) 9

declarar *v.* to declare; to say

dedo *m.* finger 10

deforestación *f.* deforestation 13

dejar *v.* to let 12; to quit; to leave behind

dejar de *(+ inf.)* *v.* to stop (*doing something*) 13

dejar una propina *v.* to leave a tip 9

del (*contraction of* **de** + **el**) of the; from the 1

delante de *prep.* in front of 2

delgado/a *adj.* thin; slender 3

delicioso/a *adj.* delicious 8

demás *pron.* the rest 5

demasiado *adv.* too much 6

dentista *m., f.* dentist 10

dentro de within

dependiente/a *m., f.* clerk 6

deporte *m.* sport 4

deportista *m.* sports person 1

deportivo/a *adj.* sports-loving 4

depositar *v.* to deposit 14

derecha *f.* right 2

derecho/a *adj.* straight 14

derechos *m.* rights

desarrollar *v.* to develop 13

desastre natural *m.* natural disaster

desayunar *v.* to have breakfast 8

desayuno *m.* breakfast 8

descafeinado/a *adj.* decaffeinated 15

descansar *v.* to rest 2

descompuesto/a *adj.* not working; out-of-order 11

describir *v.* to describe 3

descrito/a *p.p.* described 14

descubierto/a *p.p.* discovered 14

descubrir *v.* to discover 13

desde from; since 6

desear *v.* to wish; to desire 2

desempleo *m.* unemployment

desierto *m.* desert 13

desigualdad *f.* inequality

desordenado/a *adj.* disorderly 5

despacio *adj.* slowly 8

despedida *f.* farewell; good-bye

despedir (e:i) *v.* fire

despedirse (de) (e:i) *v.* to say good-bye (to) 7

despejado/a *adj.* clear (*weather*) 4

despertador *m.* alarm clock 7

despertarse (e:ie) *v.* to wake up 7

después *adv.* afterwards; then 7

después de after 7

después (de) que *conj.* after 14

destruir *v.* to destroy 13

detrás de *prep.* behind 2

día *m.* day 1

día de fiesta holiday 9

diario *m.* diary 1; newspaper

diario/a *adj.* daily 7

dibujar *v.* to draw 2

dibujo *m.* drawing

dibujos animados *m., pl.* cartoons

diccionario *m.* dictionary 1

dicho/a *p.p.* said 14

diciembre *m.* December 5

dictadura *f.* dictatorship

diecinueve nineteen 1

dieciocho eighteen 1

dieciséis sixteen 1

diecisiete seventeen 1

diente *m.* tooth 7

dieta *f.* diet 15

dieta equilibrada balanced diet 15

diez ten 1

difícil *adj.* hard; difficult 3

Diga. Hello. (*on telephone*) 11

diligencia *f.* errand 14

dinero *m.* money 6

dirección *f.* address 14

direcciones *f., pl.* directions 14

director(a) *m., f.* director; (*musical*) conductor

disco *m.* (computer) disk 11

disco compacto compact disc (CD) 11

discriminación *f.* discrimination

discurso *m.* speech

diseñador(a) *m., f.* designer

diseño *m.* design

disfrutar (de) *v.* to enjoy; to reap the benefits (of) 15

diversión *f.* fun activity 4

divertido/a *adj.* fun 7

divertirse (e:ie) *v.* to have fun 9

divorciado/a *adj.* divorced 9

divorciarse (de) *v.* to get divorced (from) 9

divorcio *m.* divorce 9

doblar *v.* to turn 14

doce twelve 1

doble *adj.* double

doctor(a) *m., f.* doctor 3

documental *m.* documentary

documentos de viaje *m., pl.* travel documents

doler (o:ue) *v.* to hurt 10

dolor *m.* ache; pain 10

dolor de cabeza *m.* headache 10

doméstico/a *adj.* domestic

domingo *m.* Sunday 2

don/doña title of respect used with a person's first name 1

donde *prep.* where

¿Dónde está...? Where is . . . ? 2

¿dónde? where? 1

dormir (o:ue) *v.* to sleep 4

dormirse (o:ue) *v.* to go to sleep; to fall asleep 7

dos two 1

dos veces *f.* twice; two times 6

doscientos/as *m.* two hundred 5

drama *m.* drama; play

dramático/a *adj.* dramatic

dramaturgo/a *m., f.* playwright

droga *f.* drug 15

drogadicto/a *adj.* drug addict 15

ducha *f.* shower 7

ducharse *v.* to shower; to take a shower 7

duda *f.* doubt 13

dudar *v.* to doubt 13

dueño/a *m., f.* owner; landlord 8

dulces *m., pl.* sweets; candy 9

durante *prep.* during 7

durar *v.* to last

E

e *conj.* (*used instead of* ***y*** *before words beginning with* ***i*** *and* ***hi***) and 4

echar *v.* to throw 14

echar una carta al buzón *v.* to throw a letter in the mailbox 14

ecología *f.* ecology 13

economía *f.* economics 2

ecoturismo *m.* ecotourism 13

Ecuador *m.* Ecuador 1

ecuatoriano/a *adj.* Ecuadorian 3

edad *f.* age 8

edificio *m.* building 12

efectivo *m.* cash 14

ejercicio *m.* exercise 15

ejercicios aeróbicos *m.* aerobic exercises 15

ejercicios de estiramiento stretching exercises 15

ejército *m.* army

el *m., sing.* the 1

él *sub. pron.* he 1; *adj. pron.* him 1

elección *f.* election

electricista *m., f.* electrician

elegante *adj. m., f.* elegant 6

elegir *v.* to elect

ella *sub. pron.* she 1; *obj. pron.* her 1

ellos/as *sub. pron.* they 1; them 1

embarazada *adj.* pregnant 10

emergencia *f.* emergency 10

emitir *v.* to broadcast 18

emocionante *adj. m., f.* exciting

empezar (e:ie) *v.* to begin 4

empleado/a *m., f.* employee 5

empleo *m.* job; employment

empresa *f.* company; firm

en *prep.* in; on 2

en casa at home 7

en caso (de) que in case (that) 13

en cuanto as soon as 14

en efectivo in cash 14

en exceso in excess; too much 15

en línea in-line 4

¡En marcha! Forward march! 15

en mi nombre in my name 5

en punto on the dot; exactly; sharp (*time*) 1

en qué in what; how 2

¿En qué puedo servirles?
How may I help you? 5
enamorado/a *adj.* (de) in love
with 5
enamorarse (de) *v.* to fall in love
(with) 9
encantado/a *adj.* delighted;
pleased to meet you 1
encantar *v.* to like very much; to
love (*inanimate things*) 7
encima de *prep.* on top of 2
encontrar (o:ue) *v.* to find 4
encontrar(se) *v.* to meet (each
other); to find (each other) 11
encuesta *f.* poll; survey
energía *f.* energy 13
enero *m.* January 5
enfermarse *v.* to get sick 10
enfermedad *f.* illness 10
enfermero/a *m., f.* nurse 10
enfermo/a *adj.* sick 10
enfrente de *adv.* opposite; facing
14
engordar *v.* to gain weight 15
enojado/a *adj.* mad; angry 5
enojarse (con) *v.* to get angry
(with) 7
ensalada *f.* salad 8
enseguida *adv.* right away 9
enseñar *v.* to teach 2
ensuciar *v.* to dirty; to get dirty 12
entender (e:ie) *v.* to understand 4
entonces *adv.* then 7
entrada *f.* entrance 12; ticket
entre *prep.* between; among 2
entremeses *m., pl.* hors
d'oeuvres; appetizers 8
entrenarse *v.* to practice; to train
15
entrevista *f.* interview
entrevistador(a) *m., f.* interviewer
entrevistar *v.* to interview
envase *m.* container 13
enviar *v.* to send; to mail 14
equilibrado/a *adj.* balanced 15
equipado/a *adj.* equipped 15
equipaje *m.* luggage 5
equipo *m.* team 4
equivocado/a *adj.* mistaken;
wrong 5
eres *fam.* you are 1
es he/she/it is 1
Es (una) lástima que... It's a
shame that . . . 13
Es bueno que... It's good
that . . . 12
Es de... He/She is from . . . 1
Es extraño que... It's strange
that . . . 13
Es importante que... It's
important that . . . 12
Es imposible que... It's
impossible that . . . 13
Es improbable que... It's
improbable that . . . 13

Es la una. It's one o'clock. 1
Es malo que... It's bad
that . . . 12
Es mejor que... It's better
that . . . 12
Es necesario que... It's
necessary that . . . 12
Es obvio que... It's
obvious that . . . 13
Es ridículo que... It's
ridiculous that . . . 13
Es seguro que... It's sure
that . . . 13
Es terrible que... It's terrible
that . . . 13
Es triste que... It's sad that . . .
13
Es urgente que... It's urgent
that . . . 12
Es verdad que... It's true
that . . . 13
esa(s) *f., adj.* that; those 6
ésa(s) *f., pron.* those (ones) 6
escalar *v.* to climb 4
escalar montañas *v.* to climb
mountains 4
escalera *f.* stairs; stairway 12
escoger *v.* choose 8
escribir *v.* to write 3
**escribir un mensaje
electrónico** to write an
e-mail message 4
escribir una (tarjeta) postal
to write a postcard 4
escribir una carta to write a
letter 4
escrito/a *p.p.* written 14
escritor(a) *m., f* writer
escritorio *m.* desk 2
escuchar *v.* to listen to 2
escuchar la radio to listen to
the radio 2
escuchar música to listen to
music 2
escuela *f.* school 1
esculpir *v.* to sculpt
escultor(a) *m., f.* sculptor
escultura *f.* sculpture
ese *m., sing., adj.* that 6
ése *m., sing., pron.* that (one) 6
eso *neuter, pron.* that;
that thing 6
esos *m., pl., adj.* those 6
ésos *m., pl., pron.* those (ones) 6
España *f.* Spain 1
español *m.* Spanish (*language*) 2
español(a) *m., f., adj.*
Spanish 3
espárragos *m., pl.* asparagus 8
especialización *f.* major field of
study or interest; specialization
espectacular *adj.* spectacular 15
espectáculo *m.* show
espejo *m.* mirror 7
esperar *v.* to wait for; to hope 2;
to wish 13

esposo/a *m., f.* husband/wife;
spouse 3
esquí (acuático) *m.* (water)
skiing 4
esquiar *v.* to ski 4
esquina *m.* corner 14
está he, she, it is, you are 1
Está (muy) despejado. It's
(very) clear. (*weather*) 4
Está (muy) nublado. It's
(very) cloudy. (*weather*) 4
Está bien. That's fine. It's okay.
11
esta(s) *f., adj.* this; these 4
esta noche tonight 4
ésta(s) *f., pron.* this (one); these
(ones) 6
Ésta es... *f.* This is . . .
(*introducing someone*) 1
establecer *v.* to establish
estación *f.* station; season 5
estación de autobuses
bus station 5
estación del metro subway
station 5
estación de tren train
station 5
estacionar *v.* to park 11
estadio *m.* stadium 2
estado civil *m.* marital status 9
Estados Unidos *m.* (EE.UU.;
E.U.) United States 1
estadounidense *adj.* from the
United States 3
estampado/a *adj.* print 6
estampilla *f.* stamp 14
estante *m.* bookcase; bookshelf 12
estar *v.* to be 2
**estar a (veinte kilómetros)
de aquí.** to be (20 kilometers)
from here 11
estar a dieta to be on a diet
15
estar aburrido/a to be
bored 5
estar afectado/a por to be
affected by 13
estar bajo control to be under
control 7
estar cansado/a to be tired 5
estar contaminado/a to be
polluted 13
estar de acuerdo to agree
estar de moda to be in
fashion 6
estar de vacaciones *f., pl.* to
be on vacation 5
estar en buena forma to be in
good shape 15
estar enfermo/a to be sick 10
estar listo/a to be ready 15
estar perdido/a to be lost 14
estar roto/a to be broken 10
estar seguro/a to be sure 5

estar torcido/a to be twisted; to be sprained 10

(no) está nada mal it's not at all bad 5

estatua *f.* statue

este *m.* east 14; umm

este *m., sing., adj.* this 6

éste *m., sing., pron.* this (one) 6

  Éste es... *m.* This is . . . (introducing someone) 1

estéreo *m.* stereo 11

estilo *m.* style 5

estiramiento *m.* stretching 15

esto *neuter pron.* this; this thing 6

estómago *m.* stomach 10

estornudar *v.* to sneeze 10

estos *m., pl., adj.* these 6

éstos *m., pl., pron.* these (ones) 6

estrella *f.* star 13

  estrella de cine *m., f.* movie star

estrés *m.* stress 15

estudiante *m., f.* student 1

estudiantil *adj. m., f.* student 2

estudiar *v.* to study 2

estufa *f.* stove 12

estupendo/a *adj.* stupendous 5

etapa *f.* stage; step 9

evitar *v.* to avoid 13

examen *m.* test; exam 2

  examen médico physical exam 10

excelente *adj. m., f.* excellent 5

exceso *m.* excess; too much 15

excursión *f.* hike; tour; excursion 4

excursionista *m., f.* hiker 4

éxito *m.* success

experiencia *f.* experience

explicar *v.* to explain 2

explorar *v.* to explore 4

  explorar un pueblo to explore a town 4

  explorar una ciudad to explore a city 4

expresión *f.* expression

extinción *f.* extinction 13

extranjero/a *adj.* foreign

extraño/a *adj.* strange 13

F

fabuloso/a *adj* fabulous 5

fácil *adj. m., f.* easy 3

falda *f.* skirt 6

faltar *v.* to lack; to need 7

familia *f.* family 3

famoso/a *adj.* famous

farmacia *f.* pharmacy 10

fascinar *v.* to fascinate 7

favorito/a *adj.* favorite 4

fax *m.* fax (machine) 11

febrero *m.* February 5

fecha *f.* date 5

feliz *adj.* happy 5

¡Felicidades! Congratulations! (*for an event such as a birthday or anniversary*) 9

¡Felicitaciones! Congratulations! (*for an event such as an engagement or a good grade on a test*) 9

¡Feliz cumpleaños! Happy birthday! 9

fenomenal *adj.* phenomenal; great 5

feo/a *adj.* ugly 3

festival *m.* festival

fiebre *f.* fever 10

fiesta *f.* party 9

fijo/a *adj.* set, fixed 6

fin *m.* end 4

  fin de semana weekend 4

finalmente *adv.* finally 15

firmar *v.* to sign (*a document*) 14

física *f.* physics 2

flan (de caramelo) *m.* baked (caramel) custard 9

flexible *adj.* flexible 15

flor *f.* flower 13

folklórico/a *adj.* folk; folkloric

folleto *m.* brochure 5

fondo *m.* end 12

forma *f.* shape 15

formulario *m.* form 14

foto(grafía) *f.* photograph 1

francés, francesa *m., f.* French 3

frecuentemente *adv.* frequently 10

frenos *m., pl.* brakes 11

fresco/a *adj.* cool 4

frijoles *m., pl.* beans 8

frío/a *adj.* cold 4

fritada *f.* fried dish (pork, fish, etc.) 8

frito/a *adj.* fried 8

fruta *f.* fruit 8

frutería *f.* fruit store 14

frutilla *f.* strawberry 8

fuente de fritada *f.* platter of fried food

fuera *adv.* outside 8

fuerte *adj. m., f.* strong 15

fumar *v.* to smoke 15

funcionar *v.* to work; to function 11

fútbol *m.* soccer 4

  fútbol americano *m.* football 4

futuro/a *adj.* future

  en el futuro in the future

G

gafas (de sol) *f., pl.* (sun)glasses 6

gafas (oscuras) *f., pl.* (sun)glasses 6

galleta *f.* cookie 9

ganar *v.* to win 4; to earn (money)

ganga *f.* bargain 6

garaje *m.* garage 12

garganta *f.* throat 10

gasolina *f.* gasoline 11

gasolinera *f.* gas station 11

gastar *v.* to spend (*money*) 6

gato/a *m., f.* cat 13

gente *f.* people 3

geografía *f.* geography 2

gerente *m., f.* manager

gimnasio *m.* gymnasium 4

gobierno *m.* government 13

golf *m.* golf 4

gordo/a *adj.* fat 3

grabadora *f.* tape recorder 1

gracias *f., pl.* thank you; thanks 1

  Gracias por todo. Thanks for everything. 9

  Gracias una vez más. Thanks again. 9

graduarse (en) *v.* to graduate (from) 9

gran, grande *adj.* big 3

grasa *f.* fat 15

gratis *adj. m., f.* free of charge 14

grave *adj.* grave; serious 10

gravísimo/a *adj.* extremely serious 13

grillo *m.* cricket 4

gripe *f.* flu 10

gris *adj. m., f.* gray 6

gritar *v.* to scream 7

guantes *m., pl.* gloves 6

guapo/a *adj.* handsome; good-looking 3

guardar *v.* to save (on a computer) 11

guerra *f.* war

guía *m., f.* guide 12

gustar *v.* to be pleasing to; to like 7

  Me gustaría... I would like . . .

gusto *m.* pleasure 1

  El gusto es mío. The pleasure is mine. 1

  Gusto de (+ *inf.*)**...** It's a pleasure to . . .

  Mucho gusto. Pleased to meet you. 1

H

haber *(aux.)* *v.* to have (*done something*) 15

  ha sido un placer it's been a pleasure 15

habitación *f.* room 5

  habitación doble double room 5

  habitación individual single room 5

hablar *v.* to talk; to speak 2

hacer *v.* to do; to make; 4

  Hace (mucho) viento. It's (very) windy. (*weather*) 4

  Hace buen tiempo. The weather is good.; It's good weather. 4

  Hace calor. It's hot. (*weather*) 4

Hace fresco. It's cool. (*weather*) 4

Hace frío. It's cold. (*weather*) 4

Hace mal tiempo. The weather is bad.; It's bad weather. 4

Hace sol. It's sunny. (*weather*) 4

hacer cola to stand in line 14

hacer diligencias to do errands; to run errands 14

hacer ejercicio to exercise 15

hacer ejercicios aeróbicos to do aerobics 15

hacer ejercicios de estiramiento to do stretching exercises 15

hacer el papel to play a role

hacer gimnasia to work out 15

hacer juego (con) to match 6

hacer la cama to make the bed 12

hacer las maletas to pack the suitcases 5

hacer quehaceres domésticos to do household chores 12

hacer turismo to go sightseeing 5

hacer un viaje to go on a trip 5

hacer una excursión to go on a hike; to go on a tour 5

hacha *f.* ax 1

hacia *prep.* toward 14

hambre *f.* hunger 3

hamburguesa *f.* hamburger 8

hasta *prep.* until; toward 1

Hasta la vista. See you later. 1

Hasta luego. See you later. 1

Hasta mañana. See you tomorrow. 1

hasta que until 14

Hasta pronto. See you soon. 1

hay there is; there are 1

Hay (mucha) contaminación. It's (very) smoggy. 4

Hay (mucha) niebla. It's (very) foggy. 18

Hay que It is necessary that 14

No hay duda que... There's no doubt that . . . 13

No hay de qué. You're welcome. 1

hecho/a *p.p.* done 14

heladería *f.* ice cream shop 14

helado/a *adj.* iced 8

helado *m.* ice cream 9

hermanastro/a *m., f.* stepbrother/stepsister 3

hermano/a *m., f.* brother/sister 3

hermano/a mayor/menor *m., f.* older/younger brother/sister 3

hermanos *m., pl.* brothers and sisters 3

hermoso/a *adj.* beautiful 6

hierba *f.* grass 13

hijastro/a *m., f.* stepson/stepdaughter 3

hijo/a *m., f.* son/daughter 3

hijo/a único/a *m., f.* only child 3

hijos *m., pl.* children 3

historia *f.* history 2; story

hockey *m.* hockey 4

hola *interj.* hello; hi 1

hombre *m.* man 1

hombre de negocios *m.* businessman

hora *f.* hour 1

horario *m.* schedule 2

horno *m.* oven 12

horno de microondas *m.* microwave oven 12

horror *m.* horror

hospital *m.* hospital 10

hotel *m.* hotel 5

hoy *adv.* today 2

hoy día *adv.* nowadays 5

Hoy es... Today is . . . 2, 5

huelga *f.* strike (labor)

hueso *m.* bone 10

huésped *m., f.* guest 5

huevo *m.* egg 8

humanidades *f., pl.* humanities 2

huracán *m.* hurricane

I

ida *f.* one way (*travel*) 5

idea *f.* idea 4

iglesia *f.* church 4

igualdad *f.* equality

igualmente *adv.* likewise 1

impermeable *m.* raincoat 6

importante *adj. m., f.* important 3

importar *v.* to be important to; to matter 7

imposible *adj. m., f.* impossible 13

impresora *f.* printer 11

imprimir *v.* to print 11

improbable *adj. m., f.* improbable 13

impuesto *m.* tax

incendio *m.* fire

increíble *adj. m., f.* incredible 5

individual *adj.* private (*room*) 5

infección *f.* infection 10

informar *v.* to inform

informe *m.* report; paper (*written work*)

ingeniero/a *m., f.* engineer 3

inglés *m.* English (*language*) 2

inglés, inglesa *adj.* English 3

insistir (en) *v.* to insist (on) 12

inspector(a) de aduanas *m.* customs inspector 5

inteligente *adj. m., f.* intelligent 3

intercambiar *v.* exchange

interesante *adj. m., f.* interesting 3

interesar *v.* to be interesting to; to interest 7

internacional *adj. m., f.* international

Internet *m.* Internet 11

inundación *f.* flood

invertir (i:ie) *v.* to invest

invierno *m.* winter 5

invitado/a *m., f.* guest (*at a function*) 9

invitar *v.* to invite 9

inyección *f.* injection 10

ir *v.* to go 4

ir a (+ *inf.*) to be going to do something 4

ir de compras to go shopping 5

ir de excursión (a las montañas) to go for a hike (in the mountains) 4

ir de pesca to go fishing 5

ir de vacaciones to go on vacation 5

ir en autobús to go by bus 5

ir en auto(móvil) to go by auto(mobile); to go by car 5

ir en barco to go by ship 5

ir en metro to go by subway 5

ir en motocicleta to go by motorcycle 5

ir en taxi to go by taxi 5

ir en tren to go by train 5

ir en avión to go by plane 5

irse *v.* to go away; to leave 7

italiano/a *adj.* Italian 3

izquierdo/a *adj.* left 2

a la izquierda de to the left of 2

J

jabón *m.* soap 7

jamás *adv.* never; not ever 7

jamón *m.* ham 8

japonés, japonesa *adj.* Japanese 3

jardín *m.* garden; yard 12

jefe, jefa *m., f.* boss

joven *adj. m., f.* young 3

joven *m., f.* youth; young person 1

joyería *f.* jewelry store 14

jubilarse *v.* to retire (*from work*) 9

juego *m.* game 5

jueves *m., sing.* Thursday 2

jugador(a) *m., f.* player 4

jugar (u:ue) *v.* to play 4

jugar a las cartas *f. pl.* to play cards 5

jugo *m.* juice 8

jugo de fruta *m.* fruit juice 8

julio *m.* July 5

jungla *f.* jungle 13

junio *m.* June 5

juntos/as *adj.* together 9

juventud *f.* youth 9

K

kilómetro *m.* kilometer 11

L

la *f., sing., d.o. pron.* her, it, *form.* you 5
   la *f., sing.* the 1
laboratorio *m.* laboratory 2
lago *m.* lake 5
lámpara *f.* lamp 12
lana *f.* wool 6
langosta *f.* lobster 8
lápiz *m.* pencil 1
largo/a *m.* long (*in length*) 6
las *f., pl.* the 1
   las *f., pl., d.o.pron.* them; *form.* you 5
lástima *f.* shame 13
lastimarse *v.* to injure oneself 10
   lastimarse el pie to injure one's foot 10
lata *f.* (*tin*) can 13
lavabo *m.* sink 7
lavadora *f.* washing machine 12
lavandería *f.* laundromat 14
lavaplatos *m., sing.* dishwasher 12
lavar *v.* to wash 12
lavarse *v.* to wash oneself 7
   lavarse la cara to wash one's face 7
   lavarse las manos to wash one's hands 7
le *sing., i.o. pron.* to/for him, her, *form.* you 6
   Le presento a... *form.* I would like to introduce . . . to you. 1
lección *f.* lesson 1
leche *f.* milk 8
lechuga *f.* lettuce 8
leer *v.* to read 3
   leer el correo electrónico to read e-mail 4
   leer el periódico to read the newspaper 4
   leer la revista to read the magazine 4
leído/a *p.p.* read 14
lejos de *prep.* far from 2
lengua *f.* language 2
   lenguas extranjeras *f., pl.* foreign languages 2
lentes de contacto *m., pl.* contact lenses 6
   lentes de sol sunglasses 6
lento/a *adj.* slow 11
les *pl., i.o. pron.* to/for them, *form.* you 5
letrero *m.* sign 14
levantar *v.* to lift 15
   levantar pesas to lift weights 15

levantarse *v.* to get up 7
ley *f.* law 13
libertad *f.* liberty; freedom
libre *adj. m., f.* free 4
librería *f.* bookstore 2
libro *m.* book 2
licencia de conducir *f.* driver's license 11
limón *m.* lemon 8
limpiar *v.* to clean 12
   limpiar la casa *v.* to clean the house 12
limpio/a *adj.* clean 5
línea *f.* line 4
listo/a *adj.* smart 5; ready 15
literatura *f.* literature 2
llamar *v.* to call 7
   llamar por teléfono to call on the phone 11
   llamarse *v.* to be called; to be named 7
llanta *f.* tire 11
llave *f.* key 5
llegada *f.* arrival 5
llegar *v.* to arrive 2
llenar *v.* to fill 11; to fill out a form 14
   llenar el tanque to fill the tank 11
   llenar un formulario to fill out a form 14
lleno/a *adj.* full 11
llevar *v.* to carry; to take 2; *v.* to wear 6
   llevar una vida sana to lead a healthy lifestyle 15
   llevarse bien/mal con to get along well/badly with 9
llover (o:ue) *v.* to rain 4
   Llueve. It's raining. 4
lluvia *f.* rain 4
   lluvia ácida acid rain 13
lo *m., sing. d.o. pronoun.* him, it, *form.* you 5
   lo mejor the best (thing)
   lo pasamos de película we had a great time
   lo peor the worst (thing)
   lo que what; that which 12
   lo siento I'm sorry 1
loco/a *adj.* crazy 6
locutor(a) *m., f.* TV or radio announcer
lomo a la plancha *m.* grilled flank steak 8
los *m.pl.d.o.pron.* them, *form.* you 5
   los *m., pl.* the 1
luchar (contra), (por) *v.* to fight struggle (against), (for)
luego *adv.* afterwards, then 7; *adv.* later 1
lugar *m.* place 4
luna *f.* moon 13
lunar *m.* polka dot 6

lunes *m., sing.* Monday 2
luz *f.* light; electricity 12

M

madrastra *f.* stepmother 3
madre *f.* mother 3
madurez *f.* maturity; middle age 9
maestro/a *m., f.* teacher (*elementary school*)
magnífico/a *adj.* magnificent 6
maíz *m.* corn 5
mal, malo/a *adj.* bad 8
maleta *f.* suitcase 3
mamá *f.* mom 1
mañana *f.* morning, A.M. 1; tomorrow 1
mandar *v.* to order 12; to send; to mail 14
manejar *v.* to drive 11
manera *f.* way
mano *f.* hand 1
   ¡Manos arriba! Hands up! 15
manta *f.* blanket 12
mantener *v.* to maintain 15
   mantenerse en forma to stay in shape 15
mantequilla *f.* butter 8
manzana *f.* apple 8
mapa *m.* map 1
maquillaje *m.* make-up 7
maquillarse *v.* to put on makeup 7
mar *m.* sea; ocean 5
maravilloso/a *adj.* marvelous 5
mareado/a *adj.* dizzy; nauseated 10
margarina *f.* margarine 8
mariscos *m., pl.* shellfish 8
marrón *adj. m., f.* brown 6
martes *m., sing.* Tuesday 2
marzo *m.* March 5
más *pron.* more 2
   más de (+ número) more than (+ *number*) 8
   más tarde later 7
   más... que more . . . than 8
masaje *m.* massage 15
matemáticas *f., pl.* mathematics 2
materia *f.* course 2
matrimonio *m.* marriage 9
máximo/a *adj.* maximum 11
mayo *m.* May 5
mayonesa *f.* mayonnaise 8
mayor *adj.* older 3
   el/la mayor *adj.* oldest 8
me *pron.* me 5
   Me duele mucho. It hurts me a lot. 10
   Me gusta... I like . . . 2
   No me gustan nada. I don't like . . . at all. 2

Me gustaría(n)... I would like . . . 7
Me llamo... My name is . . . 1
Me muero por... I'm dying to (for) . . . 1
mecánico/a *m., f.* mechanic 11
mediano/a *adj.* medium 6
medianoche *f.* midnight 1
medias *f., pl.* pantyhose, stockings 6
medicamento *m.* medication 10
medicina *f.* medicine 10
médico/a *m., f.* doctor 3; *adj.* medical 10
medio/a *adj.* half 3
 medio ambiente *m.* environment 13
 medio/a hermano/a *m., f.* half-brother/half-sister 3
 mediodía *m.* noon 1
 medios de comunicación *m., pl.* means of communication; media
 y media thirty minutes past the hour (time) 1
mejor *adj.* better; best 8
 el/la mejor *m., f.* the best 8
mejorar *v.* to improve 13
melocotón *m.* peach 8
menor *adj.* younger 3
 el/la menor *m., f.* youngest 8
menos *adv.* less 10
 menos cuarto... menos quince... quarter to . . . (time) 1
 menos de (+ *number*) less than (+ *number*) 8
 menos... que less . . . than 8
mensaje electrónico *m.* e-mail message 4
mentira *f.* lie 9
menú *m.* menu 8
mercado *m.* market 6
 mercado al aire libre open-air market 6
merendar *v.* to snack in the afternoon; to have an afternoon snack 15
merienda *f.* afternoon snack 15
mes *m.* month 5
mesa *f.* table 2
mesita *f.* end table 12
 mesita de noche night stand 12
metro *m.* subway 5
mexicano/a *adj.* Mexican 3
México *m.* Mexico 1
mí *pron. obj. of prep.* me 8
mi(s) *poss. adj.* my 3
microonda *f.* microwave 12
 horno de microondas *m.* microwave oven 12
miedo *m.* fear 3
mientras *adv.* while 10
miércoles *m., sing.* Wednesday 2
mil *m.* one thousand 4
 mil millones billion 5

Mil perdones. I'm extremely sorry. (*lit.* A thousand pardons.) 4
milla *f.* mile 11
millón *m.* million 5
millones (de) *m.* millions (of) 5
mineral *m.* mineral 15
minuto *m.* minute 1
mío/a(s) *poss.* my; (of) mine 11
mirar *v.* to watch 2
 mirar (la) televisión to watch television 2
mismo/a *adj.* same 3
mochila *f.* backpack 2
moda *f.* fashion 6
módem *m.* modem 11
moderno/a *adj.* modern
molestar *v.* to bother; to annoy 7
monitor *m.* (computer) monitor 11
 monitor(a) *m., f.* trainer 15
montaña *f.* mountain 4
montar *v.* **a caballo** to ride a horse 5
monumento *m.* monument 4
mora *f.* blackberry 8
morado/a *adj.* purple 6
moreno/a *adj.* brunet(te) 3
morir (o:ue) *v.* to die 8
mostrar (o:ue) *v.* to show 4
moto(cicleta) *f.* motorcycle 5
motor *m.* motor 11
muchacho/a *m., f.* boy; girl 3
mucho/a *adj., adv.* many; a lot of; much 2, 3
 muchas veces many times 10
 Muchísimas gracias. Thank you very much. 9
 Mucho gusto. Pleased to meet you. 1
 (Muchas) gracias. Thank you (very much). Thanks (a lot). 1
muchísimo very much 2
mudarse *v.* to move (from one house to another) 12
muebles *m., pl.* furniture 12
muela *f.* tooth 10
muerte *f.* death 9
muerto/a *p.p.* died 14
mujer *f.* woman 1
 mujer de negocios *f.* business woman
 mujer policía *f.* female police officer 11
multa *f.* fine 11
mundial *adj.* worldwide 5
mundo *m.* world 11
municipal *adj. m., f.* municipal 4
músculo *m.* muscle 15
museo *m.* museum 4
música *f.* music 2
musical *adj. m., f.* musical
músico/a *m., f.* musician
muy *adv.* very 1
 Muy amable. That's very kind of you. 5

Muy bien gracias. Very well, thank you. 1

N

nacer *v.* to be born 9
nacimiento *m.* birth 9
nacional *adj. m., f.* national
nacionalidad *f.* nationality 1
nada nothing 1; not anything 7
 nada mal not bad at all 5
nadar *v.* to swim 4
nadie *pron.* no one, nobody, not anyone 7
naranja *m.* orange 8
nariz *f.* nose 10
natación *f.* swimming 4
natural *adj. m., f.* natural 13
naturaleza *f.* nature 13
navegar (en) *v.* to surf (*the Web*) 11
Navidad *f.* Christmas 9
necesario/a *adj.* necessary 12
necesitar *v.* to need 2
negar (e:ie) *v.* to deny 13
negativo/a *m.* negative 7
negocios *m., pl.* business; commerce
negro/a *adj.* black 6
nervioso/a *adj.* nervous 5
nevar (e:ie) *v.* to snow 4
 Nieva. It's snowing. 4
ni...ni neither... nor 7
niebla *f.* fog 4
nieto/a *m., f.* grandson/granddaughter 3
nieve *f.* snow 8
ningún, ninguno/a(s) *adj.* no; none; not; any 7
ningún problema no problem 7
niñez *f.* childhood 9
niño/a *m., f.* child 3
no no; not 1
 No cabe duda (de) que... There is no doubt that . . . 13
 No es así. That's not the way it is
 No es para tanto. It's no big deal. 12
 No es seguro que... It's not sure that . . . 13
 No es verdad que... It's not true that . . . 13
 No está nada mal. It's not bad at all. 5
 no estar de acuerdo to disagree
 No estoy seguro. I'm not sure. 1
 no hay there is not; there are not 1
 No hay de qué. You're welcome. 1
 No hay duda (de) que... There is no doubt that . . . 13

¡No me diga(s)! You don't say! 11

No me gustan nada. I don't like them at all. 2

no muy bien not very well 1

¿no? right? 1

no quiero I don't want to 4

no sé I don't know 1

No se preocupe. Don't worry. 7

no tener razón to be wrong 3

noche *f.* night 1

nombre *m.* name 5

norte *m.* north 14

norteamericano/a *adj.* (North) American 3

nos *pron.* us 5

Nos vemos. See you. 1

nosotros/as *sub. pron.* we 1; *ob. pron.* us 8

noticias *f., pl.* news

noticiero *m.* newscast

novecientos/as *adj.* nine hundred 5

noveno/a *adj.* ninth 5

noventa ninety 2

noviembre *m.* November 5

novio/a *m., f.* boyfriend/girlfriend 3

nube *f.* cloud 13

nublado/a *adj.* cloudy 4

Está (muy) nublado. It's very cloudy. 4

nuclear *adj. m. f.* nuclear 13

nuera *f.* daughter-in-law 3

nuestro/a(s) *poss. adj.* our 3

nueve nine 1

nuevo/a *adj.* new 6

número *m.* number 1

número (shoe) size 6

nunca *adj.* never; not ever 7

nutrición *f.* nutrition 15

O

o or 7

o... o or; either . . . or 7

obedecer (c:zc) *v.* to obey

obra *f.* work (*of art, literature, music, etc.*)

obra maestra *f.* masterpiece

obtener *v.* to obtain; to get

obvio/a *adj.* obvious 13

océano *m.* ocean; sea 5

ochenta eighty 2

ocho *m.* eight 1

ochocientos/as *adj.* eight hundred 5

octavo/a *adj.* eighth 5

octubre *m.* October 5

ocupación *f.* occupation

ocupado/a *adj.* busy 5

ocurrir *v.* to occur; to happen

odiar *v.* to hate 9

oeste *m.* west 14

oferta *f.* offer 12

oficina *f.* office 12

oficio *m.* trade

ofrecer (c:zc) *v.* to offer 8

oído *m.* sense of hearing; inner ear 10

oído *p.p.* heard 14

oír *v.* to hear 4

oigan *form., pl.* listen (*in conversation*) 5

oye *fam., sing.* listen (*in conversation*) 1

ojalá (que) *interj.* I hope (that); I wish (that) 13

ojo *m.* eye 10

olvidar *v.* to forget 10

once eleven 1

ópera *f.* opera

operación *f.* operation 10

ordenado/a *adj.* orderly; well organized 5

ordinal *adj.* ordinal (*number*)

oreja *f.* (outer) ear 10

orquesta *f.* orchestra

ortográfico/a *adj.* spelling

os *fam., pl. pron.* you

otoño *m.* autumn 5

otro/a *adj.* other; another 6

otra vez again 15

P

paciente *m., f.* patient 10

padrastro *m.* stepfather 3

padre *m.* father 3

padres *m., pl.* parents 3

pagar *v.* to pay 9

pagar a plazos to pay in installments 14

pagar al contado to pay in cash 14

pagar en efectivo to pay in cash 14

pagar la cuenta to pay the bill 9

página *f.* page 11

página principal *f.* home page 11

país *m.* country 1

paisaje *m.* landscape; countryside 5

pájaro *m.* bird 13

palabra *f.* word 1

pan *m.* bread 8

pan tostado *m.* toasted bread; toast 8

panadería *f.* bakery 14

pantalla *f.* screen 11

pantalones *m., pl.* pants 6

pantalones cortos *m., pl.* shorts 6

papa *f.* potato 8

papas fritas *f., pl.* fried potatoes; french fries 8

papá *m.* dad 3

papás *m., pl.* parents 3

papel *m.* paper 2; *m.* role

paquete *m.* package 14

par *m.* pair 6

para *prep.* for; in order to 11

para que so that 13

parabrisas *m., sing.* windshield 11

parar *v.* to stop 11

parecer *v.* to seem; to appear 8

pared *f.* wall 12

pareja *f.* (married) couple; partner 9

parientes *m., pl.* relatives 3

parque *m.* park 4

párrafo *m.* paragraph 5

parte: de parte de on behalf of 11

partido *m.* game; match (*sports*) 4

pasado/a *adj.* last; past 6

pasado *p.p.* passed 15

pasaje *m.* ticket 5

pasaje de ida y vuelta *m.* roundtrip ticket 5

pasajero/a *m., f.* passenger 1

pasaporte *m.* passport 5

pasar *v.* to go by 5; to pass 12;

pasar la aspiradora to vacuum 12

pasar por el banco to go by the bank 14

pasar por la aduana to go through customs 5

pasar tiempo to spend time 4

pasarlo bien/mal to have a good/bad time 9

pasatiempo *m.* pastime 4

pasear *v.* to take a walk; to stroll 4

pasear en bicicleta to ride a bicycle 4

pasillo *m.* hallway 12

pastel *m.* cake; pie 9

pastel de chocolate *m.* chocolate cake 9

pastel de cumpleaños *m.* birthday cake 9

pastelería *f.* pastry shop 14

pastilla *f.* pill; tablet 10

patata *f.* potato; patatas 8

patatas fritas *f., pl.* fried potatoes; french fries 8

patinar (en línea) *v.* to skate (in-line) 4

patio *m.* patio; yard 12

pavo *m.* turkey 8

paz *f.* peace

pedir (e:i) *v.* to ask for; to request 4; to order (*food*) 8

pedir prestado *v.* to borrow 14

pedir préstamo *v.* to apply for a loan 14

peinarse *v.* to comb one's hair 7

película *f.* movie 4

peligro *m.* danger 13

peligroso/a *adj.* dangerous

pelirrojo/a *adj.* red-headed 3
pelo *m.* hair 7
pelota *f.* ball 4
peluquería *f.* beauty salon 14
peluquero/a *m., f.* hairdresser
penicilina *f.* penicillin 10
pensar (e:ie) *v.* to think 4
   pensar (+ *inf.*) *v.* to intend to;
     to plan to (*do something*) 4
   pensar en *v.* to think about 4
pensión *f.* boardinghouse 5
peor *adj.* worse; worst 8
   (el/la) peor *adj.* the worst 8
pequeño/a *adj.* small 3
pera *f.* pear 8
perder (e:ie) *v.* to lose 4
perdido/a *adj.* lost 14
Perdón. Pardon me.;
   Excuse me. 1
perezoso/a *adj.* lazy
perfecto/a *adj.* perfect 5
periódico *m.* newspaper 4
periodismo *m.* journalism 2
periodista *m., f.* journalist 3
permiso *m.* permission 1
pero *conj.* but 2
perro *m.* dog 13
persona *f.* person 3
personaje *m.* character
   personaje principal *m.* main
     character
pesas *f. pl.* weights 15
pesca *f.* fishing 5
pescadería *f.* fish market 14
pescado *m.* fish (*cooked*) 8
pescador(a) *m., f.* fisherman/
   fisherwoman 5
pescar *v.* to fish 5
peso *m.* weight 15
pez *m.* fish (*live*) 13
pie *m.* foot 10
piedra *f.* stone 13
pierna *f.* leg 10
pimienta *f.* black pepper 8
piña *f.* pineapple 8
pintar *v.* to paint
pintor(a) *m., f.* painter
pintura *f.* painting 12
piscina *f.* swimming pool 4
piso *m.* floor (*of a building*) 5
pizarra *f.* blackboard 2
placer *m.* pleasure 15
   Ha sido un placer. It's been a
     pleasure. 15
planchar la ropa *v.* to iron
   clothes 12
planes *m., pl.* plans 4
planta *f.* plant 13
   planta baja *f.* ground floor 5
plástico *m.* plastic 13
plato *m.* dish (*in a meal*) 8; *m.*
   plate 12
   plato principal *m.* main dish 8
playa *f.* beach 5

plazos *m., pl.* periods; time 14
pluma *f.* pen 2
población *f.* population 13
pobre *adj. m., f.* poor 6
pobreza *f.* poverty 3
poco/a *adj.* little; few 5
poder (o:ue) *v.* to be able to;
   can 4
poema *m.* poem
poesía *f.* poetry
poeta *m., f.* poet
policía *f.* police (force) 11; *m.*
   (male) police officer 11
política *f.* politics
político/a *m., f.* politician
pollo *m.* chicken 8
   pollo asado *m.* roast chicken 8
ponchar *v.* to go flat 11
poner *v.* to put; to place 4; *v.* to
   turn on (*electrical appliances*) 11
   poner la mesa *v.* to set the
     table 12
   poner una inyección *v.* to give
     an injection 10
ponerse (+ *adj.*) *v.* to become
   (+ *adj.*) 7; to put on clothing 7
por *prep.* due to; in exchange for;
   for the sake of 11; for; by; in;
   through 11
   por aquí around here 11
   por avión by plane 5
   por ejemplo for example 11
   por eso that's why;
     therefore 11
   Por favor. Please. 1
   por fin finally 11
   por la mañana in the
     morning 7
   por la noche at night 7
   por la tarde in the afternoon 7
   por lo menos at least 10
   ¿por qué? why? 2
   por supuesto of course
   por teléfono by phone; on the
     phone 7
   por último finally 7
porque *conj.* because 2
portátil *m.* portable 11
porvenir *m.* future
posesivo/a *adj.* possessive 3
posible *adj.* possible 13
postal *f.* postcard 4
postre *m.* dessert 9
practicar *v.* to practice 2
   practicar deportes *m., pl.* to
     play sports 4
precio (fijo) *m.* (fixed; set)
   price 6
preferir (e:ie) *v.* to prefer 4
pregunta *f.* question 2
preguntar *v.* to ask (*a question*) 2
premio *m.* prize; award
prender *v.* to turn on 11
prensa *f.* press

preocupado/a *adj.* worried 5
preocuparse (por) *v.* to worry
   (about) 7
preparar *v.* to prepare 2
preposición *f.* preposition
presentación *f.* introduction
presentar *v.* to introduce 1; to put
   on (*a performance*)
presiones *f., pl.* pressures 15
prestado/a *adj.* borrowed 14
préstamo *m.* loan 14
prestar *v.* to lend 6
primavera *f.* spring 5
primer, primero/a *adj.* first 5
primo/a *m., f.* cousin 3
principal *adj. m., f.* main 8
prisa *f.* haste 3
probable *adj. m., f.* probable 13
probar (o:ue) *v.* to taste; to try 8
probarse (o:ue) *v.* to try on 7
problema *m.* problem 1
profesión *f.* profession
profesor(a) *m., f.* teacher;
   professor 1
programa *m.* 1
   programa de computación
     m. software 11
   programa de entrevistas *m.*
     talk show
programador(a) *m., f.* programmer 3
prohibir *v.* to prohibit; to
   forbid 10
pronombre *m.* pronoun 8
pronto *adj.* soon 10
propina *f.* tip 9
propio/a *adj.* own
proteger *v.* to protect 13
proteína *f.* protein 15
próximo/a *adj.* next
prueba *f.* test; quiz 2
psicología *f.* psychology 2
psicólogo/a *m., f.* psychologist
publicar *v.* to publish
público *m.* audience
pueblo *m.* town 4
puerta *f.* door 2
Puerto Rico *m.* Puerto Rico 1
puertorriqueño/a *adj.* Puerto
   Rican 3
pues *conj.* well 2
puesto *m.* position; job
puesto/a *p.p.* put 14
puro/a *adj.* pure 13

Q

que *pron.* that; who 12
¡Qué...! How . . . ! 3
¡Qué dolor! What pain! 10
¡Qué gusto + *inf.*! What a
   pleasure to . . . !
¡Qué ropa más bonita!
   What pretty clothes! 6

¡Qué sorpresa! What a surprise! 9
¿qué? what? 1
¿Qué día es hoy? What day is it? 2
¿Qué hay de nuevo? What's new?; What's happening? 1
¿Qué hora es? What time is it? 1
¿Qué les parece? What do you (*pl.*) think? 9
¿Qué pasa? What's going on? 1
¿Qué pasó? What happened?; What's wrong? 11
¿Qué precio tiene? What is the price? 6
¿Qué tal...? How are you?; How is it going? 1; How is/are . . . ? 2
¿Qué talla lleva/usa? What size do you take? 6
¿Qué tiempo hace? What's the weather like? 4
quedar *v.* to be left over; to fit (*clothing*) 7; to be left behind; 10; to be located 14
quedarse *v.* to stay; to remain 7
quehaceres domésticos *m., pl.* household chores 12
quemado/a *adj.* burned (out) 11
querer (e:ie) *v.* to want; to love 4
queso *m.* cheese 8
quien *pron.* who; whom 12
¿Quién es...? Who is . . . ? 1
¿Quién habla? Who is speaking? (*telephone*) 11
¿quién(es)? who?; whom? 1
química *f.* chemistry 2
quince fifteen 1
menos quince quarter to (time) 1
y quince quarter after (time) 1
quinceañera *f.* young woman's fifteenth birthday celebration 9
quinientos/as *adj.* five hundred 5
quinto/a *adj.* fifth 5
quisiera *v.* I would like 8
quitar la mesa *v.* to clear the table 12
quitarse *v.* to take off 7
quizás *adv.* perhaps 5

R

racismo *m.* racism
radio *f.* radio (*medium*) 2
radio *m.* radio (set) 2, 11
radiografía *f.* X-ray 10
rápido/a *adj.* fast 8
ratón *m.* mouse 11

ratos libres *m., pl.* spare time 4
raya *f.* stripe 6
razón *f.* reason 3
rebaja *f.* sale 6
recado *m.* (telephone) message 11
receta *f.* prescription 10
recetar *v.* to prescribe 10
recibir *v.* to receive 3
reciclaje *m.* recycling 13
reciclar *v.* to recycle 13
recién casado/a *m., f.* newly-wed 9
recoger *v.* to pick up 13
recomendar (e:ie) *v.* to recommend 8
recordar (o:ue) *v.* to remember 4
recorrer *v.* to tour an area 5
recurso *m.* resource 13
recurso natural *m.* natural resource 13
red *f.* network; Internet 11
reducir *v.* to reduce 13
refresco *m.* soft drink 8
refrigerador *m.* refrigerator 12
regalar *v.* to give (*as a gift*) 9
regalo *m.* gift; present 6
regatear *v.* to bargain 6
región *f.* region; area 13
regresar *v.* to return 2
regular *adj. m., f.* so so.; OK 1
reído *p.p.* laughed 14
reírse (e:i) *v.* to laugh 9
relaciones *f., pl.* relationships
relajarse *v.* to relax 9
reloj *m.* clock; watch 2
renunciar (a) *v.* to resign (from)
repetir (e:i) *v.* to repeat 4
reportaje *m.* report
reportero/a *m., f.* reporter; journalist
representante *m., f.* representative
resfriado *m.* cold (*illness*) 10
residencia estudiantil *f.* dormitory 2
resolver (o:ue) *v.* to resolve; to solve 13
respirar *v.* to breathe 13
respuesta *f.* answer 9
restaurante *m.* restaurant 4
resuelto/a *p.p.* resolved 14
reunión *f.* meeting
revisar *v.* to check 11
revisar el aceite *v.* to check the oil 11
revista *f.* magazine 4
rico/a *adj.* rich 6; *adj.* tasty; delicious 8
ridículo *adj.* ridiculous 13
río *m.* river 13
riquísimo/a *adj.* extremely delicious 8
rodilla *f.* knee 10

rogar (o:ue) *v.* to beg; to plead 12
rojo/a *adj.* red 6
romántico/a *adj.* romantic
romper (con) *v.* to break up (with) 9
romper(se) *v.* to break 10
romperse la pierna *v.* to break one's leg 10
ropa *f.* clothing; clothes 6
ropa interior *f.* underwear 6
rosado/a *adj.* pink 6
roto/a *adj.* broken 10
rubio/a *adj.* blond(e) 3
ruso/a *adj.* Russian 3
rutina *f.* routine 7
rutina diaria *f.* daily routine 7

S

sábado *m.* Saturday 2
saber *v.* to know; to know how to 8
sabrosísimo/a *adj.* extremely delicious 8
sabroso/a *adj.* tasty; delicious 8
sacar *v.* to take out 10
sacar fotos to take photographs 5
sacar la basura to take out the trash 12
sacar(se) una muela to extract a tooth; to pull a tooth 10
sacudir *v.* to dust 12
sacudir los muebles dust the furniture 12
sal *f.* salt 8
sala *f.* living room; room 12
sala de emergencia emergency room 10
salario *m.* salary
salchicha *f.* sausage 8
salida *f.* departure; exit 5
salir *v.* to leave; to go out 4
salir con to go out with; to date (*someone*) 4, 9
salir de to leave from 4
salir para to leave for (*a place*) 4
salmón *m.* salmon 8
salón de belleza *m.* beauty salon 14
salud *f.* health 10
saludable *adj.* healthy 10
saludar(se) *v.* to greet (each other) 11
saludo *m.* greeting 1
saludos a... greetings to . . . 1
sandalia *f.* sandal 6
sándwich *m.* sandwich 8
sano/a *adj.* healthy 10

se *ref.pron.* himself, herself, itself, *form.* yourself, themselves, yourselves 7

se *impersonal* one 10

Se nos dañó... The . . . broke down on us. 11

Se hizo... He/she/it became . . . 5

Se nos pinchó una llanta. We had a flat tire. 11

secadora *f.* clothes dryer 12

sección de (no) fumar *f.* (no) smoking section 8

secretario/a *m., f.* secretary

secuencia *f.* sequence

sed *f.* thirst 3

seda *f.* silk 6

sedentario/a *adj.* sedentary; related to sitting 15

seguir (e:i) *v.* to follow; to continue 4

según according to

segundo/a *adj.* second 5

seguro/a *adj.* sure 5

seis six 1

seiscientos/as *adj.* six hundred 5

sello *m.* stamp 14

selva *f.* jungle 13

semáforo *m.* traffic signal 11

semana *f.* week 2

fin *m.* **de semana** weekend 4

semestre *m.* semester 2

sendero *m.* trail; trailhead 13

sentarse (e:ie) *v.* to sit down 7

sentir(se) (e:ie) *v.* to be sorry; to feel 7; to regret 13

señor (Sr.) *m.* Mr.; sir 1

señora (Sra.) *f.* Mrs.; ma'am 1

señorita (Srta.) *f.* Miss 1

separado/a *adj.* separated 9

separarse (de) *v.* to separate (from) 9

septiembre *m.* September 5

séptimo/a *adj.* seventh 5

ser *v.* to be 1

ser aficionado/a (a) to be a fan (of) 4

ser alérgico/a (a) to be allergic (to) 10

ser gratis to be free of charge 14

serio/a *adj.* serious

servilleta *f.* napkin 12

servir (e:i) *v.* to serve 8; to help 5

sesenta sixty 2

setecientos/as *adj.* seven hundred 5

setenta seventy 2

sexismo *m.* sexism

sexto/a *adj.* sixth 5

sí *adv.* yes 1

si *conj.* if 4

SIDA *m.* AIDS

sido *p.p.* been 15

siempre *adv.* always 7

siete seven 1

silla *f.* seat 2

sillón *m.* armchair 12

similar *adj. m., f.* similar

simpático/a *adj.* nice; likeable 3

sin *prep.* without 13, 15

sin duda without a doubt

sin embargo however

sin que *conj.* without 13

sino but 7

síntoma *m.* symptom 10

sitio *m.* **Web;** Web site 11

situado/a *p.p.* located 14

sobre *m.* envelope 14; *prep.* on; over 2

sobrino/a *m., f.* nephew; niece 3

sociología *f.* sociology 2

sofá *m.* couch; sofa 12

sol *m.* sun 4

solar *adj. m. f.* solar 14

solicitar *v.* to apply (*for a job*)

solicitud (de trabajo) *f.* (job) application

sólo *adv.* only 3

soltero/a *adj.* single; unmarried 9

solución *f.* solution 13

sombrero *m.* hat 6

Son las... It's . . . o'clock. 1

sonar (o:ue) *v.* to ring 11

sonreído *p.p.* smiled 14

sonreír (e:i) *v.* to smile 9

sopa *f.* soup 8

sorprender *v.* to surprise 9

sorpresa *f.* surprise 9

sótano *m.* basement; cellar 12

soy I am 1

Soy yo. That's me. 1

soy de... I'm from . . . 1

su(s) *poss. adj.* his; her; its; *form.* your; their; 3

subir(se) *v.* to go up; to get on/in (*a vehicle*) 11

sucio/a *adj.* dirty 5

sucre *m.* Ecuadorian currency 6

sudar *v.* to sweat 15

suegro/a *m., f.* father-in-law; mother-in-law 3

sueldo *m.* salary

suelo *m.* floor 12

sueño *n.* sleep 3

suerte *f.* luck 3

suéter *m.* sweater 6

sufrir *v.* to suffer 10

sufrir muchas presiones to be under a lot of pressure 15

sufrir una enfermedad to suffer (from) an illness 10

sugerir (e:ie) *v.* to suggest 12

supermercado *m.* supermarket 14

suponer *v.* to suppose 4

sur *m.* south 14

sustantivo *m.* noun

suyo/a(s) *poss.* (of) his/her; (of) hers; (of) its; (of) *form.* your, (of) yours, (of) their 11

sentir *v.* to feel 7

T

tal vez *adv.* maybe 5

talentoso/a *adj.* talented

talla *f.* size 6

talla grande *f.* large 6

taller *m.* **mecánico** mechanic's repairshop 11

también *adv.* also; too 2

tampoco *adv.* neither; not either 7

tan *adv.* so 5, 8

tan pronto como as soon as 14

tan... como as . . . as 8

tanque *m.* tank 11

tanto *adv.* so much 12

tanto... como as much . . . as 8

tantos/as... como as many . . . as 8

tarde *adv.* late 7

tarde *f.* afternoon; evening; P.M. 1

tarea *f.* homework 2

tarjeta *f.* (post) card 4

tarjeta de crédito *f.* credit card 6

tarjeta postal *f.* postcard 4

taxi *m.* taxi(cab) 5

taza *f.* cup 12

te *fam. pron.* you 6

Te presento a... I would like to introduce you to . . . 1

¿Te gustaría? Would you like to? 7

¿Te gusta(n)... ? Do you like . . . ? 2

té *m.* tea 8

té helado *m.* iced tea 8

teatro *m.* theater

teclado *m.* keyboard 11

técnico/a *m., f.* technician

tejido *m.* weaving

teleadicto/a *m., f.* couch potato 15

teléfono (celular) *m.* (cell) telephone 11

telenovela *f.* soap opera

teletrabajo *m.* telecommuting

televisión *f.* television 11

televisión por cable *f.* cable television 11

televisor *m.* television set 11

temer *v.* to fear 13

temperatura *f.* temperature 10

temprano *adv.* early 7

tenedor *m.* fork 12

tener *v.* to have 3

tener... años to be . . . years old 3

Tengo... años. I'm . . . years old. 3

tener calor to be hot 3
tener cuidado to be careful 3
tener dolor de to have a pain in 10
tener éxito to be successful
tener fiebre to have a fever 10
tener frío to be cold 3
tener ganas de (+ *inf.*) to feel like (*doing something*) 3
tener hambre *f.* to be hungry 3
tener miedo de to be afraid of; to be scared of 3
tener miedo (de) que to be afraid that 13
tener planes *m., pl.* to have plans 4
tener prisa to be in a hurry 3
tener que (+ *inf.*) *v.* to have to (*do something*) 3
tener razón *f.* to be right 3
tener sed *f.* to be thirsty 3
tener sueño to be sleepy 3
tener suerte to be lucky 3
tener tiempo to have time 4
tener una cita to have a date, an appointment 9
tenis *m.* tennis 4
tensión *f.* tension 15
tercero/a *adj.* third 5
terminar *v.* to end; to finish 2
  terminar de (+*inf.*) *v.* to finish (*doing something*) 4
terremoto *m.* earthquake
terrible *adj. m., f.* terrible 13
ti *prep., obj. of prep., fam.* you 8
tiempo *m.* time; weather 4
  tiempo libre free time 4
tienda *f.* shop; store 6
  tienda de campaña tent 5
tierra *f.* land; soil 13
tinto/a *adj.* red (wine) 8
tío/a *m., f.* uncle; aunt 3
tíos *m.* aunts and uncles 3
título *m.* title
tiza *f.* chalk 2
toalla *f.* towel 7
tobillo *m.* ankle 10
tocadiscos compacto *m.* compact-disc player 11
tocar *v.* to play (*a musical instrument*); to touch 13
todavía *adv.* yet; still 5
todo *m.* everything 5
  todo el mundo the whole world; all over the world 13
  Todo está bajo control. Everything is under control. 7
  (todo) derecho straight ahead 14
  ¡Todos a bordo! All aboard! 1
todo/a *adj.* whole; all 4
todos *m., pl.* all of us 1; *m., pl.* everybody; everyone 13
todos los días every day 10

tomar *v.* to take; to drink 2
  tomar clases to take classes 2
  tomar el sol to sunbathe 4
  tomar en cuenta take into account 8
  tomar fotos to take photos 5
  tomar la temperatura to take someone's temperature 10
tomate *m.* tomato 8
tonto/a *adj.* silly; foolish 3
torcerse (el tobillo) *v.* to sprain (one's ankle) 10
torcido/a *adj.* twisted; sprained 10
tormenta *f.* storm
tornado *m.* tornado
tortilla *f.* kind of flat bread 8
  tortillas de maíz flat bread made of corn flour 8
tos *f., sing.* cough 10
toser *v.* to cough 10
tostado/a *adj.* toasted 8
tostadora *f.* toaster 12
trabajador(a) *adj.* hardworking 3
trabajar *v.* to work 2
trabajo *m.* job; work; written work
traducir *v.* to translate 8
traer *v.* to bring 4
tráfico *m.* traffic 11
tragedia *f.* tragedy
traído/a *p.p.* brought 14
traje *m.* suit 6
  traje de baño *m.* bathing suit 6
tranquilo/a *adj.* calm; quiet 15
  ¡Tranquilo! Stay calm! 7
transmitir to broadcast
tratar de (+ *inf.*) *v.* to try to (*do something*) 15
Trato hecho. It's a deal.
trece thirteen 1
treinta thirty 1
  y treinta thirty minutes past the hour (time) 1
tren *m.* train 5
tres three 1
trescientos/as *adj.* three hundred 5
trimestre *m.* trimester; quarter 2
triste *adj.* sad 5
tú *fam. sub. pron.* you 1
  Tú eres... You are . . . 1
tu(s) *fam. poss. adj.* your 3
turismo *m.* tourism 5
turista *m., f.* tourist 1
turístico/a *adj.* touristic 5
tuyo/a(s) *fam. poss. pron.* your; (of) yours 11

U

Ud. *form. sing.* you 1
Uds. *form., pl.* you 1
último/a *adj.* last 15
un, uno/a *art.* a; one 1
  una vez más one more time 9
  una vez once; one time 6
único/a *adj.* only 3
universidad *f.* university; college 2
unos/as *pron.* some 1
urgente *adj.* urgent 12
usar *v.* to wear; to use 6
usted *form. sing.* you 1
  ustedes *form., pl.* you 1
útil *adj.* useful 1
uva *f.* grape 8

V

vaca *f.* cow 13
vacaciones *f. pl.* vacation 5
valle *m.* valley 13
vamos let's go 4
vaquero *m.* cowboy
  de vaqueros *m., pl.* western
varios/as *adj. m. f., pl.* various 8
vaso *m.* glass 12
veces *f., pl.* times 6
vecino/a *m., f.* neighbor 12
veinte twenty 1
veinticinco twenty-five 1
veinticuatro twenty-four 1
veintidós twenty-two 1
veintinueve twenty-nine 1
veintiocho twenty-eight 1
veintiséis twenty-six 1
veintisiete twenty-seven 1
veintitrés twenty-three 1
veintiún, veintiuno/a *adj.* twenty-one 1
vejez *f.* old age 9
velocidad *f.* speed 11
  velocidad máxima *f.* speed limit 11
vendedor(a) *m., f.* salesperson 6
vender *v.* to sell 6
venir *v.* to come 3
ventana *f.* window 2
ver *v.* to see 4
  ver películas *f., pl.* to see movies 4
  a ver *v.* let's see 2
verano *m.* summer 5
verbo *m.* verb
verdad *f.* truth 9
  ¿verdad? right? 1
verde *adj., m. f.* green 6
verduras *pl., f.* vegetables 8
vestido *m.* dress 6
vestirse (e:i) *v.* to get dressed 7
vez *f.* time 6

viajar *v.* to travel 2
viaje *m.* trip 5
viajero/a *m., f.* traveler 5
vida *f.* life 9
video(casete) *m.* video (cassette) 11
videocasetera *f.* VCR 11
videoconferencia *f.* video conference
vidrio *m.* glass 13
viejo/a *adj.* old 3
viento *m.* wind 4
viernes *m., sing.* Friday 2
vinagre *m.* vinegar 8
vino *m.* wine 8
  vino blanco *m.* white wine 8
  vino tinto *m.* red wine 8
violencia *f.* violence
visitar *v.* to visit 4
  visitar monumentos *m., pl.* to visit monuments 4
visto/a *p.p.* seen 14
vitamina *f.* vitamin 14
viudo/a *adj.* widowed 9
vivienda *f.* housing 12
vivir *v.* to live 3
vivo/a *adj.* bright; lively; living 4
volante *m.* steering wheel 11
volcán *m.* volcano 13
vóleibol *m.* volleyball 4
volver (o:ue) *v.* to return 4
volver a ver(te, lo, la) *v.* to see (you) again
vos *pron.* you 1
vosotros/as *form., pl.* you
votar *v.* to vote
vuelta *f.* return trip 5
vuelto/a *p.p.* returned 14
vuestro/a(s) *poss. adj.* your 3

W

walkman *m.* Walkman 11

Y

y *conj.* and 1
  y cuarto quarter after (time) 1
  y media half-past (time) 1
  y quince quarter after (time) 1
  y treinta thirty (minutes past the hour) 1
  ¿Y tú? *fam.* And you? 1
  ¿Y Ud.? *form.* And you? 1
ya *adv.* already 6
yerno *m.* son-in-law 3
yo *sub. pron.* I 1
  Yo soy... I'm . . . 1
yogur *m.* yogurt 8

Z

zanahoria *f.* carrot 8
zapatería *f.* shoe store 14
zapatos (de tenis) *m., pl.* (tennis) shoes 6

English–Spanish

A

A.M. **mañana** *f.* 1
able: be able to **poder (o:ue)** *v.* 4
aboard **a bordo** 1
accident **accidente** *m.* 10
accompany **acompañar** *v.* 14
account **cuenta** *f.* 14
accountant **contador(a)** *m., f.*
accounting **contabilidad** *f.* 2
ache **dolor** *m.* 10
acid **ácido/a** *adj.* 13
   acid rain **lluvia ácida** 13
acquainted: be acquainted with
   conocer *v.* 8
action **acción** *f.*
active **activo/a** *adj.* 15
actor **actor** *m.,* **actriz** *f.*
addict (*drug*) **drogadicto/a**
   adj. 15
additional **adicional** *adj.*
address **dirección** *f.* 14
adjective **adjetivo** *m.*
adolescence **adolescencia** *f.* 9
adventure **aventura** *f.*
advertise **anunciar** *v.*
advertisement **anuncio** *m.*
advice **consejo** *m.* 9
   give advice **dar un consejo** 9
advise **aconsejar** *v.* 12
advisor **consejero/a** *m., f.*
aerobic **aeróbico/a** *adj.* 15
   aerobic exercises **ejercicios**
      aeróbicos 15
   aerobics class **clase de**
      ejercicios aeróbicos 15
affected **afectado/a** *adj.* 13
   be affected by **estar** *v.*
      afectado/a por 13
affirmative **afirmativo/a** *adj.*
afraid: be afraid (of) **tener miedo**
   (de) 3
   be afraid that **tener miedo**
      (de) que 13
after **después de** *prep.* 7
   después (de) que *conj.* 14
afternoon **tarde** *f.* 1
afterward **después** *adv.* 7; **luego**
   adv. 7
again **otra vez** 15
age **edad** *f.* 8
agree **concordar** *v.*
agree **estar** *v.* **de acuerdo**
agreement **acuerdo** *m.*
AIDS **SIDA** *m.*
air **aire** *m.* 6
   air pollution **contaminación**
      del aire 13
airplane **avión** *m.* 5
airport **aeropuerto** *m.* 5
alarm clock **despertador** *m.* 7
alcohol **alcohol** *m.* 15

alcoholic **alcohólico/a** *adj.* 15
all **todo/a** *adj.* 4
   All aboard! **¡Todos a bordo!** 1
   all of us **todos** 1
   all over the world **en todo el**
      mundo 13
allergic **alérgico/a** *adj.* 10
   be allergic (to) **ser alérgico/a**
      (a) 10
alleviate **aliviar** *v.* 15
almost **casi** *adv.* 10
alone **solo/a** *adj.*
along **por** *prep.* 11
already **ya** *adv.* 6
also **también** *adv.* 2
alternator **alternador** *m.* 11
although *conj.* **aunque**
aluminum **aluminio** *m.* 13
   (made of) aluminum **de**
      aluminio 13
always **siempre** *adv.* 7
American (*North*) **norteameri-**
   cano/a *adj.* 3
among **entre** *prep.* 2
amusement **diversión** *f.*
and **y** 1, **e** (*before words beginning*
   with **i** *or* **hi**) 4
   And you? **¿Y tú?** *fam.* 1; **¿Y**
      Ud.? *form.* 1
angry **enojado/a** *adj.* 5
   get angry (with) **enojarse** *v.*
      (con) 7
animal **animal** *m.* 13
ankle **tobillo** *m.* 10
anniversary **aniversario** *m.* 9
   (wedding) anniversary **aniver-**
      sario *m.* **(de bodas)** 9
announce **anunciar** *v.*
announcer (*TV/radio*) **locutor(a)**
   m., f.
annoy **molestar** *v.* 7
another **otro/a** *adj.* 6
answer **contestar** *v.* 2; **respuesta**
   f. 9
answering machine **contestadora**
   f. 11
antibiotic **antibiótico** *m.* 10
any **algún, alguno/a(s)** *adj.* 7
anyone **alguien** *pron.* 7
anything **algo** *pron.* 7
apartment **apartamento** *m.* 12
apartment building **edificio de**
   apartamentos 12
appear **parecer** *v.* 8
appetizers **entremeses** *m., pl.* 8
applaud **aplaudir** *v.*
apple **manzana** *f.* 8
appliance (*electric*) **elec-**
   trodoméstico *m.* 12
applicant **aspirante** *m., f.*
application **solicitud** *f.*
   job application **solicitud de**
      trabajo
apply (*for a job*) **solicitar** *v.*
   apply for a loan **pedir** *v.*
      préstamo 14

appointment **cita** *f.* 9
   have an appointment **tener** *v.*
      una cita 9
appreciate **apreciar** *v.*
April **abril** *m.* 5
aquatic **acuático/a** *adj.* 4
archaeologist **arqueólogo/a**
   m., f.
architect **arquitecto/a** *m., f.*
area **región** *f.* 13
arm **brazo** *m.* 10
armchair **sillón** *m.* 12
army **ejército** *m.*
around here **por aquí** 11
arrange **arreglar** *v.* 5
arrival **llegada** *f.*
arrive **llegar** *v.* 2
art **arte** *m.* 2
   fine arts **bellas artes** *f., pl.*
article *m.* **artículo**
artist **artista** *m., f.* 3
artistic **artístico/a** *adj.*
arts **artes** *f., pl.*
as **como** 8
   as . . . as **tan… como** 8
   as a child **de niño/a** 10
   as many . . . as **tantos/as…**
      como 8
   as much . . . as **tanto…**
      como 8
   as soon as **en cuanto** *conj.* 14;
      tan pronto como *conj.* 14
ask (*a question*) *v.* **preguntar** *v.* 2
   ask for **pedir (e:i)** *v.* 4
asparagus **espárragos** *m., pl.* 8
aspirin **aspirina** *f.* 10
at **a** *prep.* 1
   at + *time* **a la(s)** + *time* 1
   at home **en casa** 7
   at least **por lo menos** 10
   at night **por la noche** 7
   at the end (of) **al fondo (de)** 12
   At what time . . . ? **¿A qué**
      hora…? 1
   At your service. **A sus**
      órdenes. 11
attend **asistir (a)** *v.* 3
attic **altillo** *m.* 12
attract **atraer** *v.* 4
audience **público** *m.*
August **agosto** *m.* 5
aunt **tía** *f.* 3
   aunts and uncles **tíos** *m., pl.* 3
automatic **automático/a** *adj.* 14
   automatic teller machine (ATM)
      cajero automático 14
automobile **automóvil** *m.* 5;
   carro *m.;* **coche** *m.* 11
autumn **otoño** *m.* 5
avenue **avenida** *f.* 11
avoid **evitar** *v.* 13
award **premio** *m.*

B

backpack **mochila** *f.* 2
bad **mal, malo/a** *adj.* 3
   It's bad that . . . **Es malo
      que...** 12
   It's not at all bad. **No está
      nada mal.** 5
bag **bolsa** *f.* 6
bakery **panadería** *f.* 14
balanced **equilibrado/a** *adj.* 15
   balanced diet **dieta
      equilibrada** 15
balcony **balcón** *m.*12
ball **pelota** *f.* 4
ballet **ballet** *m.*
banana **banana** *f.* 8
band **banda** *f.*
bank **banco** *m.* 14
bargain **ganga** *f.* 6; **regatear** *v.* 6
baseball (*game*) **béisbol** *m.*4
basement **sótano** *m.* 12
basketball (*game*) **baloncesto** *m.*
   4
bathe **bañarse** *v.* 7
bathing suit **traje** *m.* **de baño** 6
bathroom **baño** *m.* 7; **cuarto de
   baño** *m.* 7
be **ser** *v.* 1; **estar** *v.* 2
be . . . years old **tener... años** 3
beach **playa** *f.* 5
beans **frijoles** *m., pl.* 8
beautiful **hermoso/a** *adj.* 6
beauty **belleza** *f.* 14
   beauty salon **peluquería** *f.* 14;
      salón *m.* **de belleza** 14
because **porque** *conj.* 2
   because of **por** *prep.* 11
become (+ *adj.*) **ponerse (+ *adj.*)**
   7; **convertirse** *v.* 6
bed **cama** *f.* 5
   go to bed **acostarse (o:ue)** *v.* 7
bedroom **alcoba** *f.* 12; **cuarto** *m.*
   12; **recámara** *f.*
beef **carne de res** *f.* 8
   beef soup **caldo de patas** 8
been **sido** *p.p.* 15
beer **cerveza** *f.* 8
before **antes** *adv.* 7; **antes de**
   prep. 7; **antes (de) que**
   conj. 13
beg **rogar (o:ue)** *v.* 12
begin **comenzar (e:ie)** *v.* 4;
   empezar (e:ie) *v.* 4
behalf: on behalf of **de parte
   de** 11
behind **detrás de** *prep.* 2
believe (in) **creer** *v.* **(en)** 3
bellhop **botones** *m., sing.* 5
beloved **enamorado/a** *adj.* 5
below **debajo de** *prep.* 2
belt **cinturón** *m.* 6
benefit **beneficio** *m.*
beside **al lado de** *prep.* 2
besides **además (de)** *adv.* 10

best **mejor** *adj.* 8
   the best **el/la mejor** *m., f.* 8 **lo
      mejor** *neuter*
better **mejor** *adj.* 8
   It's better that . . . **Es mejor
      que...** 12
between **entre** *prep.* 2
bicycle **bicicleta** *f.* 4
big **gran, grande** *adj.* 3
bill **cuenta** *f.* 9
billion: billion **mil millones** 5
biology **biología** *f* . 2
bird **ave** *f.* 13; **pájaro** *m.* 13
birth **nacimiento** *m.* 9
birthday **cumpleaños** *m., sing.* 9
   birthday cake **pastel de
      cumpleaños** 9
   have a birthday **cumplir** *v.*
      años 9
biscuit **bizcocho** *m.* 9
black **negro/a** *adj.* 6
blackberry **mora** *f.* 8
blackboard **pizarra** *f.* 2
blanket **manta** *f.* 12
block (city) **cuadra** *f.* 14
blond(e) **rubio/a** *adj.* 3
blouse **blusa** *f.* 6
blue **azul** *adj. m., f.* 6
boarding house **pensión** *f.* 5
boat **barco** *m.* 5
body **cuerpo** *m.* 10
bone **hueso** *m.* 10
book **libro** *m.* 2
bookcase **estante** *m.* 12
bookstore **librería** *f.* 2
boot **bota** *f.* 6
bore **aburrir** *v.* 7
bored **aburrido/a** *adj.* 5
   be bored **estar** *v.* **aburrido/a** 5
   get bored **aburrirse** *v.*
boring **aburrido/a** *adj.* 5
born: be born **nacer** *v.* 9
borrow **pedir prestado** 14
borrowed **prestado/a** *adj.* 14
boss **jefe** *m.,* **jefa** *f.*
bottle **botella** *f.* 9
   bottle of wine **botella de
      vino** 9
bother **molestar** *v.* 7
bottom **fondo** *m.* 12
boulevard **bulevar** *m.* 11
boy **chico** *m.* 1; **muchacho** *m.* 3
boyfriend **novio** *m.* 3
brakes **frenos** *m., pl.* 11
bread **pan** *m.* 8
break **romperse** *v.* 10
   break a leg **romper(se) la
      pierna** 10
   break down: The . . . broke
      down on us. **Se nos dañó
      el/la...** 11
   break up (with) **romper** *v.*
      (con) 9
breakfast **desayuno** *m.* 8
   have breakfast **desayunar** *v.* 8

breathe **respirar** *v.* 13
bring **traer** *v.* 4
broadcast **transmitir** *v.*;
   emitir *v.*
brochure **folleto** *m.*
broken **roto/a** *adj.* 10
   be broken **estar roto/a** 10
brother **hermano** *m.* 3
   brother-in-law **cuñado** *m., f.* 3
   brothers and sisters **hermanos**
      m., pl. 3
brought **traído** *p.p.* 14
brown **café** *adj.* 6; **marrón** *adj.*6
brunet(te) **moreno/a** *adj.* 3
brush **cepillar** *v.* 7
   brush one's hair **cepillarse el
      pelo** 7
   brush one's teeth **cepillarse los
      dientes** 7
build **construir** *v.* 4
building **edificio** *m.* 12
bullfight **corrida** *f.* **de toros** 4
bump into (*meet accidentally*)
   darse con 10
burned (out) **quemado/a** *adj.* 11
bus **autobús** *m.* 1
   bus station **estación** *f.* **de
      autobuses** 5
business **negocios** *m. pl.*
   business administration **admi-
      nistración** *f.* **de empresas** 2
   business-related **comercial**
      adj.
businessman **hombre** *m.* **de
   negocios**
businesswoman **mujer** *f.* **de
   negocios**
busy **ocupado/a** *adj.* 5
but **pero** *conj.* 2; **sino** *conj.* (*in
   negative sentences*) 7
butcher shop **carnicería** *f.* 14
butter **mantequilla** *f.* 8
buy **comprar** *v.* 2
by **por** *conj.* 11
   by phone **por teléfono** 7
   by plane **en avión** 5
bye **chau** *interj. fam.* 1

C

cabin **cabaña** *f.* 5
cable television **televisión** *f.*
   por cable *m.* 11
café **café** *m.* 4
cafeteria **cafetería** *f.* 2
cake **pastel** *m.* 9
calculator **calculadora** *f.* 11
call **llamar** *v.* 7
   call on the phone **llamar por
      teléfono** 11
   be called **llamarse** *v.* 7
calm **tranquilo/a** *adj.* 15
   Stay calm! **¡Tranquilo!** *adj.* 7
calorie **caloría** *f.* 15

camera **cámara** *f.* 11

camp **acampar** *v.* 5

can **lata** *f.* 13

can **poder (o:ue)** *v.* 4

Canadian **canadiense** *adj.* 3

candidate **aspirante** *m. f.*; candidate **candidato/a** *m., f.*

candy **dulces** *m., pl.* 9

capital (city) **capital** *f.* 1

car **coche** *m.* 11; **carro** *m.* 11; **auto(móvil)** *m.* 5

caramel **caramelo** *m.* 9

card **tarjeta** *f.* 4; (*playing*) **carta** *f.* 5

care **cuidado** *m.* 3

take care of **cuidar** *v.* 13

career **carrera** *f.*

careful: be careful **tener** *v.* **cuidado** 3

carpenter **carpintero/a** *m., f.*

carpet **alfombra** *f.* 12

carrot **zanahoria** *f.* 8

carry **llevar** *v.* 2

cartoons **dibujos** *m, pl.* **animados**

case: in case (that) **en caso (de) que** 13

cash (a check) **cobrar** *v.* 14; **efectivo** *m.* 14

cash register **caja** *f.* 6

pay in cash **pagar** *v.* **al contado** 14; **pagar en efectivo** 14

cashier **cajero/a** *m., f.* 14

cat **gato/a** *m., f.* 13

celebrate **celebrar** *v.* 9

cellar **sótano** *m.* 12

cellular **celular** *adj.* 11

cellular telephone **teléfono celular** *m.* 11

cereal **cereales** *m., pl.* 8

certain **cierto** *m.*; **seguro** *m.* 13

chalk **tiza** *f.* 2

champagne **champán** *m.* 9

change **cambiar** *v.* **(de)** 9

channel (*TV*) **canal** *m.* 11

character (*fictional*) **personaje** *m.*

main character *m.* **personaje principal**

chauffeur **conductor(a)** *m., f.* 1

cheap **barato/a** *adj.* 6

check **comprobar** *v.*; **revisar** *v.* 11; (*bank*) **cheque** *m.* 14

check the oil **revisar el aceite** 11

checking account **cuenta** *f.* **corriente** 14

cheese **queso** *m.* 8

chef **cocinero/a** *m., f.*

chemistry **química** *f.* 2

chest of drawers **cómoda** *f.* 12

chicken **pollo** *m.* 8

child **niño/a** *m., f.* 3

childhood **niñez** *f.* 9

children **hijos** *m., pl.* 3

Chinese **chino/a** *adj.* 3

chocolate **chocolate** *m.* 9

chocolate cake **pastel** *m.* **de chocolate** 9

cholesterol **colesterol** *m.* 15

choose **escoger** *v.* 8

chop (*food*) **chuleta** *f.* 8

Christmas **Navidad** *f.* 9

church **iglesia** *f.* 4

citizen **ciudadano/a** *adj.*

city **ciudad** *f.* 4

class **clase** *f.* 2

take classes **tomar clases** 2

classical **clásico/a** *adj.*

classmate **compañero/a** *m., f.* **de clase** 2

clean **limpio/a** *adj.* 5; **limpiar** *v.* 12

clean the house *v.* **limpiar la casa** 12

clear (*weather*) **despejado/a** *adj.* 4

clear the table **quitar la mesa** 12

It's (very) clear. (*weather*) **Está (muy) despejado.** 4

clerk **dependiente/a** *m., f.* 6

climb **escalar** *v.* 4

climb mountains **escalar montañas** 4

clinic **clínica** *f.* 10

clock **reloj** *m.* 2

close **cerrar (e:ie)** *v.* 4

closed **cerrado/a** *adj.* 5

closet **armario** *m.* 12

clothes **ropa** *f.* 6

clothes dryer **secadora** *f.* 12

clothing **ropa** *f.* 6

cloud **nube** *f.* 13

cloudy **nublado/a** *adj.* 4

It's (very) cloudy. **Está (muy) nublado.** 4

coat **abrigo** *m.* 6

coffee **café** *m.* 8

coffee maker **cafetera** *f.* 12

cold **frío** *m.* 4; (*disease*); **resfriado** *m.* 10

be (*feel*) cold **tener frío** 3

It's cold. (*weather*) **Hace frío.** 4

college **universidad** *f.* 2

collision **choque** *m.*

color **color** *m.* 6

comb one's hair **peinarse** *v.* 7

come **venir** *v.* 3

comedy **comedia** *f.*

comfortable **cómodo/a** *adj.* 5

commerce **negocios** *m., pl.*

commercial **comercial** *adj.*

communicate (with) **comunicarse** *v.* **(con)**

communication **comunicación** *f.*

means of communication **medios** *m. pl.* **de comunicación**

community **comunidad** *f* .1

compact disc (CD) **disco** *m.* **com-**

pacto 11

compact disc player **tocadiscos** *m. sing.* **compacto** 11

company **compañía** *f.*; **empresa** *f.*

comparison **comparación** *f.*

completely **completamente** *adv.*

composer **compositor(a)** *m., f.*

computer **computadora** *f.* 1

computer disc **disco** *m.* 11

computer monitor **monitor** *m.* 11

computer programmer **programador(a)** *m., f.* 3

computer science **computación** *f.* 2

concert **concierto** *m.*

conductor (*musical*) **director(a)** *m., f.*

confirm **confirmar** *v.* 5

confirm the reservation **confirmar la reservación** 5

congested **congestionado/a** *adj.* 10

Congratulations! (*for an event such as a birthday or anniversary*) **¡Felicidades!** 9; (*for an event such as an engagement or a good grade on a test*) *f., pl.* **¡Felicitaciones!** 9

conservation **conservación** *f.* 13

conserve **conservar** *v.* 13

consume **consumir** *v.* 15

contact lenses **lentes** *m. pl.* **de contacto** 6

container **envase** *m.* 13

contamination **contaminación** *f.* 13

content **contento/a** *adj.* 5

contest **concurso** *m.*

continue **seguir (e:i)** *v.* 4

control **control** *m.* 7; **controlar** *v.* 13

be under control **estar bajo control** 7

conversation **conversación** *f.* 2

converse **conversar** *v.* 2

cook **cocinar** *v.* 12; **cocinero/a** *m., f.*

cookie **galleta** *f.* 9

cool **fresco/a** *adj.* 4

It's cool. (*weather*) **Hace fresco.** 4

corn **maíz** *m.* 5

corner **esquina** *m.* 14

cost **costar (o:ue)** *v.* 6

cotton **algodón** *m.* 6

(made of) cotton **de algodón** 6

couch **sofá** *m.* 12

couch potato **teleadicto/a** *m., f.* 15

cough **tos** *f.* 10; **toser** *v.* 10

counselor **consejero/a** *m., f.*

count (on) **contar** *v.* **(con)** 12

country (*nation*) **país** *m.* 1
countryside **campo** *m.* 5; **paisaje**
  m. 5
couple (married) **pareja** *f.* 9
course **curso** *m.* 2; **materia** *f.* 2
courtesy **cortesía** *f.*
cousin **primo/a** *m., f.* 3
cover **cubrir** *v.* 14
covered **cubierto** *p.p.* 14
cow **vaca** *f.* 13
cowboy **vaquero** *m.*
crafts **artesanía** *f.*
craftsmanship **artesanía** *f.*
crater **cráter** *m.* 13
crazy **loco/a** *adj.* 6
create **crear** *v.*
credit **crédito** *m.* 6
  credit card **tarjeta** *f.* **de**
    crédito 6
crime **crimen** *m.*
cross **cruzar** *v.* 14
culture **cultura** *f.*
cup **taza** *f.* 12
currency exchange **cambio** *m.* **de**
  moneda 8
current events **actualidades**
  f., pl.
curriculum vitae **currículum** *m.*
curtains **cortinas** *f., pl.* 12
custard (*baked*) **flan** *m.* 9
custom **costumbre** *f.* 1
customer **cliente** *m., f.* 6
customs **aduana** *f.* 5
  customs inspector **inspector(a)**
    m., f. **de aduanas** 5
cycling **ciclismo** *m.* 4

D

dad **papá** *m.* 3
daily **diario/a** *adj.* 7
  daily routine **rutina** *f.* **diaria** 7
damage **dañar** *v.* 11
dance **bailar** *v.* 2; **danza** *f.*; **baile**
  m.
dancer **bailarín/bailarina**
  m. f.
danger **peligro** *m.* 13
dangerous **peligroso/a** *adj.*
date (*appointment*) **cita** *f.* 9; (*cal-
  endar*) **fecha** *f.* 5; (*someone*)
  salir *v.* **con (alguien)** 9
  date: have a date **tener una**
    cita 9
daughter **hija** *f.* 3
  daughter-in-law **nuera** *f.* 3
day **día** *m.* 1
  day before yesterday **anteayer**
    adv. 6
deal **trato** *m.*
  It's a deal. **Trato hecho.**
  It's no big deal. **No es para**
    tanto. 12

death **muerte** *f.* 9
decaffeinated **descafeinado/a**
  adj. 15
December **diciembre** *m.* 5
decide **decidir** *v.* 3
decided **decidido/a** *adj.* 14
declare **declarar** *v.*
deforestation **deforestación** *f.*
  13
delicious **delicioso/a** *adj.* 8;
  rico/a *adj.* 8; **sabroso/a** *adj.* 8
delighted **encantado/a** *adj.* 1
dentist **dentista** *m., f.* 10
deny **negar (e: ie)** *v.* 13
department store **almacén** *m.* 6
departure **salida** *f.* 5
deposit **depositar** *v.* 14
describe **describir** *v.* 3
described **descrito/a** *p.p.* 14
desert **desierto** *m.* 13
design **diseño** *m.* 3
designer **diseñador(a)** *m., f.*
desire **desear** *v.* 2
desk **escritorio** *m.* 2
dessert **postre** *m.* 9
destroy **destruir** *v.* 13
develop **desarrollar** *v.* 13
diary **diario** *m.* 1
dictatorship **dictadura** *f.*
dictionary **diccionario** *m.* 1
die **morir (o:ue)** *v.* 8
died **muerto/a** *p.p.* 14
diet **dieta** *f.* 15
  balanced diet **dieta equilibrada**
    15
  be on a diet **estar a dieta** 15
difficult **difícil** *adj. m., f.* 3
dining room **comedor** *m.* 12
dinner **cena** *f.* 8
  have dinner **cenar** *v.* 8
directions **direcciones** *f., pl.* 14
  give directions **dar**
    direcciones 14
director **director(a)** *m., f.*
dirty **ensuciar** *v.* 12; **sucio/a**
  adj. 5
  get dirty **ensuciar** *v.* 12
disagree **no estar de acuerdo**
disaster **desastre** *m.*
discover **descubrir** *v.* 13
discovered **descubierto** *p.p.* 14
discrimination **discriminación**
  f.
dish **plato** *m.* 8
  main dish *m.* **plato principal** 8
dishwasher **lavaplatos** *m.,
  sing.* 12
disk **disco** *m.* 11
disorderly **desordenado/a** *adj.* 5
dive **bucear** *v.* 4
divorce **divorcio** *m.* 9
divorced **divorciado/a** *adj.* 9
  get divorced (from) **divorciarse**
    v. **(de)** 9

dizzy **mareado/a** *adj.* 10
do **hacer** *v.* 4
  do aerobics **hacer ejercicios**
    aeróbicos 15
  do errands **hacer diligencias**
    14
  do household chores **hacer**
    quehaceres domésticos 12
  do stretching exercises **hacer**
    ejercicios de estiramiento
    15
doctor **doctor(a)** *m., f.* 3; **médi-
  co/a** *m., f.* 3
documentary (*film*) **documental**
  m.
dog **perro/a** *m., f.* 13
domestic **doméstico/a** *adj.*
  domestic appliance **elec-
    trodoméstico** *m.* 12
done **hecho/a** *p.p.* 14
door **puerta** *f.* 2
dormitory **residencia** *f.* **estudiantil** 2
double **doble** *adj.* 5
  double room **habitación** *f.*
    doble 5
doubt **duda** *f.* 13; **dudar** *v.* 13
  There is no doubt that . . . **No**
    cabe duda (de) que... 13;
    No hay duda (de) que...
    13
Down with . . . ! **¡Abajo el/
  la...!** 15
downtown **centro** *m.* 4
drama **drama** *m.*
dramatic **dramático/a** *adj.*
draw **dibujar** *v.* 2
drawing **dibujo** *m.*
dress **vestido** *m.* 6
  get dressed **vestirse (e:i)** *v.* 7
drink **beber** *v.* 3; **bebida** *f.* 8;
  tomar *v.* 2
  Do you want something to
    drink? **¿Quieres algo de**
    tomar? 8
drive **conducir** *v.* 8; **manejar**
  v. 11
driver **conductor(a)** *m., f.* 1
drug *f.* **droga** 15
  drug addict **drogadicto/a**
    adj. 15
due to **por** *prep.* 11
  due to the fact that **debido a** 3
during **durante** *prep.* 7; **por**
  prep. 11
dust **sacudir** *v.* 12
  dust the furniture **sacudir los**
    muebles 12
dying: I'm dying to (for) . . . **me**
  muero por... 1

E

each **cada** *adj. m., f.* 6
eagle **águila** *f.* 1
ear (outer) **oreja** *f.* 10
early **temprano** *adv.* 7
earn **ganar** *v.*
earthquake **terremoto** *m.*
ease **aliviar** *v.* 15
east **este** *m.* 14
  to the east **al este** 14
easy **fácil** *adj.* 3
eat **comer** *v.* 3
ecology **ecología** *f.* 13
economics **economía** *f.* 2
ecotourism **ecoturismo** *m.* 13
Ecuador **Ecuador** *m.* 1
Ecuadorian **ecuatoriano/a** *adj.* 3
effective **eficaz** *adj. m., f.* 8
egg **huevo** *m.* 8
eight **ocho** 1
eight hundred **ochocientos/as** 5
eighteen **dieciocho** 1
eighth **octavo/a** 5
eighty **ochenta** 2
either . . . or **o... o** *conj.* 7
elect **elegir** *v.*
election **elecciones** *f. pl.*
electrician **electricista** *m., f.*
electricity **luz** *f.* 12
elegant **elegante** *adj. m., f.* 6
elevator **ascensor** *m.* 5
eleven **once** 1
e-mail **correo** *m.* **electrónico** 4
  e-mail message **mensaje** *m.*
    electrónico 4
  read e-mail **leer** *v.* **el correo**
    electrónico 4
embarrassed **avergonzado/a**
  adj. 5
embrace (each other) **abrazar(se)**
  v. 11
emergency **emergencia** *f.* 10
  emergency room **sala** *f.* **de**
    emergencia 10
employee **empleado/a** *m., f.* 5
employment **empleo** *m.*
end **fin** *m.* 4; **terminar** *v.* 2
  end table **mesita** *f.* 12
energy **energía** *f.* 13
engaged: get engaged (to) **com-**
  prometerse *v.* **(con)** 9
engineer **ingeniero/a** *m., f.* 3
English (*language*) **inglés** *m.* 2;
  inglés, inglesa *adj.* 3
enjoy **disfrutar** *v.* **(de)** 15
enough **bastante** *adj.* 10
entertainment **diversión** *f.* 4
entrance **entrada** *f.* 12
envelope **sobre** *m.* 14
environment **medio ambiente**
  m. 13
equality **igualdad** *f.*
equipped **equipado/a** *adj.* 15
eraser **borrador** *m.* 2

errand *f.* **diligencia** 14
establish **establecer** *v.*
evening **tarde** *f.* 1
event **acontecimiento** *m.*
every day **todos los días** 10
everybody **todos** *m., pl.* 13
everything **todo** *m.* 5
  Everything is under control.
    Todo está bajo control. 7
exactly **en punto** 1
exam **examen** *m.* 2
excellent **excelente** *adj.* 5
excess **exceso** *m.* 15
  in excess **en exceso** 15
exchange **intercambiar** *v.* 8
  in exchange for **por** 11
exciting **emocionante** *adj. m., f.*
excursion **excursión** *f.* 4
excuse **disculpar** *v.* 8
Excuse me. (*May I?*) **Con per-**
  miso. 1; (*I beg your pardon.*)
  Perdón. 1
exercise **ejercicio** *m.* 15
  hacer ejercicio 15
exit **salida** *f.* 5
expensive **caro/a** *adj.* 6
experience **experiencia** *f.*
explain **explicar** *v.* 2
explore **explorar** *v.* 4
  explore a city/town **explorar**
    una ciudad/pueblo 4
expression **expresión** *f.*
extinction **extinción** *f.* 13
eye **ojo** *m.* 10

F

fabulous **fabuloso/a** *adj* 5
face **cara** *f.* 7
facing **enfrente de** *prep.* 14
fact: in fact **de hecho** 5
fall (down) **caerse** *v.* 10
  fall asleep **dormirse (o:ue)** *v.* 7
  fall in love (with) **enamorarse**
    v. **(de)** 9
fall (season) **otoño** *m.* 5
fallen **caído** *p.p.* 14
family **familia** *f.* 3
famous **famoso/a** *adj.*
fan **aficionado/a** *adj.* 4
  be a fan of **ser aficionado/a**
    a 4
far from **lejos de** *prep.* 2
farewell **despedida** *f.*
fascinate **fascinar** *v.* 7
fashion **moda** *f.* 6
  be in fashion **estar de moda** 6
fast **rápido/a** *adj.* 8
fat **gordo/a** *adj.* 3; **grasa** *f.* 15
father **padre** *m.* 3
father-in-law **suegro** *m.* 3
favorite **favorito/a** *adj.* 4
fax (machine) *fax* *m.* 11

fear **miedo** *m.* 3; fear **temer** *v.* 13
February **febrero** *m.* 5
feel **sentir(se) (e:ie)** *v.* 7
  feel like (*doing something*) **tener**
    v. **ganas de (+ *inf.*)** 3
festival **festival** *m.*
fever **fiebre** *f.* 10
  have a fever **tener** *v.* **fiebre** 10
few **pocos/as** *adj. pl.* 5
field: major field of study **espe-**
  cialización *f.*
fifteen **quince** 1
fifth **quinto/a** 5
fifty **cincuenta** 2
fight **luchar** *v.* **(por)**
figure (*number*) **cifra** *f.*
file **archivo** *m.* 11
fill **llenar** *v.* 11
  fill out a form **llenar un**
    formulario 14
  fill the tank **llenar** *v.* **el**
    tanque 11
finally **finalmente** *adv.* 15; **por**
  último 7; **por fin** 11
find **encontrar (o:ue)** *v.* 4
  find (each other) **encontrar(se)**
    v. 11
fine arts **bellas artes** *f., pl.*
fine **multa** *f.* 11
  That's fine. **Está bien.** 11
finger **dedo** *m.* 10
finish **terminar** *v.* 2
  finish (*doing something*)
    terminar *v.* **de (+*inf.*)** 4
fire **incendio** *m.*; **despedir (e:i)**
firefighter **bombero/a** *m., f.*
firm **compañía** *f.*; **empresa** *f.*
first **primer, primero/a** *adj.* 5
fish (*food*) **pescado** *m.* 8; **pescar**
  v. 5; (*live*) **pez** *m.* 13
  fish market **pescadería** *f.* 14
fisherman **pescador** *m.* 5
fisherwoman **pescadora** *f.* 5
fishing **pesca** *f.* 5
fit (*clothing*) **quedar** *v.* 7
five **cinco** 1
five hundred **quinientos/as** 5
fix (*put in working order*) **arreglar**
  v. 11
fixed **fijo/a** *adj.* 6
flag **bandera** *f.*
flank steak **lomo** *m.* 8
flat tire: We had a flat tire. **Se nos**
  pinchó una llanta. 11
flexible **flexible** *adj.* 15
flood **inundación** *f.*
floor (*story in a building*) **piso** *m.*
  5; **suelo** *m.* 12
  ground floor **planta** *f.* **baja** 5
  top floor **planta** *f.* **alta** 5
flower **flor** *f.* 13
flu **gripe** *f.* 10
fog **niebla** *f.* 4
foggy: It's (very) foggy. **Hay**
  (mucha) niebla. 4

folk **folklórico/a** *adj.*
follow **seguir (e:i)** *v.* 4
food **comida** *f.* 8
foolish **tonto/a** *adj.* 3
foot **pie** *m.* 10
football **fútbol** *m.* **americano** 4
for **para** *prep.* 11; **por** *prep.* 11
  for example **por ejemplo** 11
  for me **para mí** 8
forbid **prohibir** *v.* 10
foreign **extranjero/a** *adj.*
  foreign languages **lenguas**
   f. pl. **extranjeras** 2
forest **bosque** *m.* 13
forget **olvidar** *v.* 10
fork **tenedor** *m.* 12
form **formulario** *m.* 14
forty **cuarenta** *m.* 2
forward **en marcha** *adv.* 15
four **cuatro** 1
four hundred **cuatrocientos/as** 5
fourteen **catorce** 1
fourth **cuarto/a** *m., f.* 5
free **libre** *adj. m., f.* 4
  be free (of charge) **ser gratis** 14
  free time **tiempo libre** 4; **ratos**
   libres 4
freedom **libertad** *f.*
freezer **congelador** *m.* 12
French **francés, francesa** *m., f.* 3
  french fries **papas** *f., pl* **fritas** 8
   patatas *f., pl* **fritas** 8
frequently **frecuentemente** *adv.*
  10; **con frecuencia** *adv.* 10
Friday **viernes** *m., sing.* 2
fried **frito/a** *adj.* 8
  fried potatoes **papas** *f., pl.*
   fritas 8; **patatas** *f., pl.*
   fritas 8
friend **amigo/a** *m., f.* 3
friendly **amable** *adj. m., f.* 5
friendship **amistad** *f.* 9
from **de** *prep.* 1; **desde** *prep.* 6
  from the United States *adj.*
   estadounidense 3
  from time to time **de vez en**
   cuando 10
  He/She/It is from . . . **Es de...** 1
fruit **fruta** *f.* 8
  fruit juice **jugo** *m.* **de fruta** 8
  fruit store **frutería** *f.* 14
full **lleno/a** *adj.* 11
fun **divertido/a** *adj.* 7
  fun activity **diversión** *f.* 4
  have fun **divertirse (e:ie)** *v.* 9
function **funcionar** *v.* 11
furniture **muebles** *m., pl.* 12
furthermore **además (de)** *adv.* 10
future **futuro** *adj.;* **porvenir** *m.*

G

gain weight **aumentar** *v.* **de peso**
  15; **engordar** 15
game **juego** *m.* 5; *(match)*
  partido *m.* 4
  game show **concurso** *m.*
garage **garaje** *m.* 12
garden **jardín** *m.* 12
garlic **ajo** *m.* 8
gas station **gasolinera** *f.* 11
gasoline **gasolina** *f.* 11
geography **geografía** *f.* 2
German **alemán, alemana** *adj.* 3
get **conseguir (e:i)** *v.* 4; **obtener**
  v.
  get along well/badly with
   llevarse bien/mal con 9
  get bored **aburrirse** *v.*
  get off (a vehicle) **bajar** *v.* **(de)**
   11
  get on/in (a vehicle) **subir(se)** *v.*
   a 11
  get up **levantarse** *v.* 7
gift **regalo** *m.* 6
girl **chica** *f.* 1; **muchacha** *f.* 3
girlfriend **novia** *f.* 3
give **dar** *v.* 9; *(as a gift)* **regalar** 9
glass *(drinking)* **vaso** *m.* 12;
  vidrio *m.* 13
  (made of) glass **de vidrio** 13
glasses **gafas** *f., pl.* 6
  sunglasses **gafas** *f., pl.*
   oscuras/de sol 6
gloves **guantes** *m., pl.* 6
go **ir** *v.* 4
  go away **irse** 7
  go by bus **ir en autobús** 5
  go by car **ir en auto(móvil)** 5
  go by motorcycle **ir en**
   motocicleta 5
  go by plane **ir en avión** 5
  go by ship **ir en barco** 5
  go by subway **ir en metro** 5
  go by taxi **ir en taxi** 5
  go by the bank **pasar por el**
   banco 14
  go by train **ir en tren** 5
  go by **pasar** *v.* **por** 5
  go down; **bajar(se)** *v.* 11
  go fishing **ir** *v.* **de pesca** 5
  go for a hike (in the mountains)
   ir de excursión (a las
   montañas) 4
  go out **salir** *v.* 9
  go out with **salir** *v.* **con** 4, 9
  go through customs **pasar** *v.*
   por la aduana 5
  go up **subir** *v.* 11
  go with **acompañar** *v.* 14
  Let's go. **Vamos.** 4
goblet **copa** *f.* 12
going to: be going to *(do some-*
  thing) **ir a (+ inf.)** 4
golf **golf** *m.* 4

good **buen, bueno/a** *adj.* 1, 3
  Good afternoon. **Buenas**
   tardes. 1
  Good evening. **Buenas**
   noches. 1
  Good morning. **Buenos días.** 1
  Good night. **Buenas noches.** 1
  I'm good, thanks. **Bien,**
   gracias. 1
  It's good that . . . **Es bueno**
   que... 12
good-bye **adiós** *m.* 1
  say good-bye (to) **despedirse** *v.*
   (de) (e:i) 7
good-looking **guapo/a** *adj.* 3
government **gobierno** *m.* 13
graduate (from) **graduarse** *v.*
  (en) 9
grains **cereales** *m., pl.* 8
granddaughter **nieta** *f.* 3
grandfather **abuelo** *m.* 3
grandmother **abuela** *f.* 3
grandparents **abuelos** *m. pl.* 3
grandson **nieto** *m.* 3
grape **uva** *f.* 8
grass **césped** *m.* 13; **hierba** *f.* 13
grave **grave** *adj.* 10
gray **gris** *adj. m., f.* 6
great **fenomenal** *adj. m., f.* 5
green **verde** *adj. m., f.* 6
greet (each other) **saludar(se)**
  v. 11
greeting **saludo** *m.* 1
  Greetings to . . . **Saludos a...** 1
grilled *(food)* **a la plancha** 8
  grilled flank steak **lomo a la**
   plancha 8
ground floor **planta baja** *f.* 5
guest *(at a house/hotel)* **huésped**
  m., f. 5 *(invited to a function)*
  invitado/a *m., f.* 9
guide **guía** *m., f.* 12
gym(nasium) **gimnasio** *m.* 4

H

hair **pelo** *m.* 7
hairdresser **peluquero/a** *m., f.*
half **medio/a** *adj.* 3
  half-brother **medio hermano**
   3; half-sister **media hermana** 3
  half-past . . . *(time)* **...y**
   media 1
hallway **pasillo** *m.* 12
ham **jamón** *m.* 8
hamburger **hamburguesa** *f.* 8
hand **mano** *f.* 1
Hands up! **¡Manos arriba!** 15
handsome **guapo** *adj.* 3
happen **ocurrir** *v.*
Happy birthday! **¡Feliz**
  cumpleaños! 9
happy **alegre** *adj.* 5; **contento/a**
  adj. 5; **feliz** *adj.* 5
  be happy **alegrarse** *v.* **(de)** 13

hard **difícil** *adj. m., f.* 3
hard-working **trabajador(a)**
　adj. 3
hardly **apenas** *adv.* 10
haste **prisa** *f.* 3
hat **sombrero** *m.* 6
hate **odiar** *v.* 9
have **tener** *v.* 3
　have to (*do something*) **tener**
　　que (+ *inf.***)** 3; **deber**
　　(+ *inf.***)** 3
head **cabeza** *f.* 10
headache **dolor de cabeza** *m.* 10
health **salud** *f.* 10
healthful **saludable** *adj. m., f.* 10
healthy **sano/a** *adj.* 10
　lead a healthy life **llevar** *v.* **una**
　　vida sana 15
hear **oír** *v.* 4
heard **oído** *p.p.* 14
hearing: sense of hearing **oído**
　m. 10
heart **corazón** *m.* 10
heat **calor** *m.* 4
Hello. **Hola.** 1; (*on the telephone*)
　Aló. 11; **¿Bueno?** 11; **Diga.** 11
help (to) **ayudar** *v.* **(a)** 12; **servir**
　(e:i) *v.* 5
　help each other **ayudarse** *v.* 11
her **su(s)** *poss.* 3; hers **suyo/a(s)**
　poss. 11
here *adv.* **aquí** 1
　Here it is. **Aquí está.** 5
　Here we are in . . . **Aquí**
　　estamos en... 2
Hi. **Hola.** 1
highway **autopista** *f.* 11;
　carretera *f.* 11
hike **excursión** *f.* 4
　go on a hike **hacer una excur-**
　　sión; ir de excursión 5
hiker *m., f.* **excursionista** 4
hiking **de excursión** 4
hire **contratar** *v.*
his **su(s)** *poss. adj.* 3; **suyo/a(s)**
　poss. pron. 11
history **historia** *f.* 2
hobby **pasatiempo** *m.* 4
hockey **hockey** *m.* 4
holiday **día** *m.* **de fiesta** 9
home **casa** *f.* 4
　home page **página** *f.*
　　principal 11
homework **tarea** *f.* 2
hood **capó** *m.* 11
hope **esperar** *v.* 2
　I hope (that) **Ojalá** 13
horror **horror** *m.*
hors d'oeuvres **entremeses** *m.,*
　pl. 8
horse **caballo** *m.* 5
hospital **hospital** *m.* 10
hot: be hot (*weather*) **hacer calor**
　4; (*feel*) **tener calor** 3
hotel **hotel** *m.* 5
hour **hora** *f.* 1

house **casa** *f.* 4
household chores **quehaceres** *m.*
　pl. **domésticos** 12
housewife **ama** *f.* **de casa** 12
housing **vivienda** *f.* 12
How . . . ! **¡Qué...!** 3
　how **¿cómo?** *adv.* 1
　How are you? **¿Qué tal?** 1
　How are you? **¿Cómo estás?**
　　fam. 1
　How are you? **¿Cómo está**
　　usted? *form.* 1
　How did it go for you . . .?
　　¿Cómo le/les fue...? 15
　How is it going? **¿Qué tal?** 1
　How is/are . . . ? **¿Qué tal...?** 2
　How many? **¿Cuánto/a(s) ?** 1
　How may I help you? **¿En qué**
　　puedo servirles? 5
　How much does it cost?
　　¿Cuánto cuesta...? 6
　How old are you? **¿Cuántos**
　　años tienes? *fam.* 3
however **sin embargo**
hug (each other) **abrazar(se)** *v.* 11
humanities **humanidades** *f., pl.* 2
hunger **hambre** *f.* 3
hundred **ciento** *m.* 2
hungry: be hungry **tener** *v.*
　hambre 3
hurricane **huracán** *m.*
hurry **apurarse** *v.* 15
　be in a hurry **tener** *v.* **prisa** 3
hurt **doler (o:ue)** *v.* 10
　It hurts me a lot . . . **Me duele**
　　mucho... 10
husband **esposo** *m.* 3

I

I am . . . **Yo soy...** 1
I hope (that) **Ojalá (que)** *interj.*
　13
I wish (that) **Ojalá (que)** *interj.* 13
ice cream **helado** *m.* 9
　ice cream shop **heladería** *f.* 14
iced **helado/a** *adj.* 9
　iced tea **té** *m.* **helado** 8
idea **idea** *f.* 4
if **si** *conj.* 4
illness **enfermedad** *f.* 10
important **importante** *adj.* 3
　be important to **importar** *v.* 7
impossible **imposible** *adj.* 13
improbable **improbable** *adj.* 13
improve **mejorar** *v.* 13
in **en** *prep.* 2
　in the afternoon **de la tarde** 1;
　　por la tarde 7
　in the evening **de la noche** 1;
　　por la noche 7
　in the morning **de la mañana**
　　1; **por la mañana** 7
　in love with **enamorado/a de**
　　5

in front of **delante de** *prep.* 2
increase **aumento** *m.*
incredible **increíble** *adj.* 5
inequality **desigualdad** *f.*
infection **infección** *f.* 10
inform **informar** *v.*
injection **inyección** *f.* 10
　give an injection *v.* **poner una**
　　inyección 10
injure (oneself) **lastimarse** 10
　injure (one's foot) **lastimarse** *v.*
　　(el pie) 10
inner ear **oído** *m.* 10
insist (on) **insistir** *v.* **(en)** 12
installments: pay in installments
　pagar *v.* **a plazos** 14
intelligent **inteligente** *adj.* 3
intend to **pensar** *v.* **(+** *inf.***)** 4
interest **interesar** *v.* 7
interesting **interesante** *adj.* 3
　be interesting to **interesar** *v.* 7
international **internacional**
　adj. m., f.
Internet **red** *f.* 11; **Internet** *m.* 11
interview **entrevista** *f.*; interview
　entrevistar *v.*
interviewer **entrevistador(a)** *m., f.*
introduction **presentación** *f.*
invest **invertir (i:ie)** *v.*
invite **invitar** *v.* 9
iron (clothes) **planchar** *v.* **la**
　ropa 12
Italian **italiano/a** *adj.* 3
its **su(s)** *poss. adj.* 3, **suyo/a(s)**
　poss. pron. 11

J

jacket **chaqueta** *f.* 6
January **enero** *m.* 5
Japanese **japonés, japonesa** *adj.*
　3
jeans **bluejeans** *m., pl.* 6
jewelry store **joyería** *f.* 14
job **empleo** *m.*; **puesto** *m.*; **tra-**
　bajo *m.*
　job application **solicitud** *f.* **de**
　　trabajo
jog **correr** *v.* 3
journalism **periodismo** *m.* 2
journalist **periodista** *m., f.* 3;
　reportero/a *m., f.*
joy **alegría** *f.* 9
　give joy **dar** *v.* **alegría** 9
joyful **alegre** *adj.* 5
juice **jugo** *m.* 8
July **julio** *m.* 5
June **junio** *m.* 5
jungle **selva, jungla** *f.* 13
just **apenas** *adv.* 10
　have just (*done something*)
　　acabar de (+ *inf.***)** 6

K

key **llave** *f.* 5
keyboard **teclado** *m.* 11
kilometer **kilómetro** *m.* 11
kind: That's very kind of you. **Muy amable.** 5
kiss (each other) **besar(se)** *v.* 11; **beso** *m.* 9
kitchen **cocina** *f.* 12
knee **rodilla** *f.* 10
knife **cuchillo** *m.* 12
know **saber** *v.* 8; **conocer** *v.* 8

L

laboratory **laboratorio** *m.* 2
lack **faltar** *v.* 7
lake **lago** *m.* 5
lamp **lámpara** *f.* 12
land **tierra** *f.* 13
landlord **dueño/a** *m.*, *f.* 8
landscape **paisaje** *m.* 5
language **lengua** *f.* 2
laptop (computer) **computadora** *f.* **portátil** 11
large (*clothing size*) **talla grande** 6
last **durar** *v.*; **pasado/a** *adj.* 6; **último/a** *adj.* 15
    last name **apellido** *m.* 9
    last night **anoche** *adv.* 6
late **tarde** *adv.* 7
later **más tarde** 7
    See you later. **Hasta la vista.** 1; **Hasta luego.** 1
laugh **reírse (e:i)** *v.* 9
laughed **reído** *p.p.* 14
laundromat **lavandería** *f.* 14
law **ley** *f.* 13
lawyer **abogado/a** *m.*, *f.*
lazy **perezoso/a** *adj.*
learn **aprender** *v.* 3
leave **salir** *v.* 4; **irse** *v.* 7
    leave a tip **dejar una propina** 9
    leave for (*a place*) **salir para** 4
    leave from **salir de** 4
    leave behind **dejar** *v.*
left **izquierdo/a** *adj.* 2
    be left over **quedar** *v.* 7
    to the left (of) **a la izquierda (de)** 2
leg **pierna** *f.* 10
lemon **limón** *m.* 8
lend **prestar** *v.* 6
less **menos** *adv.* 10
    less . . . than **menos... que** 8
    less than (+ *number*) **menos de (+ *number*)** 8
lesson **lección** *f.* 1
let **dejar** *v.* 12
let's see **a ver** 2
letter **carta** *f.* 4

lettuce **lechuga** *f.* 8
liberty **libertad** *f.*
library **biblioteca** *f.* 2
license (*driver's*) **licencia** *f.* **de conducir** 11
lie **mentira** *f.* 9
life **vida** *f.* 9
    of my life **de mi vida** 15
lifestyle: lead a healthy lifestyle **llevar una vida sana** 15
lift **levantar** *v.* 15
    lift weights **levantar pesas** 15
light **luz** *f.* 12
like **como** *prep.* 8; **gustar** *v.* 7
    I like . . . **me gusta(n)...** 2
    I like . . . very much *v.* **Me encanta...** 7
    Do you like . . . ? **¿Te gusta(n)...?** 2
likeable **simpático/a** *adj.* 3
likewise **igualmente** *adv.* 1
line **línea** *f.* 4; **cola** (*queue*) *f.* 14
listen to **escuchar** *v.* 2
    Listen! (*command*) **¡Oye!** *fam.*, *sing.*1; **¡Oigan!** *form.*, *pl.* 5
    listen to music **escuchar música** 2
    listen to the radio **escuchar la radio** 2
literature **literatura** *f.* 2
little (*quantity*) **poco/a** *adj.* 5
live **vivir** *v.* 3
living room **sala** *f.* 12
loan **préstamo** *m.* 14 **prestar** *v.* 6, 14
lobster **langosta** *f.* 8
located **situado/a** *adj.*
    be located **quedar** *v.* 14
long **largo/a** *adj.* 6
look for **buscar** *v.* 2
lose **perder (e:ie)** *v.* 4
    lose weight **adelgazar** *v.* 15
lost **perdido/a** *adj.* 14
    be lost **estar perdido/a** 14
lot of, a **mucho/a** *adj.* 2
love (*another person*) **querer (e:ie)** *v.* 4; (*things*) **encantar** *v.* 7; **amor** *m.* 9
    in love **enamorado/a** *adj.* 5
luck **suerte** *f.* 3
lucky: be lucky **tener suerte** 3
luggage **equipaje** *m.* 5
lunch **almuerzo** *m.* 8
    have lunch **almorzar (o:ue)** *v.* 8

M

ma'am **señora (Sra.)** *f.* 1
mad **enojado/a** *adj.* 5
magazine **revista** *f.* 4
magnificent **magnífico/a** *adj.* 6
mail **correo** *m.* 14; **enviar** *v.*, **mandar** *v.* 14

mail carrier **cartero** *m.* 14
mailbox **buzón** *m.* 14
main **principal** *adj. m.*, *f.* 8
maintain **mantener** *v.* 15
make **hacer** *v.* 4
    make the bed **hacer la cama** 12
make-up **maquillaje** *m.* 7
man **hombre** *m.* 1
manager **gerente** *m.*, *f.*
many **mucho/a** *adj.* 2, 3
    many times **muchas veces** 10
map **mapa** *m.* 1
March **marzo** *m.* 5
margarine **margarina** *f.* 8
marinated fish **ceviche** *m.* 8
    marinated shrimp **ceviche** *m.* **de camarón** 8
marital status **estado** *m.* **civil** 9
market **mercado** *m.* 6
marriage **matrimonio** *m.* 9
married **casado/a** *adj.* 9
    get married (to) **casarse** *v.* **(con)** 9
marvelous **maravilloso/a** *adj.* 5
marvelously **maravillosamente** *adv.*
massage **masaje** *m.* 15
masterpiece **obra maestra** *f.*
match (*sports*) **partido** *m.* 4
    match **hacer** *v.* **juego (con)** 6
mathematics **matemáticas** *f.*, *pl.* 2
matter **importar** *v.* 7
maturity **madurez** *f.* 9
maximum **máximo/a** *m.* 11
May **mayo** *m.* 5
maybe **tal vez** 5; **quizás** 5
mayonnaise **mayonesa** *f.* 8
meal **comida** *f.* 8
means of communication **medios** *m. pl.* **de comunicación**
meat **carne** *f.* 8
mechanic **mecánico/a** *m.*, *f.* 11
    mechanic's repair shop **taller mecánico** 11
media **medios** *m.*, *pl.* **de comunicación**
medical **médico/a** *adj.* 10
medication **medicamento** *m.* 10
medicine **medicina** *f.* 10
medium **mediano/a** *adj.* 6
meet (each other) **encontrar(se)** *v.* 11
meeting **reunión** *f.*
menu **menú** *m.* 8
message (*telephone*) **recado** *m.* 11
Mexican **mexicano/a** *adj.* 3
Mexico **México** *m.* 1
microwave **microonda** *f.* 12
    microwave oven **horno** *m.* **de microondas** 12
middle age **madurez** *f.* 9
midnight **medianoche** *f.* 1
mile **milla** *f.* 11

milk **leche** *f.* 8
million **millón** *m.* 5
million of **millón de** *m.* 5
mine **mío/a(s)** *poss.* 11
mineral **mineral** *m.* 15
   mineral water **agua** *f.*
    mineral 8
minute **minuto** *m.* 1
mirror **espejo** *m.* 7
Miss **señorita (Srta.)** *f.* 1
mistaken **equivocado/a** *adj.* 5
modem **módem** *m.* 11
modern **moderno/a** *adj.*
mom **mamá** *f.* 1
Monday **lunes** *m., sing.* 2
money **dinero** *m.* 6
monitor **monitor** *m.* 11
month **mes** *m.* 5
monument **monumento** *m.* 4
moon **luna** *f.* 13
more **más**
   more . . . than **más... que** 8
   more than (+ *number*) **más de**
    (+ number) 8
morning **mañana** *f.* 1
mother **madre** *f.* 3
mother-in-law **suegra** *f.* 3
motor **motor** *m.* 11
motorcycle **moto(cicleta)** *f.* 5
mountain **montaña** *f.* 4
mouse **ratón** *m.* 11
mouth **boca** *f.* 10
move (*to another house/city/coun-
try*) **mudarse** *v.* 12
movie **película** *f.* 4
   movie star **estrella** *f.* **de**
    cine
   movie theater **cine** *m.* 4
Mr. **señor (Sr.)** *m.* 1
Mrs. **señora (Sra.)** *f.* 1
much **mucho/a** *adj.* 2
municipal **municipal** *adj. m., f.* 4
murder **crimen** *m.*
muscle **músculo** *m.* 15
museum **museo** *m.* 4
mushroom **champiñón** *m.* 8
music **música** *f.* 2
musical **musical** *adj.*
musician **músico/a** *m., f.*
must: It must be . . . **Debe ser...** 6
my **mi(s)** *poss. adj.* 3; **mío/a(s)**
   poss. pron. 11

N

name **nombre** *m.* 5
   in the name of **a nombre de** 5
   last name *m.* **apellido** 9
   My name is . . . **Me llamo...** 1
   be named **llamarse** *v.* 7
napkin **servilleta** *f.* 12
national **nacional** *adj. m., f.*
nationality **nacionalidad** *f.* 1
natural **natural** *adj. m., f.* 13

natural disaster **desastre** *m.*
   natural
natural resource **recurso** *m.*
   natural 13
nature **naturaleza** *f.* 13
nauseated **mareado/a** *adj.* 10
near **cerca de** *prep.* 2
necessary **necesario/a** *adj.* 12
   It is necessary that . . . **Hay**
    que... 14
neck **cuello** *m.* 10
need **faltar** *v.* 7; **necesitar** *v.* 2
negative **negativo/a** *adj.*
neighbor **vecino/a** *m., f.* 12
neighborhood **barrio** *m.* 12
neither . . . nor **ni... ni** *conj.* 7;
   neither **tampoco** *adv.* 7
nephew **sobrino** *m.* 3
nervous **nervioso/a** *adj.* 5
network **red** *f.* 11
never **nunca** *adj.* 7; **jamás** 7
new **nuevo/a** *adj.* 6
newlywed **recién casado/a**
   m., f. 9
news **noticias** *f., pl.;* **actualidades** *f., pl.*
newscast **noticiero** *m.*
newspaper **periódico** 4; **diario**
   m.
next **próximo/a** *adj.*
nice **simpático/a** *adj.* 3; **amable**
   adj. m., f. 5
niece **sobrina** *f.* 3
night **noche** *f.* 1
   night stand **mesita** *f.* **de**
    noche 12
nine **nueve** 1
nine hundred **novecientos/as** 5
nineteen **diecinueve** 1
ninety **noventa** 2
ninth **noveno/a** 5
no **no** 1; **ningún, ninguno/a(s)**
   adj. 7
   no one **nadie** *pron.* 7
   No problem. **Ningún**
    problema. 7
   no way **de ninguna**
    manera
none **ningún, ninguno/a(s)**
   adj. 7
noon **mediodía** *m.* 1
nor **ni** *conj.* 7
north **norte** *m.* 14
   to the north **al norte** 14
nose **nariz** *f.* 10
not **no** 1
   not any **ningún, ninguno/a(s)**
    adj. 7
   not anyone **nadie** *pron.* 7
   not anything **nada** *pron.* 7
   not bad at all **nada mal** 5
   not either **tampoco** *adv.* 7
   not ever **nunca** *adv.* 7; **jamás**
    adv. 7
   not very well **no muy bien** 1

not working **descompuesto/a**
   adj. 11
notebook **cuaderno** *m.* 1
nothing **nada** 1
noun **sustantivo** *m.*
November **noviembre** *m.* 5
now **ahora** *adv.* 2
nowadays **hoy día** *adv.* 5
nuclear **nuclear** *adj. m., f.* 13
number **número** *m.* 1
nurse **enfermero/a** *m., f.* 10
nutrition **nutrición** *f.* 15

O

o'clock: It's . . . o'clock **Son**
   las... 1
   It's one o'clock. **Es la una.** 1
obey **obedecer (c:zc)** *v.*
obligation **deber** *m.*
obtain **conseguir (e:i)** *v.* 4;
   obtener *v.*
obvious **obvio/a** *adj.* 13
occupation **ocupación** *f.*
occur **ocurrir** *v.*
ocean **mar** *m.* 5; **océano** *m.* 5
October **octubre** *m.* 5
of **de** *prep.* 1
   of course **claro que sí; por**
    supuesto
offer **oferta** *f.* 12; **ofrecer (c:zc)**
   v. 8
office (*medical*) **consultorio** *m.*
   10; **oficina** *f.* 12
often **a menudo** *adv.* 10
Oh! **¡Ay!** 10
oil **aceite** *m.* 8
okay **regular** *adj.* 1
   It's okay. **Está bien.** 11
old **viejo/a** *adj.* 3; old age **vejez** *f.*
   9
older **mayor** *adj. m., f.* 3
   older brother, sister **hermano/a**
    mayor *m., f.* 3
oldest **el/la mayor** 8
on **en** *prep.* 2: **sobre** *prep.* 2
   on behalf of **por** *prep.* 11
   on the dot **en punto** 1
   on time **a tiempo** 10
   on top of **encima de** 2
once **una vez** 6
one **un, uno/a** 1
   one hundred **cien(to)** 5
   one million **un millón** *m.* 5
   one more time **una vez más** 9
   one thousand **mil** 4
   one time **una vez** 6
   one way (*travel*) **ida** *f.* 5
onion **cebolla** *f.* 8
only **sólo** *adv.* 3; **único/a** *adj.* 3
   only child **hijo/a único/a**
    m., f. 3
open **abierto/a** *adj.* 5; **abrir** *v.* 3
open-air **al aire libre** 6

opera **ópera** f.
operation **operación** f. 10
opposite **en frente de** prep. 14
or **o** conj. 7
orange **anaranjado/a** adj. 6;
    naranja f. 8
orchestra **orquesta** f.
order **mandar** 12; (food) **pedir
    (e:i)** v. 8
    in order to **para** prep. 11
orderly **ordenado/a** adj. 5
ordinal (numbers) **ordinal** adj.
other **otro/a** adj. 6
our **nuestro/a(s)** poss. adj. 3;
    poss. pron. 11
out of order **descompuesto/a**
    adj. 11
outside **fuera** adv. 8
outskirts **afueras** f., pl. 12
oven **horno** m. 12
over **sobre** prep. 2
own **propio/a** adj.
owner **dueño/a** m., f 8

P

P.M. **tarde** f. 1
pack the suitcases **hacer** v. **las
    maletas** 5
package **paquete** m. 14
page **página** f. 11
pain **dolor** m. 10
    have a pain in the (knee) **tener** v.
        dolor de (rodilla) 10
paint **pintar** v.
painter **pintor(a)** m., f.
painting **pintura** f. 12
pair **par** m. 6
pants **pantalones** m., pl. 6
pantyhose **medias** f., pl. 6
paper **papel** m. 2; (report)
    informe m.
    paper money **billete** m. 8
paragraph **párrafo** m. 5
Pardon me. (May I?) **con per-
    miso** 1; (Excuse me.) Pardon
    me. **Perdón.** 1
parents **padres** m., pl. 3; **papás**
    m., pl. 3
park **estacionar** v. 11; **parque**
    m. 4
partner (one of a married couple)
    pareja f. 9
party **fiesta** f. 9
pass **pasar** v. 12
passed **pasado/a** p.p. 15
passenger **pasajero/a** m., f. 1
passport **pasaporte** m. 5
past **pasado/a** adj. 6
pastime **pasatiempo** m. 4
pastry shop **pastelería** f. 14
patient **paciente** m., f. 10
patio **patio** m. 12

pay in cash **pagar** v. **al contado;
    pagar en efectivo** 14
pay in installments **pagar** v. **a
    plazos** 14
pay the bill **pagar la cuenta** 9
pea **arveja** m. 8
peace **paz** f.
peach **melocotón** m. 8
pear **pera** f. 8
pen **pluma** f. 2
pencil **lápiz** m. 1
penicillin **penicilina** f. 10
people **gente** f. 3
pepper (black) **pimienta** f. 8
perfect **perfecto/a** adj. 5
perhaps **quizás** 5; **tal vez** 5
periods **plazos** m., pl. 14
permission **permiso** m. 1
person **persona** f. 3
pharmacy **farmacia** f. 10
phenomenal **fenomenal** adj. 5
photograph **foto(grafía)** f. 1
physical (medical examination)
    examen m. **médico** 10
physics **física** f. sing. 2
pick up **recoger** v. 13
picture **cuadro** m. 12
pie **pastel** m. 9
pill (tablet) **pastilla** f. 10
pillow **almohada** f. 12
pineapple **piña** f. 8
pink **rosado/a** adj. 6
place **lugar** m. 4; **poner** v. 4
plaid **de cuadros** 6
plan (to do something) **pensar** v.
    (+ inf.) 4
plans **planes** m., pl. 4
    have plans **tener planes** 4
plant **planta** f. 13
plastic **plástico** m. 13
    (made of) plastic **de plástico**
        13
plate **plato** m. 12
    platter of fried food **fuente** f.
        de fritada 8
play **drama** m.; **comedia** f.;
    jugar (u:ue) v. 4; (a musical
    instrument)
    tocar v.; (a role) **hacer el
    papel**; (cards) **jugar a
    (las cartas)** 5; (sports)
    practicar deportes 4
player **jugador(a)** m., f. 4
playwright **dramaturgo/a**
    m., f.
plead **rogar (o:ue)** v. 12
pleasant **agradable** adj. m., f. 5
Please. **Por favor.** 1
Pleased to meet you. **Mucho
    gusto.** 1; **Encantado/a.** adj. 1
pleasing: be pleasing to **gustar** v. 7
pleasure **gusto** m. 1; **placer** m. 15
    It's a pleasure to . . . **Gusto de
        (+ inf.)**

It's been a pleasure. **Ha sido un
    placer.** 15
    The pleasure is mine. **El gusto
        es mío.** 1
poem **poema** m.
poet **poeta** m., f.
poetry **poesía** f.
police (force) **policía** f. 11
    police officer **policía** m., **mujer
        policía,** f. 11
political **político/a** adj.
politician **político/a** m., f.
politics **política** f.
polka-dotted **de lunares** 6
poll **encuesta** f.
pollute **contaminar** v. 13
polluted **contaminado/a**
    m., f. 13
    be polluted **estar contami-
        nado/a** 13
pollution **contaminación** f. 4
pool **piscina** f. 4
poor **pobre** adj. 6
population **población** f. 13
pork **cerdo** m. 8
    pork chop **chuleta** f. **de
        cerdo** 8
portable **portátil** adj. 11
    portable computer **computa-
        dora** f. **portátil** 11
position **puesto** m.
possessive **posesivo/a** adj. 3
possible **posible** adj. 13
post office **correo** m. 14
postcard **postal** f. 4; **tarjeta
    postal** f. 4
poster **cartel** m. 12
potato **papa** f. 8; **patata** f. 8
practice **entrenarse** v. 15;
    practicar v. 2
prefer **preferir (e:ie)** v. 4
pregnant **embarazada** adj. f. 10
prepare **preparar** v. 2
preposition **preposición** f.
prescribe (medicine) **recetar** v. 10
prescription **receta** f. 10
present **regalo** m. 6; **presentar** v.
pressure: be under a lot of pressure
    sufrir muchas presiones 15
pretty **bonito/a** adj. 3; **bastante**
    adv. 13
price **precio** m. 6
    fixed price **precio** m. **fijo** 6
print **estampado/a** adj. 6;
    imprimir v. 11
printer **impresora** f. 11
private (room) **individual** adj. 5
prize **premio** m.
probable **probable** adj. 13
problem **problema** m. 1
profession **profesión** f. 3
professor **profesor(a)** m., f. 1
program **programa** m. 1

programmer **programador(a)** *m., f.* 3
prohibit **prohibir** *v.* 10
promotion (*career*) **ascenso** *m.*
pronoun **pronombre** *m.*
protect **proteger** *v.* 13
protein **proteína** *f.* 15
provided that **con tal (de) que** *conj.* 13
psychologist **psicólogo/a** *m., f.*
psychology **psicología** *f.* 2
publish **publicar** *v.*
Puerto Rican **puertorriqueño/a** *adj.* 3
Puerto Rico **Puerto Rico** *m.* 1
pull a tooth **sacar una muela** 10
purchases **compras** *f., pl.* 5
pure **puro/a** *adj.* 13
purple **morado/a** *adj.* 6
purse **bolsa** *f.* 6
put **poner** *v.* 4; **puesto/a** *p.p.* 14
  put a letter in the mailbox **echar una carta al buzón** 14
  put on (*a performance*) **presentar** *v.*
  put on (*clothing*) **ponerse** *v.* 7
  put on makeup **maquillarse** *v.* 7

Q

quality **calidad** *f.* 6
quarter **trimestre** *m.* 2
  quarter after (*time*) **y cuarto** 1; **y quince** 1
  quarter to (*time*) **menos cuarto** 1; **menos quince** 1
question **pregunta** *f.* 2
quickly **rápido** *adv.* 8
quiet **tranquilo/a** *adj.* 15
quit **dejar** *v.*
quiz **prueba** *f.* 2

R

racism **racismo** *m.*
radio (*medium*) **radio** *f.* 2; radio (*receiver*) **radio** *m.* 2, 11
rain **llover o:ue** *v.* 4; **lluvia** *f.* 13
  It's raining. **Llueve.** 4
raincoat **impermeable** *m.* 6
rainforest **bosque** *m.* **tropical** 13
raise (*salary*) **aumento de sueldo**
read **leer** *v.* 3; **leído/a** *p.p.* 14
ready **listo/a** *adj.* 15
reap the benefits (of) *v.* **disfrutar** *v.* (**de**) 15
reason **razón** *f.* 3
receive **recibir** *v.* 3
recommend **recomendar (e:ie)** *v.* 8

recycle **reciclar** *v.* 13
recycling **reciclaje** *m.* 13
red **rojo/a** *adj.* 6
red-headed **pelirrojo/a** *adj.* 3
reduce **reducir** *v.* 13
  reduce stress/tension **aliviar el estrés/la tensión** 15
refrigerator **refrigerador** *m.* 12
region **región** *f.* 13
regret **sentir (e:ie)** *v.* 13
related to sitting **sedentario/a** *adj.* 15
relationships **relaciones** *f., pl.*
relatives **parientes** *m., pl.* 3
relax **relajarse** *v.* 9
remain **quedarse** *v.* 7
remember **acordarse (o:ue)** *v.* (**de**) 7; **recordar (o:ue)** *v.* 4
remote control **control remoto** *m.* 11
rent **alquilar** *v.* 12; **alquiler** *m.* 12
repeat **repetir (e:i)** *v.* 4
report **informe** *m.*; **reportaje** *m.*
reporter **reportero/a** *m., f.*
representative **representante** *m., f.*
request **pedir (e:i)** *v.* 4
reservation **reservación** *f.* 5
resign (from) **renunciar (a)** *v.*
resolve **resolver (o:ue)** *v.* 13
resolved **resuelto/a** *p.p.* 14
resource **recurso** *m.* 13
responsibility **deber** *v.*
rest **descansar** *v.* 2
  the rest **lo/los/las demás** *pron.* 5
restaurant **restaurante** *m.* 4
résumé **currículum** *m.*
retire (from work) **jubilarse** *v.* 9
return **regresar** *v.* 2; **volver (o:ue)** *v.* 4
  return trip **vuelta** *f.* 5
returned **vuelto/a** *p.p.* 14
rice **arroz** *m.* 8
rich **rico/a** *adj.* 6
ride a bicycle **pasear** *v.* **en bicicleta** 4
ride a horse **montar** *v.* **a caballo** 5
ridiculous **ridículo/a** *adj.* 13
right **derecha** *f.* 2;
  right here **aquí mismo** 11
  right now **ahora mismo** 5
  right there **allí mismo** 14
  right away **enseguida** *adv.* 9
  be right **tener razón** 3
  to the right (of) **a la derecha (de)** 2
  right? (*question tag*) **¿no?** 1; **¿verdad?** 1
rights **derechos** *m.*
ring (*a doorbell*) **sonar (o:ue)** *v.* 11
river **río** *m.* 13
road **camino** *m.* 11

roast chicken **pollo** *m.* **asado** 8
roasted **asado/a** *adj.* 8
rollerblade **patinar en linea** *v.* 4
romantic **romántico/a** *adj.*
room **habitación** *f.* 5; **cuarto** *m.* 7; (*large, living*) **sala** *f.* 12
roommate **compañero/a** *m., f.* **de cuarto** 2
roundtrip **de ida y vuelta** 5
  roundtrip ticket **pasaje** *m.* **de ida y vuelta** 5
routine **rutina** *f.* 7
rug **alfombra** *f.* 12
run **correr** *v.* 3
  run errands **hacer diligencias** 14
  run into (*have an accident*) **chocar (con)** *v.* 11; (*meet accidentally*) **darse con** 10
rush **apurarse** *v.* 15
russian **ruso/a** *adj.* 3

S

sad **triste** *adj.* 5
said **dicho/a** *p.p.* 14
sake: for the sake of **por** 11
salad **ensalada** *f.* 8
salary **salario** *m.*; **sueldo** *m.*
sale **rebaja** *f.* 6
salesperson **vendedor(a)** *m., f.* 6
salmon **salmón** *m.* 8
salt **sal** *f.* 8
same **mismo/a** *adj.* 3
sandal **sandalia** *f.* 6
sandwich **sándwich** *m.* 8
Saturday **sábado** *m.* 2
sausage **salchicha** *f.* 8
save (*on a computer*) **guardar** *v.* 11; save (*money*) **ahorrar** *v.* 14
savings **ahorros** *m.* 14
  savings account **cuenta** *f.* **de ahorros** 14
say (that) **decir (que)** *v.* 9;
scarcely **apenas** *adv.* 10
scared: be scared (of) **tener miedo (de)** 3
schedule **horario** *m.* 2
school **escuela** *f.* 1
science *f.* **ciencia** 2
  science fiction **ciencia ficción** *f.*
scientist **científico/a** *m., f.*
scubadive **bucear** *v.* 4
screen **pantalla** *f.* 11
sculpt **esculpir** *v.*
sculptor **escultor(a)** *m., f.*
sculpture **escultura** *f.*
sea **mar** *m.* 5; **océano** *m.* 5
season **estación** *f.* 5
seat **silla** *f.* 2
second **segundo/a** *adj.* 5

secretary **secretario/a** *m., f.*
sedentary **sedentario/a** *adj.* 15
see **ver** *v.* 4
   see (you) again **volver a**
    ver(te, lo, la)
   see movies **ver películas** 4
   See you. **Nos vemos.** 1
   See you later. **Hasta la vista.** 1;
    Hasta luego. 1
   See you soon. **Hasta pronto.** 1
   See you tomorrow. **Hasta**
    mañana. 1
seem **parecer** *v.* 8
seen **visto/a** *p.p.* 14
sell **vender** *v.* 6
semester **semestre** *m.* 2
send **enviar; mandar** *v.* 14
separate (from) **separarse** *v.*
   (de) 9
separeted **separado/a** *adj.* 9
September **septiembre** *m.* 5
sequence **secuencia** *f.*
serious **grave** *adj.* 10
serve **servir (e:i)** *v.* 8
set (*fixed*) **fijo** *adj.* 6
   set the table **poner la mesa** 12
seven **siete** 1
seven hundred **setecientos/as** 5
seventeen **diecisiete** 1
seventh **séptimo/a** 5
seventy **setenta** 2
sexism **sexismo** *m.*
shame **lástima** *f.* 13
   It's a shame that . . . **Es (una)**
    lástima que... 13
shampoo **champú** *m.* 7
shape **forma** *f.* 15
   be in good shape **estar en**
    buena forma 15
share **compartir** *v.* 3
sharp (*time*) **en punto** 1
shave **afeitarse** *v.* 7
shaving cream **crema** *f.* **de**
   afeitar 7
shellfish **mariscos** *m., pl.* 8
ship **barco** *m.* 5
shirt **camisa** *f.* 6
shoe **zapato** *m.* 6
   shoe size **número** *m.* 6
   shoe store **zapatería** *f.* 14
   tennis shoes **zapatos** *m., pl.* **de**
    tenis 6
shop **tienda** *f.* 6
shopping, to go **ir de compras** 5
   shopping mall **centro**
    comercial *m.* 6
short (*in height*) **bajo/a** *adj.* 3; (*in
   length*) **corto/a** *adj.* 6
short story **cuento** *m.*
shorts **pantalones cortos**
   m., pl. 6
should (*do something*) **deber** *v.*
   (+ *infin.*) 3

show **espectáculo** *m.;* **mostrar
   (o:ue)** *v.* 4
shower **ducha** *f.* 7; **ducharse** *v.*
   7; **bañarse** *v.* 7
shrimp **camarón** *m.* 8
sick **enfermo/a** *adj.* 10
   be sick **estar enfermo/a** 10
   get sick **enfermarse** *v.* 10
sightseeing: go sightseeing **hacer
   turismo** 5
sign **firmar** *v.* 14; **letrero** *m.* 14
silk **seda** *f.* 6; (*made of*) **de
   seda** 6
silly **tonto/a** *adj.* 3
silverware **cubierto** *m.* 12
since **desde** *prep.* 6
sing **cantar** *v.* 2
singer **cantante** *m., f.*
single **soltero/a** *adj.* 9
   single room **habitación** *f.*
    individual 5
sink **lavabo** *m.* 7
sir **señor (Sr.)** *m.* 1
sister **hermana** *f.* 3
sister-in-law **cuñada** *f.* 3
sit down **sentarse (e:ie)** *v.* 7
six **seis** 1
six hundred **seiscientos/as** 5
sixteen **dieciséis** 1
sixth **sexto/a** 5
sixty **sesenta** 2
size **talla** *f.* 6
   shoe size *m.* **número** 6
skate (in-line) **patinar (en
   línea)** 4
ski **esquiar** *v.* 4
skiing **esquí** *m.* 4
   water-skiing **esquí** *m.*
    acuático 4
skirt **falda** *f.* 6
sky **cielo** *m.* 13
sleep **dormir (o:ue)** *v.* 4; **sueño**
   m. 3
   go to sleep **dormirse
    (o:ue)** *v.* 7
sleepy: be sleepy **tener sueño** 3
slender **delgado** *adj.* 3
slim down **adelgazar** *v.* 15
slow **lento/a** *adj.* 11
slowly **despacio** *adv.* 8
small **pequeño/a** *adj.* 3
smart **listo/a** *adj.* 5
smile **sonreír (e:i)** *v.* 9
smiled **sonreído** *p.p.* 14
smoggy: It's (very) smoggy. **Hay
   (mucha) contaminación.** 4
smoke **fumar** *v.* 8, 15
smoking section **sección** *f.* **de
   fumar** 8
   (no) smoking section *f.* **sección
    de (no) fumar** 8
snack (in the afternoon) **merendar** *v.* 15; afternoon snack
    merienda *f.* 15
   have a snack **merendar** *v.* 15
sneeze **estornudar** *v.* 10

snow **nevar (e:ie)** *v.* 4; **nieve** *f.* 8
snowing: It's snowing. **Nieva.** 4
so (*in such a way*) **así** *adj.* 10;
   tan *adv.* 8
   so much **tanto** *adv.* 12
   so so **así así** 1, **regular** 1
   so that **para que** *conj.* 13
soap **jabón** *m.* 7
   soap opera **telenovela** *f.*
soccer **fútbol** *m.* 4
sociology *f.* **sociología** 2
sock **calcetín** *m.* 6
sofa **sofá** *m.* 12
soft drink **refresco** *m.* 8
software **programa** *m.* **de
   computación** 11
soil **tierra** *f.* 13
solar **solar** *adj., m., f.* 13
solution **solución** *f.* 13
solve **resolver (o:ue)** *v.* 13
some **algún, alguno/a(s)** *adj.* 7;
   unos/as *pron.* 1
somebody **alguien** *pron.* 7
someone **alguien** *pron.* 7
something **algo** *pron.* 7
sometimes **a veces** *adv.* 10
son **hijo** *m.* 3
song **canción** *f.*
son-in-law **yerno** *m.* 3
soon **pronto** *adj.* 10
   See you soon. **Hasta pronto.** 1
sorry: be sorry **sentir (e:ie)** *v.* 13
   I'm sorry. **Lo siento.** 1
   I'm extremely sorry. **Mil
    perdones.** 4
soup **caldo** *m.* 8; **sopa** *f.* 8
south **sur** *m.* 14
   to the south **al sur** 14
Spain **España** *f.* 1
Spanish (*language*) **español** *m.* 2;
   español(a) *adj.* 3
spare time **ratos libres** 4
speak **hablar** *v.* 2
specialization **especialización**
   f.
spectacular **espectacular** *adj. m.,
   f.* 15
speech **discurso** *m.*
speed **velocidad** *f.* 11
   speed limit **velocidad** *f.*
    máxima 11
spelling **ortográfico/a** *adj.*
spend (*money*) **gastar** *v.* 6
   spend time **pasar tiempo** 4
spoon (*table or large*) **cuchara**
   f. 12
sport **deporte** *m.* 4
   sports-loving **deportivo/a**
    adj. 4
spouse **esposo/a** *m., f.* 3
sprain (an ankle) **torcerse (o:ue)**
   v. **(el tobillo)** 10
sprained **torcido/a** *adj.* 10
   be sprained **estar torcido/a** 10
spring **primavera** *f.* 5
stadium **estadio** *m.* 2

stage **etapa** *f.* 9
stairs **escalera** *f.* 12
stairway **escalera** *f.* 12
stamp **estampilla** *f.* 14; **sello** *m.* 14
stand in line **hacer** *v.* **cola** 14
star **estrella** *f.* 13
start (*a vehicle*) **arrancar** *v.* 11
state **estado** *m.* 5
station **estación** *f.* 5
statue **estatua** *f.*
status: marital status **estado** *m.* **civil** 9
stay **quedarse** *v.* 7
   Stay calm! **¡Tranquilo!** *adj.* 7
   stay in shape **mantenerse en forma** 15
steak **bistec** *m.* 8
steering wheel **volante** *m.* 11
step **etapa** *f.* 9
stepbrother **hermanastro** *m.* 3
stepdaughter **hijastra** *f.* 3
stepfather **padrastro** *m.* 3
stepmother **madrastra** *f.* 3
stepsister **hermanastra** *f.* 3
stepson **hijastro** *m.* 3
stereo **estéreo** *m.* 11
still **todavía** *adv.* 5
stock broker **corredor(a)** *m., f.* **de bolsa**
stockings **medias** *f., pl.* 6
stomach **estómago** *m.* 10
stone **piedra** *f.* 13
stop **parar** *v.* 11
   stop (*doing something*) **dejar de (+ *inf.*)** 13
store **tienda** *f.* 6
storm **tormenta** *f.*
story **cuento** *m.*; **historia** *f.*
stove **estufa** *f.* 12
straight **derecho** *adj.* 14
   straight ahead **(todo) derecho** 14
strange **extraño/a** *adj.* 13
   It's strange that . . . **Es extraño que...** 13
strawberry **frutilla; fresa** *f.* 8
street **calle** *m.* 11
stress **estrés** *m.* 15
stretching **estiramiento** *m.* 15
   stretching exercises **ejercicios** *m. pl.* **de estiramiento** 15
strike (*labor*) **huelga** *f.*
stripe **raya** *f.* 6
   striped **de rayas** 6
stroll **pasear** *v.* 4
strong **fuerte** *adj.* 15
struggle (for) **luchar** *v.* **(por)**
student **estudiante** *m., f.* 1; **estudiantil** *adj.* 2
study **estudiar** *v.* 2
stuffed-up (*sinuses*) **congestionado/a** *adj.* 10
stupendous **estupendo/a** *adj.* 5
style **estilo** *m.* 5

suburbs **afueras** *f., pl.* 12
subway **metro** *m.* 5
   subway station **estación** *f.* **del metro** 5
success **éxito** *m.*
successful: be successful **tener éxito**
such as **tales como** 4
suddenly **de repente** *adv.* 6
suffer **sufrir** *v.* 10
   suffer from an illness **sufrir una enfermedad** 10
sufficient **bastante** *adj.* 10
sugar **azúcar** *m.* 8
suggest **sugerir (e:ie)** *v.* 12
suit **traje** *m.* 6
suitcase **maleta** *f.* 3
summer **verano** *m.* 5
sun **sol** *m.* 4
sunbathe **tomar** *v.* **el sol** 4
Sunday **domingo** *m.* 2
sunglasses **gafas** *f., pl.* **oscuras/de sol** 6; **lentes** *m. pl.* **de sol** 6
sunny: It's (very) sunny. **Hace (mucho) sol.** 4
supermarket **supermercado** *m.* 14
suppose **suponer** *v.* 4
sure **seguro/a** *adj.* 5
   be sure **estar seguro/a** 5
surf (*Internet*) **navegar** *v.* **(en)** 11
surprise **sorprender** *v.* 9; **sorpresa** *f.* 9
survey **encuesta** *f.*
sweat **sudar** *v.* 15
sweater **suéter** *m.* 6
sweep (the floor) **barrer (el suelo)** 12
sweets **dulces** *m., pl.* 9
swim **nadar** *v.* 4
swimming **natación** *f.* 4
   swimming pool **piscina** *f.* 4
symptom **síntoma** *m.* 10

T

table **mesa** *f.* 2
tablespoon **cuchara** *f.* 12
tablet (*pill*) **pastilla** *f.* 10
take **llevar** *v.* 2; **tomar** *v.* 2, 8
   take care of **cuidar de** 13
   take (someone's) temperature **tomar la temperatura (a alguien)** 10
   take (*wear*) a shoe size *v.* **calzar** 6
   take a bath **bañarse** *v.* 7
   take a shower **ducharse** *v.* 7
   take into account **tomar** *v.* **en cuenta** 8
   take off **quitarse** *v.* 7
   take out (the trash) *v.* **sacar (la basura)** 10

   take photos **tomar fotos** 5; **sacar fotos** 5
talented **talentoso/a** *adj.*
talk *v.* **hablar** 2; **conversar** *v.* 2
   talk show **programa** *m.* **de entrevistas**
tall **alto/a** *adj.* 3
tank **tanque** *m.* 11
tape (audio) **cinta** *f.* 11
   tape recorder **grabadora** *f.* 1
taste **probar (o:ue)** *v.* 8
tasty **rico/a** *adj.* 8; **sabroso/a** *adj.* 8
tax **impuesto** *m.*
taxi(cab) **taxi** *m.* 5
tea **té** *m.* 8
teach **enseñar** *v.* 2
teacher **profesor(a)** *m., f.* 1; (*elementary school*) **maestro/a** *m., f.*
team **equipo** *m.* 4
technician **técnico/a** *m., f.*
telecommuting **teletrabajo** *n.*
teleconference **videoconferencia** *f.*
telephone **teléfono** *m.* 11
   cellular telephone **teléfono** *m.* **celular** 11
television **televisión** *f.* 11
   television set **televisor** *m.* 11
tell (that) **decir** *v.* **(que)** 9
temperature **temperatura** *f.* 10
ten **diez** 1
tennis **tenis** *m.* 4
   tennis shoes **zapatos** *m., pl.* **de tenis** 6
tension **tensión** *f.* 15
tent **tienda** *f.* **de campaña** 5
tenth **décimo/a** 5
terrible **terrible** *adj. m., f.* 13
terrific **chévere** *adj.* 1
test **prueba** *f.* 2; **examen** *m.* 2
Thank you. *f., pl.* **Gracias.** 1
   Thank you (very much). **(Muchas) gracias.** 1
   Thank you very much. **Muchísimas gracias.** 9
   Thanks (a lot). **(Muchas) gracias.** 1
   Thanks again. **Gracias una vez más.** 9
   Thanks for everything. **Gracias por todo.** 9
that **que** *conj.* 12
   that (one) **ése, ésa, eso** *pron.* 6; **ese, esa,** *adj.* 6
   that (*over there*) **aquél, aquélla, aquello** *pron.* 6; **aquel, aquella** *adj.* 6
   that which **lo que** *conj.* 12
   that's why **por eso** 11
theater **teatro** *m.*
their **su(s)** *poss. adj.* 3; **suyo/a(s)** *poss. pron.* 11

then **después** (*afterward*) *adv.* 7;
   entonces (*as a result*) *adv.* 7;
   luego (*next*) *adv.* 1; **pues**
   adv. 15
there **allí** *adv.* 5
   There is/are . . . **Hay...** 1;
   There is/are not . . . **No hay...**
   1
therefore **por eso** 11
thin **delgado/a** *adj.* 3
thing **cosa** *f.* 1
think **pensar (e:ie)** *v.* 4; (*believe*)
   creer *v.* 3
   think about **pensar en** *v.* 4
third **tercero/a** 5
thirst **sed** *f.* 3
thirsty: be thirsty **tener sed** 3
thirteen **trece** 1
thirty **treinta** 1; thirty (*minutes
   past the hour*) **y treinta; y
   media** 1
this **este, esta** *adj.*; **éste, ésta,
   esto** *pron.* 6
   This is . . . (*introduction*)
   Éste/a es... 1
   This is he/she. (*on telephone*)
   Con él/ella habla. 11
thousand **mil** *m.* 5
three **tres** 1
three hundred **trescientos/as** 5
throat **garganta** *f.* 10
through **por** *prep.* 11
throw **echar** *v.* 14
Thursday **jueves** *m., sing.* 2
thus (*in such a way*) **así** *adj.* 10
ticket **boleto** *m.*; **entrada** *f.*;
   pasaje *m.* 5
tie **corbata** *f.* 6
time **vez** *f.* 6; time **tiempo** *m.* 4
   buy on time **comprar a plazos**
   m., pl.
   have a good/bad time **pasarlo
   bien/mal** 9
   We had a great time. **Lo
   pasamos de película.**
times **veces** *f., pl.* 4
   many times **muchas veces** 10
tip **propina** *f.* 9
tire **llanta** *f.* 11
tired **cansado/a** *adj.* 5
   be tired **estar cansado/a** 5
title **título** *m.*
to **a** *prep.* 1
toast (*drink*) **brindar** *v.* 9
   toast **pan** *m.* **tostado** 8
toasted **tostado/a** *adj.* 8
toaster **tostadora** *f.* 12
today **hoy** *adv.* 2
   Today is . . . **Hoy es...** 2
together **juntos/as** *adj.* 9
tomato **tomate** *m.* 8
tomorrow **mañana** *f.* 1
   See you tomorrow. **Hasta
   mañana.** 1
tonight **esta noche** *adv.* 4

too **también** *adv.* 2
   too much **demasiado** *adv.* 6;
   en exceso 15
tooth **diente** *m.* 7; tooth **muela**
   f. 10
tornado **tornado** *m.*
tortilla **tortilla** *f.* 8
touch **tocar** *v.* 13
tour an area **recorrer** *v.* 5; **excursión** *f.* 4
   go on a tour **hacer una
   excursión** 5
tourism **turismo** *m.* 5
tourist **turista** *m., f.* 1; **turísti-
   co/a** *adj.* 5
toward **hacia** *prep.* 14
towel **toalla** *f.* 7
town **pueblo** *m.* 4
trade **oficio** *m.*
traffic **circulación** *f.* 11; **tráfico**
   m. 11
   traffic signal **semáforo** *m.* 11
tragedy **tragedia** *f.*
trail **sendero** *m.* 13
   trailhead **sendero** *m.* 13
train **entrenarse** *v.* 15; **tren** *m.* 5
   train estation **estación** *f.* **(de)
   tren** *m.* 5
trainer **monitor** *m., f.* 15
translate **traducir** *v.* 8
trash **basura** *f.* 12
travel **viajar** *v.* 2
   travel agency **agencia** *f.*
   de viajes 5
   travel agent **agente** *m., f.*
   de viajes 5
   travel documents **documentos**
   pl. m. **de viaje**
traveler **viajero/a** *m., f.* 5
   traveler's check **cheque de
   viajero** 14
tree **árbol** *m.* 13
trillion **billón** *m.* 5
trimester **trimestre** *m.* 2
trip **viaje** *m.* 5
   take, go on a trip **hacer un
   viaje** 5
tropical forest **bosque** *m.*
   tropical 13
truck **camión** *m.*
true **cierto/a** *adj.* 13
trunk **baúl** *m.* 11
truth **verdad** *f.* 9
try **intentar** *v.* 8; **probar (o:ue)**
   v. 8
   try (*to do something*) **tratar de
   (+ inf.)** 15
   try on **probarse (o:ue)** *v.* 7
t-shirt **camiseta** *f.* 6
Tuesday **martes** *m., sing.* 2
tuna **atún** *m.* 8
turkey *m.* **pavo** 8
turn **doblar** *v.* 14
   turn off (*electricity/appliance*)
   apagar *v.* 11

turn on (*electricity/appliance*)
   poner *v.* 11; **prender** *v.* 11
twelve **doce** 1
twenty **veinte** 1
twenty-eight **veintiocho** 1
twenty-five **veinticinco** 1
twenty-four **veinticuatro** 1
twenty-nine **veintinueve** 1
twenty-one **veintiún, vein-
   tiuno/a** 1
twenty-seven **veintisiete** 1
twenty-six **veintiséis** 1
twenty-three **veintitrés** 1
twenty-two **veintidós** 1
twice **dos veces** 6
twisted **torcido/a** *adj.* 10; be
   twisted **estar torcido/a** 10
two **dos** 1
   two hundred **doscientos/as** 5
   two times **doce veces** 1

U

ugly **feo/a** *adj.* 3
uncle **tío** *m.* 3
under **bajo** *adv.* 7; **debajo de**
   prep. 2
understand **comprender** *v.* 3;
   entender (e:ie) *v.* 4
underwear **ropa interior** 6
unemployment **desempleo** *m.*
United States **Estados Unidos** *m.
   pl.* 1
university **universidad** *f.* 2
unless **a menos que** *adv.* 13
unmarried **soltero/a** *adj.* 9
unpleasant **antipático/a** *adj.* 3
until **hasta** *prep.* 1; **hasta que**
   conj. 14
up **arriba** *adv.* 15
urgent **urgente** *adj.* 12
use **usar** *v.* 6
useful **útil** *adj. m., f.*

V

vacation **vacaciones** *f. pl.* 5
   be on vacation **estar de
   vacaciones** 5
   go on vacation **ir de
   vacaciones** 5
vacuum **pasar** *v.* **la aspiradora** 12
   vacuum cleaner **aspiradora**
   f. 12
valley **valle** *m.* 13
various **varios/as** *adj. m., f. pl.* 8
VCR **videocasetera** *f.* 11
vegetables **verduras** *pl., f.* 8
verb **verbo** *m.*
very **muy** *adv.* 1
   very much **muchísimo** *adv.* 2
   Very good, thank you. **Muy
   bien gracias.** 1

vest **chaleco** *m.* 6
video **video** *m.* 11
    video(cassette) **video(casete)** *m.* 11
    video conference **videoconferencia** *f.*
    videocamera **cámara** *f.* **de video** 11
vinegar **vinagre** *m.* 8
violence **violencia** *f.*
visit **visitar** *v.* 4
    visit monuments **visitar monumentos** 4
vitamin **vitamina** *f.* 15
volcano **volcán** *m.* 13
volleyball **vóleibol** *m.* 4
vote **votar** *v.*

W

wait for **esperar** *v.* 2
waiter **camarero/a** *m.*, *f.* 8
wake up **despertarse (e:ie)** *v.* 7
walk **caminar** *v.* 2
    take a walk **pasear** *v.* 4
walkman **walkman** *m.* 11
wall **pared** *f.* 12
wallet **cartera** *f.* 6
want **querer (e:ie)** *v.* 4
war **guerra** *f.*
warm (oneself) up **calentarse** *v.* 15
wash **lavar** *v.* 12
    wash one's face/hands **lavarse la cara/las manos** 7
    wash oneself *v.* **lavarse** 7
washing machine **lavadora** *f.* 12
watch **mirar** *v.* 2; **reloj** *m.* 2
    watch television **mirar (la) televisión** 2
water **agua** *f.* 8
    water pollution **contaminación del agua** 13
    water-skiing *m.* **esquí acuático** 4
way **manera** *f.*
weak **débil** *adj. m.*, *f.* 15
wear **llevar** *v.* 6; **usar** 6
weather **tiempo** *m.* 4
    It's bad weather. **Hace mal tiempo.** 4
    It's good weather. **Hace buen tiempo.** 4
weaving **tejido** *m.*
Web site **sitio** *m.* **Web** 11
wedding **boda** *f.* 9
Wednesday **miércoles** *m.*, *sing.* 2
week **semana** *f.* 2
weekend **fin** *m.* **de semana** 4
weight **peso** *m.* 15
    lift weights **levantar** *v.* **pesas** *f.*, *pl.* 15
welcome **bienvenido/a(s)** *adj.* 12
well **pues** *adv.* 2; **bueno** *adv.* 2

well-being **bienestar** *m.* 15
well organized **ordenado/a** *adj.* 5
west **oeste** *m.* 14
    to the west **al oeste** 14
western (*genre*) **de vaqueros**
what **lo que** 12
    what? **¿qué?** 1;
    At what time . . . ? **¿A qué hora...?** 1
    What a . . . ! **¡Qué...!** 1
    What a pleasure to . . . ! **¡Qué gusto (+ *inf*.)...**
    What a surprise! **¡Qué sorpresa!** 9
    What day is it? **¿Qué día es hoy?** 2
    What did you say? **¿Cómo?** 1
    What do you think? **¿Qué le/les** *form.* **parece?** 9
    What happened? **¿Qué pasó?** 11
    What is the date (today)? **¿Cuál es la fecha (de hoy)?** 5
    What is the price? **¿Qué precio tiene?** 6
    What pain! **¡Qué dolor!** 10
    What pretty clothes! **¡Qué ropa más bonita!** 6
    What size do you take? **¿Qué talla lleva (usa)?** 6
    What time is it? **¿Qué hora es?** 1
    What's going on? **¿Qué pasa?** 1
    What's happening? **¿Qué pasa?** 1
    What's like? **¿Cómo es...?** 3
    What's new? **¿Qué hay de nuevo?** 1
    What's the weather like? **¿Qué tiempo hace?** 4
    What's wrong? **¿Qué pasó?** 11
    What's your name? **¿Cómo se llama (usted)?** *form.* 1
    What's your name? **¿Cómo te llamas (tú)?** *fam.* 1
when **cuando** *conj.* 7
    When? **¿Cuándo?** 2
where **donde**
    where? (*destination*) **¿adónde?** 2; (*location*)**¿dónde?** 1
    Where are you from? **¿De dónde eres (tú)?** (*fam.*) 1; **¿De dónde es (Ud.)?** (*form.*) 1
    Where is . . .? **¿Dónde está...?** 2
    (to) where? **¿adónde?** 2
which? **¿cuál(es)?** 2; **¿qué?** 2
while **mientras** *adv.* 10
white **blanco/a** *adj.* 6
    white wine **vino blanco** 8
who **que** *pron.* 12; **quien(es)** *pron.* 12
    who? **¿quién(es)?** 1

Who is . . . ? **¿Quién es...?** 1
    Who is calling? (*on telephone*) **¿De parte de quién?** 11
    Who is speaking? (*on telephone*) **¿Quién habla?** 11
whole **todo/a** *adj.* 4
whose **¿de quién(es)?** 1
why? **¿por qué?** 2
widower/widow **viudo/a** *adj.* 9
wife **esposa** *f.* 3
win **ganar** *v.* 4
wind **viento** *m.* 4
window **ventana** *f.* 2
windshield **parabrisas** *m.*, *sing.* 11
windy: It's (very) windy. **Hace (mucho) viento.** 4
wine **vino** *m.* 8
    red wine **vino tinto** 8
    white wine **vino blanco** 8
wineglass **copa** *f.* 12
winter **invierno** *m.* 5
wish **desear** *v.* 2; **esperar** *v.* 13
    I wish (that) **Ojalá que** 13
with **con** *prep.* 2
    with me **conmigo** 4, 8
    with you **contigo** *fam.* 8
within **dentro de** *prep.*
without **sin** *prep.* 13, 15; **sin que** *conj.* 13
    without a doubt **sin duda**
woman **mujer** *f.* 1
wool **lana** *f.* 6
    (made of) wool **de lana** 6
word **palabra** *f.* 1
work **trabajar** *v.* 2; **funcionar** *v.* 11; **trabajo** *m.*
    work (*of art, literature, music, etc.*) **obra** *f.*
    work out **hacer gimnasia** 15
world **mundo** *m.* 11
worldwide **mundial** *adj. m.*, *f.* 5
worried **preocupado/a** *adj.* 5
worry (about) **preocuparse** *v.* **(por)** 7
    Don't worry. **No se preocupe.** *form.* 7
worse **peor** *adj. m.*, *f.* 8
worst **el/la peor, lo peor**
Would you like to? **¿Te gustaría?** 4
write **escribir** *v.* 3
    write a letter/post card/e-mail message **escribir una carta/(tarjeta) postal/ mensaje electrónico** 4
writer **escritor(a)** *m.*, *f*
written **escrito/a** *p.p.* 14
wrong **equivocado/a** *adj.* 5
    be wrong **no tener razón** 3

X

X-ray **radiografía** *f.* 10

Y

yard **jardín** *m.* 12; **patio** *m.* 12
year **año** *m.* 2
   be . . . years old **tener . . .**
     años 3
yellow **amarillo/a** *adj.* 6
yes **sí** *interj.* 1
yesterday **ayer** *adv.* 6
yet **todavía** *adv.* 5
yogurt **yogur** *m.* 8
You don't say! **¡No me digas!**
   fam.; **¡No me diga!** *form.* 11
You're welcome. **De nada.** 1; **No**
   hay de que. 1
young **joven** *adj.* 3
   young person **joven** *m., f.* 1
   young woman **señorita** *f.* 2
younger **menor** *adj. m., f.* 3
younger: younger brother, sister *m.,*
   f. **hermano/a menor** 3
youngest **el/la menor** *m., f.* 8
your **su(s)** *poss. adj. form.* 3
   your **tu(s)** *poss. adj. fam. sing.* 3
   your **vuestro/a(s)** *poss. adj.*
     form. pl.
   your(s) *form.* **suyo/a(s)**
     poss. pron. form. 11
   your(s) **tuyo/a(s)** *poss.*
     fam. sing. 11
youth *f.* **juventud** 9; (young person) **joven** *m., f.* 1

Z

zero **cero** *m.* 1

Text Credits

414-415 © Marco Denevi, *Falsificaciones*, Buenos Aires, Corregidor, 1999, pág. 52, reprinted by permission of Ediciones Corregidor.

440-441 © María Velázquez, "Noviembre 24, 1992" from *Aun sin saber quién eres*, 1998, reprinted by permission of the author.

Illustration Credits

Cover Illustration: José Ortega

Herman Mejía: 5, 12, 13, 15, 16, 20, 21, 44, 51, 55, 65, 73-b, 76, 84, 85, 103, 107, 110, 131, 134, 138, 139, 143, 155, 171, 182, 190, 195, 200, 219, 244, 254, 271, 282, 283, 310, 313, 316, 340, 349, 353, 374, 412, 433, 435, 438, 440-441.

Pere Virgili: 2-3, 32-33, 52, 62-63, 73 (t), 94-96, 112, 113, 122-124, 149, 152-154, 180-181, 202, 203, 208-210, 242-243, 268-269, 296-298, 326-328, 360-362, 392-394, 422-424

Yayo: 9, 39, 69, 101, 129, 159, 187, 217, 249, 275, 303, 333, 367, 384-385, 399, 414-415, 429

Photography Credits

AP: 293 (r) Wide World. 356 (ml).

Martín Bernetti: 1, 2, 6 (b), 10, 14, 17, 28, 31, 36 (b), 42, 47, 48, 56, 57, 61, 63, 64, 66 (b), 72, 74, 77, 79, 80, 86, 87, 88, 89, 90, 91 (ml, bmr, b), 93, 95, 98 (b), 111, 117, 121, 133, 151, 163, 166-169, 174, 175, 179, 184 (b), 189, 191, 194, 204 (tl, tr, m, mr), 205, 207, 213, 220, 241, 245, 267, 272 (b), 279, 295, 300 (b), 307, 312, 325, 329, 352, 359, 361 (tl, bl), 370, 375, 391, 396 (b), 406, 409, 421, 442, 443, 444-445.

Corbis Images: 28 (tr), (tl) Robert Holmes, (m) Phil Schermeister. 29 (mr) Tony Arruza, (ml) Owen Franken, (b) Patrick Ward. 58 (tl, tr) Patrick Ward, (m) Elke Stolzenberg, (b) Reuters New Media Inc. 59 (tl) Paul Almasy, (tr) Jean-Pierre Lescourret, (ml) Francis G. Mayer, (mr) Tony Arruza, (b) Dave G. Houser. 116 118 (tl) George Lepp. 119 (tr) Bettmann, (br) Sergio Dorantes. 126 (b) David Lees. 148 (b) Dave G. Houser. 149 (tr) Steve Chenn. 177 (br) Ariel Ramerez. 204 (fl) Colita, (b) Yann Arthus-Bertrand. 214 (b) Macduff Everton. 238 (t) Bob Winsett, (ml, mr, b) Dave G. Houser. 239 (tl) Craig Lovell, (tr) Michael and Patricia Fogden, (bl) Jan Butchofsky-Houser, (br) Owen Franken. 260 (b) Pablo Corral. 261 Patrick Ward. 264 (tl) Dave G. Houser, (ml) Pablo Corral, (bl) Bettmann, (tr, mr) Macduff Everton, (bmr) Charles O'Rear, (br). 265 (tl) Wolfgang Kaehler, (bl) Roger Ressmeyer, (tr) Duomo, (br) Charles O'Rear. 289 Galen Rowell. 290 (tl) Martin Rogers, (tr) Dave G. Houser, (ml) Jan Butchovsky-Houser, (mr) Buddy Mays, (bl) Bill Gentile, (br) Bob Winsett. 291 (t) Wolfgang Kaehler, (mr) Dave G. Houser, (ml) Jacques M. Chenet, (b) Martin Rogers. 292 (tl) Jeremy Horner, (tr) Bill Gentile, (m) Kevin Schafer, (b) Stephen Frink. 293 (tl) Jeremy Horner, (mr) AFP, (bl) Tony Arruza. 320 (t) Stephanie Maze, (ml) Arvind Garg, (mtr, mbr) Galen Rowell, (b) Pablo Corral. 321 (t, r, b) Pablo Corral, (ml) Owen Franken. 322 (tr) Wolfgang Kaehler, (tl) Dave G. Houser, (m) Diego Lezama Orezolli, (b) Miki Kraftsman. 323 Dave G. Houser, (mr) Temp Sport, (b) Wolfgang Kaehler. 330 (b) José F. Poblete. 350 Danny Lehman. 353 Tony Arruza. 354 (tl) Kevin Schafer, (tr, b) Danny Lehman. 355 (tl) Amos Nachoum, (mr) Bettmann, (ml) Ralph A. Clevenger, (b) Danny Lehman. 356 (tl) Lynda Richardson, (tr) José F. Poblete, (mr) Lake County Museum, (b) AFP. 357 (l) Guy Motil, (r) Frank Lane Picture Agency. 361 (tr) Stephanie Maze, (br) Roger Tidman. 364 (b) Wolfgang Kaehler. 387 (r) 388 (tl) Tom Brakefield, (tr) Macduff Everton, (ml) Owen Franken, (mr) Tony Arruza. 389 (l) Kevin Shafer, (r) Owen Franken. 416 (t) Pablo Corral, (ml) Paul A. Souders, (mr) Neil Rabinowitz. 417 (t) Caroline Penn, (mr, ml, b) Pablo Corral. 426 (b) Pablo San Juan. 446 (t) Peter Guttman, (m) Paul Ammasy, (b) Archivo Iconográfico, S.A. 447 (mr) Joel Creed.

DDB Stock: 447 (tl) Chris R. Sharp, (bl) Francis E. Caldwell.

Carlos Gaudier: 146-147, 148 (tl, tr, ml, mr), 149 (tl, bl).

Lenin Martell: 262.

Odyssey/Chicago: 176 (tl, mrb) Robert Frerck. 177(tl, bl) Robert Frerck, (tr) Barry W. Baker.

PhotoDisc: 29 (tl), 149 (br), 176 (t, b).

Tony Stone Images: 246 (b) Bertrand Rieger. 416 Ken Fisher.

The Viesti Collection: 323 (ml) Joe Viesti.

Mar Caribe

Barranquilla
Maracaibo
Caracas
Puerto España
Trinidad

Venezuela

Medellín
Colombia
Bogotá
Cali
Pasto

R. Orinoco

Georgetown
Guyana
Paramaribo
Cayena
Surinam
Guayana
Francesa

R. Negro

R. Amazonas

Belém

Quito
Ecuador
Guayaquil
Iquitos
Manaus

Perú

R. Madeira

Recife

Cordillera de los Andes

Lima
Cuzco
Lago Titicaca

Salvador

Brasil

Arequipa
La Paz
Brasilia

Arica
Sucre
Bolivia

Iquique

Belo Horizonte

R. Paraguay

Océano
Pacífico

Antofagasta

Paraguay
Asunción

R. Paraná

São Paulo
Rio de Janeiro
Santos

Salta

Chile

R. Uruguay

Porto Alegre

Córdoba
Valparaíso
Mendoza
Rosario
Santiago
Buenos Aires
Uruguay
Montevideo

R. Paraná

Océano
Atlántico

Concepción
Argentina

Bahía Blanca

Cordillera de los Andes

Puerto Montt

N

O   E

S

Estrecho de
Magallanes
Islas Malvinas
Punta Arenas

Tierra
del Fuego

América del Sur